THE COMMERCE OF NATIONS

THE COMMERCE OF NATIONS

By J. B. CONDLIFFE
PROFESSOR OF ECONOMICS
THE UNIVERSITY OF CALIFORNIA

W · W · NORTON & COMPANY · INC · *New York*

PRINTED IN THE UNITED STATES OF AMERICA
FOR THE PUBLISHERS BY THE VAIL-BALLOU PRESS, INC., BINGHAMTON, N. Y.

CONTENTS

Part IV. THE MODERN PROBLEM

CHARTS

FOREWORD

THIS BOOK had its origin in the Henry E. Howland Memorial Lectures at Yale University in January, 1939. Through the long years of preparation and writing I have tried to remember the standards of research and expression set by the founder of this lecture series, Dr. Charles P. Howland.

Like all such books, this owes much to the help and encouragement of many friends. Jacob Viner has gone beyond what one might have expected even from an old friend by reading the whole manuscript and criticising it in detail with his accustomed vigor. My colleagues William Fellner and George H. Guttridge have read large parts of the manuscript as have J. Maurice Clark and my former colleagues Antonin Basch, Alexander Gerschenkron, Folke Hilgerdt, and Louis Rasminsky. The book has been much improved by the comments of these generous friends; but I have not always accepted their suggestions and criticisms, and they cannot be held responsible for my statements.

My thanks are due to the Alfred P. Sloan Foundation, Inc., for the grant which made possible the Teaching Institute of Economics at the University of California. I have discussed the argument of this book at great length with my associates in the Institute—Robert L. Gulick, Jr., John B. Harbell, Don R. Harris, and Raymond P. Powell—and I have profited greatly from their criticisms. I am grateful to them, to George Ramos who drew the maps and charts, to Max Knight for the index, and to Mrs. Maria Feder for the quiet method by which she kept order in an untidy and ever-changing manuscript. My sincere thanks go also to my wife for her patient endurance over a very long time.

J.B.C.

1950

THE COMMERCE OF NATIONS

INTRODUCTION

THIS BOOK is concerned with international economic questions that are vital at the present time and will be vital in the immediate future. These questions differ from any faced by earlier generations in this or any other country. The most important of them arise from the action and reaction between private economic activity and government policy. Both private activity and government regulation must be studied. Both today are very different from what they were a century, or even a generation, ago.

The scope and administrative power of government are greater, particularly in the economic field, and the economic activity of private citizens is much influenced by this fact. Moreover, technical inventions, notably in transport and communication, have widened the scope and increased the efficiency of private enterprise, as well as of government.

Economic activity proceeds in an atmosphere of credit. The control of credit policy is among the most powerful instruments which governments can use to regulate economic activity. The most difficult questions of international economic relations at the present time are those connected with the balancing of payments between national economies, and these questions cannot be fruitfully discussed except in relation to monetary and fiscal policy.

There is no parallel in history to the problems which we must solve in our generation. The combination of circumstances in our time is unique. History will not provide us with ready-made answers for them. Yet they are the product of historical development and cannot be understood except in the light of their origins. The economic structure of the modern world is what it is, population is where it is, and production is specialized along its present lines, largely because of past trading developments.

Even more important is the fact that ideas now current are the result of long and slow development. Human relations and human conduct have been studied for many centuries. Out of that study have developed explanations of behavior and codes of conduct that still shape our thinking, perhaps more than we realize. A comparative study of economic systems is therefore helpful in gaining perspective on modern problems. Even today the greater number of the world's peoples live in a pre-mechanical age, at stages of economic development that are broadly parallel with those which the more advanced industrial communities passed through many generations earlier in their history. We must not assume, as it is so easy to do, that other people respond to the same stimuli as we do and have the same means of responding. And it is wise to reflect that our current attitudes and beliefs may not comprehend the sum of human wisdom. A large part of this book is therefore concerned, directly or indirectly, with examining the assumptions upon which current explanations of international economic questions rest.

One of the best ways to become conscious of the assumptions implicit in our beliefs and practices is to approach the study of modern problems historically. To do so within a reasonable compass one must select the facts and ideas to be emphasized. To write a history of international economic relations would be equivalent to writing a history of civilization. Even to collate the opinions of those who have left a record of their attitudes to these economic facts would be a task far beyond the purpose of this book.

Selecting the facts and ideas to be used as illustrative material, however, should not consist of picking out of the record such material as will support the case to be presented. The historian interprets the past in the light of present interests and needs, and such interpretation naturally varies from historian to historian. It is therefore necessary to state at the outset why this text—intended for the elucidation of modern problems—begins with a brief analysis of primitive trade and to set out the criteria used in selecting the points to emphasize as the story moves rapidly up the centuries.

The main reason for adopting an historical approach is that academic discussion of international economic questions has been set for more than a century in the mold created by a school of economic writers who worked out their system of thought to cope with the problems faced by England in the period of change and stress during and just after the Napoleonic Wars. Their contribution to economic thought was notable and still deserves serious study. Within the limits of its assumptions, it was complete and rigorous. But those assumptions, not all of which were clearly stated, excluded very important aspects of economic policy that were clearly revealed in earlier thought, and have never ceased to be influential in practice.

In particular, ethical considerations were not expressly taken into account. Nor were the complexities of international politics. Social policy, and particularly the welfare of the laboring masses, was not ignored by the classical economists, but they tended to take an optimistic view of the power of the workers to defend their interests in a system of free competition. The controversial issues of present-day economic policy arise largely from these ethical, political, and social factors, which were very obvious to earlier writers on political economy, but were neglected by the classical school.

Another reason for the historical approach is to demonstrate the close connection that has always existed between economic fact, economic policy, and economic theory. As new discoveries or inventions, shifts in political power, or new means of communication opening up new areas and making new commodities available have changed the conditions of trade, new policies have necessarily been improvised.

In general, economic theory has followed both fact and policy, as it still does. But there have never been wanting bold thinkers whose innovating ideas corresponded with or were even ahead of the needs of their times. Those economists who, in times of rapid change, defended the status quo are mostly forgotten. Those whose ideas were consistent with the forces of change have come to be regarded as creative thinkers, and in fact they did hasten the process of change by providing a theoretical basis on which it could be justified. In great crises of history such as that presented in the early nineteenth century by the victory of England's sea power over Napoleon's continental forces, those who correctly divined the trends of the future contributed most to the reshaping of economic thought. Great economists, therefore, though their theories may survive to become the catchwords of reaction, have generally been regarded as radicals by the conservatives of their day.

Still another reason for the historical approach lies in the fact that international economic developments can never be dissociated from domestic economic questions. The assumption of the classical theory that international trade differed radically from domestic trade, since labor and capital could not be transferred between national economic systems, was a valid assumption for purposes of theoretical analysis. But it has never been quite realistic. It is true that there are difficulties in transferring the factors of production across national boundaries. However, no small part of the controversy on international economic policy has arisen from varying estimates of the extent to which enterprise, skilled labor, and capital can be transferred from one country to another.

In its original form, the classical theory based on this assumption was clearly static. It analyzed the situation at a given moment, assuming the economic conditions existing at that moment. But the major interest of international economic questions lies in their dynamic developmental aspects. Later economists widened the classical theory to take problems of economic change and development into account. But it still remains necessary to emphasize the fact that, as far back as the record goes, international trade has been the dynamic force changing local economic conditions, rather than the contrary. There has been action and reaction. International contacts do not arise in a vacuum. Trade begins in a search for greater profit in distant markets than can be gained in the home market. In this search scant account is taken of the disturbance likely to be caused to established industries and occupations.

Authority has often endeavored to hold back the tide, but with little success. The decay of the European towns in the Dark Ages, their revival after the Crusades, the American Revolutions against monopolistic colonial policies, and many other earlier and later examples, bear witness to the influence exerted on national economies by external trading developments. The land enclosures, unemployment and vagrancy problems of Elizabethan England were the domestic counterpart of the struggle to share in the profits generated by rising prices as Spanish gold poured into Europe from the Americas. The violent economic fluctuations through which all countries passed in the years between the two world wars, and the profusion of domestic economic problems in every country which resulted from those fluctuations, were too widespread and too obviously similar to have been the results of local causes. They marked in fact the collapse of the methods by which international economic relations had been regulated in the nineteenth century and which, when partially restored after the first World War, proved incapable of coping with the strains of a distorted and disrupted trading world.

International economic relations, therefore, ought not to be studied as a relatively unimportant and largely independent branch of political economy, concerned mainly with the conditions and consequences of commodity trade, and set in a theoretical framework devised to illuminate the problems of a past age. They constitute a vital, and often explosive, element of all economic questions, domestic as well as international. Monetary, price, agricultural, labor, fiscal, and investment policies, as well as commodity trade, must be taken into consideration, and will in turn be influenced, perhaps drastically, by international developments. In a world such as ours, linked through the air rather than separated by the seas, even psychological states of mind or political developments as well as scientific and economic inventions, communicated from one country to another, may have far-reaching economic consequences.

It is the purpose of this book to trace the ever-quickening pace with which such international forces have operated throughout history. It has been claimed that the frontier wars and financial troubles which disturbed the Roman Empire at the beginning of the Christian era and finally culminated in its downfall were connected with interruptions of trade occasioned by political disturbances in the Near East or faraway China. The chain of causation between such events was tenuous, and its operation was slow. But the historical record grows clearer as trade revived in the Mediterranean after the Crusades, and along the Baltic shores as the Germanic peoples pushed their frontiers east and north to exploit the trade which had gone overland until blocked by the advance of the Mongols into central Russia. Ever since, there has been a continuous acceleration in the pace at which the effects of political and economic change have been communicated from country to country. Now that the whole world can be linked by almost instantaneous transmission of news and vastly improved means of transport, it does not seem likely that the force of international influences or the speed with which they act will diminish. Unless, indeed, trade which has been the main carrier of change is suppressed.

The historical chapters of this book, however, ought not to be read as an economic interpretation of history, stressing the international aspects of economic change. It would be equally possible to pick out, from the immense panorama of past human behavior, incidents and forces to stress the gradual evolution of capitalist enterprise, the developing influence of credit, class exploitation, the successive realization of what once were regarded as utopian ideas, the influence of scientific discoveries, the primacy of political over economic motives, the philosophic backgrounds of changing political ideas, or any number of other theses. None of these accounts would be adequate in itself to explain what has happened, or to afford conclusive guidance for the future. Each would contain part of the truth. And all could help, as this account of past trading developments can help, to free our minds from the set pattern of current ideas and prejudices.

The lesson of history is that a constant effort of creative thought is required to understand and control changing circumstances. Fresh patterns are constantly being woven in the social fabric, and many strands are combined in different ways, as circumstances change, to make these patterns. International trade is one such strand, and at the moment a troublesome but important strand, in the weaving of a satisfactory pattern for the postwar world.

PART I

HISTORICAL ORIGINS

"INFERENCE may be as exact and dispassionate as logic can make it, but it is a wise philosopher who knows the source of his own premises. Like other sciences, economic science tends normally to take for granted the assumptions from which it starts, for, unless it did so, it would find it difficult to start at all. These assumptions, however, have not always been submitted to a very rigorous criticism. They are apt to reflect the views as to the manner in which man may be expected to behave that happen to be accepted, or rather—for they are often somewhat belated —to have been accepted, by a particular society at a given moment; and while the economist is aware that they are provisional and abstract, the publicist who popularizes him not seldom treats them as established truths which it is irrational, or even immoral, to question."

R. H. Tawney, Introd. to Raymond W. Firth, *Primitive Economics of the New Zealand Maori,* New York, E. P. Dutton and Co., Inc., 1929.

CHAPTER I

THE BEGINNINGS OF TRADE

THE COMMERCE OF IDEAS

PONDERING the long and fascinating story of early trading development, Adam Smith was led to postulate his whole discussion of the division of labor—the first really successful attempt at a comprehensive analysis of economic behavior—upon what he called "a certain propensity in human nature . . . the propensity to truck, barter, and exchange one thing for another."

Later anthropological inquiries have gone far to answer the question which he set aside as irrelevant to his theme—"whether this propensity be one of those original principles of human nature, of which no further account can be given, or whether, as seems more probable, it be the necessary consequence of the faculties of reason and speech." [1] The verdict is that the propensity to trade is not an original principle of human nature, but a painfully acquired accomplishment. It grew out of gift exchange which is still practiced by isolated and backward peoples such as the Polynesians in the South Seas, and survives in our own day in the ceremonial gift-giving on holidays and anniversaries.

The stages by which "silent trade," in which wary tribesmen would expose commodities to be taken and replaced by other products of which they had need, passed into overt barter, and the part played

[1] Adam Smith, *An Inquiry into the Nature and Causes of the Wealth of Nations*, London, 1776, Book I, Ch. II.

by military forces guarding trading expeditions, need not detain us here. Only gradually did the notion of valuation based on utility, rather than good will, enter into the equivalence of return gifts. The very word *trade,* derived from *tread* or *track,* has passed through many meanings such as a course, a way of life, a habit, an occupation, communication, fuss, trouble, or commotion. Some of these meanings survive in dialect, as for instance in the Yorkshire saying, "They'll have plenty o' trade on afore they mak' t' business pay." Many of these words, such as *trade goods* and *trade upon,* convey a sense of sharp practice. The companion word *truck,* which comes from an old French word meaning barter, also has these senses of worthless exchange, while the word *barter* comes from a root which literally means to outwit or to cheat. This sense has survived in maritime law in the term *barratry,* meaning a fraudulent or wrongful act by the master of a vessel against her owners or insurers.

Thus, basic notions in economic thought, such as utility, value, and (later) price, developed out of trade with strangers. It became necessary to find an objective basis of measurement in economic transactions with those outside the family or neighborhood group. Not only units of valuation, but reliable measures of weight, volume, length, and area are an outgrowth of trading transactions. The art of weighing was first used for gold which gradually replaced the ox as the universal standard of value in ancient Europe, Africa, and Asia. The standard against which the gold (and later other articles) was weighed was literally a grain—in the language of 12 Henry VII, Chapter V, "the bushel is to contain eight gallons of wheat, and every gallon eight pounds of wheat, and every pound twelve ounces of Troy weight, and every ounce twenty sterlings, and every sterling to be of the weight of thirty-two grains of wheat that grew in the midst of the ear of wheat according to the old laws of this land."

This statute is comparatively modern, enacted nearly at the end of the fifteenth century. However, Professor William Ridgeway has collected from many ancient sources irrefutable evidence to support his view that standards of weight and of coinage were established to serve the convenience of traders by traders themselves, long before governments stepped in to regulate those standards. In his words "we may be certain that untold sums of gold had been weighed by means of natural seeds and according to a standard empirically obtained before ever the sages of Thebes or Chaldaea had dreamed of applying to metrology the results of their first gropings in Geometry or Astronomy."[2]

The regulation of weights and measures by authority came later. It developed partly because the traders proved to be more expert and often less scrupulous than their customers, and partly because the rulers themselves were interested in taxing the trade, and even in manipulating the coinage. The authoritative standards of weights and measures usually conformed to and followed the established practice of the traders.

It is, indeed, obvious that trade, and more particularly foreign trade, has played a very large part in shaping all our economic and social institutions. In great periods of stress when expanding trade has disrupted conventional relationships, economic thought has been stimulated, and new theories have been projected. These periods have usually been marked by great wars which have deranged the fiscal systems and price structures. But the wars, though primarily political in character, can hardly be dissociated from their economic setting.

One can associate trading expansion with almost every institution, good or evil, that has given us the kind of society in which we live. Lewis Mumford, for example, opens his *Technics and Civilization* with a suggestive review of the way in which the clock, measuring and disciplining the use of time, became "the key-machine of the modern industrial age." He goes on to recount how "between the fourteenth and the seventeenth century a revolutionary change in the conception of space took place in Western Europe," and how new machines invented to conquer space and new instruments to measure it were made possible by mathematical development. In the same period there was a great elaboration of monetary systems and credit devices, including the use of bills of exchange. These Mumford connects with the growing mastery of abstract ideas. "The power that was science and the power that was money were, in final analysis, the same kind of power: the power of abstraction, measurement and quantification."[3]

This line of analysis leads easily to the demonstration of a logical connection between the technology that was so intimately linked with expanding trade and the various aspects of our essentially mechanical civilization. The growth of luxury and what Thorstein Veblen has

[2] William Ridgeway, *The Origin of Metallic Currency and Weights and Standards,* Cambridge, 1892, p. 232.

[3] Lewis Mumford, *Technics and Civilization,* New York, 1934, pp. 14, 20 and 25.

called "conspicuous consumption," the increasing mechanization of war, the militarization of industry, the dominance of the physical over the biological sciences, and the neglect of ultimate and organic values in the fragmentary research which breaks up the unity of life to discover how it is put together—all were facilitated by the expansion of economic activity in which trade played so large a part.

Commercial practices and the art of mathematics as well as devices of measurement were encouraged, if not actually provoked, by trading needs. The knowledge of scientific discoveries and of their practical applications spread along the trade routes. Adaptations of these discoveries using Arabic numerals made possible the systems of bookkeeping which have proved indispensable to both corporate and state administration.

The methods and devices of modern economic life, the sciences upon which they rest, and the spirit of their organization have been greatly influenced by the activity of traders, constantly widening the boundaries of human intercourse. It is possible to treat the evolution of our modern world as a history of political and economic expansion—a moving frontier of trade, investment, settlement, colonization, and missionary enterprise, preceded by maritime exploration in which trade was a dynamic impulse. The expansion did not cease until the whole world, the unoccupied temperate grasslands as well as the ancient civilizations of Asia and Africa, had been brought within the orbit of the dominant western European trading civilization. The political structure and the economic organization of our modern world were created in this vast process of commercial expansion.

From the earliest times, traders have spread knowledge and transplanted plants, animals, products, processes, and ideas. It would require many volumes to give an adequate account of these by-products of trading development. One needs only to cite such fragmentary examples as the way in which coffee conquered Europe after its introduction by the Arabs and the Turks, the Arab peoples having originally obtained it from Ethiopia, and its subsequent commercial development by the Dutch in Java and the Portuguese in Brazil, whence it spread widely over Latin America. Wheat and its baking have spread from ancient Egypt over the whole world and have become the symbol of mystical communion in many religions. The grasses, edible roots and grains, fruits, fibers, trees, and domestic animals brought by European settlers have transformed the landscape of the New World. Nor has the traffic been one way. Potatoes, corn, and tobacco are among the long list of American products now spread over the trading world. Asia and Africa contributed heavily also to the products and processes upon which European economic development was based.

In the nature of things, it is not possible to document the even more important commerce of ideas along the trade routes. The busy medieval roads, where scholars, minstrels, pilgrims, clerics, crusaders, and merchants jostled each other, were highways of ideas as well as of trade. The great trading centers have always attracted explorers and adventurers, artists and heretics, and men with new ideas. Columbus found his backing and El Greco his market in Spain, Cabot became an Englishman, Erasmus was attracted to Cambridge, and John Law to Paris. A good case might be made for the argument that learning and artistic creation have always accompanied economic expansion. New creation, as distinct from the masterpieces of the past, is commonly to be found in the bustling cities of commercial importance, rather than in those which have become museums living on the memory of past greatness.

There are those who would claim that merchants have led the struggle for freedom, self-government, and peace. City air, it has been claimed, is free air. But the freedom medieval merchants fought for was freedom from the tyrannous claims of monarchs or nobles and was quite compatible with a rigid oligarchic control by the town merchants themselves. The privileges they extorted from rulers were, in fact as well as name, private laws. Their scope was extended in later ages to become the traditional basis of democratic government, but not without struggle and sometimes revolution.

As to peace, trade in its lusty youth was often difficult to distinguish from piracy, and merchant bankers from the Fuggers onward have played a role in the financing of war. Yet capitalists are timid folk, mostly concerned with safeguarding their wealth. As the scale of their operations grows and its scope extends across national boundaries, they tend increasingly to become pacifist. Indeed they are often charged, as Pitt charged the merchants of his day, with what we now call appeasement, the pursuit of peaceful and profitable trading connections, and the endeavor to postpone or avert war. This charge has been made down the ages by those bent on adventurous policies to extend the power and influence of the state. Its substance was proudly accepted by the free traders of the nineteenth century, who identified their cause with that of peace. Their attitude persists. The history of the International Chamber of Commerce was published under the title *Merchants of Peace,* and there is little doubt that modern commerce stands to lose heavily from modern war and its consequences. But the historical record is not clear. It is evident that more than free trade is necessary if we are to grapple successfully with the scourge of war.

THE CARAVAN AND THE CARAVEL

The enterprising merchant of ancient or medieval times, whether he came from a near-by town or from farther afield, was regarded as a foreigner. He was met with suspicion or open hostility by the local producers and traders. Nearly always he had to pay dearly for protection by the local rulers. But his wares were much sought after by the wealthy, and the very fact that trade survived is evidence of mutual benefit. Many odd instances and quaint survivals of early trade could be cited in the layout of cities, street names, and other relics of the past. Thus the little street called Poultry connects Cheapside with Lombard and Threadneedle Streets in the heart of the city of London.

The main reason why this study of the economic relations between modern peoples begins with a brief outline of early trade is not to find curious historical origins, but to emphasize the fact that trade is rooted in individual and group enterprise rather than in state regulation. Such emphasis is necessary because so much history is written in political terms, in terms of war, crisis, and breakdown rather than of the slow construction of organized facilities for co-operation.

It is also necessary to stress the fact that the long history of trade is by no means confined to Europe and to the settlements of Europeans overseas. Modern trade derives from the beginnings of capitalist enterprise in western Europe from the twelfth century onward, but there was trade and international intercourse long before the era of industrial capitalism. The development of this trade proved to be abortive, often because it was taxed or regulated out of existence, or because political disturbances caused its disruption. Nevertheless, it was a potent force in economic improvement and in the spread of technical knowledge and ideas. African dealers in gold, slaves, and ivories, the Chinese and Arabian traders who met in Ceylon or on the coast of Burma, the adventurous and hardy folk who led their caravans over the silk route from China to the Near East across what we now call "the hump," those who made Palestine a highway between Mesopotamia and Egypt,[4] the Phoenicians, Carthaginians, and Greeks who pioneered trade in the Mediterranean—all of these made their contribution to the spreading of plants, processes, and products, and to the interchange of ideas.

Twice in the ancient world—under Alexander (356–323 B.C.), and again when the Romans consolidated their rule over the Mediterranean and its hinterlands (roughly from the fall of Carthage in 146 B.C. to the capture of Rome by Alaric the Visigoth in 410 A.D.)—there was an approach to Mediterranean, if not world, unity. European historians have always been primarily concerned with the origins of their own civilization. Therefore, it is important to emphasize the fact that Asia and Africa also have long histories. During most of human history—until the trading expansion of Europe began from about the twelfth century—China, India, Egypt, and even Ethiopia were more advanced in economic development and had a richer trade than Europe. Europe maintained contact with these markets across the Near Eastern land bridge, which has always been a region of economic and strategic importance. Every period of European trading expansion has been stimulated by renewed contacts with Asia.

When the Phoenician ports of Tyre and Sidon were at the height of their power and trading influence (850–550 B.C.), they drew upon a wide range of products from near and far. The variety of their commerce is attested by frequent references to it in the writings of the Old Testament prophets.[5] Imperial Rome drew large supplies of wheat for its urban proletariat from Egypt, Spain, north Africa, Sicily, Sardinia, and even England. In the same way successive capitals of imperial China depended upon continuous and large shipments of rice along the ancient canals.

The trade of China with other parts of Asia and with Africa was extensive and gave rise to trading controversies and controls very similar to the mercantilist ideas and practices which were to prevail later in Europe from the sixteenth century on and which, though submerged during the nineteenth century, were never lost and have re-emerged in our own time. Whenever the development of foreign trade has appeared to threaten the stability of local industries, attempts at regulation have followed. Many examples can be cited of

[4] Cf. Genesis 37:25.
[5] Cf. Ezekiel 27.

trade and enterprise escaping from the regulations within which governments tried to confine them. A notable case is that cited by Edward Gibbon in his *Decline and Fall of the Roman Empire.* Justinian tried to establish a state monopoly of silk manufacture on the basis of silkworm eggs smuggled from China. However, his regulations had the effect of driving the manufacture out of his realm.

As long as transport was slow, trade conducted by sea or land was subject to great risks, and the lack of settled government increased its risks. Only those articles the demand for which was capable of giving them great value in small bulk were worth the risk, expense, and labor of transport. Such demand could come only from powerful ruling classes or groups of newly enriched merchants, traders, and financiers. This luxury trade was fair game not only for pirates, but also for rulers hungry for revenue. Moralists were disturbed by the economic and social consequences of such expenditures. Thus the vehemence with which the medieval church often denounced the practices of traders derived in large part from the nature of the trade they carried on. This despite the fact that churchmen were among the most important customers of the traders.

It is difficult to trace with any approach to completeness the early trade across the land bridge connecting Europe, Asia, and Africa. The trade itself was intermittent and subject to many hindrances. It was often conducted by chains of transactions involving many exchanges rather than directly from producer to final consumer. The sources from which information can be gleaned are scattered and fragmentary. As with all the records of ancient peoples, legend and history are mingled. Nevertheless it seems clear that even in antiquity there was trading communication by water from the western Mediterranean through the Black Sea and up the Russian rivers to the fur-bearing regions of the north, or up the Danube and by way of its tributaries to within a short distance of the Adriatic. The Mediterranean was a highway to the trade of the Near and Far East. In the Indian Ocean, Chinese junks and Arabian vessels could meet. The great silk route which was later traversed by Marco Polo afforded a land route from China and India through Mesopotamia to the Levant.

The study of ancient trade and early medieval commerce is a story full of fascinating pictures of vanished but once-flourishing empires, of men living by their wits and quick reactions, of continuous conflicts and occasional compacts between thrusting new adventurers and conservative local groups, of the avarice of rulers, torn between their desire to pluck and their fear of killing the trade, the profits of which were nearly always exaggerated, and of the equal avarice of merchants who bewailed and exaggerated the tolls levied upon them.

In the Near East particularly, the caravan trade, though costly, was safer than the sea-borne trade. "Transport by camel across the desert," writes Rostovtzeff, "was reckoned a far safer and more trustworthy method of conveyance than that by ship, and it was mostly by means of caravans that the products of India, of Arabia, and even those of central Africa were dispatched from Arabia to Babylonia, to Syria, to Egypt, or even much further to north and south." [6]

Ships there were, on the Indian Ocean and in the trade between China and the Near East. The Mediterranean also was a highway for the Phoenicians. Their tiny boats crept along the shores and even out into the Atlantic through the Straits of Gibraltar. The amount of trade by water up the rivers of Europe is doubtful, but a good deal seems to have come down the rivers, and the overland trails naturally followed the river valleys. Much of the development, not only of the trade but of the taxation and regulation to which trade was subjected, was governed by this fact. The castles along the Loire and the Rhine bear witness that lucrative tolls could be extorted from passing merchants. It was out of such local tolls that customs systems developed, and out of the compromises between kings, traders, and local merchants that the pattern of national finance and self-government was largely woven.

While it is possible to trace the remote origins of modern trading practices and to discover early illustrations of customs taxation, commercial law, currency and trade agreements, international trade as we know it today is a comparatively recent development. Parallels with modern international trade can be found in inter-city or inter-regional trade. However, the rise of the nation-state from the fourteenth century on brought new emphasis to the regulation of trade passing across national frontiers. But for regulation such as this, there would be little point in making any distinction between national and international trade. The growing effectiveness of national organization from the late fourteenth century on facilitated trade within national

6 M. Rostovtzeff, *Caravan Cities*, Oxford at the Clarendon Press, 1932, p. 13.

boundaries, but it added new complications to trade across them. Moreover state regulation of such trade enabled national authorities to increase their revenues and to enhance their military power.

The study of international trade must therefore be more than an exercise in the localization of industry and in the advantages of exchanging products between different regions. It must be an exercise in political economy. Indeed political economy was evolved as an art rather than a science from the study of international economic relations. The ancient and medieval world did not offer more than rudimentary possibilities for such an art. But from about the fourteenth century on there is a definite and continuous chain of development in international economic relations. The expansion of the modern world began with the explorations that first crept around the African coast, and then plunged boldly across the Atlantic in search of the fabled wealth of the Indies.

THE DISRUPTION OF THE ANCIENT WORLD

Between the high development of ancient trade, in which Asia and Africa preceded Greece and Rome, and the development of our modern trading systems there was an interlude which was disastrous for the older civilizations. From the sixth to the eighth century the Roman Empire suffered a series of onslaughts that led to a period of confusion which historians, with some exaggeration, have called the Dark Ages. In this period, raiding parties from Scandinavia descended repeatedly upon the wealthier and more advanced western European countries and even penetrated to the Mediterranean. Nomadic Mongol tribes swept in from central Asia to gain footholds in east central Europe. The Moslems established themselves along the north coast of Africa and important areas of the south coast of Europe.

The ravages of the Northmen went far to destroy what was left of Roman civilization in the outlying western parts of the Empire. The destruction was exaggerated by the chroniclers of the time who bewailed the sacking of churches and libraries. Social life is tenacious and men find ways and means to live in the face of repeated disasters. But much of the heritage of Roman law and order was lost and there seems little doubt that urban life and trade were set back over a large part of western Europe during the Dark Ages. The primitive Asiatic peoples who plundered, and then settled, along and within the eastern frontiers of the Empire wrought similar disturbance.

The Moslems did the greatest damage of all to the more highly developed Mediterranean countries. In their first crusading zeal, soon after the death of Mahomet in 632, the Moslems from their central strongholds in the Arabian peninsula extended their sway as far east as India, Indonesia, and even parts of China. African civilization never recovered from their onslaught. In the Mediterranean they conquered most of that part of the Roman Empire which extended along the shores of northern Africa and southern Europe. They were able to do so not only because they were united in an evangelical crusade, but also because they could make use of the higher learning and the advanced economic development in the lands of their first conquests. The contributions which they made to the economic and cultural life of Europe are suggested by the many Arabic words now in common use—*candy, cotton, damask, gauze, muslin, taffeta, alcohol, algebra, divan, jar, lemon, mattress, sherbet, syrup, julep, sofa, spinach, sugar, tariff,* and *traffic.* There were musical words also such as *lute* and *guitar,* and military titles such as *captain* and *admiral,* and *morris* (moorish) dances.

Some historians ascribe the plight of western Europe in the Dark Ages mainly to the fact that the Moslems stopped up the trade of the Mediterranean so that ports decayed. With this decay, town life and Roman civilization, being cut off from the more advanced centers of economic activity, lapsed again into barbarism. This deterioration, however, is quite compatible with the fact that in the great period of Islam, its resources and techniques were so superior to those of contemporary Europe that Europeans later used them as the bases for developing modern production and trade. This is true not only of the creative activity of the Moslems themselves, but also of the spreading of the creative knowledge derived from the ancient civilizations which followed in the wake of their conquests. Greek, Assyrian, and Egyptian science, and particularly the mathematical language which was the main instrument of its development came into modern Europe—as the word *algebra* reminds us—by way of Arabia. The same story can be told of economic life.

Henri Pirenne, the Belgian historian, notes that Moslem commerce circulated "from the Straits of Gibraltar to the Indian Ocean, through the Egyptian ports, which were in communication with the Red Sea, and the Syrian ports, which gave access to the caravan route to Baghdad and the Persian Gulf." Within the brief span of their trading dominance in the Mediterranean, mainly in the latter half of the seventh century, they introduced many revolutionary products and ideas into Europe from the East—sugar cane, rice, cotton, silk, the manufacture and use of paper (without which the invention of printing would have been valueless), and the magnetic compass.

Thus what was destroyed in the Dark Ages was the Roman administrative system and whatever depended upon it, including some of the economic power of the churches and monasteries. As always happens when war breaks established trading connections, city life was set back. New overlords took the place of the old, and for a time social co-operation was disorganized. But the Europe which emerged from the Dark Ages was enriched with new learning and vigor. It gathered strength, at first slowly, and later, after the Atlantic discoveries, at an accelerating pace, until it brought the whole world under the domination of its economic power.

THE REVIVAL OF EUROPEAN COMMERCE

The modern trading world grew from a resurgence of western European enterprise after the Dark Ages. Only the ideas and dreams of the ancient world survived to haunt the early modern age. One such dream—the wealth and splendor of the "gorgeous East"—became the driving force of the exploration and enterprise that created our trading world. But the actual trade and much of the production of the ancient world dwindled into insignificance, thus providing another example of the abortive growths with which the record of history is strewn.

The recovery of economic life in Europe after the Dark Ages was a slow and complicated process to which many forces, not all of them economic in character, contributed. With the breakup of the Roman Empire, particularly after the Moslem occupation of the Mediterranean shores divided the western from the eastern (Byzantine) Empire and sealed Europe off from trading contact with the more developed economic life of Asia and Africa, there had been a rapid deterioration of town life and trading activity in western Europe. Towns had fallen into ruin and old buildings were used as quarries by the few remaining inhabitants huddled in their shelter. Deprived of steady revenues, the medieval kings and their retinues had turned nomads again, moving from one estate to another as they ate out local supplies. When town markets failed, the countryside changed. Much of the land had gone back to forest. The Roman roads had been neglected and had become unsafe. Economic life had become decentralized and had clustered around monastic, episcopal, or baronial estates which were largely self-sufficient.

Yet, something was left even in this dark hour. The church, though split into two main groups, had become intertwined with the organization of the Roman Empire and thus preserved for posterity not only the faith but the elements of the ancient culture, and the administrative methods by which men had organized a co-operative and hence a peaceful and prosperous society. Through all the confusing squabbles and intrigues by which petty chieftains strove to establish and extend their dynasties, the church remained a unifying and civilizing social force.

Gradually men emerged to revive learning, to restore orderly administration and to provide again the opportunity for economic enterprise. Largely it came from men of the church, at least as far as teaching and administration were concerned, since they were the only medieval men who had access to the intellectual tools necessary to such technicians. Our words *clergy, cleric, clerk,* and *clerical* come from the same root, which originally meant a member of a religious order and only slowly came to mean a scholar and especially a notary, secretary, recorder, accountant, or penman. The transition from the religious to the lay use of the word *clerk* came gradually during the sixteenth century after the Reformation.

The revival of trade went parallel with, if it did not precede, the revival of ordered government. It would be wrong to believe that trade awaited the restoration of law and order. Indeed the merchants who began the process of transforming European feudal society into the commercial, democratic, international trading world of our day were merchant adventurers in the crudest sense. Unless we realize this fact, we cannot understand the continuous struggle between them and the church in its efforts to apply the doctrines of the Canon Law. They were outsiders, often aliens and even outlaws, who were in conflict with the ruling groups and often with local merchants. These foreign traders were new men, mostly drawn from the dispossessed, landless classes. There was a deep gulf between them and the landowning aristocracy whose status and privileges depended upon their rendering military service in return for their lands. This social gulf has never been completely bridged. The snobbery which excluded persons engaged in trade from social contacts with the landowning aristocracy lingered into the twentieth century, and its traces still survive.

Likewise there was a sharp conflict between the rising class of traders and the medieval churchmen. Men who had cut themselves off from dependence on the established order of society to live by their trading wits were naturally regarded with suspicion by those whose power was entrenched in that order. Neither landowners nor clerics could be expected to look with favor upon the increasing wealth of Jews, foreigners, escaped serfs, or runaway apprentices, who began by peddling imported wares and soon came to be financiers as well as merchants. The beginnings of international trade in the modern age, therefore, were marked by a class conflict different from our own.

Before turning to a consideration of the trade along the medieval roads, and of the great fairs that grew up at convenient centers, mention must be made of the greatest European waterways, the Baltic and the Mediterranean. The lands around the Baltic shores had never formed part of the civilized world in ancient times. An extensive trade had developed overland by the northern route to China, by the shorter route to India through the Near East, and down the river valleys to the great market of Byzantium and the eastern Mediterranean. The great surge of Asiatic tribes which culminated in the conquests of Genghis Khan (early thirteenth century) interrupted this trade. It was revived and developed by the Baltic route after the Germanic peoples began to multiply and spread eastward across the Baltic plain from about the twelfth century on.

While the petty German princes were losing their struggle for supremacy in the politics of the Holy Roman Empire, population growth in Germany turned into an eastward and northward expansion, lodging Germanic settlements against and even within the boundaries of the Slav peoples. In the thirteenth century the Teutonic knights, the predecessors of the modern Junkers, colonized what later became East Prussia, and forcibly converted its pagan inhabitants to Christianity and servitude. This eastern garrison of the Germanic peoples was later to become the cradle of German militarism, rocked by the incessant conflicts between Teuton and Slav. Coincident with the settlement of East Prussia, the great trading cities of old Germany —such as Bremen, Hamburg, and Lubeck—began the trading expansion which was to lead them to the height of their power as leaders of the Hanseatic League. The forest products of the Baltic states—lumber, pitch, tar—became increasingly valuable as the need for ships' stores increased.

The reopening of the Mediterranean was a by-product of the revival of political and economic life in western Europe after the confusion and deterioration which had followed the Moslem conquests. The first vigor of those conquests had ebbed. Islam lost its evangelism, and its leaders settled into the comfortable luxury of a ruling class. Their westward expansion had been checked by the Franks under Charles Martel at Poitiers in 732. After the conquest of Sicily, completed in 902, they made no further advances and it was not long before they were being attacked and driven back from frontiers that were not defensible. The recoil began in Spain before the end of the tenth century. During the eleventh century, western Christendom developed a series of attacks upon Islam.

How long this offensive might have taken before it achieved great success cannot be known. However, by the end of the century (1095), Pope Urban II proclaimed the First Crusade to rescue the holy places of Christendom from the infidel. There is no reason to doubt the conviction both of the leaders of the church and of the Crusaders. Part of their motive was a desire for reunion with the Eastern Church, which, menaced by the Turks who were later to overrun the Levant, had made overtures to Rome. Part was resentment against the maltreatment of pilgrims passing through Syria, which the Turks had already overrun. No doubt some knights and princes dreamed of establishing their rule in the Holy Land or on way stations to it as the Knights of St. John did at Malta. Primarily the Crusade was the work of the Papacy undertaken at once to unify Christendom, to dramatize the power of the church then at its temporal peak, and to rescue the shrines of the faith. As a great religious demonstration the Crusades were remarkable though, as good causes so often do, the later efforts fell into the hands of professional promoters whose motives were not completely disinterested. As military expeditions they were not conspicuously successful. Though the Holy Land was reconquered, it could not be held.

One important by-product of the Crusades remained—the Mediterranean was reopened to western trade and navigation. The fishermen of the Venetian lagoons and later the adventurous spirits of other north Italian cities found profitable openings in supplying transport and provisions to the armies. They also exploited the great markets of

Byzantium and lodged trading settlements there. Still more important, they gradually took over the trade through the Near East with Asia. Marco Polo has left a record of his journeys to China in this period, and there can be no doubt that Venice grew rich from trafficking in what was left of this ancient trade. The merchants of the Near East traveled by land across the silk route which lay over the Pamir mountains, from the borders of China. The Venetians carried this trade along the shores of the Mediterranean, and even farther, through the Straits of Gibraltar to make contact with the Hanseatic traders, first at Bruges and later at Antwerp. Thus two-way trade was developed by coastal shipping, and the ports of the Low Countries began to be important trading, manufacturing, and financial centers.

Important traffic was carried also along the medieval roads. The main roads naturally followed the course of great rivers. It is doubtful if much traffic was transported by boat up these inland waterways. Packhorse trains could carry goods more cheaply up stream and it was easier to avoid the exactions of local barons when traveling by road. As the Papacy extended its hold over western Europe in the thirteenth century, there was a remarkable growth of trade, fostered by the remittance of Papal revenues to Rome. Pilgrimages increased, universities sprang up, and scholars moved from country to country. Town life became active again and great fairs grew up at convenient stages, sometimes near a monastery or crossroads town, sometimes at a break in transport, sometimes in connection with a local market. Knit together by the church, embodying not only a common faith but a common culture and a great tradition, medieval Christendom, though split into political fragments which were widely different in economic development, had a good deal of unity. Despite opposition from moralists and conservatives, the essential features of capitalist industry and credit began to emerge in the centers of trade—notably in north Italy, southern Germany, and the Low Countries. It was a false dawn of capitalism, checked by urban protectionism, and soon to be by-passed by the Atlantic development; but by the end of the fourteenth century, the modern trading system had begun to take shape.

CHAPTER II

TOLLS, TARIFFS, AND THE NATION-STATE

THE KING'S CUSTOMS

THE BEGINNINGS of trade are to be found in the enterprise of individuals and groups of individuals, but regulation and taxation of trade are almost as old as trade itself. In trading history, if enterprise is the theme, regulation is the counterpoint. As soon as the track begins to be beaten out, established authority intervenes to control and levy tolls upon the traders.

The words which we still use to discuss the collection of revenue and the methods of controlling trade are very old, but their modern use has been standardized only since the sixteenth century. One of the oldest words is *toll* which came into England with the first Teutonic invaders in the fifth century. It has a long history back through Latin to the Greek word for a place at which local rulers exacted payment for permission to pass or to trade, or simply for protection. Of such a nature was the booth which the King James Version of the New Testament describes as the "receipt of custom" where Levi the publican collected the local taxes on produce entering the city of Capernaum.

The verb *to tax* (*taxare*) was used in Roman times. It derives its fiscal meaning from an earlier use meaning to place a burden upon. The word *fiscal* comes from *fisc,* meaning a rush basket, hence purse and later treasury. The noun *tax* signifying a definite collection of revenue was not common in English before the sixteenth century. *Duty,* now commonly used in connection with taxes on trade, reflects the royal origin of such taxes, being derived directly from *devoir,* the action and conduct due to a superior. *Tariff,* as used in English, is an even more interesting and suggestive word. It is Arabic in its derivation and originally meant a definition, a notification, or an explanation. Its adoption in Italy came after the Crusades with the development of commercial bookkeeping and double-entry accounts. At first it was used to describe any tabulated scale of charges, used as a ready-reckoner, and this general meaning is still common in Europe. But the word was introduced into English, also in the sixteenth century, as a technical customs term, denoting the list of import duties chargeable.

It would be relatively easy to cite a long and almost infinitely varied list of ancient and medieval tolls and charges to which trade was subjected in various regions. Some of these charges were paid more or less willingly by the traders as the only means of gaining protection and security, but wherever such exactions could be safely avoided new trade routes were explored. Thus, when the news reached Venice that the Portuguese explorer Vasco da Gama had returned to Lisbon with a cargo of spices from India, there was a panic among the Venetian merchants. The dues exacted on the overland traffic increased the cost of spices from sixty to a hundredfold. The Portuguese, using the route around the Cape of Good Hope, could undersell the Venetians in European markets.[1] Only when the tolls were moderate and stable and when the assurance of peaceful entry, residence, and trading facilities was an adequate return for their payment, could trade survive the numerous exactions to which it was subjected by the multiplicity of petty rulers who exercised authority after the breakup of great empires. It is not surprising that the consolidation of nation-states, which was characteristic of the period from the fourteenth century on, gave a stimulus to both local and foreign trade. The growth of trade and its regulation is correlated with a stability of government exercising authority over wide areas. There is not much point in spending time either on the arbitrary and often excessive tolls levied by petty rulers in ancient and medieval times or upon the dwindling remnants of trade that have survived in areas where settled government disintegrated into local and warring tribalisms.

[1] Cf. H. Gordon Selfridge, *The Romance of Commerce,* London, 1918, pp. 61–62.

For our purposes the consolidation of customs tariffs in England provides a sufficient illustration of the manner in which state taxation of trade began. Protected by its Channel moat, England was not disturbed by foreign invasion after 1066. Its feudal organization gradually gave way to centralized authority. The monarchy in England was stronger than elsewhere in feudal Europe and was able to assert its supremacy over the barons. This process of consolidation was slow. The king was expected to live from the revenue of the royal manors supplemented by the proceeds of such payments as were his right, especially in time of war. It was not till war exigencies forced the monarchy in the thirteenth and fourteenth centuries to ally itself with the town merchants and to enlarge their privileges, with respect first to municipal government and later to grants of national revenue, that the foundations were laid for parliamentary control over finance. The institution of a national customs service was an important element in this process.

Sporadic attempts had been made by successive medieval kings to tax the import and even more the export trade that grew steadily as Flanders became a great manufacturing and trading region and provided a market for English raw materials. The customs service, as its time-honored style—His Majesty's Customs—denotes, is one of the oldest departments of government, but it emerged only after a prolonged struggle between the crown, the barons and the town merchants. Even so, its history had become legendary by the time Adam Smith wrote his well-known passage in the *Wealth of Nations* explaining the word *customs*—"They seem to have been called customs, as denoting customary payments, which had been in use from time immemorial."

The true origin of the national customs and of commercial policy, as of national institutions in general, is to be found in local tolls and regulations.[2] As cities gradually developed, especially from the thirteenth century on, the control of such trade from other cities or from abroad as entered their markets passed into the hands of the leading citizens organized into the Gild Merchant. The Gild Merchant,

[2] This is true also of the trade itself. Cf. George Unwin, *Studies in Economic History*, London, 1927, p. 223: "It was by the use of intermediate links through which foreign commerce and local trade could freely interact upon each other, that the great expansion both of trade and commerce took place. These links were mainly furnished by the various classes of traders that arose in the mediaeval city, and for that reason the origin and organization of these classes is an important part of our subject."

though not wholly composed of local citizens, since burgesses of other towns and even foreign traders were frequently members—herein may be seen the origin of the custom of conferring the freedom of the city upon distinguished foreigners—was essentially an organization of local interests designed to stabilize and protect the town's industries. Naturally it was made up largely of craftsmen, at least in its early history.

There was a fairly considerable variation from town to town and English development differed rather widely from that on the Continent. The corporate structure of the medieval town became increasingly complex. A double process, whereby the power of the separate craft gilds weakened that of the Gild Merchant while within all these bodies democracy gave way to the oligarchic rule of the wealthier merchants, stiffened the monopolistic and restrictive policies of town regulation. Gradually these mercantile associations, although separate in their origins from the institutions of local government, became powerful factors in that government and tended to merge with it. Eventually the gilds were swallowed up by local government even where the forms of organization, as in London, remained those of the gilds.

It was the Gild Merchant which was primarily responsible for the regulation of trade in the twelfth century. That trade was local rather than international. But aliens were carefully watched. The south German merchants were subject to close supervision in Venice. Even the powerful Hanseatic League, led by Lübeck and comprising practically all the trading towns of the Baltic area, had to fight hard to breach the exclusiveness of the towns where it established depots. In this keen struggle for trading privileges the royal power was usually the main hope of intruding aliens. The Gild Merchant was thoroughly protectionist. In the long run it overreached itself, driving commerce and industry to rural districts and villages or smaller towns where the corporate organization was not so strong. Old and wealthy centers of industry—Norwich, Exeter, York, and Winchester—decayed, while little places like Worsted, aided in the fourteenth century by the immigration of alien weavers, gave their names to new cloths.

The local tolls lingered on, sometimes for centuries, but trade escaped, as it has done throughout history, from local monopolistic and restrictive control. Where such control was maintained rigorously, the town languished and decayed. Where a keener sense of values relaxed the monopoly and competed for the growing trade, or where new localities became its seat, ancient restrictions disappeared. By the middle of the fourteenth century in England, the dominance of the towns was beginning to weaken. The power of taxation and of trade regulation was beginning to pass from town to state, from Gild Merchant to Parliament.

Successive kings exercising their royal prerogatives had tried to compensate for the decline of feudal revenues by levying charges, sometimes for the privilege of entry into the kingdom, sometimes for nominal services such as the formalities of inspection, mooring, anchoring, or weighing goods. These latter often became assimilated with the local customs.[3] The royal right of purveyance or requisition exercised in the "prise" of wines has often been regarded as the origin of customs duties, but the researches of Professor Gras have discounted this theory. King John tried to levy a new tax, known as the fifteenth, but Magna Carta put an end to this.[4] Other similar attempts were made at general customs taxation until in 1275 duties, including a small tax on all articles imported and exported, were imposed by the king and agreed to by the merchants in return for a charter which exempted them from many of the ancient tolls though not from the town customs then in force. In 1347 these various duties were consolidated. By a long process of bargaining, not with Parliament as such but with local and foreign merchants, the royal right to levy customs duties was finally established. Thereafter a struggle which lasted for centuries ensued over the granting of various taxes on trade, supplementary to these agreed customs duties. It was in the course of this struggle that Parliament secured the power of the purse and thus paved the way for democratic institutions of government.[5]

[3] Cf. N. S. B. Gras, *The Early English Customs System,* Cambridge, 1918, p. 288. The term *scavage* (lit. *showing*) is paralleled by *manifest,* which survives today as the declared listing of a ship's cargo. Cf. also the word *declaration,* used for an import entry.

[4] The relevant clause of the Charter reads: "Let all merchants have safety and security to go out of England, to come into England, and to remain in and go about through England, as well by land as by water, for the purpose of buying and selling, without payment of any evil or unjust tolls, on payment of the ancient and just customs."

[5] The account in the text follows the interpretation of English commercial development given by George Unwin, rather than that of William Cunningham, *The Growth of English Industry and Commerce* (5th ed.), Cambridge, 1910, Vol. I, pp. 298 ff. The latter describes Edward III as the "Father of English Commerce" primarily because of the consolidation of the customs during his reign. R. H. Tawney in his Introductory Memoir to Unwin, *op. cit.,* draws attention to Unwin's patient research, and "gently malicious common sense" as responsible for overturning the traditional admiration for militaristic adventurers.

By the end of the fourteenth century, the local taxation and regulation of trade was breaking down in England. The foundations of a national tax system had been laid. At the same time town government was giving way to the beginnings of national government. The nation-state was in process of being born. The king, symbol of national unity, was winning authority over prelates and barons. In his struggle with churchmen and landowners, he tended increasingly to ally himself not with the common people, but with the representatives of the merchants. There was an uneasy equilibrium of forces, but as trade expanded and the merchants grew richer, this equilibrium was disturbed. The monarchy leaned more and more upon the foreign traders and the towns for financial support. It was not until the dazzling prospects opened up by the explorations of the fifteenth century precipitated a struggle for trade that the nation-state was consolidated.

THE LAW MERCHANT

Before going on to trace the exciting story of the widening horizons that provided the setting for our modern age, it is necessary to recount briefly the somewhat misty origins of commercial law. Merchants early found it to their advantage to work out rules of fair dealing, and these rules evolved by agreement were administered at first by leading and respected traders. There are records of such codes of mercantile law from very ancient civilizations. The Chaldeans on the flat plains of Mesopotamia (Iraq) had developed a complex trading system with receipts and contracts baked on clay tablets. The records not only of traders but of bankers and investment houses have been preserved in this way. Eventually the practices by which all these varied transactions were regulated and enforced were codified by Hammurabi before 2000 B.C., thereby putting the force of political authority behind established commercial practice.

Much of the law by which we regulate the vast complexity of modern production and trade, even the law of partnership and of corporate relationships, rests upon concepts of fair practice applied to intricate and ever-changing situations according to the experience of actual traders. Custom and precedent count for more than is often realized, especially in the basic relations between men. Their roots go very deep in human consciousness. Inevitably men have attached to them reverence and religious authority, or have sought to identify them with the natural order of the universe.

In modern times, as the power of the state has extended, most countries have enacted codes or statutes to regulate the increasing complexity of trading transactions. For the most part, this statute law has taken over and reinforced the practice of merchants. Case law, interpreting the statutes and applying them to new situations, continues the long process of definition and precedent. Without this continuity of definition, general principles would not be workable in the infinite variety of transactions necessary to carry on a co-operative society. The rock upon which the whole structure of law and order is built is custom, arising out of the experience of the workaday world and accepted because of its pragmatic validity. The writing of the law is important, but may fail of its purpose unless it receives acceptance based on full understanding and agreement.[6]

The medieval "Law Merchant," or rules of trading out of which our modern commercial law developed, has been described "as a particular application of the general idea of contract." However, much more than general principles was worked out, because a great deal of commercial practice was incorporated into the rules by which disputes were settled. Bills of exchange, for example, "which at first blush look like the merest contracts, are overladen with minute arbitrary rules which the most ingenious jurist could not have deduced from the idea of contract. The truth is that 'law merchant' was a body of rules laid down by merchants for regulating their conduct one with another. Economical definitions of exchange and juristic definitions of contract are derived from these rules, not vice versa. In all the great matters relating to commerce, legislators have copied, not dictated."

There was no single origin for such a body of rules nor was its development a clear, uninterrupted process. Indeed it has been justly claimed that "the grandeur and historical significance of the medieval merchant is that he created his own law out of his own needs and his own views."[7] In concert with his fellow merchants from all the trad-

[6] Cf. Euripides, *The Suppliants,* pp. 429–34 (Way's translation)

No worse foe than the despot hath a state,
Under whom, first, can be no common laws,
But one rules, keeping in his private hands
The law: so is equality no more.
But, when the laws are written, then the weak
And wealthy have alike one equal right.

[7] L. Goldschmidt, *Handbuch des Handelsrechts,* Erlangen, 1891, Vol. I, cited in Henry Higgs (ed.), *Palgrave's Dictionary of Political Economy,* London, 1926, Vol. II, pp. 577–82, from which the remaining quotations in the text are cited.

ing countries, he had to devise both the rules by which he could carry on his trade peaceably and equitably and the tribunals in which those rules could be interpreted and enforced. Medieval courts were territorial, so that the trader who left his domicile either had to carry his judge with him or create special courts.

The best-known tribunals were those set up at fairs under the picturesque name of Piepowder Courts. These were of the type of gild courts. They were set up by agreement among the merchants themselves to settle disputes and enforce standards of fair dealing. Tribunals set up in important trading centers were presided over by national consuls elected by the gild to maintain discipline over the body of merchants who were resident in those centers. Some of the most important codes, such as those which were eventually incorporated into the body of maritime law, were developed and administered by consuls elected in this way by the merchants themselves. The consuls so elected were officials of the merchant bodies. Not until the consolidation of nation-states did the title come by gradual development to signify an agent appointed and commissioned by a sovereign state to reside in a foreign town or port, to protect the interests of its traders and other subjects, and to assist in all matters pertaining to the commercial relations between the two countries.

These consular courts and those set up at fairs or at the seats of the Staple—the organization of merchants through which England's export trade was regulated—"fashioned and administered the unwritten law merchant" for two or three centuries. In so doing they evolved a body of standard practice relating to a great variety of transport and trading transactions. Even where justice was administered by municipal courts (as in many German cities), or by national courts, these tribunals commonly accepted what was called "the law pypowdrous."

The main body of this law was non-national, being evolved from the common experience of merchants in many countries. Workable definitions and practices were copied from one trading center to another. The law merchant was in many respects more liberal and more modern than the prevailing usages of royal or church courts. It was directed less against the person and more against the property of a delinquent. It was concerned less with the letter and more with the spirit of a transaction, recognizing unwritten contracts and guarantees, insisting on good faith in transactions, and granting status to married women—dismissing, in fact, pedantic distinctions of outward form, of the personality of contracting parties, of title and of sex, in order to put ideas of sale and contract on a workable basis. In doing so, it contributed greatly to the development of trade and economic progress.

Despite the view of some legal historians and the language of some jurists, it seems clear that the law merchant was largely independent of civil law in its origins. "Law merchant was built up in courts of its own; these courts were invented at a time when mercantile law had little or nothing to learn from other contemporary civil law, and the latter had everything to learn from the former." It would be a mistake to assume, however, that the merchants were always their own judges. The king's justices enforced the law of the land, and the ecclesiastical courts enforced the Canon Law. Since the practices of the merchants came increasingly in conflict with the narrow medieval interpretation of commercial ethics, it is necessary to examine the Canon Law more fully.

THE CANON LAW

It has already been pointed out that the administrative tradition of the Roman Empire was preserved in the church when the attacks of the barbarians destroyed civil authority. The revival of learning and of the arts of government drew heavily upon this tradition, and the church went far toward imposing if not a theocratic rule at least a climate of Christian morality upon the communities in which trade was again developing. As contending claimants fought to be recognized as the rightful inheritors of the Holy Roman Empire, the power of the Papacy rose to its greatest heights in the thirteenth century. The Popes were themselves temporal sovereigns. They directed also the vast finances of the universal church and collected both taxes and revenues from ecclesiastical property. But more important, they wielded universal authority at least equal to that of temporal rulers in matters of personal conduct, including many important aspects of economic behavior.

Although generalizations are dangerous and there is no reason to believe that public or private morality was higher in the Middle Ages than in our own time, the pervasive influence of Christian doctrine is a fact that cannot be ignored. The first attempts of modern men to grapple with economic questions were primarily essays in the application of Christian ethics to economic behavior. In fact, questions of economic policy are always at bottom questions of ethical conduct. This was clearly recognized in the Middle Ages, since the relationships between employer and worker, debtor and creditor, buyer and seller, were easily understood. Even in our own time when these relationships are more complicated and often call for intricate analysis their ordering in society remains an ethical question. The controversies which arise concerning economic policy are seldom rooted in differences concerning the technical methods of achieving a desired goal. They arise primarily from conflicting interests desiring different goals. Such conflicts, in the last analysis, can be resolved only by appeal to ethical standards of conduct.

The body of doctrine in which the standards of the medieval church were set forth is known as the Canon Law. Derived from scriptural texts and writings of the early Christian fathers buttressed by the teachings of Aristotle, the Canon Law was developed by commentaries, papal decisions and applications to new situations until it covered the most important aspects of economic life. It built a bridge between the moral responsibilities of the individual and the institutions of property and contract based upon the Roman Law. In so far as the economic aspects of human conduct are concerned, it was an attempt to work out in all the varied relationships that arise in economic transactions the principle of a just price—a fair reward for services rendered.

It should be said that the medieval church was never as unanimous as the writings of historical analysts sometimes make it appear. From time to time waves of protest against the luxury and demoralization of prelates, against social misrule, or even against doctrinal teaching, spread widely enough to be denounced as heresies and even to be suppressed by devout rulers.[8] There were increasing premonitions of the great revolt which was to issue in the Reformation of the sixteenth century. But in the early Middle Ages these deviations from the main body of doctrine were not significant. The teaching, if not always the practice, of the church was consistent and generally accepted.

Property was not condemned, nor riches—only the love of riches.

[8] Cf. the punishment imagined by Dante as appropriate to the sin of simony, in Canto XIX of the *Vision of Dante* (Cary's translation), Florence, n.d.

But since the purpose of man's existence was to save his soul, the use of property was to be charitable. Men had a right in this imperfect world to reap the rewards of their labors, but they had no right either to demand excessive rewards or to exploit the labor of others. In trade as in production the doctrine held, but was at first narrowly interpreted to exclude payment for what would now be called time-utility. The speculator who profited by holding goods until they were scarce committed a sin. The nature of the goods had not changed so they could not be worth more. All that had happened was the lapse of time, and time was a gift of God. Value was determined by labor cost. As Professor R. H. Tawney has suggested, "The true descendant of the doctrines of Aquinas is the labour theory of value. The last of the schoolmen was Karl Marx." [9] As trade expanded and new problems constantly arose, the schoolmen, and particularly the professors of theology at Paris, were kept busy. They stretched the definitions, found ingenious formulae, and endeavored to keep the teaching abreast of developing practice, insisting always upon the fundamental principles but modifying their application to practical situations. Out of their discussions came the first attempts at economic description and classification, if not analysis.

One aspect of trading practice more than any other became increasingly difficult to reconcile with the traditional teaching. Usury, not in the sense of excessive interest but of payment for the use of money, was forbidden. The usurer was as much detested and feared in medieval Europe as the moneylender is in primitive economic communities today and for the same reasons. Personal loans for the relief of distress or for sudden emergencies were not regarded as proper occasions for extorting profit, but rather as occasions for generous mutual aid in the spirit of bearing one another's burdens. Those who took advantage of passing necessity to extort usury were guilty not only of ruthless exploitation but of unnatural conduct since they failed to observe the natural law of working in order to live.[10] Fortified by Artistotle's view of money as barren metal yielding no natural increase and by the denunciations of the Hebrew prophets and the early

[9] R. H. Tawney, *Religion and the Rise of Capitalism,* New York, Harcourt, Brace & Co., 1926, p. 36.

[10] Cf. *The Vision of Dante,* Canto XI, 11, 113–16 (Cary's translation):

> But in another path
> The usurer walks; and Nature in herself
> And in her follower thus he sets at naught,
> Placing elsewhere his hope.

Christian fathers, the medieval church forbade not only excessive charges for loans, but all payment simply for the use of money.

In face of the developing use of capital for production and trade and of the growing complexity of exchange transactions as trade increased in volume and covered a wider area, the maintenance of this prohibition on usury was not easy. It is contended that interest payments were at all times allowable; but on the ground of just compensation to the lender for loss sustained or gain forgone by not having his capital available—never because of the profit made by the borrower from the use of that capital.

Precisely the same rule was followed in the application of the usury laws to exchange transactions—a matter of importance to the church in connection with the transmission of Papal revenues. Payment was allowable both for the exchange of currencies and for the transmission of bills of exchange, in both cases for the presumed labor of transferring the money from one place to another. But dry exchange—transactions offset in the future by opposite transactions—was forbidden as being merely a device to obtain loans under the guise of a commercial operation. In every case the church aimed its condemnation at unearned profit and sought to enforce the principle of a just reward for services rendered.

However sharp and clear the distinction between usury and interest may have been in the minds of theologians, in the practice of commercial affairs it must often have seemed a distinction without a difference. In actual attempts at enforcement the estimation of injury suffered (*damnum emergens*) or gain lost (*lucrum cessans*) must have become hypothetical. The church's war against usury was conducted by ecclesiastical lawyers and clerics with little sympathy with commerce. It must have appeared obstructive and obscurantist to men anxious to get on with their busy affairs. To the clerics these men seemed too obsessed with the sin of avarice to take time or thought for their souls.

The war was fought long and tenaciously, by exhortation and admonition, by withholding of the sacraments of the church, and by prosecution and punishment through the ecclesiastical courts. Until the power of the state grew strong enough to assert itself, and for some matters even beyond that time, these courts functioned actively. The medieval merchant therefore, in addition to the civil law and equity dispensed by the king's justices or in chancery, was subject in many matters to the law of the church. There was often a conflict of jurisdictions, but in the matter of usury in particular, the church successfully asserted its control. It may be asked how, in face of this consistent hostility to moneylending, the capitalist system of production and trade ever developed. We know that credit operations of all kinds, for the financing of trade, for the transference of purchasing power between national currencies, for productive investment, and for public loans, multiplied rapidly from the fourteenth century onward.

The answer is a simple one. However general and sweeping might be the enunciation of the Canon Law, it was in practice aimed at the petty usury that battened on the misery of the poor. The generality of the law was appropriate to the simpler conditions of localized handicraft production and trade. But economic progress moved the newer forms of organization out of the control of the Canon Law. As Professor R. H. Tawney has pointed out, "whole ranges of financial business escaped from it almost altogether. It was rarely applied to the large-scale transactions of kings, feudal magnates, bishops, and abbots. Their subjects, squeezed to pay a foreign moneylender, might grumble or rebel, but, if an Edward III or a Count of Champagne was in the hands of financiers, who could bring either debtor or creditor to book? It was even more rarely applied to the Papacy itself; Popes regularly employed the international banking houses of the day with a singular indifference, as was frequently complained, to the morality of their business methods, took them under their special protection, and sometimes enforced the payment of debts by the threat of excommunication. As a rule, in spite of some qualms, the international money market escaped from it; in the fourteenth century Italy was full of banking houses doing foreign-exchange business in every commercial center from Constantinople to London, and in the great fairs, such as those of Champagne, a special period was regularly set aside for the negotiation of loans and the settlement of debts." [11]

Here, then, is a case often repeated throughout history, where economic activity developing new forms and methods, escaped from the regulation evolved in a simpler age. The medieval church did not change its doctrine, nor has the modern church departed from it. But the methods of its application to particular situations became inappropriate as a great commercial revolution changed the character of

[11] R. H. Tawney, *op. cit.*, pp. 44–45.

economic activities. The nature of that revolution and its bearing upon the regulation of trade is the next subject to consider.

THE RISE OF THE NATION-STATE

In the early years of the fourteenth century Dante Alighieri, after a brief period of political prominence which proved his undoing, wandered in exile. His movements are not clear, but, in the custom of the time, he went to the University of Paris and possibly to the University of Oxford.[12] Returning to Italy, but not to Florence, he wrote *The Divine Comedy,* a brooding, imaginative epic of man's hereafter. Its universal appeal, spiced by the malicious and easily identifiable placement of Dante's enemies in appropriate categories of Hell, was quickly recognized by his contemporaries and has grown with the years. Projected on to an appropriate scale of divine rewards and punishments, it surveyed the medieval world—a universal world dominated by religious principle, in which the loyalties of men responded to a divinely appointed order, while their earthly allegiance was given to many competing forms of organized society.

Just two centuries later, in the early years of the sixteenth century, another Florentine, Niccolò Machiavelli, wrote a slender volume entitled *The Prince,* the fame if not the knowledge of which has rivaled that of Dante's great poem. Its qualities are in many respects the reverse of those which have attracted men to the vision of Dante. A work of realism, couched in stark prose, cynical, direct, earthy, and amoral, Machiavelli's manual of statecraft shocked his contemporaries and continues to shock all those who prefer to ignore the less attractive aspects of social struggle. His name at once became a synonym for ruthless and faithless striving after power in the relations between states.

Machiavelli wrote before the state had become identified with and reinforced by the emotional drive of nationalism. His book was dedicated to Lorenzo the Magnificent, the ruler of Florence. The struggle

[12] Dante was chosen Chief of the Priors of Florence in 1300; he was confronted by one of those factional disputes that divided many Italian towns as a by-product of the strife between Guelph and Ghibelline over the succession to the Holy Roman Empire. Despite his claim of impartiality, he was driven from office and exiled by a sudden coup of the party which he later opposed. The conjecture that he visited Oxford rests upon a passage in the Latin poems of Boccaccio, and a definite statement by Giovanni da Serravalle, Bishop of Fermo, who, writing a century after Dante, asserted that he studied theology in Oxford as well as in Paris. Cf. *The Vision of Dante* (Cary's translation), Florence, n.d., p. xix.

for power which Machiavelli analyzed was between small, dynastic, almost personal property principalities. But nationalism was a growing force, and the strategy of power-politics which he outlined has become the accepted pattern of international policy. It is indeed an inevitable pattern as long as states recognize no limits to their sovereignty and men respond to no loyalty transcending that which they owe to the nation-state.

Obviously in the two centuries which elapsed between Dante's expression of medieval ideas and Machiavelli's projection of the struggle for power between states, far-reaching changes must have occurred in the social and economic structure of western Europe. These changes came earliest in the prosperous towns of northern Italy. They preceded the political consolidation which was to find its earliest and fullest achievement on the Atlantic seaboard of western Europe. And they prepared the ground for the great conflicts of the next three centuries and for the triumph of economic expansion in the nineteenth century. They introduced the beginnings of capitalism and credit, for the structure of trade was also changing, though its modern development awaited the exploitation of the great discoveries of the fifteenth century. With these new changes in trade there also developed a new instrument of regulation—the nation-state.

The first revival of European commerce from about the twelfth century on, in the Low Countries as in the Mediterranean, stimulated the growth of cities and was centered in them. International trade provoked their expansion. The Italian ports were a gateway to the East. Bruges was an outlet for the Baltic trade. Behind these cities developed the first considerable aggregations of industrial manufacture. Their arts and crafts, the beauty and magnificence of their civic buildings, and the elaborate corporate structure developed by their gilds represent the medieval spirit at its best. By the middle of the fourteenth century, the evil effects of their corporate exclusiveness were becoming apparent. Mutual aid and protection degenerated into monopoly. The new wealth and power became concentrated in fewer hands—an oligarchy of privilege, rivaling that of the feudal landowners, put an end to progress along the civic road of economic development. The comparison to be drawn between this exaggeration of city protectionism and the very similar exaggeration in our time of national protectionism in the leading industrial countries is striking.

In what is now Germany the strength of the corporate towns, banded together in a powerful league, was sufficient to check the political evolution which resulted in the creation of nation-states over most of western Europe. Of all the experiments in government in the troubled centuries between the collapse of the Roman administrative structure and the consolidation of national governments, the federal leagues of city-states that developed in the twelfth century might have seemed to contemporaries to present the most practical alternative to national unification. Most of these experiments were an outgrowth of foreign trade. The powerful gilds merchant of the great trading cities were the active agents in the promotion of consular courts, the evolution of the law merchant, the securing of treaties guaranteeing trading privileges and even in the planting of trading posts that were in effect colonies. The grave and reverend aldermen took their responsibilities seriously and were held in great respect. In the thirteenth and fourteenth centuries, it might well have seemed a leap in the dark to risk the hard-won liberties of city government in an attempt to form a national government led by some petty princeling.

The conditions under which trade was carried on made it necessary for the merchants to concert means of securing themselves from oppression and violence. It was natural that neighboring cities should join together to present a united front in foreign lands. Of the many leagues formed in this way, the greatest and longest-lived was that formed by the German towns which became known as the Hanseatic League. Its origins are obscure, and it maintained secrecy in regard to its organization and operations. The usual number of towns cited as associated in the League is 77, but the number of cities that were members at one time or another has been counted up to 115. The major purpose of the League was to establish conditions in which its merchant-members could trade profitably. But in pursuit of that purpose it was forced into diplomacy and at times into war. It was often in difficulties with the rulers of Denmark and southern Sweden who could levy tolls upon the Baltic traffic passing through the narrow waters of the Sound. In the second half of the fourteenth century in retaliation for a raid by King Waldemar of Denmark upon the League stronghold at Wisby (on Gothland Island), deputies from 77 Baltic and inland towns drew up a declaration that "because of the wrongs and injuries done by the King of Denmark to the common

German merchant, the cities would be his enemies and help one another faithfully." After some initial setbacks, the war was carried to a successful conclusion in 1369 when the League dictated harsh terms of surrender.

At the height of its power the League maintained strongly fortified posts as far east as Novgorod and as far north as Bergen. Their depot on the banks of the Thames, known as the Steelyard, was an alien fortress in the heart of London until Queen Elizabeth evicted the merchants in 1598. The secret of the long-continued power of this organization of merchants and gilds merchant was strict discipline, ruthlessly enforced upon the whole membership. When Bremen merchants defied League rules in 1356, the town was boycotted and reduced for long years to economic distress. In the sixteenth century, however, the League lost power—partly because of the growing strength of national rulers which involved it in expensive wars, partly because other sources of ships' stores were made available by the opening up of new trade routes. Ivan the Third drove them from Novgorod at the beginning of the century. In the following decades Germany was torn by religious strife and persecutions. As the strength of the League cities waned, they lost their trading outposts and the Danes gained control of the Sound. There was dissension within the League, caused largely by the rigid discipline and monopolistic policies imposed by its leaders who were accused of favoring the interests of the stronger towns such as Lübeck. By the end of the sixteenth century, what had been in effect a federated republic of city-states dominated by merchant interests had lost the struggle to maintain its privileges in territories that had passed into the control of unified national governments. Its long and tenacious struggle had contributed to the disunity of Germany which did not become a unified nation-state until 1870.

The forces of economic change which are always liberated by expanding trade cannot be bottled up for long. In the later Middle Ages they escaped from the control both of the towns and of the church. The medium of their escape was the development of credit facilities. The pressure to use that medium was a combination of the advantages to be derived from trade and of the ambition of princes to profit from those advantages in the extension of their dominions.

Alien traders and financiers were from the beginning a constant menace to local exclusiveness. Jews, being damned in any event, escaped from the usury laws. Being outcasts, they drew together. Their wide-flung connections enabled them to function not only as traders, but as agents for the transmittal of funds, and as providers of liquid capital with which to finance trading transactions. Capital began to accumulate from trading profits, from rising land values in the towns, from large-scale production even on a handicraft basis, from mining ventures, and from the accumulation of church revenues—from all the varied sources which are opened by widening and organized specialization leading to greater productivity. The north Italian merchants conducted a thriving trade with the Orient and with the Low Countries, which absorbed increasing amounts of venture capital.[13] As early as the middle of the twelfth century, the necessary settlement of accounts had called forth the invention of bills of exchange. At the great fairs in the following century, not only was there organized money-changing, but bills were cleared (offset) so as to save the expense of transporting the precious metals. The multiplicity of coins minted by various cities and princes led to a confusion of changing values which called forth the first real piece of economic analysis when Nicole Oresme in 1360 wrote his *Treatise on the First Invention of Money.*

The Lombards, a Germanic people who had settled in northern Italy in the sixth century, gradually supplanted the Jews as financiers throughout western Europe. There are Lombard streets in the financial districts of many capitals, and the three golden balls which are the universal sign of a pawnbroker derive from the crest of the Medici. Italians were employed as financial experts not only to transmit Papal revenues and as factors or agents representing Florentine, Venetian and other Italian interests abroad, but also as farmers (collectors) of national revenues, for which privilege they paid the local rulers a fixed sum. Flemings and south Germans also participated in this process of creating an international money market with all its varying functions—deposit banking, foreign exchange, acceptance and discount, marine insurance, commercial advances, investment banking,

[13] Cf. *The Merchant of Venice,* Act III, Sc. II:

But is it true, Salerio?
Have all his ventures failed? What, not one hit?
From Tripolis, from Mexico and England?
From Lisbon, Barbary and India?
And not one vessel 'scape the touch
Of merchant-marring rocks?

municipal, corporate, and public loans. The Royal Exchange in London developed from a bourse originating with the Florentine merchants who were settled in Lombard Street from at least the twelfth century.[14]

There is not space, nor would it be pertinent, to deal in detail with these late medieval financiers many of whom rose to great wealth and international power. The Medici, Strozzi, Bardi, and other Florentine families might be cited, but the story of the great south German family, the Fuggers of Augsburg, is more relevant to our purpose. Beginning as merchant-producers, husbanding their capital, extending their ventures into factories and mining enterprises, and finally into public finance on a great scale, they were leading and typical figures in a great commercial revolution. The village peasant-craftsman Hans Fugger set up a weaving establishment in Augsburg in 1367. His younger son Jacob launched into exports of cloth and imports of spices, married a daughter of the master of the Augsburg mint and so got into mining. Jacob's son Jacob II, with his brothers, developed the business into a vast organization of mines, factories, and financial houses. Kings and emperors were among their clients and debtors, but the trust they put in princes was ill-rewarded when Philip II of Spain defaulted magnificently in 1575 and 1596. These events spelled the doom of the first crop of international financiers and the profession did not revive till the emergence of the Rothschilds at the close of the eighteenth century.

By this time however, many of the western European countries had learned the practice of finance. The Italians had pioneered and taught banking and moneylending as they had taught accounting and corporate organization all over Europe. But local traders were envious

[14] Cf. *Stow's Survey of London* (reprinted from the text of 1603), Oxford, 1908, Vol. I, p. 201: "Then have ye Lombardstreete, so called of the Longobards, and other Marchants, strangers of diverse nations assembling there twice every day, of what originall, or continuance, I have not read of record, more than that Edward the second, in the 12 of his raigne, confirmed a messuage, sometime belonging to Robert Turke, abutting on Lombard street toward the South, and toward Cornehill on the North, for the Marchants of Florence, which proveth that street to have had the name of Lombard street before the raigne of Edward the second. The meeting of which Marchants and others, there continued until the 22 of December, in the yeare 1568, on the which day, the said Marchants began to make their meetings at the Bursse, a place then builded for that purpose in the warde of Cornehill, and was since by her Maiestie, Queene Elizabeth, named the Royall Exchange."

The word *bourse,* literally a purse (cf. *bursar, bursary, disburse*), was in common English use till the early eighteenth century in the form used by Stow. It was re-introduced in modern times in its French spelling.

of their profits and jealous of their privileges. New men appeared who proved that they too could organize the finances of their sovereigns and enrich themselves in so doing.

Jacques Coeur in the first half of the fifteenth century was typical of these new men.[15] They were to be found in Flanders and in England, indeed throughout western Europe. They had escaped from the control of the towns and ignored the precepts of the church. They practiced by new financial methods a new and ruthless philosophy—*caveat emptor*—let the buyer (or borrower) take care of himself.

The day was at hand when new trading horizons would be explored. As the fifteenth century opened, the discovery of new territories and undreamed of treasure by trade was already beginning. But the foundations of the economic ethics of the Middle Ages were undermined before these new possibilities were ripe for exploitation. A new group of adventurers working within the pattern of medieval European trade had created the economic mechanisms which could be used to exploit the discoveries in the New World. These mechanisms were to become the instruments of economic warfare.

Machiavelli's precepts of aggression came just at the right time for them to be used by greater political units than he had visualized. The political strategy he outlined was to find its chief use in the field of economic warfare which he had himself neglected as beyond his interest and competence. There was as yet no economic analysis comparable with his political theory, but economic practice had been emancipated from the restraints placed upon it by medieval morality.

[15] Cf. Henri Pirenne, *A History of Europe,* New York, W. W. Norton Co., 1939, pp. 514–20, for the emergence of such adventurers in many countries. Of Jacques Coeur he writes: "Beginning with nothing, he joined a consortium, one of whose members was a bankrupt merchant, which leased the privilege of minting money from Charles VII. This was a profitable business. All the master-minters were robbers who considered that the profits which they made in minting money were as legitimate as the profits which our modern bankers make by the issuance of government loans. In 1432, having learned the ins and outs of the trade in metals, Coeur began to export silver to the East and import gold, which he disposed of in France at an enormous profit. From this time forward we see him constantly increasing his business interests. He leased the Crown mines in Lyonnais and Beaujolais, in which he employed German miners. He became 'argentier,' which made him purveyor to the court, to which he advanced considerable sums of money at from 12 to 50 per cent interest. Nevertheless, he continued to increase his business interests, acting either on his own account, or in association with other capitalists. It was estimated that he had no less than three hundred factories, from Famagust to Bruges, and into England. He was accused of ruining 'honest merchants,' presumably by speculation and forestalling. His career had nothing in common with that of those 'honest merchants,' who were faithful to the traditions of the Middle Ages."

Cf. also the accounts of the English merchants in Selfridge, *op. cit.,* Chs. X–XII.

The combination of that practice with high policy was to be characteristic of the struggle for power from the sixteenth century onward. The struggle was to be waged on the expanding front of a New World trade.

The Portuguese gropings southward along the coast of Africa had begun before Jacques Coeur broke into the profitable trade with Asia through the Near East. By the middle of the fifteenth century, Antwerp, which was to grow rich on the Portuguese spice trade, was already displacing Bruges as the meeting place of the Mediterranean and Baltic traders. In England the de la Poles of Hull, William Canynge of Bristol, and Richard Whittington of London were representative of the merchants who came to wealth and power in the fourteenth and fifteenth centuries by trading with Flanders and by financing the Hundred Years' War. These men were the precursors of those who in the sixteenth century were to enter with such zest into the conflict with Spain, and equally of Sir Thomas Gresham, whose financial ability was to lay the foundations of the London money market. It is impossible to draw a sharp line between the old and the new trade or between trade and finance.

Obviously the new and immensely profitable openings for investment offered by the financing of state expenditures in the fourteenth century contributed heavily to the growth of financial capital and to its aggregation. It would take too long to recount the incessant conflicts and shifting combinations of dynastic rulers and their effects on Papal policy as the Holy Roman Empire slowly gave way to the modern nation-states of our day. Some families—notably the Hapsburgs—by judicious use of local wars and of political marriages, built up their empires. Others were absorbed or subordinated to the dominance of one royal family whose power, at first uncertainly, came to dominate the feudal landowners. Much of the confusion of political history is concerned with these dynastic struggles. The royal courts had their importance, politically as well as economically. But in retrospect it is clear that their importance in shaping our world fades into insignificance when compared with that which followed the gradual identification of the nation and the state.

It is difficult to determine what caused the growth of national consciousness in the late Middle Ages. Language had something to do with it. Local dialects, Latin or Teutonic in origin, or a fusion of both as in English, supplanted Latin as the medium of communication and government. By the fourteenth century this process was well advanced and the vulgar tongues were being glorified by works of literary creation. Dante had written in Italian, Chaucer in English. The clergy, especially of the lower orders, began to preach in the common tongue and were increasingly conscious of a stirring of patriotism among the common folk. Joan of Arc simply expresses the feeling of the ordinary people when she takes it for granted that it is God's will that the Dauphin should be crowned at Reims and rule over the whole of France. Common language and law, the rise of a merchant class seeking freedom from local tolls, the waning power of the universal church, and the beginnings of secular education, as well as war, contributed to the idea of national unity. The disintegration of the Roman Empire left a vacuum which was filled by the nation-states. This development was clearest in the western countries—France and England—where the Holy Roman Empire had never been very real. The Papacy had been involved in the Roman Empire, and the Popes waged a successful fight to maintain absolute control over church appointments. This, however, resulted in the secularization of the state, and therefore reduced the temporal power of the church.

Monarchy was the natural form of government around which the people rallied in opposition to the rival claims of the church and of local magnates. Those peoples who were fortunate enough to be led by militant yet just rulers with a gift for administration emerged first into organized nation-states. The solitary exception to this general trend was provided by the Swiss, who sat astride the trade route using the St. Gotthard Pass between Italy and Germany. Before the end of the thirteenth century the original nucleus of the Swiss confederation had asserted its virtual independence under the suzerainty of the Empire. The original cantons were joined by neighboring cities and cantons, but the form of government remained that of a confederation with much local autonomy. The success of this essentially democratic organization rested primarily upon its strong natural defenses.

The tenacious Dutch, who had built up a great commerce and industry and by their enterprise had made Antwerp the greatest money market of the fifteenth century, had to fight desperately in the sixteenth century to establish their independence from Spain. The fight was embittered by religious controversy and marked by threats and fears of persecution. Inevitably its economic cost was heavy. The Dutch, aided by shifting alliances with the enemies of Spain, gained a share in the developing trade with the New World and built up a great colonial empire, but they never developed into a great power as did England and France. Their industrial hinterland was harried and part of it was lost. It is possible that they might have lost their independence, if in their exposed position they had not had the sagacious leadership of William the Silent, founder of the House of Orange, during the critical years of their struggle with Spain. The Dutch Republic, which came into existence during the long war with Spain, profited by the enterprise of its merchants and overseas traders. The Dutch lost much of the fruits of their first colonizing and trading ventures in their eighteenth-century wars with England; but enough was retained to make them one of the greatest colonial powers, ruled again in our day by the House of Orange to whose leadership so much was owed in the sixteenth century.

The Dutch story is an epic of courage and endurance of middle-class traders, fighting stoutly for their political, religious, and economic liberties. It constitutes a bright page in the history of the struggle for freedom, but it was not the most effective road to national survival. That road was alliance between the monarchy and the middle classes, perhaps best illustrated in England.

The new merchants found it to their interest to support the monarchy as the symbol of a united nation with power to grant and enforce freedom of trade and transit in its realm. The expenses of government increased with centralization and still more with war. Taxation was slow and difficult to collect. It was convenient for the king to have a fixed sum prepaid for the right to collect taxes and still more convenient to have a loan of ready cash to be repaid by the imposition of new taxes. The "magic of credit" was a means whereby kings could easily acquire the purchasing power with which to sustain court expenditures at the new levels of ostentation, or to go to war. The debasement of coinage was another device for raising funds to supply the royal treasury. There was in the fifteenth century a constant shortage of the precious metals; but debasement of the coinage from time to time caused a rising tendency of prices by temporarily increasing the available purchasing power.

This was a period of increasing trade and productivity. Capital accumulated and became concentrated in the hands of enterprising merchants and financiers. By lending it to the state and collecting it again with heavy interest, much of the increased productivity was gathered up into the hands of the financiers.

By the end of the fifteenth century, the new financial capitalism was centered in Antwerp, which had attracted from Bruges the profitable entrepôt trade between north and south. This it did by a policy of economic liberalism which broke the power of the local gilds. Where Antwerp led, other money markets followed—notably Amsterdam and London. As a general rule, the power of the monarchy was enlisted in support of the struggle of the merchants against feudal landowners, town gilds, and church courts. But this alliance with the state was soon to prove fatal to the liberal spirit of free and aggressive enterprise. A new form of restriction, national rather than local, was in the making.

More important—the first profits of this new organization were dissipated in war. It is clear that the Middle Ages, despite all their brilliant advances in the arts of trade, would have ended in disaster by reason of the no less brilliant inventions in the arts of war, if a new world had not been opened up by the great geographical discoveries of the fifteenth century. The extraordinary flow of wealth which fed Europe with trade and treasure as a result of these discoveries enabled the new nation-states to indulge in bigger wars. The lot of the ordinary folk was not greatly improved until after the culmination of these wars at the turn of the nineteenth century which gave the victory to England over her last rival France. Only then did there ensue a long period of peace which enabled men to profit in their daily lives from the development of world trade.

CHAPTER III

THE EXPANSION OF THE WORLD

EXPLORATION AND DISCOVERY

By the end of the fifteenth century Europe had burst its medieval bounds. The Mediterranean was no longer the center of civilization. Leadership had passed to the maritime western fringe of Europe—Portugal, Spain, the Netherlands, France, and England. Italian seamen—Columbus, Vespucci, Cabot—took service under the flags of these countries, and Italian commercial enterprise was displaced. In part this was because the Italian cities fought among themselves so desperately that they weakened their own strength and incidentally facilitated the march of the Turks across the trade routes to Asia. Constantinople fell in 1453, and the whole seaboard of the eastern Mediterranean passed into Turkish hands. There was a curious tilting of fortune in the wars between Islam and Christendom. As the western Europeans bore down on the last strongholds of the Moors, the Turks drove in the eastern frontiers of the Christian world. But long before this the maritime peoples of western Europe were seeking a way to by-pass the Venetian monopoly.

Commerce, science, and religion joined in the urge to discover new routes to the East. This was an age of travelers' tales. In the late thirteenth century, Marco Polo had gone overland from Italy to China with his elders on their return to the court of Kubla Khan and had spent seventeen years in the great Khan's service before returning by sea. His stories, which were ridiculed at first, stimulated the imagination of poets for centuries afterward. Many collections of voyages and explorations, more or less accurate, appeared in different European languages. At his new palace commanding the Atlantic, Prince Henry of Portugal, the first of the great patrons of scientific exploration, collected a library which included Marco Polo's travels and those of Ibn Battuta, the most famous of the Moslem explorers, as well as the geographical writings of the ancients.

Whatever popular opinion may have been at this time, those who planned and led the voyages of exploration were well aware that the earth was round and that there were active commerce, flourishing civilizations, and accumulated riches in the Eastern world.[1] They knew of the Moslem posts on the east coast of Africa, as well as the southern coast of Asia, and they coveted access to the cottons, silks, spices, pearls, and gold of this fabulous world. It was an entirely legitimate speculation that a route to Japan—where Marco Polo had reported roofs of gold—might be found by sailing around Africa, or even in a much bolder adventure across the Atlantic. Indeed a way might be found by braving the mists and ice of the northeastern passage, driving past Ultima Thule (Scandinavia) and north of Russia. Later, after the American continent was revealed as blocking the westward approaches, many brave efforts were made to find a passage to the northwest. These persisted even after Magellan in 1519–22 had actually found the strait that bears his name, and Drake had followed in his path.

The mariner's compass had come into use by the thirteenth century, and there was some knowledge of the stars. Instruments were primitive, and much of the modern knowledge necessary for correct navigation was unknown. Few of the great discoverers had enough mathematics to calculate their position correctly. Columbus made and recorded observations which were very inaccurate and even mistook other stars for the Polar Star. But like the other great captains, he was a practical sailor with an uncanny accuracy of dead reckoning,

1 The fifteenth and early sixteenth centuries were an age of enlightment, of renascence. The learning of the ancient world was eagerly rediscovered and there was much critical discussion. The attempt of the Inquisition to regulate scientific discussion in the late sixteenth and early seventeenth centuries was directed primarily at the Copernican theory of the movement of the earth around the sun and was most actively prosecuted in the period of the Counter Reformation. The major incidents—against Bruno (1600), Tycho de Brahe (1601), and Galileo (1633)—came in an age of reaction against the free philosophic speculation that characterized the age of Columbus.

shrewd judgment, and above all determined courage. Although such men were seldom of a scholarly cast, science gained much from them. No man who had spent a life of study could have known as much as they knew about ships, winds, and men, but he would probably have known enough to ridicule the scientific bases of the practical men's projects as did the learned men to whom Columbus' *Enterprise of the Indies* was submitted. The scholars were right. Columbus' geography was wrong. But if Queen Isabella had not taken a chance and sent him out to find the western road to Japan, he would not have discovered America.

The first impulse which started the Portuguese on their discoveries was a continuation of the crusading attacks on the Moors. An attack on their outpost at Ceuta in 1415 was successful, and Prince Henry was led on to secure his victory by exploring the west coast of Africa and its outlying islands. In the process gold, the most potent of all inducements to further exploration, was found on the Guinea coast.[2] There had been earlier ventures, but Portugal was well placed to explore the African coast systematically. The strategic purposes were far-reaching—not only to secure the western flank, but, by linking up with Prester John, the mythical Christian monarch of Ethiopia, to outflank, to surround, and to crush the Moslems. The means organized were thoroughgoing. The fishermen were trained and encouraged to become skilled navigators and seamen, shipbuilding was improved, map-makers (including the brothers Columbus) were assembled, and a great library was built up. The crusading strategy persisted even after economic motives had become dominant. As late as 1487 an expedition was sent "to discover and learn where Prete Janni dwelt, and whether his territories reached unto the sea; and where the pepper and cinnamon grew. . . . They were further charged to find out whether it were possible to sail round the southern end of Africa to India and to gather information about sailing in the Indian Ocean."[3]

For many years no captain got past that stretch of coast where the Sahara Desert comes down to the sea. However, in 1434 Cape Bojador was passed, and the ancient fears of the tropical seas were shown to be exaggerated. By the time of Henry's death in 1460 his captains had rounded the bulge of Africa and, despite the disappointment felt

[2] Later the English were to mint a new coin of African gold, which circulated at a value of 21 shillings in the older worn coinage, thus it was that a guinea came to mean 21 shillings.

[3] Cf. Sir Percy Sykes, *A History of Exploration,* New York, 1934, p. 100.

when the coastline trended south again, they pushed farther and farther till in 1486–88, Bartholomew Diaz rounded the Cape of Good Hope. A decade later (1497–99) Vasco da Gama crept cautiously up the eastern coast, fought off attacks at the Arab trading posts, picked up a Hindu pilot and made the Indian port of Calicut before returning home.

This achievement of finding the long-sought passage to India was followed up at once. In the year 1500 a powerful fleet under Cabral, which sailed as far west as the coast of Brazil, rounded the Cape and established a factory at Calicut. Within the next few decades there were trading posts along the east coast of Africa, in India and the Spice Islands, and at Macao. In 1542 commercial relations were opened up with Japan. Meantime the Portuguese captains fought the Arabs and Hindus from Aden to Hormuz and Malacca. They were a seafaring rather than a colonizing people and of all their conquests not much is left—Macao, a part of Timor, Goa, and stretches of east and west Africa. But the wealth of the Indies poured into Europe through Lisbon, and the Portuguese choice of Antwerp as the depot for the spice trade contributed heavily to that town's commercial development.

The Dutch and the British followed later to secure and retain very substantial empires and to profit enormously by the later trade with the East. Their opportunity came when Portugal passed under Spanish rule from 1580 to 1640 and was thereby subjected to the harassing restrictions of the Spanish governmental system. During this period and in the following years when Portugal fought an exhausting war for her independence, the British drove the Portuguese traders from most of India, and the Dutch picked up the rich East Indies.

It should be remembered that the trade with the East was more varied and in many ways richer than that with the Americas which, until colonization, offered little but gold, silver, and pearls. The trade with the East comprised not only spices but sugar, tea, cottons, and silks. Portugal was not a great manufacturing nation and could therefore act only as trader and middleman. But she might have monopolized this profitable trade for more than a century if it had not been for the Spanish subjugation.

After Diaz had rounded the Cape but before Vasco da Gama had reached Calicut, Columbus had sailed from Palos, reached the West Indies and returned. When the significance of this voyage dawned on the Western world, it opened floodgates of excited speculation. All the Utopias for centuries to come were placed in the brave New World. No tale was too fantastic, no project too speculative. Columbus never knew that what he had discovered was not the rich Indies but a new continent. His obstinate faith in his original purpose was a measure of the importance attached to trade with the Orient. In all his four voyages with their many disappointments, Columbus sought gold. Some gold he did find on Hispaniola (Santo Domingo)—not the rich treasure of the Indies, but sufficient to attract the Spaniards back to try again. In his disappointment he shipped home some Caribs as slaves, but the Catholic advisers of Spain vetoed this venture. The European exploitation of the slave trade was left for the Portuguese to initiate and the Dutch and British to systematize later.

In the early sixteenth century, Cortes and Pizarro plundered the accumulated hoards of the American civilizations and unloosed a flood of gold and silver upon Spain and through Spain upon Europe. This plunder was double-edged. There are those who believe that Spain was ruined by it. Dazzled by the prospect of sudden riches, the best energies of her people went into a delirious search for treasure, neglecting both the solid values of her own manufacturing outposts in the Low Countries, and in great measure the possibilities of true colonization in the Americas. It was not till after long and baffling effort that exploration of the interior and colonization—French, Dutch, British and Portuguese, as well as Spanish—began in the middle of the seventeenth century to realize the true economic value of Columbus' discovery.

Magellan's voyage in 1519–22 with its annexation of the Philippines, alarmed the Portuguese who were firmly established in the Moluccas close by. They rightly suspected that the purpose of the voyage was to breach their monopoly of the spice trade in defiance of the Treaty of Tordesillas in 1494. In successive bulls, the Pope had awarded to Portugal and to Spain sovereignty over discoveries made or to be made in the south and west of the then known world. The division of Portuguese interests in Africa and Spanish interests in the Western world had been made along a line 100 leagues west of the Azores. The Portuguese had wished to change this to 370 leagues west, so that their claim to Brazil might be validated. This they had achieved in the Treaty of Tordesillas. But how far west from America into the Pacific did Spain's right go?

The Spanish lodgment on the Philippines and claim to the Moluccas brought the matter to a head. Cortes sent a galleon to Manila across the Pacific from Mexico, and the fight was on. But in 1529 the Portuguese bought out the Spanish claim to the Moluccas for 350,000 ducats, and Spain agreed to a line extending Portuguese claims to 17 degrees east of the Moluccas—which would have barred Spain forever from the Far East. Spain, egged on by New Spain, broke the agreement by sending expeditions in 1542, and again in 1564, under Legaspi, to colonize the Philippines. Once established, the Spaniards stayed there for more than three centuries.

When Spain absorbed the Portuguese empire in 1580, it appeared as if Columbus' dream had at last come true. From Africa to Asia, across the Pacific to America and across the Atlantic to Spain, a great empire had been created dominating the trade of the world. This was the period of Manila's greatest fortune under the Spaniards, and the greatest period of Spanish imperialism. But the Dutch and the English were already at their work and within a decade the sea power of Spain was to suffer an irretrievable defeat when in 1588 the Grand Armada was dispersed in the English Channel. Thereafter the question was which of the rival nations would be able to get most of the pickings, not so much from Spain's American empire, as from trade with the Far East.

MERCHANT ADVENTURERS

When the sixteenth-century merchants and officials in Portugal and Spain, Holland, France, and England found themselves with a new and vastly expanded world on their hands, there was much speculation and promotion of new economic projects. The African route to the Indies had been discovered before the century opened, and the American route soon after. Balboa crossed the Isthmus of Panama in 1513, and Magellan sailed around South America to the Philippines, whence one of his ships continued westward to round the world for the first time in 1519–22. In the meantime many other captains had explored the North and South Atlantic and the Arctic seas, always looking for a quick passage to the wealth of Asia, but in the search discovering other opportunities for enterprise and adventure. The Newfoundland fisheries, new sources of naval stores—timber, tar, pitch, and cordage—rich furs on sea and land, and the profitable slave trade were incidental by-products of the search for gold and spices.

Any attempt to analyze the projects of this age of daring experiment or to fit them into categories of policy must inevitably lose much of the variety and color of an adventurous age. A whole new world offered opportunities for enterprise. No venture could seem foolhardy or quixotic when the boundaries of the known world had been so enlarged that none could say what fresh marvels awaited discovery. It was an age of enterprise rather than of regulation. The freer and more adventurous economies of Holland and England were to win a decisive victory over the regulated economy of Spain. Even though the trade of both the English and the Dutch was organized with state aid which would eventually harden into monopolistic regulation, the enterprise rather than the regulation of trade proved most influential in shaping the modern world.

If we are to understand how our world came to be created, it is necessary to stress the activity of traders, rather than their direction in the interests of state power or the somewhat confused theories advanced to support state policy or special privilege. Mercantilist practices and doctrines were an outgrowth of thrusting enterprise in new fields. It is necessary to understand the logic involved, but these practices and doctrines should not be regarded as the basic phenomena to be studied. The characteristic of the Elizabethan age is action rather than reflection.

Gold loomed large in the Elizabethan imagination. The search for gold, however, was only one, if the most important, phase of commercial activity. It was to give place to less spectacular, but in the long run more profitable, methods of amassing wealth even in the form of gold. The slave trade, which already had a long history, found a new and wholesale vent in the Americas. The furs, fish, and naval stores of the North Atlantic seas and coasts, the dyewoods that gave their name to Brazil, and new products such as tobacco, maize, and potatoes were added to the now familiar spices and silks of the East. Moreover there was a vast extension of the trade in cotton products. Cotton itself had come into Europe and was known by its Arabic name even before the Arabs brought gauze (from Gaza), damasks (from Damascus) and muslins (from Mosul). But as early as 1540, less than half a century after Vasco da Gama's first voyage to Calicut, the word *calico* is found in English as representing the new and cheaper Indian cottons. It quickly came to be used as a general term to describe all these fabrics which were very much sought after, though bitterly resented by the local producers of woolen cloths. A publication of the woolen interests in 1719 refers to "a tawdry, pie-spotted, flabby, low-priced thing, called Callicoe . . . made . . . by a parcel of Heathens and Pagans, that worship the Devil, and work for a half penny a day."

As the growing demands of a widening market absorbed an ever-increasing volume of luxury and semi-luxury goods, habits and modes of living changed. The heavy medieval manor house gave way to Tudor constructions, in which wood was extensively used and glass windows became common. Rugs replaced rushes on the floor. Cotton fabrics were easily washed and led to a revolution in personal cleanliness. There was much ostentation in clothing, furnishings, plate, and means of travel, as well as in shows and entertainment. The use of tobacco spread rapidly, and in the seventeenth century there were constant complaints that the working classes wasted time and money in tea-drinking.[4]

The first experiments in colonization began toward the end of the sixteenth century, partly to develop new trading opportunities and partly to secure strategic bases for further exploration or for warlike operations. True colonization, as distinct from the establishment of "factories" or trading posts, or from the riveting of an alien government upon communities more backward than their conquerors in the arts of war, was pioneered by Spanish settlers; but in the long run it became largely an achievement of the English. In 1583 Sir Humphrey Gilbert led an expedition to Newfoundland, and in 1587 Sir Walter Raleigh settled a group at Roanoke. But the true model of the later colonies that were to become the original thirteen states of the union was the plantation by Elizabeth first of Munster and then of

[4] Cf. *Stow's Survey of London, op. cit.,* Vol. I, p. 84: ". . . but now of late yeares the use of coatches brought out of Germany is taken, and made so common, as there is neither destination of time, nor difference of persons observed: for the world runs on wheeles with many, whose parents were glad to goe on foote," and Jusserand, *A Literary History of the English People,* London (2nd ed.), 1907, Vol. II, p. 297: "In these coaches and also in the play-houses, and, in fact, everywhere, gallants display their finery, they appear all embossed with gold, 'fairer in show than the tombs at Westminster,' and so do ladies, whose complicated dress is, like their admirers', a triumph for 'that smooth and glittering devil, satin.' Trimmed in lace from head to foot, the fine gentleman 'holds himself very busy about the burning of his tobacco-pipe; as there is no gallant but hath a pipe to burn about London.' "

Ulster, in order to reward those who had assisted in the conquest of Ireland. From the early seventeenth century onward colonization and trade are inseparable, and shipping is closely tied to both.

Thus it is convenient to consider the exploitation of the New World under three broad heads—first the searching after accumulated treasure or gold mines, the regulation of commodity trade, and the actual occupation of the new lands by colonists. Before taking up these aspects of policy in more detail, it is necessary to draw attention briefly to the political setting in which policy was pursued.

The loosening of the ties that had bound medieval Christendom in a common culture, the weakening of church discipline, and the decline of municipal power had left the field open for aspiring nation-states. At the same time both administrative costs and the costs of war increased by leaps and bounds. The need of governments for revenue was the key to many aspects of economic policy. The use of artillery and of massed infantry brought with them the necessity to provide supplies in greater volume. Logistics, as it is now called, began to occupy a larger and larger place in military calculations. The political history of Europe from the fifteenth through the eighteenth century was largely the story of a free-for-all struggle for survival and power, first among contending feudal princes, and then among the nation-states that were gradually consolidated. At the beginning of this period there was a special cause of bitter conflict. Discontent with the manifest abuses of the church organization, the recurring movements of social reform claiming Christian inspiration, and the inevitable resentment aroused by the accretion of economic property and power in a never-dying institution, finally issued in the great religious cleavage that we now know as the Reformation.

Religious wars, unlike those waged for limited national objectives as a matter of calculated policy, are bound to be wars to the death. To compromise is to betray the faith. Christians had fought the infidel in successive crusades. Now Protestant fought Catholic within a divided Christendom. The Wars of Religion (1562–98) paralyzed French economic initiative in the critical latter half of the sixteenth century, and after the massacre of St. Bartholomew's Day (1572) many of the Huguenots fled the country. Among the German states the conflict smouldered till it broke out in the Thirty Years' War (1618–48) which embittered, divided, and impoverished the German people for generations. In the late sixteenth century, the manufacturing and banking prosperity of Flanders was ruined by the exactions of the Spaniards and by the fear rather than the fact of their persecution of the Protestant merchants, many of whom fled north from Antwerp to Amsterdam and there fought a bitter struggle from behind their water ramparts. Spain itself was weakened in the struggle, and its great empire, the first on which it was said that the sun never set, fell a prey to the marauding Dutch and English seamen.

The political and economic successes of the Protestant countries quite naturally led to the belief that the essence of the Reformation was the repudiation of the ethical restraints placed by the church upon commercial enterprise. This belief originated quite early and still persists. It was Calvinism which made business respectable. It has been said that "The heroic age of Calvinism savored more of a collectivist dictatorship than of individualism," and that if the philosophy of laissez faire emerged from Calvinism, it emerged like the idea of religious tolerance by a somewhat indirect route. The early history not only of John Calvin's Geneva and John Knox's Edinburgh but also of John Cotton's Boston would seem to support this view.[5]

Unlike the peasant mysticism of Luther, Calvinism was born in an urban environment and drew its adherents mainly from the merchants and manufacturers. Such men could see no sense in the argument that income from labor or land was morally justifiable while income from trade or manufacture was not. Catholic doctrine did not condemn commercial gain, but it did impose moral restraint upon the pursuit of gain. It was the urban Calvinists who emphasized individual conscience and judgment. By a natural development they accepted "the necessity of capital, credit and banking, large-scale commerce and finance, and the other practical facts of business life." [6] Indeed they taught that occupation should be regarded as a vocation, pursued soberly and with diligence. They frowned upon worldly

[5] Cf. R. H. Tawney, *Religion and the Rise of Capitalism,* pp. 83–113. There has been much controversy over the connection between Calvinism and capitalism, since Max Weber first published his articles on "The Protestant Ethic and the Spirit of Capitalism" in the *Archiv für Sozialwissenschaft und Sozialpolitik* in 1904–5. The English edition (London, 1930) was introduced by R. H. Tawney who states *inter alia:* "What is significant, in short, is not the strength of the motive of self-interest, which is the commonplace of all ages and demands no explanation. It is the change of moral standards which converted a natural frailty into an ornament of the spirit, and canonized as the economic virtues habits which in earlier ages had been denounced as vices. The force which produced it was the creed associated with the name of Calvin. Capitalism was the social counterpart of Calvinist theology."

[6] R. H. Tawney, *op. cit.,* p. 104.

amusement and ostentatious expenditure and even upon the arts, as lures to tempt men from holy living. Inevitably this emphasis upon frugal living and industrious habits brought its own very substantial rewards. It would be straining the evidence to contend that Elizabethan England which was the chief instrument in the downfall of Spain, or the England of the Restoration period which beat the Dutch, or the England of George III which brought Napoleon to his knees at Waterloo, were models either of puritanism or of economic liberty. But the puritan virtues were strongest among the middle-class merchants who provided the sinews of war.

As they had accepted the new methods of business, so these Protestant communities found no difficulty in accepting the new science based upon the Copernican theories. While the Inquisition put the work of Copernicus on the Index pending its correction and restatement as an hypothesis rather than an established fact, and Galileo felt it necessary to smuggle his manuscripts out of Italy for publication in Holland, the way was being cleared in England for Robert Boyle and Isaac Newton.

The struggle for trade became a struggle to exploit the incalculable opportunities of the newly discovered, expanding world. It was waged between the original discoverers—who by the middle of the sixteenth century had become subjected to a stiff political control and at times an exaggerated religious discipline—and outsiders who could exploit new and often unscrupulous methods of piracy and plunder, free from moral inhibitions and secure in the backing of their governments. No merchant at that time, however adventurous, could sustain alone the hazards of his enterprise. The very enlargement of the trading world made the ventures more costly.[7] Those who could count upon access to a developing credit system and liberal support from government in devising new trading structures were bound to win out.

[7] Cf. Henri Hauser, *Les origines historiques des problèmes économiques actuels,* Paris, 1935, p. 37: "Pour qu'un navire parti de Lisbonne atteigne Cochin ou Diu, pour qu'il ramène dans l'estuaire du Tage sa riche cargaison d'épices, près de deux ans, parfois plus de deux années s'écoulent. Il a donc fallu, d'avance, construire ou affreter les navires, les outiller et les armer, recruter et payer les équipages, acheter les marchandises d'exportation, en imputant ces dépenses immédiates sur le produit des ventes futures. Produit très aléatoires, puisqu'au retour comme à l'aller la flotte peut être à demi detruite par un typhon, s'écraser sur un récif, subir l'attaque d'une escadre turque, des pirates malais, des corsaires de France ou d'Angleterre. Il faut donc trouver les prêteurs et leur consentir un benefice qui represente à la fois l'interêt de leur argent et une prime d'assurance."

All trade was in some measure regulated. But it is necessary to keep a sense of historical perspective. The participation of the English and Dutch authorities in the ventures of their merchants should be compared with the tight control exercised by Spain after the accession of Philip II, rather than with the private enterprise which became possible only after England had won the supremacy of seapower. Stress should be laid upon the relative freedom enjoyed by enterprise in Holland and England—upon the remarkable growth of Dutch banking and the inventive genius which developed the great English trading companies—the discernment which concentrated upon trade, shipping and colonization as more profitable than gold-hunting or plunder, and the discipline and foresight which enabled Elizabeth, when continental Europe was in the throes of a great financial crisis, to carry through on the advice of Sir Thomas Gresham the profitable recoinage of 1560.[8]

PLUNDER AND PIRACY

The traders and soldiers of fortune who pillaged their way across the Spanish Main and the Indian Ocean were not in business for their health. Treasure was what they wanted and treasure they meant to get. The dream that drove them forward was built upon the legend of the wealth and splendor of the East. It was fed by travelers' tales and notably by Marco Polo. Who could resist the opening passage of his description of Japan? Certainly not Columbus, who became obsessed with it.

The Spain to which Columbus finally resorted, after having failed to finance his "enterprise of the Indies" in Portugal, was entering a period of consolidation. The marriage of Ferdinand and Isabella had united Castile and Aragon, to which Granada was soon added by a short war. Except for Portugal and Navarre, the Iberian peninsula was consolidated under one monarchy. Aragon had a thriving Mediterranean commerce and ruled over the Balearic Islands, Sardinia, and southern Italy. There was a good deal of shipbuilding and commerce also in the Biscayan ports of Castile. The Arabs had developed the

[8] *Ibid.*, p. 33: "La reine peut se féliciter d'avoir conduit la lutte jusqu'à la victoire sur ce hideux monstre de la baisse monnaie. En realité elle avait introduit dans le monde, pour un long avenir, une puissance nouvelle: la royauté de la sterling. Royauté qui demeurera incontestée jusqu'en 1914." The recoinage was a success, but there were further periods when the value of sterling was badly depreciated. Professor Hauser exaggerates when he attributes the credit for sterling stability to Elizabeth. This was, in fact, a development of the nineteenth century.

manufactures of such cities as Toledo, and many converted Moriscos were still active in trade.

Nevertheless it is somewhat remarkable that the expansion of Spain in the New World took the form of conquest rather than of trade. Leadership was in the hands of soldiers of fortune rather than merchant-captains. It was as if Spain—a land power—used ships as floating fortresses. This was an age of incessant maritime skirmishes, in which the Spanish ships, though heavily armed and well-nigh impregnable in a convoyed Armada, were ponderous and seldom a match for their more nimble adversaries in a running fight. Unlike the captains of Portugal, Holland, and England, the Spaniards did not develop naval power and a merchant marine on principles of naval strategy.

It was a curious accident that the Portuguese found their way first to the trade of the Indies, but that it was the Spanish explorers who found gold and silver in the Americas. There were hoards in the Orient, but trade with India and China continued to drain the precious metals from Europe as it had done since Roman times. This drain, which has sometimes been advanced as a cause of the Roman Empire's decline, had been troublesome during the period when the Venetians acted as middlemen with the Levant. It increased after the Portuguese rounded the Cape to India. Part of the trading expansion which took place in the sixteenth century was an attempt both to find outlets for exports and, in so doing, to stop this drain of specie in payment for Oriental spices, silks, and cottons.

Little success attended these efforts and the East remained even into the nineteenth century a "sink for the world's precious metals." Both the Dutch and the British East India Companies had constantly to defend themselves against critics who charged that their operations drained treasure from the country.[9] Europe, however, was hungry for specie. Attempts to conserve the scanty available supplies had long been common to most of the developing states of western Europe.

In the early sixteenth century, the need for specie was rendered more acute than ever by the developing international rivalry and by the expensive diplomacy, so well characterized by the lavish hospitality offered on both sides at the meeting between Henry VIII and Francis I at the Field of the Cloth of Gold near Calais in 1520, and by Charles V's

[9] The so-called Opium War between Britain and China in 1840 was precipitated by the attempt of the Chinese to prohibit the import of opium, which had been developed along the Asiatic coast from Persia, largely as a substitute for specie payments.

wholesale bribery of the Holy Roman electors in the preceding year.

Dynastic changes had brought this scion of the Hapsburgs (Charles V) into possession of the greatest European territory since Charlemagne's empire. Thus sixteenth-century Spain became the leading territorial power in Europe. Charles V controlled not only a united Spain with Sardinia, Sicily, and Naples, but also Burgundy with the Netherlands, and extensive areas in central Europe which were later to form the nucleus of the Austro-Hungarian Empire. The discoveries of Columbus added to these great possessions a New World, and the conquistadores poured in from that New World a flood of gold and silver beyond precedent. When Philip II took over from his father Charles V in 1556, he inherited an unparalleled domain. The Holy Roman Empire and the Austrian possessions he did not get, but in 1580 he made good his claim to Portugal and its vast empire.

Meantime the treasure poured in. First came the gold of Hispaniola. Then Cortes plundered Mexico after his decisive conquest in 1521. In 1532 Pizarro captured Atahualpa, the leader of the Incas of Peru. The Inca's offer to buy his release by covering the floor of a room with gold was received incredulously, whereupon he said that "he would not merely cover the floor, but would fill the room with gold as high as he could reach"—a room about seventeen feet broad, by twenty-two feet long, to a height of nine feet, and in like manner an adjoining room of smaller dimensions twice full with silver. In his *History of the Conquest of Peru,* William H. Prescott describes the amazement of the Spaniards as the promise was redeemed with "goblets, ewers, salvers, vases of every shape and size, ornaments and utensils for the temples and royal palaces, tiles and plates for the decoration of public edifices, curious imitations of different plants and animals. Among the plants, the most beautiful was the Indian corn, in which the golden ear was sheathed in its broad leaves of silver, from which hung a rich tassel of threads of the same precious metal. A fountain was also much admired, which sent up a sparkling jet of gold, while birds and animals of the same material played in the waters at its base."

All of these works of art, save a few kept for royal inspection, were melted down into bars. The gold alone, according to Prescott, was worth the equivalent of fifteen and a half million dollars, equal to more than twenty-six million dollars today—with the silver, the greatest ransom ever paid by a prisoner, and unhappily without securing his promised release.

It was the mines, particularly the great silver mines of Potosi, Zacatecas and Guanajuato—and the mercury of Huancavelica which aided in their exploitation—that poured such a flood of treasure into Spain. This development between 1545 and 1558 was primarily the work of private enterprise, working under government protection and supervision.

The great question of economic policy for Spain in the sixteenth century was how to convoy this immense treasure home and how to keep it there. For the rest of the trading countries, the problem was how to filch it from Spain en route, or failing success in such hijacking ventures, how to trade so as to get as much of it as possible away from Spain. Even during the uneasy periods of peace, privateers were constantly at work. Sir Francis Drake took the Spaniards by surprise when in 1577 he attacked their ports and convoys on the west coast of South America in the course of his voyage around the world, and many other such instances of piracy might be cited, until Sir Henry Morgan destroyed Panama in 1670.

It is difficult to resist comparing the unhappy Philip II of Spain with Midas. Convinced that he must be unswerving in pursuance of his duties, he regarded his great possessions and the treasure which was acquired from them as instruments to use in bending his own and other peoples to the rule of an orthodoxy used to further his absolutist aims. He set up a highly centralized bureaucracy to enforce his absolute personal rule and to keep his people in the path of religious orthodoxy. It was not an easy task, and, despite the acquisition of Portugal, his persistence in it led to disaster after disaster.

Within his own kingdom the accumulation of treasure led to a great inflation. Prices rose by about 50 per cent in the first quarter of the sixteenth century, had more than doubled by the middle of the century, and had more than quadrupled at its close. The effects at first were buoyant, but the nemesis was sure.

To the sixteenth-century world, however, the idea of the most powerful state being weakened by an excess of the "sinews of war" would have seemed a paradox. The explanation of the paradox is to be found in the means used to gather and hoard this excess of treasure. At every stage the utmost care was taken to avoid any leakage. Thus minute regulations prevented intercolonial exchanges which might have led to development of fertile regions such as Argentina. The persistent effort to encourage sheep-raising in Spain itself, so as to lessen the need for imports of wool from England, resulted in overstocking and led to erosion of the soil. In the Spanish colonies the concentration on mining, and even the attempts of missionaries to safeguard the welfare of the Indians, hindered true colonization. Both at home and in the colonies in addition to high prices a multitude of harassing regulations and heavy taxation, made necessary by an expensive bureaucratic administration and a still more expensive foreign policy, crippled domestic industry and agriculture.

Other powers naturally resented the exclusiveness of Spanish policy. As early as 1562 William Cecil, Elizabeth's Clerk of the Privy Council, challenged the dominion of Spain over the newly discovered territories and made it plain that England would trade and colonize as its captains thought fit and found opportunity. Philip returned a stiff answer and soon afterward began to prepare the Grand Armada which, in 1588, set out to crush such upstart pretensions. In the preceding years of developing tension a real crusade developed in England—a compound of cupidity, national fear, indignation at the Inquisition, and religious fervor, all combined in fierce hatred of the "Spanish lyms of Antichrist" and a determination to plunder and destroy them.

The French corsairs did their share in attacking the Spanish fleets, though the Wars of Religion (1562–98) rent France and for a time destroyed the power of the middle-class Huguenot merchants. But it was Spain's attempt to dragoon the Flemish manufacturers, traders, and financiers, and later to destroy the Dutch cities to which these stiff-necked and heretical capitalists had retreated that did most to sap Spanish power. There was a double incentive for Spain to attempt the repression of these heretical traders. Not only were they obdurate in their religious beliefs but their persistence in trading was a prime cause of the leakage of treasure. By every means Spain tried to stop up the leaks and to reduce the Low Countries to the subservience of regulated production and trade that was easier to enforce in Spain. Protests broke into revolt, briefly in 1539, but determinedly in 1565. The revolt was led by William the Silent and, after draining Spanish energies for more than a generation, it ended in Spain losing the most productive area of the great Hapsburg Empire.

The sixteenth and seventeenth centuries were therefore an age when vigorous groups of enterprising capitalists were struggling to exploit the opportunities of an expanding world and doing so in a climate of practically continuous warfare. The strengthening of the nation-state and the enrichment of ruling groups—power and plenty—were the chief ends of policy and no conflict was discerned between them. Specie was a visible and potent symbol of both, the importance of which was exaggerated by a false analogy between personal and national finance. It was only gradually that clear notions as to the true functions of a monetary system emerged from a voluminous controversial literature arising for the most part in connection with specific policy measures.

TREASURE BY TRADE

There is an old debating trick of collecting scattered statements made at intervals by one's opponents and running them together as a means of ridicule. Adam Smith used a variant of this trick when he attacked the top-heavy bureaucracy and the monopolistic devices of his day by lumping them with the outworn fallacies of early writers into something he called "the mercantile system." [10]

Subsequent discussion has fallen into the habit of grouping into the mercantilist school a wide variety of writers over a somewhat indefinite period of time, usually in the sixteenth, seventeenth, and eighteenth centuries, but sometimes extending back into the later Middle Ages. The school and the system it was supposed to propagate appear, however, to be convenient fictions created by Adam Smith and his followers in an attempt to forward their own views by attacking their opposites.

Economic writing in the Middle Ages had been concerned largely with ethical questions. In the sixteenth and seventeenth centuries and well on into the eighteenth century, it was almost wholly political. There was a voluminous pamphleteering literature advocating different and often conflicting policies and incidentally offering analyses and explanations of economic development as justification for them. There was much preoccupation with foreign trade and particularly with the balance of trade. This was natural in the midst of a great struggle to gain access to the wealth of the newly enlarged world.

[10] The phrase "mercantile system" appears to have been first used by a French physiocrat in 1763. Cf. A. V. Judges, "The Idea of a Mercantile State," *Transactions of the Royal Historical Society*, London, 1939, p. 44. The view taken in the text that Adam Smith was responsible for the belief that mercantilism was "a definite, unified body of doctrine," was the considered opinion of Alfred Marshall. Cf. his *Industry and Trade*, London, 1919, App. D., especially pp. 718–19.

But in practical policy, even more than in the literature, domestic questions loomed large. The mercantilists were not concerned solely with manipulating foreign markets so as to gain an import of precious metals. They knew that the ability to export depended upon low costs of production, and they were much concerned with employment. Crude as were many of their theories, they did not dissociate the problems of foreign trade from their domestic background. Indeed the regulation of foreign trade was largely influenced by the necessity to increase the revenues of central governments.

There was a persistent tendency in the economic writings of the sixteenth, seventeenth, and eighteenth centuries (but by no means confined to those centuries) to overstress the organization of economic resources for the strengthening of state power. This was natural in the circumstances of the time. The medieval organization of economic life had broken down. The precepts which had governed economic activity were outworn. Gild ordinances and church law were no longer effective. Men were groping to explain the happenings that had followed the expansion of trading opportunities and the social upheaval consequent upon a prolonged and vast inflation of the price structure. Old trades were languishing while new merchant adventurers made unheard-of profits. The demands of the new industries displaced agricultural workers. Landowners in order to produce wool for the developing textile industries enclosed common and tenant lands and converted them to pasture. As early as 1515 an act had been passed in England to avoid the pulling down of towns. Sir Thomas More had written in his *Utopia* that "your sheep, formerly so gentle and tranquil, and such small eaters, now display a savage gluttony: they devour men themselves. They destroy, consume and swallow up fields, houses and towns." By the end of Elizabeth's reign, it had been necessary to carry through what amounted virtually to a "New Deal"—the recoinage of 1560 after a long period of debasement; the Statute of Artificers of 1563 which was intended to replace the gild regulations that had broken down in respect to wages, apprenticeship, and labor conditions; and the Poor Law system which was codified in 1601, so that the unemployed were set to work, the idle punished, children apprenticed, and the impotent and old cared for in workhouses.

The state had been forced to take over the regulation of the domestic economy. The medieval system was gone and the liberal faith in a self-regulating competitive economy had yet to be born. One of the characteristics of this whole period was acceptance, in regard to the domestic economy as well as in matters of foreign trade, of the right and the duty of the state to regulate private initiative so that it might serve the common good.

Such acceptance is always readier in time of war, and war was a chronic condition in the days of the mercantilists. Foreign trade and shipping were of crucial importance to the state. National power which at any moment might have to fight for its life, depended in this maritime age largely upon ships and ships' stores. Trade was regulated as an instrument of policy to gain national advantages and to inflict damage upon the enemy or potential enemy. The advantages to be gained were not only the import of treasure, but revenue for the state, outlets for manufactures, access to raw material supplies, and freight to employ the ships which in turn provided a nursery of seamen.

Policies designed to direct trading enterprise into channels that would maximize the power of the state emerged only as the result of long experiment. Discussion concerning them carried over the inadequate understanding and misconceptions of a simpler age. There seems little doubt that many of the mercantilists confounded the ideas of wealth and treasure, but this confusion should not be regarded as one of the central propositions of mercantilism. The confusion was prominent in the literature because it made an effective appeal to uninformed public opinion. Trade restrictions were represented as necessary to prevent treasure from being drained out of the country. But many writers were aware that national wealth was not identical with the precious metals and were careful to repudiate such identification.

The central propositions of mercantilism may be summarized as the regulation of domestic production and external trade in such a way as to build up national wealth and power, and to safeguard the possession of particularly important elements of power. As always there was some confusion between these objectives and particular policies which were defended as aimed at achieving them. Such policies often served the interest of selfish groups. Many of them were wrong, even if their objectives were right. They came to serve as a cover for privilege, inefficiency, and graft. Adam Smith had no difficulty in documenting his attack upon them. It is now generally agreed that economic writers identified wealth and power and saw no conflict between them as ends of policy. It is one of Adam Smith's distinctions that he saw clearly that the pursuit of power and the pursuit of wealth might conflict. Nationalists in all ages have believed that wealth breeds power and power breeds wealth. The sacrifices of personal convenience and wealth imposed by restrictions and regulations designed to increase the power of the state are commonly justified as leading eventually to greater wealth for the national community.

The mercantilist writers, however, were concerned both with private and with national wealth. While they sought wealth for themselves, they were also interested in the kind of wealth which increased the ability of the country to wage war. Labor to most of them was a resource. Expenditure for consumption (except by the ruling classes), especially of luxury goods and more especially of imported luxuries, was a weakening of the national power. Hence the desire for abundant population, low wages, industrious and docile habits of industry. The planners of war—and many pacific industrialists—have desired these things in all ages. *The Book of Lord Shang,* a classic of the Chinese School of Law, written between 359 and 338 B.C., puts this desire succinctly in the statement that "A weak people means a strong state and a strong state means a weak people."

The mercantilists were concerned not only with the total wealth and power of the state relative to its rivals. They were particularly anxious about certain specific elements of power. Their discussions often foreshadow the kind of analyses now made by students of political geography in calculating the military potential of a state. Three elements of power in particular were anxiously discussed—ships and ships' stores; population and particularly skilled artisans (including trained seamen); and above all, treasure. Treasure was needed for a variety of purposes—the securing of arms, munitions and naval supplies, the hiring of soldiers and sailors, the conduct of espionage, the bribery of enemy officials, and the subsidizing of potential allies, as well as a medium of circulation to facilitate production and employment.

The characteristic feature of economic policy in this period of state-building and state rivalries, therefore, was the acceptance of centralized authority in directing external trade as well as domestic production. While this often led to graft and to misdirected economic ventures, it was usually justified as being necessary for the achievement of national purposes, especially the mobilization of power. When ships were essential to gain access to the New World and to carry the exports which might purchase the desired new imports, as well as to wage war, it was regarded as desirable to foster shipbuilding and to encourage the fisheries. When supplies of tar, pitch, cordage, sail-cloth, or spars were liable to be interrupted by a hostile power, it was desirable to try out the possibilities of alternative and more reliable sources of supply by settling colonies in promising areas. It is not possible to justify mercantilism as an economic system, but in a period of economic warfare, some aspects of mercantilist policy could be justified. Pushed to extremes, as in Spain, mercantilism defeated its own purposes.

It must be admitted that national interests were easily identified, as in England, with the interests of a limited merchant class able to focus its arguments effectively even when in a political minority. In the first flush of adventure, these "new men" had broken through the traditional practices and the exclusive monopolies of town gilds that had outworn their usefulness. The great company of the Merchant Adventurers of London, for example, has been lauded by the historians of empire. The company did undoubtedly pioneer in new markets and make good use of the monopolistic privileges with which it was endowed by the state. At a very early stage there were murmurings against its exclusiveness. There were the same protests against other and later companies, culminating in the successful resistance of the American colonists to the attempts of the East India Company to exploit its tea monopoly.

Nevertheless, during this period England built up her commercial supremacy and, in a long series of wars first against the Spaniards, then against the Dutch, and finally against the French and their continental allies, she emerged as the undisputed mistress of the seas with the greatest empire of modern times, despite the loss of her first colonies. Two explanations are possible. The first is that despite the abuses of monopoly against which Adam Smith inveighed, and despite the diversion of trading profits from the enrichment of the common people, mercantilist policy built up the strength and power of the state so that the state was able, after final victory, to expand its commerce and relax restrictions upon it. This is the view advanced by many German historians in justification of recent German policy. In this view economic liberty is a luxury, possible only to the strong and secure. The discipline of state regulation is indispensable to the achievement of national power.

Though less dramatic, the alternative explanation seems to carry more conviction. It is that English economic life was much less regulated than that of its rivals. No one can read through the detailed description of internal tolls and bureaucratic regulations contained in Professor Eli F. Heckscher's survey of mercantilism without realizing how fortunate English producers and traders were in these respects as compared with their competitors.[11] From the advent of the Tudors onward England had enjoyed a long period of domestic peace, broken only by the brief Civil War in the middle of the seventeenth century. Her soil had been free from foreign invasion since the Norman Conquest. Capital accumulated, agriculture was improved, and science was cultivated.[12]

The Elizabethan code of domestic regulation, entrusted to the justices of the peace, became steadily less effective. The courts interpreted Magna Carta as a constitutional basis for the progressive enlargement of personal rights and liberties so that the privileges of feudal barons became the basis for the rights of merchants. The common law doctrine was developed that monopolies in restraint of trade were illegal. Partly by reason of lax administration and neglect, partly by disregard for laboring interests, state control of domestic economic activity which had never been as strict as in France, lapsed into ineffectiveness. The freedom thus afforded to enterprise built up the productive powers of British industry. The engineering and metallurgical knowledge which the German scholar, Georgius Agricola, had summarized in his volume, *De Re Metallica* (1556), found application in the drainage of the English fen country and in the early experiments of ironmasters like the Dudleys. As early as 1612 a German, Simon Sturtevant, obtained from James I a patent to smelt iron with coal. The Earl of Dudley and his natural son experimented along these lines from 1619 on, after Sturtevant's patent had lapsed. The Civil War (1640–49) interrupted such industrial experiments; but in 1709 the Quaker, Abraham Darby, developed a successful process of smelting with coke. In this most important of all the processes of the eighteenth century that gave Britain leadership in the Industrial Revolution Englishmen used foreign inventions. The Dudleys worked

[11] Eli F. Heckscher, *Mercantilism,* London, 1935, Vol. I, pp. 56–109.

[12] Cf. the *Diary of Samuel Pepys,* January 9, 1664: "I saw the Royal Society bring their new book, wherein is nobly writ their charter and laws, and comes to be signed by the Duke as a Fellow; and all the Fellows are to be entered there, and lie as a monument; and the King hath put his, with the word Founder."

on German discoveries, and a long line of other experimenters tried out other methods before Darby used his observations of Dutch smelting to achieve his great advance. It was the freedom of British enterprise that enabled such men to experiment successfully. The relative absence of mercantilist restrictions in Britain gave them the opportunity to pioneer new industrial processes.

Two comments, however, may be appended to this conclusion. The first is that to which even Adam Smith, in many ways the most destructive critic of mercantilist ideas, lent his support in the oft-quoted dictum—"defense, however, is of much more importance than opulence . . ." National security could not be neglected in this period when nation-states fought each other at short intervals and privateers carried on the fight even in the brief interludes of peace. In our own time we may have to pay more attention to the accumulation of strategic materials and to the fostering of strategic industries.

The second note is more controversial, but as important as the first in the light of economic policy at the present time. The preoccupation of mercantilist writers with the necessity of securing an excess of exports over imports so that treasure might be imported, was for long regarded as a rather crude fallacy based upon the identification of money with wealth. Some modern economists, more conscious of the subtle relationships between production, employment, and the monetary system, have been inclined to credit the mercantilists not indeed with a theoretical understanding of these relationships, but with an empirical knowledge of their importance.

Generalized into a restrictive system of protection to local producing, trading, and shipping interests, mercantilism broke down. Where it was pursued most logically and thoroughly, as in Spain, it weakened rather than strengthened the power of the state. There were writers in England who on moral as well as economic grounds advocated freedom of trade, even when protectionist policies were at their most popular acceptance.

The recently attempted rehabilitation of the ideas of the mercantilists in respect to their insistence upon a favorable balance of payments extends only to recognition of their awareness of a problem, which is often important in the practical short run, but which was ignored by the later economists of the classical school. Gradually in the course of the eighteenth century a clearer understanding of the relations between national price levels, the circulating medium, and the balance of trade resulted in formulation of the price specie-flow theory which explained the balancing of international payments and the distribution of the world's precious metals. But this theory, especially in its first sharp formulation by the classical economists, was a theory of long-run equilibrium, not greatly concerned with the problems that arise in short-run departures from the theoretical equilibrium. The classical economists came to believe that competition would bring automatic correctives to any departures from equilibrium. The mercantilist writers had no such faith. Their constant concern with securing a favorable balance of trade, though based on inadequate analysis and pursued by methods that led to restrictive policies, is thus justified by some modern economists as arising from a practical realization that employment was affected by the adequacy or inadequacy of monetary media. This is not a convincing justification, even though Lord Keynes lent his authority to it. The mercantilists did not have a cyclical policy. Theirs was a policy of protection equally applicable to booms and to slumps.

It should be noted that this justification extends only to the awareness by the mercantilists of a practical short-run problem. Indeed it is a criticism of later economists for neglecting this problem rather than a justification of mercantilist theory. It does not defend the faulty analysis of the mercantilists. Still less does it justify the restrictive practices of mercantilism, even in a simpler age than our own. In our day more sophisticated devices of credit regulation are available to achieve the objectives which mercantilists tried to achieve by crude regulation of the balance of trade. The emphasis now is on domestic employment and the necessity of safeguarding it from unnecessary constriction as a result of temporary pressures on the credit system resulting from fluctuations in the balance of external payments. It is not upon measures designed to restrict international trade.

COLONIES AND PLANTATIONS

Even more important in the long run than the discovery of gold and silver, or the development of new trading opportunities, was the occupation and settlement of the newly discovered lands. Spanish settlements had been established in many places; but none were as successful in the long run as the experiments that led finally to colonization by the English along the eastern coast of North America, behind which lay the richest agricultural and industrial area in the world. High as were the hopes of the first colonial enthusiasts, neither Sir Humphrey Gilbert in Newfoundland, nor Sir Walter Raleigh in Virginia, nor even the Pilgrim Fathers, foresaw the riches that lay beyond the coastal ranges. Indeed, the French from the north and the Spanish from the south first began to explore the great river systems of the interior. But the lodgment of English settlers on the eastern coast in the course of the seventeenth century made it inevitable that they should eventually control the hinterland.

There is an obvious distinction to be drawn between exploitation of the trade in spices, silks, and cottons, and permanent colonization. The first led to empire—the rule of dominant over subject peoples. Colonization led to the creation of new societies which eventually achieved independence either by breaking from the metropolitan country or by contractual association with it.[13] There are, of course, many variant developments between the two extremes of a subject people ruled by what is essentially a garrison, as in India until 1947, and the independent growth of the United States after the original colonies repudiated British rule. However, the broad distinction is clear.

When the Portuguese in the early sixteenth century established themselves in the Spice Islands (the Moluccas), so that they might have a permanent base for their trading ventures, they naturally fortified their headquarters for defense not only against the native peoples, but against marauders and pirates. The Indian Ocean was notorious for piracy by Arabs, Indians, and Malays. Moreover the French, Dutch, or British might appear from time to time. As on the African coast, by way of which they had come, way stations were built as fortified bases. Goa, Macao, and Timor survive as isolated parts of this empire. Until 1577 the Portuguese spice trade was a state monopoly, and three years later all the Portuguese possessions passed into Spanish control.

Portuguese independence from Spain was regained in 1640, but in

[13] Words change their meaning. The statement in the text follows the original meaning derived from the Roman practice of establishing permanent settlers in a newly conquered country. These settlers were *coloni*—tillers, farmers, cultivators, planters. In the sixteenth and seventeenth centuries, a *colony* was understood as a settlement in a new country, forming a community subject to, or connected with, the parent state.

The use of the words *colony* and *colonial* to signify dependent territories and peoples is more recent, and distinguishes such peoples from the self-governing, but associated, Dominions of the British Commonwealth. In the seventeenth century, the dependent territories would have been called simply possessions.

the meantime the English, Dutch, and French had made inroads both on the spice trade and on Portuguese possessions. These inroads became greater as Portugal struggled with Spain to preserve its regained independence and was exhausted in the process. Portuguese possessions in India and Indonesia were lost almost completely. Brazil was retained, though mainly by the efforts of the Brazilians themselves in fighting off the Dutch. The transatlantic slave trade had been begun by the Portuguese, and by the Assiento of 1600 they had secured a privileged position in supplying slaves to the Spanish colonies, but this too passed mainly into the hands of the British. However, toward the end of the seventeenth century the discovery of gold and diamonds in Brazil made that colony a very profitable possession. The Portuguese also retained some of their possessions on both African coasts.

Spain ruled over a large part of Central and South America from the sixteenth to the early nineteenth century and over the Philippines for nearly a century longer. The Spanish empire extended from the West Indies to the River Plate and from California to Chile. As Spanish names and the use of the Spanish tongue over this whole vast territory bear witness, there was some measure of genuine colonization. Missions were actively organized, exploration pushed up the inland rivers through semi-deserts and across the Andes. European plants and animals were introduced and there was some large-scale agriculture. But mining, particularly of the precious metals, was the main business of the Spanish rulers and settlers, and the history of Spanish-America before the colonies achieved independence bears witness to the truth of Raleigh's dictum: "Where there is store of gold, it is in effect nedeles to remember other commodities for trade."

Though the search for treasure caused neglect of some of the most fertile regions of the New World, notably the valley of the River Plate, the Spanish colonial period, especially in Mexico and Peru, achieved for the ruling Spaniards a considerable degree of economic prosperity and artistic creation. Vigorous leaders like Cortes were alive to the true values of colonization. But their efforts were largely vitiated by the use of the Indians as virtual slave labor. Agriculture was extended, manufactures were introduced, and the building of churches and palaces reached extraordinary proportions, but the Spaniards remained a ruling caste.

In the Philippines there was much the same story. In the period of Manila's splendor in the late sixteenth and early seventeenth centuries, the profits of the trade carried by the Acapulco galleon were sufficient to maintain an easy and luxurious existence for the Spanish colony. Intermediaries between the rich manufactures of the Mogul Empire and China on the one hand and the ever-flowing stream of Mexican silver on the other, they made little effort to develop the resources of the islands themselves. By the end of the seventeenth century, harassed by the restrictions of the Spanish colonial system, with the Mexican silver dwindling and Spain itself falling into economic decay, the outlying garrisons were withdrawn and the colony became moribund.

The extraordinary precautions taken by the Portuguese to preserve the secrecy of their spice monopoly kept their rivals, the Dutch and the English, from entering the Orient effectively until toward the end of the sixteenth century, and the French until much later. But in the seventeenth century as part of their conflict with Spain, the Dutch, sometimes in conjunction with the English and sometimes in competition with them, rapidly built up a great empire, the heart of which was the spice trade. Portugal had been exhausted by the struggle to maintain its newly won independence and had lost command of the eastern seas. The Dutch were then the greatest sea power in Europe. In the summer of 1667 Samuel Pepys's diary is studded with references to their defiant raid up the Thames in early June. In this period they established themselves in Java, Sumatra, Formosa, and the Spice Islands, and gradually secured territorial possession of the whole of Indonesia. They also gained footholds in India. But after William of Orange came to the English throne in 1688, there was a broad division of influence, the Dutch withdrawing from India, though not from Formosa, and the British withdrawing from the East Indies, though subsequently they took Singapore and parts of Borneo. From 1638 to 1854 the Dutch were the only Europeans permitted to trade with Japan. The only considerable permanent settlement of the Dutch was at the Cape of Good Hope and this the British took in the Napoleonic Wars also. At one time the Dutch almost secured Brazil and they did get footholds which they still retain both on the mainland of South America (Guiana) and in the West Indies (at Cuba and Curacao). On the mainland of North America they established their New Netherlands colony with its capital at New Amsterdam (New York), but lost the colony to the British in 1664, regained it briefly in 1673, and lost it finally in 1674.

As for France, Jacques Cartier had explored the St. Lawrence in 1534–35. In the sixteenth century French privateers preyed on the early Spanish and Portuguese trade and French fishermen were among the pioneers of the Newfoundland fishing banks. After Champlain founded Quebec in 1608, New France began slowly to develop along the coast of Acadia and the banks of the St. Lawrence. A flourishing trade developed, particularly in furs, but the French colonies never developed as fast as the British colonies further south. New France was laid out in great seignorial estates. The royal governors ruled autocratically. By 1756 when the conflict between Britain and France flared into the Seven Years' War there were about two million inhabitants of the English colonies but only sixty thousand French settlers in Canada. The French, however, had pushed their explorations (and left their names) west into the Great Lakes area and south down the Mississippi valley to link with Louisiana which had been colonized in 1699. Colbert (1619–83), the great French minister whose name became synonymous with mercantilism, had vigorously supported this colonial expansion, partly as a means of encircling the British colonies, partly to secure raw materials, but mainly to secure a base on the Spanish colonial frontiers.

The footholds which France (like Holland and England) had secured in the West Indies—Martinique, Guadeloupe, what is now Haiti, and smaller islands—were useful points of attack on the Spanish trade. But from about 1640 onward, sugar and rum produced by slave labor made them even more profitable. So highly were they regarded that in the settlement of the Seven Years' War it was strongly urged by many in England that Guadeloupe rather than Canada should be retained, a proposal that was defeated only by the exertions of those who had a vested interest in the British West Indian islands and feared for their monopoly. One reason urged for giving Canada back to the French was that a foreign community there would keep the New Englanders from becoming too independent!

In the East also, France established powerful trading posts and way stations to them at Madagascar and Réunion. It was not till Colbert established an East India Company in 1664 that they made a really serious bid for the oriental trade, and it was not till the middle of the eighteenth century that Joseph François Dupleix, French agent in India, by hiring native Indian troops and playing politics within the Indian states, threatened to oust British interests there until he met his match in Robert Clive.

These developments—of trading posts rather than colonies—are recalled thus summarily as a reminder of the setting for the wars of the seventeenth and eighteenth centuries, and for the revolt of the American colonists against the old colonial system. They serve also to emphasize the fact that the English alone in this period managed to establish real colonies of settlement on a grand scale. It is one of the ironies of history that the only considerable settlements of French and Dutch colonists overseas—in Canada and South Africa—now form parts of the British Commonwealth. In both cases their population growth has been due to cumulative natural increase rather than sustained immigration, and in both most of the increase has developed since they came under British rule.

The English too played the game of plunder and piracy on the Spanish Main, down the African coast, and across the Indian Ocean. They established fortified trading posts and picked up strategic bases —from the Portuguese, including Bombay which came in 1662 as a dowry with Charles II's queen; from the Spaniards, mainly in the West Indies; from the Dutch, including the Cape of Good Hope and New York; and from the French, including Canada and most of the French stations in India. By the end of the eighteenth century their empire of trade was the greatest in the world, with its defense resting upon control of strategic bases such as Gibraltar, Malta and Egypt, the Cape Colony, Aden at the entrance to the Red Sea, Ceylon, and India.

The primary objective of British maritime expansion in the Middle and Far East was trade. Territorial possession became inevitable when the Asiatic empires crumbled under the impact of trading penetration backed by superior armaments, but this acquisition of territory was largely an unsought and unwelcome extension of responsibilities. India provides a good illustration. In retrospect it is clear enough that the rivalry of French and British agents was bound to destroy the independence of the several empires governing that subcontinent. When Dupleix began in the middle of the eighteenth century to hire Indian soldiers and to intrigue among the Indian states, the British retaliated effectively. When he was recalled in 1754, the field was left open to the British who found themselves in the anomalous position of exercising rule over vast populations by the agency of a commercial concern—a form of government which Adam Smith condemned unsparingly. Illustrating his argument by reference to the destructive practices of the Dutch in Indonesia as well as the British in India who "have not yet had time to establish in Bengal so perfectly destructive a system," but whose plan of government "has had exactly the same tendency," he concluded that "such exclusive companies are nuisances, therefore, in every respect; always more or less inconvenient to the countries in which they are established, and destructive to those which have the misfortune to fall under their government." [14] His arguments were vigorously attacked, for example, by William Julius Mickle in introducing his translation of Luis de Camoëns' *The Lusiad*. Mickle defended the British and Dutch East India Companies. He showed that the Portuguese trade, which Adam Smith had mentioned as demonstrating that commercial monopoly was unnecessary, was a state monopoly with even worse consequences. But the future lay with Adam Smith's arguments for the separation of government from commerce. The inconvenience at home and the destruction in India grew. In 1784 the British East India Company was subjected to control by the India Office, and a royal board of control was established in London, but it was not till 1858, after the Mutiny, that the British government superseded the Company.

Important as was this imperial expansion, it was less important for the future of international trade than the steady growth of settlement in the North American colonies. These were, especially at first, organized settlements promoted for reasons of state as well as the hope of

[14] Cf. *Wealth of Nations,* Bk. IV, Ch. VII. Lord Macaulay's *Essay on Warren Hastings,* written in 1841, is a brilliant example of a political tract. Recounting a historical episode, not in an effort to weigh the evidence impartially, but in order to emphasize the facts which supported the author's political philosophy, it should be regarded as documentation for the electoral campaigns of the mid-nineteenth century, rather than history of the late eighteenth century. When the British beat the French in exploiting the break-up of the Mogul Empire, there was undoubtedly much plunder, and for his share in this plunder Warren Hastings was tried by his peers. But the amounts involved were small, as compared with the trading profits of the East India Company or with the plunder garnered by the Spanish rulers in the Americas.

Professor Viner has called my attention to the criticism of Adam Smith contained in William Julius Mickle's translation of *The Lusiad* (3d ed.), London, 1798, Introduction, pp. ccxxiii–ccxlvi. It has been suggested, for example, by Robert Southey in the *Quarterly Review,* Vol. 27 (1822), pp. 29–30, that Mickle's attack on Adam Smith was prompted by a hope of reward or patronage from the East India Company. Cf. Sister M. Eustace Taylor, *William Julius Mickle: A Critical Study,* Washington, D.C., 1937.

profit. Some of them were expensive ventures, criticized because they drained capital from the motherland. At a somewhat later stage the loss to England of population, especially of trained artisans, was deplored. There was an effort to limit emigration to paupers, criminals, and unemployed.

Besides this controlled development, however, there was a steadily increasing number of immigrants who came to the American Colonies as a result of religious persecution, social conflict, and economic oppression, or merely in search of land to cultivate. Those who came in an ever-increasing stream of migration to search for livelihood and to make their homes in the New World included many who were independent of government assistance. Many of the indentured laborers found opportunity in the New World also. Long before the Revolution there was a frontier community of aggressive individuals, by no means wholly of British extraction, to whom their own economic welfare was more real and more important than the perpetual wars or the economic advantage of the ruling power.

Colonial policy, in the strict sense of the word, was based upon the ideas of nationalism then current. A mixture of motives operated. The desirability of securing assured access to strategic raw materials loomed large. New outlets for manufactured goods and enlargement of the carrying trade were important also. In the first stage of colonization the acquisition of strategic bases and bases for further exploration could not be ignored, and there was always the possibility of discovering treasure. In many a case the missionary motive cast an aura of divine sanction over commercial enterprise. In considering any or all of these matters, or in debating whether the loss of manpower at home was recompensed by greater productivity in the colonies, there was no illusion in the minds of those responsible for policy. The colonies were planted in order to enrich the mother country. It would be absurd if their development were allowed to trench upon established interests at home.

The restrictions of the British colonial system were in fact much less onerous than those imposed by other powers on their colonies. The very fact that immigration of political and religious dissenters had been tolerated is significant of this greater freedom. Immigrants had come in also from many other European countries to lay the foundation of the very mixed population of the United States today.

It was the emergence of the spirit of enterprise and independence among these colonists which burst the shackles not only of the old colonial system but of the whole mercantilist system.

The settlement of the New World by people who were not content to remain under monopolistic regulation was therefore an essential element both in the freeing of trade and in the evolution of economic doctrine. The trade between England and her colonies came to be the most important kind of trade, not only quantitatively, but also because it was forming the pattern of future world trade. The controversies to which it gave rise were of more importance than those which attacked or defended the East India trade for causing a drain of specie. It would therefore be unrealistic to attempt an understanding either of commercial policy or of the development of economic doctrine in the latter part of the eighteenth century, without placing colonial policy in the center of discussion.

CHAPTER IV

THE INSTRUMENTS OF ECONOMIC NATIONALISM

THE FASHIONING OF TARIFF PROTECTION

THE SEVENTEENTH and eighteenth centuries witnessed a great development of protection and of bureaucracy in the strictest sense of that word. To find the fullest expression of detailed regulation, one must go to the France of Jean Baptiste Colbert (1619–83). Colbert built upon a revived and reorganized gild system an apparatus of central inspection and enforcement and a series of experiments in state-operated and state-licensed monopolies. It is true that like all of his mercantilist contemporaries he attached as great importance to external as to domestic trade and made eloquent statements advocating "liberty of trade." This did not mean what was then regarded as the anarchy of individual liberty, but rather an active trade conducted within the framework of centralized regulation, freed from the ancient restrictions of local tolls and regulations. Colbertism was an attempt at detailed regulation of the national economy. Its enforcement at times was ruthless. In the eighteenth century, France had become the leading industrial country of Europe, producing about twice as much iron as England and more cotton goods. The minute regulations to which its producers were subjected were often evaded, while its positive experiments were by no means an unqualified success. They did, however, go a long way toward freezing the pattern not only of social classes and of regional location but of manufacturing methods, while in Britain the new manufacturers were escaping from the remnants of the Elizabethan domestic regulation which was enforced only spasmodically by local justices.

By 1776 when Adam Smith gathered up and systematized contemporary criticism of regulative practices, the internal economic structure of England was beginning to take on the characteristics of modern industrial capitalism. The first stages of the Industrial Revolution were well under way. The new differentiation of social classes was far advanced. The manufacturers were beginning to draw upon the pool of pauperized labor for their factories in the industrial north. Joint-stock financing had passed through its first experimental period. Craft organization had broken down and the regrouping of social classes was preparing the way for trade-union organization. The currency was on a firm basis and the institutions of credit were developing fast. The stage was thus being set for the emergence of industrial capitalists whose pressure to export finally swept away the restrictions on external as well as internal trade.

This chapter is devoted to a review of the major instruments of economic nationalism as they developed during the seventeenth and eighteenth centuries. It is, of course, impossible to separate the external from the domestic aspects of policy in any realistic way. Control of external transactions has always—in our own day as throughout history—involved interference with the domestic organization. The converse is equally true. Domestic regulation is bound to involve control of the external balance of payments.

In the period we are now considering, the balance of trade was the central preoccupation of those responsible for public policy. The maxim of Thomas Mun published in 1664 was generally accepted: "The ordinary means therefore to increase our wealth and treasure is by foreign trade, wherein we must ever observe this rule; to sell more to strangers yearly than we consume of theirs in value." Mun himself was an official of the East India Company, concerned to defend the India trade from the charge that it resulted in a direct drain of specie. His arguments, taking account of invisible imports and exports and also of triangular trade, were directed toward proving that the outlay of specie in the East Indian trade was the means, in the long run, of securing a more favorable balance than might otherwise have been possible.

It is interesting to note that in discussing the balance of trade some of the Spanish mercantilists used an approximation to modern terminology. Thus Bernardo de Ulloa, writing in 1740, defines active commerce as an excess of exports compensated by an inflow of gold and silver. Passive commerce he defines as an excess of imports resulting in an outflow of the precious metals. This, he complained, was the state of Spanish trade. When imports and exports were in equilibrium so that there was no movement of the precious metals, a state of reciprocal trade existed. Mercantilist policy was directed toward achieving an active commerce, since in Ulloa's view the nation which enjoyed an inflow of gold and silver would enrich itself and impoverish its rivals.

In the devices to which they resorted mercantilist statesmen displayed a good deal of ingenuity. In the period of economic warfare preceding the outbreak of hostilities in 1939, methods for regulating and restricting trade were highly elaborated. But for most of these methods analogous practices can be found in the sixteenth, seventeenth, and eighteenth centuries, and even earlier. To trace the development of these devices even in one country would be a tedious and for our purpose unnecessary task. But it should be recognized that the restrictive trade methods developed by the Nazis in particular, as well as the arguments advanced in their support, were not a new refinement of economic policy. They constituted a reversion to practices well-known for centuries. All that was new was the more efficient administration made possible by modern governmental methods, and the subsuming of crude efforts at direct restriction and discrimination in commodity trade relations and specie flows by control of the credit system and of the foreign exchanges.

The mercantilists were familiar with import and export prohibitions and licensing systems, with retaliatory duties and tariff wars.[1] They urged that exchange transactions should be monopolized and that the national currency should be maintained at a high official rate. They tried to conserve raw materials and discourage the export of machinery and know-how. Export bounties and drawbacks (refunds)

[1] Cf. Stephen Dowell, *History of Taxation and Taxes in England* (2nd ed.), London, 1888, Vol. 1, pp. 77–78: ". . . Henry VII received, in 1490 . . . a grant of a special duty on malmsey imported by any merchant stranger from Crete. In this island, then called Candia, the Venetians . . . had recently imposed new duties on wines of Candia laden by Englishmen and in English ships. Our duty on malmsey was retaliatory . . . it was to continue 'until the Venetians should abate their new impositions of four ducats at Candy,' and thus formed a first step in the international war of tariffs which, in future years adopted as a system, fills so large a space in our fiscal history."

of duty to encourage the re-export of manufactured goods were among their favorite devices. Discrimination was characteristic of their policies, both as concerned the industries which they desired to encourage or discourage and as concerned the countries whose trade yielded a favorable or unfavorable balance. Discrimination led to bilateralism and proved the most restrictive of all regulatory practices. They were led, as many protectionists still are led, to emphasize the desirability of exporting manufactured rather than crude products so as to maximize employment, and they were perfectly familiar with the infant-industry argument.

Their most important contribution to the development of national economic policy is to be found in the elaboration of customs tariffs, in the evolution of administrative methods for the collection of customs revenue, and the enforcement of trade regulations. Inevitably the story of these developments differs from country to country. Only the broadest and most summary treatment of the English customs developments can be given here.

The first major development to be noted is a gradual shift in the seventeenth century from reliance primarily upon export duties to reliance upon import duties. In the Middle Ages the collection of revenue mainly from the export trade (principally wool and somewhat later woolen cloths) was consistent with what has been called the policy of provision. Before the advent of a money economy, when production was mostly for local consumption and was concentrated largely on such necessities as food and clothing, it was natural to welcome imports and discourage exports. The need for revenue rather than any policy of state was the prime reason for imposing duties. Duties were easier to collect on exports and could be defended as hindering the loss of valuable raw materials.

There was a brief period of transition in the latter part of the sixteenth century when the older policy of provision remained powerful enough to neutralize the growing clamor for a policy of protection. In this period many writers attacked export prohibitions and duties with arguments that came surprisingly close to those by which free trade was later advocated. By the middle of the seventeenth century, the protectionist trend was clear. Emphasis was being placed on the regulation of imports rather than exports, and there was more readiness to impose import duties when greater revenue was needed. In certain respects the old policy of provision persisted, notably in regulation or prohibition of the export of wheat even after import duties had been imposed to protect the English farmers. In any case, no Tudor or Stuart monarch was ready to forgo the revenue derived from export duties.

It was not until 1649 that the old export duties lapsed. The Parliamentary party was strongest in London and depended largely on the London merchants. The Civil War (1642–49) had interrupted the export trade in woolen cloths and the merchants seized upon the opportunity to reinforce the principle of protection by imposing more import duties. Even then many export duties survived till they were reduced in 1700, and finally abolished by Sir Robert Walpole in 1721–24. With the exception of certain raw materials—some minerals, leather, and rabbit fur for hatmaking—the repeal was designed to allow "all goods and merchandise of the product or manufacturers of Great Britain to be exported duty free." [2]

By the beginning of the eighteenth century the tariff of duties chargeable on imported goods had come to be both the chief source of revenue and an elaborate instrument of protection to English manufacturing industries. This twofold aspect of tariff development was characteristic of the mercantile age. In some respects the twin objectives—revenue and protection—were inconsistent since the more revenue that was obtained, the less the protection. But the merchants were quick to utilize the necessities of the Crown to forward their own interests and the result was a compromise in which the Crown gained new revenues while the merchants received more protection. The duties imposed were much lower on the whole than the tariff levels which have been imposed in modern times, so that the compromise was easier to achieve.

The Parliamentary party had the support of the London merchants and therefore the effective control of the customs revenue. The Civil War was expensive and duties were raised. After the restoration of Charles II in 1660, the tariff continued to be complicated by specific duties on particular products and by additional levies. Imports were valued for duty purposes at conventional valuations contained in the *Book of Rates,* which was first issued in 1558, and frequently revised. From time to time additional duties were added so that the tariff became complicated. Thus in 1721, pepper and spices were subject to seven separate duties, levied on their value as assessed in the current

[2] Stephen Dowell, *op. cit.,* Vol. II, p. 92.

Book of Rates. These duties had been imposed to provide revenue to meet the subsidies granted in 1660, 1698, 1703, and 1704, to which were added "the new duty, the additional duty, and the further new duty." The proceeds of these impositions, under appropriation clauses in the several acts, were appropriated for paying off different loans.

Sir Robert Walpole, who held office most of the time from 1712 to 1742, was a peace minister and was able to introduce a measure of simplification into the tariff. But the increasing severity of the wars of the later eighteenth century caused greater confusion than ever in the whole tax system. The war with France waged at intervals over most of the second half of the century caused special discriminations against French imports, and these were the chief incentives to smuggling in England. The attempts to tax the colonial trade and to channel it through English ports for that purpose also led to a good deal of colonial smuggling. In addition, there was much speculation and graft from time to time. In fact, the system of trade regulation became too burdensome and complicated for effective enforcement. Private interests naturally took advantage of this situation.

It has been argued that the development of a customs tariff was in itself an improvement over the older methods of prohibitions, and in that sense a necessary step toward freer trade. But it was created out of the exploitation of the government's financial necessities by the private interests of those who stood to gain by protection. The theoretical arguments by which protection was justified were mainly a cover for private privilege and profit. In 1776 Adam Smith attacked the whole complicated system on grounds of administrative inefficiency, inconsistency of aims, and monopolistic greed. He had no difficulty in documenting his criticism. The paragraph with which he concludes his analysis is as applicable to modern tariffs as it was to those which existed in his own time: "It cannot be very difficult," he says, "to determine who have been the contrivers of this whole mercantile system; not the consumers, we may believe, whose interest has been entirely neglected; but the producers, whose interest has been so carefully attended to; and among this latter class, our merchants and manufacturers have been by far the principal architects. In the mercantile regulations which have been taken notice of in this chapter, the interest of our manufacturers has been most particularly attended to; and the interest, not so much of the consumers, as that of some other sets of producers, has been sacrificed to it."

This, it may be noted, is a criticism of the political working of protectionism. The economic case for interference with private interest in order to promote the common good must always reckon, however, with the political realities. In a system of economic nationalism what tends to emerge is not the common good, but a government of producers, by producers, and for producers.

THE EVOLUTION OF JOINT-STOCK COMPANIES

The international conflicts of the seventeenth and eighteenth centuries, and to some extent the political battles also, were largely fought by chartered companies. A clear case is the struggle between the British, Dutch, and French East India Companies which were the spearheads of economic penetration in the Orient. American colonization was promoted by a succession of companies which in their origins were primarily commercial. A great array of companies endeavored also to pioneer and monopolize the trade in various regions from Russia to Africa and from Hudson Bay to the South Seas. This form of commercial organization leading ultimately to the limited-liability joint-stock corporation of modern industry was built upon earlier associative experiments and went through a very complicated series of developments in this period. This type of organization played a large role in the transformation of trade and was intimately linked with almost every aspect of economic development. No discussion of trade policy can neglect the companies—indeed the more powerful companies contributed heavily to the promotion of policy and their officials were prominent in the controversies concerning policy. Moreover the characteristic form of modern large-scale corporations and such important institutions as permanent national debt, deposit banking, and the stock exchange are outgrowths of this evolution of joint-stock enterprise.

The development of the joint-stock company came late in England and when it came was characteristically cast in a traditional form. But the amplitude of its development in that country was greater than in Italy or in Germany and is of particular importance. This is not only because of its use in colonization and in developing world trade, but also because it provided the basis of modern commercial organization. It is necessary, therefore, to outline the main stages through which it passed.

The first organization which must be noticed is the Fellowship of

Merchant Adventurers, which from the fifteenth century on fought both the Hanseatic League and the Venetians. It finally ousted them both from their privileged position in England and followed up this victory by establishing itself in Hamburg. The connection with Hamburg remained important until, in 1806, Napoleon broke up the "English Court" there.

The Merchant Adventurers and most of its offshoots were regulated companies—associations of merchants chartered to trade in a given area but trading individually. This form of organization survived long after the more modern form of joint-stock companies had appeared. Indeed some of the most important of the companies—notably the East India Company—changed from joint stock to the regulated form and back again. This was a period of experiment and there was strong pressure always from interlopers and new men, especially from the ports outside London, to share in the trade of new regions. The regulated companies, in theory, were open to all who could qualify, and from time to time they were forced to modify their monopolistic tendencies to admit interlopers. But a variety of causes gradually brought the joint-stock form into common use. More distant voyages called for greater capital over longer periods. Joint funds were needed to make the loans to needy monarchs in order to secure monopolistic privileges or preferential duties, to buy concessions from foreign rulers, or to erect overseas fortified posts.

There was always resentment of any monopoly that was granted and interlopers would immediately cut in illegally on newly opened markets. The arguments that were used for and against the granting of monopolies are curiously akin to those used in our own time regarding cartels, and particularly regarding patent agreements. Those who had put capital into development of a new trade would argue that they were entitled to protection from the competition of those who had risked nothing. They would point to the unscrupulous way in which interlopers, once the trade was established as profitable, rushed in to exploit its richest opportunities without contributing to the overhead, such as the cost of fortified posts, and with no concern for orderly development. The Africa Company, for example, complained bitterly of the way in which Sir John Hawkins' slave raids in 1562, 1564, and 1567 had ruined its business, and in fact the company did little business after 1566.

There was a close connection between the development of joint-stock companies and state policy. In two important respects the grant of exclusive privileges to a compact group of merchants was convenient to the crown. In the first place, no Tudor or Stuart monarch was able to meet the growing expenses of centralized administration and recurrent wars, let alone protect English merchants abroad. Thus it was natural that small groups of wealthy and enterprising merchants who offered not only to protect themselves but to pay to the Crown loans or cash advances for a charter would meet with royal favor. It is true that a financial expert like Sir Thomas Gresham, the financial adviser of Queen Elizabeth, could squeeze even a regulated company as he did when in 1588 he extracted £20,000 from the Merchant Adventurers, and then manipulated the exchange rates against them to gather more profit for Elizabeth. But it was easier to get gifts or loans from a joint-stock company which had common capital than to force a regulated company to collect them by subscription from its members. In the extravagant and corrupt administration of the Stuarts the practice of securing concessions by bribing court favorites grew to amazing proportions.

In the second place, where secrecy was necessary for diplomatic reasons, as in numerous privateering ventures against the Spanish or where important defense industries were concerned, it was wise to entrust the business to a small group working with a joint-stock fund. Some of the privateering expeditions were very profitable. Drake, for example, in his famous voyage around the world (1577–80), during which he plundered the unprepared Pacific outposts of Spain, used about £5,000 to outfit and man his ships. The returns from his venture which can be definitely traced amounted to at least £600,000 (of which Elizabeth received about half while the venturers got 4700 per cent on their capital) and have been estimated as high as £1,500,000 to £1,750,000.

The ultimate gain from such ventures was more than offset by the crippling of normal trade, which resulted both from the destruction of trading facilities and from the diversion of enterprise and capital to plunder rather than to trade. But it is obvious in a period of economic warfare that joint-stock privateering ventures were attractive. In the same way both at home and abroad, joint-stock companies were used for purposes of state such as the promotion of defense industries, for the planting of colonies, and for the prosecution of trade in competition with similar organized foreign groups in areas where the struggle for power was waged relentlessly, as in India. No small part of the favor accorded to the joint-stock form of enterprise came as a result of its service in power-politics.[3]

The colonizing companies which in the seventeenth century laid the foundation of what is now the United States broke new ground in more senses than one. Their origins are to be found in ventures such as those of Gilbert to Newfoundland and Raleigh to Roanoke and in joint ventures for single voyages to various West Indian Islands. Sums sufficient to equip an expedition and support adventures on an unknown shore were expected to be recouped by shipments of marketable products—perhaps of treasure. There were many early disappointments. Relief expeditions had to be sent and projects abandoned. But after the peace with Spain in 1604, there was a constant resurgence of colonizing enterprise. There was in addition a great hunger for land and opportunity in a new country as well as for religious freedom, shared by Catholics and Protestant dissenters.

There was from the beginning a potential clash between state policy and the private interests, not so much of the commercial promoters as of the colonists themselves. Support of colonization was urged on government for many reasons—to secure naval stores, to create strategic outposts, to secure both freight and sea power, to forestall territorial expansion by the Spanish, Dutch, and French, to develop markets for English manufactures and, until mercantilist population theories became dominant, to find outlets for the idle, the poor, and the criminal surplus of population.

[3] "From 1553, little as the names of the Fellowship for the Discovery of New Trades, the societies of the Mines Royal and of the Mineral and Battery Works suggest it, these enterprises find their unity in relation to the equipment of the navy. The first imported masts and cordage, while the Mines Royal discovered and worked the copper from which the Mineral and Battery Works made bronze or brass, which again was cast into cannon. Moreover the flexibility of the system was such that from 1568 to 1588 its dominant manifestation was in the financing of the earliest colonizing expeditions. Thus, during the first half-century of its existence, the joint-stock company was the requisite for obtaining both sea-power and colonial possessions. . . . From 1600 to 1635 the main activity of joint-stock enterprise consisted in the following up of the tentative efforts of the previous decade, in a vigorous planting of colonies, joined with the prosecution of trade to tropical countries, such as the East Indies. . . . Thus, during the first century of its existence in England, the joint-stock company was the organization that provided funds for the growth of maritime enterprise and for the beginnings of colonization. Thereafter, for about thirty years, it was instrumental in extending and consolidating certain distant foreign trades, and in the remaining quarter of a century it laid the foundations of an organization of credit on a new and augmented basis."—W. R. Scott, *The Constitution and Finance of English, Scottish and Irish Joint-Stock Companies to 1720,* Cambridge, Cambridge University Press, 1912, Vol. I, pp. 440–41.

The first charter of the Virginia Company contained the seeds of future conflict. On the one hand, its administration was entrusted to a royal council in England and resident councils in each colony. On the other hand the colonists were regarded as Englishmen and as such were expressly guaranteed all liberties, franchises, and immunities under the law that Englishmen were at the time enjoying at home. These included trial by jury, benefit of clergy, and all the rights of possession and inheritance of land as in England.

Between the colonists and the Crown, the companies were soon in a difficult situation. State policy and the private interests of the colonists themselves combined to make it impossible for the colonies to be operated as commercial enterprises in the interests of their proprietors or shareholders. The Virginia Company was the first to succumb. In 1623 its charter was terminated, and Virginia became a royal colony—the first of a long series. The reasons for the Company's failure were complicated, but, despite dissensions and political rivalries in its management, they were primarily economic. The investment demanded to bring a new colony into production and profit was too great and extended over too long a period. Reluctantly, its officers had accepted the colonists' neglect of a diversified agriculture and their concentration upon a staple cash crop—tobacco. Both the colonists and the companies encountered trouble, however, when foreign markets were shut off by the requirement of the Navigation Acts that all tobacco be brought to England to pay duty there before being re-exported. The Company was forced into virtual receivership and its charter was soon terminated. Other experiments were made, and there is no clear-cut pattern of development to be summarized in a phrase. But thus early in colonial history it was evident that the formative factors of policy and of later conflict would be the clashing interests of the colonists and of the Crown.

The most successful of the joint-stock trading companies were those which pioneered the distant trades. Of these the most important was the East India Company, which was formed in 1600 by a group of merchants active in the Levant Company. Until its dissolution in 1858, the East India Company was to bear the brunt of British expansion in India and the Far East. Its evolution illustrates the experiments in organization of joint-stock enterprises as well as many aspects of economic nationalism and imperialism. Originally it was a joint venture, with a varying number of shares of fixed amount, subscribed at first for a single voyage, and later for a limited term of years. The device of issuing shares of a fixed amount which could be bought and sold was adopted early in the seventeenth century. These shares were later made permanent, and in 1662 liability was limited to the value of the shares subscribed. Thus before the end of the seventeenth century the essential principles of modern joint-stock organization had been developed.

It is difficult if not impossible to discover exactly how profitable the East India Company and its contemporaries actually were. Dividends on successive capital subscriptions made accounting difficult until the share capital was made permanent. The chronic necessities of government, always seeking to appropriate the proceeds of any profitable enterprise, made it advisable to minimize returns, and the public statements of the companies are a melancholy series of pleas for greater privileges and more lenient exactions. Nevertheless, the first returns seem to have been large and the persistence of capital seeking investment in these trades indicates that subsequent profits were substantial. While it seems probable that the British East India Company did not fare as well as its Dutch rival in the early seventeenth century, there was a great trade boom after civil conflict ended in 1649. In the course of that boom large dividends were distributed. Before the boom burst in the great speculative operations of the South Sea Bubble, the East India Company doubled, the Hudson's Bay Company trebled, and the Royal African Company quadrupled their nominal capital by way of bonus out of reserved profits.

This record was not established without trouble or criticism. There were always interlopers who picked the eyes out of the trade, took no share in its continuing costs, and often ruined its prospects by greedy, unscrupulous, and ruthless dealings with the native peoples. Successive kings and their courtiers were not above raiding the profits of the companies, sometimes by measures that were in the nature of blackmail, as when in 1635 Charles I chartered a rival East India Company. After various reorganizations the East India Companies were combined in 1657 and a new charter was granted by Cromwell. Successive reorganizations register political difficulties. Sir Josiah Child, one of the most famous of the mercantilist economists, threw the East India Company to the support of the Stuarts after the Restoration and thus opened it to retaliation when in 1688 his Whig opponents came into power with William III.

The chief problems of the Company from that time forward were its gradual drift into unwieldy bureaucracy, the greed of its shareholders for dividends, and the difficulty of controlling its officials in India. Such control was particularly difficult after the struggle with the French Company involved it in the politics of the Indian states, and subsequently in assuming the responsibilities of government over great territories. In the course of the eighteenth century it became a massive and somewhat hidebound monopoly as profitable and seemingly as secure as the Bank of England. It was influential enough to exert considerable influence on state policy as was illustrated by its attempt to assert its monopolistic control over the tea market in the American colonies.

Whatever its early enterprise may have been, and however compelling the reasons for its initial monopoly, by the end of the eighteenth century it invited the attack made upon it by Adam Smith. To understand why he made such a violent attack, not only upon the East India Company but upon the whole method of joint-stock organization a brief statement should be made of the connection of joint-stock enterprise with banking developments and public finance in the early eighteenth century. It is, at first, surprising to find such an acute observer as Adam Smith declaring that the corporate form of organization is suitable only for routine business operations.

The attack concludes an extended analysis of the East India Company's operations and is no doubt pivoted upon the parenthetical clause "without an exclusive privilege." Why was it that joint-stock companies, which in our day are the accepted form of private enterprise, were in the eighteenth century confined to monopolistic trading concerns or to a few routine businesses—banking, insurance, canals, and water companies? The answer is to be found in the great outburst of speculation which led up to John Law's experiments with paper money and to the South Sea Bubble in 1720, as a result of which joint-stock enterprises were severely restricted by law.

It would take us too far afield to trace the evolution of credit instruments in the latter half of the seventeenth century. Primarily because of peace at home and abroad, profits were accumulating in England. Capital began to flow into agricultural development and industrial experiments as well as trade. Goldsmiths began the practice of accepting deposits and issuing bank notes, the first private banks began to operate, and checks were used. Still the governments were chronically short of cash. The Stuarts mortgaged future claims to public revenues, big and little, sold honors, patents and monopolies, and extracted whatever they could for the renewal of company charters. Even then the floating debt—unpaid bills—grew steadily.

In 1694 a company of Whig merchants had loaned £1,200,000 to William III and had received a charter as the Bank of England. In 1711 another enterprising group was incorporated as the South Sea Company, using floating-debt claims on the government as capital to the amount of over nine million pounds, which was soon increased to ten million pounds. On this capital, returning 6 per cent interest secured by various taxes, the company was able to borrow for developing its trading privileges. Actually it had little to develop. It might have been just another debt-financing scheme if the credit boom started by John Law's financial operations in Paris in the early decades of the eighteenth century had not spread to London. The South Sea Company, but not the Bank of England, was swept into a tide of speculation which was remarkable for the flotation of fantastic and fraudulent schemes. As the speculation developed, the South Sea Company was guilty of fraudulent statements and of bribing ministers and public officials. Its operations can best be understood by comparing them, as Professor Eli F. Heckscher has done, with the recent financial operations of Kreuger and Toll. The speculative boom ended in disaster in 1720, and one result was legislation to prohibit the formation of joint-stock companies except by charter or act of Parliament. Passed in 1719 at the instance of the South Sea Company itself, to protect it and the public against fraudulent promotions, the Act was not repealed till 1825, and the full privilege of limited liability was not allowed to such companies until 1862.

Thus when Adam Smith wrote, the joint-stock form of enterprise as a result of the excesses of the South Sea Bubble had been outlawed from the field in which it has since had its greatest successes. The South Sea Company remained only an echoing memory.

The South Sea Bubble was a serious blow to English credit, though it was not as bad as the convulsions into which John Law's Mississippi Bubble ultimately led France. For more than a century its memory prevented the use of joint-stock enterprise and cast discredit upon stockbroking and jobbing in all their forms. The low repute into which corporate financing had fallen was reflected in an Act of 1734 passed "to prevent the infamous practice of stock-jobbing," and in Dr. Johnson's dictionary definition of a stockjobber as "a low wretch." Those who dealt in stocks and bonds were reduced to conducting their operations in private. The Stock Exchange rule against intruders on the floor of the "house" dates from this period, a relic of the secrecy necessary when dealings were illegal and there was a danger from informers.

THE NAVIGATION ACTS

In the age of maritime expansion and colonial warfare throughout the seventeenth and eighteenth centuries, shipping and naval power were constant objects of state policy. The regulations by which governments attempted to build up their power at sea were a cornerstone of the whole protective system. While there was some conflict of contemporary thought concerning their wisdom and effectiveness, they soon won the support of the great body of public opinion. So relentless a critic of mercantilism as Adam Smith expressly exempted England's efforts to protect shipping from his attack on restrictive and monopolistic practices. He was aware of the charge that the Navigation Acts which had been passed from 1651 onward were restrictive of commerce, and he had no illusions as to their political purposes. But he went out of his way not only to defend them but to claim that they were "the wisest of all the commercial regulations of England." There was a long history of shipping regulation behind them in England and in every other trading country. Both to protect shipbuilding and shipping (including fisheries) as important industries in their own right, and to protect other industries by controlling seaborne competition, many experiments had been tried for centuries. These early experiments had not been satisfactory since they imposed direct burdens on traders and consumers and had proved difficult to administer. From time to time they had been relaxed or abandoned, though the shipping interest worked incessantly for protection.

What Professor L. A. Harper has called "the basic formula . . . destined to govern English navigation for two centuries" was put forward in 1651 at a time of great tension with the Dutch.[4] Whether, from the viewpoint of immediate policy, it was a wise and statesmanlike piece of economic preparedness or a provocative blunder is difficult now to judge. There are strong opinions on both sides. Adam Smith's has been quoted. Most economic historians, however, agree with Pro-

[4] L. A. Harper, *The English Navigation Laws*, New York, 1939, p. 34.

fessor W. R. Scott that "in spite of the statement of Adam Smith, it may well be questioned whether, on the whole, the Act was wise, and especially whether it was desirable at this particular time." [5] It is not proven that war was inevitable, and evidence can be cited to show that the Dutch were prepared to negotiate. They had been allies and were linked with England by many ties, economic, political, and religious.

It is in any case certain that the war which followed (1652–54), whether precipitated by the Navigation Act or not, had the effect of reducing English trade, straining the public finances, and rendering inevitable the retention and stiffening of the measures aimed at crippling Dutch shipping. Once committed to the struggle, English statesmen had little choice but to pursue it relentlessly. Controversy concerning the Navigation Acts turns largely upon estimates of the necessity for launching the struggle.

The original Act of 1651 was aimed primarily at the carrying and entrepôt (warehousing) trade of the Dutch. For example, this trade infringed the monopolistic position of the Levant Company, which could not compete with the importation of Turkish goods from Holland, because the Dutch ships were built and operated more cheaply. The Act of 1651, however, was not very firmly administered, especially while England was at war with Spain and found Dutch ships useful.

The acts which were to be operative for more than a century and a half were the Navigation Act of 1660 and the Act of Frauds of 1662. The guiding principle was to control the imports carried in foreign ships. For this purpose a reasonably effective administration had been developed. The customs service was by no means perfect, but it was the best organized, because it was the oldest of the fiscal departments. The customs officials whose supervision of arrivals was supplemented by the agents of those to whom various revenues had been farmed out, and by the agents of the companies whose monopolies might be infringed, had been able to watch the import trade, though they could not well enforce control of the export trade without installing a large foreign service. The Act of 1660 incorporated a new idea by confining the control to a specified list of enumerated articles, so that supervision was made easier. The articles enumerated were important products comprising bulky goods such as grain, strategic items such as naval stores, and commodities where Company interests sought protection. Altogether it has been estimated that the enumerated commodities

[5] W. R. Scott, *op. cit.*, pp. 250–51.

constituted about half Europe's trade with England both in weight and in value. These goods had to be shipped in English-built vessels, manned by English masters and English crews to the extent of three-fourths, or in ships built in the country from which the goods originated and manned by crews of that country.

Contemporary opinion was divided as to the economic consequences of the Acts upon European trade. Adam Smith admitted that they were restrictive. The full text of his statement is worth quoting since it sheds a flood of light upon the whole political situation in the seventeenth century.

"When the act of navigation was made, in 1651, though England and Holland were not actually at war, the most violent animosity subsisted between the two nations. It had begun during the government of the long parliament, which first framed this act, and it broke out soon after in the Dutch wars during that of the Protector and of Charles II. It is not impossible, therefore, that some of the regulations of this famous act may have proceeded from national animosity. They are as wise, however, as if they had all been dictated by the most deliberate wisdom. National animosity at that particular time aimed at the very same object which the most deliberate wisdom would have recommended, the diminution of the naval power of Holland, the only naval power which could endanger the security of England. The act of navigation is not favourable to foreign commerce, or to the growth of that opulence which can arise from it. The interest of a nation in its commercial relations to foreign nations is, like that of a merchant with regard to the different people with whom he deals, to buy as cheap and sell as dear as possible. But the act of navigation, by diminishing the number of sellers, must necessarily diminish that of buyers; and we are likely thus not only to buy foreign goods dearer, but to sell our own cheaper, than if there was a more perfect freedom of trade. As defence, however, is of much more importance than opulence, the act of navigation is, perhaps, the wisest of all the commercial regulations of England."

During the period when the Navigation Acts were in force, there was a considerable decline in the Mediterranean and Baltic trade; but many factors were at work. England ultimately won in the struggle with the Dutch; but there were many who believed that English sea power was injured rather than helped by the Navigation Acts and that Dutch sea power declined for domestic rather than international reasons.[6] These domestic difficulties arose in large part out of the effects of successive wars, and it may be argued that Holland was finally outpaced in a long and exhausting struggle with a power that could draw upon greater resources.

If a longer view be taken covering the eighteenth as well as the seventeenth century, it is apparent that trade and shipping with the colonies in America had gradually come to play a much larger role in British commercial development. Despite murmurings from time to time and some smuggling, particularly to and from the foreign colonies in the West Indies, the colonists did not find the restrictions of the Navigation Acts too irksome. The channeling of trade through English ports was, however, a diversion from the most economical trading arrangements, and it was so felt by the colonists. But in the first half of the eighteenth century, the colonial trade grew by leaps and bounds. There can be no doubt that it contributed greatly to the development of English and also of colonial shipping, especially after Parliament by rejecting the attempt in 1713 to open friendly trade relations with France committed England to a continuance of economic warfare with that country.

The colonists for the most part acquiesced in the progressively stricter enforcement by which the Navigation Acts were used to foster English exports, to develop English and colonial shipping and shipbuilding, and to funnel colonial exports through English ports to be taxed. Few would contend that these protective measures, devised in the interest of English merchants rather than that of the colonists, were responsible for the steady growth of the colonial trade. To do so would be to ignore the initiative and enterprise within the colonies and the rapid growth of population, which were to make them at a later date the most productive community in the whole world.

What the restrictions did was drain off some of the profit of this developing trade for the benefit of the English revenue. Occasionally, the mercantilists overreached themselves as when the Navigation Acts gravely impaired the competitive power of British West Indian sugar in the European market by making the British sugar more expensive. In general however, the forces of expansion were strong enough to

[6] J. R. McCulloch, in an elaborate note (XII) to his edition of the *Wealth of Nations* published in 1828, cites evidence that the Acts had neither crippled Dutch nor improved English shipping, and quotes Dutch authorities to support his view that "excessive taxation and not our navigation law was the principal cause of the fall of profits, and of the decline of manufactures, commerce and navigation in Holland."

carry the additional burden imposed on them by mercantilist policy. One of these burdens was the requirement that the most important export products from the colonies should be carried in English or colonial ships to an English port and should be subject to duty before they could be re-exported. The freight costs were higher than those on most foreign ships. Part of the burden imposed on the colonial trade, therefore, was in effect a subsidy to shipping and shipbuilding. This can be defended as Adam Smith defended it, as a wise measure of national defense, but it cannot be defended as a means of promoting trade. Moreover the colonists came to feel that they were paying, indirectly but substantially, too heavy a price for maintaining the English connection.

It is questionable whether this concealed subsidy was necessary to develop shipping and thereby the sea power which enabled the English to defeat first the Dutch and then the French. They had defeated the Spanish without the aid of the Navigation Acts in a period when there were various attempts made to encourage national shipping, but these were largely by means of partial and often indirect devices. It was effectively argued by J. R. McCulloch that "navigation and naval power are the children, not the parents—the effect, not the cause—of commerce. If the latter be increased, the increase of the former will follow as a matter of course. More ships and more sailors become necessary, according as the commerce between different and distant countries is extended."

At a later date, when British commercial and shipping pre-eminence was clearly established, McCulloch could add to this argument by way of concession that: "A country, situated like Great Britain in the reign of Charles II, when her shipping was comparatively limited, might perhaps be warranted in endeavoring to increase its amount, by excluding foreign ships from her harbors. But it is almost superfluous to add that it is not by any such regulations, but solely by the aid of a flourishing and widely extended commerce, that the immense mercantile navy we have accumulated can be supported." [7]

Toward the close of the nineteenth century when Germany was preparing to challenge British commercial and maritime supremacy, German nationalists would argue that England had built up its sea power as well as its trade by well-directed policies of economic nationalism, and was then able to kick away the ladder by which it had

[7] J. R. McCulloch, *loc. cit.*

climbed. The validity of this argument which opened the way to a new struggle for power is more than doubtful. If this was true for England, it was not true for Spain or France, which also tried the same devices. There must have been something in the geographical, political, economic, and social situation of England which enabled it to emerge victor in the struggle. The best judgment of economic historians is that domestic peace and internal freedom were among the principal causes of England's success. If this is true, these conditions could have been even more effective if so much wealth and energy had not been diverted to the destructive techniques of economic warfare and armed conflict.

Perhaps economic warfare was inevitable at the time, but this does not prove either that it was profitable or that it must remain inevitable. Defense of the Navigation Acts on the ground that they were a necessary instrument of economic warfare in a period of international anarchy is possible. To defend them on the ground that they enabled the victor in the struggle to reap rich rewards is an entirely different proposition. Such an argument would need to prove that the gains outweighed the costs of the struggle and could not have been secured by peaceful means. It is in any case an argument based upon the presumed gains to the victor, not the losses to the vanquished. There is in fact no valid economic case for the Navigation Acts. Their only justification was as a weapon of power-politics.

THE OLD COLONIAL SYSTEM

The "old colonial system" was an aspect of mercantilist policy which has been distinguished for separate treatment largely because of its importance in the history of the United States. Like every other aspect of mercantilist policy, it was a mixture of great ideals and petty prejudices. What constituted the peculiar aspect of colonial trade policy was the manner of applying mercantilist devices to the trade, and less effectively to the production, of settlements overseas which were rapidly developing their own economic interests.

Because the English colonies in America were the most considerable permanent settlements of Europeans and because of the significance of their eventual achievement of independence, there is a natural tendency to think of the old colonial system as something peculiar to them. In fact, they became the most considerable settlements largely because of their relative freedom, and their independence came as a development from their staunch defense of that freedom. The struggle was primarily political and was facilitated by the fact that a large measure of self-government had been attained by the thirteen original states while they were still colonies. Other colonial empires—the Portuguese, Spanish, Dutch, and French—were administered very strictly in the interests of the metropolitan country and had no development of local self-government comparable with the legislatures of the English colonies in North America. New France was governed directly by a viceroy until it passed under the rule of England. The Spanish and Portuguese colonies in Central and South America were governed in the same way and did not achieve their independence for more than half a century after the United States, largely because they had no elected legislatures to focus popular discontents.

Also it should be remembered that the economic controls to which all colonial empires were subjected in the seventeenth and eighteenth centuries were milder in the English colonies than elsewhere. They were milder indeed in North America than in Ireland or the West Indies even though, from a strict mercantilist viewpoint, the New England settlements were the least productive and the most troublesome of all the colonies.

It is true that many statements may be quoted along the lines of the well-known official memorandum of 1726: "All advantageous projects or commercial gain in any Colony which are truly prejudicial to, and inconsistent with, the interests of the Mother country, must be understood to be illegal and the practice of them unwarrantable; because they contradict the end for which the Colonies had a being." This was accepted doctrine, common to all colonial systems. It became intolerable to the colonists only when the manner of its execution infringed what they held to be their inalienable political rights. In so far as it was taxation to which they objected, it was to being taxed without representation.

Contemporary opinion both in the colonies and in Britain was emphatic that the rapid development of the North American colonies was the result, in Adam Smith's words, of "plenty of good land, and liberty to manage their own affairs in their own way." Good land was to be found elsewhere, but "the political institutions of the English colonies have been more favourable to the improvement and cultivation of this land."

"In everything, except their foreign trade, the liberty of the English colonists to manage their own affairs in their own way is complete. It is in every respect equal to that of their fellow citizens at home and is secured in the same manner, by an assembly of representatives of the people, who claim the sole right of imposing taxes for the support of the colony governments."

These institutions of local self-government derived from the belief of the original colonists that they had lost none of their rights and privileges as Englishmen. There was a brief period during which the early Stuarts maintained that the colonies and the companies which founded them lay within the royal prerogative. The legal form of their constitution followed this theory which curiously foreshadows the modern association of the British Commonwealth, the independent Dominions of which owe allegiance to the King, but not to the British Parliament. But the Crown had power in the seventeenth century, and the Stuart claim was largely based on the desire to find sources of revenue outside parliamentary control.

After the Civil War, Parliament reasserted its control over all aspects of commercial policy and taxation so that the claims of the colonial legislatures came to be regarded as a challenge to the supreme authority of Parliament. These claims were never admitted, and it required long and painful experience before other British colonies were able to work out a political formula of independent association in a Commonwealth. The utmost concessions made to colonial demands, even by opponents of mercantilist policy, took the form of proposals from the colonies and from liberals in Britain for representation of the colonies in Parliament. Such proposals led to no practical result and the legal supremacy of Parliament was firmly upheld. However, the same disintegration of domestic regulation that earlier took place in England itself, coupled with the difficulty of creating effective organs of administration in the colonies, led at a very early date to an effective degree of colonial self-government in domestic affairs, which included local taxation. It was the attempt of Parliament to reassert its right to tax the colonies directly that led to armed resistance and ultimately to independence.

It was not easy to apply the English tariff to the distant American colonies so that the main device used was the diversion of the most significant part of the export trade to be taxed as it passed through English ports. This was done in pursuance of the Navigation Acts which also served other purposes. They created a virtual monopoly of the colonial markets in favor of the English manufacturer, while assuring English ships (and in the eighteenth century, colonial ships also) of a preferential demand for freight. These were hardships imposed upon the colonists, but they were not without some justification and compensation. The costs of defense against the Indians and the French, on land as well as on sea, fell upon the British Treasury, and it was felt that the colonists should contribute to these costs, if only indirectly. Moreover, colonial exports were assured a virtual monopoly of the English market by the imposition of high duties against competing products from foreign colonies, and further in the case of tobacco, their most important crop, by prohibition of its cultivation in England.

The enforcement of the regulations governing the external trade of the colonies was progressively strengthened. The Act of 1651 provided no machinery of enforcement in the colonies, but relied solely on informers. In any case its administration was lax. In 1660 the colonial governors were instructed to require colonial shippers to give bonds which were forfeited if it were found that the laws had been evaded. In 1663 import declarations were required in an attempt to control foreign imports. But it was not until 1675 that the governors were given staffs of English officials to enforce the law, and not until 1696 that these officials were given effective powers to enforce their control over colonial trade and shipping. Thereafter enforcement seems to have been reasonably efficient. The channels of trade were established between Britain and the North American colonies. Ireland and the Isle of Man, which were outside the customs area of Great Britain, for a time provided loopholes for evasion. There was also some smuggling to and from the foreign colonies in the West Indies in contravention of such legislation as the Molasses Act of 1733. However, the great bulk of the trade went through British ports. Bristol and Glasgow grew rich on tobacco, and later Liverpool was to grow rich on cotton.

The harshest effects of the old colonial system were in fact felt by Ireland, which was nearest to the seat of enforcement and could most easily be supervised. In 1667 the importation of Irish cattle was prohibited, and when Ireland turned to wool its export elsewhere than to England was prohibited, so that English manufacturers could gain from cheap raw materials. The export of butter and cheese to England was prohibited, and in 1699 the export of Irish woolens was confined to England. As Arthur Young, an acute observer, wrote nearly a century later, "the Irish woolen fabrics were destroyed by one of the most infamous Statutes that ever disgraced a legislature."

The West Indian colonies also suffered heavily by the diversion of their sugar exports to be taxed in English ports, before they could be re-exported to foreign countries. Their sugar became too expensive to compete with the products of French and Dutch plantations in the West Indies, and England could not absorb the growing production. In 1739 the mercantilists suffered a partial defeat when sugar was allowed to be exported directly to foreign ports south of Cape Finisterre; but the permission was hedged about with restrictions and was only partially effective.

In the effort to prevent or retard the development of manufactures in the North American colonies—an effort which Adam Smith attacked as "a manifest violation of the most sacred rights of mankind"—mercantilist policy was difficult to enforce. The woolen manufacturers had much influence in England and an Act of 1699 endeavored to prohibit the export of colonial wool, woolen yarn, or woolen manufactures to foreign countries, or even from one colony to another. There was not at that time much prospect of colonial woolen goods competing in European markets, but the local trade flourished despite the prohibition. Attempts of the English ironmasters to prohibit the manufacture of iron were met by the opposition not only of the colonists but of English manufacturers. After 1750 pig iron and bar iron were admitted to England from the colonies duty free, but the manufacture of iron products was forbidden in the colonies. Hatmaking from beaver felts was also forbidden in 1732. But like all of these laws it was unnecessary as far as the export trade was concerned and ineffective as far as it concerned the colonial market.

It should be noted that as the colonies grew in population and the wealth of their resources became more evident, the notion gradually emerged of a self-sufficient empire. This notion was as far as liberal thought and political invention went in the eighteenth century. Politically, it involved both the maintenance of civil rights in the colonies and colonial representation in Parliament. Economically, it went to the length—as stated by Adam Smith—of proposing imperial free trade. This notion has never been lost. Though proposed too late and resisted too strongly to be of serious importance in the conflict which gave the American colonies their independence, it remains a living idea in other imperial systems, including the modern British Empire, and has even in the stress of war been proposed as a means of reintegrating the English-speaking peoples. For the greater part of the nineteenth century it was overshadowed by the dominant belief in laissez faire. This, it was hoped, would lead to world-wide free trade and peaceful co-operation among independent states content to give free rein to economic competition—the ideal upon which the League of Nations ultimately rested. In default of a world federation with centralized authority, this looser form of association was the arrangement which idealists aimed at. But there have always been powerful groups aiming at the closer integration of kindred peoples.

It was the struggle with France which prompted the British Parliament to tighten the old colonial system in an effort to force the colonists to pay at least the costs of their own defense. The measures chosen raised constitutional issues on which the colonists were prepared to fight, and the alternatives proposed were inadequate to avert the conflict. Most economic historians now conclude that the restrictions of the old colonial system, though burdensome and officious, were neither so onerous nor, over the greater part of the eighteenth century, so effectively administered as to foment rebellious attitudes. They were not wholly one-sided. The colonies had preferential access to the English market and to the West Indies, and shared in the shipping monopoly created by the Navigation Acts. Until the passing of the Stamp Act in 1765 and the subsequent stiffening of political and legalistic attitudes, the restrictions on colonial trade were a cause of grumbling and evasion rather than of rebellion.

Nevertheless what is important for an understanding of modern problems is the fact that the ultimate test of mercantile policy, complicated by the pressure of private-interest groups, raised political issues on which the colonists were prepared to fight. It is a weak defense of the restrictive policies outlined in this chapter to argue that, as long as they were not too rigidly enforced, they did not cause discontent to break out in open rebellion. Their object was to strengthen the military potential of the mother country, but their result was hardship equally severe to the colonists and to the consumers in the mother country. Adam Smith was a close observer of these events and made a careful analysis of the "colony trade" and of the monopoly to which it was subjected. The "natural good effects" of the trade he rated highly as contributing heavily to the expansion of English manufactures and shipping. But he argued this beneficial result was achieved not "by means of the monopoly of that trade, but in spite of that monopoly." For the old colonial system itself he had nothing but contempt, despite his firm belief that the colonies ought to contribute to the cost of their own defense.

His condemnation of the system was emphatically summed up: "The monopoly of the colony trade, therefore, like all the mean and malignant expedients of the mercantile system, depresses the industry of all other countries, but chiefly that of the colonies, without in the least increasing, but on the contrary diminishing, that of the country in whose favour it is established."

With the justice of this verdict, there are few who would now quarrel.

CHAPTER V

THE EMERGENCE OF ECONOMIC THEORY

THE RELATIVITY OF ECONOMIC THOUGHT

THE PRECEDING chapters have dealt with the complementary themes of trading enterprise and regulation as they were manifested in the progressive widening of markets. Beginning in antiquity the story has been brought rapidly up to the end of the eighteenth century. Necessarily it has dealt not only with trading developments but also with the broader aspects of changing economic organization, and even with the main outlines of the historical setting in which those developments occurred. While these references were intended to be no more than illustrative of the general setting, they were necessary to indicate that neither trading enterprise nor its regulation can be fruitfully studied except in relation to contemporary thought and action.

So far little has been said of economic theory. This is because the development of theoretical economic analysis, and still more its systematization, came long after commercial practice had been well developed.[1] That there is action and reaction between theory and practice

[1] Cf. the passage with which John Stuart Mill, the most systematic expositor of classical economic theory, opened his *Principles of Political Economy,* London, 1848: "In every department of human affairs, Practice long precedes Science: systematic enquiry into the modes of action of the powers of nature is the tardy product of a long course of efforts to use those powers for practical ends. The conception, accordingly, of Political Economy as a branch of science is extremely modern; but the subject with which its enquiries are conversant has in all ages necessarily constituted one of the chief practical interests of mankind, and in some a most unduly engrossing one."

is obvious. Ideas shape events and the brilliant formulation of a generalized thesis may influence thought and policy for generations. The thesis of Adam Smith which is the main subject of this chapter was influential in this way. But generally it is ideas rather than their formulation into a systematic theory that are most apt to be influential.

The experimental scientists by providing a basis for new technology have been the innovators responsible for revolutionary economic changes. Social studies have to deal with human behavior, and therefore are concerned with ends as well as means. Examples could easily be cited to prove that the organization of enterprise is at least as important as the technical methods of production. But organization immediately raises questions of social purpose—organization for what and by whom? The controversies of economic analysis and still more clearly those of economic policy arise primarily from disagreements as to ends and as to the practicability of attaining desired ends, rather than from disagreement on the technical means of attaining them.

In an effort to emulate the rapid advancement of the experimental sciences, some modern economists have attempted to limit the field of analysis by excluding consideration of the social purposes for which economic activity is organized. This, however, means that certain purposes must be assumed as the motives of economic activity. These theoretical assumptions are made explicitly or implicitly, usually by definition—a process that excludes the conflicts and controversies which are of major interest in social policy, and opens the door to unreality, since "no science can be more secure than the unconscious metaphysics which tacitly it presupposes." [2]

There are, in fact, two streams of thought in economic discussion. The one which corresponds most nearly to the processes of the experi-

[2] Cited from A. N. Whitehead by R. W. Souter, *Prolegomena to Relativity Economics,* New York, 1933, p. 1.

For an exposition of economics as a science, cf. Lionel C. Robbins, *An Essay on the Nature and Significance of Economic Science,* London, 1936. Lancelot Hogben attacks passages in this *Essay* such as the statement (p. 72) that: "In the last analysis, therefore, our proposition rests upon deductions which are implicit in our initial definition of the subject-matter of Economic Science." In his *Retreat from Reason,* New York, 1937, Hogben uses this passage to attack economic theory as consisting of "statements solely based on logical manipulations of verbal assertions," and cites Bacon's dictum that, "It cannot be that axioms established by argumentation can suffice for the discovery of new works, since the subtlety of nature is greater many times over than the subtlety of argument."

Much of the argument advanced by Hogben in his *Retreat from Reason* is textually reproduced in his *Political Arithmetic,* New York, 1938, pp. 13–46, and again in his *Dangerous Thoughts,* London, 1939.

mental sciences, but which is debarred by the very nature of human behavior from their most productive experimental methods, is an attempt to classify, describe, and explain the relations of human beings in the production and exchange of goods and services. The other, which is an offshoot of moral philosophy, is a critical evaluation of those relations. It is possible for clarity of analysis to separate what is from what should be; but in doing so account must be taken of the fact that what is, is governed in some measure by men's notions of what should be.

The standards by which economic behavior has been evaluated have changed from time to time. They still differ widely between different types of society. In China for example, the family rather than the community is the basis of social organization, and economic behavior tends to be judged by community opinion as to whether or not it is moral by its effect on the family rather than on the community as a whole. In every society there are some standards and these influence the motives which prompt men to economic activity. If economic analysis is to be realistic it must assume motives which correspond essentially with the prevailing motives in the society being studied and these are affected by, though they may not correspond with, prevailing standards of behavior. On the other hand the evaluation of economic relations easily becomes unrealistic if it is not correlated closely with scientific analysis. The peculiar difficulty of economic studies is to be found in this interdependence of two modes of thought, both of which are essential to an understanding of economic behavior. Economic thought—if its primary purpose is to provide a basis for action, and not simply intellectual exercise—must use both analysis and evaluation, and neither is fruitful without the other.[3]

If these views are correct, it is clearly important to relate the development of economic theory both to the scientific knowledge of the particular period under consideration (or at least to the industrial applications of that knowledge) and to the prevailing beliefs as to

[3] Cf. the letter from Marshall cited in A. C. Pigou (ed.), *Memorials of Alfred Marshall*, London, 1925, p. 427. " . . . I had a growing feeling in the later years of my work at the subject that a good mathematical theorem dealing with economic hypotheses was very unlikely to be good economics: and I went more and more on the rules—(1) Use mathematics as a shorthand language, rather than as an engine of inquiry. (2) Keep to them till you have done. (3) Translate into English. (4) Then illustrate by examples that are important in real life. (5) Burn the mathematics. (6) If you can't succeed in 4, burn 3. This last I often did."

man's responsibility in society. There was little need of theory when the organization of economic activity was simple and confined both in time and space, and when standards of conduct were laid down by religious belief. It was only when co-operative activity became complicated, extended over wider areas and, by the increasing use of instrumental capital, linked future production with that of the preceding period in which the capital was produced, that it became necessary to go into elaborate explanations of the economic relations of men in society.

The seventeenth-century writers on political arithmetic who were closely connected with the founding of the Royal Society foreshadowed the inductive, statistical approach to social questions. The best-known members of this group were William Petty and the astronomer, Edmund Halley. It has been claimed that they began the application of statistical methods to economic analysis, and especially to the study of population, and came close to formulating the concepts of national income and national expenditure which now loom so large in the most modern economic theories. But they did not achieve much more than fragmentary studies, and those were warped by their uncritical acceptance of state revenue and state power as the criterion by which economic activity should be judged. Even Adam Smith, who had "no great faith in political arithmetic," devoted much of his work to political economy in this original sense of state housekeeping. In his hands, however, the organization of private economic activity became the principal object of study.

The major contribution of scientific research to economic thought in this formative period was not in regard either to method or to subjects of inquiry. It was the philosophic concept of a self-operating and self-correcting equilibrium achieved by a balance of forces in a rational universe. In the eighteenth century the connection between social science and philosophy was closer than that between experimental and social science. It was as a branch of moral philosophy that political economy emerged as an academic discipline in its own right, and the men who shaped its development were philosophers.

John Locke had prepared the way for a scientific approach to the study of political economy when he set forth his exposition of a society based on the natural rights of individuals. Among those rights property loomed large. Locke was the philosopher of the middle-class revolution of 1688. He represented the views of the men who founded the Bank of England. The fight against the divine right of kings was won, and the new social order was dominated by the sacred right of individual property.[4]

Thus by the time Adam Smith wrote, the political setting was prepared for a philosophy of individualism. His thesis is clearest in the field of commercial policy with which we are more particularly concerned, and subsequent generations have rightly construed his main teaching as an attack upon the monopolistic regulation of international trade. Here he was able, in the circumstances of the time and using the economic analysis of the time, to demonstrate to the satisfaction of his contemporaries that government interference with trading enterprise was futile and harmful. His arguments were not an unreasoning defense of individual freedom in all circumstances, but a reasoned attack upon specific limitations of that freedom which in his time led to manifest abuses. However, before proceeding to a closer examination of his views it is necessary to recapitulate the progress made up to his time in the formulation of economic theory.

A SELF-REGULATING MECHANISM

The piecemeal emergence of a better understanding of different parts of the economic mechanism may be outlined very briefly. It was a product of controversy, and the literature to be sifted is both voluminous and uneven in quality. Here and there scattered statements, sometimes merely passing references and sometimes more systematic expositions in letters, pamphlets, treatises, or official reports, indicate that clearer insight was being gained into the essential relationships of economic phenomena.

As trade expanded and took new forms, attempts to apply the Canon Law had led to discussion of particular cases in which the foundation was laid for theoretical generalizations. As early as the latter part of the thirteenth century a better understanding of what we should now

[4] One of the main arguments advanced to prove the sacredness of property was that all value was created by labor and men had an inalienable right to the products of their labor. This doctrine, rooted in ancient and medieval philosophy, has plagued economic thought by attempts to found analytical systems upon a labor (cost of production) theory of value. In its strict form, as elaborated by Karl Marx, this theory leads to a denial of certain forms of property rights; but John Locke argued (*Treatise on Civil Government,* ii, 27, 28) that "The grass my horse has bit, the turf my servant has cut, and the ore I have digged in any place where I have a right to them in common with others, become my property without the assignation or the consent of anybody." Cf. Ivor Brown, *English Political Theory,* London, 1920, pp. 62–67.

call place-utility was evident. It was realized that traders increased the value of goods by moving them from where they were plentiful to where they were scarce. The concept of time-utility was slower in receiving recognition at the hands of theorists, though practical men were paying for time as soon as the widening range of transactions demanded the use of short-term credits in the financing of international trade.

Already in the latter part of the fourteenth century the confusion of local coinages and their circulation at varying rates of exchange had led Nicole Oresme to analyze the relation of the supply of money to commodity prices and to formulate the theory, later known as Gresham's law, that bad money drives good money from circulation. In the early sixteenth century Copernicus made his famous report analyzing the conditions of a sound monetary policy, and before the end of that century Jean Bodin, studying the effects of the inflow of treasure from the New World, had formulated the quantity theory of money. It is evident also that the Italian, French, Flemish, and Dutch bankers from the twelfth century on had a reasonably clear insight into the nature of trading and exchange transactions, and even into the relation of the supply of money to prices. Sir Thomas Gresham when urging on Queen Elizabeth the opportunity of a favorable occasion for the recoinage of 1560, or astutely manipulating the Antwerp exchange market so as to raise revenue, or to compound Elizabeth's debts, was dealing in operations that he understood. It is not so evident that men of this type knew the significance for the community of what they were doing.

Early in the seventeenth century Antonio Serra wrote *A Brief Treatise on the Causes Which Can Make Gold and Silver Plentiful in Kingdoms Where There Are No Mines.* This work attempted to formulate the theory of trade and of money. But it was clearly dominated by what was then the new touchstone of policy, the necessity of state revenue. For a century and a half economic thought was to be dominated and in many respects distorted by this and similar overriding political considerations. The ideas of an earlier age persisted and were complicated by economic warfare waged with new instruments and by new methods. Even those who had some insight into the realities of trading and monetary relationships were far from consistent either in their thought or in their recommendations of policy.

The calculations of the political arithmeticians in the seventeenth century did little to elucidate theoretical relationships. The title of William Petty's first work is sufficient to indicate the discursive nature of their inquiries.[5] The close association of scientific theory and social practice, which Lancelot Hogben in *Dangerous Thoughts* refers to as being a feature of the "adventurous hopefulness" of early English capitalism, was stimulating but as yet undisciplined. In the hands of Adam Smith that association was to yield a rich harvest of specific investigations and illustrations illuminating a central hypothesis. But the hypothesis was as necessary as the investigations, and both were relative to the times.

The clearest insight as to the working of international trade continued to be displayed by men of affairs who used it practically to conduct their own operations, or theoretically, as did the officers of the East India Company, to defend those operations by ex parte arguments. This judgment is buttressed by the rediscovery in quite recent times of a remarkable work published early in the eighteenth century, which modern economists have hailed as the first systematic treatise on economic theory. The *Essai sur la Nature du Commerce en Général* is attributed to Richard Cantillon, "a financier of Irish extraction who had business in Paris, and was murdered by his servant in London in 1734."[6]

No one can read this remarkable work, which was almost completely neglected for more than a century, without being struck by its modernity, particularly in regard to matters where Cantillon himself had exact knowledge either through his own business or as a result of personal inquiries. One can well believe the description of him found in a manuscript written about 1750 by the elder Mirabeau, describing

[5] "A treatise of Taxes and Contributions, showing the Nature and Measures of Crown-Lands, Assessments, Customs, Poll-Moneys, Lotteries, Benevolences, Penalties, Monopolies, Offices, Tythes, Raising of Moneys, Hearth-Money, Excize, etc., With several intersperst Discources and Digressions concerning Warres, The Church, Universities, Rents and Purchases, Usury and Exchange, Banks and Lombards, Registries for Conveyances, Beggars, Ensurance, Exportation of Money, Wool, Free-Ports, Coins, Housing, Liberty of Conscience, etc. The same being frequently applied to the present State and Affairs of Ireland, 1662."

[6] Edwin Cannan, *A Review of Economic Theory*, London, 1929, p. 19. The French text, apparently translated by Cantillon himself from the original English manuscript, has been printed, with a re-translation into English, by the Royal Economic Society in Richard Cantillon's *Essai sur la Nature du Commerce,* London, 1931. The English version has been collated with the long extracts, apparently from the original MS, used by Postlethwayt in 1749 and 1751, for his *Dictionary of Commerce.* The editor (Henry Higgs) has also included the article by W. S. Jevons in the *Contemporary Review* of January, 1881, which restored a knowledge of Cantillon's work, and his own article in the first volume of the *Economic Journal,* 1891, giving the results of subsequent research.

his great mental activity, the insight with which he foresaw the course of John Law's monetary manipulations and made an immense profit from them, and the tireless curiosity which led him to investigate the details of economic activity wherever he traveled.

He was doubtless an exception among businessmen, particularly in the degree to which he was articulate and in his power to generalize from his practical experience. Though in parts of his essay he repeats the shibboleths of his time, wherever he treats of what he knows at firsthand, he is convincingly realistic. Thus he has a clear notion of what we should now call idle balances and of the quantity theory of money, concerning which he remarks acutely that "the great difficulty consists in knowing in what way and in what proportion the increase of money raises prices." He expounds the practice and theory of the foreign exchanges in precise terms of specie flows, mint par, and the specie points, and adds that "for those who have practical knowledge of it nothing is easier to understand, and they are rightly astonished that those who govern States and administer the Finances of great kingdoms have so little knowledge of the nature of exchanges as to forbid the export of bullion and of specie of gold and silver. The only way to keep them in a State is so to conduct foreign trade that the balance is not adverse to the State."

Adam Smith knew of his work, though his only citation of it is a passing reference to a small point on wages. What is more important is that the kind of practical knowledge which Cantillon analyzed in a systematic treatise must have been fairly well dispersed among his business contemporaries. There is little doubt that Adam Smith learned such facts from the businessmen with whom he dined regularly at Glasgow. And, though his ideas were formed before he traveled to France, they were reinforced by his contacts with the Physiocrats upon whom Cantillon exercised a considerable influence. It is as an unusually intellectual example of the businessmen and financiers of the eighteenth century that Cantillon is important. The book in which his ideas were set down in such succinct form was practically without influence, except indirectly through such writers as the Physiocrats and Malachi Postlethwayt. But those ideas were drawn from the progressive business methods which were becoming widespread in his day.

The Physiocrats who were active in France toward the end of the eighteenth century are important in the history of liberal thought, since they attacked the feudal land system and the toll which it levied upon the peasants and upon the domestic trade of France. It was one of their number, Jean Claude Marie Vincent de Gournay, who is credited with the phrase which has now become an international synonym for free competition—*laissez faire, laissez passer*—in protest against the vexatious regulation which was throttling the economic life of France.[7] John Rae, the biographer of Adam Smith, has described the rooms of their leader, François Quesnay as "a little sanctuary of free speech pitched by an odd chance in the heart of a despotic court." Here they earnestly discussed the catastrophe which they saw impending and tried to work out the bases for freeing landed property from the burdens under which it labored. France, like most countries of continental Europe, had not gone through the agrarian revolution which England had experienced in the sixteenth century. The Physiocrats were attempting to work out the applications of the idea of natural liberty to landed property, while their English contemporaries were applying the same idea to industrial property. This preoccupation with the land as the sole source of wealth, apparently reinforced by descriptions of China brought by returning Jesuit missionaries, stultified their economic analysis. In their attacks upon the regulations and tolls which interfered with the free flow of trade, they were in accord with the English philosophers of the time.

However it is to the English writers of the eighteenth century, and notably to David Hume (1711–76), that we must turn for the general ideas that finally led to a clearer understanding of the nature of international trade, and particularly of the balancing of payments between national economies. Professor Viner has given a clear account of the way in which the essential ideas and pieces of the reasoning were developed until they were fitted into a coherent synthesis by Hume. Viner shows first that the fact that "net international balances of payments must be settled in specie" was a commonplace of mercantilist discussion, and second, that the concept that "the quantity of money is a determinant of the level of prices" had gradually become accepted until by the eighteenth century it was not the subject of much dispute. It remained to prove that the volume of imports and exports depended upon relative prices at home and abroad and to demonstrate the connection between the flow of specie and the flow

[7] For the history of the phrase, cf. Henry Higgs (ed.), *Palgrave's Dictionary of Political Economy*, London, 1926, Vol. II, pp. 534–35.

of trade. Steps in this direction were taken by many writers. The credit, however, for the first complete formulation of a satisfactory theory is given to Hume.

Hume's exposition is as sharp and as clear as it is, partly because it is based upon the assumption of simple conditions. It assumes that money consists of coins exchangeable at their bullion value and that the quantity of money available has a simple and direct relation to the prices of commodities. Upon these assumptions Hume proceeds to show that, if a country loses a large part of its money in payment for an excess of imports over exports, commodity prices in that country will inevitably fall sharply. This will enable foreigners to buy goods cheaply in that country by paying for them in specie. On the other hand, the nationals of the country which has lost the specie will not be able to buy so much abroad because foreign prices will be too high. Therefore exports will increase and imports will decrease. The net balance due for these greater exports will be met by an inflow of specie until the transfer of metallic money reduces prices abroad and raises them at home to the levels at which in and out payments will once again be in equilibrium.

This states the barest elements of the price specie-flow analysis by which Hume for the first time demonstrated the working of a self-regulating mechanism for the balancing of payments between national economies. It proved that, if not interfered with by government regulation, the competitive operations of traders would keep commodity prices in equilibrium and would automatically distribute the available supplies of precious metals in accordance with the needs of trade. It is important to note that Hume's argument applies within a country as well as between countries. If left alone the money supply will flow where the needs of trade determine, so that commodity prices will be evened out.

The simple statement above omits many elements in the balancing of payments. Of some of these Hume was aware, and later economists have elaborated them. It is necessary to consider not only the effects of a loss of specie upon the price level of a country which imports more than it exports, but also the effects which result from the loss of income to producers in that country. The uneven incidence of both effects upon different classes in the community cannot be ignored. Moreover, account must be taken of other elements in the balance of payments besides commodity trade and specie flows. Much more than commodity trade must be considered, since invisible items and especially capital movements both on short and on long term greatly complicate the actual balancing process. That process must be analyzed as it operates when various kinds of money, not necessarily circulating at their bullion value, are used; when the use of paper money and of bank credit is greater than the use of actual coin; and finally when exchange rates fluctuate or are held at parities not determined by the ratio of the bullion values of national monies. All of these complications became of increasing importance as the organization of international trade took unprecedented leaps in the nineteenth century. Analysis of them is still founded upon Hume's exposition of the simplest case.

The importance of Hume's explanation of the balancing of payments between national economies extended far beyond a refutation of mercantilist ideas concerning the importance of treasure. What Hume did was of supreme importance for the future because he provided what appeared to be convincing proof that the free extension of international trade was possible without involving ruin to the national economy by deflating it of its money supply and creating uncontrollable dislocations of employment. Within national boundaries, in England particularly, considerable progress had been made toward reliance on a free market economy, unhampered by local or national regulation. The price specie-flow theory demonstrated that this kind of economy need not be hampered by concern for the balance of external payments. Coming just on the eve of that great burst of industrial invention which we now call the Industrial Revolution, Hume's theory of a self-regulating mechanism for the balancing of international payments enabled industrialists to demand freedom for their increasing volume of manufactured exports and for the equilibrating imports of raw materials.

THE LIMITS OF LAISSEZ FAIRE

The year 1776 was as memorable a year in the annals of thought as of action. Besides the Declaration of Independence, it was marked by the publication of Adam Smith's *An Inquiry into the Nature and Causes of the Wealth of Nations,* by Edward Gibbon's *History of the Decline and Fall of the Roman Empire,* by Jeremy Bentham's first work, the *Fragment on Government,* and by John Cartwright's *Take Your Choice,* the first step in his fight for annual parliaments and universal suffrage. The importance of these literary formulations of explosive ideas was not evident at the time, but they were to shape the political, legal, and economic development of the nineteenth century. The coincidence of these events was, of course, not fortuitous. The time was ripe for political change. Indeed it is probable that such change might have come even more rapidly if the excesses of the French Revolution had not frightened timid people.[8]

It is an interesting fact that the major interest and effect of Adam Smith's work was in the realm of political action, rather than in the development of economic ideas. Though his name is the best known of all writers on economic subjects, later generations of economists have built their theoretical systems and even the theory of international trade primarily upon the work of David Ricardo, who in turn drew largely upon Smith's predecessor, David Hume. It is, indeed, possible to pick out from earlier writers all the important ideas which Adam Smith used, and at the same time to demonstrate that Ricardo gave a logical precision to those ideas which is not to be found in *The Wealth of Nations*. Walter Bagehot, in his *Economic Studies*, refers to the way in which Adam Smith "describes at length, and in an interesting way, what we should now call non-economical phenomena; and, therefore, he *is* more intelligible than modern economists, and seems to be more practical." [9]

Bagehot, however, then goes on to assert that in fact the later economists, and especially Ricardo, were really more practical because they omitted all but strictly economic considerations and took "the most business-like step towards real practice—that of dealing with things one at a time." This assertion raises a difficult question. By basing his theory upon assumptions which excluded complicating social factors, Ricardo and his followers gave point and precision to the analysis of conduct governed solely by individual desire for gain in a society where no check is imposed upon such desire. This analysis was

[8] Cf. Elie Halevy, *The Growth of Philosophic Radicalism*, London, Faber & Faber, Ltd., 1928, p. 106: "The great historical fact, of which Adam Smith's doctrine is the theoretical equivalent, is the American Revolution. This, in a sense by force, converted the English public to the new doctrine of commercial liberalism, and showed the possibility of establishing commercial cosmopolitanism in the near future. The idea of free-trade spread first among isolated reformers, then among the most enlightened part of the public, then among an ever-increasing section of the population, whose immediate interests were suffering from a prolonged war." Cf. also John Rae, *Life of Adam Smith*, London, 1895, pp. 292–93.

[9] Walter Bagehot, *Economic Studies*, London, 1880.

a valuable exercise, yielding much insight into the working of a pure economic system, but it omitted aspects even of economic conduct that are vital to an understanding of society as a whole.

Adam Smith was not a scientific economist in this sense. Rather he was a social philosopher. Because of the range of his illustrations and of the many qualifications to his main thesis, widely differing schools of thought later claimed his authority. Such claims are nearly all unfounded and unjustified. The very essence of Adam Smith's work was its application to the problems of his own day. His great influence in his own time, and upon later generations, derives primarily from his sagacity and judgment of practical affairs rather than from any abstruse or involved reasoning. Because of his priority and eminence, and since his experience throws a flood of light upon the nature of economic studies, it is worth while to recall the main facts of his life and work.

He was born in 1723 and received a sound Scottish education. After passing under the influence of the philosopher Francis Hutcheson at Glasgow, he spent seven years at Oxford mainly concerned with his own reading and by his own account gaining little or nothing from the university teaching. When he returned to Edinburgh his first ambition apparently was in the field of literature. He offered, at the invitation of Lord Kames, a course of lectures on what we should now call political economy, and these lectures contained the main principles which he afterward elaborated in the *Wealth of Nations*. There was a great ferment of scientific activity in Edinburgh at this time, and Smith absorbed the current ideas as he had earlier absorbed Hutcheson's teaching of natural liberty. In 1750 at the age of 27, he was appointed Professor of Logic at Glasgow, and two years later transferred to the Chair of Moral Philosophy which he held till 1764. His first book, *The Theory of Moral Sentiments*, which appeared in 1759, must have occupied much of his time during these years, but he was actively interested also in current economic discussions. Hume consulted him on his publications, and he was a regular participant both in Glasgow and in Edinburgh in dinner discussions of business and academic groups.

In 1761 he made his first visit to London, where he met the notable intellectuals of the time. In 1764 he became tutor to the young Duke of Buccleuch, a post that was not only well paid, but carried a life pension. From 1764 to 1766, he was in France with his pupil first at

Toulouse where he began to write *The Wealth of Nations,* and then for several months in Paris where he became familiar with the most stimulating intellectual circles in Europe, and particularly with the Physiocrats. A first draft of *The Wealth of Nations* was apparently completed in 1770 after his return to Scotland where he was appointed a Commissioner of Customs.

He worked on the book for another six years. For three of these years he was in London, a man of considerable fame with access to the most distinguished intellectual and political society of England, having been elected a Fellow of the Royal Society in 1767. There is much evidence that he drew heavily upon these opportunities for consultation and criticism. Benjamin Franklin was among his acquaintances, and it has been claimed that this goes far to account for the authenticity of the many references to colonial conditions which are scattered through *The Wealth of Nations.* Later research, however, indicates that the acquaintance may not have been quite as close as biographers of Adam Smith and of Franklin have sometimes claimed. Colonial questions were topical in the 1770's and Adam Smith could have learned from many other sources than Franklin.

It is no detraction from the originality and achievement of Adam Smith to lay stress upon his debt to others. His fame is secure, both because of the ammunition he furnished to economic reformers, and because he was the first to set out a systematic and consistent explanation of economic behavior. This he did by applying to economic questions the theory of natural liberty already worked out by political philosophers and theologians. The animus of *The Wealth of Nations* is an attack upon specific cases of exploitation and interferences with the free and beneficient working of a system of natural liberty. In particular it is an attack upon mercantilist restrictions on trade. Without the elaboration of this attack, made realistic by his abundant references to practical detail, the book would not have been the influential work it is.

Indeed one may go further and doubt whether Adam Smith was as thorough a believer in laissez faire as his followers and popularizers came to be. He had intended to complete his lifework by a volume on the functions of government. It is probable that notes for this volume or even a draft of it were among the sixteen volumes of manuscript which, at his insistence, were destroyed a week before he died. However, there is enough evidence to indicate that if such a volume had been written, it might not have supported the extreme case for laissez faire even in his own time, while its argument would have been primarily in pragmatic rather than absolute terms.

In stating the case for laissez faire Adam Smith took account of administrative procedures, which in his day had reached a very low point of efficiency. In his pragmatic view no weakness of laissez faire could be worse than the specific abuses of the government controls and monopoly practices at which his attack was directed. He was ready to concede that where government was efficient it could perform useful economic functions. Moreover, as Professor Viner has indicated, there are passages even in *The Wealth of Nations,* upon which it would be possible to make an argument for state intervention to ensure defense, to control investment through the usury laws, to use taxation as a means of social reform, to ensure economic justice, and to promote public works, public health, education, and even commercial enterprises if they do not entail a burden upon the public finances.

It would of course be absurd to push this argument too far. We can only surmise what Adam Smith might have written in his projected volume on the functions of government, and the main drift of *The Wealth of Nations* is clearly an attack upon government intervention. This section has been written to emphasize two main points. First, Adam Smith's writing was positive. If we are to interpret correctly his great contribution to the formulation of economic theory, we must remember that it was an attack upon specific evils of his day, not a defense of economic anarchy in later and vastly different circumstances.[10]

Secondly, it begins to be clear that his pragmatic and sagacious

10 Arnold Toynbee, *Lectures on the Industrial Revolution of the 18th Century in England,* London, 1884, pp. 13–14: "Whether he writes as a pamphleteer or a historian; whether he is pursuing a grave investigation into the influence of political institutions on economic progress, or dogging tedious and confused advocates of the mercantile system through all the weary windings of their arguments; whether he is engaged in learned research, fierce denunciation, dubious refutation, every page of Adam Smith's writings is illumined by one great passion, the passion for freedom. . . . All around were the signs of an obsolete system of restriction, cramping and choking political and industrial life. . . . Whilst Turgot, the governor of a province, was labouring day and night to improve the conditions of down-trodden peasants, Adam Smith, the professor, was shielding from the effects of obsolete privileges the greatest mechanical genius of the age. Nothing can be more interesting than that story of James Watt, refused permission to practise his trade by the corporation of hammermen, but admitted by the professor within the walls of the University of Glasgow, and allowed there to set up his workshop. Thus in Glasgow . . . and in Limousin . . . the same lesson was being forced into men's minds—the need of liberty; and at the same time great mechanical inventions were preparing the way for a new age."

wisdom rested in no small measure precisely upon his attention to those non-economical phenomena to which Bagehot made deprecatory reference. In Bagehot's words, since he considered "the natural progress of opulence as an item in greater studies, as part of the natural growth of human civilization, Adam Smith always thought how it had been affected by human nature, taken as a whole." He knew that factors other than selfish acquisitive motives were influential even on economic behavior. Because he knew this, he did not limit too narrowly the premises upon which his reasoning was based, and he checked that reasoning by frequently appealing to concrete instances. Thus he was saved from the false generalizations to which more rigorous logicians were later led by the unguarded inadequacy of their assumptions.

THE CHALLENGE OF REVOLUTION

The last quarter of the eighteenth century began with the American Revolution. The full political import of this event was not recognized quickly, and it was not till a few years later when the French Revolution passed into a reign of terror that the decay of the old political order became evident. Between these political revolutions, an economic incident of far-reaching significance passed almost unnoticed. In 1785 the firm of Boulton and Watt installed a steam engine to power a cotton mill. This was the year when Arkwright's patents on his textile inventions expired and the new spinning processes became freely available to the textile industries. Mechanical methods of production powered by steam called forth the factory system which was to set a new pattern of urban life. The rapidity with which manufacturing towns were to develop could hardly be foreseen, but in retrospect this economic incident appears as no less revolutionary than the opening shots at Lexington or the storming of the Bastille. By the end of the century, therefore, the political and economic forces which were to shape modern life were already discernible.

Among the ruling classes, it was a period of great complacency, and serious thought on the consequences of these events hardly penetrated. Samuel Johnson was the arbiter of literary London. Tattered copies of Tom Paine's pamphlets might circulate among the almost equally tattered revolutionary armies. But if his ideas ever penetrated to the best circles they could be dismissed with a rotund aphorism. John Wesley knew that "you cannot be too superficial in addressing a polite audience," and his remark measures the intellectual standards of the English upper classes in his time. The universities and with them the church and Parliament had sunk very low. Politics, not yet quite set in constitutional practice nor organized along party lines, was largely a struggle between those who looked for preferment to the king and those who pinned their hopes on his heir. The Crown competed with other interests in the purchase of boroughs. Appointments were made for good or ill mainly by nepotism and patronage. Adam Smith, for example, owed his well-paid post as Commissioner of Customs in Scotland to Lord North, whose budgets to finance the war against the American colonies had drawn upon *The Wealth of Nations* for new tax ideas. Local administration was in the hands of the country landowners and clergy, whom Henry Fielding caricatured so savagely in his novels.

Even so Englishmen took pride in their Constitution, in the well-being and independence of their people, and in the freedom of their institutions. They looked across the Channel to the elegance of Versailles and the misery upon which its splendid extravagance rested, and to less elegant centers of absolutism beyond. They felt that foreigners like Montesquieu had been no more than just in holding British institutions up to admiration. Despite independence, there was a good deal of this feeling in the United States also. The Constitution was written by substantial men who drew heavily upon the philosophy of the English Revolution of 1688. Tom Paine and Sam Adams had no part in its drafting.

The industrial changes which clustered about the introduction of the factory system were slower in their development and less dramatic than the political revolutions. But they were even more revolutionary in their ultimate effect upon the daily lives of common people all over the world. The Industrial Revolution, as we now call these changes, is not easy to define or describe, or even to date. It is not easy to diagnose its origins, its main forces, or its social consequences. Eminent authority can be quoted today for the view that it was primarily the result of a series of mechanical inventions, culminating in James Watt's steam engine, or of canal and road construction widening market areas, or of credit expansion, or of a liberation of commercial enterprise exploiting cheap labor pauperized by the maladministration of the Poor Law. One school of economic historians emphasizes the social dislocation, poverty, and human degradation of the new manufacturing towns. Another school emphasizes the increased productivity and higher wages of the workpeople in the new industries.

Those who lived through this period seem to have had as little recognition of the revolutionary import of the new industrial methods as even professional observers have had in our time of the dramatic acceleration of organized research in the experimental sciences. Adam Smith knew James Watt and helped to provide him with facilities for his experiments in the University of Glasgow, but *The Wealth of Nations* does not anticipate the momentous consequences of steam power. Indeed instances could be multiplied to show that the extent and the pace of economic and social change caught even the shrewdest observers off guard. They were unable to comprehend the revolutionary nature of the changes whose beginnings they were witnessing. No one should be surprised at this. Prophecy can never be precise, except in the short run, and those who know most of current happenings are inevitably bound by their knowledge.

It has recently been argued that the apparent facts on which the principles of the classical economists—Malthus, Ricardo, and James Mill—were grounded "reflected merely paradoxical tendencies prevailing during a sharply defined period of transition." This argument echoes the protests made throughout the nineteenth century, not so much against the logic of the classical economists as against the applications made of their logic to practical affairs. It is a protest against the concept of the "economic man" and the neglect of those aspects of civic association that are not implied in the division of labor—against the "smashing up of social structures in order to extract the element of labor from them." [11]

How did it happen that a group of mildly reformist individuals as the classical economists were, all of them "left of center" in their

[11] K. Polanyi, *The Great Transformation,* New York, 1944, p. 104 and p. 164. Cf. also Arnold Toynbee, *op. cit.,* p. 23: "The conception of men, not as members of families, associations and nations, but as isolated individuals connected only by pecuniary interests, is essentially the conception of them which pervaded economic science. And not only was this conception the peculiar characteristic of Political Economy as a theoretical science, but it determined its whole bearing as a practical science . . . the fatal confusion between laws and precepts which made Political Economy appear as the gospel of self-interest . . . did without doubt practically assert that pecuniary interest was a sufficient bond between men. . . . No wonder, then, that against the economists were arrayed philosophers, moralists, even statesmen. All these saw in the doctrine of individualism a solvent of domestic political and national union—a great disintegrating element of social life."

personal opinions, came to be regarded as prophets of a soulless, reactionary, antisocial creed? Jeremy Bentham, who devoted his life and fortune to the search for practical means of achieving the greatest happiness of the greatest number, came at last to acceptance of political democracy as the means of achieving it. James Mill, a young Scot trained for the ministry, lived a laborious life as a London journalist, tilting against every aspect of reactionary legislation and very active in progressive educational movements. Francis Place began his public career as a strike organizer, and after he had himself become an employer worked for every reform cause. David Ricardo, the most abstract of all the theorists, was a generous personality and was associated with Joseph Hume in the successful campaign for removal of the iniquitous Combination Acts that rendered the organizers of trade unions liable to prosecution for conspiracy. The Reverend Thomas Robert Malthus wrote his *Essay on Population,* one of the basic pillars of the classical system, in protest against the illusions of William Godwin, the radical philosopher whose public views seemed to his contemporaries no less unscrupulous than his private extravagance. Malthus himself never accepted the deductions which Ricardo drew from his essay. Obviously such men as these, high-minded, conscientious, and able, did not set out to become the high priests of a grinding, conscienceless, materialistic social order.

They wrote in an era of transition. Their attack was on the privilege and exploitation of the social order which was crumbling into decay. They were optimistic enough to believe that the new order would not have need of social restraints against the strong and of protection for the weak. At least they did not pay much attention to the possibility that such needs would arise. Moreover they were in the grip of current events and doctrines more than they realized. It is as unfair to blame them for accepting the poverty and degradation they saw around them and for relying upon the individual's own efforts to avoid these evils, as it would be to blame John Wesley for stressing individual salvation, with its concomitant of resignation in this life and reward hereafter. It is not necessary to accept such attitudes as valid, even for their own times and still less for ours, but they can be understood.

The bridging of the gap between the empirical, and not always consistent, social philosophy of Adam Smith and the more rigid assumptions from which the precise analyses of the classical economists were deduced, has been described by Halevy almost as a kind of self-hypnotism.[12] In his view the economists set themselves to disguise naturalism (a view of the world and of man's relation to it in which only the operation of natural, as opposed to supernatural or spiritual, laws and forces is admitted or assumed) as rationalism (a system based solely on reasoning). This is another way of saying that the assumptions on which their reasoning was built were derived from the natural laws which seemed to them to be operative in their own time. Hence such deductions as Malthus' principle that population would always tend to increase up to the limits of subsistence.

A case can be made for believing that this "principle of population" was, indeed, the foundation upon which the whole structure of classical economics was erected. Malthus himself formulated the law of rent. As a logical consequence of increasing pressure of population upon limited natural resources, inferior land would be brought into cultivation and diminishing returns would be received from successive applications of labor and capital to all land. Hence there would be a differential return, leading to an increased value of the best or the most favorably situated land, and this return or rent would be the ultimate repository of increased productivity.[13]

Upon these foundations Ricardo was egged on by James Mill to work out his theories of the distribution of wealth. His *Principles of Political Economy and Taxation,* in 1817, was the first general economic treatise to be published in England since *The Wealth of Nations.*[14] Its style is dry, its reasoning is abstract, and its illustrations

[12] Elie Halevy, *op. cit.,* pp. 105–6.

[13] Cf. Elie Halevy, *A History of the English People in 1815* (Penguin ed.), London, Ernest Benn, Ltd., 1938, Vol. 3, p. 203: "Little by little he had reached an original theory of rent which he regarded as the direct consequence of the *Principle* which he had formulated in 1798. . . . When the restoration of peace was followed by an agricultural crisis, a Parliamentary Commission was appointed to investigate its causes. A large proportion of the witnesses before this Commission maintained, almost unconsciously, the theory of Malthus. Buchanan, in his edition of the *Wealth of Nations* published in 1814, and the economist West in an essay published in 1815, maintained theories closely akin to the theories of Malthus. Malthus decided that, if he were not to lose his property in the theory, he must no longer delay its publication. He therefore published [1815] his essay on the *Nature and Progress of Rent.*

"This was the signal for Ricardo to intervene . . . he accepted the two laws which Malthus had formulated and of which the latter depended on the former, his law of population and his law of rent. But he rejected the protectionist consequences which Malthus deduced from his laws in his essay of 1815. And to prove his own doctrine of Free Trade he built upon both an original system of laws regulating the distribution of wealth."

[14] Jean Baptiste Say published a systematic treatise, *Traité d'Economie Politique,* at Paris in 1802, and its logical arrangement went far to set the pattern of subsequent treatises. Its English translator, in 1821, referred to the work in England of "Malthus

are hypothetical. As Ricardo's contemporary, himself a famous economist and one of the main authors of the reform of the Poor Laws, Nassau Senior was later to assert: "Political Economy is not greedy of facts; it is independent of facts." The assumptions of Ricardo's logic are not clearly stated, but the conclusions are set out dogmatically, as if they applied not only to Ricardo's England, as indeed he believed they did, but were universally true. Industriously plugged by James Mill and his associates in London, and by J. R. McCulloch, the Scottish journalist in Edinburgh, the publication rapidly gained an almost scriptural authority among those who were out to destroy the chief remaining barriers to manufacturing expansion—relief of the laboring poor, regulation of the labor market, and protection to shipping and agriculture.

Ricardo's earlier essays had been in fields where his assumptions were closer to reality. The generalizing of his arguments, particularly in regard to income distribution, developed into what Ferdinand Lassalle, the German socialist and precursor of Karl Marx, later called "the iron law of wages" and the tendency of the rate of profits to diminish. In this view, the unfortunate plight of the laborer was held to be the working out of inescapable natural law and the creative capitalist became a public benefactor, while the privileged landlord secured the ultimate profit of improved production. In the technical analysis of specific aspects of this general scheme and notably in regard to the working of the monetary system at the time, Ricardo's acute mind and wealth of practical experience enabled him to make valuable contributions to economic thought. It was the general economic philosophy derived from his writings that won him recognition.[15]

on Population; Young, Torrens, and numberless others on Agriculture; Thornton on Credit; Ricardo on Money; Blake on Exchanges; Cobbett on Fluctuation of Price; Hamilton on National Debt; Brougham on Colonial Policy," and to Ricardo's *Principles* which he described as "limited in range, involved in the style and defective in the arrangement." Say's work is therefore presented as containing "the best and most methodical view of the general theory of wealth that has yet appeared."

[15] Cf. J. R. McCulloch, *The Works of David Ricardo,* London, 1846 (new edition, 1888), pp. xxv and xxvii: "The establishment of general principles being Mr. Ricardo's great object, he has paid comparatively little attention to their practical application, and sometimes, indeed, he has in great measure overlooked the circumstances by which they are occasionally countervailed . . . The change that has taken place in the public opinion respecting the financial and commercial policy of the country, since the period when Mr. Ricardo obtained a seat in the House of Commons, is as complete as it is gratifying. Not only are the most enlarged principles advocated by all the leading members of both Houses; not only are they now ready to admit that the exclusive system is founded on vicious principles; but they are about to make these doctrines a part of the law of the land, and to give them the sanction of parliamentary authority."

Appalled by the prevailing social distress, the paternalistic and sentimental Tories clung to such remnants of the Elizabethan state controls as had survived, and particularly to the system of poor relief which in 1795 had become a vast system of indiscriminate wage subsidies. The political economists would have none of this, and much of the invective leveled against them came from the harsh surgery they proposed and ultimately carried through in an effort to restore independence and self-respect to the laborer by throwing him upon his own resources. It was necessary to cut away the remnants of an outworn system of labor regulation which had degenerated into an appalling instrument of pauperization. It was also necessary to cut away the privileges of the landowners, and especially the burdensome import duty on wheat. There were many other survivals of the old mercantile system that had outlived any usefulness they may ever have had only to become obstructions to new enterprise and shelters for privilege, inefficiency, and unearned income.

Gradually the mass of the more informed workers swung away from paternalism and accepted the doctrines of self-reliant and self-respecting freedom. The intellectuals led the way. William Wilberforce, agitating for reforms such as the abolition of the slave trade, was surprised to find that his most potent allies were the philosophic radicals. Francis Place brought contacts with those workers and radicals who were active in promoting electoral reform. The philosophic radicals on their part accepted the logic of political democracy. Before the first quarter of the nineteenth century had ended, a formidable mass movement was in the making, aiming at parliamentary reform, popular education, abolition of the Poor Laws, repeal of the Navigation Acts, and ultimately also of the Corn Laws. Though criticism of the harshness of economic doctrine was not stilled, laissez faire became the creed of all but a minority of reformers.

It is true that Robert Owen laid the foundations of modern socialist thought and that after him a group of obscure writers were to provide ammunition for Karl Marx. The Swiss economist de Sismondi visited England in 1818 and was shocked both by the anarchy of economic conditions and by the optimistic advocacy of anarchic economic principles. But these were voices crying in the wilderness. James Mill and Francis Place in London and J. R. McCulloch in Edinburgh had constituted themselves a lobby and propaganda agency to spread the gospel according to Ricardo. Such was their energy and skill that, when the great surge of expanding trade carried England to commercial and industrial supremacy, it had become heretical to challenge Ricardo's authority.

Yet this teaching rested upon a curious mixture of pessimistic resignation to the supposed facts of nature and of optimistic belief that in the long run nature, if left alone, would do better than governments could do by interfering with her processes. The Ricardians, however, were keenly interested in education. Men, they held, should be equipped with knowledge (especially it must be said of the current political economy) so that they might know their interest in a competitive society. Hence the interest of James Mill and Jeremy Bentham in school and university reform, and of Francis Place in popular education. Place, and in his youth John Stuart Mill, included a knowledge of contraception in this educational process, but until very recent days such knowledge continued to be almost universally regarded as impious and antisocial.

Education, however, proved too frail and slow-growing a reed for the working people to cling to in the catastrophic changes of the Industrial Revolution. Laissez faire, whether based upon the harmony of egoisms ordained by an all-wise providence or, after Darwin, upon belief in the survival of the fittest, became a destructive creed. Propagated as an instrument to clear away the debris of an outworn system of state regulation, it was used to obstruct the erection of needed safety devices in the new mechanical age. Not only displaced farm laborers and craft workers in England, but peasants in India, and wherever the industrial system spread, were ground through its "dark, satanic mills." What came out in the long run was an immense increase of production, unevenly distributed, but adequate to provide better living standards for much larger numbers. In the process, however, great misery was inflicted on individuals and groups. England was the center and testing ground of this development, but its effects spread over the whole trading world.

PART II

THE NINETEENTH CENTURY

"THE London discount market where the whole world was both borrower and lender was the crux of the one-centered, pre-war world credit system. This market was from the world point of view an international credit mechanism under expert British control. . . . The way in which normal pre-war London was geared to the economic activity of the world was admirably epitomized by B. M. Anderson, Jr., three years ago:

" 'More commodities were dealt in in London than in any other single center. There was a great community of expert students of commodities, of recognized integrity, whose grading of commodities was accepted throughout the world. There was an admirable warehouse system. There was a great body of expert speculative buyers, who knew their outlets, and who were prepared to buy, at a concession in price, almost any commodity, on very short notice. The merchants of the world trusted this machinery, and the British banks could safely trust it. They could make loans which were truly liquid loans, against virtually any commodity. The London stock market also was a wide and dependable stock market, which readily made marketable a greater range of securities than would be marketable in any other center and which consequently made good collateral out of securities which could not serve as collateral, safely, in other financial centers. The foreign exchange of every country in the world was freely dealt in in London, and could consequently be made the basis of bank credit. What came to London became liquid, and everything came to London.' "

William Adams Brown, Jr., *The International Gold Standard Reinterpreted, 1914–1934,* New York, 1940, Vol. I, p. xvii.

CHAPTER VI

LAISSEZ FAIRE: PRACTICE AND THEORY

THE NEGATIVE VIRTUES OF LAISSEZ FAIRE

To understand the tremendous expansion of international trade during the nineteenth century, the controversies over commercial policy to which that expansion gave rise, and the theories of international trade which emerged from those controversies, it is necessary first to trace the outlines of the industrial system that was developing as the nineteenth century opened. The use of steam power was just being mastered. Soon it would be applied to transport both on sea and on land. Metallurgy had reached the point where the new power could be harnessed. Textile machines had been invented which were to open the way to new methods of factory production.

The out-thrust of these industrial changes was felt in every land where the industrializing nations of western Europe sought raw materials to supply the developing factories, and food to feed the growing populations of their factory towns. The impact of factory exports was almost as immediate and even more widespread. The handicrafts of India crumbled under the competition of cheap machine-made cottons and metalwares. As momentum was gathered, trade grew by leaps and bounds. The steam locomotive opened up vast inland areas, the cultivation of which transformed the world's food supplies. The tramp steamer ploughed its way into remote ports and brought not only the newly colonized lands but also the ancient civilizations of Asia into the network of world trade that was centered on London. The whole world was linked in a series of intersecting markets.

The dream developed of a great republic of world commerce, in which national boundaries would cease to have any great economic importance and the web of trade would bind all the peoples of the world in the prosperity of peace. The optimistic idealism which was characteristic of the bustling commercial prosperity of the mid-nineteenth century took its furthest leap in respect of international trade. Peace was the ultimate utopia toward which progress and prosperity were to lead the free peoples of the world. Tennyson, in *Locksley Hall,* wrote his lines about aerial commerce and airy navies raining a ghastly dew, as preliminary to the organization of peace and universal law created by "the common sense of most."

The social philosophy of laissez faire was derived from the somewhat naïve optimism discussed in the preceding chapter as the background of classical economic theory. Self-interest pursued in a competitive society, it was believed, would achieve the greatest good for the greatest number, internationally as well as nationally. The Indian or the Chinese peasant, equally with the new factory workers, would gain in the long run by being drawn into this beneficent circle of exchange. He might be living in what Bagehot called a "pre-economic age," and the process of shifting from such an age to modernity might involve some passing discomfort but the gains of economic maturity could be speeded by resort to the kindly, practical aid of the money market. As Bagehot remarked: "We press upon half-finished and half-civilized communities incalculable sums; we are to them what the London money-lenders are to students at Oxford and Cambridge."

The notion of world-wide competitive specialization leading to mutual prosperity and a common interest in peace was a noble and plausible dream, grounded in reality. For a brief period in the third quarter of the century it caught the imagination of enlightened leaders of public opinion in every country. The costs of transition, however, came too high. The advocates of laissez faire in the early nineteenth century were successful in their attack upon outworn and cumbrous forms of social regulation that were impeding the use of new technical processes. They were able to sweep away much of the old system by which government had endeavored to regulate wages, employment, and prices, but they put nothing in its place, and the workers in India as in Lancashire proved unable to safeguard their interests in the new competitive struggle. English political history in the nineteenth century was largely concerned with the creation of new safeguards for the economically weak, beginning with the first Factory Act in 1819. By the end of that century, the dream was fading. Men began to doubt the ultimate achievement of peace through prosperity, and the twentieth century has lived through the death agonies of the laissez-faire system.

The virtues and achievements of the age of laissez faire should not, however, be forgotten. The nineteenth-century faith in free competition may have been utopian, but it was lusty and long-lived, and in many respects productive of immense social gains. It gave scope to invention and enterprise that transformed methods of production, trade, and transport, and this transformation is still in process. The use of new techniques gave subsistence at higher levels of well-being to a world population that more than doubled in the interval. Under its impact the Americas gained independence and strength and the British Dominions gained independence in an associative commonwealth. Representative government, popular education and trade unionism were among the by-products of this age. The common man, wherever industrialism spread, gained more in material welfare and ultimately in social status and political power than in any previous century.

As the eighteenth century drew to its close, a great industrial transformation was changing the aspect of the English countryside, particularly in the northern counties. Wordsworth's solitary wanderer took a poetic view of this transformation. He noted the disappearance of

> The foot-path faintly marked, the horse-track wild,
> And formidable length of plashy lane.

These, under the vigorous engineering of Telford and Macadam, were giving way to "stately roads." Canals also were being built, and the poet notes the ceaseless traffic gliding "along the low and woody dale, or on the naked mountain's lofty side."

But what really caught his imagination was the rapid growth of the new industrial towns.

> Meanwhile, at social industry's command,
> How quick, how vast an increase! From the germ

Of some poor hamlet, rapidly produced
Here a huge town, continuous and compact,
Hiding the face of earth for leagues—and there,
Where not a habitation stood before,
Abodes of men irregularly massed
Like trees in forests—spread through spacious tracts
O'er which the smoke of unremitting fires
Hangs permanent, and plentiful as wreaths
Of vapour glittering in the morning-sun.[1]

This is a pretty picture, and so is the description which follows of bustling ports crowded with shipping, "freighted from every climate of the world." In the comfortable perspective of history, it is clear that poetic imagination laid hold of important aspects of the changing economic scene.

After the price inflation of the Napoleonic war period had been worked off, there was a tremendous increase of productivity and the purchasing power of wages steadily increased. During most of the nineteenth century real standards of living rose greatly, though not evenly nor equitably. Especially in the latter part of the century, after railroads had begun to open up great inland food-producing areas, not a little of this improvement in living standards was due to the widening of consumer's choice made possible by the vast increase in world trade. The price of food declined sharply and many important commodities became available to wider circles of consumers. Among these commodities were tea, coffee, cocoa, sugar, rice, tapioca, raisins, currants, oranges, and lemons, which had formerly been luxuries of the rich, but in the second half of the nineteenth century became conventional necessities to all classes.

These were the ultimate gains from a long process of change and development. They were reaped not by those who suffered in the process but by those who inherited the gains from trade. The suffering was immediate in its impact, particularly upon the working classes. Social historians have laid stress upon the deterioration of working conditions—the tyranny of the factory whistle and the monotony of the new machine processes which made factory workers out of independent craftsmen. Hours were long enough and wages low enough in the new factories, but they were better than in the declining handicraft and rural industries. To contemporary observers, the worst ef-

[1] William Wordsworth, *The Excursion*, Book VIII.

fects of the new industrial processes were the prolonged decay of what had been prosperous crafts, the abuse of child labor in some factories, and, worst of all, the deplorable working and housing conditions and lack of decent living facilities in the factory towns.

Whatever gains were made in the long run, there can be no doubt that the Industrial Revolution accelerated the break-up of the balanced and reasonably prosperous village economy, while for the working population in the factory towns life became more drab, less healthful, more insecure, and less self-respecting. Much of this deterioration is directly traceable to the fact that the towns grew rapidly in a haphazard fashion. In the deplorably ineffective conditions of municipal government at the close of the eighteenth century, there was no authority capable of restraining the greed of speculators or of providing essential public services. Urban life became set in a pattern from which it has not yet been possible to break completely free.

The Industrial Revolution made its first, and perhaps its worst, impact upon living conditions in northern England. The story of its excesses has been revealed in the evidence given before successive royal commissions on factory legislation, as well as in the contemporary protests of social workers. Karl Marx drew heavily upon this material to support his analysis of capitalist development. Wherever urban industrialism has spread, the story has been repeated.

The significance of these developments for an understanding of modern international questions lies in the fact that trade, by introducing either the cheapened products of machine processes, or the processes themselves, dislocated employment and living conditions all over the world. When the new textile inventions became freely available to enterprising capitalists just as steam power was being successfully harnessed, a great new cotton industry developed, drawing its raw materials more and more from the United States and sending its cheap manufactures all over the world. There was a sharp reversal of the trade currents between England and Asia. Instead of drawing cotton cloths from the handicraft looms of the Orient, England loosed a flood of cheap cotton goods into Eastern markets. The impact of the textile inventions was closer home in the woolen industry. The handicraftsmen of the southern and western counties of England found it hard to meet the competition of the Yorkshire factories and the handloom weavers went through a long period of depression which ended in the virtual elimination of their craft. Such a disturbance of markets is, of course, inevitable with every advance in the methods of production and marketing, but the pace of change caught, and still catches, most communities unprepared. The pace of change has constantly accelerated, and business enterprise has always moved faster than governments could cope with its consequences.

David Ricardo, confining himself to the purely economic aspects of the changes brought about by machinery, admitted that the earning power of the workers might be reduced. The wider social consequences of rapid industrial change must also be taken into account. Ricardo was a man of generous feeling and it is hard to believe that he would have remained unmoved by the conditions in which factory operatives lived and worked, or content to ignore them. He was typical of his time in taking poverty for granted. Economic writers since Aristotle had accepted the subsistence theory of wages—that unskilled workers would never for long receive much more than was necessary to keep them alive and reproducing. The heart of Ricardo's economic reasoning is to be found in his *Essay on the Influence of a Low Price of Corn on the Profits of Stock,* published in 1815. In this essay he commits himself to the statement that "experience demonstrates that capital and population alternately take the lead, and wages in consequence are liberal or scanty." If this assertion is granted, it follows that the essential conflict of interest which determines the division of the national income is between the landowner and the capitalist—and that nothing can be done about increasing the share of labor, except temporarily, since the population will always increase up to what he calls its "natural limit." In the harsher language of many of his followers, the improvidence of the workers in thus multiplying their numbers was stated in terms very curiously akin to those sometimes used in our own time to describe the less wealthy sections of the population of our own or other countries.

In order to understand this attitude, it is necessary to appreciate the effect produced upon the minds of thinking men by the sudden and alarming increase of the laboring population toward the end of the eighteenth century. The basic cause of this increase was the agricultural revolution that had been developing gradually in England from the seventeenth century on. Improved methods of drainage, cultivation, fertilizing, and animal breeding had increased food supplies. More abundant and varied nutrition brought greater resistance to disease and there was a slow decline in the death rate, particularly in the rate of infant mortality. Statistics are available from 1780 to measure this decline, but it must have been proceeding steadily for decades because population increased substantially throughout most of the seventeenth and eighteenth centuries. The increased numbers were welcomed as a source of national power. Agriculture was prosperous and the handicrafts, particularly woolen spinning and weaving, shared in the prosperity.

The population increase was cumulative. Larger numbers in one generation gave birth to still larger numbers in the next. In the last quarter of the eighteenth century, new possibilities of reducing the death rate, particularly from epidemic diseases, began to be evident. The "great sanitary awakening" did not produce its most marked effects until the latter half of the nineteenth century; but towns like London were bringing in fresh water from outlying streams quite early in the eighteenth century. Better nutrition, improved sanitation, and improved medical knowledge—as evidenced by Edward Jenner's publication, in 1798, of his experiments in vaccination for smallpox—seemed likely to reduce the death rate further and further.

Meantime the handicrafts had been struck a mortal blow by the application of steam power to machines in the new factories. Just when the agricultural population had swelled to alarming proportions, the economic balance of the countryside in the south of England was disturbed by loss of the supplementary earnings from such crafts as spinning and weaving. To relieve the distress of the farm laborers and their families, the country justices who administered the Poor Law system began in 1782 to dole out payments in cash to indigent applicants, and to make such payments proportionate to the number of children in the family. There seems little doubt that this indiscriminate relief, given without any requirement to work, contributed to the demoralization of the rural workers and to their more rapid increase in numbers.

Malthus published his *Essay on Population* in 1798 to draw attention to the social problems thus being created. He based his argument on the fact that population was capable of increasing in a geometrical ratio, every increase producing a greater increase in the succeeding generation, while food could be increased only in an arithmetical ratio, which diminished as poorer land had to be brought into cultivation. A cumulative increase of numbers would therefore press down the level of subsistence. Unless voluntary restraint was exercised, by the postponement of marriage and strict morality outside of marriage, the tendency of population to increase would inevitably lead to what Malthus described as the harsh natural checks imposed by war, pestilence, and famine. Malthus was a clergyman, whose main objective was to press home the moral argument for voluntary restraint of numbers; but the harsh teaching became accepted as economic doctrine. More and more it was used as an alibi, a convenient argument against higher wages or any other social reform.

The classical economists ascribed responsibility for the despair and demoralization of the English laboring classes at the beginning of the nineteenth century primarily to the indiscriminate charity of the Poor Law system of cash payments for relief of the indigent laborers. There is no doubt that the granting of outdoor cash relief proportioned to the size of families operated as a depressing influence on wage rates. It sapped the self-respect and independence of large masses both of the displaced agricultural laborers and of the skilled craftsmen who were thrown out of work by the new machine processes. As the number of paupers on relief increased, their shiftlessness and apathy appeared to justify the belief that they were incapable of raising their material or moral standards. They came to constitute a diseased section of the body politic and drastic surgery became necessary. In 1834 the advocates of reform carried through the Poor Law Reform Act which stopped outdoor relief, created workhouses, and generally imposed both a moral stigma and harsh discipline upon paupers. The severity of this regime caused great suffering and led to strong protests. It was defended as necessary to restore independence and self-respect to the workers. In the long run, a great increase of productivity carried all classes to higher living levels. But the costs of transition were thrown upon those least able to bear them.

It should not be forgotten that the worst and most widespread misery came from 1815 onward, at the close of the Napoleonic Wars. The fact is too often forgotten that the waste, and still more the economic distortion, of war was an important cause of social distress. During the actual war effort there was vigorous productivity and a high level of employment, though scarcities developed and consumption was restricted. When the war ended the transition to peace revealed impoverishment. Taxation was high. Unemployment accompanied reconversion in a succession of sharp industrial and financial crises. The credit expansion necessary to finance war expenditures had led to a

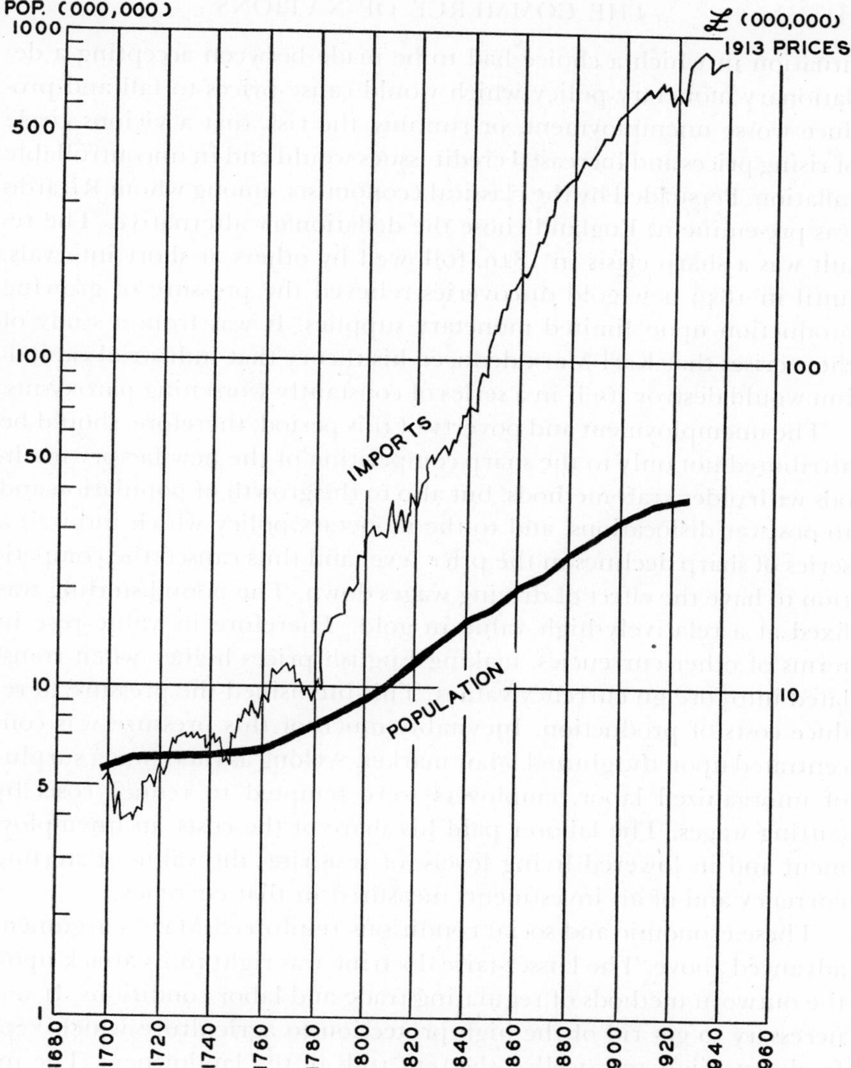

BRITISH TRADE AND POPULATION, 1700–1925

Note the trading set-backs caused by the American Revolution (ca. 1780) and the economic crises following the Napoleonic Wars (ca. 1800–1820). The rapid rise of imports more than offset the growth of population.

Sources: For population data, 1700–1841—G. Talbot Griffith, *Population Problems of the Age of Malthus,* Cambridge University Press, 1926, pp. 18, 21; 1841–1931—*Encyclopedia Britannica.* For the trade data—Werner Schlote, *Entwicklung und Strukturwandlungen des englischen Aussenhandels von 1700 bis zur Gegenwart,* Gustav Fischer, Pub., Jena, 1938, p. 48.

situation in which a choice had to be made between accepting a deflationary monetary policy which would cause prices to fall and produce worse unemployment, or running the risk that a vicious circle of rising prices and increased credit issues would end in uncontrollable inflation. Persuaded by the classical economists, among whom Ricardo was pre-eminent, England chose the deflationary alternative. The result was a sharp crisis in 1819, followed by others at short intervals, until in 1849 new gold discoveries relieved the pressure of growing production upon limited monetary supplies. It was from a study of these crises that Karl Marx deduced his theory that industrial capitalism would destroy itself in a series of constantly worsening paroxysms.

The unemployment and poverty of this period, therefore, should be attributed not only to the sharp competition of the new factory methods with older craft methods, but also to the growth of population and to postwar dislocations, and to the monetary policy which induced a series of sharp declines in the price level and thus caused the competition to have the effect of driving wages down. The pound sterling was fixed at a relatively high value in gold. Therefore its value rose in terms of other currencies, making English prices higher when translated into foreign currency values. This intensified the pressure to reduce costs of production. Inevitably much of this pressure was concentrated upon the glutted labor market. As long as there was a surplus of unorganized labor, employers were tempted to reduce costs by cutting wages. The laborer paid his share of the costs, in unemployment and in lowered living levels, of restoring the value of sterling currency and of all investments measured in that currency.

These economic and social conditions reinforced Marx's argument advanced above. The laissez-faire doctrine was right in its attack upon the outworn methods of regulating trade and labor conditions. It was necessary to get rid of the high protection to agriculture which kept food costs high and swelled the rent rolls of the landowners. The indiscriminate distribution of outdoor relief was not in fact a benefit to the laborers, but operated to depress wage levels while demoralizing and pauperizing those workers displaced by the new machine processes. The Elizabethan machinery for regulating the labor market had long outlived its usefulness and had lapsed into ineffective and obstructive regulations enforced only spasmodically by country justices. There was a mass of legislation which protected privileged groups, including shipowners and shipbuilders. The machinery of government was cumbrous and corrupt.

The classical economists were the agents of reform in agitating that the whole mess should be discarded. The weakness of their position was that it was almost completely negative. In colonial policy, the laissez-faire doctrine sought to resist further domination of native peoples, but provided no means of protecting them against exploitation by unscrupulous individuals. In international affairs, it advocated the support of nationalist movements aimed at the unification of divided peoples, but it did not foresee that the need would arise for international means of regulating disputes between nation-states. In international trade, it launched a great crusade for world-wide competition, but ignored the dislocation of industry and agriculture induced by such competition. It failed to create the necessary safeguards against industrial exploitation of the young and the weak in economic bargaining power. In a word, it took refuge in a facile reliance upon the enlightened selfishness of the individual in safeguarding his own interest in a competitive society, and therefore failed to create a new framework of social order in place of that which was destroyed.

A major defect of laissez faire was this concentration upon negative aims—the abolition of outworn systems of regulation—to the neglect of the complementary constructive aim of erecting a new framework of social order. It was good to facilitate the introduction of new technical processes, but safeguards against the abuse of child labor should have been adopted earlier. The new factory towns were able to produce by more efficient methods, but more efficient local government was needed to forestall the speculative builder and to provide community services. It would have been wrong and probably futile to attempt to preserve the pattern of handicraft employment, but the cost of its transformation ought not to have been thrown on to the workers. The deflation which followed the wars gave England a sound monetary system, but it was unnecessarily harsh in its impact on employment and wages.

The record of the economists on all these matters was at least no worse than that of the bishops and of other influential groups. It is easy to take a constructive attitude after history has revealed what might have been attempted. It is not clear that better results could have been achieved by alternative methods, given the low levels of national income and the heavy pressures of increasing population. The economists were insistent upon the need for greater productivity, and it was the achievement of this greater productivity that ultimately made possible a more humane approach to the social problems that always arise in any period of rapid industrial change.

Today, we have better administrative machinery of government and more knowledge of monetary policy at our disposal. There is no need to repeat the failures of the past. But there is danger in building policies upon a misreading of history, and particularly in sacrificing the very real gains of enterprise pursued on an international scale for fear that such enterprise may entail a recurrence of the miseries which in fact sprang from other causes, and which were not remedied until increasing productivity brought a general increase of living standards.

THE GROWTH OF A MONEY MARKET

As the nineteenth century opened Great Britain was favorably placed to profit from the opportunities of expanding trade. Her geographical position as an island off the coast of the European continent gave her security from invasion and immediate access to the sea routes. Even after the American colonies had won their independence, trade between them and Britain continued to increase. They provided an expanding market of high purchasing power for the new manufactures, particularly of iron. India, from which England's last rival France had been ousted in the course of the Seven Years' War (1756–63), offered an apparently insatiable market for cheap cotton goods. When in the early years of the nineteenth century Nelson destroyed the French and Dutch fleets, the sea lanes of the world were opened freely to British commerce.

No other European power was as happily situated for rapid economic development. Russia and Austria-Hungary, which emerged with Britain as victors over Napoleon, were continental powers with limited access only to inland seas. Both were backward in industrial development and with their agriculture still organized on a feudal basis. Prussia, another victor, was more favorably placed; there was no unified Germany and no Italy. France, the greatest of the western European powers, with a far larger population than Britain, had suffered from the rigorous controls elaborated by Colbert and continued by his successors. For a brief period Napoleon's dazzling conquests had seemed to restore and expand her prestige, but when his

Continental System collapsed in 1815, not only France but her continental allies also were handicapped in the race for world trade. The essence of the Continental System had been counterblockade against the British sea blockade. It was essentially designed to cut Britain off from trade with Europe. In this it was unsuccessful. But it had helped take France and her allies out of overseas markets.

Britain and the United States were favorably located to expand their oceanic trade. But the opening up of the American continent was soon to offer even more glittering opportunities, and the best energies of America turned to the expansion of the inland frontier rather than to more distant trading ventures. Thomas Jefferson, in the first of many efforts to maintain American neutrality by withdrawing from contact with European quarrels, had in 1807 secured the passing of embargo legislation restricting trade with the belligerents and so had stimulated the growth of manufactures within the United States. In 1816 at the close of the wars, protective tariffs were imposed.

The same factors which made possible the industrial inventions and new production processes in Great Britain at the close of the eighteenth century also facilitated the development of institutions for mobilizing and distributing capital resources. The financial and engineering aspects of the Industrial Revolution were closely connected. Considerable capital outlay was needed for the construction first of canals and then of roads, as well as for the new factories, for housing in the factory towns, for the iron and steel industry, and in the 1840's for railway construction. Capital was needed also to finance the greatly expanded volume of trade—imports of raw material, particularly of cotton, and exports of manufactured goods.

During the eighteenth century, Britain had enjoyed tranquillity at home and had been free from the necessity of providing large standing armies to defend her frontiers. Although remarkably successful in acquiring new territories, her wars overseas had been fought cheaply, and long periods of peace, notably under Sir Robert Walpole (1721–42), had fostered the accumulation of capital. Much of this capital had gone into drainage, improved methods of cultivation and stockbreeding, resulting in increased food production on great estates. Much too had gone into industrial experiment and construction.

In exploiting her unparalleled and almost uncontested openings for world trading development, Britain profited greatly from her ability to mobilize her increasing capital resources. She profited also because Napoleon's anti-Semitism and the unfavorable economic conditions in most European countries during the wars of 1793–1815 attracted enterprising traders and financiers to London. In the course of the nineteenth century the London money market came to be the controlling nerve center of world trade and investment. It is therefore essential to recount briefly the stages by which the various mechanisms of this market came into existence. It is the more important to do so since the basic theorems of modern economic analysis were hammered out in the course of controversy over monetary, commercial, and financial policy during the confused period of economic expansion and international conflict that ushered in the nineteenth century.

Other peoples had preceded the British in the establishment of banking and credit facilities. The bill of exchange was an Italian invention in the twelfth century. The origins of the Bank of St. George at Genoa can be traced back to this period also. National banks to finance government expeditures, or—as at Amsterdam—to facilitate exchange and commercial transactions were well established at Venice (1584), Amsterdam (1609), Hamburg (1619), and Stockholm (1656), long before the Bank of England was founded in 1694. Indeed the Bank of Amsterdam and the Bourse with which it was closely linked were the envy of traders throughout the sixteenth- and seventeenth-century world. In 1568 Sir Thomas Gresham had founded the Royal Exchange in emulation of the Amsterdam Bourse, and the various national bank schemes proposed in many countries during the seventeenth century were prompted largely by the advantages derived by the merchants, particularly of Amsterdam and of Hamburg, from their banks.

Private banks were functioning in many continental towns, and financiers were borrowing to relend, exchanging various kinds of money, and transmitting funds from country to country by means of bills of exchange, long before these facilities were developed in London. As early as 1658, the Bank of Sweden (now the Riksbanken) had issued notes payable to bearer at sight and thus claims to have been the first "bank of issue." Its note issue was short-lived, however, and the Bank of England was the first national bank to develop the issuing function into a powerful instrument of central control over the money market.

As the nineteenth century opened, the Bank of England had completed its first checkered century. It had been formed on the initiative of a group of professional promoters, among whom the Scot, William Paterson, was prominent. It had the backing of substantial merchants who from the first exercised the real power, as Paterson's short life as a director bears witness. The part played in its foundation by the necessity of securing new sources of revenue for the government is sufficiently indicated by the title of the Act by which the Bank was constituted—"An Act for granting to their Majesties several Rates and Duties upon Tunnages of Ships and Vessels, and upon Beer, Ale, and other liquors; for securing certain Recompenses and Advantages, in the said Act mentioned, to Such persons as shall voluntarily advance the sum of Fifteen hundred thousand Pounds towards carrying on the war against France."

A total of £1,200,000 was advanced to William III and Mary, interest on which was to be paid at 8 per cent, with an annual payment to the Bank of £4,000 for management. The corporation was given the privileges of a bank for twelve years. The original intention was to form a bank of issue, but this was a novel proposal and the House of Commons did not authorize note issue. By this time the practice of issuing notes was well established among the goldsmith-bankers of London. These were promissory notes—promises to pay standard coin on demand. The goldsmiths had found that it was possible to accept deposits, issue these notes, and invest the bulk of the deposits, as long as a sufficient reserve was kept on hand to redeem all notes presented for payment. The Bank of England adopted this practice, and in its first year bearer-notes, "without which the Bank could hardly have carried on business," were in circulation. Sir John Clapham, the historian of the Bank, records that as early as 1696 a critic charged that these notes seemed "to be a Credit beyond the intention of the Act . . . and never practised before by any Corporation, and almost a Fraud on the subject."

Nevertheless the practice grew, was gradually developed into its present standardized form, and was formally authorized in successive renewals of the charter. It came to be the pivot upon which the Bank gained the power to regulate the monetary system. The privilege was so highly valued that the Bank sought and gained, somewhat vaguely in 1709, but more precisely in 1742, the exclusive right among corporate organizations to issue notes. This was regarded as giving to the

Bank the exclusive right of joint-stock banking. Lacking the privilege of note issue, no joint-stock bank was projected in England till 1826 outside London, and till 1833 within the London radius.

By the end of the eighteenth century the Bank was well entrenched. It had survived numerous crises and many rival banking schemes. Several times, notably in 1720 during the South Sea Bubble, it had been pushed very close to failure, but successive renewals of its charter had enabled it to strengthen its relations with government, to which it had advanced large sums. It had had staunch friends at court, notably William Lowndes, Secretary of the Treasury from 1695 to 1724, and later the great Whig peace minister, Robert Walpole (1721–42). Its conduct had been steady and conservative, so that by 1794, after a hundred years of operation, it had accumulated solid reserves and was in an almost impregnable position.

Yet it remained a private corporation, pursuing commercial banking practices and jealous of its competitors. Indeed its functions as a central bank as we now understand the term were a fortuitous development in the course of the nineteenth century. The most famous of all the acts renewing its charter, that of 1844, in effect constituted it the repository of the gold reserve upon which rested not only its note issue, but by convention and precedent, the commercial banking deposits upon which checks could be drawn.

Even then the Bank by its practice, as well as by its rare statements of policy, disclaimed responsibility for positive action to regulate the supply of monetary media. It regarded itself as a cog in the competitive monetary mechanisms, the untrammeled operation of which was relied upon to bring about an equilibrium in the money and capital markets. No small part of the controversies concerning the Bank's policies during the Napoleonic war period turns upon the extent to which it should have accepted the public responsibilities in regard to monetary and credit regulation which later were recognized as a corollary of its privileges and powers. As late as 1873, Bagehot wrote his famous analysis of the London money market, *Lombard Street,* as a tract to insist that the Bank did in fact have a responsibility for positive regulatory action, particularly in times of crisis. However it was only in the last quarter of the nineteenth century that this responsibility was fully accepted and that appropriate policies were developed for discharging this public trust.

Thus it was to a private banking corporation, which had a semimonopolistic position by virtue of the privileges conferred upon it in return for financial aid to successive governments, that William Pitt turned in 1793 for help in financing the war that broke out against France. In the course of the next four years he secured short-term advances from the Bank cumulatively totaling almost £10,000,000. He was enabled to do so by reason of the Indemnity Act passed in 1793 legalizing past and future advances against Treasury bills payable at the Bank. The initiative in promoting this Act had been taken by the Bank directors in an effort to safeguard their own legal position. The limit of advances to the government which they originally proposed was omitted from the Act and thus the government secured access to an elastic new source of ready money.

As a result of government expenditures financed in this way, supplemented by an incautious expansion of note issues by the private country banks that were beginning to develop, prices rose and the exchange rate of sterling fell to the point where it became cheaper to export gold than commodities in settling the balance of foreign payments. The drain of gold was increased by naval and military payments abroad and by subsidies to Britain's uncertain allies on the Continent. The point was soon reached, therefore, when only a reduction of the Bank's short-term advances to the government, and of notes in circulation, could have maintained it in a position to redeem its notes when presented for payment. Such a restriction of credit was difficult in time of war, and when a run on the banks began early in 1797, there was no alternative to suspending the convertibility of the Bank of England's notes. Thenceforward until the resumption of specie payments (1819–21), Britain operated on an inconvertible currency.

During this period known as the "Restriction of Payments," there developed a lively discussion of monetary policy, primarily concerned with the policies followed by the Bank of England. Except for a brief but sharp depreciation of the sterling exchange rate in 1801–3, there was little further rise of commodity prices or exchange depreciation until 1808. After that year the rise of prices was marked until the end of the war against France in 1815, when there ensued a sharp fall in prices.

The controversy aroused by these price fluctuations was motivated by intensely practical disagreements on policy; but much of it inevitably was concerned with analyzing the reasons for the inflationary rise of prices and for the subsequent sharp decline. The crux of the controversy was whether the Bank was responsible, or partly responsible, for aggravating both the rise and the subsequent fall of prices.

It is clear that, in so far as government expenditure was financed by short-term advances, the Bank was not a free agent. The question at issue, therefore, was whether it could or should have exercised a restraining influence upon the note issues—its own and those of the private banks—for industrial and commercial purposes, or whether it refrained from doing so because it did not wish to curtail its own profits. Subsequent experience has shown that a true central bank, operating primarily as a public service rather than a profit-making institution, can in fact regulate an inconvertible currency, even during the strain of a great war; but this was too advanced a concept to expect in the early years of the nineteenth century. The same can be said of the plan advanced by Ricardo for making the Bank's notes payable in bullion rather than coin; a plan by which the Bank would not have had to depress prices still further by gathering gold for coinage as well as for its reserves. This is the system that many central banks operated between the wars, but a century and more ago it was still a rather daring proposal and the Bank did not accept it.

It should be recognized that the instruments of central banking developed slowly and many of them were not available in the first quarter of the nineteenth century. The amalgamation process by which town and country banks were absorbed into a few powerful institutions practicing branch banking had not yet made checks the main monetary medium, and relegated notes to the monopolistic control of the Bank of England. The Bank was inhibited by the Usury Laws from raising its discount rate above 5 per cent. Still more important, the civil service was not then available which could collect heavy taxation, float large loans at low interest rates at par, and administer a complex system of price controls and rationing to prevent commodity prices from rising.

Subsequent generations of economists have found in the controversial literature of this period a great clarification both of policy issues and of monetary theory, including the theory of the foreign exchanges. In both fields the argument has never really died down, since the early nineteenth-century debates constitute the first really constructive discussions on many points that have not ceased to be important current issues. The doctrines that emerged were based upon the acceptance of gold as the standard of value. Bank notes and other substitutes for gold were regarded as mere conveniences, to be strictly limited and always convertible on demand into gold. In 1810 David Ricardo elaborated some letters written to a newspaper into a tract, *The High Price of Bullion a Proof of the Depreciation of Bank Notes.* He showed that sterling was depreciated on the Hamburg exchange, that the price of gold as measured in bank notes had risen, and that the prices of goods had risen proportionately. He argued that the overissue of bank notes was the common cause of all of these phenomena. His arguments were accepted by the majority of the famous Bullion Committee of the House of Commons which reported in that year. But there were many doubters of Ricardo's monetary theories, including Malthus, and neither the government nor the Bank accepted the deflationary implications of his analysis.

In the postwar period of deflation which began even before the resumption of specie payments in 1819, the distress and unemployment which ensued called forth a wide range of protest, including Thomas Attwood's advocacy of inconvertible currency as a means of ensuring full employment. Repeated financial crises followed upon the failure of private banks, as in 1825. These crises and a growing interest in international trade led to increasing popular acceptance of the gold standard and to the monetary theories on which it was based. By the middle of the century the Ricardian orthodoxy was established, and questionings or qualifications of it were swept aside as ill-considered heresies. From time to time, an economist would revive the old issues and question the infallibility of the Ricardian doctrines. It was not till the monetary disturbances following the war of 1914–18 that the critics, as well as the exponents, of these doctrines were again given the attention they merited.

The situation of the Bank of England was complicated by the demands made upon it by government, as well as by the operations of the many private banks that sprang up in the rapidly developing industrial and commercial districts outside of London. The date usually given for the expansion of private banking enterprise in the provinces is 1760, the same year as that in which the Industrial Revolution began to accelerate. This is of course more than a coincidence. The two developments were intimately connected.

Of the many illustrations that might be given, Yorkshire, while not the earliest, has the special interest that it attracted the attention of Adam Smith. He referred in strong terms to some of its "beggarly bankers," who issued notes of very small denominations. The historians of the Midland Bank refer to Yorkshire's unenviable reputation for "harbouring numerous irresponsible issuers of notes for very small amounts—an obvious means of exploiting the poorer members of the community." Such small banks grew up to meet a recognized need for financing trade between the provinces and London, and with overseas countries. Until this time, both the exchange and clearing functions (transmitting and offsetting funds between trading centers) and the provision of short-term credit to finance the transference of goods had been discharged by the merchant-manufacturers themselves.

The appearance from 1760 onward of specialized institutions to take over these functions was one of the major steps in creating the basis for a competitive system of private enterprise. Any individual, or group of not more than six partners, could set up a bank, accept deposits, issue notes, and deal in bills of exchange. The liability of the partners was unlimited, but there was no requirement to maintain adequate cash reserves to meet a sudden presentation of notes. When prices were rising and trade was expanding, the temptation to overissue and overlend was great. It was not until 1776 that an Act was passed prohibiting the issue of notes for sums less than £1, and not until 1808 that a license with its implication of control was required before notes could be issued.

Periodically sudden panics brought down scores of the weaker banks, but always their numbers increased again, and their activities constituted a speculative, uncontrolled weakness in the monetary system until in the 1830's the first joint-stock banks began to operate successfully. Soon thereafter a process of amalgamation began, linking the joint-stock banks with London private bankers who were members of the Clearing House which had been organized between 1750 and 1770, and the country banks with both. As this process went on till the number of banks fell to a score or so, the note-issue privileges of the country banks lapsed, since they became merged with joint-stock banks and the Bank of England was the only joint-stock bank empowered to issue notes.

Even more important for a study of international trade than the evolution of central banking or the development of commercial, deposit banking, was the emergence of specialized dealers in the money market. Of these, the most important were the dealers in bills of exchange. They had their precursors in the seventeenth-century money scriveners (writers), who had acted as go-betweens, bringing together the lenders and borrowers for whom they wrote loan contracts of various kinds. The specialized business of bill-broking did not become important until the emergence of country banks, which in agricultural districts usually had surplus funds on deposit. These they sought to use either in London or, through London, in the industrial districts with their growing need of short-term capital. The instrument by which such funds came to be transferred was the "inland bill," a bill of exchange modeled upon those which had long been used in foreign trade. In the period from 1760 to 1797, when funds were relatively scarce, London banking houses had paid interest on the balances of their country bank correspondents; but after the suspension of payments in 1797 there was a plethora of paper money and interest rates fell. It was difficult to use short-term money in London and the banks ceased to pay interest on balances. The country bankers, therefore, turned to these bill-brokers who, by their enterprise, could find a use for surplus funds, largely in financing domestic and international trade.

The Bank of England operating as a commercial bank had its own discount department. Its regulations were stiff, and its rate of discount remained unchanged at 5 per cent from 1746 to 1822. Enterprising individuals with country connections could cut this price when after 1797 money became abundant and could, with their specialized knowledge, take risks on bills that did not meet the Bank's regulations. The domestic transfer of funds was an important, and largely new, economic function to be discharged, and private enterprise found an efficient and profitable means of discharging it. The Bank, by reason of its close relations with government and its privilege of note issue, became the occasional lender of last resort, in the sense that when funds were scarce the brokers might be driven to discount their bills at the Bank; but it lost the bulk of the current bill discounting business. Thus was laid the basis for the later development by which the Bank rate of discount became an instrument whereby the credit structure of the country could be regulated in a crisis. In normal times the financing of trade and private investment was carried out by private agencies, but in a depression these agencies had to turn to the Bank of England.

These pioneer operations laid the foundations of the discount market in which bills from the whole trading world were later dealt with so as to provide the revolving fund which enabled world trade to be financed on an expanding scale. An exporter could receive payment when goods were shipped, but the importer did not need to pay till goods were received—the market advancing the necessary funds to finance the goods in transit. It has been said that the bill-brokers who began this process were evading the Bank's regulations. This is true in the sense that the Bank was conducting the business by rules which the brokers did not need to observe. But it is not true in the sense that the Bank had any power to make statutory regulations.

The vitality of competitive enterprise, as British merchants and financiers strove to exploit the opportunities for profit in a time of rapidly rising prices and expanding trade, is especially well illustrated by the emergence of these specialized brokers who found new and efficient means of financing trade. As the nineteenth century wore on, many other specialized markets developed within the general framework of the money market. These markets were created by individual initiative. They remained highly competitive, with little organization beyond contiguity and contact among independent operators.

Central banking institutions and even commercial banking do not suffice to constitute a money market, and it was the peculiar distinction of London that it gradually fitted together the specialized mechanisms which enabled it in the nineteenth century to function as the reservoir and clearing center of the world's trading, credit, and currency systems. The development of three of the most important of these mechanisms—the Bank of England, the private banks, and the discount market—has been outlined above. The discount market became an essential link in the capital, and exchange, as well as the money, markets. It pioneered the specialization by which distinctive functions such as acceptance, foreign exchange, bullion-broking, new issues, underwriting, insurance, and the various commodity exchanges, came to be organized in highly technical markets—each with its own peculiar skills, but each geared into the whole complex of financial mechanisms.

Two great mechanisms, which developed later, need to be added to this list—the Stock Exchange and joint-stock deposit banking. Joint-stock banking in its modern form did not develop till after 1833. The Stock Exchange, at least as far as dealings in the public funds are concerned, had had a longer history going back to the late seventeenth century. But the speculative mania of 1720 known as the South Sea Bubble had cast discredit upon its function in respect of private capital. Penal legislation had been passed against joint-stock organization and against stock-jobbers. Dealings in government bonds, however, continued to be active as successive wars added to the public debt, and stock-jobbing was carried on surreptitiously in the coffee-houses of Change Alley. The Bubble Act of 1720 proved to be obscure and unenforceable, and the case-law that was developed in the eighteenth century to regulate partnerships and incorporation was very complex and unsatisfactory. Though the law in the eighteenth century was hostile to joint-stock organization and to dealings in shares, the Stock Exchange had been formally organized as early as 1773 and had moved to its own building in Capel Court next to the Bank of England in 1802. The railway developments of the 1840's were undertaken by companies incorporated by charter or by acts of Parliament, so that investment in railroad shares became widespread and the Stock Exchange began to be a really important factor in the money market. Limited liability was not generally legalized until 1855–57, and there still remained a long process of legislation and judicial interpretation before company law was modernized. It was not until the Companies Act of 1862 generalized the practice of limited liability that the Stock Exchange was able to function effectively as a means of co-ordinating the value of existing capital with the price of new issues and with the rate of interest.

It is significant that David Ricardo who became the accepted authority on economic questions was a product of the money market. It became common in the nineteenth century to describe the whole economic system as a market economy. The market visualized was the keen, competitive bargaining of relative equals in monetary operations where rapid figuring of fine margins of profit was the test of efficient operation. This concept of the market was a very imperfect picture of the real world of agricultural and industrial production—it pictured a money economy rather than a product or skill economy. In course of time finance came to be the dominating factor of economic activity to a greater degree than ever before on a national, and even an international, scale. The facts of human co-operative effort in the production of goods never have approximated this competitive model, but economic theory has assumed that they do.

THE CLASSICAL ECONOMISTS

The violent controversies which shaped economic thought in the first quarter of the nineteenth century were intensely practical. Even when they were conducted in abstract terms and were concerned with what might seem to be purely theoretical issues, they arose from sharp disagreements on practical issues. As Arnold Toynbee later asserted, "as a matter of fact, while affecting the reserved and serious air of students, political economists have all the time been found brawling in the market-place." [2]

In the period of controversy at the beginning of the century, political economy had not yet emerged as an academic discipline in its own right. The classical economists were in a sense amateurs. Among them were businessmen and bankers, such as David Ricardo, Thomas Tooke, Henry Thornton, and Francis Place. Others were active politicians, as were Francis Horner, and after 1819, Ricardo himself.[3] Among the most influential in their own day were the journalists, James Mill and J. R. McCulloch. But there were also noblemen (Lords Lauderdale and King), soldiers (Robert Torrens and the elder Wakefield), lawyers (Jeremy Bentham and Nassau Senior), and clergymen (Malthus). Some of these, it is true, became professors of political economy, as did Malthus (at Haileybury in 1807), Senior (at Oxford in 1825), and McCulloch (at University College, London, in 1828). The latter is generally regarded along with James Mill as being responsible for the generalization of Ricardo's ideas into the

[2] Cf. Arnold Toynbee, *The Industrial Revolution,* London, 1884, p. 23.

[3] Ricardo lent an Irish landowner £20,000 free of interest, and so was elected to the House of Commons to represent a constituency he never saw. From 1819 till his death in 1823 he found that "by an accident of history, . . . he had become at once the representative, the theorist and the orator of a class which was optimistic by profession—the great manufacturers who dreamt of making the economic conquest of the world. They needed to be freed from all regulations regarding labour: they needed, in the historical conditions in which England found itself placed about the year 1820, to see the customs barriers broken down: they needed to believe that overproduction was impossible, and that all production created a corresponding demand: they took over a doctrine which seemed to justify their claims as against the interests of the class of landlords—claims which were on some points identical with those of their workmen: and the temperament of the men of action gave its tone to the doctrine of the thinker." (Elie Halevy, *The Growth of Philosophic Radicalism,* London, Faber & Faber, Ltd., 1928, p. 342.) It is said that Ricardo gained the ear of the House and was highly regarded by his fellow members; but the record of his votes shows that he was usually on the minority side in divisions. (Cf. E. Cannan, "Ricardo in Parliament," *Economic Journal,* June and Sept., 1894.)

extreme and rigid statements that are the usual targets of attack by critics of the school.

The bestowal upon this group of the title "classical" is comparatively recent, dating from the 1860's. Karl Marx was largely responsible for its popularization.[4] Its usual connotation is flattering, as meaning "economic writers of the rank who have left models which all others must follow." As early as 1888 Lujo Brentano suggested another meaning when he compared classical economics with classical sculpture. He suggested that both ignored personal peculiarities in favor of broad general human characteristics, creating an abstract man without scars or wrinkles.

The issues on which the classical economists fought have passed into history. Primarily they were concerned with public policy. In order to demonstrate the evil effects of government interference, it became necessary to analyze the nature of economic activity. In this respect the early nineteenth-century writers followed and built on the work of Adam Smith. In two important respects, however, they broke from his influence. They relied more upon abstract methods of formal logic, and they were concerned less with the production and more with the distribution of wealth. Ricardo recognized this. In 1820 he wrote in a letter to Malthus, "Political economy you think is an enquiry into the nature and cause of wealth; I think it should rather be called an enquiry into the laws which determine the division of the produce of industry amongst the classes who concur in its formation." The conflict of class interest which Ricardo stressed grew out of a struggle for power between the landowning aristocracy and the middle-class merchants and manufacturers. Karl Marx later rounded out the pattern by stressing the interest of the industrial wage earners.

It is important to stress the background of class struggle in order to understand why it became necessary for the classical economists to create a distinctive theory of international trade. There is abundant evidence that the major theoretical contributions of the Ricardian

[4] Cf. Henry Higgs (ed.), *Palgrave's Dictionary of Political Economy,* London, 1926, Vol. I, p. 303. Karl Marx in *Das Kapital* (1867) uses the term. J. M. Keynes in his *General Theory of Employment, Interest, and Money,* New York, 1936, p. 3 n., credits Marx with inventing the term. This may be right in so far as its application to the school was concerned. It is possible, however, to cite earlier references, e.g., Jerome Adolphe Blanqui, *Précis elementaire d'économie politique,* Paris, 1826 (3rd ed., 1857), p. 8: "M. J.-B. Say, le plus classique, assurement, de tous les économistes qui aient paru depuis Smith."

school arose from the controversies connected with the passing in 1815 of an act to protect the wheat-growing industry, and that "it was inevitable that Ricardo's thought during this period should take the form of a theory of distribution and that it should center about the rate of profits." [5] This period at the end of the Napoleonic Wars marked a turning point in the economic development of England, which was ceasing to be an agricultural exporting country and becoming an industrial exporting country. Wheat exports had ceased during the Napoleonic Wars. Importing was difficult as long as the war lasted and the demands of a growing home market maintained prices at a high level. In 1815, the landowners had sought to protect themselves against the competition of increased imports by raising a higher tariff barrier. Ricardo argued that higher food prices protected by the new tariff would merely increase the unearned income which accrued to landowners in the form of rent and would not by raising wages cause a general increase in prosperity. This ran counter to accepted doctrine and he was forced to re-examine the theory of value.

The theory of value is the heart of any theoretical economic system. It explains why men are willing to produce goods and services, how they come to rate them for trading purposes, and how in doing so the incomes of individuals are determined. Ricardo attempted to give precision to the long-accepted idea that labor cost was the effective measure of value. As he probed deeper just before his death, his honest mind found itself in difficulties which his less rigorous colleagues were willing to ignore. But the formulation of his ideas, systematized and simplified by James Mill and J. R. McCulloch, proved immensely influential.

In one respect however, the labor-cost theory of value raised serious doubts concerning the premise from which Ricardo's reasoning began. If labor cost determined value, production would shift to areas where labor cost was low. Did this mean that industries would migrate to

[5] Jacob H. Hollander, *David Ricardo,* Baltimore, 1910, pp. 72–73. Cf. also on p. 118: "Not until Parliament was called upon to determine whether legislative policy should be shaped, first in the matter of the Bank, in the interest of debtor or creditor; second, in the matter of the corn laws, in the interest of agriculturalists, rather than that of the manufacturers; third, with respect to taxation and funding, in the interest of consumer instead of property owner—not until then was it that the economic thinker, deriving his philosophical creed from the new utilitarianism, felt impelled to inquire what will be the natural shares of these several classes, destined to be affected in one way or another by this contemplated legislation."

countries of cheap labor? This was precisely what the mercantilists had long argued, and what advocates of tariff protection still argue.

Ricardo's answer was a new theory of international trade, based not on absolute but on comparative costs of production. This theory involves some measure of circular reasoning. In order to prove that international trade arises because of comparative differences in the costs of production, one has to assume that labor and capital are not able to migrate between countries. Much of the controversy, however, arises precisely from the fact that capital is more easily moved than labor. In the circumstances of Ricardo's day, the assumption that capital and labor did not move freely because of what he described as "the natural disinclination which every man has to quit the country of his birth and connections" was in general sufficiently realistic, though his own family history might have been cited against it. Granted this assumption, the value of goods traded between nations depends not upon labor costs, but, as John Stuart Mill later demonstrated, upon the reciprocal intensities of demand for the products exchanged.

Thus the Ricardian economic system came to have two hearts, a domestic theory of value based upon cost of production, and an international theory of value based upon the opposite principle of demand. The failure to put these theories together is proof enough that Ricardo's theoretical structure was not complete. Both theories, however, led him to the same conclusion—that trade should be freed from restraints and governmental interference.

It would, of course, be wrong to assume that the practical issues of commercial and monetary policy were decided solely upon intellectual grounds. A large element in the decision was a struggle for political power among contending interest groups.[6] As the controversy de-

[6] Cf. Edwin Cannan, *Theories of Production and Distribution* (2nd ed.), London, 1903, pp. 391–92: "For the basis of an argument against the Corn Laws it would have been difficult to invent anything more effective than the Ricardian theory of distribution. The divergence of interests with regard to the Corn Laws was really a divergence of the interests of classes, and not of individuals. It was not a question of the classes against the masses, or, in other words, of the rich against the poor, but of the landowning class against the commercial and manufacturing class. . . .

"At a later period, when political power had passed in some measure to the wage-earning classes, it would doubtless have been more effective to show that the Corn Laws diminished real wages, but at the time it simplified the matter to declare the comforts of the labourers a nearly constant quantity, and consequently outside the problem."

Cf. also E. R. A. Seligman, "On Some Neglected British Economists," *Economic Journal,* Vol. XIII, Sept. and Dec. 1903, pp. 533–34.

veloped, the growing but as yet weak power of the laboring masses was enlisted in support of the rising class of manufacturers in their attack upon the privileges of the landowners who were so strongly entrenched in Parliament. The landowner became the villain responsible for the high price of food and for almost every other social evil. The low level to which Parliament, the universities, the church, the "public" schools, and the civil service had fallen gave liberal orators a vulnerable target. It is not an accident that Jeremy Bentham and James Mill were active in the founding of University College at London as a secular institution organized on different lines from the two old universities, and that they attacked the church directly. But it is more significant that a growing proportion of the new manufactures sprang up in the north, which was ill-endowed with churches and schools and therefore became a fertile field for John Wesley and his followers. The reform of the Poor Laws and the repeal of the Corn Laws did not come until electoral reform in 1832 made the House of Commons responsive to popular opinion in the manufacturing districts. Effective factory legislation also followed electoral reform. The class interest which Karl Marx was to throw into sharp relief against both manufacturer and landowner was stirring even while the labor leaders made common cause with the former against the latter.

In the currency controversies that loomed so large from 1797 to 1816 the influence of the economists was perhaps more direct, but even here it was belated. The reasoning of the Bullionists, as the followers of Ricardo came to be known, under the skillful handling of one of their number, Francis Horner, carried conviction with the Bullion Committee in 1810. But the Bank had the ear of government, and the government had the votes in Parliament. Ricardo may have been right in his opinion that the Bank Directors who in his view mismanaged the resumption of specie payments from 1816–19 were "a very ignorant set of men." But his attacks had little practical effect at the time, and it was not till long after his death that his followers had the satisfaction of seeing the principles of currency regulation he advocated score at least a partial victory when the Bank next sought a renewal of its charter in 1844.

In the formation of the classical doctrine, it is convenient to distinguish three stages of development. The first may be said to have closed with the third edition of Ricardo's *Principles* in 1821. By this time, the analysis of economic ideas was on a new basis, and many leading practitioners were expressing great confidence that its remaining controversies would quickly be resolved. The second stage of development was largely that of elaboration and consolidation, beginning with such general treatises as that of James Mill (1821) and J. R. McCulloch (1825). The third stage of the classical doctrine was inaugurated by the publication of John Stuart Mill's *Principles* in 1848 and lasted till about 1870. A distinguished philosopher-statesman, A. J. Balfour, later sneered at the "thin lucidity" of John Stuart Mill. But for a generation Mill's work was regarded as the crowning achievement of the classical school. This period was marked by an extraordinary complacency, which was remarkable in its belief that the major issues of economic controversy had been settled for all time. This was soon indeed to be shattered.

In 1867 Karl Marx published *Das Kapital.* About 1870 the ideas of the German historical economists were introduced into England by T. E. Cliffe Leslie. In 1871 John Stuart Mill abandoned the wages-fund doctrine which had been one of the pillars of the classical system. In the same year Walter Stanley Jevons published his *Principles of Political Economy* and prefaced it by a violent attack on both Ricardo and Mill. The authority of the Ricardian teachings was undermined almost before their canonization as classical doctrine had been completed.

It is difficult to accept as valid the definition of the classical school which includes Adam Smith. It is true that his great work was profoundly influential in the early years of the nineteenth century, as it still is. But the most characteristic theories of the Ricardians were either new—for example, the comparative-cost theory and the theory of reciprocal demand—or were derived from the predecessors of Adam Smith—for example, David Hume's price specie-flow theory of the balancing of payments. Ricardo's abstract logic gave a precision for which Adam Smith did not seem to strive. The monetary and fiscal problems to which it was applied were very different from those confronting Adam Smith, and the shift of emphasis from production to distribution changed the character of the discussion.

The doctrine of natural liberty did, indeed, link the generations. But the sharper economic analysis of Ricardo constitutes the foundation of a new school rather than the elaboration of already known ideas. In his *Autobiography* John Stuart Mill makes it very clear that he wrote his *Principles* to systematize and clarify the ideas he had gained from Ricardo, either directly or through the teaching of his father, James Mill. Nor have the critics of Ricardo failed to note his originality and eminence. W. S. Jevons, indeed, urged economists "to fling aside, once and for ever, the mazy and preposterous assumptions of the Ricardian School," and was emphatic in his view that "that able but wrong-headed man, David Ricardo, shunted the car of Economic science on to a wrong line, a line, however, on which it was urged further towards confusion by his equally able and wrong-headed admirer, John Stuart Mill."

By the testimony of friend and foe, Ricardo was the founder of a new school. Some explanation is needed for the authority which the doctrines of this school came to command. The insularity of English intellectual life is perhaps sufficient explanation for the comparative neglect in England even of French economic thought. In 1802, the French economist Jean Baptiste Say had cast economic ideas into the logical arrangement in which they are still studied. A succession of able French writers was later described by Jevons in the passage cited above as the line of succession through which "the true doctrine" was developed. In Germany also, von Thünen published in 1826 an important treatise adding greatly to our understanding of the theory of rent, of exchange between non-competing groups, and of monetary theory. Yet it was the Ricardians who became canonized as the classical school, not in England only but over the greater part of the economic world. Their authority was derived largely from acceptance of their doctrine by those who led the free-trade movement to triumph and thus set the stage for the great trading expansion which enabled the manufacturers and financiers of Britain to achieve leadership, and even domination in world trade, shipping and investment. It became the creed of success.

While the theories of the classical school were being formulated, there was a constant and vivid interchange of ideas. Ricardo founded the Political Economy Club in 1821 and intimate friendships developed among the principal members of the group. The result was a fertile elaboration and precision of new ideas, but until about 1821 it can hardly be said that these ideas were crystallized into what we now regard as the classical system. In particular, Ricardo has suffered gross misinterpretations and misunderstandings of his views at the hands of later critics who read only the *Principles*. In many respects his best work is to be found in his early pamphlets. For a full understanding of his honest, inquiring mind, which was by no means as rigid as his later critics have maintained, it is necessary to read these pamphlets and his correspondence and speeches, as well as such hints of his views as may be gleaned from contemporary accounts of the discussions in which he participated.

The crystallization of classical doctrine and its reduction to a system were begun by James Mill and completed by his son, John Stuart Mill. In the process it was perhaps inevitable that the ideas, which to the humble-minded Ricardo were his "present views" to be earnestly discussed and tested, came to be stated as established truths. McCulloch wrote them into a Supplement of the *Encyclopedia Britannica,* and Malthus protested "at the general adoption of the new theories of my excellent friend Mr. Ricardo into an Encyclopedia, while the question was yet *sub judice.*" McCulloch swept aside such protests. By the time Bagehot wrote in the 1870's Malthus had come to be regarded as an amiable, but not very clear-headed, contemporary and friend of the great master, who added very little to economics except a somewhat mistaken theory of population.[7] It has been left for our own time to discover that the doubts and disagreements expressed by Malthus were based on an appreciation of factors in economic activity which were brushed aside by the Ricardians, but have persistently obtruded themselves and have now become the basis of the newest economic theories.

It is difficult to overstress the importance of the secondary writers of the classical school in disseminating and incidentally crystallizing economic theory and doctrine. Every prophet must have his disciples. Ricardo's disciples were an uncommonly energetic set of propagandists whose activities somewhat disturbed him in his lifetime and after his death, in their zeal to establish his authority, went far to ruin his scientific reputation. James Mill was perhaps the most influential in persuading Ricardo to set down his ideas in systematic form and labored incessantly both to complete the logic and to spread a knowl-

[7] Cf. W. Bagehot, *Economic Studies* (1st ed.), 1880, p. 148: "The truth is, that Mr. Malthus had not the practical sagacity necessary for the treatment of Political Economy in a concrete way, or the mastery of abstract ideas necessary to deal with it in what we should now call a scientific way. He tried a bad mixture of both. There is a mist of speculation over his facts, and a vapour of fact over his ideas."

edge of it. He was a pedantic, industrious Scot, an active journalist during most of his working life.[8] He was also an assiduous logician and propagator of fixed ideas, largely derived from Bentham and Ricardo.

His son, John Stuart Mill, was the recipient of most of these ideas and the subject of a remarkable educational experiment. James Mill by personal tuition trained the boy in the classic languages, in ancient history, logic, and political economy. Beginning with Greek at the age of three, and Latin at eight, logic at twelve, and political economy at thirteen, the boy's formal lessons ended when he was fourteen. He was being prepared to be the expositor and final draftsman of the gospel according to Ricardo. In the process his father took occasion to expound to him the doctrines in Ricardo's newly published *Principles* and the boy's homework, recounting each day's lesson, became the basis for James Mill's *Elements of Political Economy,* published in 1821.[9]

This was the first of a long series of secondary treatises, articles, and reviews, expounding, simplifying, and hardening Ricardo's ideas. In 1824, James Mill and Jeremy Bentham founded the *Westminster Review,* which Mill used to expound the Ricardian philosophy. J. R. McCulloch contributed the article in the Supplement to the *Encyclopedia Britannica* in which Ricardo's ideas were enshrined, and as editor of the *Scotsman* did much to popularize these ideas. In 1825, he too produced a book of *Principles.* Robert Torrens, a retired Colonel of Marines, and a Fellow of the Royal Society, was an indefatigable and somewhat voluminous writer also, overshadowed somewhat unfairly by Ricardo's greater repute. It has been argued that he was the

[8] His biography, written by another Scot (Alexander Bain, *James Mill: A Biography,* London, 1882) is one of the dullest catalogs of a busy detailed life ever to be printed. It gives year by year a meticulous record of correspondence, articles, reviews, political activity and promptings of Bentham, Ricardo, and other original minds, until in 1819 a highly paid post in the East India Company diverted his energies to administration and to the completion of his *History of British India,* written not from firsthand acquaintance with the country, but primarily as an exposition of his philosophy of history.

[9] John Stuart Mill, *Autobiography* (5th ed.), London, 1875, pp. 27–28: "Though Ricardo's great work was already in print, no didactic treatise embodying its doctrines, in a manner fit for learners, had yet appeared. My father, therefore, commenced instructing me in the science by a sort of lectures, which he delivered to me in our walks. He expounded each day a portion of the subject, and I gave him next day a written account of it, which he made me rewrite over and over again until it was clear, precise, and tolerably complete. In this manner I went through the whole extent of the science; and the written outline of it which resulted from my daily *compte rendu,* served him afterwards as notes from which to write his *Elements of Political Economy.*"

true discoverer of the theory of comparative costs; but this claim is disputed by the admirers of Ricardo. Thomas Tooke and his younger associate William Newmarch propounded their theses on monetary questions through a succession of letters, pamphlets, and statements of parliamentary committees, much of which is incorporated in their monumental *History of Prices.*

Even more important, perhaps, at this stage was the work of the popularizers. Beginning with Mrs. Marcet's *Conversations on Political Economy,* the first edition of which was published in 1816 (and praised by McCulloch as "perhaps the best introduction to the science that has yet appeared"), and Harriet Martineau's *Illustrations of Political Economy* (1832–34), a stream of storybook economics became increasingly lyrical in praise of the classical doctrines. Never before or since has economics been, in Maria Edgeworth's words, "so much the fashion that distinguished ladies before engaging a governess for their children inquired about her competence to teach political economy." Miss Harriet Martineau became the most prolific of these popularizers of what were deemed to be the unassailable truths of political economy. The scope of her writings, which after a brief visit to the United States extended into American affairs, challenges comparison with the confident omniscience of columnists and radio commentators in our own day. Her tone became increasingly admonitory as she scolded the "philo-operative cant" of Charles Dickens, the "meddling legislation" of the Factory Acts, and the "inquisitorial annoyance" of the inspectors who, for the first time, were trying to enforce compliance with the laws requiring the fencing of machinery to prevent industrial accidents. Her plea "to leave to workers in factories, as to other workers, the care of their own lives and limbs," was published first in the *Westminster Review* and was reissued as a pamphlet by the National Association of Factory Occupiers.

There is, of course, a great gap between the dignified, impersonal analysis of the economists and the popular literature which purported to translate their principles into simple language, and to apply those principles to current issues. In 1848, John Stuart Mill had published his *Principles.* This at once became the standard economic text whose authority was almost unchallenged for the better part of a generation. Studiously trained from his earliest infancy, Mill carried throughout his adult life the impress of his father's and Ricardo's influence. A noble and sympathetic figure himself, he is characteristic of the liberal philosophy at its best. He did not hesitate to admit error when convinced of it, or to espouse unpopular causes. His essay *On Liberty* will long be read as an authoritative statement of the liberal creed. Another of his essays, *On the Subjection of Women,* in which he advocated political and economic equality of the sexes, was a courageous break with convention, and he lent the great weight of his authority in later life to a sympathetic attitude toward social reform. No small part of this later development was clearly due, as he himself bore witness, to the influence of Mrs. Harriet Taylor, whom he married in 1851.[10]

Nevertheless, the economic argument of Mill's *Principles* was primarily a restatement of the classical political economy. This is particularly true of the chapters on international trade. The summary statement of the classical theory which follows in the next chapter is based upon Mill's exposition. It is important to restate this theory, both because it was the accepted and authoritative doctrine upon which the free-trade movement rested its case in the latter half of the nineteenth century; and because it contains all the essential theorems which are still repeated in modern textbooks. The modern equilibrium theory is stated more broadly than the classical theory of international trade, and must take account of many complications arising from the changed conditions of present-day economic activity and its regulation. But it is still cast in the classical mold, the outline of which was roughed out by Ricardo and polished by John Stuart Mill.

[10] Cf. John Stuart Mill, *Autobiography,* p. 247: "What was abstract and purely scientific was generally mine; the properly human element came from her: in all that concerned society and progress, I was her pupil, alike in boldness of speculation and cautiousness of practical judgment."

CHAPTER VII

THE CLASSICAL THEORY OF INTERNATIONAL TRADE

ITS ASSUMPTIONS AND CONTENT

No OTHER aspect of economic activity has led to more confused argument at cross-purposes than has foreign trade. The confusion arises largely because the questions at issue are so often discussed from the angle of particular experience and interest. The individual producer, trader, or consumer, however practical and expert he may be in his own affairs, cannot from his own experience give a complete answer to the questions that are under discussion. These questions are concerned with the social consequences of trading activities, with the effects of trading transactions upon the community as a whole.

There are three main groups of questions to be answered. The first is concerned with the reasons why trade becomes possible. Individual traders import and export because they can buy goods cheaply in one country and make profits by selling them in another. Their profits, made by transporting goods from where they are cheap to where their price is higher, are to them a sufficient reason for trading. But how does it happen that the prices of these goods are cheaper in one country than in another? Why is it that in recent decades the United States has tended to export manufactured goods rather than agricultural products? Why is Brazil a great exporter of coffee, Australia of wool, Denmark of butter, and India of tea?

The second group of questions is concerned with the way trade is financed. Every producer expects to be paid, promptly and in his own currency, for the goods he sells. Some of these goods may be exported to a foreign country. The foreign importer who receives them does not expect to pay for them until they are in his hands, and then he does so by payment in his currency. When a Frenchman pays francs for American cotton, how are these francs transformed into dollars which the American cotton grower can use? The individual trader need not worry about the processes by which payments are transferred from one currency to another. Even the bankers who handle the bookkeeping are not directly concerned with the effect which their bookkeeping has on the national currencies, on the prices of goods and services measured in them, and ultimately on economic activity and employment in the countries concerned. But these are the main topics of popular argument. Should we lend dollars for reconstruction and development of foreign countries, so that they may import from us and help keep employment at a high level in the United States? How will the expenditure of these dollars affect prices in the United States? Should we insist upon the other members of the International Monetary Fund co-operating with us to keep the exchange rates stable?

The third set of questions is concerned with the advantages to be gained by trading, and with the division of these gains among the trading countries. Here again the trader's answer is simple but inadequate for our purposes. He imports because he can buy foreign goods cheaply and sell them at a profit. He exports because he can get higher prices in the foreign than in the home market. In either case he makes a profit. But what effect do his transactions have on his fellow citizens, and on the national community as a whole? The imported goods compete, directly or indirectly, with home products. These home products are displaced to some extent or their prices are lowered. Is the community as a whole better off by reason of the cheaper imports, or worse off because the home products have been cheapened?

The producer whose goods have suffered from the competition of imports has no doubt of the injury he has received. The benefits have accrued to someone else. How is the balance to be struck for the community as a whole? The answer to this question would be simpler if it could be confined to a balancing of benefits and of injuries to groups within the same national community. But in fact there is always a cross-conflict so that the argument becomes confused by reference to national as well as to group interests. The producers in the exporting country and the consumers in the importing country obviously want to increase their trade; while the consumers in the exporting country and the producers in the importing country share a contrary interest. Thus, in the first half of the nineteenth century the English cotton manufacturers led the free-trade movement and finally persuaded Parliament that the national interest demanded abolition of the protective duties on wheat. The cotton growers in the United States were free traders also, but in the long run they failed to persuade Congress that it was in the national interest to reduce the duties on British manufactured goods.

These then are the three main aspects of the theory of international trade—first, an explanation and delimitation of the conditions which make it profitable for individuals to trade across national boundaries; second, an explanation of the way payments are transferred or offset between national currency systems, and also of how these currencies and the economic activity they serve react to the balancing process; and finally, an analysis of how the gain from trade is divided between the trading countries.

It is not surprising that economic theory developed first in the field of foreign trade. The complicated conflicts of interest within and across national boundaries; the subtle and often delayed or hidden reactions of international payments upon national currencies and price levels, and ultimately upon production and employment; and the baffling difficulties of any attempt to estimate the national interest as a whole and to measure the division of the gains from trade—these are questions that cannot be answered by reference to the limited and partial experience of individuals or interested groups.

The main reason why it is necessary to devote special attention to international, as distinct from domestic, trade lies in the fact that the political organization of the world into sovereign nation-states leads to a conflict between national and cosmopolitan interests or values. Apart altogether from such obstacles as import and export duties deliberately imposed by governments to check or control dealings with foreigners, there are many difficulties in international trade. These arise from differences in legal and tax systems, in standards, weights and measures, in technical equipment and industrial structure, in consumers' preferences, and often in language. It is true that many of them arise to some extent in the domestic trade of most countries. But there is sufficient difference of degree in the difficulties which traders must face in dealing with citizens of another country, to constitute a difference in kind.

The mere fact that each sovereign state operates a uniform currency system within its territory independent of all other currencies is sufficient to distinguish international from domestic trade. Indeed, the major interest of international trade theory is and always has been centered on the balancing of international payments, and on the repercussions of this balancing process upon the monetary systems, and therefore on the domestic economic activity of the trading countries.

As long as nation-states retain their sovereignty there can be little substance in the assertion that the theory of international trade is simply an aspect of the theory which explains the location of industry. In regard to the conditions in which international trade arises and the limits within which such trade is possible, there is something to be learned from the theory which analyzes the forces determining industrial location. Economists have studied the forces that have caused industries to develop in particular regions. Climatic factors are important. Transport costs must be minimized, so that manufacturing sometimes develops at the source of raw materials, or close to the market, or at a midway point between the source of raw materials and the main market for the manufactured product. The availability of power, the supply of labor, and many other factors must be considered. All these considerations enter into the international as well as the national location of industry. But this is by no means the whole or even the most important aspect of international trade theory.

Increasingly, modern economists have come to feel that the most direct and realistic approach to a discussion of the whole theory of international trade is to treat it simply as a special and somewhat more complicated case of interregional trade. There is much to be said for this approach. The classical treatment of international trade which will be summarized in this chapter was based upon assumptions different from those used in discussing domestic trade. Many of those assumptions were implicit, rather than explicit, in the writings of the classical economists, and their implications are often overlooked. It is necessary, therefore, to make these assumptions explicit before proceeding to discuss the main theorems by which the classical economists explained the nature and consequences of international trade.

Anyone who for the first time reads David Ricardo, or even John Stuart Mill, must be struck with the brevity and elliptical character of their arguments. In Ricardo's *Principles* only one short chapter is devoted specifically to international trade, and that chapter starts with the categorical statement, "No extension of foreign trade will immediately increase the amount of value in a country, although it will very powerfully contribute to increase the mass of commodities, and therefore the sum of enjoyments." This in itself demands a whole series of definitions and explanations before it can be intelligible to the ordinary reader. In his *Principles of Political Economy,* John Stuart Mill treats the various problems at greater length, but even his treatment is based on assumptions that need to be made explicit. To state this is not a criticism of the classical theory. All theory must be abstract. Thinking is necessarily a process of abstraction from the immaterial and irrelevant aspects of a question in order to concentrate on essentials. The assumptions must be examined to discover how far they achieve this concentration.

The theory of international trade first outlined by Ricardo and later systematized by John Stuart Mill was based upon three major, and a number of minor, assumptions. What the classical economists constructed was an abstract model. They defined international trade for the purpose of their analysis, as the exchange of goods which took place in the conditions which they assumed to represent the fundamental, irreducible skeleton of essential trading relationships. Such a model could never be and was not intended to be realistic. Its purpose was to discard the unessential detail which complicates and obscures the working of fundamental principles. The conclusions drawn from analysis of such an abstract model must always be modified before they can be safely applied to actual conditions in the world of reality. The usefulness of the model depends upon the skill of the theorists in choosing assumptions and definitions which correspond with the essential realities of the trading world.

The three major assumptions of classical theory were: (1) that within a country labor and capital moved freely and without friction; (2) that between countries they did not move at all; and (3) that the supply of money consisted of gold or gold substitutes which necessarily were adjusted automatically to trading needs.

It should be emphasized that the classical economists were trying to discover the fundamental and permanent relationships of cause and effect in trading across national boundaries. Therefore they confined their analysis to the long-run conditions that would be established when temporary dislocations of production and employment had been resolved. They did not concern themselves with these short-run temporary dislocations, since they believed that in a competitive system the labor and capital displaced by imports would find alternative employment. This is the meaning of their first major assumption—that within a country labor and capital moved freely and without friction. As early as 1819 however, Mathew Carey was impressed by the fact that the flood of imports into the United States, with the expansion of British production and trade at the close of the Napoleonic Wars, had caused widespread unemployment among American craftsmen.

He therefore attacked this first assumption of the classical theory with great vigor. Where, he asked, were these craftsmen to find alternative employment? The reply of the classical economists was that they were concerned with the long run, and that in the long run the displaced craftsmen would be absorbed into other industries in which the United States had a comparative advantage in production costs. In their view, the appearance of temporary unemployment was a complicating detail which did not invalidate the logical conclusions of their theory. These conclusions were unassailable, granted the assumptions upon which the theory rested. Carey's view was that, theory or no theory, the unemployment was real. Hence, he argued, the assumptions were so unrealistic as to make the theory useless and misleading.

In regard to the second assumption, John Stuart Mill made it clear that he was aware that the assumptions of the classical theory did not correspond with reality. He recognized that there was a growing tendency for both labor and capital to move more freely between countries, so that in practice the distinction between domestic and international trade was not as sharp as it was assumed to be in the model set up for analysis.[1] For the purpose of this analysis, he defined

[1] Cf. J. S. Mill, *Principles of Political Economy* (Ashley ed.), London, 1921, p. 575: "If capital removed to remote parts of the world as readily, and for as small an inducement, as it moves to another quarter of the same town; if people would transport their manufactories to America or China whenever they could save a small percentage in their expenses by it; profits would be alike (or equivalent) all over the world, and all things would be produced in the places where the same labour and capital would produce them in greatest quantity and of best quality. A tendency may, even now, be observed towards such a state of things; capital is becoming more and more cosmopolitan; there is so much

international trade as the exchange of goods between areas among which labor and capital could not be transferred. This definition led him to remark that certain kinds of international trade which did not conform to his definition should be discussed as if they were species of domestic trade. Thus he considered the trade between England and the West Indies as being similar to the trade between town and country, rather than to international trade as he defined it. Obviously this almost casual exclusion of certain categories of international trade from the model being analyzed limited the validity of the conclusions drawn from the analysis. A great and growing part of the international trade of the latter nineteenth century was of the kind which Mill excluded by his definition from consideration in the classical analysis.[2] The fact is that the precision of the classical doctrines was achieved only by defining international trade in a way which was highly limited and artificial, even in Ricardo's own time. The model constructed for analysis was admirably fitted to throw light upon the questions which the classical economists were concerned to study. These were the fundamental principles of international trade in the conditions assumed. But those conditions excluded much of the developing trade even of their time.

Since by definition the classical theory arbitrarily excluded the transference of capital and labor between nations, it was, in terms commonly though not very appropriately used, a static rather than a dynamic theory. It was confined to a consideration of the long-run consequences of trade between two communities at a given moment, given the resources available to each community at that moment. It did not attempt to deal with the development of trade over a period of time. It is true that John Stuart Mill admitted as an exception the validity of the argument for protection in appropriate circumstances to growing industries—the infant-industry argument—but this formed no part of the classical doctrine. The infant-industry argument had

greater similarity of manners and institutions than formerly, and so much less alienation of feeling, among the more civilized countries, that both population and capital now move from one of those countries to another on much less temptation than heretofore."

[2] Cf. John H. Williams, "The Theory of International Trade Reconsidered," *Economic Journal*, Vol. XXXIX, No. 154, June 1929, p. 208: "On these precise principles, England had found it convenient to produce wheat and meat (and for that purpose to export capital) in Argentina, gold and wool in Australia, minerals and food products in Africa, raw materials and foods in the United States and Canada through the greater part of their history; nor was her nineteenth century trade with Western Europe devoid of these same characteristics, though there the goods trade and the movement of capital were not so directly and obviously linked together."

been common in mercantilist literature; but the Ricardian theory excluded it from consideration by defining international trade in such a way as to exclude the possibility that capital and labor might be attracted to a developing country of abundant resources. Thus the classical theory was a snapshot rather than a movie—an explanation of why and how international trade is carried on at a particular moment of time rather than an explanation of economic development over a period of time.

The third major assumption was that the money used as a standard of value consisted of coins, or notes redeemable in coin or bullion, and that the coins circulated at their value as bullion. This money was assumed to be convertible into gold or silver bars and to be freely exchangeable either as coin or as bullion between countries. Its value was fixed at its bullion value, and the rate of exchange between two currencies was easily calculated by comparing the intrinsic value of the precious metal in their coins. In these conditions, the supply of the precious metals would automatically adjust itself to the needs of trade in each country.

This is one of the key positions of both Ricardo and John Stuart Mill.[3] They believed that there was nothing that governments could do about this. If they issued paper money beyond the amount that the public would accept in the belief that these notes could at any moment be converted into gold, the surplus issue would be cashed and the government would have to redeem it with gold or silver from its reserves. If the notes were made inconvertible, their value would fall and the price of gold (and of all commodities) as measured in the paper money would rise in proportion to their overissue. This was Ricardo's argument in his first pamphlet (1810) entitled *The High Price of Bullion a Proof of the Depreciation of Bank Notes.* The conclusion drawn by the classical theorists was that governments must accept the fact that the only true money (gold and silver) was beyond

[3] Cf. J. S. Mill's *Principles,* p. 625: "The result of the preceding discussion cannot be better summed up than in the words of Ricardo. 'Gold and silver having been chosen for the general medium of circulation, they are, by the competition of commerce, distributed in such proportions amongst the different countries of the world as to accommodate themselves to the natural traffic which would take place if no such metals existed, and the trade between countries were purely a trade of barter.' Of this principle, so fertile in consequences, previous to which the theory of foreign trade was an unintelligible chaos, Mr. Ricardo, though he did not pursue it into its ramifications, was the real originator. No writer who preceded him appears to have had a glimpse of it: and few are those who even since his time have had an adequate conception of its scientific value."

their control. All the elaborate mercantilist devices for increasing the national supplies of treasure were self-defeating. Money accommodated itself to the needs of trade. If governments issued inferior monetary substitutes, their value would depreciate. There was no place, therefore, in the classical theory for positive monetary policies designed to maintain full employment or to combat depressions.

The classical theory of international trade made use, implicitly or explicitly, of many other assumptions which can be regarded as being necessary in order to simplify the analysis. This is the usual procedure in a complicated problem. It is the only available procedure in the analysis of economic questions; but it must be used cautiously since it assumes that many of the factors in the problem remain unchanged. Thus the classical economists assumed that trade was conducted between two countries only, and that each of them produced only two commodities. Later economists have shown that trade between more than two countries, covering a wide range of commodities, introduces complications that are important; but they have been able to restate the classical theory so as to take these questions into consideration. In the same way transport costs were ignored by the classical economists who assumed also that the goods traded were produced at a constant cost per unit—that there were no cost advantages or disadvantages in increasing or decreasing the scale of production. Another assumption of the classical theory was that costs could be measured in labor time. This was in accordance with the theory of value held at the time—that labor time expended in production was the cause and the measure of value. As with the other working assumptions this assumption of labor cost may be replaced by more modern concepts of value without changing the essential character of the classical analysis.

What is important for our purpose is the fact that the theories of the classical school are valid only upon the basis of the three major assumptions stated above. The main theorems that were built upon these assumptions constituted a complete system of thought answering the three major groups of questions set forth at the beginning of this chapter. The first theorem, known as the theory of comparative costs, explains the conditions in which trade will arise. The second theorem, known as the price specie-flow theory, explains how payments are made between national currency systems. A corollary of this theorem explains how, in the process of making payments, the precious metals are distributed among countries in accordance with trading needs. The third theorem, to which Mill gave the name of the theory of international values, is now known as the theory of reciprocal demand. It explains how the terms of trade are arrived at, and how the gains from trade are divided between nations. Together, these three theorems constituted a closed and rigorous system. It was the first and until quite recently the most useful, indeed the only, complete and rigorous theory available to explain the workings of international trade.

Given the assumptions on which it is based, this classical theory is unassailable. It is very helpful in explaining how trade is carried on between mutually exclusive, non-competing groups. It is important to present the classical theory here in its complete form because it formed the basis of the practical arguments by which the laissez-faire case for free trade was carried to practical triumph in England in the course of the nineteenth century. It was therefore immensely influential in shaping our modern trading world. Moreover, the classical theory, though never lacking critics, was then generally accepted as valid by economists. Today there is an increasing recognition of the extent to which its assumptions were chosen to throw light upon the questions of policy selected for study. There is also a growing rejection of the laissez-faire philosophy on which these assumptions ultimately rest. Most economists would still urge the case for international economic co-operation, but few would now rest that case upon the classical theory. However, it is necessary to understand that theory, both because it was so powerful in the past and because a thorough understanding of it is the best point of departure from which to construct a theory more appropriate to present circumstances.

THE TERRITORIAL DIVISION OF LABOR

A trader, alert for profit, will buy wherever he can do so cheaply. If he buys outside his own country for sale within it, or buys at home to sell abroad, he must calculate many extra costs—transport, taxes, the cost of transferring payment, and usually a great deal of paper work in meeting tax and statistical requirements at the frontiers. In new or poorly organized trades, he must often take a risk on the quality of the product or on its acceptance by consumers. The difference in price between the home and foreign market must usually be considerable if he is to face all these expensive complications in trading across national frontiers.

In course of time, however, international trade tends to become canalized and to some extent standardized. The quality of the product and the sources of supply become known; trading connections are organized; the consumers' demand can be estimated; transport, duty, and other costs are known; and the paper work can be reduced to routine. Goods can then move from country to country along established routes whenever a somewhat narrow price differential makes such movement profitable.

Whether the trade is new and somewhat hazardous or well-established and moving as the result of close profit calculations based on long experience, it is this price differential which causes it to move. Apart from exceptional cases where the market is miscalculated, no trader ever goes to the trouble of buying in a foreign market goods he can buy more cheaply at home. He buys abroad because the price of a commodity is cheaper there in the simple and absolute sense.

The classical economists were practical men. They knew how trade was carried on. Ricardo, for example, stated clearly that trade arose as a result of absolute price differences.[4] After all he was a successful stock-exchange broker, perfectly familiar with practical business methods, and not likely to invent a theory which would seem nonsensical to his business associates. But unlike the majority of them, he was concerned to probe into the reasons why cloth could be bought cheaply in England and sold in Portugal at a profit. The conclusion to which he came was this. If traders were left alone to pursue their own profit by buying in the cheapest and selling in the dearest market, the result of their activities in the long run would be that each country would come to specialize on producing and exporting those commodities in which its comparative advantage, as measured in labor cost, was greatest.

[4] David Ricardo, *Principles of Political Economy and Taxation,* Ch. VII, "Every transaction in commerce is an independent transaction. Whilst a merchant can buy cloth in England for £45, and sell it with the usual profit in Portugal, he will continue to export it from England. His business simply is to purchase English cloth and pay for it by a bill of exchange, which he purchases with Portuguese money. It is to him of no importance what becomes of this money: he has discharged his debt by remittance of the bill. His transaction is undoubtedly regulated by the terms on which he can obtain this bill, but they are known to him at the time; and the causes which may influence the market price of bills, or the rate of exchange, is no consideration of his."

This theory, or law of comparative cost or of comparative advantage, is now associated with Ricardo's name, though Robert Torrens was perhaps the first to state it. Ricardo himself did not use this exact phraseology. His followers regarded it as his greatest contribution to economic science, and the case for free trade came to be postulated upon it. It is of some importance, therefore, to get a clear understanding of what this theory of comparative cost purported to prove.

Earlier economists, notably Adam Smith, had made a strong case for free trade by demonstrating the advantages of specialization, or of what Torrens in a happy phrase later called the territorial division of labor. But they had been content to argue their case for free trade on the broad ground of the advantages of specialization. It is relatively easy to demonstrate the simple truth that it pays to specialize. Individual experience can be drawn upon to show that any person can maximize his productivity by concentrating upon those things which yield the best return for his time.

Within any country, as between countries, there are clear cases of regional specialization based on the advantages offered by climatic or other assets. In California for example, agriculture is highly organized on the basis of a scientific appraisal of soil, climate, and other production factors. Around each specialized industry appropriate services are organized, often co-operatively. Castroville concentrates on artichokes, advertising itself as "the artichoke center of the world," and buying from other areas many products which it could grow from its own soil. This is a good example of the exploitation of comparative advantages based on natural conditions. In the same way, Hawaii cultivates its three major crops—tourists, sugar, and pineapples—and imports most of its vegetables from California.

Regional specialization, leading to a territorial division of labor between countries, was the basis of Adam Smith's argument for free trade. He argued that if competition is not interfered with, it will lead to this kind of specialization and will thereby maximize production within each country, and in the whole trading world. It is an essential part of the free-trade argument that every country which specializes upon the production of those commodities which enable it to participate in international trade will share to some extent in the gains from trade. The division of the gains may be unequal and may vary from time to time, but every trading country will find its national income increased by trading.

Many of the earlier mercantilist writers had noted the advantages of specialization, but, as Adam Smith did, they based their discussion upon such natural advantages as climate and geographical situation. Unlike Ricardo, they did not assume that enterprise, labor, and capital were confined within national boundaries. Indeed, Adam Smith pointed out that merchants were not necessarily citizens of any particular country and commented upon the lack of patriotic sentiment in business. It is true that he wrote before the advent of factories dependent on steam power. But he was very emphatic that "a very trifling disgust will make him (the merchant) remove his capital, and together with it all the industry which it supports, from one country to another."

The conclusion that goods would be produced in the countries where their real costs of production were lowest, and that labor and capital would be attracted to those countries where production costs were low, was unpalatable to those who like Ricardo were concerned to make a case for free trade. In order to make this case on laissez-faire grounds, it was necessary to meet the protectionist argument that under free trade industries might move to countries where natural resources were abundant and labor costs cheap. Such movement clearly took place within national boundaries, but the Ricardians assumed that labor, capital, and enterprise were immobile internationally. International trade was defined as taking place between areas where such transfers were impossible. Upon the basis of this definition, the Ricardians developed the law of comparative cost. The international distribution of productive resources was taken as fixed.

The novelty of the classical theory of international trade was this contention embodied in the law of comparative cost. That is to say, if traders were left free, their activities would result in each country concentrating upon the production and export of those commodities in which its costs (as measured in labor time) were lowest as compared with other commodities which it might produce. Each country would import those commodities in which its labor costs were greatest. It would import such commodities, even if they could be produced at a lower real cost at home, in order to gain the greater advantage of specializing upon those commodities whose labor costs were still lower. This did not necessarily mean that commodities would always be produced in the country of lowest real costs. Indeed Ricardo was at pains to deny this conclusion, and if his assumption of international immobility of the factors of production is granted, his denial is clearly logical.

The law of comparative cost is best stated by using Ricardo's own arithmetical illustration. He assumed that England could produce a quantity of cloth with the labor of 100 men for a year, and a quantity of wine with the labor of 120 men for a year. In Portugal the same quantities of cloth could be produced by the labor of 90 men and of wine by the labor of 80 men. Both cloth and wine, therefore, could be produced more cheaply (in terms of real cost measured in labor time) in Portugal. Upon the reasoning of earlier economists, there would be a tendency for the production of both to increase in Portugal. Ricardo, however, assuming that capital and labor could not move from England to Portugal, demonstrated that both countries would gain if England concentrated on cloth and Portugal on wine. If each country was of the same size, enough cloth for both could be produced in England by the labor of 200 men, leaving the labor of 20 men to be used for other purposes. In Portugal enough wine for both countries could be produced by the labor of 160 men, leaving the labor of 10 men free. Assuming the complete mobility of labor and capital within each country, it followed that this freed labor would be quickly absorbed in other employment. Each country would then be better off by concentrating on the kind of production in which it had the greatest comparative advantage.

This is the arithmetic which critics have called "unreal." Later economists have challenged this reasoning, based upon the simple case of two countries and two commodities, in that it ignores transport costs and other frictions and hindrances, and assumes constant costs per unit of production. These critics do not deny that, even in the case of trade with a third country, where one country might expand its exports at the other's expense, trade would continue. But they claim that the displaced country's trade would have to be conducted on less favorable terms than in the absence of the new competition. Much of the controversy pivots on the question of how the gains from trade will be divided. This aspect of the classical doctrine will be considered later. Here we are concerned only with the general validity of the law of comparative cost.

It is clear that whatever validity the classical theory may have depends upon the assumption that labor costs correspond, at least roughly, with the money costs by which trade is operated in practice.[5] Economists have long since abandoned the notion that labor cost, however measured, is the ultimate determinant and measure of value. Labor cost has become a kind of symbol or token of real costs, as distinct from money costs, of production. These real costs consist of the actual labor, resources, capital, and organizing skill devoted to producing a particular commodity. But how are these real costs to be measured unless by assuming that they are reflected in money costs? And if we assume this, why not make the analysis of real costs directly in terms of money costs? The classical economists did not give much more than passing attention to this question. They were mostly content with the simple demonstration of the comparative-cost theory based only on labor costs which seemed to afford a conclusive justification of the free-trade doctrine.

Modern economists however are not content with this attitude. They are aware that the measurement of comparative advantage in terms of money costs is more complicated, and that it blurs the simple argument for free trade. They prefer, however, to seek the true and more complex explanation of the conditions in which trade arises, even though the case for free trade may seem less clear in consequence.

It is not necessary to abandon the case for territorial specialization, or the theory of comparative cost, simply because it can be shown that even in Ricardo's day the factors of production were not entirely immobile between countries. The modern explanation of international trade runs in terms of the most profitable combination of the factors of production in different countries. Thus where labor is abundant and capital is scarce, there is likely to be a comparative advantage in producing goods with a high proportion of labor cost. Where technical and organizing skills are lacking, the export of simple raw materials is more likely than that of highly manufactured commodities. And where capital is abundant and organization is at a high level, there will tend to be a comparative advantage in concentrating upon complex manufactures.

The modern theory takes into account the advantages of speciali-

[5] Jacob Viner, *Studies in the Theory of International Trade,* New York, 1937, p. 493: "Unless the prices of commodities within a country are at least roughly proportional to their real costs, the doctrine of comparative costs is insufficient to establish a presumption of free trade and, in fact, may provide a presumption in favor of interference with trade in order to bring it into conformity with comparative real costs."

zation based not only upon climatic and geographical differences in the endowment of various countries, but upon economic organization. It recognizes that economic organization (and therefore the utility of the natural endowment) depends in part upon trade, as trade depends upon the endowment. What may be useless rock in a country without transport may be valuable ore when trade develops. Conversely, valuable ore may become useless rock if trade ceases. Thus comparative cost or comparative advantage is more complex, more flexible, less easily determined, and more fleeting, than the simplified teaching derived from the analysis of the classical economists often made it appear to be.

Even a relative immobility of the factors of production—greater difficulty in transferring resources between countries than within a country—is sufficient to warrant the formulation of a theory of comparative advantage. As long as there is a relative immobility of the factors of production, it is clear that, in the absence of government restrictions, trade will continue because it brings mutual benefits. If labor and capital cannot move, the goods they produce will be exchanged. In many important respects the recent strengthening of nationalism has made this assumption of immobility more realistic than it was in the nineteenth century. Men and equipment are now less free to move between countries.

The theory of comparative advantage, therefore, contains a truth that ought not to be lost—the truth that the territorial division of labor brought about by allowing economic forces to operate brings the best total use of the world's resources and the maximum of total productivity. The benefits may be divided differently among the countries concerned as trading conditions change, but trade will continue because of the uneven proportions in which the factors of production are combined in different countries. The mere fact of continuance is prima-facie proof of mutual benefit. Indeed, if there is a definite limit to some factor of production—for example, a limited amount of agricultural land—the extreme case of the comparative-cost theory may occur. It may pay a community to specialize on the most advantageous use of its limited factor, such as land, even if this means importing goods and services which might be produced more cheaply on the spot.

It would seem wise not to be too hasty about rejecting the practical deductions drawn from the classical theory because of the imperfections we can now see in the manner of its first presentation. The experimental scientists have gone beyond Newtonian physics, but they do not reject the law of gravity, or speak disrespectfully of its author. We cannot expect the classical formulation of the theory to suit our modern needs. In more than a century, it would be strange indeed if we had not come to a fuller understanding of the phenomena involved, and if the phenomena themselves had not changed.

In two important fields of inquiry the classical theory was precluded by its assumptions from taking into account problems which we now recognize as important. The first is the distributive problem. If enterprise and capital can in fact move with relative freedom, while labor is less mobile, it is obvious that trade may lead to a shift in the distribution of income to the detriment of the labor which is immobile. Thus New England capital and enterprise may find it profitable to set up cotton mills in Puerto Rico to supply the local market. What then happens to the cotton worker in Nashua? The classical economists could not attack this problem as long as they assumed that all the factors of production were immobile. When the problem was forced on their successors, it was argued that the displaced labor would be absorbed in other industries in which New England had a comparative advantage. But these other industries tend more and more to consist of financial, commercial, and shipping services which do not offer employment opportunities to the displaced cotton operatives.

The second field of inquiry from which classical theory was debarred by its assumptions is that of economic development, which is now much discussed as many countries seek to industrialize. It is true that the followers of the classical school broadened the theory of international trade somewhat so as to take the movement of capital into account. It is also true that some preliminary effort has been made to develop a separate theory of capital movements. But the complicated economic relations between advanced and backward economic areas are only now being studied scientifically. It seems rather silly to start by assuming that the phenomenon we wish to study does not exist, and then proceed to modify our conclusions by admitting that it does. Clearly a new approach is necessary, and this approach is being worked out by considering international trade as a special complicated case of trade in general.

This new approach is undoubtedly practical. Yet, it seems clear that some residue of the classical theory will survive. In that residue will be found the truth embodied in the theory of comparative advantage—that the best results for the trading world will in the long run accrue from working out a pattern of territorial specialization and interchange that makes the most efficient use of available resources and capacities in the different trading countries. These resources and capacities are in part determined by natural causes—there is not a great deal man can do about climate, or about the uneven distribution of minerals and soil fertility. But man can do a good deal about the numbers and technical capacity of the world's peoples, their capital equipment, and their institutional arrangements. In our own time we have seen startling examples of this fact, and a modern theory of international economic relations must take such processes of change and development into consideration.

THE BALANCING OF PAYMENTS

In order to explain how payments are balanced between national economies, the classical economists elaborated David Hume's price specie-flow theory. Thereby they explained the balancing of international payments and demonstrated how the precious metals were distributed in accordance with the needs of trade. This price specie-flow theory was the second major theorem of the classical theory of international trade. Together with its corollary it provided an answer to the second group of questions noted earlier in this chapter. That is to say those connected with the balancing of payments between national economies.

In this field the classical economists had less need to resort to hypothetical and somewhat tortuous reasoning. In 1752 David Hume had shown how national currency systems and price levels were connected by a pipeline through the balance of payments. He demonstrated that the flow of specie along this pipeline would automatically adjust the supply of currency, and thereby the level of prices in each trading country so that in and out payments for exports and imports would offset each other. What Hume had shown was that there were two aspects of this proposition. The movement of the precious metals adjusted prices and regulated the flow of trade, but at the same time that movement was responsive to trading needs. If prices went up in any country, bullion was then employed to purchase commodities in other countries and, when bullion thus moved out of a country, prices came down. This neat counteraction was produced by reason of the fact that the commodity value of gold was the same in all countries.

The classical economists refined and elaborated both aspects of this theory—the processes by which the flow of specie effected the balancing of payments, and the manner in which this balancing distributed the precious metals appropriately among the national currency systems. Ricardo knew his money market. The money market, however, was to undergo great change, particularly in the latter part of the nineteenth century. It is necessary now to revise Ricardo's theory, and to modify the practical policies to which it pointed. But in the confusion of the early nineteenth century the basic analysis was illuminating, and it remains a good starting point from which to approach a study of the balancing of payments in modern circumstances.

In their exposition of the price specie-flow theory, the classical economists assumed that money consists of coined precious metals. John Stuart Mill put it quite succinctly: "I shall use the terms Money and the Precious Metals indiscriminately. This may be done without leading to any error; it having been shown that the value of money, when it consists of the precious metals, or of a paper currency convertible into them on demand, is entirely governed by the value of the metals themselves: from which it never permanently differs, except by the expense of coinage when this is paid by the individual and not by the state."

Actually Ricardo wrote when the monetary circulation of England was inconvertible into gold. He was concerned with showing that when bank notes ceased to be convertible, their value in terms both of gold and of goods depended upon the extent of their issue. He was right in this thesis that the high price of bullion was proof of the depreciation of bank notes through overissue. The dependence of depreciation upon overissue was not as direct and simple as he believed, but it was a fact and the most important fact to emphasize. In analyzing the balancing of international payments, however, the classicists abstracted from the complication of inconvertible paper money. They were concerned with demonstrating that imports paid for exports. To do so they assumed that money consisted of coin or of paper currency convertible into coin.

The classical economists did not concern themselves with the complications in the balancing process that arose from fluctuations between the precious metals—gold and silver. Gresham's Law—that if two coinages circulated at their bullion value, the cheaper would drive the dearer from circulation—was well known. It had been made clear from centuries of experience that if an attempt was made to use both gold and silver as standard money, the result was likely to be that one or the other would disappear from circulation because it was more valuable as bullion. Thus alternating shortages of gold and of silver would occur. England had come to rely on gold when the Coinage Act of 1816 made gold the single standard of value. When specie payments which had been suspended in 1797 were resumed in 1819, it was gold into which bank notes were made convertible. In the English monetary system silver became a subordinate element, coined at a token value. There was however an active market for silver. In India and the Far East it was the medium of circulation and of hoarding. Any temporary surplus of silver was likely to find its way to the East on a relatively slight cheapening of the price. Moreover France and most of the continental countries were still at this time on a double standard, as was the United States until 1873.

Alterations in the gold price of silver, therefore, affected and reflected the exchange between England and other countries. As long as current production of gold and silver was small in relation to the total accumulation available for monetary use, such price changes were small and did not put too great a strain on the exchange rates. However, the gold rush in California in 1849 and in Australia in 1851 changed this situation abruptly. With the increased production of gold, there was an appreciation of silver which began to disappear from circulation. Although these developments, which were to disturb the relative values of the precious metals so seriously and to end in the virtually complete abandonment of silver as a monetary standard, began in 1849—the year after John Stuart Mill published his *Principles*—and were in full swing before Mill made his last revision in 1862, he did not take them into account. Primarily this was because he was concerned with the fundamental principles and with keeping his exposition simple and concentrated on fundamentals.

After the great gold discoveries in California and Australia, silver was an expensive metal and hard to keep in circulation. The Latin Union, formed in 1865, united France and some of its neighboring countries in an agreement to maintain their currencies at par, and to keep the larger denominations of silver coins as standard money equally with gold. One incidental result was that England, the only country then on the gold standard, secured a passing advantage in its exchange rates. Using the temporarily cheapened metal, its exports of commodities were encouraged and it built up its gold reserves. Soon, however, an abrupt reversal took place. From 1842 on, metallurgical processes were discovered which improved the recovery of silver from lead ores. These were widely used after what are now the Rocky Mountain States were taken over by the United States from Mexico in 1848 and 1853. A flood of silver cheapened the metal in relation to gold, and silver was progressively demonetized. In 1873 the United States went on to the gold standard. In the second half of the nineteenth century there was a great debate which extended over many countries over the use of silver. The efforts of silver producers, notably in the United States, to restore the monetary demand for silver are an echo of this debate which was one of the burning issues of the time. Despite such passionate utterances as William Jennings Bryan's famous Cross of Gold speech (1896), one country after another was forced to rely on gold as the single standard.

John Stuart Mill wrote extensively on the development of deposit banking, but his exposition of the balancing of international payments did not deal adequately with the important influence exerted by the growing use of credit as a means of payment. It will be recalled that the first joint-stock bank organized primarily as a bank of deposit had been established outside London in 1826, and the first within the city had been established in 1833. The practice of making payments by check had rapidly increased. Though economists hesitated to admit that checks were currency if not money, a great proportion of payments were being made by check in England by the middle of the nineteenth century.[6]

The Bank Charter Act of 1844 had incorporated the principle that beyond a fixed amount equal to the Bank of England's long-standing advances to the government, every note issued by the Bank was to be backed by deposit of an equal value of gold in the reserve. This Act set a pattern which was to be followed in principle, though not in detail, by most other countries. The Act achieved, in a characteristi-

[6] Despite the British economist, H. D. Macleod's description of the word as "a mischievous Yankeeism," the use of the word *currency* as a synonym for money is at least as old as Adam Smith. The definition of *money* as consisting of legal tender, as distinct from *currency* (bank notes) and *credit*, was not made by the classical economists, has never been accepted in popular usage, and is now difficult to justify. It seems to have derived from the attempts of neo-classical writers to grapple with the new credit developments without abandoning the classical theory.

cally English way—by the use of historical precedents—what in other countries became a definitely proportioned reserve of gold against note issue. The bank notes supplemented by coin were used as till money and cash in circulation among banks and private individuals. The deposit banks, as a result of custom based on experience, kept as "cash on hand or in the Bank of England" an amount of notes, coin, or deposits in the Bank, equal at that time to about 15 per cent of their deposits subject to call. These deposits subject to call were in fact largely created by the advances of the banks to their customers. Thus was developed an elastic credit system. If advances and deposits grew to the point where additional notes were needed in order to maintain the conventional cash ratio, such notes could be issued only by the deposit banks selling to the Bank of England an equivalent amount of gold. By convention and custom the credit available to the community came to be proportioned to the amount of notes issued and this amount was in turn regulated by the gold placed in the reserve.

There was flexibility in these relations, particularly because not only the amount of credit but the rapidity of its turnover had to be reckoned in calculating the effectiveness of its use. The Bank of England began gradually to develop methods—primarily the alteration of its discount rate, supplemented by purchases or sales of government securities in the open market (open-market operations)—to keep credit expansion or contraction within bounds. The inflow and outflow of gold into the Bank reserve was largely influenced by the balance of payments. Thus were developed the delicate, and on the whole, effective mechanisms of the balancing of payments under the gold standard.

The classical analysis of the balancing of payments, however, remained the simple price specie-flow theory that had been first clearly stated by David Hume. According to this theory, if a surplus of exports over imports caused a demand for inward payments greater than for outward payments, the rate of exchange would turn toward the gold import point. If this rate did not encourage importers to buy more freely and discourage exporters from selling abroad, sufficiently to rectify the balance, the rate would eventually reach the point where gold would be imported as the cheapest means of settling the payments for the surplus exports. The classical economists realized, but did not greatly stress, what modern economists call the "income effect." When a country has an active export balance, the mere fact that exporters have more purchasing power tends in itself to right the balance of payments, since this larger purchasing power—apart altogether from the effects of an inflow of specie to pay for the export balance—causes prices to rise and imports to increase. The classical economists laid greater stress upon the fact that the country gaining gold would thereby have a larger monetary circulation, so that prices would tend to rise. The country losing gold would experience a contrary pressure on its prices as a result of reduced monetary circulation.

A practical illustration will demonstrate the simplicity of this relationship. As long as the gold standard was in operation, the English pound contained the same weight of gold—allowance being made for fineness and for minting charges—as was worth $4.8665 in United States currency. This was the "mint par of exchange." As long as dollar bills and Bank of England notes were freely exchangeable for gold, it followed that the exchange rate would not depart from this figure by more than the cost of shipping gold across the Atlantic. This might have been from 5 to 6 cents to the pound. The gold "export point" for the United States therefore was about $4.92 to the pound. The gold "import point" was about $4.80 to the pound.

If the United States had an exceptionally good harvest and was thus able to ship to England larger exports than usual, Englishmen would have more debts to pay in the United States than Americans had debts to pay in England. Competition in the exchange market would then force up the price of dollars. English bankers would be willing to pay £1 for $4.80. But if the price went above this, it would be cheaper for them to arrange for gold to be sent to the United States. Actually the arbitrage operators who specialized in foreign exchange would anticipate this situation and gold would begin to flow from England to the United States. The flow of American exports would then be checked in some measure by the movement of the exchange rates. For example, a shipment of 100,000 bushels of wheat which sold in England for a net return of five shillings a bushel (£25,000), would bring the exporter $123,000 if the exchange was at $4.92 to the pound, but only $120,000 if the exchange was at $4.80, a difference of three cents on the bushel. It was this kind of calculation that Ricardo had in mind when he wrote of "the causes which may influence the market price of bills, or the rate of exchange."

The classical theory was a theory of long-run equilibrium. It dealt with fundamental and permanent rather than transitory situations. Ricardo in particular was somewhat impatient with short-run, exceptional cases and sought to push his inquiries beyond them into the essential, basic forces that are determinant in the long run. Much modern discussion of the terms of trade and of the adjustments brought in a national economy by fluctuations in the balance of payments is concerned with short-run departures from equilibrium and with exceptional situations and pockets of advantage that may be exploited. The classical economists refused to be diverted from their main theses by such temporary complications. They enunciated, and drove home relentlessly, elementary truths in simple statements that are now regarded in many quarters as somewhat naïve and platitudinous. If a platitude is a truth that is in some danger of being forgotten, their teaching on the balancing of payments was by no means a platitude in their day. They had to fight hard before it was accepted by popular opinion. The essential point the classical economists wanted to drive home was that imports pay for exports—this is a truth which still needs emphasizing.

In order to demonstrate this truth Mill first analyzed international trade as a form of barter. He then showed how the precious metals enter into trade as commodities and went on to consider their movement from country to country as part of the process of balancing payments between national currency systems. After a discussion in rather simple terms of the effect of specie movements upon the exchange rates and upon national price levels, he tried to demonstrate that trade conducted on a monetary basis must, in the long run, come to the same equalization of imports and exports as in the case of barter.

There is a majestic simplicity about these elementary truths which seems to irritate those who prefer to concentrate upon peculiar and aberrant exceptions to the general case. But interest in peculiarities ought not to obscure the essential basic phenomena. An intelligent blinded person will beg his sighted guide to give him first the essential facts—the size, shape, color, material, and general proportions of a building—before describing some odd piece of decoration. Otherwise he gets a quite distorted impression of what his guide is describing. It was this concentration upon the essential phenomena that made the work of the classical economists so effective in bringing home to popular opinion a clear understanding of the nature of trading relationships.

The obverse of their explanation of the balancing of payments was their demonstration of the way in which the precious metals were distributed throughout the world in accordance with the needs of trade. The most elaborate exposition of this aspect of the classical doctrine was contained in Nassau Senior's *Three Lectures on the Transmission of the Precious Metals from Country to Country* (1828). In the course of that exposition Senior assumed that gold to the value of £5,000,000 was exported from England to France in payment for imports and considered what the effect of such a movement would be. He asked what to him was a rhetorical question: If this amount of gold did not enter into the French monetary system and cause an expansion of the circulation, what good would it do to France?[7] Unless it was allowed to raise prices and thus attract a greater volume of imports into France, all that the French people would receive in return for their exports would be a useless commodity which is expensive to store and guard. The English people, on the contrary, would have received French exports to the value of £5,000,000, goods they could use and enjoy. Senior put this question in a rhetorical form because he did not believe that any nation would ever be so foolish as to exchange the useful products of its labor for gold which it would proceed to inter in expensive vaults. The United States, however, has done just that in recent years. The piling up of large inactive reserves, reflecting a maldistribution of the world's gold supplies is prima-facie evidence that the trading world is out of joint—that the tail is wagging the dog.

The mechanism which the classical economists analyzed in these simple terms envisaged a world in which traders were free to import and export as they saw opportunities for profit. If prices in one country were low, foreign traders would increase their purchases in that country and cause an expansion of its exports. This would result in an inflow of the precious metals to the country where prices were

[7] Cf. London School of Economics *Reprints* No. 3, p. 12: "To suppose that the level of the precious metals in the commercial world can be permanently disturbed by taking money from one country to another, is as absurd as to suppose that the level of a pond can be altered by taking a bucket-full of water from one place, and pouring it in at another. The water instantly rushes to the place from which the bucket-full has been drawn, just as it rushes from the place into which it has been poured. Every country to which France exported any of the money she received from England would, to that extent, have more money than her habitual state of prices could allow. It would flow from her either directly back to England, or to those countries which were in want of money in consequence of having previously exported to England."

low. That inflow would raise prices and bring trade into an equilibrium where the payments due for imports would offset those receivable for exports. New supplies of the precious metals coming from the mines would be distributed in the same way.

The California gold rush in 1849 offered a dramatic illustration of their thesis. The abundance of gold and shortage of commodities caused very high levels of prices in California.[8] The gold producers and those who supplied them with goods had larger incomes. Dollar bills were brought to San Francisco by the banks which bought the newly mined gold. The gold found its way eastward to pay for the dollar bills so that the higher income levels and the rising trend of prices were diffused over the whole United States. This encouraged imports, depressed the exchanges, and so gold flowed out of the United States, to be distributed around the trading world. In 1851 gold was discovered in Australia and a similar sequence of events was produced. Ten years later, in 1861, gold was discovered in New Zealand, and the trade statistics of that little country show clearly the jump in imports—from £1,500,000 in 1860 to £7,000,000 in 1863—which followed the higher income levels and higher prices induced by the temporary abundance of gold.

As long as the currency systems of the world consisted primarily of gold or gold substitutes circulating at their bullion value, the classical explanation of the balancing of payments was valid. Briefly summarized, this explanation was that changes in a nation's price level (and therefore in the volume of its imports and exports) were determined by the amount of gold available to it for monetary purposes, and that changes in the amount of gold available were determined primarily by international gold movements. There was a reciprocal relationship between the movements of trade and the movements of specie. The same mechanism which adjusted price levels so that in- and out-

[8] Cf. the volume in which (*inter alia*) Herbert Asbury described the effect of the gold rush in 1849 upon economic conditions in San Francisco, *The Barbary Coast,* New York, Alfred A. Knopf, Inc., 1933, pp. 5–6: "Apples found a ready market at one to five dollars each, and eggs varied from ten to fifty dollars a dozen. In the restaurants a boiled egg was never less than a dollar and quite often several times that amount. Other foods sold at equally high prices. Tea and coffee cost from three hundred to four hundred dollars a barrel, and from four to five dollars a pound in small quantities. Wheat flour and salt pork each brought forty dollars a barrel, and a small loaf of bread, such as sold in New York for four cents, cost fifty to seventy five cents in San Francisco. The same price was paid for a pound of common cheese."

payments were balanced also distributed the precious metals among national monetary systems as the needs of trade determined.

The monetary mechanisms have now been greatly modified by the increasing use of credit—convertible and inconvertible paper money and bank deposits subject to check. The balancing of international payments is therefore a more complex and subtle process, but the essential truth of the classical theory is not dependent upon the accidents of its historical setting. What the classical economists were insistent upon was the fact that imports pay for exports, and that the use of monetary media, such as gold, facilitated but did not alter this process of offsetting goods and services. This truth remains valid, even though gold has now ceased to be the basis upon which national monetary systems are organized.

THE GAINS FROM TRADE

The third major group of questions to be considered in a theory of international trade is concerned with the nature of the gains from trade, and with their division among the trading nations. The classical economists took a broad view of these questions. They were not much concerned with national advantages. They propounded the theory of reciprocal demand to explain the division of the gains from trade. But they were much more interested in the volume of trade to be shared than they were in determining precisely how its gains were divided. The reason for this was their belief that each nation would get the share to which it was entitled by the competitive efficiency of its industries.

The mercantilist writers, however, had been much concerned with national wealth and power. Adam Smith, their severest contemporary critic, did not attack this preoccupation. What he was concerned to demonstrate was that—provided adequate precautions were taken against sudden overwhelming attack—the wealth of a community was best promoted by allowing individual merchants to trade freely for their own profit. It might sometimes be necessary in exceptional situations to sacrifice wealth in order to maintain national power. Such an exceptional situation, he believed, was the necessity for maintaining the Navigation Acts in order to build up naval strength.

On the assumption that a nation maintained the defenses necessary to ward off sudden attack, he always returned to his contention that a nation would grow strong by becoming rich. Subsequent experience has borne out his wisdom. During the nineteenth century England grew rich and powerful as her trade expanded. Even in the preceding centuries her natural defenses had enabled her to develop a freer economy than any of her continental rivals. That freedom gave her a long start in developing the new industrial methods that assured her leadership in the Industrial Revolution.

Throughout the nineteenth century Britain's strong power position cost her little. Secure from land attack, she was able to avoid the heavy burdens of universal military service. A small professional army (incredibly small in retrospect), backed by naval power, sufficed to garrison a great empire. The navy dominated the narrow seas around the British Isles and policed the trade routes of the world. In a crisis, therefore, Britain was sure of having time to mobilize all her power. In doing so, she could draw upon the resources of the whole trading world except that part closed off by a continental enemy.

The classical economists and their followers were not unpatriotic. Some of them in fact were professional soldiers. By contrast with the mercantilists, there was in classical writings a significant lack of concern for national power. During the first years of the war with France —before Napoleon established his dictatorship—there was a strong antiwar party in England. The economists were not active in this political opposition, but their criticism of the financial policies pursued by the Treasury and the Bank showed a surprising lack of interest in the war effort. If the monetary policy advocated by the Bullion Committee—a return to convertibility of bank notes in gold—had been followed in 1810, England would have been plunged into deflation and a severe financial crisis. No government could have accepted such monetary advice at such a critical stage of the war.

When the wars were at last ended in 1815, most of the economists and the overwhelming majority of the business community displayed consistent critical opposition to almost all increases in government expenditures, including those for military and naval purposes. Reduction of taxes to a minimum, abolition of all interference with private enterprise, and the elimination of discriminatory preferences for national shipping and for colonial trade, were among their cardinal doctrines.

England grew rapidly in wealth, power, and prestige. The growth of the United States was even more rapid. Despite some friction, there was a strong sentiment in both countries that any difficulties between them could and should be settled without resort to war. This sentiment grew and widened until those who worked for free trade came to identify their cause with the cause of peace.[9] They came to believe that universal free trade would promote peaceful prosperity among all nations. The belief that free competitive trade would bring peace with prosperity may have been naïve, but at least it demonstrates the completeness with which the free traders had dissociated themselves from the mercantilist preoccupation with economic warfare as a means of achieving national power.

The classical economists likewise displayed little interest in employment, which had also been a preoccupation of the mercantilists. They discarded the fear of imports, the fear that an adverse balance of payments would result in a loss of gold, reduce the monetary circulation, lower prices, and so cause periodic industrial depression and social distress. This was in part because they were concerned with the analysis of long-term equilibrium, and therefore brushed aside the incidental consequences of short-term departures from that equilibrium as irrelevant and unimportant. However, their attitude was largely based upon a robust belief in the virtues of competition.

In discussing the division of the gains from trade it is necessary first to stress these broad conceptions of the classical economists. Their complete rejection of mercantilist philosophy, and their adoption of completely opposite attitudes explain their indifference to specific calculations of the exact or even approximate division of the gains from trade. What they were interested in was the most efficient use of the productive resources of the world leading to an expanding world trade. In this trade, they were confident, each country would get its share according to its efficiency. The eloquent passage from his *Prin-*

[9] In 1842, Richard Cobden wrote to a friend: "It has struck me that it would be well to try to engraft our Free Trade agitation upon the Peace movement. They are one and the same cause. It has often been to me a matter of the greatest surprise that the Friends have not taken up the question of Free Trade as the means—and I believe the only human means—of effecting universal and permanent peace. The efforts of the Peace Societies, however laudable, can never be successful so long as the nations maintain their present system of isolation. The colonial system, with all its dazzling appeals to the passions of the people, can never be got rid of except by the indirect process of Free Trade, which will gradually and imperceptibly loosen the bands which united our Colonies to us by a mistaken notion of self-interest. Yet the Colonial policy of Europe has been the chief source of wars for the last hundred and fifty years. Again Free Trade, by perfecting the intercourse, and securing the dependence of countries one upon another, must inevitably snatch the power from the governments to plunge their people into wars."—John Morley, *The Life of Richard Cobden* (14th ed.), London, 1910, pp. 23–24.

ciples of Political Economy in which John Stuart Mill summarized this view is quoted below:

. . . the only direct advantage of foreign commerce resides in the imports. A country obtains things which it either could not have produced at all, or which it must have produced at a greater expense of capital and labour than the cost of the things which it exports to pay for them. . . .

But there are, besides, indirect effects, which must be counted as benefits of a high order. . . . A country which produces for a larger market than its own, can introduce a more extended division of labour, can make greater use of machinery, and is more likely to make inventions and improvements in the processes of production. Whatever causes a greater quantity of anything to be produced in the same place, tends to the general increase of the productive powers of the world. . . .

But the economical advantages of commerce are surpassed in importance by those of its effects which are intellectual and moral. It is hardly possible to overrate the value, in the present low state of human improvement, of placing human beings in contact with persons dissimilar to themselves, and with modes of thought and action unlike those with which they are familiar. Commerce is now what war once was, the principal source of this contact. Commercial adventurers from more advanced countries have generally been the first civilizers of barbarians. And commerce is the purpose of the far greater part of the communications which take place between civilized nations. Such communication has always been, and is peculiarly in the present age, one of the primary sources of progress. . . .

Finally, commerce first taught nations to see with good will the wealth and prosperity of one another. Before, the patriot, unless sufficiently advanced in culture to feel the world his country, wished all countries weak, poor and ill-governed, but his own: he now sees in their wealth and progress a direct source of wealth and progress to his own country. It is commerce which is rapidly rendering war obsolete, by strengthening and multiplying the personal interests which are in natural opposition to it. And it may be said without exaggeration that the great extent and rapid increase of international trade, in being the principal guarantee of the peace of the world, is the great permanent security for the uninterrupted progress of the ideas, the institutions, and the character of the human race.

Impelled by such beliefs and confident of their own competitive power, the merchants who led the free-trade movement in the second quarter of the nineteenth century pushed vigorously ahead with their campaign for unilateral economic disarmament. They were not unaware that it was necessary to reduce tariffs all over the world, but they were determined to begin this reduction at home. Their attack was first and foremost on monopoly and privilege in England. Whether other nations had the good sense to follow their example or not, they were resolved to take away the protection which the tariff on wheat gave to the landowners and thus to cripple the political power of the aristocracy. Therefore they had little interest in using the tariff as a bargaining weapon in trading deals with other nations. Nor were they interested in narrow calculations to discover which of two trading countries had the better of any particular bargain or of trade in general. The enormous expansion of trade which they confidently and rightly prophesied would give opportunities to all. How much of the benefit would accrue to their own country they were content to let rest upon its efficiency and enterprise.

This was a strong political attitude for the merchants to take in their struggle for free trade. But economists are concerned with the "nicely calculated less or more." Quite early in the discussions that centered about the meetings of the Political Economy Club which Ricardo had founded in 1820, the question was raised as to how the gains from trade were divided. Ricardo had neglected this question. His arithmetic worked out to an equal division of the gains. In correcting a misleading summary of his position in which James Mill had given figures indicating that all of the gain would accrue to one country, several of the classical economists appear to have arrived at the conclusion that there is a fairly wide range of bargaining positions between the limits set by comparative costs. They worked out the law of comparative costs first. It was the basis upon which they could justify their advocacy of free trade. The theory of international values was an afterthought, necessary to complete the theoretical analysis. John Stuart Mill demonstrated that the point at which values would settle within the limits set by comparative cost depended upon the relative intensities of demand for the traded articles. In economic jargon, "the terms of trade are determined by reciprocal demand."

The first elaboration of the theory of reciprocal demand was made by John Stuart Mill in essays written in 1829 and 1830. In 1844, Mill published these in a book entitled *Essays on Some Unsettled Questions of Political Economy*. Interest had been revived in the question by renewed controversy as to the wisdom of unilateral tariff reduction.

Mill did not "claim to himself the original conception, but only the elaboration, of the fundamental doctrine." However, he has been generally credited with it.

The occasion of publication of these essays was an argument raised by Robert Torrens. He contended that British retaliation against foreign tariffs, even if it did not lead other countries to reduce their tariffs, would cause price changes that would be beneficial to British trade. This argument was not welcome to those who were within sight of success in their campaign to get rid of the Corn Laws. Torrens must have been a difficult colleague. Voluble in print, sometimes arrogant, and always ready to claim priority for his theories, he was also obstinate. His reputation has suffered from his own prolix and often confused arguments, and even more from the fact that his views were often unpalatable to those who preferred elegant theoretical demonstrations that could be used to support a course of political action on which in any case they were determined.

There ensued a complicated controversy over the theoretical possibilities of the bargaining process. A great creditor country, with undoubted industrial and commercial leadership such as Britain enjoyed in the middle of the nineteenth century, had much to gain by opening up the channels of trade. It is probable that by reducing her own tariff, even though she could not at once be sure of reciprocal concessions, she turned the terms of trade somewhat in favor of her rivals and clients. Torrens' argument was theoretically sound. But the advocates of free trade regarded this worsening of the terms of trade as a small price to pay for the great expansion both in cheaper imports and in greater exports. A timid policy of making quite sure that Britain gained reciprocal concessions for every tariff reduction would have slowed up the hoped-for trade expansion. She might have gained a larger relative share of the gains from trade if she had insisted on other countries making equivalent tariff concessions, but the gains to be shared would have been smaller. A great industrial and creditor nation which aspires to be the center of a world trading system must work on both methods—reduce its own tariff boldly and use every possible means to persuade other countries to reduce their tariffs also.

It is now generally agreed by economists that circumstances may occur—and in practice they do frequently occur—where judicious and well-timed interference with the free flow of competitive trade may secure at least passing advantages to a country by turning the terms of trade in its favor. The classical economists, if they had been aware of this refined analysis, would probably have tossed it aside. They would have scoffed at the possibility that any government would be wise enough, possess enough knowledge, and be sufficiently independent of political pressures to manipulate the regulation of trade so delicately as to secure its maximum advantages, without provoking reprisals leading to a general constriction of trade. They were interested less in quibbling over division of the gains than in making sure that there would be the maximum of gains to be quibbled over. The objective sought by them and by those who translated their doctrines into practical politics was as great an expansion of world trade as possible.

In any case, the final conclusion of modern theory seems to be that there is no way in which the gains from trade or their division among the trading countries can be measured.[10] Various statistical devices have been suggested to measure the terms on which a country exchanges its efforts for imported goods. These measurements have some practical value as indicating the way in which, for example, raw material exporting countries may find themselves with export prices moving favorably or unfavorably as compared with the prices of the manufactured goods they import. Such measurements can be made only after the statistics have been compiled, and their chief use is in demonstrating the international aspects of business-cycle fluctuations. They are useless as a guide to current policy, and in any case they do

[10] The slow steps by which academic writers broadened the discussion—considering trade between more than two countries and in more than two commodities, under the varied conditions of increasing or decreasing, as well as constant, costs of production—have been reviewed in F. Y. Edgeworth, *Papers Relating to Political Economy,* London, 1925, Vol. II, pp. 3–50, and in Jacob Viner, *op. cit.,* pp. 444–593. Cf. Viner, p. 534: "Free trade, therefore, always makes more commodities available, and, unless it results in an impairment of the distribution of real incomes substantial enough to offset the increase in the quantity of goods available, free trade always operates, therefore, to increase the national real income. That the available gain is ordinarily substantial there is abundant reason to believe, but the extent of the gain cannot in practice be measured in any concrete way. These conclusions, which are little more than a paraphrase of some words of Cairnes's, are, in my opinion, very nearly as far as the argument can be carried."

Cf. also Gottfried Haberler, *The Theory of International Trade,* New York, 1936, p. 166: "But these discussions about the 'gain' from international trade and from changes in the international economic situation of a country ignore such important factors as changes in distribution and gains or losses due to the fact that a cumulative process of expansion or contraction might be started or interrupted, retarded or accelerated. Therefore, these considerations have such an unreal air that there is little point in pursuing them further."

not measure the division of the gains from trade, still less the extent of the gains.

The conclusions of this chapter may be briefly summarized. Despite the laborious attempts that have been made by some modern writers to discuss modern problems within the framework of the classical theory, there is a growing consensus that it is better to approach modern problems with the more developed analytical methods now available. This, however, does not detract from the services rendered by the writers of the classical school. Given their assumptions, they developed a convincing, rigorous, and complete theoretical system which answered the major questions to be faced—the conditions in which trade arises, the processes by which payments are balanced and the precious metals are distributed, and the nature of the benefits of trade. While their theoretical apparatus was cumbersome and most of its analytical concepts are now discarded, the core of truth which they established remains valid. It is still important to allow specialization to maximize the economic resources of the different trading regions of the world. It is perhaps more necessary than ever to emphasize the fact that, in the last resort, trade is barter, and that imports are paid for by exports. In the confused and complicated disorganization of trading relationships that always follows a great war, there is danger that the gains of trading expansion may be underestimated in striving for reciprocity of bargaining advantages. The classical viewpoint may have been unduly simple, but it concentrated on essential truths that are in some danger of being forgotten in our more sophisticated age.

CHAPTER VIII

THE FIGHT FOR FREE TRADE

RECONSTRUCTION AFTER NAPOLEON

THE POSITION of Britain at the end of the Napoleonic Wars offers many parallels to the position in which the United States found itself at the close of the second World War. Sea power had defeated a continental system. Britain had been safe from invasion and had developed productivity, technical skills, and financial strength. Instead of a debtor, it had become practically the sole creditor country in the world. In the course of a long and exhausting struggle, France, then the greatest power on the continent of Europe, and its reluctant allies, had been cut off from the expanding overseas world and impoverished. Refugee capital had flowed to Britain, and London had taken the place of Amsterdam as the leading money market of the world. Britain had been the arsenal and the paymaster of the enemies of Napoleon. The credit to restore their currencies and the skilled workmen to reorganize their industries could come only from her. British business and financial leaders were bent on developing world markets and needed peace to bring their plans to profit. Economic policy, and above all an expansion of international lending, suddenly became powerful factors in diplomacy. " 'There are Six Powers in Europe,' the Duc de Richelieu is reported to have said, 'Great Britain, France, Russia, Austria, Prussia and Baring Brothers.' And Barings were a synonym for the investment market at London." [1]

[1] Cf. Leland H. Jenks, *The Migration of British Capital to 1875,* New York, Alfred A. Knopf, Inc., 1927, p. 36.

Cf. also C. K. Webster, *The Foreign Policy of Castlereagh, 1815–1822,* London, 1934, pp. 49–50.

From the recent experience of the United States, it is now easier to understand the processes by which Britain in a comparatively short time was transformed from a debtor to a creditor nation. Right up to the outbreak of the war with France in 1793, the Dutch had been the leading financiers of Europe. Rates of interest were lower at Amsterdam than at any other commercial center. Much Dutch capital was laid out in shipping, in the financing of international trade, and even in long-term productive enterprises abroad, such as the draining of fens and the construction of canals in England. But England had enjoyed a long period of domestic peace and security from invasion. Capital had begun to accumulate, not only from increased domestic production and rising land values as population increased, but also from trading profits. Some of these profits were amassed by methods we should now condemn—the slave trade until 1807, the exploitation of slave labor in the profitable sugar plantations of the West Indies, and the trade and governance, hardly less than the spoliation practiced by the East India Company. Officials, or retired traders, living on newly and often ill-gotten wealth, became known as nabobs, whether they had acquired their money in India or elsewhere, and a whole terminology of nabobery sprang up to characterize such new rich as Thackeray satirized in *Vanity Fair*. It has often been said that the European peoples became rich by the impoverishment of other parts of the world, and there is truth in the charge. No quantitative measurement is available, however, and it seems probable that the larger part of the British capital accumulation in the eighteenth century was derived from trafficking in loans to the home government, from legitimate trade particularly with the American colonies, and from increased agricultural production as a result of improved methods of cultivation. In any case, it was not till the Industrial Revolution was well under way and the large-scale financing of the Napoleonic Wars offered opportunities for exceptional profits, that London developed the financial mechanisms that were to make it the center of world trade and investment.

It was to London that the impoverished European countries turned at the close of the Napoleonic Wars for financial aid. The reparation payments and occupation costs imposed on France were paid from a loan floated in 1817 by Baring Brothers. The firm of Baring, founded by German immigrants, became a pillar of the London money market and its stature grew throughout the nineteenth century until it was brought down by the Argentine crisis of the early 1890's. Another pillar of the London market was the house of Rothschild, represented by a first generation immigrant, Nathan M. Rothschild. Thus early in its rise to international power, the London money market was thoroughly cosmopolitan. As always, international financiers chose to conduct their operations under the shelter of the most stable government, which was also the center of the most thriving trade and of the most rapidly accumulating capital fund in Europe.

In the course of the decade, 1815–25, public loans were floated in London or through London for most of the countries of Europe and for many in Latin America. Thirty-one public loans were floated between 1818 and 1825, in favor of 17 different governments. Of the total nominal amount of these loans, over £70,000,000, more than £50,000,000 was subscribed in England. This was only a small part of the capital that began to flow through the London market to finance trade, promote land settlement, develop mining enterprises, build railroads and establish mercantile houses abroad.

Perhaps the most significant of all these developments was the rapid evolution of mechanisms for financing and clearing the payments on account of international trading transactions. Giving evidence before a Parliamentary Committee in 1832 Nathan Rothschild had declared that "this country in general is the Bank for the whole world; . . . all transactions in India, in China, in Germany, in the whole world, are guided here and settled through this country." It is hardly possible to lay too much stress on this development of facilities for short-term international lending and for the clearing of international payments. Without such facilities the rapid expansion of trade and investment would have been impossible. It was in this field that private banking enterprise achieved its greatest triumphs in the early nineteenth century. The creation of similar facilities, soundly based on intimate personal knowledge of world markets and geared to twentieth-century needs, is an essential service that must be provided if trade and investment are again to expand.

The beginnings of foreign investment are to be found mainly in the establishment of mercantile houses, in capital carried abroad by emigrants, in the development of plantations and land settlement, and in mining. There was a boom in such enterprises after 1820, which contributed heavily to the failures of the private banks when the boom collapsed in 1825. There was a growing amount of private direct investment particularly in textile factories. But facilities for investment in the shares of foreign enterprises did not develop on a great scale until after limited liability had been written into the company legislation of 1862, which provided a sound legal basis for joint-stock organization. The need to protect small investors became evident in the British railroad era of the forties and fifties, but joint-stock organization was not broadened till the sixties. The earlier construction even of such large undertakings as canals, roads, and docks had been financed by private subscription. In the first half of the nineteenth century, the Stock Exchange did not function in regard to such enterprises, nor in regard to industrial concerns.

A marked characteristic of investment in the first half of the nineteenth century was the degree to which it was associated with the emigration, temporary or permanent, of both organizers and skilled workmen. Much more was involved than mere lending. Loans were the vehicle by which enterprise, efficient commercial organization, new means of transport, power-driven machinery, and the technical dexterity necessary for its construction and operation were transferred to countries that had lagged behind in industrial development. British technology had made such rapid advances during the wars that its machines and its workmen had far outdistanced their competitors. Abortive attempts were made to keep this know-how—particularly the new cotton machinery—from being exported, so that Britain might have a monopoly, but enterprise easily found ways of circumventing the export prohibitions. A witness before the Parliamentary Committee on Artisans and Machinery (1824) estimated that in the two preceding years no fewer than 16,000 skilled workers had gone to France alone. This industrial development was in addition to the great number of merchant houses, insurance, shipping, coaling, gas, and, later, railroad undertakings that were being established in Europe, Latin America, the United States, and wherever opportunity seemed to beckon.

The lesson of this outpouring of technical skills is obvious. In the succeeding decades British overseas trading connections were firmly established. Moreover there were few markets concerning which reliable information could not be obtained from trusted sources. The continuous maintenance of personal contacts and the ebb and flow of personnel replacements provided British commercial and financial houses with commercial intelligence that was unrivaled. This intelligence in turn provided a solid basis for investment and trading decisions. The credit even of individuals in distant markets could be judged almost as accurately in London as on the spot.

At the same time as this great extension of British enterprise was taking place, emigration and with it capital export poured out to the United States and to the British colonies of settlement. British shipping and British trade grew in an expanding world. Capital was transferred, in the only possible way in the long run, by a great expansion of commodity trade. Britain was in an advantageous position to export the manufactured products of her newly mechanized industries, and to draw in return raw materials and foodstuffs from an expanding empire of trade. Other European nations later shared in this expansion, but by the middle of the century the foundations of British shipping and commercial supremacy had been firmly laid. Accessible steam coal provided a great advantage since outward cargoes to coaling stations, or to ports whose local supplies were as yet inaccessible for lack of railroad transport, made it possible to quote cheap return freights for bulky cargoes of raw materials. Contractors, of whom Thomas Brassey was the prototype, built ports and railroads all over the world. Mining engineers opened up new sources of the minerals which a mechanized world was beginning to consume in geometrically increasing quantities. The first public utilities—gas companies, street railways, waterworks, and sewage systems—were installed in many countries by British engineers, using British capital and often British workmen.

The greatest openings for British enterprise and trade in the first half of the nineteenth century were found in the developing markets of America, the British colonies, and Asia, rather than in Europe. Cotton manufactures bulked large at this stage of the Industrial Revolution. Imports of raw cotton from the United States provided Americans with sterling exchange that could be used to buy British goods. Large markets for cotton goods developed in India and China. On the other hand, the Napoleonic Wars had impoverished Europe and had stimulated the growth of European tariffs. The British Corn Laws hindered the import of wheat which was then derived mainly from Europe. Increasingly the trade of Britain was channeled to India and to the United States. Many German economic historians have maintained, largely on the basis of the colonial adventures in the eighteenth century and of trade developments in the early nineteenth century, that British economic progress was based primarily upon the exploitation of colonial markets. It is significant, however, that the increase in British exports to the United States in the first half of the nineteenth century was greater than the increase to Asia.

Care must be exercised in interpreting the very scarce and defective statistics of international trade in this period. From 1819 to 1849 there was a general downward tendency of prices, punctuated by severe financial crises. It says a great deal for the vitality of British financial and commercial enterprise that it made headway against almost universal trade barriers. To all British protests against trade restrictions, the European statesmen could and did reply that as long as the Corn Laws remained in force, there was no means of paying for larger British exports.[2]

The Corn Laws were to the nineteenth century what the Hawley-Smoot tariff passed by the United States in 1930 is to the twentieth. British imports and exports rose steadily, but they might have risen still more and might have been less directed toward India, China, the West Indies, and other colonial areas, if other markets had been more readily accessible. In the third quarter of the nineteenth century after Britain had adopted free trade, and tariffs had been lowered generally over a large part of Europe, the statistics tell a different story. A large, and the most rapidly growing, sector of world trade was that exchanged between the great industrial countries.

It is difficult to realize how great a transformation was wrought by the processes of international trade and investment which had thus been set in motion. A considerable effort of imagination is now required to re-create the picture of the trading world at the close of the Napoleonic Wars—a sprinkling of settlement on the Atlantic seaboard of the United States, small penal settlements at Sydney and Hobart, no white settlement in New Zealand, a handful of Dutch at the Cape and of French in Canada, Japan a hermit kingdom, and China almost as unknown, India governed uneasily from the scattered coastal

[2] Cf. J. H. Clapham, *An Economic History of Modern Britain*, Cambridge, Cambridge University Press, 1926, Vol. I, Ch. XII, esp. p. 476: "In 1836, an informal agent of the Board of Trade, who was 'exploring the possibilities' of a commercial treaty with the recently established Germanic Customs Union was told that England must begin 'with a reduction of her corn duties' which were far more unreasonable than the Zollverein taxes on manufactures. When the agent suggested alternatives, the Prussian stubbornly 'took his stand upon corn.' "

forts of the East India Company, Spanish America in its undeveloped colonial status, and Africa still the Dark Continent. In Europe the British were a nation of thirteen million. There was no Germany and no Italy. The Ottoman Empire was still intact. Austria-Hungary and Russia were the greatest continental powers, and Prussia had not yet begun to organize the German Reich.

The development of world trade in the nineteenth century transformed not only the economic but the political world pattern. It was the activities of bankers and traders, not simply a political gesture, that called a new world into existence to redress the balance of the old.

THE TRIUMPH OF FREE TRADE

In the second quarter of the nineteenth century the merchants of Britain, notably of Manchester, organized and carried to success a campaign for free trade, which was one of the most effective and practical campaigns for political and economic change ever undertaken. The philosophical principles upon which their campaign rested may be traced back to Adam Smith and even to earlier writers. The classical economists gave useful support on the theoretical side. Essentially however, the campaign for free trade was organized, financed, and led to success by the merchants themselves. After the crucial victory had been won by the repeal of the Corn Laws in 1846, the completion of their campaign required a long period before detailed administrative reforms could become fully effective. In the course of a century this historical episode has come to be treated primarily as a political struggle between the landowning aristocracy and the middle-class merchants, culminating in the abolition of the Corn Laws. But the true importance of this great reform and its lesson for our own time, cannot be understood unless an effort is made to recapture the less obvious, but more fundamental and lasting, practical aspects of the movement as a whole.

The lesson of the free-trade agitation is that enduring reform is the result of patient mastery of detailed issues, registered not merely in broad legislative acts but in practical procedures of administration. The gap between legislation and administration is wide. Administrative regulations, executive decisions and interpretations often at a subordinate level of administrative authority, and the spirit in which they are applied, can be themselves among the most important barriers to trade. Without a sympathetic and competent administration, the noblest reforms may fail of their intended effect.

The free-trade movement was much more than an attack on the Corn Laws. It was both an attempt to organize an idealistic system of international relations and a painstaking reform of the public finances and of the regulations by which trade was controlled.[3] Disraeli laughed at Richard Cobden, the leader of the free-trade movement, "as the successor of the Abbé St. Pierre, Rousseau and Robespierre in the dreams of perpetual peace." At the same time, both popular audiences and the House of Commons recognized Cobden's mastery of commercial and administrative detail. He was not a grandiloquent orator. His speeches were delivered in a conversational tone, building up unanswerable arguments from specific examples. Under his leadership, the Anti-Corn Law League conducted a long, complicated, and detailed agitation to reduce the tariff, reform the administrative regulations, and extend the reforms into related fields such as shipping. Necessarily, such reforms entailed a reorganization of the public finances and a drastic shift in the incidence of taxation.

Not the least important aspect of the free-trade movement was its reliance upon democratic procedures of discussion and education. The leaders of this movement were themselves merchants. They relied upon the detailed information brought to them by practical men of business, and took to the public such a convincing and detailed case that there ensued a complete reversal of public opinion. No longer was it presumed that trade ought to be regulated. Instead, trade was presumed to be beneficial and the onus of making a case for any specific piece of regulation was thrown upon the protectionists. The result was a vast simplification and cheapening of the administrative procedures to which imports and exports were submitted. This was the most lasting, as it was certainly the most widespread, consequence of the agitation.

In order to understand the magnitude of the free traders' achievement, it is necessary to realize the jungle of legislation and administrative decisions to which trade was subject when they began their work. A customs handbook, published in 1730, illustrates the complexity which had even then resulted from the combination of wholesale

[3] Cf. John Morley, *The Life of Richard Cobden,* p. 319: "They [his speeches in 1844 and 1845] show how completely Cobden had worked out the whole conception of economic policy and the whole scheme of statesmanship, of which the repeal of the Corn Law was only a detail and a condition precedent." For the Disraeli statement, see p. 497.

protectionism, graft, and the needs of impecunious governments.[4] Though only 34 categories of imports were then listed, the calculations of duty were formidable. After setting forth the duties payable under these varied headings, the author prints the Book of Rates containing the valuations to be used for various commodities. He then gives an index system of references by which the various charges may be looked up, and follows this with 44 pages of illustrations of how various combinations of duties may be calculated. It says much for the value of trade and for the enterprise of traders, that they could surmount these complex rules and regulations. The rules applied, for example, to goods coming from different countries, imported by an alien or by a citizen, to goods carried in British or in alien ships and, if the latter, belonging to the country of export or to some other country. Though rates were low, the calculations of duty became exceedingly complex and mounted in the aggregate to large sums.

If it is tedious now to read about this administrative complexity, it must have been more than tedious to the importers, who in addition had to pay the duties, as well as fees for several other services. In practice they must often have been tempted to smuggle the goods, or to bribe the officials to interpret the regulations with a somewhat lenient eye or in desperation to give up such a troublesome business.

The regulations in 1730 were by no means as bad as they had become by 1815. In 1784, under the influence of Adam Smith's teaching, Pitt had indeed lowered some duties, and the Eden Treaty with France in 1786 had aimed at a further relaxation of trade barriers. Pitt was prepared to reduce and simplify the tariff still further, but from 1793 to 1815 war finance made confusion worse than ever. Only

[4] Henry Crouch, *A Complete View of the British Customs,* London, 1730. I am indebted to my colleague Professor L. A. Harper for access to a photostatic copy of this manual, from which I cite the following (summarized) prefatory list of types of duty then payable: "The several particular Branches of the Revenue, at present payable to his Majesty in Great Britain, upon Goods and Merchandises imported, exported and brought Coastwise, the which are distinguished by the following Denominations; viz,

"1. Customs i. Old Subsidy ii. Petty Custom iii. Additional Duty iv. One Per Cent Inwards v. Composition on Petty Seizures 2. New Subsidy 3. One Third Subsidy 4. Two Thirds Subsidy 5. Imposts on Wines and Vinegar 6. Impost on Tobacco 7. Impost 1690 8. Impost 1692/3 9. New Duty on Whalefins 10. Fifteen Per Cent on Muslins 11. New Duty on Spice and Pictures 12. Additional Duty on Spice and Pictures; And New Duty on Drugs, White Callicoes, Dimities, and other Manufactures of Cotton; and China Ware. 13. Second 25 Per Cent on French Goods 14. Coinage 15. New Duty on Pepper and Raisins, And a further New Duty on Spice 16. New Duty on Candles Imported 17. New Duties on Coals, Culm and Cinders 20. Additional Duty on Candles Imported"—and so on through 34 classifications.

in one respect did the war lead to some fiscal improvement. British shipping was engaged in a life and death struggle with the French fleet. In 1796 the Navigation Acts were relaxed in favor of American ships, and this concession was extended in 1815.[5] Meanwhile the traders had become restive. In 1820 the merchants of London and of Edinburgh sent memorials to the House of Commons pleading for a reduction of duties.

In 1823, William Huskisson, the member for Liverpool, became President of the Board of Trade and began the triple task of reducing some of the more restrictive tariff duties especially on raw materials, of simplifying the customs regulations, and of modifying the Navigation Acts. In 1823 he carried through a general relaxation of the Navigation Acts on a reciprocal basis. From 1823 to 1825 he reduced or abolished the duties on many raw materials. When he began to revise the regulations, he found no fewer than 1,500 acts in operation. He reduced their number to eleven. At the same time he began to consolidate the duties that were chargeable and to simplify the methods of clearing and inspecting imports and exports, assessing them for duty, accounting for the duties collected and for the many official fees charged to merchants.

As a result of Huskisson's reforms, the free-trade movement made its first ground—enough to encourage a considerable expansion of trade particularly in cottons. British policy was not yet completely emancipated from mercantilist ideas. Huskisson was a follower of Adam Smith, but he was sympathetic also to the preferential policies advocated by the colonial reformers, and the brief period of his leadership at the Board of Trade saw some progress toward Empire free trade. His political career was cut short by an unfortunate accident—he stepped onto the track at the opening of the Liverpool and Manchester railroad in 1830, to greet the Duke of Wellington, and was killed. The later free traders became cosmopolitan rather than imperialist in their outlook. The agitation for imperial preference was not revived in Britain until after the Boer War and did not register any political success until the first World War.

In 1832 the first Reform Act was passed, giving votes to a consider-

[5] Cf. G. M. Trevelyan, *British History in the Nineteenth Century,* London, 1922, p. 203. The relaxation of the Navigation Acts was largely the result of the legislation passed by the United States by way of reprisal, an example followed by several European countries. Britain had more to lose from being shut out of the carrying trade to these countries than she had to gain from protecting the carrying trade to and from her own islands.

able number of middle-class people. The Reform Act also abolished many of the rotten boroughs that were the strongholds of the landowners and gave seats to the growing industrial towns in the north. As a result it was not long before businessmen began to win seats in Parliament. Effective action, however, was not possible during the relatively prosperous years that followed. It was not until after a sharp crisis occurred in 1837 that the newly enfranchised merchants began to organize seriously. High food prices and unemployment were the conditions that called the Anti-Corn Law League into existence in 1838 [6] and carried it to triumph after the severe crises of the forties and the Irish potato famine in 1845–46 had lent redoubled emphasis to the League's propaganda.

Conflict developed between the leaders of the free-trade movement and those of the Chartist agitation. In the beginning of the Chartist movement, for example at the mass meeting in 1819 which ended tragically in the Peterloo massacre, freer trade and electoral reform had been advocated as the economic and political aspects of a democratic program. In 1838, these movements began to diverge. In that year the Anti-Corn Law League was founded and led by merchants. It was well-financed and organized, and relied wholly upon democratic processes of agitation—tracts, newspapers, public meetings, parliamentary motions, petitions, and personal canvass. *The Economist,* for example, was founded in 1844 as an independent journal, in sympathy with the Anti-Corn Law League.

Chartism, on the other hand, was a purely working-class movement. It arose among the new class of factory workers and had much in common with the modern development of industrial, as distinct from craft, trade unionism. Its original program, as worked out by leaders of the London Working Men's Association, was idealistic though in some respects impractical in detail. Most of it has now been incorporated into democratic procedures. The original Chartist program

[6] An Anti-Corn Law League was founded by a group of radicals in London early in 1838, but it was overshadowed and soon absorbed by the League founded a few months later in Manchester by a group of businessmen, among whom Richard Cobden soon emerged as the organizing leader, sacrificing his business as he became increasingly engaged in organizing and speaking. Cobden entered Parliament in 1841. For the story of his enlistment of John Bright in active work, after the death of Bright's wife, see John Morley, *Life of Richard Cobden,* p. 190. Bright entered Parliament in 1843. In 1846, Cobden's health and finances were broken. A national subscription enabled him to purchase the small farm on which he was born. His house is now maintained as a memorial to his work.

became overlaid with other causes—repeal of the Poor Laws, Land Reform, Paper Currency—and Chartism collapsed in 1848, whereas the free traders had kept steadily to their program and had gained a complete victory in 1846.

The conflict which developed between the movements was at first almost entirely on the Chartist side. The Chartist leaders were suspicious of manufacturers like Cobden, who were opposed to trade unionism and factory legislation though resolute for municipal as well as parliamentary reform. They were fearful that cheap food would in practice mean low wages. Many of them were opposed to factory work as destructive of the crafts, and others were afraid of agricultural unemployment. Because they were never able to raise enough money to organize a continuous and expert campaign of education, their main effort was exhausted in sporadic mass meetings. The time had not yet arrived when proletarian revolutionary movements could sustain a long campaign of organization and agitation, and in England there was not such desperate misery as gave occasion for a sudden popular uprising like the French Revolution.

After failing to win over the Chartists, the free traders continued their campaign in and out of Parliament and gradually won over to their support the mass of the factory workers. Chartism drifted into the hands of extremists. These leaders struggled among themselves and vied in putting forward new schemes of economic reform. The end of Chartism as an organized movement came in the revolutionary year, 1848, when a mass meeting was to march with a petition to Parliament. There was a general fear of revolt and troops were mobilized; but when the Chartist leaders lost their nerve and delivered the petition in a cab, the movement expired in ridicule. Thereafter the British working-class movement merged again with the free traders and became the backbone of the Liberal party.

The country-wide educational campaign conducted by the Anti-Corn Law League from 1838 to 1846 presents an instructive contrast to the failure of Chartism. It was led by capable organizers, it could command substantial funds, and it was never allowed to depart from its clear and simple original purpose. In many respects it remains a model of democratic agitation. Every year a motion was made in the House, and the occasion was used for speeches. There was also a continuous agitation throughout the country, directed skillfully and purposefully by able and resolute men. Opponents of the League charged

Cobden and Bright with promoting the interests of their fellow manufacturers. They cheerfully admitted the charge, but maintained that their interests were identical not only with the national interest but with the cause of peace. They hammered away at the inefficiencies and injustices of the tariff, deluged their hearers with statistics and practical examples, refused to identify their cause with party politics, and gradually by sheer sincerity, persistence, and logic won the majority of public opinion and later of the House of Commons to their support.

It was this educational campaign, rather than a dramatic parliamentary decision at a moment of acute social distress, that changed the course of events. The free traders were shrewd enough tacticians to realize the debating value of concentrating upon the most vulnerable point in their opponents' case. By the time the country was threatened with famine in 1846, the privileged landlords had little support for their policy of high food prices. Even more important there was widespread popular acceptance of the case for free trade in general. Whereas before, protection had been the rule and free trade the exception, the majority of the British people had come to believe that trade should always be completely free. In 1840 a parliamentary committee had reported that of 1,150 items in the tariff, ten produced 90 per cent of the customs revenue, and eight more produced 5 per cent. Clearly if tariffs were to be levied for revenue only, sweeping reforms could be carried out, leaving all but a very few articles completely free of tariff restrictions. At the same time the customs procedure could be vastly simplified.

These reforms were in fact made within the next two decades. The Act of 1846 abolishing the Corn Laws did not become fully effective until 1849. In the same year the Navigation Acts were abolished. The political confusion which ensued after Sir Robert Peel, the Tory Prime Minister, had wrecked his party by abolishing the Corn Laws in 1846, prevented any very clear party alignment for some years. In 1853 William Ewart Gladstone, originally a Peelite Tory, carried through further tariff reductions. The necessity of financing the Crimean War (1854–56) delayed further progress toward free trade. In 1860 Gladstone began the great series of budgets which completed the free-trade movement.

These budgets laid out a systematic plan by which all but a few tariff items were transferred to the free list, the revenue being supplemented by re-introduction of the income tax. At the same time vigorous economy of public expenditure was enforced, especially upon the armed services. The result was a shift from indirect to direct taxation, paid more heavily by the wealthier classes. In 1860, the number of dutiable items in the tariff was reduced to 48, and all preferential duties admitting imports from British possessions at favorable rates were abolished. In Gladstone's own words there was "a sweep—summary, entire, and absolute—of what are known as manufactured goods from the face of the British tariff." Timber was put on the free list in 1866, the last small registration duty on corn went in 1869, and sugar became free in 1875.

By the end of the nineteenth century, the British tariff contained only fifteen items, the duty on all of which was imposed for revenue and countervailed by excise duties on domestic manufacture. Nine-tenths of the customs revenue was derived from tobacco, tea, spirits, and wines. For all other goods entry was free, and statistical and inspection formalities were kept to a minimum. In consequence Britain became the greatest market of the world—a dumping ground for the world's surpluses, as the protectionists grumbled—the greatest importer of foodstuffs and raw materials and even of manufactures. Though she lost the commanding leadership in manufactures with which she had started the century, her export trade continued to expand. The shipping, commercial, insurance, and financial commissions which were gained from acting as the clearinghouse of world trade and investment were very considerable.

As long as the earnings from exports and services enabled her to support an increasing population on a plane of living which was the highest in Europe and which rose steadily, there could be no effective challenge to the free-trade policy that had made her rich and powerful. It was not until the world trading system and its monetary mechanisms were seriously impaired by the first World War that any breach was made in the completeness of her free-trade policy.

THE TREATY BASIS

The movement toward freer trade achieved its greatest victory when Britain abolished all protective duties. The movement spread to other countries through the negotiation of commercial treaties and tariff agreements. Commercial treaties have a long history. Early instances can be adduced from the Old Testament and from classical history.

Some of the British commercial treaties still in force date back to the seventeenth century. The principles of international law established by such treaties, and the detailed application of those principles to particular situations, have been highly elaborated. Standardized phraseology has been worked out and precedents have been established for the interpretation of specific treaty provisions. This extension of commercial treaties in the nineteenth century constitutes one of the most useful branches of international law, precisely because it was worked out in practical detail. The impairment of this nineteenth-century treaty network was one of the most serious consequences of the period of economic warfare between the great depression and the outbreak of hostilities in 1939. And its restoration on a new basis is one of the most urgent tasks which confronts statesmen in this postwar period.

The establishment of the legal rights of alien traders is the first and the most fundamental objective of commercial treaty negotiations. Though negotiations to reduce the impediments to trade, such as tariff duties, are often combined with agreements to establish the legal rights of alien traders, tariff reduction by treaty is a distinct and in some ways less important objective of treaty-making. The rights of aliens do not depend wholly upon treaties, still less upon commercial treaties. National legislation in most countries gives them a defined status, which tends to approximate that of nationals. It has become the custom of most civilized states to observe the well-established principles of international law in their treatment of resident aliens. Obviously the simplest way to do so is to afford them the protection accorded to citizens as long as they observe the laws of the country.

In the nineteenth century however, there was a great extension of the process by which the legal rights of aliens were specifically elaborated in the Treaties of Commerce and Navigation negotiated by practically all countries of any trading importance. A long list of rights was covered in different commercial treaties, ranging from conditions of residence, travel, and trade, to the right of burial with suitable decorum and respect. Treaties differed a good deal in comprehensiveness, but the trend in the nineteenth century was definitely toward the full acceptance of what came to be known as "national treatment." Indeed in the latter half of the century this came to be taken so much for granted that its importance was almost forgotten. By that time an alien could travel over a large part of Europe without passport visas, and could buy or rent property, employ labor, and invoke the protection of the law almost as securely as in his own country. There was no exchange control, and customs inspections at the frontier were perfunctory.

Much of this cosmopolitanism has been lost in recent years. Obviously it was an attribute of the laissez-faire system. The increasing extent to which states intervene in economic activity diminishes the freedom of international transactions. The mere fact of higher taxation, particularly of income, opens the door to discrimination against aliens. National taxation can be levied in a general form which bears with special severity on alien incomes. Schemes of nationalization may in practice affect mainly alien enterprises. It becomes increasingly difficult to maintain individual rights when the state operates or regulates a large sector of economic activity. In a system of complete nationalization of industry the alien trader or investor has no place at all. Inevitably trade is subjected to a state monopoly.

It is not surprising to find that a similar impairment of individual rights has affected various forms of property. In the nineteenth century international conventions were negotiated concerning the use of patents, copyrights, trade-marks, and other forms of industrial property. While national legislation differed a good deal, particularly in respect to the validity of patents, the general principle of property rights was widely recognized. There has been a notable weakening of this principle in recent years, particularly in countries where the state has enlarged its functions. Even if patents, for example, remain valid, the opportunity for their use may be circumscribed or the transfer of payments may be blocked.

It is important to realize, therefore, that the trading system of the nineteenth century was built up in a world where the rights of the private trader and of private property were guaranteed by an extensive network of treaties. A substantial body of international law worked out in specific detail was accepted and implemented over the larger part of the trading world. This provided the legal security necessary for international enterprise and international investment, just as the world-wide practice of exchange stability provided security against monetary depreciation. It was a stable world, in which traders were free to come and go, to organize and invest abroad, almost as freely and as safely as in their own countries. The treaties which guaranteed this freedom and security were entered into for long terms and were normally renewed with a constantly extending scope.

The United States negotiated its first commercial treaty with France as early as 1778. Other treaties were signed with the Netherlands in 1782, with Sweden in 1783, and with Prussia in 1785. In 1794 a treaty with Britain provided a clear indication of reconciliation. All these treaties, with the exception of the Prussian, are still in force, having been renewed and extended at long intervals. From its earliest independence, the United States demonstrated its desire to trade with the rest of the world upon a basis of legal rules embodied in treaty commitments. It still remains a protagonist, and is now the outstanding protagonist, of the rule of law in this as in every other aspect of international relations.

At the beginning of the nineteenth century, the United States was still a minor factor in the world's trade. Discerning eyes might see, as Richard Cobden did, its promise of future greatness, but that greatness was still in the future. In 1836 Cobden predicted that the United States would become the most productive and powerful country in the world because of "its boundless expanse of the most fertile soil in the world and its inexhaustible mines," and because of "the quality and position of a people universally instructed and perfectly free, and possessing, as a consequence of these, a new-born energy and vitality very far surpassing the character of any nation of the old world." This prediction, so different from the supercilious criticisms of many other visitors, demonstrates the deep understanding which Cobden had of the springs of social progress. It was to be abundantly fulfilled; but in the mid-nineteenth century the influence of the United States in world affairs was still slight.

Leadership in establishing the rule of law lay then, as it always lies, in the hands of the great trading nations—at that time Britain and France. Even in the preceding period of mercantilism, efforts had been made at intervals to negotiate treaties that would place trade between the two countries on a more secure basis. A notable example was the Eden Treaty negotiated at the insistence of William Pitt in 1786, in an effort to restore trade with France after the Seven Years' War. The revolution intervened and the two countries were again at war from 1793 to 1815, with only a brief truce in 1802.

After peace returned, there was little opportunity for satisfactory commercial negotiations between France and Britain. Both countries maintained a high protectionist tariff. Even after Huskisson's reductions of duties and simplification of tariff formalities in 1823–25, the high British duties on French wines and brandies remained a stumbling block. Moreover, as long as the Corn Laws remained in force there was chronic complaint that Britain would not import from the continental countries where her manufacturers were pressing their exports. British manufactures were technically superior to those of any other country. British trade also was becoming more conspicuously multilateral—drawing from the New World imports of raw materials (such as cotton from the United States) and exporting manufactured goods to many markets. The less developed industry of France in its struggle toward recovery after the long and exhausting war feared the competition of British steel and woolens and cotton goods. There were periodic overtures for a treaty both to establish national treatment for traders and to achieve the secondary objective of trade negotiations, a reduction of tariff duties, but all overtures proved abortive.

As the great struggle for free trade rose to its climax in Britain during the forties, there were attempts in France to emulate the work of the Anti-Corn Law League. The professional economists, Jean Baptiste Say, Jerome Adolphe Blanqui, and Michel Chevalier especially, were convinced free traders. Frederic Bastiat came to Paris from the south of France to devote his witty pen to the cause, and turned to ridicule the constant search of the manufacturers for further protection. His petition of the candlemakers against the competition of the sun remains a classic satire on the protectionist faith. But the French manufacturers unlike those of Britain were not ready to face the bracing winds of competition. There was little popular support for a reduction of trade barriers and the Chamber of Deputies under Louis Napoleon (1852–70) as under his predecessors remained staunchly protectionist. Chevalier was driven to the conclusion that the only way to get the French tariffs down was by concluding a commercial treaty with England. He made repeated overtures to the leaders of the free-trade movement in England, but without effect until 1859.

In that year the recurrent political tension between the two countries was working up to a crisis. They were allies and only a few years before had fought together against Russia in the Crimean War. But

Louis Napoleon had ambitions to play off the nationalist movement in northern Italy against Austria-Hungary and in doing so to add to French security by annexing Savoy and Nice. Queen Victoria and her Prince Consort were resolutely opposed both to the weakening of the Austro-Hungarian monarchy and to the strengthening of France. Lord Palmerston, the Prime Minister, was suspicious of designs not his own and alert to safeguard British security from invasion. There were alarmist reports of the fortification of Cherbourg, of new French naval construction, and of barges being prepared for a cross-Channel invasion.

At the height of this tension, John Bright, who shared with Cobden the leadership of the free-trade movement, spoke in the House and asked "why, instead of lavishing the national substance in armaments, they did not go to the French Emperor and attempt to persuade him to allow his people to trade freely with ours." [7] Bright was even more resolute than Cobden in his opposition to Palmerston's diplomacy and to expenditure upon the army and navy. His speech was Chevalier's opportunity to realize his long-cherished dream of a commercial treaty between England and France. A follower of the socialist-technocrat Saint-Simon, Chevalier retained his belief in benevolent autocracy. He knew that under the French constitution the treaty-making power was vested in the Emperor. He therefore pleaded with Cobden to visit France and urge the value of a treaty upon Louis Napoleon.

Cobden, like most of the free traders, had been opposed to using commercial treaties as a means of tariff bargaining. In this view, treaties should guarantee the conditions of free-trading enterprise, and tariffs should be reduced unilaterally as a sovereign act in the national interest, not on a basis of reciprocity.[8] Chevalier, however, was able to convince Cobden that a treaty was the only practical means

[7] John Morley, *The Life of Richard Cobden*, p. 702. For Bright's own account of this incident see G. M. Trevelyan, *Life of John Bright*, London, 1913, p. 285. The exact text of this passage in Bright's speech is given by A. L. Dunham, *The Anglo-French Treaty of Commerce of 1860*, Ann Arbor, 1930, p. 49.

[8] The doctrinaire free traders continued to hold this view. Villiers criticized the treaty in the House. McCulloch, in a long Note XIV to his edition of *The Wealth of Nations* in 1863, and maintained in the revised edition of 1870 (p. 546), argued that: "When a few general rules are agreed upon for the security of trade and navigation . . . all is done that ought to be attempted in a commercial treaty. . . . It is an abuse and a perversion of commercial treaties to make them instruments for regulating duties or prescribing Custom-house regulations. The commercial treaty with France negotiated in 1860, strikingly illustrates what has now been stated."

of moving toward free trade in France. Clearly the peace motive was uppermost in the minds of Cobden and Bright, as well as of Gladstone who as Chancellor of the Exchequer had the political power to put the treaty through. Preliminary conversations first with officials in Paris and then with the Emperor at Compiègne, convinced Cobden that a treaty was possible. As he warmed to his task, the magnitude of the opportunity grew upon him. After receiving Gladstone's blessing, he wrote to Chevalier: "I utterly despair of finding peace and harmony in the efforts of Governments and diplomatists. The *people* of the two Nations must be brought into mutual dependence by supplying each other's wants. There is no other way of counteracting the antagonism of language and race. It is God's own method of producing an *entente cordiale,* and no other plan is worth a farthing." [9]

The treaty that was signed in 1860 represented substantial concessions on both sides. Britain would in any case have given up the duties on French manufactures, but she would probably not have reduced the duties on wines, which represented a substantial loss of revenue. The opportunity to do this was presented by the maturing of some annuities. The obligation to pay these annuities came to an end in 1860 and the saving thus made was set off against the loss of revenue caused by the reduction of duties on French wines. This was a victory for the peace party since there had been a strong demand that the saving on the annuities should be devoted to fortifications. Gladstone incorporated the tariff reductions in his great budget of 1860, and this went a long way toward completing the free-trade program. The most difficult concession for the British to make was a pledge not to obstruct the export of coal—a difficult pledge to carry through a House suspicious of French invasion plans and irritated by Louis Napoleon's seizure of Nice and Savoy.

The British action was the more courageous since the Emperor, in fulfillment of a prior commitment to the Chamber of Deputies, was able to promise only a future reduction of duties. This promise however was soon redeemed, and the British manufacturers of cottons and woolens and of iron and steel and metal wares as well found a

[9] This is the first recorded use of the phrase *entente cordiale* which became the standard description of the increasingly intimate relations between England and France. Cf. J. A. Hobson, *Richard Cobden: The International Man,* London, 1919, p. 242: "Cobden's mission to France in 1859–60 for the negotiation of a commercial treaty with Great Britain was not in its first intent a business mission. It was a peace mission."

great market opened to them. Louis Napoleon made loans available to the French manufacturers to tide them over the first severe impact of competition from the cheaper British imports. Thus they were enabled to start a process of modernization. It was not long before French industry, specializing upon the commodities for which its people had peculiar skills, notably in design, were competing effectively in world markets including the British market. In its main objective the negotiation achieved a considerable measure of success. The political tension was dissipated and the *entente cordiale* gradually became a reality. Since 1860 there has only once—the Fashoda incident in 1898—been any possibility of war between France and England.

Two other results warrant the fame of this treaty. The first was that for a brief period it inaugurated a chain of other tariff treaties. Within a few years after 1860 France negotiated similar agreements with all the other European countries except Russia, and Britain, despite her inability to offer tariff concessions once she had completed the free-trade program, secured treaties with Belgium (1862), Italy (1863), the Zollverein and Austria (1865).

The second and even more important result was that the use of the already standard most-favored-nation clause was copied in practically all the treaties signed thenceforward among the European countries. This clause—by which each contracting party to a trade agreement assures the other of tariff duties at the lowest level granted to any third country—ought in fact to be called equally-favored-nation treatment, or in the modern American phrase "equality of trading opportunity." The unconditional form of the clause, by which each country receives without any question of reciprocal concessions whatever tariff reductions are granted by every country with which it has a treaty, was a potent means of restraining tariff increases during the latter part of the nineteenth century. In addition many important treaties which ran for long periods contained provisions binding tariff items against increase. These had the effect of preventing, during the currency of the treaty, any increase of duties on a large list of imports. Since every country had many treaties containing such provisions and expiring at different dates, it became difficult to embark upon wholesale tariff increases.

The Anglo-French treaty of 1860 left a permanent mark on commercial policy. It demonstrated that bilateral negotiations are the most effective of all methods of tariff reduction, provided they aim at multilateral trade. Indeed, the effectiveness of this treaty owes much to the unilateral determination of Britain to complete her free-trade policy. Bilateralism—the attempt to canalize trade between each pair of trading countries—has been a growing evil in recent years. But no one should confuse the objective of bilateralism with the method of negotiating bilaterally to open up markets for multilateral trade. Cobden and Chevalier showed once and for all in 1860 that the bilateral method of negotiation can be used effectively to stimulate a world-wide expansion of multilateral trade, and that in doing so good use can be made of the unconditional form of most-favored-nation treatment.

The fundamental requirement of a treaty basis is a body of international legal rules by which trade may proceed freely and securely. In the nineteenth century this was achieved somewhat slowly and haphazardly by the negotiation of a network of bilateral treaties. In the more urgent and rapid pace of events at the present time, it has been found necessary to negotiate a multilateral agreement between many nations in order to create a means to restore order and sanity to the confused and anarchic world market.

THE RETURN TO PROTECTION

Coming after a long and grueling struggle that had ended in the final round with a knockout blow in 1815, the second quarter of the nineteenth century had been a period of political and economic exhaustion. Not only the victors and the vanquished, but the spectators as well, needed time to build up their emotional reserves and physical energy. In such periods nationalism falls to a low ebb. Economic necessities take precedence over political aspirations. Impoverished and exhausted peoples dream of peace, retrenchment, and reform. A bold initiative on the part of the great trading countries can at such times restore international economic co-operation. But if that initiative is lacking, exhaustion and despair may—as after the war of 1914–18—breed a more virulent nationalism.

Free trade was a British concept, and Britain was the predominant economic power in the nineteenth-century trading world. By the middle of the century her leadership in manufactures, finance, trade, and shipping was at its peak. The middle-class manufacturers and traders, aided at the last by the financiers of the city of London, had won a resounding victory over the landowning aristocracy.[10] The working classes had been persuaded that it was important to concentrate on ensuring abundant supplies of cheap food before struggling for the vote. John Bright, for whom free trade had always been a "condition of the people" question, had begun to lead the fight for electoral reform as soon as the free-trade victory was won. Money wages had not fallen when food was cheapened. Indeed they had risen sharply in the prosperous years following abolition of the Corn Laws. In the twenty years 1846–66, money wages rose by 30 to 40 per cent and hours were shortened, but the greatest gain was in the improved purchasing power as food prices fell sharply. The free traders could point to a prosperous England as proof of the soundness of their policies.

The British renunciation of economic nationalism was complete. But the free traders knew that this was merely the foundation upon which a peaceful world might be built. They confidently expected that public opinion in other countries would be so impressed by British prosperity that other governments would be forced into parallel reforms. In the decade following 1860 there was some reason to hope that their confidence would soon be justified. There was a scaling down of tariffs all over Europe, a network of trade treaties was negotiated, and most-favored-nation treatment was widely accepted. It really seemed as if universal free trade was only a matter of time. To men who believed passionately in the power of rational argument to enlighten public opinion and whose belief had been so triumphantly vindicated in their own country, it seemed inevitable that all other peoples would join Britain in the quest of peace and prosperity.

Meanwhile the liberal free traders fought steadily for conciliatory foreign policies and for restraint in the use of Britain's naval and military strength. They opposed every item of expenditure on the armed services, and extended their opposition to government expenditure in general. The basis of their opposition to the successive Factory Acts and to the shortening of hours by legislation was buttressed by their fear of increasing the power of the bureaucracy. Bright was

[10] Cf. G. M. Trevelyan, *The Life of John Bright,* pp. 69 and 74. The Anti-Corn Law League orators had made effective use of such flippancies as the couplet attributed to Lord Manners (later Duke of Rutland):

> Let trade and commerce, laws and learning die,
> But leave us still our old nobility,

and the unfortunate advice by a "Protectionist Duke" offered apparently in good faith. He had recommended the operative classes to take an occasional pinch of curry powder in a little water to allay their inconvenient craving for food.

indignant that Lord Ashley, the leader of the movement for factory legislation, who drew his income from rents and represented a rural county, "said nothing about the abject condition of the labourer there at six shillings to eight shillings a week, while he raised a hue and cry against masters who, like Bright himself, paid sixteen shillings a week to their men. And at the same time Ashley was still refusing to better the condition of Lancashire and Dorsetshire alike, by repealing the Corn Law."

We may agree with Professor G. M. Trevelyan that in the long run it was fortunate that the condition of the agricultural laborers was exposed by the manufacturers and that of the industrial laborers was exposed by the landlords. In the end both free trade and factory legislation were achieved. We may agree also that it was impossible to rely at that time upon "the common sense and benevolence of masters and the bargaining power of the employee," [11] and that state intervention in the labor market was justified and necessary. But the free traders were right in fearing the arbitrary extension of state power.

In two important fields of diplomacy the Cobdenite free traders fought traditional policies. In the first place, they were wholeheartedly opposed to meddling in the affairs of other countries, even for righteous causes. They recognized that tyranny was widespread, but they did not believe that Britain either could or should rescue freedom by force of arms. John Bright was a Quaker, but he was not a pacifist. Both he and Cobden, however, were staunch in their opposition to saber-rattling and threatening gestures, and still more to war on balance-of-power principles.[12] When Russia in 1849 attacked the followers of Kossuth who were fighting for the independence of Hungary, and Turkey gave asylum to Hungarian refugees, the merchants who knew the incredible corruption of the Ottoman Empire could not be deceived into believing that Turkey was a liberal power

[11] Citations from G. M. Trevelyan, *Life of John Bright,* pp. 155–59.

[12] Bright expressly repudiated the pacifist position of non-resistance. The best illustrations of this fact are found in his correspondence with Charles Sumner during the Civil War period. He was active in conciliation during the affair of the Confederate envoys Mason and Slidell and during the Alabama negotiations. But he was wholeheartedly on the antislavery side. Many of his letters were read in meetings of Lincoln's Cabinet, including his appeal against a compromise peace. In January, 1864, President Lincoln pardoned a twenty-year-old British subject who had been convicted by the California courts of trying to outfit a privateer in San Francisco Bay. The pardon was given at Bright's request and was stated by Lincoln to be intended as "a public mark of the high esteem held by the United States of America for the high character and steady friendship of the said John Bright." Cf. Trevelyan, *ibid.,* Ch. XIV.

to be defended against the might of Tsarist Russia. They held no brief for the Tsar, but when in 1854 a dispute between Turkey and Russia led to the Crimean War, they refused to join in the clamor to defend Turkey.

In the second place, the liberal free traders protested against the promotion of trade by force and the exaction of economic privilege from colonial peoples and weaker nations. Their record in this respect is unblemished. John Bright in particular is still remembered gratefully in Ireland for his long struggle in an unsympathetic House of Commons against what Disraeli pithily described as "an alien church and an absentee aristocracy." But the free traders fought also against exploitation in India, Burma, China, Borneo, and other areas. They were staunchly and consistently anti-imperialist. As long as their ideas were reflected in government policy, the clamor of special interests for more aggressive diplomatic support of trading ventures was resisted.[13]

These facts have been recalled briefly, not only to emphasize the political aspects of the liberal philosophy, but also because it was defeat on these issues that destroyed all hope of extending the free-trade movement internationally. The dream of a world-wide commercial system in which economic competition would bring about the maximum of specialized production may have been an illusion based upon a naïve and idealistic belief in the essential rationality and common sense of men. It may have counted unduly upon traders being wise

[13] Cf. R. Barry O'Brien, *John Bright*, London, 1910, p. 1: "Why should I write a monograph on John Bright? What is there in common between the English Puritan statesman and an Irish Catholic Nationalist? Had a stranger entered my father's house in the West of Ireland forty years ago, the first object which would have met his eye was a bust of John Bright. Why was it there? Because alone among leading English statesmen, at that time, Bright fearlessly identified himself with the Irish popular cause. His speeches were a revelation to me. They breathed, one might almost say, a spirit of revolt against English injustice in Ireland, and defiantly demanded that the wrongs of the people should be redressed."

Cf. also John Morley, *Life of Richard Cobden*, p. 519, citing a letter from Cobden to Bright (December 6, 1849): "You must get Captain Mundy's edition of 'Brooke's Diary'. . . . There are details of bloodshed and executions which, if they had appeared in the first edition, would have checked the sentimental mania which gave Brooke all his powers of evil. . . . We as a nation have an awful retribution in store for us if Heaven strike a just reckoning, as I believe it does, for wicked deeds even in this world. There must be a public and solemn protest against this wholesale massacre. The Peace Society and the Aborigines Society are shams if such deeds go unrebuked. We cannot go before the world with clean hands on any other question if we are silent spectators of such atrocities."

For the pressure of vested interests, cf. Nathan A. Pelcovits, *Old China Hands and the Foreign Office*, New York, 1948.

enough to see that their true long-run interest lay in promoting the common welfare, and in being generous enough to abstain from attempts to exploit the weakness and ignorance of their fellow men. But it was never tested in practice. Before it could get well under way, economic nationalism had recaptured the seats of power, from which indeed it had never been completely displaced.

The closing decades of the nineteenth century witnessed a steady, if cautious, extension of tariff warfare. National economic rivalry found vent in renewed imperialism. Africa was partitioned, and China was divided into spheres of influence. New empires were carved out and old empires consolidated in southeast Asia and the Middle East. There was a scramble even for the scattered islands of the Pacific. As this new imperialism developed, shipping and naval rivalries were exacerbated, and the tension thus provoked finally broke into war in 1914. The revival of tariff protection to which the remainder of this section is devoted was the first symptom of ultimate conflict.

Tariff history is largely a record of interested groups seeking a privileged position in the national economy and advancing patriotic reasons for so doing. Employment, living standards, national welfare, and national power are the stock in trade of the protectionist argument. There are cases where the argument is plausible, though the self-interested promotion of protection in the public interest is inevitably suspect. If this was the worst aspect of tariff protection, however, not too much damage would be done. The experience of the latter part of the nineteenth century, when there was a widespread increase of tariff duties, is sufficient to prove that moderate and stable tariffs, while they hamper, do not destroy trade. This is primarily because they are compatible with the working of the competitive price mechanism, and not destructive of it. Imposed at the most competitive point of the trading process, the contact of wholesale buyer and seller, the effect of a tariff duty is diffused by the bargaining processes of the market over a wide range of producing and consuming interests of the commodity taxed, its component materials, and auxiliary and competing products. Spread in this way, moderate duties have not, in the past, prevented trade expansion.

The really dangerous use of tariffs, as of other impediments to trade, occurs when they are imposed primarily for reasons of state, usually as an instrument of economic warfare. When protection is advocated as a means of strengthening the power of the state—by making the national economy more self-sufficient, by establishing strategic industries, by building up trade connections less vulnerable in case of war—when national power and prestige are thus invoked, even though private interests profit by the protection, then it becomes difficult to operate a specialized, interdependent, world trading system. Power takes many forms. It is always liable to be abused. But the most dangerous of all concentrations of power occurs when economic and political power is fused into a single instrument. What finally destroyed the nineteenth-century trading system was economic policy pursued in a spirit of nationalism, for political rather than economic reasons.

In the decade of the seventies there was a resurgence of protectionism in Europe. The most important evidence of this was the German tariff of 1879, incorporating Bismarck's "compact of iron and rye." It is true that other European countries, including France, had recoiled in the early seventies from the trend toward freer trade. It is also true that after the Civil War the United States rapidly developed a high protective tariff, and that other independent countries in the New World began to raise their tariffs also. The British colonies of settlement used their newly granted powers of self-government to begin the process of industrial development behind the shelter of protective tariffs. For the most part these colonial tariffs were moderate. In any case they were erected largely at the expense of the local consumers, since it was not feasible at that time to develop any great industries in such small markets, and the export trade continued to be a dominant preoccupation.

After the Civil War the United States tariff became an important barrier to trade. There had not been much protectionist sentiment in Congress in the forties and fifties. The struggle over nullification and the Compromise tariff of 1833 had shown the political dangers of high-tariff proposals. The tariff of 1842 raised duties somewhat. Those of 1846 and 1857, to take the more outstanding of frequent revisions, were downward. The United States was embarked upon its westward expansion and there is a general consensus of opinion that tariff legislation in this period was unimportant and did not arouse great public interest.

High tariffs came with the outbreak of war between the States in 1861, and then primarily because of the need for revenue. An elaborate system of excise taxes, covering a wide variety of commodities, was countervailed by corresponding increases in the tariff on imports.

After the war the southern opposition to protection, formerly so potent, could be disregarded. The dominant northern states, their manufactures expanded by the stimulus of war demands and by inflationary war finance, faced great difficulties when deflation set in. They demanded and obtained the abolition of the excise taxes, while the higher import duties were maintained and even increased. The identification of the Republican party with high tariff policy and of the Democrats with tariff reduction was strengthened in this postwar period and has not yet wholly disappeared. This identification became clear when President Cleveland advocated a sharp reduction in the tariff and this became the main issue of the election of 1888. Cleveland lost the election and the McKinley tariff of 1890 marked a new phase of still higher protection. By this time the infant-industry argument was somewhat threadbare, and the protectionist case began to be based upon the home market and self-sufficiency. The full dinner-pail made its appearance as an effective slogan.

The popular reaction to the McKinley tariff, however, was hostile, especially in the western states. In 1892 Cleveland was again elected and the tariff of 1894 lowered duties. This was a short-lived victory for the low-tariff party. In the next election, fought mainly on free silver, the Republicans were returned and the Dingley tariff of 1897 marked a new high level of protection. The Dingley tariff remained the basic law until in 1913, under President Wilson, there was again some reduction. Then after the first World War, the Fordney-McCumber tariff of 1922 and the Hawley-Smoot tariff of 1930 carried protection to higher levels than ever.

Throughout these decades the issue was fought in the United States almost wholly on economic grounds. The tariff was primarily a domestic issue. Considerations of national defense were unimportant and hardly mentioned. The United States was not yet a creditor country, nor was it a great industrial exporting country until after 1918. Even after 1918, the international economic aspects of the tariff question continued to be neglected almost as completely as its international political aspects, until the severe crisis of 1929–33 brought home to its citizens the changed position of the United States in the world economy. The first indication of a changing policy had been the switch from conditional to unconditional most-favored-nation treatment in 1923. The great depression brought in its train the Reciprocal Trade Agreements Act of 1934.

Unlike the increase of protection in the United States, the return to protection in Europe after 1879 was very definitely influenced by international politics. The rise of Germany as a great power and the quick strokes by which Bismarck had consolidated the German Empire under Prussian leadership disturbed the balance of power in Europe. This process of consolidation had begun when Frederick the Great had taken Silesia with its coal fields from Austria-Hungary in 1740 and part of Poland in 1772. This was the first partition of Poland. The second and third partitions in 1793 and 1795 had added further territory to Prussia.

The process thus begun was furthered by the nationalist reaction evoked by Napoleon's rough treatment of the smaller German states. There were more than 300 of these states and Napoleon reduced their number to 39. It was in the early nineteenth century that the philosophers Johann Gottlieb Fichte and G. W. F. Hegel, enunciated the theories which were to provide an intellectual basis for the revival of German nationalism. The process of consolidation was carried on by the negotiations which finally led to the formation of the Customs Union (Zollverein) in 1834. A century later Germans would recall this step as the inauguration of an era of national unity, freedom, and development.[14]

The movement that led to this most important customs union was largely inspired by free-trade principles, though as always in such movements power-politics entered in. Prussia was contending for leadership among the German states and conducted what almost amounted to economic warfare against Hanover, partly because of Hanover's British connection. The very liberal Prussian tariff of 1818 had inaugurated free trade within the scattered Prussian territories and had levied only moderate duties on foreign imports. There was a strong liberal movement in Prussia led by H. F. K. Stein and Karl August Hardenberg. Its main emphasis was on domestic reforms, particularly in regard to agricultural serfdom. But Stein and Hardenberg were disciples of Adam Smith, and Smithianismus was widespread.

[14] Cf. W. Röpke, *German Commercial Policy,* Longmans, Green & Co., Inc., New York, 1934, p. 1: "It was one of the merriest New Year's Eves which the German nation had seen. Precisely at the moment when the church bells all over the country chimed in the new year the good old turnpikes were lifted from the Baltic Sea down to the Bodensee, to the infinite enjoyment of the people who got rid thereby of the internal customs barriers which otherwise would have strangled the growth of the later colossus of German industry. Everybody was happy except the smugglers because everybody was to gain except the smugglers. An era of freedom and unimpeded enterprise had been initiated."

The weight of Prussia was thrown behind liberal opinion in regard to tariff policy.

On the other hand, Prussia lay across most of the trade routes, and the temptation to use high transit duties, not only as a lucrative source of revenue but as an instrument of trade rivalry, was too great. Pressure to remove these duties helped along the movement toward a customs union. It is significant to recall that the Zollverein was primarily a liberal movement and for many years was dominated by liberal, almost free-trade, principles. But in the long run it became the nucleus of an aggressive imperial development. The history of customs unions shows that they seldom endure unless they lead to closer political union. When this happens there is a considerable chance that a new, enlarged nationalism finds expression in restrictive commercial policies.

Palmerston and other European statesmen were not very sympathetic with the Zollverein negotiations. Fearing the creation of a new center of power, which might eventually embark upon a high protective policy, Palmerston coquetted with the idea of a rival union or alternatively of special arrangements with some of the smaller German states. The British free traders opposed to Palmerston were secure in their belief that common sense would dictate a low-tariff policy and were wholehearted in support of the Zollverein. From 1834 to 1870 events seemed to bear out their judgment. Despite the nationalist teachings of Friedrich List, the Zollverein maintained a low tariff, and after the repeal of the British Corn Laws, German landowners found a profitable market in Britain for their agricultural exports. The dominant Prussian Junkers grew grain on their great estates and were therefore strong advocates of free trade until the opening up of the Middle Western plains of the United States began in the early seventies to pour a flood of cheap grain into Europe. This flood not only ruined the Junkers' market in Britain, but spilled over into their own home markets.

The German tariff revision of 1879 which marked the end of the Zollverein low-tariff policy, followed tariff increases in many other countries. Before this, however, Bismarck had struck suddenly at Denmark in 1864, securing the Schleswig-Holstein territory, through which the Kiel Canal was later to be cut; at Austria in 1866, disposing once and for all of the latter's influence among the Germanic states; and, finally, at France in 1870, securing Alsace and Lorraine, and also the final unification of the German states. The German Empire was proclaimed at Versailles in January, 1871. In 1870 Italy, too, achieved unification but it was the union of Germany which reversed the free-trade current and set every continental power on the search for security and self-sufficiency. The alarm felt by the manner in which the German Empire had been created was further enhanced in 1879 when Bismarck negotiated the agreement known as the compact of iron and rye between the grain-growing Junkers east of the Elbe and the rising group of manufacturers whose power was centered in the Rhineland. This agreement by which tariff protection was extended both to grains and to manufactures enabled him to shift his political support from the liberal to the conservative groups in the Reichstag, and committed Germany to policies of industrial expansion and agricultural protection. The detailed steps by which European tariffs were raised are less important than the fact that commercial policy became subordinate to diplomatic and power considerations.

The tariff history of Europe thenceforth was influenced by the diplomatic struggle that finally ended in the first World War. It would be difficult to cite specific cases of tariffs being used for political bargaining. Actual tariff schedules resulted in the main from protectionist pressures. But a reawakened nationalism made their acceptance easier. In one respect—the struggle for markets in colonial areas—tariff barriers appear to have contributed directly to the drift toward war. In the last quarter of the nineteenth century Europe became more and more of an armed camp. Every aspect of international economic relations—the building of railroads and telegraphs, loan policies, and commercial policy—was influenced by this fact.

Despite these developments Britain remained faithful to free trade and a group of smaller powers in western Europe followed her example. Denmark adapted her agriculture to the use of imported grain and foodstuffs. Switzerland, Belgium, and Holland specialized upon the production of commodities in which they had a comparative advantage, and upon the transit trade between the outside world and continental Europe in which their geographical position gave them advantages. More and more, Britain came to specialize upon the production of commodities such as textiles in which she had long held a commanding position, and upon highly efficient shipping, commercial, and financial services she could render by reason of her free commodity and money markets. Though her own trade was world-wide, and the great bulk of world trade was cleared and largely financed through London, many of her important markets were being walled about by tariffs. The area in which trade could proceed freely shrank virtually to the undeveloped colonial, or semi-colonial areas of Asia, Africa, and Latin America. The weight of trade restrictions gradually began to tell, and about 1910 economists were discussing the extent to which the terms of trade were turning against Britain.

In the latter decades of the nineteenth century there had been a renewed scramble among the industrial powers for colonial territories and for assured access to raw materials. The British crown had taken over the direct responsibility for the governance of India after the Mutiny in 1857. Despite the check to colonial expansion imposed by the American Revolution, and the theory so tenaciously held by the free traders that access to markets was preferable to annexation of territory, the boundaries of the British and other empires were steadily extended. Clashes with native peoples or weak governments, resulting from the activities of traders, investors, and even missionaries, often resulted in punitive expeditions and ultimate annexations. In the same way trading enterprise, supported by diplomatic pressure and armed force, resulted in the imposition of unequal treaties and the granting of territorial concessions by weak nations. Foreign settlements were lodged in Japan, China, and Siam. Turkey was put under a regime of capitulations. Egypt and much of the Middle East became a sphere of British influence after Disraeli secured effective control of the Suez Canal in 1875. Malaya, Burma, Borneo, and much of Africa became British territory also.

The scramble for Africa had begun anew when the Belgian king, Leopold II, in the seventies acquired what later became the Belgian Congo. Using harsh methods which had been all too common in earlier colonial ventures, the Belgians found that the public conscience in civilized countries had become more sensitive. A century of humanitarian teaching had not been without effect. As different European nations joined in the scramble, there was strong condemnation of ruthless methods, and not a little condemnation of imperialism in general. Such protests were inadequate. Modern industrialism was beginning to devour mineral raw materials in constantly increasing quantity. The older centers of industrial manufacture were exhausting their reserves of all but the commoner metals, and new supplies were being sought in undeveloped areas all over the world.

Italy began in the eighties to push toward Ethiopia from the Red Sea as well as from Libya. Following the Belgian example France extended her control from the north African coast across the Sahara, and west until in 1898 General Marchand was checked at Fashoda by the British who had pushed their control south from Egypt. The price paid by the British for French withdrawal from the Sudan was recognition of French claims in Morocco. The British were also expanding inland from their holdings on the east and west coasts of Africa and northward from the Cape till in 1899 they clashed with the Boer republics. Cecil Rhodes, who had amassed a great fortune in South African gold mining, was dreaming of the Cape to Cairo railroad. In the Near East the Ottoman Empire was crumbling, the Balkan states asserting their independence, while British enterprise was opening up the territory around the Persian Gulf, and Germany was pushing a project for the Berlin to Bagdad railroad.

The United States, as a result of the Spanish-American War, acquired the Philippines and Porto Rico in 1898. Hawaii was also annexed in 1898 and part of Samoa in 1899. In 1903 the Canal Zone was acquired, and the Panama Canal was built across the isthmus where the newly created Republic of Panama proved to be more complaisant than Colombia had been. Most of the other Pacific Islands fell to Britain, though France had acquired Tahiti and New Caledonia, and Germany the Marianas and—to the great alarm of Australia and New Zealand—part of New Guinea and the rest of Samoa. In 1899 the United States with British support had promulgated the doctrine of the Open Door in China as supplement to the earlier Monroe Doctrine. In simple terms the Open Door doctrine was the rule of most-favored-nation treatment, a prohibition of exclusive or preferential concessions in China. It did not safeguard the independence or economic interest of China but merely ensured an open field for foreign enterprise.

By the end of the nineteenth century the conquest of the non-European world was virtually complete, and over a large part of it, annexation had completed the process of subjugation of the native peoples. Except in regard to minerals in certain areas—such as the gold of South Africa, the copper of Rhodesia and the Belgian Congo, and the tin of Malaya—and to the less valuable opportunities for capital investment in other areas, this latest period of imperialism failed to yield as rich returns as did the earlier ventures of Spain in

South and Central America, of Portugal in Brazil, of the Dutch in the Far East and the British in India. If the costs of war and war preparation and of a broken world trading system are reckoned in, the balance sheet of imperialism shows a poor return.

It was the misfortune of Germany, Italy, and Japan to enter the scramble after the richest prizes had already been taken. Germany's colonial quest yielded little more than inferior colonies in the interior of Africa and a barren stretch of its southwest coast, a few Pacific islands, and some concessions in China. A colonial and world trading power must also have ocean shipping, and shipping must be protected by naval power. Germany added to its already formidable military expenses an expanding naval budget. Steel orders for shipping and shipbuilding were part of the compensation received by the heavy industries for their consent to increased agricultural protection. The armament race was on, and it was inevitable that one incident or another would precipitate a greater war than the world had ever seen.

The outcome of this venture in forceful diplomacy—the reliance upon blood and iron—was what might have been foreseen. German diplomacy was inept because the iron hand was too plainly visible. The decision in 1914 to attack France through Belgium was merely the last in a long chain of decisions that finally mobilized the larger part of the democratic world in opposition to German aspirations. Cobden, a true friend and staunch admirer of the German people, would have regarded this ultimate defeat as the inevitable consequence of relying upon armed diplomacy rather than peaceful trading penetration. The Germany he knew had laid the educational and scientific foundations for industrial leadership. Upon those foundations subsequent generations had erected an imposing industrial and trading structure. Germany might have become the greatest trading power in Europe, but the challenge to war was accepted, and in the struggle the whole structure of German trade so carefully erected crumbled into ruin.

CHAPTER IX

THE DISSENTERS

THE CLASSICAL ORTHODOXY

IMMEDIATELY after the free-trade campaign had been carried to triumph, there ensued in England a tremendous burst of prosperity and trading expansion. In retrospect this seems to have come in part from the inflationary effects of the great gold discoveries in the middle of the nineteenth century. For one brief decade at the close of this period of prosperity—from 1860 to 1870—there seemed a reasonable prospect that all the great trading nations would follow the example of England and accept free trade. That dream came to a sudden end. In the first reaction from it Walter Bagehot was driven to explain the "obvious reasons why English Political Economy should be thus unpopular out of England." His explanation was a double one. It was difficult, he thought, for most people to understand that political economy is an abstract science. It was particularly difficult for those whose economic environment was less developed than in England and hence more remote from the assumptions of political economy.

The classical economists had been perfectly aware that their analytical models were abstractions, deliberately designed to reveal certain forces they wished to emphasize. As an oculist uses atropine to dilate the pupil of an eye he wishes to examine, they were concerned to throw into sharp relief the working of the economic forces they wished to emphasize. John Stuart Mill in an eloquent justification of the deductive method had been at pains to define political economy as an abstract science, akin to mathematics. He had ridiculed the notion that "any political economist was ever so absurd as to suppose that mankind are really thus constituted," and was emphatic in his statement that "the mere political economist, he who has studied no science but Political Economy, if he attempt to apply his science to practice, will fail."

Contemporary writers in other countries were somewhat puzzled by the narrow emphasis which in England gave political economy "a physiognomy and a tendency exclusively industrial." Jerome Adolphe Blanqui, who had succeeded J. B. Say in his chair at the Collège de France, first published his survey of economic thought in 1837. In characteristically French style, he attempted to summarize the nature of the various national schools of political economy in his day. The Italian school, he wrote, "has been at all times philosophic and reformatory," concerned with wealth not "from an abstract and positive point of view, but in its relation to the general welfare." In Spain, political economy "was always considered an ally of the treasury . . . it covered with flowers the edge of the precipice over which that monarchy was one day to be plunged." In France, it "assumed an organizing and social character," with "generous voices being raised for the triumph of the eternal principles of justice in the distribution of the profits of labor." In Germany "political economy comes near being the science of administration, the science of the state."

Only the English "have treated political economy like algebra, and have ventured to maintain that all the propositions of the science could be demonstrated with mathematical certainty. This tendency has not led them to the most philanthropic solutions, but it has permitted them to follow out the consequences of their principles with inflexible logic. They have thus succeeded in giving to economic language a precision which has contributed much to the progress of ideas. It is the English who have best defined the words *production, capital, competition, credit,* and a host of others not less important. They have created a nomenclature, which has finally been adopted by all the economists of Europe, and which will serve as a starting point for their future labors."

By the last quarter of the nineteenth century the reaction against free trade was all but universal. The developing countries of the New World had resorted to protective devices as soon as they achieved self-government. Europe, where the Cobden-Chevalier treaty had opened a breach in the tariff walls, reverted again to economic nationalism after 1870. Only England and some of the smaller western European states—Denmark, Belgium, Holland, and Switzerland—maintained low-tariff policies approximating to free trade. It was therefore an unbalanced trading world in which the great expansion of international trade and investment took place in the closing decades of the nineteenth century—in many respects a travesty of the "great commercial republic," which had been the dream of Cobden and his free-trade followers.

In economic theory, as distinct from policy, the classical doctrine steadily won its way. This was even truer in the United States than in England. The pattern of thought worked out to buttress the case for freedom of enterprise found ready acceptance in the United States where Bagehot's "great commerce" became a more definite reality than in his England. In the United States, commerce found its vent largely in the development of a new continent and was therefore less concerned with the frontiers of world trade. But it was essentially of the same character as English commerce. Continental European preoccupations with economic strategy, misgivings as to the moral consequences of free enterprise, historical criticism of economic institutions, and socialist theories of more equitable distribution and more humanistic production, did not find much echo in the bustling exploitation of the American frontier.

This chapter draws attention to some of the more important dissenting voices that were raised in the first half of the nineteenth century against the classical doctrines. These voices were drowned in the rising clamor for free trade. At least they were drowned in England. On the continent of Europe what came to be known as English political economy—in the effective German phrase, national economy—could be represented as a rationalization of policies which Britain alone among the nations could afford and profit from. Even though, as Blanqui had foreseen, the classical terminology and analytical methods of English writers steadily won their way to acceptance as the tools of economic science, those who rejected the narrow definition of economics as a science could dispute the validity of the classical theories when applied to conditions different from those in England. There was never such unqualified international acceptance of the Ricardian doctrines as might be inferred from the orthodoxy of English economic thought in the last half of the nineteenth century, or from the influence which this orthodoxy exerted on academic economics in practically all countries.

In recent years it has been recognized that many contemporaries of Ricardo refused to accept either the validity of his theoretical analysis or the conclusions of practical policy which he derived from it. J. M. Keynes has emphasized the independence of Malthus and has credited him with recognizing many of the facts upon which Keynes's own theories were built in recent years. But Malthus did not stand alone in this respect. Of the dissenters whose theories are important for the study of international trade the first group to be noticed are those who, in new countries or in countries of backward economic development, disputed the free-trade doctrines on economic grounds. Primarily these writers relied on the infant-industry argument as the core of a theory of economic development. The *locus classicus* of their argument is to be found in Alexander Hamilton's *Report on the Subject of Manufactures,* presented to the House of Representatives in December, 1791. Though not immediately recognized at its full importance, this report came to be regarded as authoritative when the first American tariff campaigns were vigorously organized at the close of the Napoleonic Wars. These campaigns, supported by local manufacturers particularly in Pennsylvania and energetically promoted by the tireless activity of Mathew Carey, had an influence far beyond the borders of the United States. As soon as they achieved self-government, Canada, Australia, and New Zealand followed the example of the United States in adopting protective tariffs to foster their infant industries. Today, wherever the question of economic development is raised, as in India, China, and Latin America, the arguments of Alexander Hamilton and the example of the United States are invoked.

The second group to be considered is the colonial reformers. The guiding spirit of these was Edward Gibbon Wakefield. Their monument is the association of self-governing nations in the British Commonwealth. Its political importance in our world needs no emphasis, but its economic importance is also considerable. Current ideas of regional economic organization are clearly foreshadowed in the colonial theories worked out by this group of colonial reformers.

The third group of dissenters were those responsible for the steady growth of socialist doctrine from the earliest decades of the nineteenth century. There was a growing protest against the theory and practice of laissez faire. This may be seen in the indignant protests of the Romantic poets, the earliest demonstrations of the efficacy of high wages and good working conditions by the philanthropist-manufacturer Robert Owen, the denunciations of the early English factories upon which Karl Marx drew so heavily, the Swiss economist Sismondi's criticism of the economic anarchy that he found in England at the close of the Napoleonic Wars, and the utopian socialism of the French aristocrat Saint-Simon. Not the least important criticism was contributed by monetary reformers—cranks as they were then regarded—protesting against the rigors of deflation.

Working in the library of the British Museum, Marx digested both the Ricardian orthodoxy and the complaints of its critics. With thorough German scholasticism, he fitted them all into the strait jacket of his philosophy, to furnish an even more abstract inversion of the classical doctrines. By thus turning the weapons of the laissez-faire theorists against themselves, he created an inexhaustible arsenal of argument. His system was not cosmopolitan. It took scant account of nationality as such, but it recognized the necessity of organization in large political units. His interest was in the development of such political conditions as would give room for industrialized economic development in which the proletariat could use scientific methods of production. His emphasis was on technical progress. And nowhere was it more clearly argued than in his *New York Tribune* articles where he preferred British to Russian imperialism in India.[1]

In this body of dissent, whether expressed in the evolutionary sentiments of utopian socialism or in the revolutionary accents of Marxism, are to be found the ideas of technical efficiency, of planned economies for full employment, and of distributive justice, which are today among the most important elements in all discussions of national policies affecting international relations.

The challenge to free trade on political grounds constituted a fourth body of dissent from the classical economic doctrines. This

1 Cf. the citation of the article by Marx on June 25, 1853, in Solomon F. Bloom, *The World of Nations: A Study of the National Implications in the Work of Karl Marx*, New York, 1941, p. 53: "England, it is true, in causing a social revolution in Hindostan was actuated only by the vilest interests, and was stupid in her manner of enforcing them. But that is not the question. The question is, can mankind fulfill its destiny without a fundamental revolution in the social state of Asia? If not, whatever may have been the crimes of England, she was the unconscious tool of history in bringing about that revolution."

challenge proved to be crucial. The revival of protectionist ideas in Europe—notably in Germany—sprang from political even more than from economic causes. Friedrich List was the prophet of economic nationalism and his arguments fell on fertile ground as the integration of the German states into a great new empire in the heart of Europe disturbed the balance of power. The rise of Germany was the most portentous development of the latter half of the century, but nationalism was not confined to Germany.[2] Trade can surmount tariff barriers. But it cannot cope with the suspicions and uncertainties created by economic warfare waged as a supplement to diplomacy based on armaments.

The contributions of these dissenting groups to economic thought have been obscured by the acclaim given to the classical economists whose theories had been carried into practice in the free-trade experiment which seemed to be the foundation of England's predominant commercial and financial position in the nineteenth century. The influence of the classical economists was further increased because their theories provided a logical, analytical framework on which later economists could build. The heresies were never wholly forgotten. Throughout the nineteenth century they were repeated from time to time. But they could not win intellectual recognition as long as the policies advocated by the orthodox school seemed to be vindicated in practice. In our own time, however, when regional blocs are developing, when full employment and national economic development are accepted slogans, and when economic strategy can be neglected only at the risk of national survival, a more attentive hearing may perhaps be given to these voices from the past.

PROTECTION FOR ECONOMIC DEVELOPMENT

The beginnings of tariff protection in the United States coincide with the formation of the Union. The first tariff of 1789 was deliberately, though mildly, protectionist. Indeed the desire for protection

[2] Cf. John Morley, *Life of Richard Cobden,* p. 470: "The substitution of Lord Palmerston for Lord Aberdeen at the Foreign Office was instantly followed by the active intervention of the British Government in the affairs of other countries. There was an immediate demand for increased expenditure on armaments. Augmented expenditure meant augmented taxation. Each of the three items of the programme was the direct contradictory of the system which Cobden believed to be not only expedient but even indispensable. His political history from this time (1847) down to the year when they both died (1865) is one long antagonism to the ideas which were concentrated in Lord Palmerston."

and the need for revenue were among the factors which hastened union. Local and sectional clamor for protection went far back into the colonial period. The struggle of colonial manufacturers against the attempts of the British government to repress their activities was an important part of the reaction against the old colonial system.

Free-trade theorists were strongly represented in the Constitutional Convention, and in the First Congress James Madison attempted to introduce a tariff intended primarily as a revenue measure. He was defeated. The first tariff of 1789 was copied from the state tariff that had been adopted by Pennsylvania during the period of confederation. Pennsylvania, despite Benjamin Franklin, was already the home of protectionism. In due course its faith in the tariff became so definitely accepted a creed that loyal Pennsylvanians found it hard to believe that their great common-sense philosopher had not advocated it.

The reasons for this early resort to protectionism were mixed. At the beginning, they arose from the need for revenue to finance the Union, and the reluctance of the dominant landowners to accept direct taxation. These were the reasons stressed by Franklin himself and given pride of place later by Charles A. Beard in his analysis of the economic influences that helped shape the Constitution. Beyond these fiscal reasons there were definite political motives arising from the necessity to establish the strength of the Union both against the internal forces of division and against external dominance. There had been a long record, stretching back into the earliest colonial years, of state protectionism and retaliation. In the period of confederation, many states, burdened by debt and uncertain of finding other revenues, had imposed tariffs. There was a good deal of local protective rivalry and some tariff warfare among the states. It was evident that the Confederation could not long survive such rivalries; but, as in Australia more than a century later, the price of union was federal adoption of the protective tariff that some states were unwilling to give up.

Even so, union might have been delayed if British policy had been less threatening. At the conclusion of the Revolutionary war there was over-importation of the familiar British manufactured goods that had been lacking while the war lasted. The British government promptly imposed on imports from the United States the higher duties appropriate to a foreign country. The United States in consequence suffered an adverse trade balance and a drain of specie. Many theoretical free traders—among them James Madison and Thomas Jefferson—were led to conclude that for political reasons free trade was not a practical policy. As early as 1784, Jefferson had put his signature to a report which advocated retaliation against British measures destructive of American commerce. The report urged that: "Unless the United States in Congress assembled shall be vested with power competent to the protection of commerce, they can never command reciprocal advantages in trade; and without these our commerce must decline and eventually be annihilated."[3] The British protective policy undoubtedly hastened the necessity of replacing the Articles of Confederation by a federal constitution, in which the regulation of external commerce would be placed in the hands of Congress.

While these fiscal and political reasons were conclusive in the passing of the first tariff, and even earlier in the very formation of the Union, it must not be forgotten that there was strong pressure for protection emanating from industrial groups in several states. Appeals from "mechanics and manufacturers" were frequent. There were many meetings and a considerable pamphlet literature developed. On the other hand, the shipping and commercial interests of New England, and to some extent the tobacco and the cotton exporting interests of the Southern States were opposed to the demands of the manufacturers who were especially strong in Pennsylvania and New York. Congress as early as January 15, 1790, referred the question of increased protection to the Secretary of the Treasury, for report.

In December, 1791, Alexander Hamilton submitted his *Report on the Subject of Manufactures,* which has become a classic statement of the case for protection. This remarkable document, written by a young and busy official in the intervals of establishing the finances of a new and still weak nation, is a closely reasoned and cogent brief, summarizing ideas that were well known to the mercantilists but found no place in the first statements of the classical theory of international trade. While the report is an arsenal of arguments, upon

[3] *Journals of Continental Congress,* IX, 1186, cited by William Hill, *The First Stages of the Tariff Policy of the United States,* Philadelphia, 1932, p. 153. This, it may be noted, antedates by more than thirty years the well-known letter of Jefferson to Jean Baptiste Say, cited by E. M. Earle (ed.), *Makers of Modern Strategy,* Princeton, 1943, p. 137, in which Jefferson justifies his departure from free-trade principles by the necessity of retaliation in order that an infant state may preserve its independence.

which later writers drew freely and to which they added little that was valid, its essence is a dynamic if embryonic theory of economic development.

Stripped of its polemic against the depreciation of manufactures as unproductive, which reflected the contemporary interest in physiocratic doctrines, the *Report* is much more than a recapitulation of mercantilist doctrine, as William Graham Sumner and many later economists have declared it to be. The critical review of physiocratic arguments was directed against the Jeffersonian doctrines of agricultural democracy. Hamilton had no difficulty in proving that manufactures were at least as productive as agriculture. The strength of the *Report* lies in its recognition of the potentialities of development in a new country of rich resources.

There is much in the *Report* that has stood the test of time. But on one point Hamilton was strangely wrong. Concerned to argue that there was no division of interest between the agricultural South and the manufacturing North, he committed himself to the statement that, "the extensive cultivation of cotton can perhaps hardly be expected, but from the previous establishment of domestic manufactories of the article." He had previously used the English cotton industry to illustrate his argument that machinery created employment, but he did not foresee the immense market which that industry would create for American cotton. The foreign demand for a commodity in which the United States had a comparative advantage was the rock on which the first high-tariff campaigns came to grief in 1832. This is always an obstacle to the realization of protectionist ambitions in new countries, as the wheat exports of Canada and the wool exports of Australia give evidence today.

In some respects Hamilton's argument anticipated Wakefield's. He too had stressed "the field of enterprise," and made the point repeatedly that the home market "is more to be relied upon." His argument took on some of the aspects of regionalism, a sheltered and assured market, safe from the uncertain demands and restrictive policies of foreign governments. As the United States developed, this was no mean argument. The reaction in the forties against Jacksonian low-tariff and hard-money policies came when the frontier communities of the expanding West became convinced by the home market argument and swung their support to the eastern manufacturing interests in their renewed campaigns for higher tariffs. Within this expanding home market, it should be noted, the Federal Constitution provided a guarantee of almost complete free trade.

The so-called infant-industry argument for the protection of newly established manufactures was by no means original with Hamilton. It was well known to the mercantilists. So was its corollary that in favorable circumstances competition might and should reduce rather than increase prices to the consumer. But Hamilton's *Report* is more than a plea for temporary help to establish industries that might otherwise be throttled in their infancy by the competition from already established competitors in foreign countries. It challenges the three basic assumptions of the classical theory of international trade. This it does by rejecting the static analysis of immediate advantage in favor of a dynamic analysis of future development.

Hamilton did not lay much stress upon the point of which Mathew Carey later made such telling use—that within a country the factors of production, and especially labor, are not transferable between industries without a good deal of friction. Hamilton did emphasize the transferability of factors between national economic systems. He made repeated reference to the desirability of encouraging immigration, especially of skilled labor, and he had a clear vision of the importance of technical skills—"a much more powerful mean of augmenting the fund of national industry than may at first sight appear." He pleaded also for the importation of foreign capital—"every farthing of foreign capital which is laid out in internal melioration and in industrial establishments of a permanent nature is a precious acquisition." In addition, much of his discussion of ways to augment the available capital of the country, particularly by the introduction of banks and by the use of the funded debt "as a species of capital," opens the way to positive national monetary policies in contrast to the classical theory that the supply of money inevitably accommodated itself to the needs of trade.

It is worth noting that tariff agitation flared up in successive periods of financial crises. Whatever the validity of protectionist arguments may have been in times of prosperity, it was unemployment and the idea that home industry must be protected to stabilize employment that proved the potent and visible reason for putting pressure on legislators. The need for revenue; considerations of national unity and even of national defense; resentment against foreign discrimination; desire for retaliation, particularly against Britain in the early years of the Union, and notably after the war of 1812–14; the desire for economic independence as well as military strength; the argument for diversified industries, using a variety of technical skills and developing a great home market—all these could be presented persuasively and buttressed by what was inevitably a tendentious selection of statistics. But they had little political effect in the period of war prosperity. It has been argued and with good reason that protectionism naturally arises in a period of warfare, but it is in the economic distortion which follows great wars that it becomes most firmly established.

The early history of the United States tariff is no exception to this general rule. England went to war with France in 1793, and from that time forward until the end of the wars in 1815, business prospered in the United States and there was not much interest in protectionism. Memorials and petitions came to Congress between 1789 and 1809, when Jefferson's nonintercourse system went into effect. For the most part they were the complaints of unprofitable firms in industries that were generally prosperous. During the peace of Amiens (1802–3) there was a brief flurry of excitement, but the peace proved little more than a truce, and the demand for protection died down. During this whole period, until the embargo was imposed by the United States on British shipping in December, 1807, there was a diminishing pressure of British exports, while the favorable markets for United States exports and above all for shipping made available ample foreign exchange to pay for such imports as came in. Prices of agricultural produce were kept high by export demand. This was the period when ships out of Boston, Salem, and other New England ports opened up the tea and silk trade with the Orient, when the whalers and sealers depleted the Pacific Ocean fisheries from Alaska to the Antarctic, and when the shores of Tripoli first made the acquaintance of American marines.

With the establishment of the embargo, followed in 1809 by the Nonintercourse Act, and soon thereafter by the disputes which led to declaration of war on England in 1812, domestic manufactures had little competition in the home market. The volume of foreign trade in 1814 was little more than one-tenth of what it had been in 1807.

From 1808 to 1815 the British blockade of Europe and the demands of the war upon British industries gave American manufactures virtually complete protection from imports.

Peace in Europe in 1815 brought a double threat to United States industry. The stiffening of the English Corn Laws in 1815 (which brought forth Ricardo's economic analysis) provoked resentment among the grain-exporting states on this continent. The political influence of the exporting and shipping interests in the United States was weakened by the virtual closing of the British market and by the revival of British shipping. Agricultural prices fell heavily and shipping was depressed. Despite a brief postwar reconstruction boom and a moderate increase of protection in the tariff of 1816, the economic situation in the United States precariously supported by credit expansion was clearly unstable.

Across the Atlantic the British manufacturers were producing greater and greater quantities of the new textile and iron manufactures without any clear notion of where these goods were to be sold. Production was in the saddle, and consumption had to adjust itself. It was to quiet the concern expressed by many conservative folk that Jean Baptiste Say enunciated at this time his famous theory that there could never be general overproduction. But markets were not easy to find. Europe was exhausted by the wars. The thoughts of the British manufacturers naturally traveled to the large market that had been closed to them for so long. They were conscious that American manufactures had developed, but confident they could meet their competition. Indeed Henry Brougham, never noted for his tact, urged in the House of Commons in 1816 that it was wise for English merchants to take a loss upon exports to America in order, "by the glut, to stifle in the cradle those rising manufactures in the United States which the war had forced into existence contrary to the natural course of things." [4]

The flood of imports into the United States, which reached its peak in the crisis year 1819, brought Mathew Carey (1760–1839) into the ring. The motives animating him are clear. As an Irishman he loved a fight, especially if it was against the English. He was much attached to his adopted country and very confident of its future greatness. He was keenly alive to the suffering of those less fortunate than himself.

[4] Cited by K. W. Rowe, *Mathew Carey: A Study in American Economic Development*, Baltimore, 1933, p. 48.

The widespread economic distress and unemployment in 1819 disturbed him and he "commenced writing on political economy." [5] The animus of his first attacks on the free-trade doctrine was against the easy assumption that producers displaced by imported goods could always find employment in collateral branches of industry. This is the classical assumption of complete mobility of the factors of production within a country. To Carey its absurdity was manifest in the person of unemployed workers for whom there was no collateral employment. It is interesting to note the long list of occupations he cites, for which no collateral employment could be found. It is a list of specialized craftsmen, the skilled workers who are always intent upon protecting their status, and from whom the strongest support of the tariff has always been drawn.[6]

From 1819 on, the protectionist agitation began to be organized. Carey was its prophet. Later generations have remembered his name, and that of his son Henry C. Carey, as responsible for protectionist theories. No doubt this is due to the elder Carey's incessant pamphleteering. By his own account he wrote 45 tracts totaling 2,020 pages between 1819 and 1831, and another 14 of 302 pages in the next two years, before nullification put an end to the first tariff drives. This formidable labor was that of a propagandist, not of a theorist. One can read long in Carey's diffuse, repetitive, and often confused writings without coming across an idea that had not been more concisely and accurately expressed by Hamilton. Of this Carey himself was so conscious that he referred to his own work as an exposition of the Hamiltonian school of political economy. The *Report on the Subject of Manufactures* he described as "the most perfect and luminous work ever published on the subject," which, in his judgment "more richly

[5] The free traders in the cotton South regarded him as an irresponsible theorist and were confirmed in their view by the passage in his autobiographical letters (later reprinted as Mathew Carey's *Autobiography*, New York, 1942) which confessed: "I had been five or six years writing on the subject of Cotton Crops—Cotton Manufactures—Cotton Tariffs—and Cotton prices current when. . . . I saw a plant, of a species I had never seen before, and asked Mr. Gales what it was. He satisfied my curiosity by the information that it was the very plant which had furnished matter for so many of my lucubrations."

[6] Mathew Carey, *op. cit.*, pp. 103–4: "Where will he [Adam Smith] or any of his disciples find 'collateral manufactures,' to employ printers, coachmakers, watchmakers, shoemakers, hatters, paper-makers, bookbinders, engravers, letter-founders, chandlers, saddlers, silver-platers, jewellers, smiths, cabinet-makers, stonecutters, glass-makers, brewers, tobacconists, potters, wire-drawers, tanners, curriers, dyers, rope-makers, calico-printers, paper-stainers, engine-makers, turners, wheelwrights, and the great variety of other artists and manufacturers?"

deserved the title of The Wealth of Nations than the celebrated work which bears the name." There can be no doubt that his organizing initiatives were fruitful, but, being quarrelsome and demanding, he nearly always lost control of the movements he started. The manufacturers did not come through with the financial support he felt that he had a right to expect. He had the mortification of being thrust aside at the moment of triumph, when the practical men and politicians were capitalizing the results of his long agitation. The only individuals whose services to the protectionist cause could challenge comparison with his were Hezekiah Niles, whose widely read *Register,* in season and out, repeated the Hamiltonian arguments; and the Kentucky senator, Henry Clay, who built these arguments into what he called an American System, in his ambitious campaigns for the Presidency.

By the time the protectionist movement had been sufficiently organized to call a great convention at Harrisburg in July, 1827, it had become deeply involved in politics. The drawing of the political battle lines is curiously illustrated by the careers of John Calhoun and Daniel Webster. In 1816, Calhoun had been among the most prominent advocates of a protective tariff, but he was responsive to the views of his constituents who began to profit by the ever-growing demands for cotton to supply the looms of Lancashire, and feared the loss of these exports if British manufactured exports to the United States were cut off by a protective tariff. He ended as the champion of nullification, threatening to break up the Union if a halt was not put to the raising of tariff barriers. Webster started from the opposite side and much of his early eloquence was devoted to a lofty defense of commercial liberty. The manufacturing interest of New England, however, had begun to overshadow shipping and commerce. The majestic careers of these two great orators therefore moved in opposite directions. By 1824 Webster was advocating protection.

A powerful combination of manufacturers secured the passing of the high tariffs of 1828 and 1832. The former, which became known as the Tariff of Abominations, issued from a political maneuver that recoiled on its inventors. The opponents of high protection joined in supporting duties that they thought would prove to be preposterous and intolerable, while successfully opposing protection on some items that were among those most desired by the manufacturers. Their hope that such a tariff would be rejected by the protectionists was disappointed, and the subsequent tariff of 1832 gave the manufacturers practically everything they had desired. But this was too much for the Southern States, and in 1832 they carried their protest to the point of threatening secession from the Union. Soon thereafter the Jacksonian administration carried through a series of tariff reductions as well as an effective check to the credit expansion which was the counterpart of manufacturing development. The successful struggle against the Bank of the United States was consistent with tariff reduction, and both were defeats for the American System.

As in all such conflicts of economic policy, theories were of less immediate influence than the play of interests originating in sectional and group pressures to secure privileged positions in the economy. These pressures became rationalized in political programs which used the language of idealism, usually by identifying the particular with the national interest. When unemployment is widespread, as it was in the United States in the crises following the Napoleonic Wars, it is easy to argue that imports are taking the bread out of the mouths of local workers.

Yet it is also true that such passing crises are resolved along the trend of prevailing philosophies. In England unemployment during this period proved a powerful argument for free trade. In the United States on the contrary, it was used as an argument for protection. The protectionists always fell back upon Alexander Hamilton's *Report on Manufactures* for their final arguments. A quarter of a century had hallowed its authority since it was a product of the heroic age of the Union which had been supported by the pragmatic wisdom of Washington.

It is as a theory of economic development that Hamilton's *Report on Manufactures* has exercised such a lasting influence. As such, it had a peculiarly favorable environment in the United States. The later American protectionists could point to a growing home market, in which manufactured prices did in fact decline and to which foreign labor and capital were increasingly attracted. It was a market in which competition remained keen and technical invention was pronounced. How much of all this was due to the continuance of protective policies beyond the initial stages of establishing new industries may well be questioned.

That Hamilton's arguments were valid at the time and in the circumstances of their presentation has long been admitted. Whether they can be taken over and applied to the vastly different circumstances of other countries at the present time is another question. They no longer apply to the United States which is itself the powerful competitor that other countries most fear. Caution must be exercised in applying them to countries which lack the rich resources, coupled with a relative scarcity of population, as well as a shortage of capital and technical skills, that were characteristic of the infant United States. There is a case for the economic development of backward industrial areas, but it is not as strong a case as Hamilton made for the United States, and it must be argued on different grounds.

THE COLONIAL REFORMERS

In 1778 the issue of the struggle between the British government and the American colonists was still doubtful. In London there was much discussion of colonial policy. A recently discovered memorandum, apparently written by Adam Smith, considers four possible ends to the conflict. These were: the complete submission by all the colonies to the offer of a conciliatory settlement; the complete emancipation of all the colonies; a complete British victory resulting in the restoration of the old colonial system, or, finally, the submission by conquest or by treaty of some of the colonies, the remainder being successful in establishing their independence.

The author of this memorandum considered that conciliation, the first of these, was the most desirable but the least likely. Neither the third nor the fourth of these alternatives—restoration of the old colonial system, or the partial recovery by conquest or by treaty of some colonies—appealed to the memorialist as a satisfactory solution, though he confessed he thought the latter the most likely outcome of the war. Indeed the second solution—that of complete emancipation—he regarded as in many ways a more agreeable prospect. If the colonies were to gain full independence, Great Britain would be freed from the cost of governing them, and of the still greater cost of defending them in time of war. Their "antient affection" and their trade with Britain might revive. In order to help toward this desirable end, Britain should freely concede their independence. If at the same time Canada should be restored to France and the two Floridas to Spain, the newly emancipated colonies would more readily turn to Britain for alliance. As the memorialist observed, "we should render our own colonies the natural enemies of those two monarchies and consequently the natural allies of Great Britain." [7]

As British trade with the United States revived strongly after their achievement of independence, the view that colonial emancipation should be welcomed gained ground among liberals in Britain. A great many contemporary observers concluded that the whole colonial system, as it had been built up by mercantilist rivalries, had received its death blow. Trade was being developed on the basis of new and more enlightened principles. Cotton was pouring in from the United States to feed the hungry looms of Lancashire. The tobacco trade was more flourishing than ever. Wheat was beginning to come in to Britain from New York and New England. There was more trade and shipping between Britain and the independent United States than there ever had been with the dependent colonies. Moreover there was no expense and bother with colonial governments, and no risk of being dragged into Indian wars or frontier skirmishes. In retrospect the whole colonial effort looked like an expensive blunder. Colonies were definitely at a discount.

Such a philosophy might seem like making the best of a humiliating defeat, but it fitted the trend of economic thought at the time. Confident of their competitive power, the British industrialists were turning their minds to the building up of a great trading system. Markets, rather than territorial possessions, were their goal. They took much the same attitude as the United States officially takes at the present time—for much the same reasons. They disclaimed territorial ambitions, but sought to open competitive world markets.

As the political influence of the merchants and manufacturers grew, so did their resistance to ambitious foreign policies, to military and naval expenditures, and to colonial expansion. As early as 1793, Bentham had written his tract, *Emancipate Your Colonies*. The liberal free traders accepted this attitude and became known as "Little Englanders." Their arguments were clear. The burden of colonial defense, the constant temptation to war with other colonizing powers, and the lurking danger of monopoly in the colonial trade, all made it advisable to get rid of colonial obligations as quickly as possible. This line of argument fitted perfectly with the opposition of the Man-

[7] G. H. Guttridge, "Adam Smith on the American Revolution: an Unpublished Memorial," *American Historical Review*, Vol. XXXVIII, No. 4, July 1933, pp. 714–20.

chester merchants to balance-of-power politics as the antithesis of free trade.

These remained the views of an enlightened minority of public opinion, even in England. The Spanish and Portuguese colonies had secured their effective independence while the Napoleonic Wars were in progress. A volunteer army of British Peninsular veterans had helped Bolivar, and the British Navy by its blockade and as a war measure had facilitated the achievement of independence. The military, it is true, were not always clear as to their objectives. For example, an unauthorized British expedition from South Africa had landed on the River Plate in 1806 and had annexed what is now Argentina, holding Buenos Aires for the better part of a year before the Argentinians compelled them to withdraw. After the war ended in 1815, British diplomacy favored insurgent movements. In Europe there was a revival of absolutism. The Holy Alliance had set itself to repress liberal movements in Europe and in European colonies overseas. The British Foreign Secretary, George Canning, however, supported the doctrine laid down in President Monroe's famous message to Congress in 1823, and next year formally recognized Mexico, Buenos Aires, and Colombia as independent states. This step was clearly directed against France, a move in the game of power-politics in Europe. This was the occasion of George Canning's oft-quoted statement—"contemplating Spain as our ancestors had known her, I resolved that if France had Spain, it should not be Spain with the Indies. I called the New World into existence to redress the balance of the Old."

Despite the views of the Little Englanders, after the loss of the American colonies administration was not relaxed, but rather was tightened in the colonies that remained to Britain. Economists and philosophers might analyze the lessons of defeat. Manufacturers might protest against the costs of war and preparations for war, but the majority of Englishmen stubbornly maintained their faith in sea power and their pride of empire. There were, moreover, large vested interests at stake. The shipping interest fought against any relaxation of the Navigation Acts. The Army and Navy had a professional interest in maintaining the services, and a personal interest in colonial patronage.[8] Such small and compact interest groups were apt to exercise a disproportionate influence in politics.

[8] Cf. Charles Buller's statement cited in R. C. Mills, *The Colonization of Australia*, London, Sidgwick and Jackson, Ltd., 1915, p. 14: "The patronage of the Colonial Office is

It can be argued that, from a national standpoint, the narrow views of the economists and the merchants were proven wrong by those who clung stubbornly to traditional attitudes. If the views of the economists and of the Manchester free-trade school had prevailed there would have been no second British Empire. Even after the loss of the American colonies a good deal remained—Canada, India, Australia and New Zealand, the Cape Colony, the West Indies, and trading stations on the west coast of Africa, besides strategic bases such as Gibraltar, Malta, Aden, and Singapore. They proved a valuable basis for the expansion of British trade in the nineteenth century.

As the frontier of trade, prospecting, missionary effort, investment, and settlement was steadily pushed forward by private enterprise, situations arose which invited or compelled government intervention. Almost insensibly, Britain was drawn again into a considerable extension of her colonial empire. There may be a warning in this development for the United States. Despite sustained opposition from missionary groups, from economic theorists, and from industrialists, Britain was gradually drawn into a new colonial struggle. No American has ever used stronger language than Cobden did against those who, like Palmerston, were in favor of interventionist foreign policies.[9] Yet Cobden protested in vain against the wars and "butcheries" in Burma, and lost his seat in Parliament because of his violent opposition to the "Arrow" war in China. His pamphlet, *How Wars Are Got Up in India,* fell on deaf ears, and before he died he was sadly convinced that he had lost the battle against colonial expansion and balance-of-power politics.

During the first half of the nineteenth century while the influence of the mission boards was strong in the Colonial Office, intervention was reluctant, and indeed was often delayed too long for the welfare of the native peoples involved. This was notably the case in New Zealand, where earlier intervention might have averted a bloody

the prey of every hungry department of our Government. On it the Horse Guards quarters its worn-out general officers as governors; the Admiralty cribs its share; and jobs which even Parliamentary rapacity would blush to ask from the Treasury, are perpetrated with impunity in the silent realm of Mr. Mother Country."

[9] Cf. John Morley, *op. cit.*, p. 474, citing Cobden's letter to John Bright, in 1847: "But you must not disguise from yourself that the evil has its roots in the pugnacious, energetic, self-sufficient, foreigner-despising and pitying character of that noble insular character, John Bull. Read Washington Irving's description of him fumbling for his cudgel always the moment he hears of a row taking place anywhere on the face of the earth, and bristling with anger at the very idea of any other people daring to have a quarrel without first asking his consent or inviting him to take a part in it."

series of inter-tribal wars as well as a long list of massacres and reprisals. In the latter half of the nineteenth century, however, there was a definite revival of imperialism led by Benjamin Disraeli. The revival was undoubtedly buttressed by pride in the growing strength of the colonies of settlement which are now known as the Dominions. Those colonies owed their development, and in some cases their very existence, to the group of enthusiasts known as the Colonial Reformers.

The moving spirit of the Colonial Reformers was Edward Gibbon Wakefield (1796–1862), the son of one of Ricardo's friends and contemporaries. In the late twenties Wakefield found himself in Newgate prison, as a result of abducting an heiress and carrying her off to a clandestine marriage at Gretna Green. Realizing that the normal avenues to a political or professional career had been closed by his indiscretion, and perhaps prompted by the fact that many of his fellow prisoners were destined for the convict settlements in Australia, he began to study colonial policy. In 1829 he issued anonymously a small book entitled, *A Letter from Sydney*. This purported to be a description, written from firsthand experience, of life in Australia. It was so vivid and authentic that many well-known Australian settlers were suspected of its authorship.

The ideas developed in this remarkable publication were to serve from the moment of Wakefield's release from prison as the basis for his incessant activity in the field of colonial policy. Though debarred from any official position, in private meetings, in evidence before parliamentary committees, in tracts, pamphlets, books and journal articles, and above all, in the organization of group settlement schemes, he carried through a strenuous agitation for organized colonization. The first of his schemes to bear practical fruit resulted in the settlement of South Australia. But it was in New Zealand that Wakefield achieved his greatest triumphs. The New Zealand Company which sent immigrants to Wellington in 1840, and its successors, the Otago Association (1848), and the Canterbury Association (1852), were his handiwork. He went himself to New Zealand in 1853, soon after the colony had received self-government, and almost immediately threw himself into local politics. His political career was stormy and brief and he died in 1862, largely discredited and almost forgotten. The magnitude of his achievement was not realized until historians from the Dominions he had done so much to create began to study their origins.

Besides Wakefield's success in organizing actual colonization there must be put to his credit the almost complete overhaul of the policies by which the unoccupied lands, not only of Australia and New Zealand, but of Canada, South Africa, and other parts of the British Empire, were disposed of. His main objective was to prevent these lands from being sold at nominal prices to monopolists. His insistence upon the policy of a "sufficient price" for land was embodied in the Waste Lands Act of 1842, which went far toward checking the speculative purchases of large areas. But his greatest claim to fame was his contribution to the establishment of responsible self-government in the colonies. In 1839 he went with Lord Durham to inquire into the unrest in Upper and Lower Canada. Though he held no official post in Durham's mission, he is generally credited with a large share of responsibility for the Durham report, which laid the foundations of the British Commonwealth.[10] This report recommended a federal constitution conveying the right of self-government—a pattern that has since been followed not only in Canada, but in New Zealand, Australia, and South Africa.

Wakefield strove to find a theoretical basis for colonial policy. He rejected the callous disregard of colonial interests shown equally by the reactionaries and by the liberals.[11] He was scornful of the plan for settling the colonies by "shoveling out paupers" which Wilmot Horton conducted as a crusade, and of the very similar policy of convict transportation. Bitterly he contested the orthodox liberal view, expressed by the economist J. R. McCulloch, that it did not much matter where the convicts and paupers went, so long as England was rid of them. Instead he contended that it was necessary to build up colo-

[10] Cf. E. M. Wrong, *Charles Buller and Responsible Government*, Oxford at the Clarendon Press, 1926, p. 32: "Historical gossip, for it is little more, often regards Buller as the chief author of the Report. Brougham spread and possibly originated this story. On 13th February, 1839, he said of the Report to Macaulay, 'it was a second-rate article for the *Edinburgh Review,* the matter came from a swindler, the style from a coxcomb; and the dictator furnished only six letters, DURHAM.' This sounds like the origin of the epigram, 'Wakefield thought it, Buller wrote it, Durham signed it.' "

[11] Cf. R. C. Mills, *op. cit.*, p. 26: "James Mill's article on Colonization in the *Encylopaedia Britannica* in 1822 was a Malthusian essay on population, an economic argument against the monopoly of colonial trade, and a denunciation of the government of the 'many' in the interests of the 'few,' rather than an account of the principles and practice of colonization."

nies where England could be sure of her trade connections. He did not share the optimistic faith of the free traders that all peoples would come to see that it was to their advantage to adopt free trade. He and his associates pleaded for the free admission of colonial grain and for "the direction of our over-flowing capital towards the Dependencies of the British Crown." They were thus the forerunners of modern advocates of economic regionalism, of imperial tariff preference, and of a sterling area bloc.[12]

Moreover his speculations in this field drove him to criticize the classical economic theories of wages and profits in ways that anticipate modern analysis. He pointed out, for example, that "it does not follow that, because labour is employed by capital, capital finds a way in which to employ labour." In his repeated emphasis on this point he comes very close indeed to the concept of the national income which has been emphasized by J. M. Keynes and his followers since 1936. John Stuart Mill accepted Wakefield's argument, but failed to see that it was far more than a corollary, as he thought, of the classical principles.[13] There are many passages in Wakefield's writings which anticipate the views of such modern economists as Alvin H. Hansen who emphasize the employment problems of mature economies. Wakefield's emphasis on the necessity for regulating the price of land so as to maintain a due proportion between the supply of land and of labor displays a partial, if one-sided, anticipation of the emphasis laid now upon the availability of production factors in determining comparative trading advantage.

It was on this point he built his theory of colonization. Land should be sold at a "sufficient price." The proceeds should be used as an

[12] Cf. the article cited by R. C. Mills, *op. cit.*, pp. 93–94 n.: "The argument in favour of preferring trade with independent states to colonizing for the sake of trade, rests altogether on one great fallacy. It is taken for granted that the world abounds in independent states, having wants which England can supply, producing commodities which England wants, and desirous of making the exchange. Where be they? . . . More or less in all the countries of Europe, trade with England is impeded—in some it is almost prohibited—by restrictions imposed by independent governments. The tariff of the independent United States is the most serious impediment that exists in the world to the extension of the trade of England."

For the advocacy of imperial preference, cf. C. R. Fay, *Life and Labour in the Nineteenth Century*, Cambridge, 1920, pp. 14–17, and *Great Britain from Adam Smith to the Present Day* (4th ed.), London, 1947, pp. 52–56.

[13] Cf. Wakefield's statement (*England and America*, Vol. I, p. 115) that "the modern economists, in treating of the production and distribution of wealth, have overlooked the chief element of production, namely, the field in which capital and labour are employed," and Mill's comment in his *Principles, op. cit.*, pp. 727–28. For the whole theory see R. C. Mills, *op. cit.*, Ch. V, in which the preceding references are cited.

immigration fund. If the price was properly calculated, the system would become self-regulating—the demand for land being equated to the supply of labor. This semi-automatism will not stand close examination, but Wakefield had put his finger on an important weakness in the colonial systems of his day. The weakness of most colonial experiments had been that large areas of land were allowed to pass at a nominal price into the possession of monopolist and often absentee owners without adequate capital to work the land, while convict or pauper labor was dumped into unprepared areas without adequate employment opportunities. Wakefield fought for planned group settlements in which the class structure of England would be reproduced. Capitalist landowners would provide employment openings. Workers would not be able to take up unoccupied land. Sale of this land at a fixed and sufficient price would supply a fund to finance immigration. Wakefield's theory clearly depended upon the concept of a wages-fund which was accepted economic theory in his day. Karl Marx was quick to pounce upon his analysis as proof of the capitalistic assumptions of economic theory.[14] Obviously if the cure for a disproportion between the supply of land and of labor in a colony was to raise the price of land, it could be argued that the cure for a disproportion between the supply of labor and of land in an old country, was to raise the price of labor.

In practice the solution found was for the colonists to specialize upon forms of production in which an abundance of land was an advantage, while a scarcity of labor did not greatly affect production. In the case of Australia and New Zealand, wool fulfilled these conditions. Wakefield had seen from the beginning that this might ruin his theory, and he went to great pains in *A Letter from Sydney* to prove that there were limits to the increased consumption of wool. He was, however, completely wrong in his forecasts, and the profits of woolgrowing in New Zealand as well as Australia wrecked his elaborate plans for group colonization of concentrated agricultural settlements.

Like many another prophet, Wakefield was on stronger ground in

[14] Cf. the closing paragraph of *Capital,* Vol. I: "The only thing that interests us is the secret discovered in the new world by the political economy of the old world, and proclaimed on the housetops: that the capitalist mode of production and accumulation, and therefore capitalist private property, have for their fundamental condition the annihilation of self-earned private property; in other words, the expropriation of the labourer."

his denunciation of existing evils than in his remedies for them. His incessant agitation worked a revolution in colonizing methods, but his theoretical system broke down. The practical consequences of his agitation have left a permanent impress on our world—the abandonment of convict transportation, the orderly disposal of the waste lands "held in trust, not merely for the existing colonists, but for the people of the British Empire collectively," a careful selection of emigrants, the abolition of the worst evils of the emigrant ships, a cleaning-up of patronage in colonial appointments, and above all, the concept of colonial self-government leading to the association of self-governing nations in a loose commonwealth. These developments flowed directly from the activity of the Colonial Reformers, inspired and largely directed by Wakefield.

Later in this book an account will be given of the prolonged and complicated negotiations undertaken since the second World War to organize a world trading system. These negotiations grew out of the master agreement between Britain and the United States for the settlement of lend-lease obligations. Both countries have joined with others to develop an International Trade Charter, but there has been strong opposition in Britain to this attempt to restore a multilateral, non-discriminatory system of world trade. The alternative advocated is a system of imperial preference, the organization of a regional trading bloc of which the associative commonwealth of British nations would be the nucleus. That such an alternative is conceivable is due to the work of the Colonial Reformers. Without their efforts there would not have been the nucleus of self-governing dominions. No study of international economic relations in the modern world can afford to neglect this regional aspect of nineteenth-century economic development. The existence of the British Commonwealth is an important political and economic fact. The theory which led to its creation constitutes an important variant of the classical economic theory and of the political theory which was its counterpart. In this respect Wakefield's ideas are perhaps more important today than they were in his own time.

THE SOCIALIST CHALLENGE

The elaboration of socialist doctrines in the nineteenth century clearly challenged the thesis of laissez faire. Although social responsibility for individual welfare was not a new concept, it gained new importance in the violent economic changes of the early nineteenth century. It is never easy to date such developments. Economic history is continuous and untidy. For our purposes it is sufficient to draw attention to the unusual severity of financial crises and the widespread dislocation of employment immediately following the Napoleonic Wars. In part, this was the consequence of these wars; in part also, the dislocation was caused by the sudden application of factory methods of production to wider market areas. For some decades mechanical inventions had been accumulating in England. After 1815, they became available for production by factory methods for world markets. Almost simultaneously, the application of steam power extended their range and amplitude. The result was a vast series of shifts in employment and recurring periodic crises of overproduction and unemployment. A large part of the economic and social history of the nineteenth century is concerned with attempts to assert social control over the new productive forces thus released, and to protect the individuals and classes who were threatened with disaster by the suddenness of their impact.[15]

In the following pages the elements of socialist thought are grouped —first, into the humanitarian and utopian criticism of the workings of capitalist society; second, into the gropings of monetary reformers who perceived dimly that all was not well with the mechanism by which the marketing process functioned, and finally into the scientific socialism so-called, crystallized in the work of Karl Marx.

The humanitarian protest was often perplexed and inconclusive, as when Sismondi confessed that great as were the defects of competitive capitalism, a better system seemed to him "beyond the wit of man to devise." Often it consisted of generous but unhelpful out-

[15] The origins of modern socialist thought are to be found mainly in England and France. Cf. the statements of two Austrian historians of socialism, Anton Menger, *The Right to the Whole Produce of Labor,* translated with an Introduction by H. S. Foxwell, London, 1899, p. cxv: "This almost complete ignorance of English and French Socialism, especially of the older period, has contributed not a little to the disproportionate esteem which the writings of Marx and Rodbertus now (1886) enjoy in Germany. . . . I shall show in this book that Marx and Rodbertus borrowed their most important theories without any acknowledgement from English and French theorists." And M. Beer, *A History of British Socialism,* translated with an Introduction by R. H. Tawney, George Allen & Unwin, Ltd., London, 1920, Vol. I, p. v: "From the thirteenth century to the present day the stream of socialism and social reform has largely been fed by British thought and experiment. Mediaeval schoolmen and statesmen, modern political philosophers, economists, poets and philanthropists of the British Isles have explored its course and enriched its volume, but left it to writers of other nations to name and describe it."

bursts of sentiment. William Wordsworth wrote of the glowing hopes raised by the French Revolution:

> Bliss was it in that dawn to be alive,
> But to be young was very heaven.

Coleridge and Southey hatched Pantisocracy, a plan for a socialist community. In the next generation of poets, Shelley died in the revolutionary faith and Byron for it, but neither contributed much more than invocations to revolt. In a still later generation, Charles Dickens did much to arouse sympathy for "the parish apprentice, the debtor in prison, the pauper in the workhouse, the criminal by profession, and all the rest of that pitiful gallery." He had, as John Morley remarked, "hardly any solution beyond a mere Christmas philanthropy, but he stirred the sense of humanity in his readers, and from great imaginative writers we have no right to insist on more."

There was much room for indignation at the abuses only too prevalent in the unregulated labor market. The Poor Laws demoralized a large part of the working population—the laboring poor as they were called. Small boys crawled through still hot chimneys to clean flues; women and children were driven to heavy and degrading work in the coal mines; cottage workers who worked on contract in their own homes were miserably sweated; factory workers were cheated in company shops and houses. The worst exploitation was not in the efficient new factories; but on the fringe of industrialization and in the displaced cottage industries. Often the hardest taskmasters were parents whose own livelihood was imperiled and who were therefore forced to exploit the labor of their children. Contemporary observers compared the lot of these unhappy families with those of the parish children who were apprenticed in large groups to unscrupulous manufacturers.[16]

Pity for the victims of the factory system—the women who crowded into the textile mills and the children who began work at a tender age—was mingled with a false idealizing of a mythical golden age of agri-

[16] Cf. the considered judgment of Alfred Marshall on these facts, *Industry and Trade*, London, 1919, pp. 71–77, and his refutation of the common belief that the laissez-faire economists opposed factory legislation, pp. 747–50. Ricardo did not write on the subject. Tooke, Torrens, McCulloch, and Newmarch actively supported the legislation, as did John Stuart Mill. Senior at first opposed the acts, but later was one of their leading advocates. The main opposition among economic writers came from the popularizers, and notably from Miss Harriet Martineau.

cultural and handicraft prosperity. There was always a strain of backward-looking sentiment in the protest against industrial development. Machines were taking away employment from skilled handicraft workers. Weavers had been independent producers, reasonably prosperous in the good times just before and during the Napoleonic Wars. In the great crises that followed, their skill was thrown on the junk heap. It was significant that one of the earliest protests against the new system was the organized smashing of machines by the Luddites, a movement that took its name from the half-wit Ned Ludd. It enlisted widespread support among the displaced workers, and not a little sympathy among the more fortunate classes. There was fear also that abolition of the Corn Laws would destroy rural employment and the amenities of country life.

The social improvement made possible by the new factory methods was demonstrated in the early years of the nineteenth century by Robert Owen, who rose quickly from humble origins to great wealth and influence by applying essentially modern ideas of labor relations in the rapidly expanding cotton industry. The various phases of his career embodied most of the elements of social reform that were to be influential in the development of utopian socialist thought—the improvement of factory conditions in order to achieve efficient production, factory legislation to enforce such conditions and to restrain the abuses of the labor market, currency reform, experiments in co-operative communities, consumers' co-operative societies, universal education, and parliamentary reform.[17] The basis of Owen's ideas of social reform is to be found in his belief that a man's character is

[17] Cf. M. Beer, *A History of British Socialism,* pp. 160–81. Owen, the son of a Welsh saddler, was born in 1771 and went to work as a shop boy at the age of nine. After some years in London and Stamford he came to Manchester and by the age of twenty-two was in a position to start his own mill for the manufacture of fine cotton yarn. He was already recognized as one of the rising men in the new industry, and when, in 1799, he married the daughter of a wealthy banker and cotton spinner, he was able to take over the mills at New Lanark which he turned into a model and very profitable industrial concern, the type and forerunner of the modern factories which have found that it pays to enlist the loyalty and improve the efficiency of their workers. From 1815–18 he devoted much time and money to the advocacy of factory reforms and the first Factory Act of 1819 owed much to his efforts. The severe postwar crises drew him into the advocacy of co-operative communities to provide work for the unemployed and he received much influential support for this idea until he frightened his supporters by avowing his disbelief in organized religion. In 1824 he bought the Rappist community Harmony, in Indiana, and reorganized it as New Harmony. In three years the community failed and Owen returned to England. He lived till 1858, active in the Chartist and other working-class movements.

molded by his environment. He attacked organized religion because many leaders of the churches opposed factory reforms and insisted that character was formed by grace. He thus anticipated Marx's attack on religion as "the opiate of the masses." He also anticipated Marx in his insistence on the necessity of machine production to provide the abundance necessary for higher living levels.

Robert Owen and many other high-minded reformers were interested in the creation of voluntary communities, in which high productivity might be combined with frugal and egalitarian personal outlays and wise community expenditures. The early nineteenth century saw many experiments in such communities, in old and new countries. They failed, but they left an important legacy in the destructive analysis of capitalist society by which they were justified, an analysis which was built into the later theories of Marxian socialism. Saint-Simon's emphasis on the rule of the elite was particularly influential.

Moreover the social protest of the early nineteenth century left enduring practical legacies, particularly in Britain. The political temper of the British people has generally been cautious and distrustful of theories carried to logical extremes. Socialist communities did not appeal to them, but the idea of voluntary association found expression in a solidly organized trade-union movement, in the consumers' co-operative movement that began at Rochdale in 1844, and in the powerful friendly society movement which pioneered in the field of group health insurance. All of these voluntary associations found room to grow within the capitalist order of society.

In addition the capitalist order was gradually brought under some measure of control by legislation. Factory conditions were regulated and the abuses of truck (payment of wages in kind) abolished. There was a gradual but sure evolution of the public finances along what were essentially socialist lines—progressive taxation bearing more heavily on the rich and expenditures meeting general needs. Not only education but social services were steadily improved and widened. Many countries in both the Old and the New World, have followed this evolutionary line of socialist development. In many respects this is divergent from and alternative to the Marxian policies, since it is in fact reformist and conservative, rather than revolutionary.

In recent years this evolutionary socialism has tended to incorporate within its program the second body of social protest noted above—

the monetary theories and policies which at their first formulation were dismissed as the ignorant illusions of monetary cranks. The world-wide appeal of the slogan of full employment at the present time is intimately connected with reliance upon monetary manipulation to stabilize production and employment within national communities.

It is not surprising to find that the heretics who blamed the prevailing social distress after the Napoleonic Wars upon rigid adherence to deflationary monetary policies were the objects of scorn among the followers of Ricardo. However, had they known of it the heretics might have quoted Ricardo's own letter declaring against the deflationary policy necessary to restore sterling to parity at its former gold value. Sterling was depreciated by 30 per cent and Ricardo would have stabilized it at that value in terms of gold. The depreciated currency had in fact been restored in 1819 to its old parity and this was undoubtedly a cause of severe price deflation. Thomas Attwood, a Birmingham banker, led a crusade against the gold standard thus inaugurated, and rallied a group of Birmingham businessmen to his cause.[18] He and his brother Matthias had opposed the resumption of specie payments in 1819, and, in the subsequent period of falling prices and severe crises, they never ceased to advocate an inconvertible managed paper currency as a monetary standard superior to gold. Some minor writers supported them, but the dominant school of economists, impressed by the advantages of an internationally exchangeable money, treated them with contempt and derision. They, and still more their followers, were not always convincing in their positive arguments. Schemes for monetary reform always attract the support of cranks. But modern economists are now aware that the Attwoods

[18] Though a Tory M.P., and by no means a democrat, Attwood, despairing of carrying his currency reforms through the first reformed House of Commons (1832), associated himself with the revival of the Chartist movement. His influence was sufficient for a time to commit prominent individuals, including Robert Owen and Feargus O'Connor, to paper money schemes. But the primary aim of the Chartists was electoral reform; and currency became one of a number of associated and complicating planks in the platform. Attwood presented a Chartist petition to Parliament in 1838, but Lord John Russell was able to quote against him a manifesto of the real Chartist leaders and to ridicule the movement in the person of Attwood, who shortly afterward disappeared from political life. Cf. Mark Hovell, *The Chartist Movement,* Manchester, 1918, pp. 100–10. The trade-union movement on the whole steered clear both of Chartism and of its currency wing. (Cf. Sidney and Beatrice Webb, *The History of Trade Unionism, 1666–1920* (rev. ed.), London, 1920, pp. 174–79.) Finally in the person of Philip Snowden, it provided the last-ditch defender both of free trade and of the gold standard, when they were abandoned in 1931.

did have hold of a real problem and that their attempts to state it anticipated modern monetary theories.

The management of currency and credit as a means of implementing national policies of full employment and social security is now advocated, for example in Britain, as a practical alternative to the laissez-faire, free-trade policy based upon an international gold standard. Under the gold standard, employment, prices, and the whole economic structure were bound to accommodate themselves, at times painfully, to fluctuations in world markets transmitted to the national economies through the balance of payments. Now many national economies endeavor to maintain a high and stable level of employment and a wide variety of social services, by managing their credit systems and insulating them from the fluctuations of the balance of payments. This very characteristically British evolution, based upon what Sidney Webb once called the inevitability of gradualness, has gathered up the elements of voluntary association, legislative reform, and monetary manipulation into what it is becoming the fashion to describe as a social-service state.

The third and in many respects more formidable current of socialist thought—the so-called scientific socialism—also had its roots in early nineteenth-century Britain. It was hammered into a system by Karl Marx and has finally been used as the theoretical justification for the political and economic experiments of the Union of Soviet Socialist Republics. Of even more importance for our purpose here, this system of socialist thought has formulated a body of doctrine regarding international economic relations, and particularly those between developed and undeveloped economies. And this has become a potent force in the modern world.

Obscure writers, access to whose works is now difficult, evolved the ideas which Karl Marx was to rediscover and forge into a system. Of the men who were important in the formulation of these ideas only William Godwin, the author of *Political Justice,* is reasonably well known. The others—Charles Hall, William Thompson, John Gray, Thomas Hodgskin, and John Francis Bray—were, respectively, a physician, an Irish landowner, a wholesale merchant, a journalist, and a compositor. They were active in the early decades of the nineteenth century and most of them had associations with the fermenting social movements of the time. The reason for mentioning them rather than many others is that their writings form a chain of logical ideas of which Marx's synthesis was the culminating achievement.

Godwin, following Jean Jacques Rousseau, attacked private property as an instrument of social injustice. Hall maintained that the worker was entitled to the whole product of his industry. William Thompson elaborated this thesis that the worker was the sole producer and should receive the whole product of labor. He developed the idea which Marx later was to call surplus-value. Gray's *Lecture on Human Happiness* was influential both in Britain and in the United States. It was an attempt to document the case against the inequalities of income distribution. Hodgskin developed from the Ricardian analysis what is essentially the Marxian theory of value, and Bray took the final step of advocating a communist system.

Karl Marx was probably the most widely read and learned economic writer of his time. In the library of the British Museum he had access to pamphlet and periodical literature, as well as to treatises, both well-known and obscure. He lived in the thick of the working-class agitation and maintained close contact with its leaders all over Europe, so that he was familiar with the revolutionary ideas that were simmering at the time. Marx brought to the analysis and co-ordination of these ideas an intellectual equipment and training that was unusual among labor leaders.

He was born in 1818 at Trier (Trèves), which had been a fortress commanding the Lorraine gate since Roman times and is still an important strategic point in a cultural borderland. The son of a minor German official, Marx went through school and university in training for an academic career. Here he was exposed to one of the most active and brilliant intellectual environments in Europe at that time. After a thorough training in jurisprudence and philosophy, he realized that he could not conform to the political and religious orthodoxy demanded in the state universities of Germany. At the age of 24 he began to edit a radical journal at Cologne, but the journal was soon suppressed. Marx then moved to Paris where he became associated with a weekly named the *Vorwärts*. Expelled from Paris at the request of the Prussian government with his friend Friedrich Engels he next went to Brussels, and it was there that the first of their collaborative documents was produced. Engels became a successful cotton manufacturer. But he continued to collaborate with Marx and was responsible, after Marx's death, for the completion of *Das Kapital,* the study which expounded the theory of Marxian economics and its application to economic history and analysis.

It was as a theorist that Marx finally achieved his greatest reputation and influence. He did not achieve immediate success as an agitator and failed to create in his own time an effective international working-class movement. Expelled from Brussels in 1848, he went back to Germany, but was expelled from there, and again from Paris. He finally came to London in 1849 and spent the rest of his life there, except for brief visits to congresses. He died in 1883. *The Communist Manifesto* in 1848 launched Marx and Engels as revolutionary agitators and organizers. The invective and abusive style which Marx in particular developed in the course of violent argument with his opponents in the course of a stormy career is one of the reasons why his work has always been regarded with dislike, and until recently with contempt, in academic circles. Neither this polemic style, nor the often cloudy philosophic jargon with which Marx clothed his analysis, ought now to obscure his contribution to economic thought. He should be regarded neither as a malevolent portent of all that is evil nor as a prophet whose literal inspiration it would be impious to question, but as a serious student molded by the circumstances of his time. Opinions may differ as to the validity of his theories and of the practical conclusions he drew from them, but there can be no doubt that he is one of the great economic writers, in the direct line of descent from Ricardo.[19]

In essence Marx—using G. W. F. Hegel's method of dialectic, but standing it, as he said, on its head—interpreted history as reflecting the struggle between economic classes.[20] His argument was that at

[19] Cf. the comments cited by Gide and Rist, *A History of Economic Doctrines* (rev. ed.), London, 1948, p. 467, from the later neo-Marxians—Labriola: "*Das Kapital,* instead of being the prologue to the communal critique, is simply the epilogue of *bourgeois* economics," and Sorel: "Marxism is really much more akin to the Manchester doctrine than to the Utopian. We must never forget this." For a brief exposition of the Marxian theoretical system written in modern economic language, cf. Joan Robinson, *An Essay on Marxian Economics,* London, 1942.

[20] In its original meaning, the word *dialectic* used as a noun was synonymous with *logic,* the art of critical examination into the truth of an opinion. Kant used the word in a special philosophical sense to mean the criticism which reveals the mutually contradictory character of scientific principles when employed to explain matters beyond the limits of experience. Hegel applied the term to the process by which such contradictions are resolved in a more adequate understanding of the truth. The process thus becomes thesis, antithesis, and finally synthesis, the synthesis in turn developing an antithesis and being resolved in a new synthesis. Marx accepts this definition, but instead

any period there is a class whose interests coincide with those of society as a whole. In the early stages of industrial capitalism this class consisted of the organizers of the new method of capitalist production. It was their historic mission to smash the power of the feudal land-owning class and to organize the more effective methods of production. There was no point, in Marx's view, in denouncing capitalism or in bewailing the suffering it caused—all this was mere sentimentality. Thus in his uninvited and undelivered address on Free Trade to the Brussels Free Trade Congress in 1847, after belaboring the free-trade arguments with heavy sarcasm, Marx concluded in favor of free trade and against protection. This was not for the orthodox reasons but solely because it would prove a step toward the social revolution.[21]

The advent of industrial capitalism, he argued, especially when it produced for a world market, was of no benefit to the workers. Marx held the view of the extreme Chartists that all the free traders wanted was cheap food to enable them to pay lower wages and produce at lower costs. This deduction followed inevitably from the Marxian theory that all value is produced by labor, but that labor receives only the minimum necessary for subsistence, the remaining surplus-value being withheld by the owners of capital. He maintained that the accumulation of this surplus-value caused periodic overinvestment which broke down in recurring cyclical crises or paroxysms of industry, the severity of which inevitably increased. The struggle for markets, in his view, also led inevitably to war since the dominant class of bourgeoisie directed and used the powers of the state to protect and advance its own interests as such dominating classes have done throughout history. War and the intensified crises which it provokes, he believed, would eventually destroy capitalism. As society moved from crisis to crisis in cycles of increasing severity, so his argument ran, the contradic-

of agreeing with Hegel that the economic reorganization of society reflects the thought process, he reverses this view and argues that prevailing beliefs and ideas reflect the conflicts of economic classes.

[21] The text of this address, which was later delivered before the Democratic Association of Brussels, is printed with an introduction by Friedrich Engels as an appendix to Karl Marx, *The Poverty of Philosophy*. Engels, writing in 1884, after traversing the reasons for renewed protectionism comes to the same conclusion as Marx. The latter ends his address with the paragraph: "But, in general, the protective system of our day is conservative, while the free trade system is destructive. It breaks up old nationalities and pushes the antagonism of the proletariat and the bourgeoisie to the extreme point. In a word, the free trade system hastens the social revolution. It is in this revolutionary sense alone, gentlemen, that I vote in favour of free trade."

tions inherent in capitalism would eventually force resort to the socialist alternative.

This brief summary inevitably telescopes ideas that Marx developed, not always consistently, during a long life of revolutionary agitation and polemic writing. The later German historian, Werner Sombart, used to speak of two Marxes. The younger Marx was an active revolutionary. The analysis of his more mature years emphasized the evolutionary character of capitalism, and there was a good deal of gradualism in his analysis of the tendency toward capitalist concentration which, he contended, would lead to the inevitable expropriation of the expropriators. However, the temperament of a lifelong revolutionary and a great hater prevented him from accepting the full implications of his own later analysis.

At times he seemed to believe that in Britain and the United States there was a chance that the revolution might come peacefully. But as amelioration and evolutionary reform took the revolutionary spirit out of the workers' organizations, he reverted to his earlier view that the only way to a socialist society was by revolution. Toward the end of his life, he realized that American labor was still provided with an outlet on the frontier. The organized British working class was firmly in the liberal camp. The weakness of French radicalism had been revealed in the short-lived commune of 1870. German social democracy had set out to gain control of, rather than to supplant, the machinery of the nation-state. Marx's eyes therefore began to turn toward the Russian revolutionary movements, but he was disappointed in the immediate outlook. Though revolution finally came in Russia, it was long delayed.

The Marxian doctrine was presented as a scientific explanation of inevitable developments. The vehicle of these developments was to be the proletariat—an awakened and organized working class. The leaders might come from other classes, but they would become leaders only by identifying themselves with the class which had the historic mission of expropriating the capitalist expropriators. Marx believed that demarcation of class interest had taken its final form, since capitalism had arrayed the masses of the workers against the owners of landed and industrial property. This conflict, in his view, would lead to the final synthesis. Once accomplished, the class war would end in a classless state. The historic state, in which political power was used by a dominant class as an instrument of exploitation, would wither away.

There would still be administrative functions to be performed in the general interest. Whatever privileges the administrators might secure, there could be no mass exploitation since ownership of the means of production would be communized and there would be no inheritance of economic or political power.

The incompatibility of the Marxian doctrines thus developed with the ideal world of the laissez-faire free traders is obvious. The latter visualized a world in which trade was organized by private enterprise, and in which competition in free markets would maximize wealth by bringing about co-operation among specialized producers. The distribution of this wealth would be achieved competitively so that everyone would receive a share proportionate to his contribution to the total production.

Marx did not deny the effectiveness of the capitalist system in the sphere of production. As between Tsarist Russia and capitalist England, he preferred the latter because of its greater efficiency. He even applauded its imperialism. This was because, though he declared that it "was actuated only by the vilest interests," he argued that it was fulfilling the "double mission" of annihilating the traditional society and "laying the material foundations of Western society in Asia." His main complaint was not that the British were destroying the organized society of India, but that they were not destroying it fast enough. In later years he began to doubt whether the process of exploitation would bring its own nemesis of revolution quite as fast as he had expected. But he never wavered in the conviction that economic progress—mechanization as his followers would later call it—should not be impeded by archaic social organization or by concern for political independence, which in his view always meant the rule of a dominant class interest.

But if he agreed, for his own reasons, with the capitalist free traders' emphasis on productivity, he differed with them violently and profoundly in regard to its distributive implications. Private property and class government, he maintained, secured the whole of the increased productivity for the capitalist. This was perhaps a necessary phenomenon when capital equipment had to be built up. But with economic progress there would come monopoly and struggles for power and profit within the capitalist system. The time would inevitably come when the workers would realize the fatal weaknesses of capitalism and would feel confident enough in their own skills and political power to put an end to these weaknesses. Then the workers would rise in their massed strength, expropriate and eliminate those who had robbed them for so long, and take the means of producing wealth into their own hands, not as individuals but as a community.

Between these extremes of belief—the free traders' belief in competitive capitalism, and the Marxian creed of an invitable class war and catastrophic revolution ending in a communist state—there is a middle way. The idea of reforming the abuses without destroying the foundations of capitalism has appealed to large numbers of those concerned with the avoidance both of reaction and of revolution. Since these middle-of-the-road reformers deny the scientific inevitability of the Marxian analysis, they are naturally the target of the most abusive Marxian hostility.

Much has, however, been achieved by the method of reform. The Marxian sequence of events is not inevitable. In many countries it has been upset by raising living standards, generalizing educational opportunities and thereby giving scope for creative work, relieving and preventing poverty and distress, and checking exploitation. Taxation and control of public expenditure have proved potent instruments in raising the real incomes of the masses of the people. Monetary and fiscal policy may prove equally potent in maintaining employment and preventing the periodic recurrence of destructive crises. New experiments have been made in the control of vital industries and public services.

All of these experiments have involved recourse to the machinery of national government. German state socialism, urged by a trade-union movement, staffed largely by men trained as non-commissioned officers in the German Army, ended by tame submission to a totalitarian state. In the British countries, notably Australia and New Zealand, as well as in Scandinavia, the democratic tradition has been strong enough to experiment with state socialism without disaster. Even in the United States, much has been done to supplement private enterprise and bring it under some measure of public control. It is clear that, if either the reformist or the Marxian socialist theories retain the hold they have now gained in so many countries, international economic relations must be organized on a different basis from the free competitive markets postulated by the laissez-faire free traders.

THE REVIVAL OF ECONOMIC NATIONALISM

The preceding sections of this chapter have dealt with ideas that have found expression in the economic development of the United States, in the regionalism and social service organization of the British Commonwealth, and in the revolutionary social protest which resulted ultimately in the creation of the U.S.S.R. These bodies of dissent from the classical free-trade doctrine have been summarized here as they were expressed by the men with whose names they are most clearly connected—Alexander Hamilton, Edward Gibbon Wakefield, and Karl Marx. The importance of these ideas today may be judged by the fact that it is tempting to identify them directly with the policies of the greatest powers in the modern world.

However, to identify them so directly is to simplify unduly what are inevitably complex ideas, which are not the exclusive possession of any one person or any one country. Nor can national policies at a time of flux such as the present be labeled so simply. The creation of regional trading blocs is not necessarily a British idea, nor is it inevitable that British Commonwealth policy will continue in that pattern. Economic development has become an excuse for protectionism in many countries of backward industrial organization, but can no longer be applied to the United States. The social protest against laissez faire based on the popular slogan of full employment is practically world-wide. And it is possible and even probable that the particular form of socialist organization now operating in the U.S.S.R. may continue to evolve.

In this section attention is devoted to the revival of economic nationalism. This was in fact the most effective body of dissent from free-trade doctrine in the nineteenth century, since it brought about the collapse of the nineteenth-century world trading system. The revival of economic nationalism is described with particular reference to the doctrines of Friedrich List and to the economic policies followed in Germany. This is not to identify economic nationalism exclusively with the teaching of List or with German economic diplomacy, though they offer the best illustrations of it. There are elements of nationalism in the policies of every country, and it is probable that List would have been shocked by the perversions of his teaching in later German practice.

Two important arguments will be developed in the pages that follow. The first is that the phenomenal growth of German industry in the latter part of the nineteenth century was primarily the result of an early development of general and scientific (including technical) education, and only secondarily of state aid and protection to industry. This industrial progress was foreseen by foreign observers long before Germany adopted a high-tariff protective policy, before cartels were envisaged, and before industrial banks with government support fostered both production and trade. As early as 1840 an official representative of the Board of Trade, Sir John Bowring, reporting to the British government on the industrial arts in Germany, laid stress on the high level of education, and particularly of technical education, in the principal German states, and foretold Germany's future leadership in many lines of manufacture.

It is true that it was enlightened government in many of the German states which promoted and subsidized both universal general and vocational education and so laid the foundation for future industrial progress, before other countries had realized the necessity of educating their peoples. In the second quarter of the nineteenth century, when England still relied primarily upon apprenticeship or actual factory experience, young Germans were being trained not only in craft skills, but in design, modeling, elementary science, drawing, mathematics, languages, and geography. This investment in human capital yielded a rich return, as it has done in every country where an effort has been made to develop the capacities and skills of the whole population. It is the true secret of the rapid industrialization of countries as diverse as Germany, the United States, Japan, and the U.S.S.R. And it provides the only method by which countries which have hitherto lagged behind in the technical processes of production —including Britain in the twentieth century, as well as China and India—may hope to draw abreast of the industrial leaders.

The second argument to be made is that reliance upon state aid and protection to industry has in the past proved a dangerous experiment. The danger arises because the power of the state is apt to become an end in itself, rather than an instrument for the expression of the common will and for the promotion of individual welfare. In Germany glorification of the state eventually led to the Hitlerian tyranny.

In the early years of the nineteenth century the petty kingdoms which had survived from the feudal age were a serious obstacle to national unity in Germany. As a matter of record, it may be noted in passing that the greatest revival of the arts in modern Germany came in the period before unification. Bach and Beethoven were born in small dynastic states. It was these states that led the way in general and vocational education. But there was great emotional appeal in the idea of a nation-state, combining all those who felt the ties of a common culture derived from language, kinship, or historical tradition. National unity and self-determination were felt to constitute the first condition of political liberty. The humiliations imposed upon the German people by Napoleon had provoked a strong patriotic reaction which took the form of a movement for national unification. In Germany more than in any other country the idea of the nation-state became the symbol of unity and power. It is always fatally easy to confuse an idea with the machinery created for its expression. In particular it is easy to confuse the idea of a national community with the machinery of state, and to erect the latter into a personified incarnation of the common will, existing independently, as the highest expression of human values.

German writers in the early nineteenth century contributed more than their share to this confusion. The philosopher, G. W. F. Hegel, who became the semi-official mouthpiece of the Prussian government, wrote of the state as if it had a life of its own, transcending that of its citizens. Those who fought for national unity were led to idealize the nation-state as "the ultimate unit in human organization and, accordingly, the ultimate unit in human allegiance." [22] The state which Hegel rationalized in this way was a Germany united under Prussian leadership. Friedrich List accepted the Hegelian state philosophy, and contributed to it a comprehensive and effective economic program.[23]

[22] Cf. Harold J. Laski, *A Grammar of Politics,* London, 1925, p. 222. Cf. also Ivor Brown, *English Political Theory,* London, 1920, p. 144.

[23] Cf. Edward M. Earle, *op. cit.,* Ch. 6, "Adam Smith, Alexander Hamilton, Friedrich List: The Economic Foundations of Military Power." For a more critical appraisal of Hamilton, cf. Frank A. Fetter in Leverett S. Lyon and Victor Abramson, *Government and Economic Life,* Washington, D.C., 1940, Vol. II, pp. 536–42. Cf. also Gide and Rist, *op. cit.,* Bk. II, Ch. IV, for a sympathetic account of List's philosophy, stressing "his love of individual liberty," and "the importance which he attaches to moral, political and intellectual liberty as elements of productive efficiency." M. Rist argues that the later development of economic warfare differs fundamentally from List's ideas; but it must be recognized that there are passages, particularly in the latter part of *The National System of Political Economy* which specifically make suggestions for an aggressive commercial policy to combat Britain's "insular supremacy" and the doctrine of free trade

List was born in Württemberg in 1789 and rose rapidly in the civil service of that kingdom. In 1816 he was appointed also to a chair of public administration (Staatspraxis) in the University of Tübingen. Soon thereafter he became president of an association formed to work for the abolition of the customs tariffs by which trade between the German states was then impeded. Thus in his middle twenties, he was a leader in the movement for a German customs union. Because of these activities, the King of Württemberg soon dismissed him from his official positions and when he was elected to the Diet, vetoed his election. In 1822 after a period mainly occupied in traveling through Germany agitating for the customs union he was again elected to the Diet. This time, not only was his election vetoed, he was also sentenced to imprisonment with hard labor. He escaped but, being unable to get permission to settle in other German states, went to Paris where he met Lafayette. A few months later he went back again to Württemberg to plead his case, was thrown into prison but released after some months, only on condition of leaving Württemberg and renouncing his citizenship. He was not allowed to settle either in Germany or in Paris. In 1825 he came to the United States.

While in the United States he took an active part in the protectionist agitation, being sponsored and honored by the Pennsylvania Association for the Promotion of Manufacturing Industry. Like Carey, he was an ardent admirer of Alexander Hamilton though his ideas had been formed before he left Germany. He made money by conducting a successful German language newspaper, and by discovery of a new and important coal field in Pennsylvania. Though he became an American citizen and went back to Germany in 1832 as a United States consul, his main interest was always in German politics. As early as 1828 while still in America, he began to write essays advocating the construction of a national system of railroads in Germany. It was while he was United States consul at Leipzig that he successfully urged on Saxony the first steps toward realization of this railroad system. He left Leipzig and his consulate in 1837 but remained in Germany and devoted his energies thenceforward mainly to urging upon German authorities more positive policies to counter what he

---

which, in a famous phrase, he describes (p. 295) as a "clever device that when anyone has attained the summit of greatness, he kicks away the ladder by which he has climbed up, in order to deprive others of the means of climbing up after him."

termed "the crafty and spiteful commercial policy of England." In 1846 after a period of ill health, he committed suicide.

It is the stress List laid upon nationality as the dominating fact and organizing principle of international economic relations that made him the prophet of later nineteenth-century developments and that put him in sharp opposition to the cosmopolitan attitudes of the laissez-faire, free-trade school.[24] In order to understand the later influence of his theories and their perversion into aggressive economic nationalism, it is necessary to consider briefly the conflict between the philosophy of individual welfare and that of state power.

The political philosophy of the classical economists and of the free-trade school stressed individual enterprise and individual welfare. Emphasis has been laid in a preceding chapter upon the evil consequences which flowed from their neglect of the important fact that individuals exist only as members of a community. A great part of List's argument is directed to this fact. His plea for protection to manufactures (but not to agriculture) was based on his belief that manufacturing was necessary for the industrial education of a nation. He did not dispute that, given the distribution of skills and resources among the nations at any moment, free trade would maximize wealth. But he was interested in building up the productive powers of the German people. To him the wealth of the moment was less important than the prospects of economic development—the power of producing wealth. He saw clearly that productive power depended largely upon good government, upon developed educational facilities, impartial law, and equal justice.

List's program was many-sided. He had advocated the abolition of internal frontiers and customs barriers among the German states, which had been achieved in the Customs Union (Zollverein) of 1834. Even more important in many ways was his systematic and successful campaign for the construction of railroads.[25] The network of German

[24] Cf. Friedrich List, *The National System of Political Economy,* translated by Sampson S. Lloyd, new edition with introduction by J. Shield Nicholson, London, 1922, p. xliii: "I would indicate, as the distinguishing characteristic of my system, NATIONALITY. On the nature of *nationality,* as the intermediate interest between those of *individualism* and of *entire humanity,* my whole structure is based." (Capitals and italics as in the author's original preface.)

[25] Cf. the citation from Treitscke, *Deutsche Geschichte,* IV, 581–82, in J. H. Clapham, *The Economic Development of France and Germany, 1815–1914,* Cambridge, 1921, p. 150: "It was the railways which first dragged the nation from its economic stagnation;

communications was planned as an instrument of unification and an aid to industrial development, but also specifically for troop movements in frontier zones. This proved effective in the wars by which Bismarck consolidated Prussian leadership and created the Reich, and contributed a good deal to the humiliation of France in 1870.[26]

List's emphasis on the nation-state as a basic natural phenomenon led him almost insensibly to the concept of the state as an end in itself and the major end of policy, rather than as an instrument for the promotion of individual welfare. The inevitable consequence was that he contemplated both the unification and the expansion of the German state. He came to regard economic policies directed to the strengthening of state power, as a necessary stage in the development of a nation-state. Bismarck, and later the Nazis, could find in List's writings authority for practically all of their policies. List held that a large population and an extensive territory of varied natural resources were essential to a developed nation-state, both for intellectual activity and for material development and political power. Therefore he proposed to incorporate Denmark, Belgium, Holland, and Switzerland within a unified Germany, partly on grounds of race and language, partly because Germany needed access to the sea and colonial possessions, and partly to secure easily defensible frontiers.

He also foreshadowed the German drive to the Balkans and its economic penetration of Turkey. He advocated the acquisition by a united Germany of overseas colonies in Australia and New Zealand. An enterprising shipping policy and a vigorous German consular and diplomatic system were equally important in his projects for a greater Germany, and he did not shrink from the conclusion that execution of these projects would entail war with Britain. He looked forward to the time when the United States would surpass Great Britain in industrial and naval power, and therefore counseled Britain to appease Germany and to seek the friendship of continental Europe as a shield against American power. In his view, Britain "should practise resig-

they ended what the Zollverein had only begun; with such power did they break in upon all the old habits of life, that already in the forties the aspect of Germany was completely changed."

[26] The resistance to railroad development in France is well characterized by the remark of Thiers, cited by Clapham, *op. cit.*, p. 144, regarding a line projected from Paris to St. Germain: "Il faut donner ça à Paris, comme un joujou; mais ça ne transportera jamais un voyageur ni un colis." This was in 1835, two years after List had published his pamphlet outlining a system of national railroads for Germany.

nation betimes," and "by timely renunciations gain the friendship of European Continental powers." [27]

Much of the invective that List used against British policies sprang from his resentment of Palmerston's attempts to thwart the negotiations that led in 1834 to the formation of the Zollverein. Scattered throughout List's writings, and particularly in the historical chapters of the *National System of Political Economy* (1841), there are statements which are a curious compound of admiration, resentment, and envy of British achievements. List's account of the Hanseatic League is a condemnation of the exclusive and selfish jealousies of the German cities in contrast with what List regarded as the enlightened nationalism that had made Britain a strong and united nation. For him the all-important aspect of history was the timely intervention of the state to direct economic activity toward the strengthening of its own power. His view is aptly stated in his attack on those who stressed enterprise rather than regulation as the source of British strength.

"The theorists," he maintained, "have since contended that England has attained to wealth and power not by means of, but in spite of, her commercial policy. As well might they argue that trees have grown to vigour and fruitfulness, not by means of, but *in spite of,* the props and fences with which they had been supported when they were first planted." [28] He became the prophet of those who laid stress on the props and fences of state support for industrial development, rather than on enterprise. But the history of Germany after 1870 has provided a tragic commentary on the confusion between state power and community development. In the last quarter of the nineteenth century, the rise of German industry was phenomenal. Its foundations had been securely laid in the educational and social system. After 1870 it owed much, as indeed it had earlier, to state encouragement and direction. But in the end this connection with state power caused its ruin.

It is important, therefore, to re-emphasize the fact that it was scientific education rather than protection or cartel organization that enabled Germany to develop so rapidly and to pioneer the new applications of science to industry. A curious reflection of the hold which the idea of the state gained over the German mind can be found in most German historians' extended accounts of various forms of state regu-

[27] Friedrich List, *op. cit.,* p. 340.
[28] *Ibid.,* p. 33.

lation and assistance, to which an altogether exaggerated importance is attached. The technical skill of the German industrial scientists, and hardly less important, of the German operatives, tends to be mentioned briefly if at all. Moreover, when these human skills are dealt with, the role played by the state is strongly emphasized.

It was one of the glories of Germany in the early and middle decades of the nineteenth century that her various state governments provided both general and technical education for the masses of the people, earlier and more adequately than did the governments of other countries. Many observers have remarked upon the close connection between German industry and German science: the laboratory facilities provided by industrial plants for pure science; the encouragement and elaboration of scientific work in the universities, especially on the applied side; the immense technical literature and abundant opportunities provided to keep industrial technicians constantly in touch with new discoveries. It is true that German education was devoted more to applied than to pure science, or more accurately, that the attitude toward science was more practical and less philosophic than it was in Britain and France. German education was devoted also to the development of technical skills rather than to democratic training for citizenship.[29] It produced an intellectual proletariat of highly trained workmen, and a numerous body of salesmen who could speak foreign languages, of chemical engineers, of electricians, and of applied research technicians. These technicians were kept always in close touch with the new discoveries of science. These were the men who, with their ability to grind and polish optical glass, to produce new chemical dyes, and to devise new instruments and new uses for them, placed Germany in the forefront of the new chemical, electrical, and mechanical industries. It was salesmen, equipped with technical skills as well as languages and detailed knowledge of their foreign customers, who extended Germany's trade so widely and so rapidly.

29 The historical school of German economists rejected the universalism of the British and French school, but their effort tended to be spent in diffuse and detailed studies (cf. Gide and Rist, *op. cit.*, Bk. IV, Ch. I). Cf. also W. F. Bruck, *Social and Economic History of Germany from William II to Hitler, 1888–1938: A Comparative Study*, London, 1938, p. 3: "It was the fate of this school that it followed the blind alleys of detailed research. But it is recognized, especially in Germany, that this school contributed much to the empirical research which led to the creation of economic sociology." Alfred Marshall, however, believed that "it would be difficult to overrate the value of the work which they and their fellow-workers in other countries have done in tracing and explaining the history of economic habits and institutions. It is one of the great achievements of our age . . ." (*Principles of Economics*, App. B and C).

By the end of the nineteenth century the pressure of German competition was felt in every market. The export effort was massive and integrated. Diplomatic and consular officials, bankers, technicians and salesmen, teachers and research workers, supplemented and supported what became a concerted national drive for markets. But without the technical skills that drive could not have been as successful as it was. The co-ordinating governmental support—so effective when contrasted with the individualistic and secretive competition particularly of British firms before 1914—in the end provoked retaliation from many countries in the form of subsidized competition and of increased tariff protection. The alliance between industry and the state was purchased at a high price.

In the early years of the twentieth century, the German state was dominated by the Prussian agrarians who ruled largely by exerting their power through non-parliamentary channels such as the dynasty, the army, the bureaucracy, and the educational system. It was their dominance which rendered so fateful the confusion between the nation and the state. It is true that this confusion was by no means a German monopoly. The marriage of militarism and protectionism which became such a formidable challenge in Germany, found in the policies of other countries, and still more in the utterances and actions of power groups in those countries, justification for representing its own designs as the struggle of a poor nation against the selfish and exclusive attitude of richer peoples. Economic nationalism proved the most formidable of all the bodies of dissent from the classical economic doctrines. Ultimately it wrecked the world trading system of which those doctrines were a rationalization.

CHAPTER X

THE NETWORK OF WORLD TRADE

THE COMMERCIAL REVOLUTION

THE PURPOSE of this chapter is to describe the nineteenth-century and early twentieth-century trading system, to analyze the strength and weakness of the international pricing of major commodities and the linking of national price structures, and to reveal the conditions which made it possible for the highly organized but free commodity markets to function as long and as well as they did. There was a pattern in multilateral trade. It was not consciously organized. Its details are only now being revealed by painstaking research. Like an organic growth it functioned successfully even though its mechanisms were not fully understood.

In 1942 the Economic Intelligence Service of the League of Nations published an illuminating study of world trade. This work, which was based upon a statistical survey of world trade from 1928 to 1938 comprised much more than a well-arranged collection of statistics. The figures themselves were collated from national sources of varying accuracy, using methods that differ a good deal. It was a laborious task to adjust them so that they might be broadly comparable, reduce them to a common monetary unit, and rearrange them into significant economic groupings. The title of this chapter has been copied from that of the League of Nations publication.

This significant study by Folke Hilgerdt could have been written only by an international civil servant who had spent long years mastering the intricacies of the movements of world trade, until the secrets of their relationships had become clear to him. The relationships laid bare by his analysis reveal in his words "the essential unity of world trade, a unity which is due to the complexity of the trade of each separate area." Such an analysis, based not upon hypothetical assumptions but upon the actual facts, lays a solid foundation for a theory of international trade adequate to explain modern problems.

The trading areas of the world are finally grouped into six broad categories. These are arranged in an order which clearly reveals the currents of trade and the processes by which payments used to be balanced before the second World War. The symmetry of this arrangement is such that it can be represented in a neat circular diagram which is not just a theoretical design, but a summation of the actually recorded values of world trade. The tropical countries exported more to the United States than they imported from it; the United States sent more to the British Dominions and non-tropical Latin America than it received from those areas; they in turn exported more to continental Europe; continental Europe exported more to Britain, and the circle was closed by Britain exporting more to the tropics than it imported from them.

This was the main arterial system of the world's commerce, as revealed by the trade statistics of 1928. The expansion and world-wide development of that system, multilateral in its balancing of payments, was the crowning economic achievement of the nineteenth century. It was damaged by the war of 1914–18. But the world trade that was restored between the wars fell into the same pattern—which is indeed the pattern dictated by the distribution of population, skills, resources, and therefore of wants that resulted from nineteenth-century trading developments. When restored between the wars, this world trading system did not function with full efficiency. It was broken by the depression of 1929–33 and its destruction was completed by the ensuing period of economic nationalism which culminated in the second World War. The monetary mechanism by which it had functioned before 1914 was the international gold standard. An attempt was made to restore this monetary mechanism after the first World War ended, but trade moved stiffly and the mechanism did not function well. It broke down, probably for the last time, in 1931 when Britain abandoned both its free-trade policy and gold parity for its currency.

The network of world trade was not as simply, as fully, or as smoothly organized as the preceding paragraphs might seem to suggest. Nor was it created suddenly. Many intricate circles of payments subsidiary to the main arterial system are revealed by the League study. One of the characteristic features of world trade before 1914 was the way in which payments were cleared, currencies were maintained at stable parities, and prices were kept in equilibrium—all without international agreements, government intervention, or even formal marketing arrangements. An immense variety of goods and services was exchanged between near and distant markets. In the great financial centers transactions were made daily that called for payments in most of the world's currencies. These payments might be for goods actually traded, or to finance investments, or they might be merely speculative—designed to make profit by offsetting transactions in different markets. Not only commodities but securities and currencies were the subjects of such speculation, and this had the effect of equalizing prices in space and time.

The whole trading process was regulated by incessant price fluctuations around shifting equilibria in intersecting and interdependent markets. From time to time there were great waves of fluctuation which seemed to carry the average level of prices from crest to crest, or from trough to trough in a cyclical pattern. There are those, indeed, who regard instability as the outstanding characteristic of the whole process. In their view, it reeled from crisis to crisis rather than moved from one point of equilibrium to another.

Yet, as long as trade was relatively free and the international gold standard was accepted, markets were cleared, goods were moved in increasing volume, payments were settled, and prices, though very sensitive, moved within narrower limits than we have become used to in recent years. One can understand why those economists and banking specialists who lived through the vast proliferation of these activities in the latter part of the nineteenth century wrote almost with awe of the way in which competition worked to bring order out of the seeming chaos of innumerable individual transactions. The principle of competition was regarded as the regulator of the world's economic activity and economic theory was elaborated upon the assumption of such competition.[1]

[1] Cf. J. R. Hicks, *Value and Capital,* Oxford, 1939, p. 84: "It is, I believe, only possible to save something from this wreck—and it must be remembered that the threat-

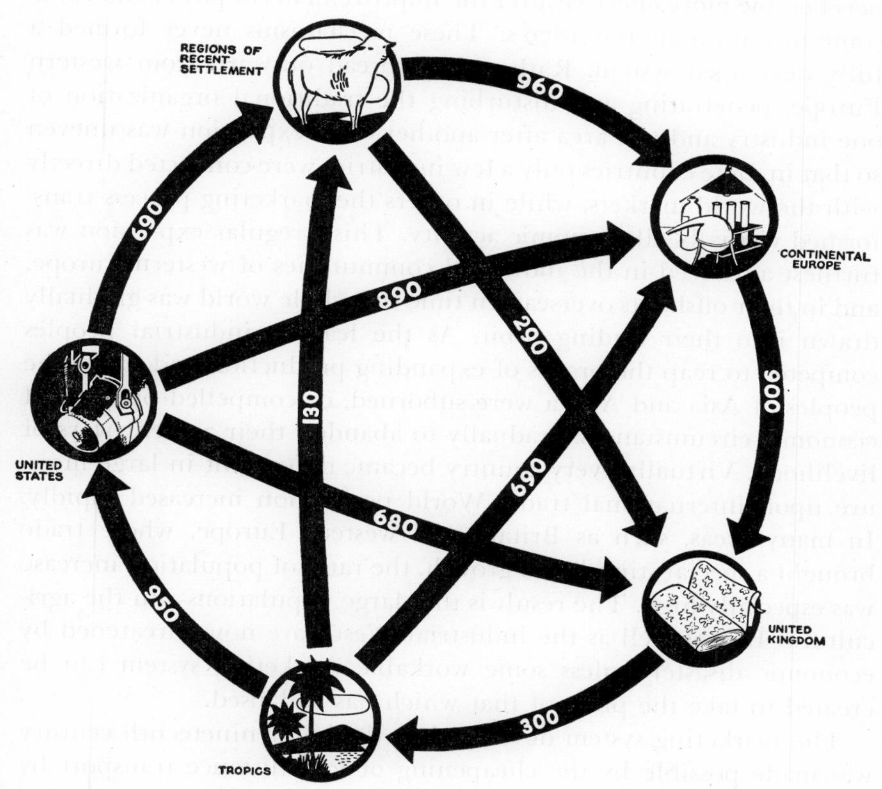

THE CIRCUIT OF PAYMENTS, 1928

Read clockwise, this diagram shows the main streams in the multilateral trading system. The arrows indicate the flow. The figures are dollar amounts of the trade balances (net).

The exports of each region exceed the imports with the next region. Thus in 1928 the United States enjoyed export surpluses to every region except the tropical raw-material producing countries.

The diagram is adapted from the similar one in the League of Nations, *The Network of World Trade,* Geneva, 1942.

The competitive mechanisms of the world markets for staple products became more effective after the improvements of postal and cable communication in the 1870's. These mechanisms never formed a fully developed system. Rather they spread outward from western Europe, penetrating and disturbing the traditional organization of one industry and one area after another. The expansion was uneven so that in some countries only a few industries were connected directly with the world markets, while in others the marketing process transformed virtually all economic activity. This irregular expansion was furthest advanced in the industrial communities of western Europe, and in their offshoots overseas. In time the whole world was gradually drawn into their trading orbit. As the leading industrial peoples competed to reap the profits of expanding production and trade, the peoples of Asia and Africa were suborned, or compelled by force of economic circumstances, gradually to abandon their ancient ways of livelihood. Virtually every country became dependent in large measure upon international trade. World population increased rapidly. In many areas, such as Britain and western Europe, where trade brought a special stimulus to growth, the ratio of population increase was especially high. The result is that large populations—in the agricultural East as well as the industrial West—are now threatened by economic disaster unless some workable marketing system can be created to take the place of that which has collapsed.

The marketing system developed in the latter nineteenth century was made possible by the cheapening of long-distance transport by sea and by land, by the invention of rapid means of communication between widely separated areas, and by practically universal acceptance of the principles of monetary policy necessary for the operation of the international gold standard. Its development was accompanied by a great expansion of international investment which brought new areas into effective production, and by the development—primarily in London—of elaborate money markets by which trade was financed and payments were cleared. These operations will be described in subsequent chapters dealing with the capital and foreign exchange markets. Here we are mainly concerned with the commodity markets which so greatly increased the availability of foodstuffs and raw ma-

ened wreckage is the greater part of economic theory—if we can assume that the markets confronting most of the firms with which we shall be dealing do not differ very greatly from perfect competitive markets."

terials, particularly to the industrial populations of the Western world.

It is necessary first to emphasize the magnitude of the trading expansion and of the changes in marketing methods brought about by improved transport and communication. There had been earlier periods of trade expansion, but never on this absolute scale.[2] Even after the discovery in the sixteenth century of the New World and of sea routes to Asia, trade, though much increased, was still on a small scale. The first stages of the Industrial Revolution brought further increase in the early nineteenth century, but as long as Britain maintained a protective system and was confronted with high protective tariffs in most other Western countries, this increased trade was in large measure channeled from Britain to Asia and to the British colonies. The really great increase in British exports came after her adoption of free trade in 1846. Their average annual value in 1870–74 was estimated as being four and a half times as great as in 1840–44, and more than fifteen times as great as in 1770. Imports rose even more after 1846, and continued to rise slowly through the twenty years of falling prices from 1873 to 1895. Exports were checked in this period of falling prices; but progress was resumed with rising prices after 1895. By 1913 British exports were ten times what they had been in 1840 and more than thirty times greater than in 1770.

This rapid expansion of British trade in the decades following free trade went hand in hand with an impressive increase in industrial production. These were the years in which railroads and steamships, gasworks and drainage systems, were coming into use in all countries which could afford them. In the five years 1870–74, the British annual output of pig iron was 6.4 million tons, as compared with Germany's 1.8 million tons and the United States' production of 2.2 million tons.[3] Some elements of the industrial leadership thus established were maintained till 1914, in face of the growing industrial strength of Germany and the United States. Shipping, which was closely allied with Britain's free-trade markets, gave her a great advantage. Right up to the first World War her ships carried more than half of the sea-

[2] Cf. Edward Gibbon, *The Decline and Fall of the Roman Empire* (Modern Library ed.), New York, 1932, pp. 49–50, for a description of the way in which "the most remote countries of the ancient world were ransacked to supply the pomp and delicacy of Rome."

[3] United States production did not overtake the British till 1890, and the German production did not overtake it till after 1900. Cf. L. C. A. Knowles, *Industrial and Commercial Revolutions in Great Britain during the Nineteenth Century*, London, 1921, p. 192: "As the builder of railways and steamships, the provider of engineering tools, rails and locomotives England was unrivalled during the years 1850–1873."

borne trade of the world, while in the twenty-five years preceding that war she built two-thirds of the new ships that were launched. In the textile industries also she retained a large measure of leadership.

But by the beginning of the twentieth century, it was clear that Britain's great rivals, Germany and the United States, had surpassed her, not only in the basic heavy industries associated with iron and steel, but in the new industries which were dependent upon the application of scientific skills—the chemical, electrical, and machine industries. This was also true in those industries where new methods of mass production cheapened costs. By that time however, the great commodity markets with their associated shipping, financial, insurance, and monetary services were taking a predominant place in Britain's contribution to world trade.

In the last quarter of the nineteenth century Britain was ceasing to be the workshop of the world, but was emerging as the organizing and regulating center of world trade, finance, and investment. Her exports continued to grow, though not as fast as those of Germany and the United States. There was room for all in the expansion of world trade, and the living levels of the British people continued to rise. London, the center of commerce and finance, outstripped Manchester, the center of industrial production. Moreover, the agricultural prosperity that had seemed to justify the confident predictions of the free traders proved to be temporary. Cobden in 1845 had argued that the wheatgrowers of Britain even under free trade would have substantial protection from the cost of transporting corn; but he did not foresee that transport costs would fall rapidly. McCulloch in 1842 had made an even more confident prediction that not an ounce of meat would ever enter Britain from South America.

In the fifties and sixties there had been nothing to indicate that these predictions of continued agricultural prosperity in Britain would not be justified. There were wars both in Europe and in the United States. Though British imports of food and raw materials increased, population and purchasing power increased faster. The California gold discoveries gave Britain, then the only country using gold as a single standard, an export advantage equivalent to a slight depreciation of her exchange rate. Trade was booming and agriculture remained prosperous.

By the early seventies, however, railroads in various parts of the world had begun effectively to open up inland continental areas of rich fertility. The first transcontinental line in the United States, for example, was completed in 1869. A gathering flood of cheap grain began to pour into the markets of industrialized western Europe, not only from the Middle Western plains of the United States, but from Australia, India, Canada, Argentina, Russia, and the Danube valley. The price of wheat fell as a result of the abundant production from the virgin prairies of the Middle West. Competition among the railroads and the lowering of ocean freights as steam replaced sail were also important elements in a long-continued fall of wheat prices. In certain years prices fell to the point where American wheat was sold not only in London, but at Hamburg and even at Odessa. The result was a sharp increase of protective duties on wheat in practically all the countries of continental Europe, and especially in Germany. Only Denmark (which transformed its agriculture and utilized the cheap imported grain to build an efficient pastoral industry), Belgium, the Netherlands, Switzerland, and other relatively small markets such as Norway, continued along with Britain to accept the cheapened wheat. There ensued a prolonged agricultural depression in Britain, which ended in virtual abandonment of the attempt to compete with imported grain.

What happened first with grain was to be many times repeated with other commodities. In the late seventies meat began to be carried from the United States in refrigerated ships. It was not long before Canada, Argentina, Australia, and New Zealand were sending increasing quantities of chilled and frozen meat to Britain. Butter and cheese followed meat, and means were found in the twentieth century to transport apples and citrus fruits.

Not only foodstuffs but agricultural raw materials were transported in growing volume from the newly opened inland areas—wool from Australia, New Zealand, South Africa, and Argentina; jute from India; kapok from the East Indies; vegetable oils from east Africa and many other tropical regions. The opening of the tropics to cultivation for industrial markets was almost as important as the opening up of the last remaining temperate plains. Vegetable oils, lumber, dyestuffs, spices, and cane sugar were important items in this trade. When rubber came into demand for automobiles a great new industry was developed. Moreover the ever-growing consumption of minerals led to a search for new sources of supply. Gold was found in South Africa, Western Australia, and Alaska; nickel in Canada; copper in Rhodesia and the Belgian Congo. Petroleum was sought all over the world.

Thus, not only did trade become much larger in volume during this period, but its character completely changed. This may be seen by comparing the list of raw materials and foodstuffs which the League study singled out for special treatment, with any description of sixteenth-, seventeenth-, eighteenth-, or even early nineteenth-century trade. As late as the seventeenth century the spice trade was the source of trading fortunes, and in the eighteenth century, sugar and tobacco became important. In the nineteenth century, particularly after Britain adopted free trade in 1846, trade came to consist largely of cheap bulky articles such as iron ore, coal, foodstuffs, and fibers. Agricultural and mineral raw materials were brought in large quantities to the manufacturing centers located near the coal fields, and in return a great variety of manufactured goods, including bulky items such as steel rails and locomotives, was exported from the industrial centers. In Hilgerdt's League of Nations study, spices do not appear in the list of twenty-six raw materials and foodstuffs whose export value in 1938 was more than $100 million. There are three categories of petroleum products, whose combined value far exceeds that of any other product. Cotton comes next, and then wheat and wheat flour, coal, meat, wool, tobacco, sugar, copper, butter, rubber, coffee, maize, tea, rice, iron ore, silk, tin, and citrus fruit. All of these commodities, it will be noted, are articles of general consumption. There has therefore been a transformation not only of the geographical distribution of world trade, but also of its commodity composition.

An important point must be added here. Trade in raw materials and foodstuffs constitutes a large segment of world trade, and the trade between advanced and less advanced industrial countries is an even larger segment of the total. But the trade in manufactured goods before 1931 constituted a great and growing proportion of world trade. The variety of these manufactures is so great that no single item bulks as large as the raw materials and foodstuffs listed above, but in the aggregate the share of world trade provided by manufactured goods steadily increased until 1931.[4]

[4] Cf. Albert O. Hirschman, *National Power and the Structure of Foreign Trade*, Berkeley, 1945, pp. 117–51. An elaborate German study by the Kiel Institut für Weltwirtschaft und Seeverkehr—"Die Aussenhandelsentwicklung und das Problem der Deutschen Aus-

These facts confirm what economists have long argued, that free trade leads to a rapidly growing interchange between industrialized countries. As they became industrialized, Germany, the United States, and later Japan, became better customers of industrial Britain, while the manufactured goods they produced were of a character that could be sold only in other industrialized countries with high purchasing power. This development clearly depended upon a reasonably free flow of competitive trade. In the period of economic nationalism after 1931, the trend described above was reversed. The percentage of world trade which consisted of the exchange of manufactures against raw materials rose steadily from 24.9 in 1931, to 33.3 in 1937, while the other kinds of trade fell. This reversed trend was a clear indication of the breakdown of international co-operation, as the great powers followed autarkic policies dictated by war preparations. The future of international trade does not lie in the creation of new empires, but in the elimination of trade barriers and, above all, in the industrial development of what have hitherto been backward economic areas.

An important qualification of this summary description of the expansion of world trade from 1850 to 1931 should be taken into account. A large part of that expansion came from the economic development of new countries in the temperate zone which were settled mostly by European immigrants. The first exports of those countries were naturally agricultural, but it was a new kind of agriculture that was developed. The highly developed rural industries of the United States, Canada, Australia, New Zealand, and Argentina have little in common with the peasant agriculture of Europe, and still less with that of Asia. In their use of mechanical power and scientific research, their reliance on credit mechanisms, and their specialized production for what is often a distant market, they are much more akin in economic structure to the manufacturing industries. The efficient, large-scale organization which reduces their production costs also gives them high yields and therefore living levels which are the highest in the world.

To class the trade in canned and dried fruits from California, in lard from the Middle West, butter from New Zealand, or wool from

fuhrpolitik," published in the *Weltwirtschaftliches Archiv,* Vol. XXXVI (July 1932)—classified the trading countries of the world into agricultural and industrial countries and showed that well over half (58.8 per cent) of the world's trade in 1913 was carried on between these groups, whereas trade between the agricultural countries accounted for only 10.7 per cent, and trade between the industrial countries for only 29.2 per cent of the total.

Australia, with that in tung oil from China, or olives from Spain, is to ignore economic categories. This new kind of agricultural production and trade ought to be classed as an aspect of industrial specialization —in that segment of world trade which is most promising for future development, the exchange of specialized manufactures against other manufactures. A clear distinction should therefore be drawn on the one hand between the trade and investment that enabled the United States, the British Dominions and parts of Latin America, as well as Germany and Japan, to develop their productivity and contribute their share to world trade, and on the other hand the colonial type of trade and investment practiced wherever inefficient governments and undeveloped economic systems made it impossible for weaker peoples to protect themselves. Americans and Australians, for example, borrowed and traded on an equal bargaining basis with the European creditor countries.

The development of the tropics and the scramble for new spheres of influence in Asia and Africa was a different story. The new imperialism with which the nineteenth century ended was a struggle to develop the old European empires in south and southeast Asia, and to carve out new empires largely in Africa. Other aspects of this imperialism were the extension of European economic influence in the Middle East, in China, and in the less developed Latin-American countries with rich mineral resources. In all these regions trade was of the colonial type. The most important exports were minerals, and in the twentieth century, the most important mineral was oil. Rubber was of increasing importance also, particularly in southeast Asia.

Out of the intense struggle from about 1880 to 1914 to secure access to raw materials and markets there came the shipping and naval rivalries and the diplomatic conflicts, which preceded the first World War. There is no denying the gravity of the issues raised by these aspects of world trade. As the factories of the industrial countries devoured greater quantities of raw materials, the widening search for new and cheaper sources of supply led not only to the political subjection (or what is substantially the same, the economic exploitation) of weaker peoples, but also to conflict among the great powers. For the political and military weakness of these colonial and semi-colonial areas invited their subjugation, and this led to quarrels among the great powers in dividing up the spoils.

In fact, the stronger countries and those which formed part of a strong empire produced more of the needed raw materials. The problem of regulating access to raw materials is not primarily economic but political. It is a problem of strengthening the ability of the peoples whose resources are coveted to develop these resources and sell them, or of devising international trusteeships capable of developing the resources to supply the world market without destroying the welfare of the peoples unable to use them. The late nineteenth-century scramble to grab and exploit natural resources brushed aside the weaker peoples and contributed to the tensions that later flared into war. It was not only politically dangerous, it was uneconomic. The largest stream of commodities that was fed into world trade came not from the regions of colonial exploitation, but from areas where settled government and efficient economic production made an abundant supply of foodstuffs and raw materials both cheap to the consumers and profitable to the producers.

This revolution in the world's commerce which was caused in the latter half of the nineteenth century by improvements in transport and communication ranks in economic importance with the Industrial Revolution. Indeed, it was the outgrowth and fulfillment of the Industrial Revolution. The steam locomotive and the steamship began to work revolutionary changes in the nature and geographical distribution of world trade from the moment of their introduction in the early years of the nineteenth century. But their full effects were not felt until the latter part of the century.

At this time also the improvements in communication, which were the result both of speedier and more regular transport and of improvements in telegraphs, telephones, and ocean cable services, widened the scope and area of markets. The first Atlantic submarine cable was opened for traffic in 1866. Networks of telegraph and telephone systems began to spread in all the industrial countries and to send out their tentacles to distant areas. A cable was laid to Pernambuco, for example, in 1874 to link Brazilian coffee production with the world markets. The Suez Canal was opened for traffic in 1869, the same year as that which linked the coasts of the United States by the first transcontinental railroad. There had already been an expansion and cheapening of postal services in most countries; but it was not till 1874 that the Universal Postal Union was founded and international correspondence became cheap and certain.

As a result, in the fifty years preceding the first World War, the everyday life of the ordinary man changed more than in many preceding centuries. Coal gas was barely established when it began to be supplanted by electric light and power. The sprawling towns became dependent on networks of transport, communication, drainage, water supply, and power. Their inhabitants enjoyed not only more abundant, varied, and regular supplies of goods and services to meet their primary needs—food, clothing, and shelter—but a growing variety of entertainment. Goods and services that had formerly been luxuries of the rich—white bread, meat, sugar, tropical cereals and fruits, tea, cocoa and coffee, leather shoes, new textile fabrics and patterns, as well as stoves, baths, and a variety of manufactures—became cheap, conventional necessities. The taxes on knowledge had been removed. Cheap newspapers and books were printed on paper produced from remote forests. Cable services made the news of the world available at every breakfast table.

THE EVOLUTION OF WORLD MARKETS

It is important to realize the interdependence of all the varied aspects of the commercial revolution in the latter half of the nineteenth century. Here stress will be laid upon three of them—the revolution in the world's food supplies, the widening search for minerals to feed into the insatiable furnaces of modern industry, and the increasing importance of manufactured goods and of the skills needed to produce, repair, and service them. This increasing mechanical development opened broad new avenues of employment. At the same time it accelerated the displacement and degradation of already existing skills. It gathered workers into factories and therefore into towns. It undercut the market for handmade products—the products of peasant agriculture, as well as hand-woven cloths and beaten metalwares. Local unemployment was created, and there was a degradation of craft skills. Selection of materials, planning and design, as well as the machine processes themselves, called for new craftsmanship, but the first effect of industrialization was to destroy the economic basis of formerly prosperous handicrafts.

Railroads and steamships, carrying bulk cargoes of raw materials to steam-powered factories and delivering their products to wholesale centers for world-wide distribution, also went far to destroy local marketing systems. The impersonal wholesale market came to be the regulating center and clearinghouse of economic activity. More and more these wholesale markets tended to become international. The prices, even of commodities produced and consumed locally, were geared to the incessant but narrow fluctuations of the world markets for goods entering into international trade. The very nature of these markets had changed. They could hardly be said any more to have a local habitation and a name. So pervasive was their influence that it ought almost to be described as an attitude of mind rather than an organized marketing system.

No previous period had produced the abundance of food which made possible both a large population increase and rapidly rising levels of living. The increase in numbers was very great and very rapid. No longer confined to a few industrial countries in western Europe, it set in motion new cycles of population increase wherever trading initiative penetrated. In the Western countries, where the increase of population was greatest during the nineteenth century, and at its peak in the latter half of that century, levels of living rose so fast that ultimately the peoples achieved conscious control of their own tendency to increase. Elsewhere the increase, though at first less rapid, was more ominous. Between the censuses of 1872 and 1911 there was, for example, a 50 per cent increase in the population of India. Some of this apparent increase doubtless reflected improved census efficiency. But no one who has studied the question seems to deny the fact of a heavy increase, with little or no rise in living levels.

In such countries as the United States and Canada, the British Dominions and the more developed regions of Latin America, where productivity kept ahead of increasing numbers, it was possible to liberate men from the soil. In medieval Europe (or in the Far East today) it had required four out of every five workers to produce a scanty supply of food. An efficient new country such as New Zealand could produce not only abundant supplies for itself, but a large export for industrialized and urbanized Europe, by the labor of one worker out of six. These New World countries were able to free a large proportion of their own people to produce manufactured goods and services, while, at the same time, they fed a large proportion of the western European peoples engaged in industry, commerce, entertainment, education, and the arts.

The commercial revolution which brought this abundant and efficient production from rich areas of virgin soil also provided a variety of foods that made possible more adequate diets. The science of nutrition is of very modern growth. The more varied diets made possible by the cheapening of staple foods gave not only more calories, but more of the elements necessary to growth and health. How much of the obvious vigor and enterprise of the better-fed peoples is the result simply of improved diet is not measurable. That workers display increased vigor and enterprise when they have access to an adequate and varied diet has been abundantly proved by the experience of many minority groups in the United States.[5]

Moreover the new marketing methods provided a more regular and dependable, as well as a cheaper and more abundant, supply of the staple foods. Professor Lilian Knowles has listed the arrival of wheat cargoes in London in 1905.[6] In January cargoes arrived from the Pacific Coast of America, in February and March from Argentina, in April from Australia, in May, June, and July from India. By July and August the winter wheat from the United States was coming in, and in September the spring wheat arrived, to be reinforced in October by Russian shipments. In November the Canadian wheat arrived. This spread of shipments over the year diminished the risk of seasonal shortages and made it possible to offset climatic failures in one region or hemisphere. It reduced the necessity for storing large stocks. In 1905, Britain had less than two and a half weeks' supply of wheat in the ports, plus three weeks' supply in the hands of millers, and another week's supply in the hands of bakers—little more than six weeks in all. But as long as trade was reasonably free, there was always wheat from some region of the world en route for England.

There were significant and large shifts in the production and trade not only of the staple foodstuffs (wheat, meat, butter, cheese, sugar, corn), but of the tropical foods, fruits, and beverages (rice, sago, tapioca, vegetable oils, coffee, tea and cocoa), of the forest products including rubber, and of the fibers (wool, cotton, silk, flax, and the hemps). It was not until 1854 that the first tea auctions were held in India, and the great production on plantations in that country, in Ceylon, in the Netherlands East Indies, and in Japan came in the last

[5] Cf. the bitter comparison of British and Dominion troops in the first World War in C. E. Montague, *Disenchantment,* London, 1922, where the men from the new countries are described as "startlingly taller, stronger, handsomer, prouder, firmer in nerve, better schooled, more boldly interested in life, quicker to take means to an end, to parry and counter any new blow of circumstance."

[6] Lilian A. Knowles, *Industrial and Commercial Revolutions in England during the Ninteenth Century,* London, 1921, pp. 201–2.

half of the nineteenth century. It was not till late in the nineteenth century that Brazil and the Central American republics, aided by their proximity to the expanding market of the United States, came to dominate the world market for coffee. Cocoa, the bean of a Central American plant, was not extensively cultivated in tropical Africa until in 1903 a railroad opened up the country, but the Gold Coast now produces about half the world crop.

Instances of shifts in crops, of the development of new varieties of plants, and of new uses for them, could be multiplied almost indefinitely. The wine industry of France was saved from the Phylloxera in the late eighties by grafting the European vine upon stocks of the native American vines which are resistant to this root disease. The tobacco, corn, and many other industries in the United States have been immensely strengthened by the breeding of new plants, often from primitive stocks gathered by botanists from different habitats. The heavy-yielding and disease-resistant sugar cane of modern commerce, the rubber plantations of southeast Asia, the cinchona of Java, the camphor of Formosa, are other examples of the scientific development of natural products.

The multiplicity of such examples serves to remind us that one of the most important attributes of the expansion of food and raw material production induced by world trade was the way in which it developed new and more efficient areas and methods of production. There were heavy losses incurred in this experimental development, losses which at times increased the severity of recurrent crises. The Baring crisis of the nineties, for example, was largely the result of overinvestment in Argentina after the potentialities of frozen meat had been demonstrated. But there were great gains also. It would not now be possible for an impoverished Europe to appeal for food from the New World if the productivity of Argentina and of the British Dominions, as well as of the United States, had not been built up by nineteenth-century trade and investment. The poverty in Asia is worse than that in Europe and less likely to be relieved, but its huge populations could not have been fed even in peacetime if increased productivity had not been available to support their growing numbers.

The whole process by which western Europe became the controlling center of world trade was interconnected. The crowding of the people into industrial towns made them dependent upon imported foods and raw materials. These were produced largely in countries that had formerly been vacant or little used. As these areas developed they absorbed capital goods as well as manufactured goods for immediate consumption. The new scientific processes of production, whether of food and raw materials, or of manufactures, competed strongly with the handicrafts and with peasant agriculture all over the world. Attempts to protect these traditional methods of production seem bound in the end to fail, since the competition that threatens them arises from the economic forces that are responsible for industrial progress.

As industrial progress accelerated in the last quarter of the nineteenth century, it devoured increasing quantities of raw materials. Ivar Högbom has calculated for the period 1880–1913 the rates at which the basic minerals were produced. The regularity and rapidity of the increase are best revealed in his calculation of the periods during which production doubled. For petroleum the doubling period was 8.6 years, for copper 13.1 years, for pig iron 15.6 years, for phosphates about 16.5 years, for coal and zinc 16.7 years, for lead 19.7 years, and for tin 20.1 years. The world production of aluminum can be calculated only for 1921–29, but a doubling period of about five years was indicated. This geometric increase did not begin till the third quarter of the nineteenth century and was interrupted by the war of 1914–18. It was resumed at an even more rapid rate from 1922–29; but was checked again by the depression and subsequently by the war of 1939–45. Such a geometric increase means that, in each period, the amount produced equals the whole earlier world production. Every 8.6 years, as much petroleum was produced as in all preceding periods.

Fortunately for mankind, the basic minerals and fossil fuels are abundant and widely distributed. The nineteenth century was the age of coal. Britain gained a great advantage from abundant coal as long as it was, on the whole, cheaper to bring raw materials to coal for their manufacture than to erect new power units close to the raw materials. The country's dependence on coal was the subject of much discussion as industrialization got into its stride. The exhaustion of available coal did not materialize as quickly as was feared, but the pace at which production increased alarmed many students, as the even more rapid acceleration in the rate of petroleum output now alarms many in the United States.

The tendency to exhaustion of the more readily available supplies of less common metals and fuels is easily demonstrable. The center of gravity of the world's production moved away from Europe and

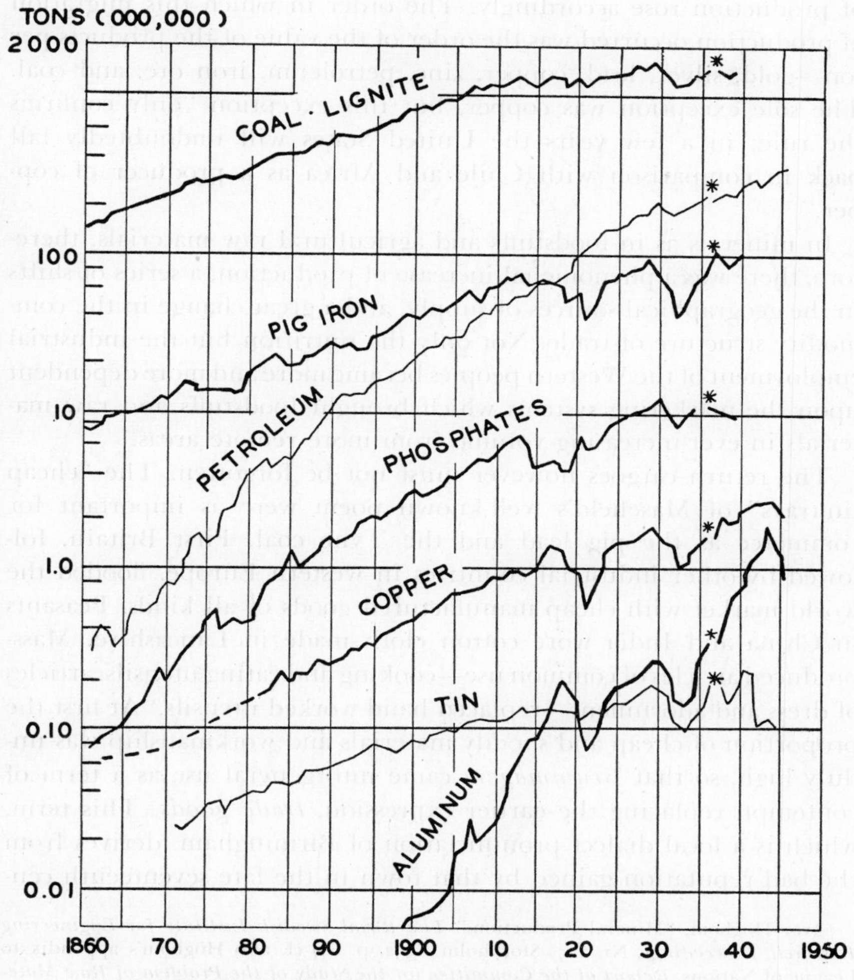

WORLD CONSUMPTION OF MINERALS, 1860–1945

Revised and brought up-to-date on the basis of the original diagram by Ivar Högbom, reproduced in League of Nations, *Report of the Committee for the Study of the Problem of Raw Materials,* Geneva, 1937, p. 39. Data for years subsequent to 1936—U.S. Department of the Interior, *Minerals Yearbook,* Washington, 1939, 1942, 1947.

the United States as the older supplies were exhausted, and the costs of production rose accordingly. The order in which this migration of production occurred was the order of the value of the products per ton—gold, silver, lead, copper, zinc, petroleum, iron ore, and coal. The sole exception was copper, but this exception "only confirms the rule; in a few years the United States will undoubtedly fall back in comparison with Chile and Africa as a producer of copper." [7]

In minerals as in foodstuffs and agricultural raw materials, therefore, there was a phenomenal increase of production, a series of shifts in the geographical sources of supply, and a great change in the commodity structure of trade. Not only the nutrition but the industrial employment of the Western peoples became more and more dependent upon the marketing systems which brought foodstuffs and raw materials in ever-increasing volume from more remote areas.

The return cargoes however must not be forgotten. The "cheap tin-trays" of Masefield's well-known poem were as important for commerce as the pig lead and the Tyne coal. First Britain, followed by other industrial countries in western Europe, flooded the world market with cheap manufactured goods of all kinds. Peasants in China and India wore cotton cloth made in Lancashire. Mass-produced articles of common use—cooking and eating utensils, articles of dress and adornment—replaced hand-worked utensils.[8] At first the proportion of cheap and shoddy materials and workmanship was unduly high, so that *Brummagem* came into general use as a term of contempt, replacing the earlier expression, *trade goods.* This term, which is a local dialect pronunciation of Birmingham, derives from the bad reputation gained by that town in the late seventeenth cen-

[7] Ivar Högbom, "Mineral Production," *The Royal Swedish Institute for Engineering Research, Proceedings,* Nr. 117, Stockholm, 1932, p. 64; cf. also Högbom's appendix to League of Nations, *Report of the Committee for the Study of the Problem of Raw Materials,* Geneva, 1937. Högbom's prediction depends for its fulfillment upon a modification of United States' excise duties giving access to the cheaper copper deposits in the Belgian Congo, Rhodesia, and Chile.

[8] Cf. Lewis Mumford, *Technics and Civilization,* New York, 1934, p. 100: "Marble was imitated in plaster, gold in gilt, handwork in moulded ornament, glass was used instead of precious stones. The reproduction for mass consumption of substitutes, as in the jewellery of Birmingham, took the place of the slow original creation of genuine handicraft; the systematic cheapening through mass production and inferior materials for the sake of achieving an effect beyond one's means, occurred in ornament long before it was applied to objects of use."

tury because of a local gang of forgers who circulated groats made from base metals instead of silver.

But the machine industries gradually developed new standards of workmanship and utility, and even new forms of beauty and design. Almost illimitable horizons of increasing prosperity and rising levels of living for the masses of the people were opened by the expansion of trade in manufactured goods. Vastly greater numbers of people were not only better fed, better housed and better clothed, but had an increasing variety of manufactured commodities available to lighten their daily toil in the home as well as the field and the factory, to widen their range of movement, to lengthen the day with artificial light, and to occupy their hours of leisure and recreation.

It has already been shown that this trade in manufactured goods was the segment of world trade that was growing most rapidly. With new forms of power—electricity, the gasoline engine, and, in the future, the power generated by nuclear fission—and with modern chemistry constantly increasing its ability to break down the structure of matter and recombine its molecules, new frontiers of industrial progress are now being opened. There seems no reason to doubt that, given freedom from war and war preparations, the trend toward interdependence and the exchange of specialized products will be resumed perhaps by different methods, but certainly in greater volume.

THE MARKETING PROCESS

The word *market* originally meant a place where traders met for the transaction of business, usually at a regular time. In the last half of the nineteenth century, as the movement of goods increased in volume and widely separated centers of production and consumption became involved, the marketing process was reduced to its essence, the making of a price by higgling between buyers and sellers. This essential function became specialized. Whole series of middlemen interposed themselves between the original producers and the ultimate consumers. They were able to do so because their expert dealings in place and time utility widened the range and lowered the cost of making connections between producers and consumers. By buying whenever and wherever commodities were cheap and selling them later or elsewhere to meet the needs of consumers they evened out and lowered the prices of commodities on the average. As long as competition was reasonably active they derived profit by providing specialized services which lowered costs. The values in which these specialists dealt were intangible. They did not need actual goods for their operations since they dealt in price differentials between regions and over periods of time.

The marketing process reduced in this way to its primary essence of dealings in price differentials became diffused throughout the whole producing world. There were meeting places—the cotton, grain, or metal exchanges and similar institutions. These, however, tended to become clearinghouses for transactions and a means of settling accounts rather than actual trading centers. The market for the staple commodities was far wider than the dealings on these exchanges. It came indeed to comprehend practically the whole extent of production, exchange, and consumption. For example, the farmer on the plains of Minnesota would be influenced to enlarge or reduce his wheat acreage by the price of wheat in the chief wholesale consuming center, usually London. This price would be influenced not only by actual supplies coming in from competing sources and by the demand in the consuming areas, but by anticipated changes in both demand and supply. A threatened drought in India might cause a rise in the price for wheat futures, and this rise would in turn decide farmers in the United States, Canada, Australia, and Argentina to plant more wheat.

There were real transfers of actual goods on a great and increasing scale. The city of London, the heart of this marketing system, illustrated the whole process. Within the square mile of the city surrounding the money market were centered the different sorts of banks and specialized financial institutions. And almost within a stone's throw of this financial district were concentrated the shipping and insurance companies, the importing houses, the various commodity exchanges, and all the apparatus of international trade. A steady and expanding stream of goods of all kinds flowed through the docks and warehouses, but the traders dealt in titles to goods. Many of their purchases and sales were offset or canceled by the payment of price differentials. The specialized brokers, as a rule, never saw the goods in title to which they dealt. Their paper transactions might add up in the aggregate to vastly greater quantities of those goods than actually existed. Many of the transactions of the commodity exchanges were purely speculative and not intended to be made good by actual deliveries—aiming only at making a profit by anticipating price changes—but behind them the tides of trade flowed strongly.[9]

Certain conditions were necessary before such markets could develop. A large volume of real transactions was the foundation, and this was facilitated by free trade—within the great area of the United States, or at free ports such as London, Liverpool, and Amsterdam. Around the leading centers there developed specialized services of transport, credit facilities, and storage. Merchants devoted themselves to specialized functions and had access not only to cheap short-term credit, but to large demands for their services. In some of the most highly developed markets there was a differentiation not only by function—primarily between brokers and jobbers—but by region and by type of commodity.

Only those commodities which met certain tests were suitable for such highly developed markets. The Stock Exchange was their prototype since it was concerned with perfectly homogeneous and interchangeable titles, which were readily transportable, durable, and identifiable. Such commodities as approximated to these qualities—the commodities which could be standardized and sold by description, whose quality could be tested by sampling and exchanged in bulk lots that were interchangeable and of which there was a large and relatively stable supply and a wide demand—such goods could be marketed by these methods. At first wheat and other grains, cotton, some of the fibers, and many of the minerals were dealt with, but later, in the last quarter of the nineteenth century, there was a surprisingly large extension of this marketing process to include a wide range of products.

It should be emphasized that the marketing process developed. It was not organized. Its essence was spontaneity. There was no central

9 The word *speculation* is derived from *speculum*—a watchtower. Constructive speculation performs a useful function by shouldering the risks of price fluctuations and leveling them. Producers and industrial consumers can plan their operations in full assurance of a firm price. Thus a cotton spinner who buys future deliveries from a broker can quote a price for the yarn he will spin some months hence. The weaver can make a price for future deliveries of cloth based upon the quoted price of yarn. The speculator is a specialist who makes his profit from his ability to estimate the risks of price fluctuations. If he gambles recklessly he will not survive; the amateur gambles without information. In an active, competitive market the chances of monopolistic operations are kept to a minimum. Speculation becomes antisocial and increases price fluctuations when markets are thin so that monopolies can be rigged at the expense of amateurs who are tempted to take risks they cannot properly estimate.

regulating authority. There were no rules, except the law of contract as enforced by national courts and such technical procedures as the merchants themselves derived for their convenience out of their practical experience. In particular there was no legislation designed to achieve price stability and no governmental machinery set up to regulate the markets. The whole process was free and therefore unstable. It relied upon competitive forces to maintain equilibrium within and between markets. The great commodity markets were merely the highest development and focusing points of a widely diffused marketing process which permeated the economic activity of the whole trading world. The full extent of this process cannot be explained until some account has been given of the capital and foreign exchange markets, but that part of it which concerns commodity prices in local and world markets is described in the following pages.

Every improvement in transport and communication has extended the area and increased the number of commodities that are potentially marketable.[10] Every cheapening of freight rates tends to alter trading relations and to influence the location of industry in new areas. Within a free-trade area economic forces are free to operate. In the last half of the nineteenth century the lowering of freight rates brought about by the use of steamships and steam locomotives, together with the opening up of a great free-trade market in Britain, made possible a great expansion in the variety of goods traded. Across the North Atlantic the shipping lanes were broad and thick with ships. This was the Main Street of world commerce, and every shipping lane led into it. The bulk of the cargoes carried were the great staple commodities that are normally thought of as internationally traded goods.

In addition to these bulk cargoes of staple goods in the latter part of the nineteenth century a great variety of products entered world trade. Bulbs, cut flowers, and early vegetables went from Holland to London; onions were hawked from house to house in England by their growers from Brittany; the street markets of Geneva were supplied

[10] The air age promises new developments. We have become used to airplanes carrying mail, passengers, and valuable express freight—gold, samples, small machine parts, and orchids—but the army transport services which carried bulky commodities and machines all over the world have led to a crop of new experiments. Spring flowers, strawberries, early vegetables, and fresh lobsters are among the goods which have been carried by air within the free-trade area of the United States. There seems little doubt that similar expansion of air transport, as freight rates are lowered, will develop internationally within the limits set by trade barriers.

with vegetables and fruit from Italy, France, and even Spain. Much trade which originated in local collections of small quantities of odd commodities was ultimately gathered up into lots suitable for international marketing. Yugoslav immigrants in New Zealand speared for fossil kauri gum which found its way to Germany; schooners collected copra and coir from scattered Pacific islands; insecticides sold to American farmers were extracted from pyrethrum flowers sent over in bales from Japan, or from the roots of Indonesian jungle plants; rat poison necessary to control the wastage of stored grain was derived from red squills, the sea onion gathered on the north African coast; Mongolian wool found its way on camel-back to Tientsin for shipment. The bristles rubbed off by wild boars in eastern European forests made the best shaving brushes; tung oil from southern China painted American houses; mother-of-pearl from northwestern Australia was made into buttons for London costers. Many of these curious trades have disappeared or diminished since trade has been subjected to an increasing degree of regulation. They were highly specialized, often risky, and generally too small in value to enter into the barter agreements negotiated by civil servants. Moreover they were essentially a part of multilateral, rather than bilateral, trade.

Wherever transport charges were low for any reason, even bulky articles might be transported over great distances. The extensive British export trade in coal was built up largely by tramp steamers carrying it at low outward freights in place of ballast. In the same way sailing ships going out to Australia and New Zealand for cargoes of wheat or wool often carried Marseilles tiles. Before 1914, Belgium had a large export of steel rails, and Wales of slate.[11]

It has been usual for economists seeking to expound "the simple arithmetic of international economics," to classify goods into those which entered into international trade and those which did not. This

[11] Cf. Viscount Gwynedd, *Dame Margaret*, George Allen & Unwin, Ltd., London, 1947, p. 53: "From Portmadoc in those days [the late nineteenth century] fleets of sailing ships [chiefly schooners of from 100 to 200 tons] made regular voyages to far-distant ports. As a boy I have counted as many as thirty of these little windjammers making their way in and out of the bay at one time. Outward bound they all carried slates, quarried from the near-by mountains, and world-famous for their lasting qualities. These they would take to such distant ports as Hamburg, Stettin, Bremen. There, having discharged the cargo, they would take on coal for delivery in an Italian port. In Leghorn, say, the new cargo would invariably be salt, with which they would cross the Atlantic to Newfoundland. Arrived there, and having discharged the salt, they would fill up with dried codfish and set a course for home."

admittedly "arbitrary simplification" for purposes of exposition distinguished between three categories of goods and services. The first category consisted primarily of staple products which were homogeneous in character and eminently suited for international trade. Wheat is the type of commodity which used to have a common world price. The second category consisted of commodities, mainly manufactured goods embodying much labor such as locomotives, so specialized in character that there could not be a common world price, since the goods could not be compared or interchanged. An increasing volume of such goods entered world trade by contract and along definite channels, rather than through the competitive world markets. The third category consisted of goods and services, such as houses and factories, railroad and public utility services, which were immovable and essentially local in character.

These categories were distinguished in order to facilitate discussion of the manner in which the market prices of goods and services were maintained in a competitive equilibrium. In practice, however, it was always difficult to classify actual commodities into these theoretical categories. Shifts in demand or supply, in import or export duties, or in transport costs were constantly bringing some marginal commodities within the range of profitable trade or shutting others out. What was true of transport was true also of technology in general. A new chemical process brought the Witwatersrand gold fields into profitable production. Another went far to destroy the market for Chilean nitrates.

Unless the explanation of international prices is to run in static terms, it is clear that the categories of goods which enter or do not enter into international trade cannot be regarded as fixed. If relative prices warranted, even the local immovable goods and services classified in the third category might become invisible exports or imports in the sense of being enjoyed by tourists. Moreover there were different market levels in relation to the consumer. Usually the discussion of international prices was confined to the prices of goods traded in wholesale markets. But the great bulk of the goods were ultimately retailed to consumers. The maintenance of equilibrium between wholesale and retail prices was an important aspect of the market process which was ignored by the analysis in terms only of goods traded at wholesale.

It is more realistic therefore, and just as enlightening, to approach these questions of international prices by picturing world markets as shading into local markets and inextricably connected with them. All goods are potentially tradable. Every commodity and service has a potential import and export point. Even a Scottish castle or an Italian church can be transferred bodily to the United States if the owner is willing to sell and someone is willing to pay the price. Australians transported the Yorkshire cottage where Captain Cook was born, and set it up stone by stone in a Melbourne park. In the case of commodities such as wheat, the import and export points were close together in the nineteenth century, so that the whole trading world became a single market. It required only a slight change of price in one area to cause such goods to move in trade. There were other commodities and services such as bricks or the printing of advertising material where for economic or other reasons the import and export points were farther apart. Some commodities, such for example as art treasures, could not be bought. Others would not repay the cost of transportation and sale.

The merit of approaching international price questions in this way is the emphasis it gives to the fact that, as world markets developed in the late nineteenth century, the whole range of price structures, local, national and international, at wholesale and at retail, for movable and immovable objects and services, formed part of one marketing process. There was a tendency toward both vertical (national) and horizontal (international) equilibrium of price levels. In other words, within each country the price structure, including retail prices and the prices of labor, of credit, and of natural resources, was kept in equilibrium by the same forces that maintained the general or average levels of prices, as well as the wholesale prices of traded goods, in equilibrium between the countries. If there was a substantial movement in the prices of internationally traded articles, the level of wages (or the amount of employment), the price of land, and the rate of interest would be affected, and vice versa.

These tendencies to equilibrium in the price levels may be illustrated by the way in which the prices not only of internationally traded goods, but of immovable goods and services also, adjusted themselves in Shanghai to fluctuations in the exchange rate. After 1870 when the major trading countries began to demonetize silver, the price of silver dropped steadily year after year. China was on a silver bullion standard so that the prices of commodities as measured by silver rose as the price of silver fell. The price of bar silver in London fell from 60.56 pence per ounce in 1870 to 25.31 pence in 1914. The index number of Chinese wholesale prices (1867–71 = 100) rose from 97.9 to 226.2 as compared with a decline from 100 to 87 in London in the same years. During the first World War the price of silver rose again practically to the levels of 1870, but war demands kept the prices of commodities from falling. When the price of silver began to fall again in 1920, commodity prices resumed their upward trend. By 1931 the price of an ounce of silver had fallen to 14.46 pence and the price index number had risen to 339.8. The adjustment was not immediate. Nor was it evenly distributed over different commodities and services, or over different regions of China. But interior markets as well as the port cities felt the influence of the falling price of silver. In Shanghai the effect of the fall was immediately reflected in the exchange rate and was quickly felt also in the prices of commodities. It spread to the retail as well as the wholesale markets and therefore affected the cost of living and wage rates. Moreover it brought about a reappraisal of rents, leases, and land values.[12]

Before cable connections were established in the early seventies, the profits to be made from acting upon early knowledge of the most recent silver quotations in London had prompted commercial firms to construct specially designed vessels to connect with the mail steamers at Hong Kong or Singapore. Designed for speed and carrying no cargo, these vessels then brought the latest news some hours earlier than the liners, so that those who had access to the earlier news gained a market advantage. When cabled advices became available, the Shanghai market became even more sensitive. This was a case of the

[12] *Report of the Hon. Mr. Justice Feetham, C.M.G., to the Shanghai Municipal Council,* Shanghai, 1931, Vol. I, pp. 338–39. "It is, I think, a generally accepted fact that, throughout the world, more particularly in seaports and populous centres, land has what may be called an international value. If the sterling/tael exchange declined to 6*d.*, and owners of land and buildings did not adjust their ideas of prices at which they were willing to sell, it would mean that Banks, Insurance Companies or other concerns from overseas would come to Shanghai and buy important properties for an amount in gold ridiculously small, having regard to the cost of the buildings, and the value of the land upon which they stand for international use by reason of its location. Were it not for the fact that the cost of living, wages, rents, etc., do not immediately, although they do almost precisely ultimately, adjust themselves to fluctuations in exchange—as in the case of China to fluctuations in the price of silver as a commodity—, values of property would react almost immediately to such fluctuations . . . We are witnessing in Shanghai now a gradual adaptation of prices, wages and rents to the lowered purchasing value of silver."

For the statistical verification of this argument, cf. Report of the Committee for the Study of Silver Values and Commodity Prices, *Silver and Prices in China,* Shanghai, 1935.

prices of local immovable goods—the category described above as not entering into international trade—being adjusted to the international equilibrium. The prices included those of the factors of production—land, labor, and capital. Retail prices and the cost of living were affected as well as commodity prices at wholesale.

The same kind of effect on local prices, however, was produced by other influences affecting the Chinese balance of payments. A fall in overseas prices for Chinese exports or a slackened demand for them, or a rise in the rates of interest in the main financial centers or in the prices of Chinese imports, would have an adverse effect on the exchange rate and through it on local conditions. In normal times these changes were not sudden or great, so that it was hard to trace their effects on land values or wages. But when the commodity, silver, depreciated sharply in relation to gold, as it did from 1870 and again from 1920 on, the whole scale of local prices was adjusted very clearly to the new exchange rate.

Every community in the world found its prices affected to the extent that its economy was geared to world markets. No doubt areas could be cited where so little trade was done with the outside world that prices were determined almost entirely by local conditions. But this was not true of any of the great trading countries. It was certainly not true, for example, of the United States. The prices of wheat and later of lard at Chicago were directly connected with world markets and exercised a considerable influence on the purchasing power of the Midwestern farmer.

In every community there were some prices that were conventional or sluggish—the price of newspapers, of public utility services such as streetcar fares, and the charges for gas, water, and electricity. Too much stress should not be laid upon the sluggishness of these conventional prices. A five-cent cigar could vary in quality. A two-cent newspaper could take up increased costs by changing its advertising rates. Though local conditions might be predominant in fixing many prices and some of these prices might appear to be independent of international influences, closer investigation reveals that over a sufficiently long period the whole economic structure was sensitive to the pressures exerted upon the price level by international trading developments.

The mere fact that news was readily transmitted all over the trading world was a powerful influence in keeping all the various sorts of prices in line. In the case of internationally traded goods, or of those which were potentially tradable, the mere quotation of prices out of line with those in other countries, was enough to initiate speculative operations. If the price differentials (allowing for transport and other costs) remained, goods would move to the most profitable markets. A fall in London wheat prices caused by a bumper crop in Argentina would depress prices and check exports from the United States. This would tend to pile up surpluses in the United States and to reduce the income of American farmers. These developments in turn would affect the real-estate and labor markets. As long as trade moved with relative freedom and markets remained price-sensitive, the prices of commodities and services were part of an international marketing process.

It followed that efforts to stabilize domestic prices were inherently impossible without restrictions on international trade. One of the most serious criticisms now made of the world trading system as it functioned in the latter nineteenth century is directed precisely at this fact. The criticism is usually directed at the international gold standard, which has been charged with transmitting the fluctuations of the business cycle from country to country. It can be more properly directed at the whole marketing process by which employment, wages, profits, land values, and the entire range of economic activity in every country were affected by fluctuations in world markets transmitted through the balance of payments.

It is often said that the characteristic feature of this whole development was instability. This is true in the sense that a widening range of prices was sensitized and made subject to incessant minor fluctuations. It is also true that local communities became part of this world marketing process, in its incessant minor changes, and in the larger rhythmical swings of the trade cycle as well. The statistical facts prove conclusively that prices and employment were more stable under this competitive system than they have been since national governments began to make such strenuous efforts to stabilize them.

Before 1914 there was, for a great and growing number of products, one world market. The price of wheat in Winnipeg, Minneapolis, Chicago, Buenos Aires, London, or Hamburg, allowing for transport and tariff differentials, could not diverge by more than a very small fraction. Since 1931, when production and trade have been regulated in order to stabilize national markets, prices have diverged very widely. In 1937 the price of wheat in France was three times the price of wheat in London, and the price of sugar in Hamburg was six times that of sugar in Amsterdam. The breaking up of the world market has been accompanied by a wide spread between prices in the separate national markets. Besides greater price fluctuations, an inevitable result has been an uneconomic use of the factors of production leaving shortages in some areas and overproduction in other areas. The nineteenth-century marketing process spread the risks of crop failures or business setbacks in different areas. As long as trade was active and speculation evened out prices between the main trading centers, the effects of a crop failure in any one area were diffused over the whole trading world.

It is natural to find, therefore, that the price variations registered in the competitive world markets of the latter nineteenth century were smaller, both in space and in time, though more frequent than those to which we have since become accustomed. This may be demonstrated very simply by comparing the fluctuations in prices as disclosed by the price of such a commodity as wheat in the United States before and after 1914.

THE PRICE OF PROGRESS

The nineteenth century had a robust belief in progress and in competition as its mainspring. There was much in the contemporary scene to justify that belief. The gains of economic development and expanding trade were real and substantial, especially to the western European communities which pioneered them. They were still more substantial to the people of the United States and to the emigrants from western Europe who peopled newly opened colonies of settlement. The extraordinary optimism so evident in the United States, where the frontier of opportunity was a living reality, sprang from a belief that enterprise was rewarded with wealth. In no other country was this belief so widely shared by all classes of the population and to all appearances so well justified. Not only were there dazzling examples of men who from modest beginnings had made great fortunes, there were hundreds of thousands who had escaped from the narrow bounds of a socially stratified society to find independence and modest fortune in a new land of free competition. There were millions more who hoped that the fortunes of their children would be greatly bettered. It is this tradition of opportunity open to enterprise which gives strength and depth to the still dominant American belief in competition.

The constructive achievements of the nineteenth century worked out in a system of relatively free enterprise ought not to be minimized. The development of these new communities of high productivity and high living standards in the United States, the British Dominions, and temperate Latin America has no parallel, at least on this scale, in history. Moreover the growth of industry in western Europe went far to break the bonds imposed by an aristocratic society, and to liberate the masses of the working population from political, economic, and social servitude. Stress has been laid earlier in this chapter upon the impressive rise in the living levels of populations that multiplied rapidly. The Malthusian bogey seemed to have been an illusion: no longer was there a pressing sense of urgency in regard to food. Numbers were increasing more rapidly than ever before in history, but these greater numbers were better fed, better clothed and better housed. The abundant supplies of food and raw materials that poured in by way of trade liberated a great and growing proportion of the population from the primary task of securing the elementary necessities of life. There was more leisure. More people were free to devote their energies to amusement, recreation, philanthropy, education, science and the arts.

The emancipation of women from economic and social, even more than political, subordination strengthened the tendency toward humanitarian attitudes. The demand for education and self-expression spread downward through the economic levels of society. Educational opportunities and political democracy became possible not merely for privileged groups but for the whole population. Life gradually became less primitive and brutal. In the more advanced countries, the grosser forms of amusement and sport did not survive the humanitarian influences that were a natural consequence of release from primitive economic pressures any more than did the exploitation of child labor or the slave trade. It should never be forgotten that social reform depends largely upon economic efficiency.

Yet a price was paid for this progress, and in some respects the progress itself was an illusion. The immense increase in productivity was the result of a combination of improved productive efficiency and of the prodigal exploitation of newly tapped natural resources. Progress was real in so far as the increased productivity was the result of greater knowledge, enhanced vigor, and improved skills. It was illusory in so far as it represented the squandering of irreplaceable natural wealth.

In some areas, such as the heavily populated parts of Asia, the benefits of increased productivity went, not into an improvement of human quality and vigor, but almost wholly into greater numbers of an already impoverished population.

The marketing process places a premium upon present or short-run values and takes little thought for the future. It is always dangerous to entrust the final decision in matters of social policy to those who stand to gain from an immediate course of action. It is not clear that political leaders are endowed with greater vision than are those responsible for economic enterprise; but uncontrolled competition has often sacrificed the future to the present. It was for this reason that John Muir described laissez faire as a gobble-gobble economy. If it had not been for John Muir and the conservationists who followed in his train, the people of the United States would have lost much more of their national heritage than they have. The national and international economic policies of the future need not sacrifice the real values of initiative and enterprise, but they may avoid some of the worst mistakes of the past, if scientific knowledge and vision are used to construct a framework of regulation and conservation within which enterprise may be utilized.

The instances of short-sighted wastage of natural resources in the nineteenth century are numerous. At the beginning of the century before the settlement of New Zealand, there were vast seal rookeries on the coast and coastal islands. These have long since vanished almost completely. The New England sealers, even more than those from Britain, were responsible for their destruction. They clubbed breeding females, as well as males, in their search for profitable cargoes to trade in China for porcelain and tea. The sandalwood of Hawaii was just as wastefully exhausted. In our own time, it has been necessary to negotiate conservation agreements to prevent the extinction of whales, seals, halibut and sockeye salmon in the north Pacific.

From many points of view the most wanton destruction in the countries of European settlement was that of the forests. Deforestation is an old story in many lands. In the new countries of European settlement it was a sudden and often a devastating process. In the United States, Canada, Australia, and New Zealand much forest was destroyed by cutting and by fire to make arable or pasture land. As a case in point, New Zealand has no longer any appreciable amount of kauri for cabinet-making, or of kahikatea, the odorless wood used for butter-boxes, and has much less lumber than is needed for construction purposes. Every one of the new countries had a similar experience— a brief period when the soil, enriched with the ashes of the forests, yielded remarkably, and then a progressive exhaustion of natural fertility. The development was not one-sided. The forests were not then valuable. The land has been turned into a valuable resource and the balance sheet of land settlement would probably show a large profit, even though some resources were sacrificed needlessly.

Where not only the good land but hilly watersheds were deforested, additional damage ensued in the form of erosion and floods. There are many historical examples—the river valleys of Mesopotamia, Cyprus, Palestine, Spain—where the loss of forests and other natural cover has brought this double disaster. Another notable case is that of northwest China. Here, not only has the topsoil long since been washed away from a great region, rendering it practically a desert, but the no-longer-fertile eroded material continues to be carried down on the periodic floods that have given the Yellow River both its name and its nickname, "China's sorrow."

Many biologists have claimed that the hastening of soil erosion was one of the worst results of the nineteenth-century marketing process. It is argued that widespread erosion has been caused by using agricultural methods suitable to the climate and soil conditions of northwestern Europe in areas where entirely different conditions prevail. It has been estimated that already "nearly a million square miles of new desert have been formed, a far larger area is approaching desert conditions and throughout the New World erosion is taking its relentless toll of soil fertility with ever-increasing speed."[13] Against this damage must be set the increased fertility of large areas of man-made soil. In the new countries of European settlement there is a growing awareness of the problems involved, and some progress has been made in arresting the further deterioration of soils. The difficulties of a thorough conservation program, however, have hardly yet been faced. They involve the reversal of some of the most fundamental principles upon which agricultural production and trade have been organized.

It would be unduly alarmist to treat soil erosion as if it threatened immediate disaster to the more advanced industrial and agricultural

[13] Cf. G. V. Jacks and R. O. Whyte, *The Rape of the Earth: A World Survey of Soil Erosion,* London, 1939.

countries. Scientific knowledge has advanced to the point where some enthusiasts at the opposite extreme have maintained that there is no longer any need for soil. If both of these extreme fantasies are discarded, there remains a substantial problem which is troublesome to the New World countries. Their scientists have at least presented the elements of a solution but political conflicts hamper the necessary steps to fulfill its realization, as the slow progress toward a Missouri Valley Authority demonstrates. In Asia and Africa, where an increasing population has failed to share in the advancement of scientific knowledge, the prospect of a solution is infinitely more remote. Indeed there the depletion of natural resources is rendered much more serious by the fact that new cycles of population increase have been initiated among their peoples.

The greater part of the increased productivity that accompanied the nineteenth-century expansion of world trade went to raise the living levels of the rapidly increasing populations of western Europe and its offshoots overseas. It is true that some relief was given to the pressure of numbers upon limited resources in the areas from which the industrial countries drew their supplies of raw materials and foodstuffs. It was not possible to turn the Gold Coast into the greatest producer of cocoa, to develop copper in the Congo, gold in South Africa, rubber and tin and petroleum in the Dutch East Indies, tea, indigo, jute, and other export commodities in India, without providing employment for a growing number of the inhabitants of those areas. Imperialism had many faults but in most colonial areas the mere fact of settled and honest government and of orderly legal procedures gave greater security to life and property.

In many colonies also, much constructive work of great value was carried through to successful operation. Indian railroads, irrigation schemes, and improved methods of cultivation removed the specter of famine for more than a century, until in the trading disorganization and accelerated population increase of recent years the specter has been revived. In the Netherlands East Indies, and indeed in most colonial areas, Western technicians were responsible for a vast increase in economic production. Colonies and colonial powers varied in the efficiency of their administration. But it would be foolish to pretend that the impact of Western influence was unconstructive in the sphere of economic development. Even in such a case as that of China where direct foreign influence was confined within the limited zones of the treaty ports, Western enterprise did much to initiate new and more efficient methods both of political organization and of economic production.

In Asia and Africa as in the European countries, measures of public health as well as more abundant production have begun to cause death rates to fall. No one can measure exactly how far the new cycles of population increase have gone in most of these countries. Where there have been reasonably efficient censuses, as in India and the Dutch East Indies, there is evidence that the rate of increase, though usually at a slower rate than in nineteenth-century Europe, has been substantial and cumulative.[14] The rate of increase in these countries is now accelerating, while in the Western industrial countries the rate of increase is declining. Moreover in the huge populations of Asia even a small rate of growth yields a tremendous increase in absolute numbers. Neither the rate of increase nor the present numbers are known in China. But a rate of increase no greater than that which prevailed for decades in many European countries could add forty or fifty millions a decade to the Chinese population.

The most important charge that can be made against the nineteenth-century trading system is that it did not operate in the colonial areas, as it did in Europe and in the countries of European settlement overseas, to transmit industrial skills to the colonial populations involved. It destroyed the market for traditional handicraft skills, upset the age-old balance of occupations, and destroyed the economic bases of the ancient society. Public works and transport systems, large-scale private enterprise, scientifically controlled plantations, as well as the less obvious but greater innovations of law and public audit certainly increased productivity. Earning power and consumption per capita were greater at the end than at the beginning of the nineteenth century in most colonial countries. But the organizing and governing skills remained in the hands of the Western peoples. The colonial peoples, with few exceptions, had not been encouraged to become competent.

It is significant that where effective adaptation was made by these

[14] For the most recent analysis of population pressures in the Pacific, cf. Warren Thompson, *Population and Peace in the Pacific,* New York, 1946. It is difficult and not very enlightening to compare the statistics for continents; but it is significant that the rate of increase shown for Asia between 1900 and 1939, though still less than that for Europe, is much closer than the rate from 1800 to 1900. If a comparison were made between industrialized western Europe and Asia, the rate of increase would now be greater in the latter.

peoples to the new mechanical methods of production, the initiative came usually from groups among them which had not suffered the first impact of Western civilization. In New Zealand the most powerful Maori tribes had held the best land—the land the settlers wanted. It was the less powerful tribes in the more remote, mountainous country who drew the correct deduction from the fate of their more prosperous neighbors. They resolved not to sell their land and at the same time to send their young people to school to learn the secrets of the white man's way of life. In Burma the rich land of the Delta region has largely passed from native ownership, but the hill peoples to the north, where economic development was slower, have kept their land. Japan's quick release from Western tutelage may be ascribed also to the fact that, by the time her ports were opened to trade, the dangers of tutelage were sufficiently evident elsewhere in Asia to stir her leaders to successful efforts of modernization.

Wherever the local peoples have made a successful adaptation to the modern world, it has been primarily by their own effort. This was easy for the new countries of European settlement overseas. Their peoples brought with them not only the scientific knowledge which is the essential basis of modern economic organization, but confidence in their ability to develop industrial and commercial skills and to adapt them continuously to new scientific discoveries. They had a fundamental understanding of what was happening as trade expanded and were able to profit from the expansion.

The case was quite different with those peoples whose ancient culture lacked modern scientific knowledge and was in any case confined to a small ruling class. Indeed the more developed the cultural background, the more difficult it proved to adapt it to modern needs. It was not too difficult to create a new industrial and social organization to recruit workers for the copper mines in the Congo. In India, on the contrary, where an elaborate and detailed social order had hardened into caste distinctions, the old rulers were displaced by those who, not understanding the subtleties of the traditional system, further crystallized the already great rigidity of political rule and land ownership. The enterprise which penetrated India was commercial. Traders bent on quick profits did not display any great anxiety for the welfare or education of the local people. They made compacts with the local rulers, or displaced them. But they took the minimum of responsibility for government or social welfare until the growing abuses, which culminated in the Mutiny of 1857, forced the British government to shoulder the burden.

Such modern production as was developed in colonial areas was primarily for the world rather than the local market. The growth of the seaports is evidence of this, as is the absence of interior communication networks. Transport in all colonial areas leads to the sea. Moreover, the higher executive posts in industry and government, as well as the technical posts, and the related services—shipping, insurance, banking, commerce—have until very recently been virtually monopolized by Europeans. In all colonial areas, the contribution of the local peoples to industrial development has mainly taken the form of labor. There are exceptions: local moneylenders have thrived upon peasant poverty and there have been notable cases of local business enterprise. By and large, such share of the increased productivity as accrued to the local populations has come mainly to wage laborers. The result naturally has been an increase in numbers rather than a rise in living levels.

The nineteenth-century trading system, organized by European commercial enterprise primarily to meet the industrial needs of the Western world, is probably at an end, but its consequences remain. In Asia not only are there vastly increased numbers threatened now with economic disaster, but a whole new series of conflicts is brewing between the Asiatic peoples themselves. Indian moneylenders in Burma and Chinese traders in Siam, Indo-China, Indonesia and the Philippines, are the object of resentment almost as marked as that directed against Europeans. The solution of colonial problems is difficult enough, but beyond them lie new quarrels and conflicts. These are certain to be exacerbated if the withdrawal or weakening of imperial governments and technical services results, as it is only too likely to do, in further impoverishment of the Asiatic peoples. These peoples are already too numerous for the limited resources and economic organization available to support their present living levels, still less to meet the rising standards they are coming to demand.

On a gigantic scale therefore—a scale indeed too great to be readily grasped—the breakdown of world trade demonstrates the argument already made concerning the negative character of laissez-faire economic policies. It was inevitable, in Asia and Africa as in early nineteenth-century England, that outworn modes of production and antiquated forms of government should be destroyed by the progress of the industrial and commercial revolutions. But failure to initiate the colonial peoples into the skills required in the modern world, and to provide new institutions of social protection has brought and will continue to bring a vast reckoning, not merely for groups or classes but for whole great communities.

CHAPTER XI

INVESTMENT AND ENTERPRISE

INTERNATIONAL CAPITAL MOVEMENTS

THE NEW MACHINE methods of production which characterized the Industrial Revolution were far more efficient than the old handicraft methods. Those who could command the means of securing already accumulated goods to be used in the process of further production became the most powerful agents of economic development. Credit facilities were developed, pledging present assets or future prospects, in order that this new class of enterprising manufacturers might secure capital resources to exploit the new mechanical inventions.

The increased power of those who could command the use of capital is the outstanding characteristic of the nineteenth-century economic system. This is quite properly described as capitalism, if attention is centered upon the location of power to make decisions in regard to the use of economic resources. In the eyes of the classical economists, this development was a benevolent and constructive shift in power from the hands of a conservative landowning aristocracy to those of new and enterprising merchant-manufacturers among whom competition operated to maximize productive efficiency and to keep profits at a minimum. In the eyes of Karl Marx, it represented a consolidation of the property-owning groups who, by their increasing control over the means of production, were able to keep wages at a subsistence level and to appropriate the surplus value in amounts that they were unable to use effectively.

Capital is an elusive concept. The economist uses it in a broader and looser sense than the accountant who is concerned with private property rights as defined and regulated by law. What the economist must be concerned with is the allocation of resources between production for current and future consumption. No attempt is made here to enter into past controversies of definition or into those of capital theory. Since these controversies are rooted in the assumptions and definitions from which analysis starts, any such attempt would involve both an extensive survey of the technical literature and an excursion into political and social philosophy. A modern approach to the question defines capital as "all those goods, existing at a particular time, which can be used in any way so as to satisfy wants during the subsequent period." [1] This definition is adequate for an economic analysis of the questions that arise in connection with the allocation of resources between production for current and for future consumption.

Before considering the questions that arise from the development of an active international capital market, it is advisable to summarize the irregular trends of international investment, particularly in the latter part of the nineteenth century. It was the scale of these transactions rather than their novelty, which made them significant. The rapid growth of international investment in the second half of the century was the flowering of the industrial revolution, the transference to an expanding world market of investment processes that had formerly been confined largely within national boundaries.

During the first half of the nineteenth century the export of capital had been primarily an outflow from Britain. There had been a growing accumulation of wealth in Britain, and this accumulation was greatly increased by the leadership of Britain in the new mechanical methods of production and in the use of steam power. Almost undisputed access to overseas markets further added to the accumulation of wealth in that country. Factory production expanded rapidly and a network of railroads was constructed which greatly facilitated the export trade. In the fifties and sixties, following the British adoption of free trade which enabled other countries to pay for a still greater volume of British exports, there was a spectacular increase in British production, trade, and capital accumulation. This led to the remark-

[1] Cf. J. R. Hicks and A. G. Hart, *The Social Framework of the American Economy*, New York, 1945, p. 99.

able increase of foreign investment which is the subject of this chapter.

It should not be forgotten that the political stability and the security of property rights in Britain stood in striking contrast with the unsettled state of Europe after the Napoleonic Wars. As always in such circumstances there was some migration of liquid capital to London. But what was more important was that cosmopolitan financiers found London the most secure base for their operations. The London capital market became international not only in the scope of its transactions, but also in the enterprise and initiative which directed them, and to an increasing extent in its ability to draw upon unused capital accumulations in many other lands.

In considering these trends of international investment it must be emphasized that statistical data are scanty and estimates are extremely hazardous. This is particularly true for the latter nineteenth century, when trade and investment were a part of the competitive marketing process which was then conducted with a minimum of regulation or even registration. Information as to individual transactions may be compiled from scattered sources so that a sufficiently accurate picture may be obtained of general trends and typical processes of investment. Estimates have been made of the amount of foreign investments for different dates, and these are sometimes divided regionally or by types of industry. Any attempt to calculate the flow of investment from year to year must rely on indirect estimates derived from doubtful statistics of imports and exports, and still more doubtful guesses as to the magnitude of invisible items in the balance of payments of the lending country. It is unwise, therefore, to rely on these estimates as revealing anything more than the broad trends of movement.[2]

Britain became a capital-exporting country after the Napoleonic Wars. From 1815 onward foreign lending, in the form both of public loans and of direct private investment, had been steadily growing. Public loans for European reconstruction and private investment in mining and land development enterprises, mainly in the United States and Latin America, attracted substantial sums made available by the

[2] The results of such calculations by L. H. Jenks, *The Migration of British Capital to 1875* (p. 414) and C. K. Hobson, *The Export of Capital* (p. 197) as to the net movement of British capital and interest payments for the decade 1871–80, the only years in which the calculations overlap, show differences in magnitude but the same general trend. Hobson's was a pioneer study published in 1914, so that it is probable that the calculations published by Jenks in 1927, with the advantage of being able to use later data in supplement of Hobson's, are more nearly accurate. Both, however, reveal the investment boom of the early seventies and its reversal in the crisis of 1874–75.

increasing profits of British industry. In the 1830's this first phase of British foreign investment culminated in a great expansion of loans to American cities and states. The economic depression of 1837–39 made it difficult to keep up interest payments, and despite strenuous efforts made by the lenders to persuade Congress to assume the burden of these city and state debts, they fell into default. Most of them were repudiated in the early forties. The credit of the United States was for a time seriously impaired and the outflow of loans from Britain was temporarily checked. In the forties, railroad construction within Britain itself absorbed practically all available capital. In this decade there was a succession of serious financial crises as a consequence of overexpansion of the credit system.

It was not till the fifties that railroad building on the continent of Europe and gold discoveries in many lands produced a renewed outflow of capital. British contractors like Thomas Brassey and Morton Peto, using permanent staffs of engineers and foremen and often large permanent corps of experienced workmen, spread a network of railroads from Belgium across Europe. By the late fifties and the sixties British capital was moving in increasing volume to transportation and industrial enterprises in the United States, Canada, India, Australia, and Argentina. There was a great stimulus to both trade and investment when in 1869 the sea route to the East was shortened by the opening of the Suez Canal. After 1869, also, the completion of transcontinental railroads in the United States and Canada stimulated investment.

By the fifties the thrifty French had recovered from the effects of revolution and war sufficiently to become active participants in the international capital market. The steady flow of small savings to Paris kept interest rates in that market low, but French industrial development was slow and limited. There was a large fund of credit available in Paris particularly for the fixed-interest loans to governments which guaranteed the stable income demanded by Frenchmen who looked forward to retirement as *rentiers*.[3] It was to reconcile this demand for fixed income with the profitable openings for industrial investment

[3] Cf. Herbert Feis, *Europe: The World's Banker,* Yale University Press, New Haven, Conn., 1930, p. 37: "Out of the small black purse of the French bourgeois, the Russian monarchy could draw the substance for its monumental plans, the Austro-Hungarian Empire equip itself with railroads, banks and factories, the Turkish Sultan spend without accounts, Italy endure the anxieties of the first years of unification, the small Balkan states establish their national existence."

abroad that the Crédit Mobilier had been founded in 1852. It pioneered the practice of investment banking until its collapse in the crisis of 1867. The preference of most French investors for a fixed return on their investments had the result that Paris became a rival to London in the flotation of government loans rather than in the pioneering of industrial development. Nevertheless French enterprise was responsible for the greatest single undertaking of this period—the Suez Canal, which was opened in 1869.

It should be noted that changes in the British laws governing incorporation, and particularly those which made possible the generalizing of limited liability of stockholders, had been made largely as a result of the inconveniences encountered in raising capital for railroad construction in the forties and fifties. By the time that the Companies Act of 1862 codified these changes, the British railroad system had been created. The time was propitious for an enlargement of the capital market. The Stock Exchange by this time was functioning as an important cog in the money market and the joint-stock banks were well begun on the amalgamations that were to center the whole credit system in London. Engineering and metallurgical advances had reached the point where Britain was able to supply railroad equipment, materials for port construction and for public utilities such as gasworks, the bulk of the world's new ships year by year, and in addition a wide variety of industrial machines. Rising price levels after 1851 and the slight exchange advantage resulting from the cheapening of gold relative to silver after the California gold rush in 1849 were helpful. But the great change in the fifties and sixties was that Britain's free trade policy put her foreign customers in the possession of sterling receipts which they used to buy in her markets the capital equipment they needed. The export trade thus stimulated increased the formation of a capital surplus available for investment. In the 1860's what had been a slowly growing capital export mainly to European countries suddenly increased and widened its range.

The early seventies saw the culmination of this expansive era in a great outpouring of investment. It was an inflationary boom fed by the demands for reconstruction and the plethora of purchasing power after the Civil War in the United States and Bismarck's wars in Europe. The public issues on the London market in the five years 1870–74 ran at twice the average levels of 1860–64. Most of the increase was in loans to the United States government and in shares of railroad corporations in the United States. A short crisis in 1874 precipitated a long period of falling prices and recurrent depression which lasted from 1874 to 1896.

It is the judgment of Professor Leland H. Jenks that the era in which Britain was able, from the expanding productivity of her manufacturing industries, both to pay for continuously increasing imports of food and raw materials and to invest new capital abroad, as well as to reinvest the returns from former capital, came to an end about 1875. For a generation thereafter there was little new investment. However, the total of British foreign investments continued to increase till 1914. Jenks estimated their value in 1875 as £1,200 million. Sir George Paish estimated them as being worth more than three times this value (about £3,763 million) in 1913, in addition to about £300 million of industrial capital directly invested. In the two decades preceding the first World War, British investments in Europe declined substantially; but there was a large increase in British investments outside Europe.[4] A substantial part of the investment, which in the decade preceding 1914 made Britain by far the world's largest creditor country, was the result of new ventures.

The major legacy of the third quarter of the century was the elaboration of the mechanisms for international lending in the London capital market. Other financial centers, notably those of western Europe, were also stimulated to activity so that the market became international. London, however, remained the largest and the dominant market, particularly in respect to industrial investment, and above all in respect to the investment which pioneered transport systems and industrial development in new countries and thereby contributed most to the expansion of international trade. Estimates of foreign capital invested in 1913 show that of the British total of £3,763 million, over 46 per cent was within the Empire, 20 per cent in the United States, and 20 per cent in Latin America.

The total of French foreign investments in 1914 was estimated at £1,800 million. Of this total 25 per cent was invested in Russia and 36 per cent in the rest of Europe. The French colonies accounted for approximately 9 per cent, Latin America for 13 per cent, and the United States, Canada and Australia together for little more than 4

[4] Cf. Herbert Feis, *op. cit.*, pp. 19–20. Fragmentary estimates from different sources cited by Feis (pp. 14 and 16) indicate that British foreign investment grew faster than British domestic investment in this period, and that the percentage of national income derived from foreign ownership grew at a still faster rate.

per cent. The German foreign investment in 1914 was smaller—a total of £1,175 million, of which 55 per cent was in Europe (14 per cent in Austria-Hungary), 16 per cent in Latin America, and approximately the same percentage in the United States and Canada.

Germany was a latecomer in the field of international investment. Its internal economic development was rapid and absorbed a large proportion of its available capital. It did not have either the accumulated profits of past production and trade or the great volume of current trade which gave London such advantages as a capital market. Nor did it have a peasantry whose saving habits assured a steady flow of new capital, such as made Paris a center of international lending. German productivity, however, increased rapidly after 1870, and the German banking system was designed to stimulate and promote industrial investment which could later be capitalized and sold to the investing public when its commercial success was assured. There was a co-ordination between German trading and banking enterprise and between both of these activities and government policy, which did not exist in any other country. German economic penetration was closely linked with diplomacy—in Austria-Hungary, eastern Europe, the Ottoman Empire, and Italy, and to some extent in Latin America and China.

The smaller creditor countries—the Netherlands and Switzerland in particular—followed the British model, though their investments were less widespread. The United States, in this period, was primarily concerned with its own development and was still a considerable debtor on international account, though there were instances of foreign investment, sometimes on a considerable scale. It is obvious from these figures that the largest volume of true industrial investment in pioneer areas was British or at least was mobilized through the London market. While French, German, Swiss, Dutch, Belgian, and American savings were growing and tending always to seek investment outlets outside national boundaries, the British until 1914 had the advantage of an early start and a tremendous volume of both short- and long-term securities available to an active market. Europe remained the world's banker, until its capital accumulations were largely dissipated in the war of 1914–18. The trends of international investment in the nineteenth century have been thus briefly summarized because the international capital market which developed to handle this investment became the organizing and controlling center

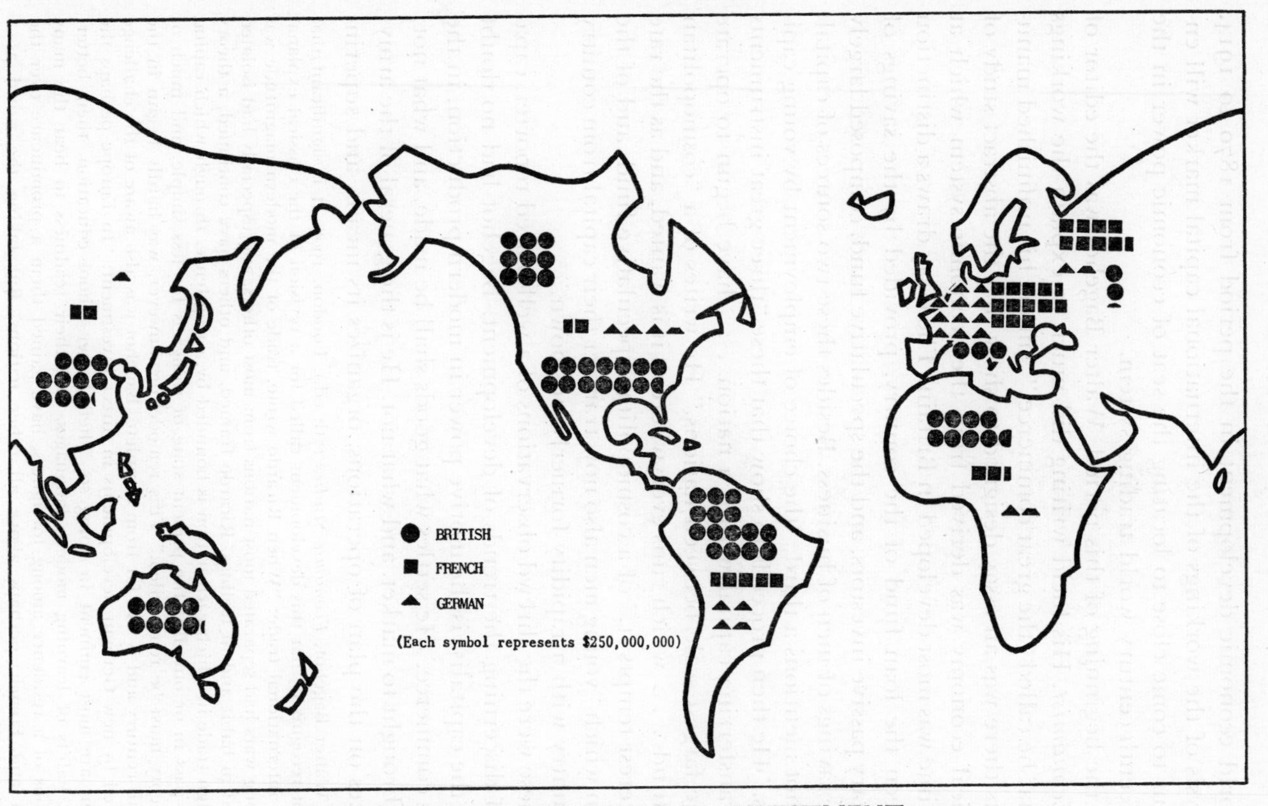

LONG-TERM INTERNATIONAL INVESTMENT, 1914

Source: Drawn from data in Herbert Feis, *Europe, the World's Banker, 1870–1914,* New Haven, 1930, pp. 23, 51 and 75.

of world economic development in the period from 1870 to 1914. Analysis of the workings of the international capital market will enable us to come close to locating the seat of economic power in the nineteenth-century world trading system.

At the beginning of this period, Walter Bagehot was the editor of the *Economist*. His lucid writing did much to explain the workings of what he called "the great commerce." Among his unfinished manuscripts there was an essay designed to show that the abstract study of political economy was derived from the economic system which at that time was most developed in Britain. The essay draws a distinction between the loan fund of the country, provided by the savings of ordinary passive investors, and the speculative fund, composed largely of the savings of men of business. Besides these two sources of capital, Bagehot mentions a third, "the choice of employment by young capitalists." He then proceeds to show that these "three great instruments for transferring capital within a nation . . . have begun to operate on the largest scale between nations." He writes of a "cosmopolitan loan fund . . . which runs everywhere as it is wanted, and as the rate of interest tempts it," of a cosmopolitan speculative fund, and of the way in which "young men also now transfer their capital from country to country with a rapidity formerly unknown." [5]

These were the shrewd observations of a well-placed reporter, capable of discerning the trends of development. Bagehot had no doubt that "the capitalist is the motive power in modern production, in the 'great commerce.' He settles what goods shall be made, and what not; what brought to market, and what not. He is the general of the army; he fixes on the plan of operations, organizes its means, and superin-

[5] Cf. Walter Bagehot, *Economic Studies* (7th ed.), London, 1908. It is significant that Bagehot recognized that this development called for a revision of the classical explanation of international trade: "When Ricardo wrote, trade of the modern magnitude was new: long wars had separated most nations from most others, and especially had isolated England in habit and in feelings. Ricardo framed, and others have continued, a theory of foreign trade in which each nation is bounded by a ring-fence, through which capital cannot pass in or out. But the present state of things is far less simple, and much of that theory must be remodelled." This remodeling, however, was hardly begun in the next half-century and is still far from complete. Bagehot was also aware of the challenge presented by new German developments in direct investment: "In Europe perhaps the Germans are most eminent in doing so. Their better school education, their better-trained habits of learning modern languages, and their readiness to bear the many privations of a residence among foreigners, have gained them a prominence over the English and French, perhaps above all other nations. But taking the world as a whole the English have a vast superiority. They have more capital to transfer, and their language is the language of the great commerce everywhere, and tends to become so more and more."

tends its execution. If he does this well, the business succeeds and continues; if he does it ill, the business fails and ceases. Everything depends on the correctness of the unseen decisions, on the secret sagacity of the determining mind."

In retrospect, we can see that the extension of the power of the capitalist to direct the flow of international investment, and therefore of production and trade, was fraught with social consequences particularly to the weaker peoples. Productivity was increased and the "unseen decisions" yielded profits, so that business was successful and continued. But this is to measure the value of economic activity by its returns to the organizers, rather than to the community as a whole. Even if the imponderable social and political consequences of the marketing process are ignored and purely economic tests are applied, considerable doubt must arise as to the wisdom of entrusting the allocation of economic resources and energies, in time and space, primarily to those who could secure access to capital.

It was so entrusted in the belief that competition would keep to a minimum the rewards of their enterprise. In the latter part of the nineteenth century over the greater part of the trading world, the ultimate decisions of economic policy lay primarily in the hands of those individual capitalists who were able to direct the flow of national and international investment. They made the significant and controlling decisions which determined what proportion of current production should be allocated to the needs of the future and in what areas. The decisions were not taken in a vacuum and they were not arbitrary. They constituted interpretations and judgments of the market for capital, and that market, on the side both of demand and of supply, was constituted by the flux of production and trade. The difficulty of gauging the market correctly was the cause of the periodic cycles of booming overinvestment and subsequent depression. But these decisions as to the proportions of current production to be allocated to capital as distinct from consumption uses, and as to the rates of interest chargeable, were the central and controlling decisions in the whole economic process.

THE INVESTMENT PROCESS

The simplest form of capital investment is the withholding of seed grain from present consumption. Much the same process takes place when a great corporation, instead of distributing all of its current earnings as dividends to its stockholders, sets aside sums adequate to finance an expansion of its capital equipment. The essence of the investment process is the allocation of goods already in existence, or of purchasing power which can be used to acquire such goods, for future as distinct from present consumption.

In all but the simplest economies this allocation is made not directly by earmarking goods to be used as capital, but indirectly by earmarking purchasing power. Investment, therefore, takes place through the medium of credit. This section is concerned with an explanation of the social as distinct from the individual effects of the credit transactions that result in international capital movements. These transactions take place in what is usually known as the money market. What we are concerned with, however, is the market for capital. This forms part of the money market in the broadest sense of that term, as used to describe all transactions which are carried through in monetary terms. The specialized market in which the moneys of different countries are exchanged and payments are balanced between national economies is known as the foreign exchange market. This also forms a part of the money market.

The international capital transactions described above involved lending across national boundaries. Governments issued bonds and corporations issued bonds or shares, for purchase by the private citizens of a foreign country. Those who subscribed to these bonds or shares received securities which entitled them to receive interest on the bonds, or dividends on the shares. The borrower received the purchase price of these bonds or shares as a credit in the currency of the lending country. This type of international lending was highly developed during the period from 1870 to 1914 when the international gold standard was functioning.

Some typical examples may serve to illustrate the process. If before 1914 the government of an Australian state decided to seek a loan in London to finance a public works program, it would first negotiate with a London banking firm which specialized in the flotation of such loans. If the state's credit was good, it could float a loan upon its general guarantee of repayment without pledging specific revenues for the purpose. The main questions to be settled would be the amount and the duration of the loan, the rate of interest to be offered, and the price at which the bonds should be issued. The banking firm might advise a loan of £3 million, at 5 per cent, to be issued at 97, for thirty years. This would mean that, in their judgment, the lowest price at which such a loan could be raised by public subscription was slightly more than 5 per cent. The bank would then underwrite, i.e., guarantee, the loan at a commission of say 1 per cent. The state would therefore be assured of receiving £96 for every £100 bond, or a total of £2,880,000, deposited to its credit in London.[6]

A corporation which wished to raise money in a foreign market would follow much the same course. It would seek advice from an issuing house as to the most attractive form of offering—bonds at a fixed interest rate; preferred shares, the fixed dividends upon which would be paid before the dividends on ordinary shares (common stock); or ordinary shares, dividends upon which would fluctuate with the earnings of the enterprise. There were many varieties of these offerings, designed to appeal to different classes of investors. Usually such issues would be underwritten before being offered for public subscription. The result, as in the case of the government loan, would be an amount of credit equal to the net value of the issue, deposited in the currency of the lending country.

This is the end of the transaction from the accountant's viewpoint, or from that of the individual borrowers. But the economist is concerned to take up the analysis at this point. Three main questions emerge: First, where did this credit come from and what effect did it have upon production and upon consumption in the lending country? Second, how was it transferred so that it could be used in the borrowing country? And third, how was interest paid upon these loans, and ultimately the loans themselves repaid? The answers to these questions cannot be simple since they involve an understanding of the complex processes of credit creation and price formation. The simplest answer to the first question is that many subscribers were able to purchase the bonds or shares by setting aside income that they might have used for current consumption. Clearly they put purchasing power at the disposal of the borrowers. They might have used this purchasing power themselves to buy clothing or luxuries for their personal use.

[6] Subscribers would pay £97 for each £100 bond carrying 5 per cent, and would therefore receive slightly more than 5.15 per cent on their actual investment.

If the price was unduly favorable, the loan might be oversubscribed, in which case bonds would be allotted, usually by filling all small subscriptions in full, and the larger holdings on a proportional basis, so as to spread the holdings as widely as possible. If the price was not attractive to investors, the loan might be undersubscribed, in which case the underwriters would take up the amount which was not bought by the public, in the expectation of selling it at a later date.

By using their income to buy securities instead of goods, they decreased the demand and therefore depressed the prices for those goods. This was the immediate, but not necessarily the ultimate, result of the loan in so far as it was subscribed by private investors from current income or liquid savings.

It is probable, however, that in order to purchase these bonds even small subscribers might have withdrawn their money from savings or deposit accounts in financial institutions which had used a substantial proportion of those deposits in their investments, or in advances to business firms. Or the subscribers might themselves have sold securities to get the cash with which to subscribe to the new loan. The new loan must always have had a tendency to reduce the credit available for capital purposes in the lending country. It would, therefore, tend to depress the market value of existing securities and to raise the interest rates in that country.

It would be too simple, however, to think of the credit available for domestic or international capital purposes and for current consumption as being a fixed amount. Both the amount of credit and the rates of interest were flexible within rather wide limits. There was an elaborate structure of interest rates, graded to meet all needs, and moving up or down as the Bank of England raised or lowered its discount rate in accordance with the balance of payments as reflected in its gold reserve.

The bank deposits upon which checks might be drawn were created largely by the advances which banks made to their clients. There were conventional rules to which bankers found it prudent, or were required, to conform. Most governments had passed legislation to control the issues of bank notes which in private hands had been the dangerous and inflationary element in the credit structure. The increasing use of checks, however, made bank advances relatively more flexible than note issues. Moreover, the rapidity with which this credit was turned over in the course of trading—what economists call the velocity of circulation—gave added flexibility to the system. When a foreign loan was floated, large subscribers, and particularly financial houses, might take up part of it, perhaps as a speculation, by borrowing from the banks and thus increasing the amount of credit in use. This would tend to cause a strain on the gold reserves and might result in raising interest rates and reducing the amount of credit available for national purposes.

Ultimately then a foreign loan, directly or indirectly, diverted purchasing power and capital from those industries producing primarily for the national market to those producing primarily for export. In so far as it was subscribed by those who otherwise might not have invested so much of their income, it also diverted purchasing power from current to future consumption. It has sometimes been argued that, if there had not been foreign capital outlets, the price of capital might have been cheaper, and that a larger proportion of the national income could have been distributed as wages, so that the distribution of income would have been more equitable. But it must be remembered that these foreign loans, as will be shown below, were always spent within the lending country. It is true that exported capital gave employment only initially, while domestic capital continued to be used within the country. Capital export tended to keep rates of interest up. The effect upon wages depended upon whether the productivity of the export industries (which were presumably the more efficient industries since they could meet international competition) was sufficiently greater than that of the industries producing only for the domestic market to offset the disadvantages of the capital export. As long as the export industries were able to compete effectively in foreign markets, the development of those markets by loans raised wage levels in the investing as well as the receiving country. The main effect of foreign lending, therefore, was not to reduce current consumption, but to divert capital and enterprise, and hence employment, from industries catering primarily to the national market, to those catering also to the export market.

This can be seen more clearly if we proceed to the second question. How were the proceeds of the loan transferred from the lending to the borrowing country? This can be explained by considering what the government or corporation which had raised a loan would do with the credit now in its possession. It could, if it needed capital goods, buy them in the lending country and pay for them with checks drawn on this credit. A substantial part of the foreign loans raised in London before 1914 was used in this way. The trade statistics show large exports of capital goods, for instance railroad equipment.

It often occurred, however, that the particular capital goods which a borrower desired to import could be procured more cheaply in some other country than in the lending country. In short, Britain might be the cheapest country in which to borrow, but other countries might produce the desired capital goods more cheaply. Thus Belgium came to specialize in the production of such goods as steel rails, and Germany produced excellent machines. These items could be bought in the best market and paid for by a draft on London. In this case while the ownership of part of the sterling credit changed hands, the credit still remained in London. The Belgian or German exporter could then get payment in his own currency by selling this draft to a bank which would use it to pay for British exports. Whether the sterling was drawn upon directly to pay for British capital goods, or indirectly to pay for British exports to a third country—perhaps woolen goods exported to Germany—it gave employment to British export industries. For this reason, it was not usual to insert a clause in the loan contract specifying that the proceeds were to be spent directly in the lending country. It was believed that since the proceeds must ultimately be spent there, it was best to leave it to competition to determine which exporting industry could most effectively transfer them in the form of goods.

Again part of the foreign loan might be used to finance expenditure in the borrowing country. The Australian state might buy its railroad equipment abroad; but it would have to employ local labor in actual construction. An American railroad which issued shares or bonds in London would have to do the same. It would, therefore, sell to an American bank part of the sterling it had acquired and receive a dollar credit with which it could pay for local labor and materials. As it made these payments, purchasing power would be increased, and prices would then tend to rise in the United States. Imports would flow in and would be paid for, directly or indirectly, by use of the sterling loan. The whole amount of the sterling would be used in England, directly or indirectly, to buy exports. Some of those exports might be machines sent to Japan, the Japanese having sent silk to the United States. Some might be whisky sent directly to the United States. However the loan was spent, its ultimate result was exports from the lending country and imports to the borrowing country.

The third question remains to be answered. How were interest payments, and ultimately repayment of the capital sum, transferred from the borrowing to the lending country? When an installment of interest or a dividend payment fell due, the borrower would have to meet it in the currency of the lending country. The owners of the bonds on which interest was due would clip the coupons attached to the bonds and present them for payment. This they usually did by handing them to their own banks which would credit their current accounts and collect the payment due from the bank at which the borrower had lodged the necessary funds. The owners of shares would receive dividend warrants which they would cash in the same way.

The funds necessary to meet these payments due in the currency of the lending country could be obtained only as a result of an export surplus from the borrowing country. In our Australian example, the building of a railroad or improvement of a seaport by use of the loan funds would reduce freight rates on wool and other exports. The woolgrowers would receive in London a larger proportion of the price for which their wool was sold. The government would receive in Australia the profits on the railroad or port dues. If these were insufficient to meet its obligations it would set aside part of its tax receipts. It would buy from Australian banks enough of the sterling received from exports to meet its interest payments, paying these banks, as the banks had already paid the woolgrowers, in Australian currency. When the loans had been wisely and productively used, there would be increased Australian exports sufficient both to meet the interest and amortization payments, and to pay for increased Australian imports. If the loans had been wastefully used, the heavier taxation necessary to meet the interest payments would reduce the proportion of export receipts that was available to pay for Australian imports.

The extraordinary flexibility of the London money market made possible this process of portfolio investment. The lenders placed purchasing power at the disposal of the borrowers. This purchasing power could be used to finance expenditures in the lending country, in some other foreign country, or in the borrowing country. The result was always the same in the long run. The lending country exported more and the borrowing country imported more. It was difficult to trace the effect of such lending upon trade because that effect was many-sided. A British loan to an American railroad might finance increased exports of Belgian locomotives to the United States, and of British woolen cloth to Belgium. Increased exports of American wheat would in due course provide the sterling out of which interest payment could be made. This whole process can best be understood by comparing it with bank loans within the United States. A borrower may use the loan to procure materials in a different locality and sell his finished products in still another. Eventually the checks in payment of these transactions are cleared through the banking system and, if the loan has been well spent, receipts will enable the borrower to repay it with interest. What the London money market did in the latter part of the nineteenth century was international banking. Loans were extended and payments were cleared through London in a world-wide trading expansion.

As the development of pioneer areas proceeded apace in the latter half of the nineteenth century, the volume of international lending increased. The extent of this increase may be gauged by the figures cited in the preceding section: between 1875 and 1913, the outstanding long-term investments of Great Britain rose from £1,200 million to over £4,000 million. These investments were made irregularly, but they average for the 43 years an amount of over £60 million annually of new capital or reinvestment of former loans. Meantime the interest due on these outstanding loans mounted steadily. At 5 per cent the £1,200 million invested in 1875 would have returned £60 million annually. Therefore, despite the additional amounts invested in this period, Britain came to have a substantial and growing surplus of interest receivable over new capital issues. This accounted for a substantial part of her continuously growing surplus of commodity imports over commodity exports.[7] A complementary development may be seen in the trade returns of the borrowing countries. In the first period of borrowing they were able to import more than they exported; but in the seventies and eighties interest payments began to mount beyond the new borrowings they were able to make, so that they began to develop surpluses of exports over imports.

These results of the investment process were of peculiar importance for Britain. A growing number of British citizens drew a substantial proportion of their incomes from overseas investments, colonial pensions, profits from financial services, and the like. These incomes gave employment in Britain, but it was employment of a different kind and in different areas from that which had increased the population

[7] Other items in her balance of payments which enabled her to import more than she exported were the sale of new ships, freight earned by British ships which in this period carried about half of the sea-borne trade of the world, the interest earned by her substantial short-term investments in the financing of trade (estimated by Hartley Withers as £350 million in 1914), financial, commercial, insurance, and foreign exchange commissions and other receipts flowing from the London money market's transactions, and the profits of British direct investments abroad (estimated by Paish as £300 million in 1914).

and productivity of the manufacturing districts in the middle of the century. In the decade preceding the first World War British exports were finding competition harder to meet. There was a sharp increase in international trading competition, one aspect of which was a very large expansion of international lending paced by German expansionist policies.

The renewed expansion of British overseas investment between 1905 and 1914 was an interruption of the trend and was caused by abnormal political developments in the sphere of economic policy. Britain, a free-trade country in a world of protection, had been tending to specialize upon the shipping, commercial, and financial services in which she was still unrivaled, and to live in greater measure upon the mounting receipts from past investments. In 1907 no less than 7 per cent of her national income was estimated to come from abroad in the form of interest and profits. By 1913, that estimate had risen to 9 per cent. Challenged by Germany in world markets, her industries proved that they were still powerful and her financial strength enabled them to make an effective reply to the challenge. Income was diverted again from domestic to export employment. The excess of imports declined sharply.[8]

Whether this spurt of energy in Britain might have led to effective modernization of her industries, and in particular to emulation of the scientific research and of the encouragement of its industrial applications that were the bases of Germany's growing competitive power, is a question that no one can answer. Before it was possible to determine whether the British effort was merely a summoning up of reserve strength that was still formidable or the prelude to a new period of industrial growth, war intervened. For Germany the economic outcome of the war was the loss of two generations of industrial expansion. For Britain it was not only the weakening of her own industrial structure, but the wreckage of the international trading

[8] Cf. F. W. Taussig, *International Trade,* New York, 1928, pp. 246–47: "The new loans—the capital exports—vary to an extraordinary degree; and no variation is so striking as the upward burst in 1904–1914. The phenomenon, it may be noted, was not peculiar to great Britain. A similar one appeared in Germany and France, indeed in all the capital-lending countries of Europe. With it went an equally striking expansion of the total volume of international trade, an accentuation of international competition, a yeasty and uneasy turmoil both in the lending and the borrowing countries—the various types of trade rivalry, fomented by nationalistic sentiment and by economic jealousies and fallacies, which contributed so largely to the ensuing war. It was in Great Britain, then still by far the most important lending country, that the capital export reached undreamed-of dimensions."

and financial system which London had built up and lived by. Though an effort was made from 1925 to 1929 to restore this system, it received its death blow during the first World War and did not survive the collapse of 1931.

The mechanisms developed in the nineteenth century for the allocation of resources between present and future consumption were an integral and indeed pivotal part of the marketing process. As they functioned in London, they were in private hands. There was little regulation by government beyond the legislation designed to prevent fraud and that which governed the issue of bank notes and thereby, indirectly and loosely, of credit. Decisions and judgments as to investment and therefore as to the development of production and trade, were left in the hands of merchant-bankers who regarded themselves as the interpreters of the impersonal forces of demand and supply.[9]

The best organized aspect of this investment process was that which developed out of the discount market. This market dealt in short-term loans on an international scale. Both the acceptance houses—the specialized bankers who endorsed and thereby guaranteed bills of exchange—and the discount houses, which bought bills of exchange for cash and collected them as they fell due, dealt in large amounts on small margins. Though possessed of considerable capital, they borrowed the major funds for their operations. Theirs was a skilled profession, judging the credit of traders all over the world. The far-flung transactions of British traders gave them a reliable intelligence service kept continuously up-to-date.

Indeed every aspect of trading, shipping, insurance, and investment was geared into the money market. There would not have been a continuous accumulation of funds available at short notice if London had not been the kind of center where banks found it convenient to maintain branches, where surpluses could be invested and yet be available at short notice, and where a market could be found for any commodity or for any kind of currency. This capital market was like

[9] Cf. Walter Bagehot, *Economic Studies,* pp. 45–46: ". . . a very great many of the strongest heads in England spend their minds on little else than on thinking whether other people will pay their debts . . . The mind of a man like Mr. Chapman, if it could be looked into, would be found to be a graduating machine marking in an instant the rise and falls of pecuniary likelihood. Each banker in his own neighborhood is the same; he is a kind of 'solvency-meter,' and lives by estimating rightly the 'responsibility of parties' as he would call it. . . . The moment any set of traders want capital, those whose promises are known to be good, get it in a minute, because it is lying ready in the hands of those who know, and who live by knowing, that they are fit to have it."

a reservoir, fed by large streams and supplemented by trickles of funds, from which there could be drawn large and small sums for short- or long-term investment in a great variety of forms. Those who controlled the outlets from this reservoir could control its level quickly by shutting or raising the sluice gates, while the streams of credit continued to pour in. This was the real secret of the measure of control which London had over the working of the international gold standard. It was, in short, a predominant power in the extension of credit, particularly for short-term lending.

The investment process has been described in terms of the competitive working of the London money market because this market handled the most important, as well as the largest, volume of investment. It was most important because it was directed to industrial and trading development in pioneer areas. The volume of French lending, though impressive, did not lead either to the same kind of trading expansion or to the development of a sensitive and flexible money market. While it is true that the French loans to Tsarist Russia financed a considerable industrial expansion, that for a time (1852–67) the Crédit Mobilier led the way to the mobilizing of venture capital, and that the Suez Canal stands as a monument to French enterprise in this period, the frontier of investment was outside Europe, and French investment did not often venture so far afield. Britain lost ground relatively in the world's manufactures, but shared in the development of the United States and the world outside Europe by its investments there.

The really serious challenge to British investment methods came from Germany. In the decade preceding 1914, Germany was pushing farther and farther afield the new methods of aggressive industrial banking which had promoted her industry at home. German bankers and businessmen might look somewhat ruefully on the weakness of their investments in Turkish railroads and Romanian oil fields, as compared with the British investments in Argentine railroads and Persian oil fields. In the appeal to arms, Britain's commercial investments overseas proved a greater source of strength than Germany's semi-political investments in Mitteleuropa. But in the years before 1914 German trade and investment abroad were developing at a rapid pace. German bankers gave longer credit and did not insist on the punctilious practices into which British short-term lending was becoming stereotyped. The close integration of consular, trading, and investment activities was giving German exports a foothold in many markets, notably in Latin America.

In many respects the direct investments of German corporations or cartels, in close co-operation with banking and with government policy, pointed to a new era foreshadowing the evolution of modern practices. The German bankers had borrowed much from the experience of the Crédit Mobilier and were passing individual investments through officially supported corporations which were given monopolistic privileges and banking support. The British methods in which individual lenders placed their capital by public subscription directly with foreign enterprises were an outgrowth of the competitive marketing processes of the nineteenth century and these methods have not survived.

THE LONDON MONEY MARKET

The financial supremacy of London became marked in the 1850's and 1860's. The tremendous pressure of manufactured exports began to facilitate capital investment on a great scale to open up new production areas. It was no longer possible to rely mainly upon imports from established sources of supply. China had exported silks, porcelain, and tea. India had paid in jute, wheat, raw cotton, and indigo for her increasing purchases of cheap cotton cloths. But after Britain adopted free trade and especially after the free-trade movement spread to western Europe following the Anglo-French treaty of 1860, more positive measures were needed to stimulate the production in foreign markets of the goods which could be exported in payment for the constantly growing exports of British manufactures. For by this time Britain was equipped to export machines, railroad equipment, and other capital goods while the London money market was ready to raise on long-term credit the funds necessary to supply these goods.

Thus the expansion of trade in the second half of the nineteenth century was largely dependent upon international investment. One of the best illustrations of this was provided by the flood of cheap grain from the Middle West of the United States, which followed upon the railroad development in the sixties. Wherever port facilities and railroads opened up new areas of agricultural or mineral production, trade developed rapidly. Wool from Australia and Argentina was supplemented by exports of frozen meat and dairy produce. The tea plantations of India and Ceylon, the gold mines of South Africa, tin dredges in Malaya, and copper mines in the Belgian Congo exemplified another kind of international investment. In the sixty years or so preceding the first World War there was a tremendous development in the amount and variety of foreign investment directed to the production of raw materials and foodstuffs entering into world trade.

This investment which was mainly responsible for developing the agricultural, mineral, and even the manufacturing resources of new countries was overwhelmingly British. In Latin America and the British Dominions, the means to build railroads and frozen-meat works were provided by London. The same was true of gold mines in South Africa, tin in Malaya, vegetable oils in east Africa, petroleum in Mexico and Iran, cotton in Egypt and the Anglo-Egyptian Sudan, and, to a surprising degree, railroad construction and mining in the United States. Belgian ventures in the Congo and Dutch enterprise in the East Indies were of the same pattern as the British, but on a much smaller scale.

Hence it follows that the structure of the London money market is of special interest in any study of international trade in this period. The aggressive entrepreneur spirit in German banking no doubt foreshadowed practices that may become important in future trading organization. The methods by which American banks promoted and participated in the mergers of giant corporations, and thereby hastened the development of international business enterprises, are even more likely to yield lessons for future development. The nineteenth-century trading world, however, was shaped by the London money market. Its highly specialized and competitive institutions developed a virtually world-wide clearing of international payments. They provided the bulk of the short-term credit needed to finance the expanding volume of international trade. They organized the largest volume of long-term investments for the construction of transport and public utilities, for land improvement, and for mining enterprises all over the world. In so doing they evolved the art of central banking which, though not confined to London, was never fully practiced in any other center.

It is highly improbable that the London money market can regain in the twentieth century the commanding position it held in world trade and investment during the latter part of the nineteenth century. After a prolonged depression and a cruelly devastating second World War, it does not have the resilience that could justify the claim, as late as

1931, that it was the most highly organized international market for money in the world. It is still a powerful and stable monetary center which functions effectively in financing trade and investment within the sterling area. But it is no longer the chief lending center in the world, and its characteristic freedom has been impaired both by the British abandonment of free trade and by the growth of economic and monetary nationalism elsewhere. The obstacles to its resumption of financial leadership may be gauged by the disrepute into which the concept of the international gold standard has fallen in so many quarters. The international gold standard was a name loosely applied to the practices centered in London, by which payments were cleared and prices were maintained in equilibrium between independent currency systems.

However, there are two reasons why it is still necessary to analyze the structure and working of the London money market when it was in its prime between 1870 and 1914.[10] The first is that it is impossible to explain the growth of international trade in the nineteenth century without stressing the role of London. The second reason is that the current methods for the clearing of international payments and the financing of international trade have grown out of the procedures developed in London.

It is important to note that many of the attributes of the London money market were the result of historical accident rather than of design. No small part of the difficulty that generations of students have experienced in the study of international monetary relations arises

[10] Cf. W. Bagehot, *Lombard Street*, London, 1873, p. 4: "The briefest and truest way of describing Lombard Street is to say that it is by far the greatest combination of economical power and economic delicacy that the world has ever seen. Of the greatness of the power there will be no doubt. Money is economical power. Everyone is aware that England is the greatest moneyed country in the world; everyone admits that it has much more immediately disposable and ready cash than any other country. But very few persons are aware *how much* greater the ready balance—the floating loan-fund which can be lent to anyone for any purpose—is in England than it is anywhere else in the world. A very few figures will show how large the London loan-fund is, and how much greater it is than any other. The known deposits—the deposits of banks which publish their accounts—are, in

		£
London	(31st December, 1872)	120,000,000
Paris	(27th February, 1873)	13,000,000
New York	(February, 1873)	40,000,000
German Empire	(31st January, 1873)	8,000,000

And the unknown deposits—the deposits in banks which do not publish their accounts —are much greater than those in any other of these cities."

from this fact. The London money market was the financial center of the nineteenth-century trading world, but it grew up in the traditional British setting. It drew most of its strength from the great volume of trade, and hence of international financial transactions, that resulted from British leadership in the Industrial Revolution and from the British experiment in free trade. It is true that some of the men who shaped its practices were cosmopolitan financiers. Names like Alexander Baring, his partner P. C. Labouchere, David Ricardo, Nathan Rothschild, G. J. Goschen, and at a later date Ernest Cassel, Edward Sassoon, Alfred Beit, and Barney Barnato bear witness to this. Such names were prominent particularly in the sections of the market concerned most directly with international trade and finance. But the majority of the operators in the market, including many of the leaders, were always English. Its institutions showed a characteristic British regard for traditional forms and practices. Thus it is not always easy to separate the essential nature of its monetary procedures from the peculiar forms and practices which were a legacy of historical precedents.

This regard for tradition had important results in practice. As Walter Bagehot was careful to explain, the Bank of England was a private bank governed by a Court of Directors, elected by the shareholders. It was owned by merchants and specialized merchant-bankers, among whom the firms dealing in foreign investment were especially prominent. But the Bank never appointed directors who were concerned with other English joint-stock banks. There was no one on the Court of Directors whose primary concern was with British banking or British industry. By long tradition, the Bank of England did not admit into its councils the other banking institutions which had been its rivals.

On the other hand, neither the Bank of England nor the specialized institutions of the London money market sought to control the development of British industry. Those who directed the powerful private institutions connected with the money market's international transactions did not as a rule accept directorates in British railroads or industrial enterprises, and only rarely in investment trusts or insurance companies. British joint-stock banks were excluded from the direction of the Bank of England, and the money market specialists on their part refrained from seeking to control British companies.

Three important aspects of the London money market need to be emphasized. First, all of its institutions were private in character and free from government control or regulation. Even the Bank of England was a private corporation and remained so until 1945. In cross-examination before the Macmillan Committee in 1931, the Deputy Governor of the Bank declared that no restrictions were placed upon the Bank except those in the Tonnage Act of 1694 (the Act which created the Bank) forbidding it to use its funds in dealing with merchandise or wares of any description. The Bank of England, the issuing houses, the acceptance houses, discount firms, and brokers, as well as the Stock Exchange, insurance companies, investment trusts, and bullion brokers, the joint-stock banks, and the London offices of colonial and foreign banks—were all privately owned and managed. There was virtually no government regulation or supervision—nothing corresponding to the Securities and Exchange Commission which now regulates security transactions in the United States. London was a free market, and it was this freedom which had attracted the cosmopolitan financiers referred to above. Such regulation as existed was self-imposed and grew out of the market's own experience and convenience. The American markets were similarly free in this period, but they were concerned almost entirely with American development and little with foreign trade or finance.

The second important aspect of the London money market was its high specialization. It was composed of a great many different types of financial institutions, both national and international. It supplied funds for all sorts of ventures—to finance the transfer of commodities or security transactions by loans ranging from overnight money to advances for a few months, or to finance long-term mining, land, or construction developments by loans without any repayment date. Its great achievement was the mobilizing of small and large sums collected from many sources, such as the small savings of individual investors or the seasonal balances of overseas banks. Institutions were created which could turn these savings and balances into investible funds. This is the essence of banking. The owner of the funds is assured of being able to withdraw them at need or by agreement. The longer the term for which he agrees to leave them, the higher the interest he receives. The banker, keeping on hand sufficient cash to meet anticipated withdrawals, uses the balance for investments of various kinds.

So great was the volume of trade flowing through London that the supply of loanable funds far exceeded that of any other center. By a natural consequence other funds were attracted to this market where such a great volume of transactions was always in process that balances could be used profitably. The joint-stock banks mobilized in London the surplus funds of their country branches. The British banks operating abroad (such as the Hongkong and Shanghai Banking Corporation and the Chartered Bank of India), the various colonial and dominion banks and most foreign banks maintained offices in London and fed the stream of funds into the market from their unused balances. London became the most convenient place to settle international payments, the market where any national currency could be bought or sold.

In this market with its far-flung connections, expert advice was always available. A group of merchant-banking firms known as acceptance houses, relying upon their specialized knowledge of the credit rating of individuals and firms abroad, would accept (literally endorse and therefore guarantee) bills drawn upon London. Another group of specialists, borrowing from the short-term funds available in the market, would discount such bills. If the available funds were not adequate, bills would be sent for discount to the Bank of England. The demands for both long-term and short-term credit were met by a variety of specialists who kept close watch on their respective segments of a world-wide commerce. They were specialists in a double sense. They confined their operations to a particular banking function—acceptance, discount, exchange, underwriting, security issues. And within that function there was specialization by area or by type of operation. Some firms, for instance, specialized in Argentine securities as did the Barings, or in Brazilian as did the Rothschilds. On the Stock Exchange the Kaffir market (in South African mining shares) was distinct from Home Rails. This, however, was a shifting, competitive specialization, and always there were free lances who undertook by various forms of arbitrage (dealings between the specialized markets) to bridge the gap between different specialties and even different markets.

Within this competitive structure might be found a way for investing large or small sums on almost any kind of terms and a means of raising funds for almost any kind of project.[11] In the characteristic

[11] Cf. Feis, *op. cit.,* p. 9: "This was the market for 'money,' the agency through which financial support was bought and sold. To its bartering, scheming, and developing was

informal British manner there was a good deal of unwritten understanding among the competitive specialists. A foreign government which tried to shop around for favorable terms would be likely to find itself referred politely to the firm with which it had formerly dealt.[12] Private entrepreneurs would find a lack of interest in their projects among all but the firms whose specialized knowledge enabled them accurately to appraise the particular kind of venture. Before 1914, there were only the rudimentary beginnings of the integration which in more recent times has gathered a great proportion of these specialized operations into the hands of great banks. These banks, in addition to their deposit banking, now undertake such varied functions as foreign exchange, security issues, governmental lending, acceptance, discount, underwriting, and even stockbroking. In the nineteenth century, the London money market was a heterogeneous collection of many specialized markets, and within these specialized markets there was the keenest of competition.

The third important aspect of the London money market grew out of this specialization. There was a rather sharp distinction between the institutions engaged in the financing of foreign and those engaged in domestic trade and investment. There was in a broad sense only one market. The supply of funds which was fed into the market from domestic and foreign sources was available for either foreign or domestic uses. But the specialized and powerful firms which han-

attracted a large part of the saving of the British people. To this market you might come with a collection of treaties bearing the smeared symbols of an African chief, a survey map of properties located in India, suitable for tea-growing, a concession for a power plant in some South American town, the prospectus of a new bond issue of the Erie Railroad, and find some door open to you, some dim office where your treaties, maps, concessions, and prospectuses would be taken as familiar chances."

[12] Cf. William Adams Brown, Jr., *The International Gold Standard Reinterpreted*, New York, 1940, Vol. I, pp. 621–22: "The business of the London money market is conducted with a minimum of formal correspondence. The men in the market do not change as readily from one connection to another as they do in other markets. This is one of those extremely important non-statistical facts that must be given weight in discussions of money market technique, for it is a force making for the type of stability that goes with 'old-established' institutions and methods. It has been said that one of the characteristics of the peculiar British business genius is that when, by a process of trial and error, a method of doing a particular type of business has been worked out that in general gives satisfactory results, the business community stops at this point and continues to use that method as long as it proves serviceable. It was by such a process of finding the appropriate means of carrying out its business and stopping short when it was found that the monopoly element in the London market had its origin and sanction. The internal organization of the London money market is evidence of the British conviction that international banking cannot be carried out under a complete laissez-faire system."

dled foreign issues dominated the market and it became a subject of complaint that it was easier to raise loans for foreign than for domestic ventures. For example, in the three years 1911–13, of the annual average of new issues amounting to £200 million, only £36 million were for British enterprises, while £164 million were for government loans and industrial ventures in the British Dominions and colonies, and in foreign countries. Friendly critics of the market, from Walter Bagehot in 1873 to the Committee on Finance and Industry over which Lord Macmillan presided in 1931, drew attention to the fact that British industry had its own methods of self-financing and its own connections with the joint-stock banks, so that it neither drew as heavily upon the resources of the market, nor had as much influence upon its organization, as was the case in most other financial centers.

The peculiar situation developed, therefore, in which the important decisions of monetary policy lay primarily in the hands of the specialists in foreign trade. Britain in the fifties and sixties was the greatest manufacturing country in the world and, even after it was surpassed by Germany and the United States, it remained a great industrial country. But neither its industrialists nor the joint-stock banks which served them were directly represented upon the Court of the Bank of England. The Court of Directors was composed primarily of merchants interested in foreign trade, among whom international investment houses were prominent and exercised an influence even greater than their numbers.

In the last quarter of the nineteenth century, London became the financial center not only of Britain and of the British Empire overseas but of the whole trading world. It conducted an immense and varied volume of financial transactions by organizing methods that made funds investible and yet available. A small investor could buy a parcel of shares, place his money on deposit with a bank, buy shares in an investment trust, or deposit what cash he had in a savings bank or building society. Insurance companies or foreign banks could place their temporary surpluses in the market for use by specialist brokers or discount houses. A foreign government or national bank might keep its reserves almost immediately available and yet earning interest in the short-term market. The Japanese government, for example, helped stimulate a boom in 1905–6 by so using part of its indemnity from Russia, until the Bank of England persuaded it to place the money in its hands. Many foreign central banks operated their monetary systems by keeping at least part of their reserves in interest-earning short-term assets in London, where gold could always be bought. Some of the British Dominions went further and frankly operated what has been called a sterling exchange standard.

The specialized operators of the market worked on slender margins, relying on their specialized knowledge to lend the maximum proportion of the funds they borrowed without being caught at any moment short of cash to meet demands for repayment. The ultimate source of cash was the Bank of England. Therefore the gold reserve of the Bank became in effect the reserve of the whole trading world. It was for this purpose minute. Bagehot, writing in 1873, reported that for some years it had averaged about £10 million but had formerly been much less. Gradually it was increased to over £100 million, and the Macmillan Committee in 1931 urged that it should be £150 million. Even these sums do not compare with the holdings of the Federal Reserve System in our own time, or even with those of the Bank of France and the Bank of Spain in earlier periods. It was a very economical system that was operated from London and one which required great skill and delicacy of judgment.

This was supplied by the experienced and informed specialists who bore the major responsibility for determining policy. In their judgments the Directors of the Bank were influenced by the financial needs of British industry only as one consideration among many world-wide factors. Their motives were not altruistic but were prompted by the fact that the liquidity, as well as the solvency, of the houses specializing in international finance was the prime determinant of monetary policy in the most important money market of the world.

It seems unlikely that such power will ever again accrue to a group of private financiers concentrated in one money market. The time has gone by when even a weak country will allow its people to be put through severe deflationary pressure in order to maintain the stability of its exchange rate. The situation where funds for economic development could be obtained only through the good offices of a specialized issuing house is not likely to be recreated. What is important, therefore, in this nineteenth-century experience, is not so much the details of its actual working but the demonstration that virtually world-wide stability of the exchange rates is possible with skillful management; that upon such stability there may be developed a great volume of international investment bringing new resources into production and expanding the volume of international trade. What the private capitalism of the London money market achieved in the half-century preceding the first World War was an impressive demonstration of economic development resulting from well-directed investment and skillfully managed monetary policies. Any attempt to repeat that demonstration must now reckon with heightened economic nationalism and must therefore proceed by international agreement. This involves a larger measure of intergovernmental control so that foreign investment and trade must in the future proceed in a different political climate. Even so it has much to learn from the great experiment of the London money market.

THE LONG AND THE SHORT

The interaction of the different types of investment, as they operated in the nineteenth-century trading system, deserves a more extended examination. It has been shown that there was a great development of international capital movements in the latter half of the century. The economic importance of these capital movements has been demonstrated and attention has been drawn to the peculiar structure of the principal money market. It remains now to show how the various forms of capital transactions were interdependent and how they operated through the credit system. This will prepare the way for an understanding of the intricate processes by which international payments were balanced, national currencies were maintained at their gold parities, and prices were maintained in equilibrium between widely separated markets.

It is necessary first to recall the emphasis placed in the preceding chapter on the extension of the marketing process in space. During the latter half of the nineteenth century the trading world was greatly expanded. A larger and larger variety of commodities entered into world trade, and the prices of a still wider range of goods and services over a widening area were influenced by trading activities. Thus the volume of transactions which involved payments across the boundaries of national monetary systems continually increased.

The elaboration of these transactions as well as their increasing volume multiplied the financial dealings that were involved. This may be illustrated by considering the shifting of the crops across the Atlantic. Each year a large volume of cotton, wheat, and other agricultural produce was shipped from the United States to Europe. Much of it was shipped directly to London and by far the larger part of it was financed through the London money market. The ultimate debt that was due was payment to the American producers by the European consumers of these foodstuffs and raw materials.

But the marketing process consisted of an elaborate specialization of dealings. It worked from both ends. The Lancashire cotton spinner, for instance, would want to be sure of his supplies of raw cotton. To be able to quote firm prices on future deliveries of yarn he needed to know what price he would have to pay for this cotton delivered at a certain date. Therefore he would be buying cotton for future delivery, and he would buy fairly continuously. The brokers and other specialized dealers in the cotton market would thus have a flow of buying orders to handle. On the side of the growers there would be a more or less parallel flow of selling orders for cotton which dealers expected to be able to deliver.

As crops became available on the market, there would be a liquidation of these transactions, the dealers on the American side handing over the actual material for shipment to London or Liverpool warehouses, and the industrial users in Lancashire drawing from these warehouses cotton of the description they needed to fill their manufacturing orders for yarn. This actual shifting of the crops was the solid core of the marketing process. At any moment the payments due for actual deliveries would form only a fraction of the total payments due on account of marketing transactions. Obviously these deliveries were the basic reality, the *raison d'être* of the whole elaborate organization. As long as trade flowed actively, the speculative transactions which were undertaken, though greater in amount than those actually implemented by deliveries of goods, were governed by those deliveries actual and prospective.

It is significant of the extent to which this marketing mechanism deteriorated during the interwar years that the only reference to commodity exchanges in J. M. Keynes's *General Theory* (1936) is one sentence in a footnote appended to an elaborate description of the way in which speculation has come to dominate the leading stock exchanges.[13] In the half-century preceding the first World War the commodity exchanges were active because trade was freer then than it was earlier, or than it has since become. The substantial reality of trading transactions formed a steady stream of enterprise, on which

[13] J. M. Keynes, *General Theory, op. cit.*, pp. 159–60 n.

an elaborate play of constructive speculation did little more than ruffle the surface. This was true even though from time to time unscrupulous and predatory individuals and groups found ways of using the marketing processes which were not only disturbing to, but actually destructive of, confidence.[14]

At any moment a great variety of transactions fell due for settlement. Practically all of them were carried through on credit, so that they represented short-term debts falling due for payment or renewal. When the London money market was at the height of its activity and influence, it dealt in a far larger volume of these commodity transactions than any other financial center. The art of central banking, which was gradually developed to a high pitch in London, operated largely by manipulating the rate of interest on the various forms of short-term credit borrowed by dealers in the commodity markets.

Who were these borrowers in the short-term market? They were first of all actual manufacturers, the Lancashire cotton spinners, for example. In a time of active trade and rising prices, they would increase their overdrafts to cover production outlays on a larger scale. Such borrowers were not very sensitive to higher interest rates, since their anticipated profits from larger sales at higher prices could easily absorb the relatively minor interest charges. But the dealers in the commodity markets, of whom there were many varieties, who worked almost entirely with borrowed short-term money were in a different category. A rise in the rate at which they could borrow would quickly induce in them a reluctance to buy at current prices. It would almost as quickly cause pressure upon them to sell and therefore to lower their prices.

Much of this pressure fell upon those who in various ways carried the stocks of goods, or titles to goods, in their progress between the original producers and the ultimate consumers. The far-flung marketing system and the round-about capitalistic methods of production, had greatly widened the distance between producer and consumer both in space and in time. This widening would not have been possible but for the emergence of new specialized dealers who handled and financed the intermediate stages. These men, working almost entirely

[14] A particularly bad example was that of an unscrupulous group which penetrated the management of the old-established discount house of Overend, Gurney & Co., whose unquestioned credit enabled them to float its losses on to those who subscribed when it was turned into a limited liability company which failed in the crisis of 1866. Cf. W. T. C. King, *History of the London Discount Market,* London, 1936, pp. 242–56.

on credit borrowed for short (and sometimes very short) terms, took over ownership of the titles to goods for the period after the producer had parted with his claim and had received payment and before the consumer took possession and closed the transaction by making payment. They dealt in titles to the goods, which moved as these titles changed hands.

This dealing in titles did not always involve possession of the actual goods. Much of it was in titles representing potential possession. This could be made actual at a settlement date, or could be liquidated by an offsetting transaction, the owners accepting or paying the price difference that had emerged in the interval. Thus a cotton-broker who anticipated a rise in prices might buy forward many times the actual quantity of cotton for which he had firm orders from the manufacturers. At the settlement date, he would deliver what was ordered and close out the remaining transactions by selling an equivalent quantity at the now higher price. In this way he would moderate price fluctuations, his purchases raising the price when it was low, and his sales moderating the rise.

There was a large volume of transactions always in process. Not only dealings on commodity account, but dealings in securities—titles to already invested capital—were involved. In the last half of the nineteenth century the legal procedures of incorporation had been carried to the point in most countries—especially in Britain and the United States—where ownership had been divided into various kinds of bonds and shares designed to attract different kinds of investors. There was also a great enlargement of the market for government loans. It so happened that these developments took place just when the use of inland bills to transfer short-term funds within Britain began to dwindle. The spread of branch banking, which from the 1840's onward was the result of the process of amalgamation by which joint-stock banks absorbed country banks, left the London bill-brokers and discount houses in a position where they had little option but to divert their operations from inland bills to international bills and to the security market.

The titles to securities—stocks and bonds—were so readily transferable, nationally and internationally, that active markets grew up in them. As with commodities, there was a superstructure of speculative purchases and sales built upon the genuine investment demand. What the stock exchanges were engaged in doing was a continuous revaluation of existing investments. Two main elements entered into this revaluation—the current rate of interest and expectations as to the state of business. The latter was the predominant influence, since investors and speculators do not usually worry much about interest charges when they are buying or selling.[15] The only dealers in securities to whom movements of the short-term interest rates were of great consequence were the stock-jobbers who used short-term credit to carry securities likely to be in demand by the public, and their holdings were not large.

At the beginning of a period of active business and rising prices, there would be a reviving demand for securities. Prices of existing securities would rise, and the prospect of a continuing rise would encourage new issues both to meet the greater demand, and because the promoters, underwriters, and issuing houses concerned with the new flotations operated largely on short-term credit and would take advantage of the low interest rates at the beginning of a business revival. If the revival went on to cause a stringency in the available cash reserves of the commercial banks so that monetary authorities fearful of a drain on their gold reserves raised interest rates, the dearer accommodation would have little effect immediately on the price of securities, but it would tend to discourage further new issues. The process of flotation was a lengthy one, so that there was delay before the rise in interest rates exerted its full effect. New issues which had passed through the preparatory stages of promotion and underwriting would still be launched.

It was this lag in the launching of new investment projects, and the still greater lag between the financing and the actual construction of new productive enterprises, that were largely responsible for the irregular rhythm of long-term investment. Decisions were made to allocate credit and thereby control over economic resources in periods when credit was cheap. These decisions usually became effective only after steps had been taken to raise interest rates because more active trade had absorbed the available cash resources of the money market. The pressure of dearer credit on dealers in the commodity markets would begin to drive commodity prices down just as production from the new ventures was coming on to the markets. The inherent instability of the credit system, therefore, found its chief expression in the irregularity of the market for new capital issues. Economic develop-

15 R. G. Hawtrey, *The Art of Central Banking*, London, 1932, pp. 162–66.

ment proceeded by fits and starts. For brief periods there would be spurts of promotion activity, during which much investment would be made that would prove unprofitable in the ensuing period of correction.

In every money market this irregular rhythm would make it necessary for the dealers in credit to be constantly adjusting the structure of interest rates in an effort to keep the supply and demand for different kinds of credit in equilibrium. It was a very complex and shifting market, or rather series of markets, with which they had to deal. For those closest to the actual transactions—the various financial specialists such as the acceptance and discount houses—the rate at which they could borrow on short term was a determining factor. For the commercial bankers who were the chief suppliers of short-term money, the ratio between their cash and their deposits was the index to watch. Their cash consisted of legal tender currency or deposits at the central bank which they could turn into legal currency. This meant ultimately that the central bank, which was the final source of cash and the lender of last resort, had to keep a watchful eye upon the trends of the market as a whole, in order to avoid being caught suddenly by such a demand for cash that its reserves would be depleted.

In Britain in the last quarter of the nineteenth century the Bank of England finally, though not very willingly, accepted this ultimate responsibility of using its powers to influence the short-term interest rates so as to control the amount of credit in proportion to the supply of cash available to the commercial banks. It came to this situation by historical accident, and there were many who thought that it would have been preferable to spread the responsibility more widely. It was in fact spread widely at this time in the United States where the banking system had no centralized control and no centralized reserve. In some other countries the national bank was by law required to keep a reserve of gold or of gold and silver which did not fall below a minimum percentage of the issues of currency. This was an onerous obligation, and toward the end of the nineteenth century many of these banks were keeping part of their reserves in the form of short-term money earning interest in London. They did so on the theory that the bullion market in London was free and these advances could therefore be turned into gold at short notice. Dominion, colonial, and foreign commercial banks also maintained balances in London which had become the chief center for the clearing and settlement of international payments.

Thus it came about that the gold reserve maintained by the Bank of England had to function not only as the reserve against the British currency, but was also liable to be drawn upon to meet the demands for gold caused by a withdrawal of foreign short-term credit. There was a constant tendency toward overtrading. Every firm operating in the market was anxious to do as much business as possible. The commercial banks were anxious to lend as much of their deposits as they could. The Bank of England regarded itself as a commercial bank and competed for certain classes of business. In the third quarter of the nineteenth century the volume of credit operations thus undertaken was too great for the very small gold reserve of the time, and the provisions of the Bank Charter Act of 1844 which required gold backing for all notes issued beyond a fixed minimum amount had to be suspended in 1847, 1857, and 1866. Gradually, however, the market learned the limits of safe operation and the Bank's reserve was increased, so that later crises were successfully weathered until the outbreak of war in 1914.

If London was a great borrower, it was also a great lender. There was a considerable body of informed opinion, from the time of Walter Bagehot at least, which expressed concern over the growing amount of foreign short-term money always liable to be withdrawn suddenly from London in a crisis. Whenever there was credit stringency abroad this short-term money was withdrawn. But London was not defenseless. On the contrary, it could by raising the short-term interest rates bring pressure upon every other financial center. The London discount market financed a large part of world trade so that it was estimated in 1914 that £350 million was out on bills of exchange falling due within at most three months. A rise in interest rates would restrict these operations. Bills falling due would be collected and new bills would not be accepted in the same volume.

It should be clearly understood that such an operation was possible only as long as foreign financial centers played the gold standard game. When London took steps to raise its interest rates, lending would be restricted in London and in other money markets. There would be an inflow of funds to London as foreign bankers took steps to increase their sterling funds in order to take advantage of these higher interest rates. This would mean that, while London was not accepting the same volume of commercial bills, other centers were buying sterling. Therefore the higher London interest rate would make sterling a more valuable currency, and other currencies would be forced down in value. If this process went on for long, it would force the value of foreign currencies to the point where gold would flow to London. Thus by the simple expedient of raising the discount rate, London could attract short-term credit and gold from every other center.

But in the peculiar circumstances of the London money market, there were many devices by which the international merchants and financial specialists who were most influential in the market and on the Court of the Bank were able to attract short-term credit or gold, without raising the Bank rate of discount. They could and they did use persuasion in London and abroad. They could vary their holdings of government securities, buying when they wanted to release cash to the market and selling when they wanted to secure control of short-term credit. They would "borrow on Consols," that is they would sell their holdings of British government securities against equivalent future purchases. They would vary the buying price for gold by forgoing or increasing the charges made for coining. There was a whole gamut of devices which could be used for the correction of minor disequilibria. And, in the complicated play of the market, it was often difficult to discover when the Bank was at work and what it was trying to do.

Every financial center at every stage of its development has worked out such devices. The ingenuity of Dr. Schacht and his advisers was responsible for a whole new series of them in the peculiar conditions of the early years of the National Socialist regime in Germany. The complicated relations between the United States Treasury, the Federal Reserve Board, the Federal Reserve Banks, and the other financial institutions in the United States have offered scope for practices very different from those which were worked out in the nineteenth-century London money market.

These details of banking mechanisms are of interest primarily to practical operators. Detailed knowledge of them is not necessary to an understanding of the principles upon which the international gold standard operated. The study of those principles has been unnecessarily obscured by a confusion between these accidental details of practical operation worked out in London, and the essential nature of the economic processes involved in the settlement of international obligations. Because there was so much regard for historical tradition in London, the details were very confusing and often misleading to those unfamiliar with that tradition. New devices of operation have now to be invented if the International Monetary Fund created by the Bretton Woods Agreement in 1945 is to act the part played by the Bank of England in the nineteenth century, as the ultimate regulator of the process through which international payments are settled.

The process of international payments reduced to its essentials was not unduly complicated. It came to a focus in the balancing of payments between national currencies. This balancing was continuous. At any moment a large volume of transactions fell due. These were of many kinds—bills drawn in payment for actual shipments of goods or securities or for speculative sales and purchases; transfers of funds to take advantage of differences in the short-term interest rates; payments of interest on long-term investment or drawings on funds subscribed for new investments; payments for shipping, insurance, financial or commercial commissions, remittances for government expenditures, philanthropic gifts, emigrants' remittances, and many other expenditures across national boundaries. If any country had more payments to make than to receive, the value of its currency would fall. This was because its citizens who wished to buy foreign currencies would compete and offer more of the local currency in exchange for the foreign currencies they needed.

In every money market this continuous balancing of payments involving other currencies was part of an equally continuous process of settling payments within the country concerned. There was only one national market and its rates of interest for various forms of credit were interrelated and competitive. But in the decades preceding 1914 when the international gold standard was in operation, the international balance of payments was of peculiar importance since heavy foreign payments would push down the international value of a national currency. If this state of affairs persisted, gold might be withdrawn from the currency reserves and exported. If there was even a possibility of this happening, the monetary authorities of the country concerned would take steps to tighten interest rates. This would quickly affect foreign traders, causing them to reduce prices. The lower prices would restrict imports and expand exports. It would also reduce incomes in the country which had raised its interest rates and this would reinforce the restriction of imports and expansion of exports. Thus the effect of higher interest rates would be to bring payments due for imports into equilibrium again with the payments receivable for exports.

The London money market was not only the agent of the greatest importing country in the nineteenth century, it was also the center where international payments were ultimately cleared. Sterling was not only an important national currency, it was also the medium for settling international payments. Therefore the movement of interest rates in London was of particular importance. Those interest rates were fixed by the bargaining processes of highly competitive specialized markets. But they clustered about one central rate—the rate at which the Bank of England would discount approved bills. Bank rate, as it was called, was fixed every Thursday and if it was changed, the structure of interest rates in the market would go up or down with it. Thus the ultimate control of the money market lay in the hands of the Bank directors, and these men were primarily interested in international trade and finance. There is no evidence that they were motivated in their decisions by any particular tenderness for other than their own interests. But those interests were far-flung and intimately connected with the economic prosperity particularly of the developing new countries. More and more the indices which they interpreted were those reflecting world trade and finance rather than national production and employment.

It was unfortunate that a by-product of this competitive regulation of the money market was the irregularity it produced in the flotation of new capital issues. The result was that investment in Britain and abroad fluctuated with a lag following the shifting state of credit in the short-term money market. The necessity of occasional pressure on the credit facilities used to finance commodity trade and the speculation connected with it imparted an irregular rhythm to investment, and this contributed to the periodic swings of overinvestment and subsequent liquidation.

As long as competition remained the dominant principle of trade and finance, such fluctuations were the price of freedom. The marvel is not that they occurred, but that they were not more violent. The whole marketing process for capital as well as for commodities was dispersed and impersonal. Nothing is more remarkable in reading over the records of the latter nineteenth century than the reliance expressed at every turn upon what was generically termed the market. The banker who foreclosed an overdraft, the trader who quoted a price, the financier who floated a loan, did not regard himself as more than the interpreter and agent of impersonal and irresistible market forces. The law of supply and demand attained an authority which the Ten Commandments never had. The unforgivable sin was to be caught short on a settlement date.

At the top of the pyramid the Bank of England directors held the same view. They were the custodians of the reserves not simply of the London money market, but of the world-wide trade and investment which were cleared through that market. The particular devices which they used in an effort to keep all the fluctuating demands on the market in equilibrium are now mainly of historical interest. What is of basic importance for an understanding of the trading system in which they were the central figures was their implicit reliance upon competitive forces to maintain market equilibrium in detail and in the aggregate —for the short as well as the long term. Even when they took positive action—by lowering or raising Bank Rate to correct what they regarded as a departure from equilibrium—they regarded themselves not as the managers of the market but as brokers or middlemen responding to market pressures.

CHAPTER XII

THE INTERNATIONAL GOLD STANDARD

THE BATTLE OF THE STANDARDS

THE PRESENT chapter explains how the foreign exchange market functioned from 1870 to 1914. It continues the theme of the two chapters immediately preceding, which have outlined the development of commodity markets and of the market for capital. What is under discussion here is the market for currencies, which was an integral part of the marketing process. In that process, the competitive pricing of goods and services made possible the comparisons of value that constituted a basis for trade. But these prices were quoted in national currencies—in dollars, francs, marks, sterling, and a variety of other monies. Thus the market in which these currencies were exchanged was an essential part of the world trading mechanism. The international gold standard was more than a monetary system. It cannot be understood, as it cannot be operated successfully except as part of the trading system in which it was developed.

Gold has exercised a fascination over the minds of men from time immemorial. It has been sought all over the world under conditions often of almost incredible hardship. It has been cherished for its beauty and for its use as ornament. Always it has been in demand as a virtually imperishable store of value. More than any other of the commodities that have at various times been used for monetary purposes—cattle, various metals, wampum beads, shells, rum, tobacco, cigarettes—it possesses the qualities that make it generally acceptable in exchange. Writing in 1875, Walter Stanley Jevons following earlier writers summed up these qualities in a catalog which has been repeated by practically every subsequent writer on the subject—utility and value, portability, indestructibility, homogeneity, divisibility, stability of value, and cognizability.

Gold and silver had been used for monetary purposes long before the nineteenth century. In Europe as trade expanded from the thirteenth century onward, these two precious metals gradually displaced all other monetary commodities. For hundreds of years they were used simultaneously without any provision for regulating their value. It was early recognized that their value fluctuated in terms of each other and as between the face value of the coins and the intrinsic value of those coins as bullion. For centuries, therefore, there was confusion in the monetary systems. One or other of the metals was constantly tending to disappear from circulation. The heavier coins would be melted down and only the worn and light coins would continue to circulate.

In 1717 Sir Isaac Newton in his capacity as Master of the Mint made a survey of the state of the British currency. He showed that the source of confusion lay in the fact that both gold and silver were used as standard coins. Gold was still a scarce commodity, too expensive for use as a medium of circulation. Practically all of the monetary legislation of the eighteenth century in Britain, and of the nineteenth century also in other countries, was aimed at maintaining the purchasing power of the silver coinages which were in common use. However in 1816, the British passed the Coinage Act which took the decisive step of limiting to forty shillings the amount of silver that could legally be tendered in payment of a debt. Gold had long been the *de facto* standard; but after 1816 silver became a subordinate coinage and gold became the legal standard of value in Britain.

The silver-producing interests naturally made strenuous efforts to retain governments as customers for their product, and they were not wholly unsuccessful, especially in the United States. The economic argument for the continued use of silver raised two issues. The first was the effect upon such countries as India and China—where the poverty of the population made gold too expensive for monetary use—of diverting to them the large quantities of silver made available by the closing of the mints in other countries to the coinage of silver.

The second was the disturbing effect upon commodity prices of valuing them in terms of a single metal which was still scarce.

The silver-producing interests had stalwart allies among statesmen, officials, and economists who were concerned for the welfare of Asia, and for European trade with Asia, as well as among those who feared the social consequences of the deflationary pressure on price levels which followed the adoption of the gold standard by one country after another in the years 1873 to 1897. Continental statesmen and economists particularly in France and Poland were deeply divided on the question. In the United States popular resentment against the agrarian consequences of a persistently falling level of prices found an eloquent spokesman in William Jennings Bryan. Even in England where the issue had long been decided, men of such eminence as A. J. Balfour and Sir David Barbour, as well as the two greatest economists of the period, W. S. Jevons and Alfred Marshall, were sufficiently impressed by the arguments of the bimetallists to give serious consideration to international plans for a regulated bimetallic standard.

Thus it is important to realize that the international gold standard did not come into existence until the 1870's and then only after vigorous dissent in many quarters and reluctantly and partially in many countries. Britain was on gold from 1816, but the international gold standard began to be a reality only in 1873 when the adherence of Germany followed immediately by that of the Scandinavian countries became effective. The decision of the United States was taken in that year also but did not become effective until 1879. France and the other countries of the Latin Union which had been formed in 1865 (Belgium, Holland, Italy, Switzerland, and later Poland and Romania) struggled to preserve the bimetallic standard. But a continuing fall in the price of silver drove them by 1876 to suspend its coinage. When Russia and Japan went on to the gold standard in 1897 the process was virtually complete. Two years later the Indian government put that country on what is now known as the gold-exchange standard, a system by which the issues of circulating paper and silver coins were regulated according to the inflow and outflow of a gold fund held in London. The period during which the international gold standard was fully operative is less than twenty years, from 1897 to 1914.

In the United States after the California gold rush in 1849, the silver dollar virtually disappeared from circulation. Both silver and gold were standard money, but the prices at which the metals were purchased for coining made silver more valuable as bullion than as coin, so that silver dollars disappeared from circulation and ceased to be offered as backing for silver certificates.[1] Coinage and legal tender of silver were limited after 1853 and from that time forward the United States was *de facto* on the gold standard. An act of 1873 legalized the gold standard and fixed 1879 as the date for resumption of specie payments which had been suspended during the Civil War. In the seventies, however, the price of silver was falling heavily. The silver mines of Nevada were beginning to add their supplies to those of Montana, Colorado, and New Mexico, while the world demand was shrinking as the mints of one country after another were closed to the coinage of silver. The silver producers, therefore, pleaded for the re-establishment in the United States of the double standard.

From 1873 to 1897, as one great country after another began to accumulate gold for monetary reserves as well as a stock of gold bullion for coining, there was good reason to fear that the suddenly increased demand for gold would force up its value in terms of commodities. This is in fact what happened. The prices of goods and services were calculated in terms of standard gold money. In order to buy gold in the bullion market the national monetary authorities had to offer the currency demanded, usually sterling, since London was the principal gold market. The price of gold, and of all currencies on the gold standard, was fixed in terms of sterling. The only way in which sterling funds could be accumulated was by building up an excess of export receipts over import payments. Germany did this in part by using a large portion of the indemnity paid by France after the war of 1870, thus passing on to France the necessity of producing an export surplus.

In general, the only way to sell abroad was to lower prices. Most of the exports to England were foodstuffs and raw materials. Supplies of grain from the Midwestern United States and many other newly developing areas were coming on to the market in ever-increasing quantities and their pressure on the market was supplemented by the competition of such countries as Germany and Russia bent on acquiring

[1] When the United States achieved its independence, there was a variety of gold and silver coins in circulation, exchangeable at their bullion value. In 1785 Congress voted to adopt the silver dollar as standard; but in 1791 Alexander Hamilton, as Secretary of the Treasury, recommended to Congress a bimetallic system. The adoption of this recommendation in 1792 did not, as Hamilton hoped, attract gold to circulation since it was undervalued at the ratio chosen. In 1834 the ratio was changed in favor of gold, and silver tended to disappear from circulation.

gold reserves. From the economic depression of 1874 until 1896 the general level of prices fell in a succession of crises which caused hardship on agricultural producers everywhere. Inevitably they connected their distress with the adoption of the new monetary standard. And they were right, at least in part. The remedy, however, did not lie, as the bimetallists argued, in a return to the double standard of gold and silver, nor in the issue of paper money as was often contended at the time. The proper cure was in the devising of more flexible instruments of check credit.

Consultations among the double-standard countries were held even before the international gold standard began to be accepted. During the period of cheap silver, France lost gold to England, but drew gold from the German states which consulted frequently in an effort to devise some means of protecting their monetary circulation and reserves. In 1865 the Latin Union was formed and held annual conferences. In 1867 the first of many international conferences on the silver question was held at Paris. The most important of these conferences was the second, held in 1878 as a by-product of the attempts in the United States to remonetize silver. A third conference met in 1881–82. In 1887 the British Royal Commission on Gold and Silver followed the commission which had reported in the preceding year on the depression in trade and industry. Other international conferences were held in Paris in 1889 and 1892–93, but without any practical result.

The conference of 1892–93 marked the end of the bimetallic agitation. The lines had been drawn fairly consistently throughout the whole agitation. Delegates from the United States, the largest producer of silver, proposed free coinage of silver at a fixed ratio with gold, to be determined by international agreement. The British recognized that the complete demonetization of silver threatened to produce an unparalleled commercial crisis but they declared that England could not consent to modify the gold standard which had served her so well. After 1871 the Germans were of this opinion also, and at each successive conference the number of countries committed to the gold standard increased. Various suggestions were debated for a limited but generous coinage of silver and for international agreement to maintain a fixed ratio with gold.

The flooding of the Asiatic countries with silver raised prices in those countries and imparted an element of instability to their trade.

On the other hand, the scramble for gold was a powerful deflationary force over the widening area of the international gold standard. But Britain was the most advanced industrial country in the world. The London money market financed the world's trade and a substantial part of the new economic development in many of the new countries. The gold standard had served Britain well, officially since 1816 and *de facto* for almost a century before that. The bankers and the trading public had come to rely upon gold as a symbol of conservative banking practice. There was never any readiness to go back to the alternating shortages of gold and silver in a double standard.

Meantime the art of central banking was being perfected, and by the early nineties it was clear that more flexible credit policies were easing the strain on price levels. The gold discoveries in the Transvaal came opportunely at this moment, and the cause of silver as a single standard or as an alternative to gold was irretrievably lost. Only China clung to it until driven at last by renewed American silver purchases at an artificial price to abandon its traditional silver bullion standard in 1935.

This phase of monetary history has been thus briefly recalled to emphasize three major points. The international gold standard was established piecemeal and with difficulty between 1873 and 1897. Its establishment was attended by deflationary pressure on the price level and by all the social hardships associated with such pressure. And what was established in the end was not a pure gold standard, in any country or internationally. Rather it was a series of credit systems based on gold and linked with each other by fixed exchange rates.

This last point needs some elaboration. In all the countries on the gold standard, the standard measure of value was a gold coin, minted within a narrow tolerance of a given weight and fineness. Thus the dollar contained 25.8 grains of gold, nine-tenths fine and the English sovereign 123.27 grains of gold, eleven-twelfths fine. These facts can be stated in another way: one ounce of gold containing one part of alloy in ten was worth twenty dollars and sixty-seven cents, while the price in English money of one ounce of gold containing one part of alloy in twelve was three pounds seventeen shillings and tenpence halfpenny. These odd amounts had been arrived at by fixing them at the market value of gold at the moment when the currencies were stabilized.

The value of one currency in terms of another was therefore defined by the gold content of the standard coins. If both coins were in the same place, the exact value of one in terms of the other could be calculated by finding how much gold it contained in comparison with the other. If allowance was made for the different fineness and for minting charges, this ratio, which is known as the mint par of exchange, worked out at $4.8665 to the pound sterling. The equation could be extended to include other currencies so that $4.8665 = £1 = M. 20.40 = Fr. 25.25.

Actual rates of exchange, that is the prices quoted in one financial center for currencies available in another, fluctuated narrowly about these ratios. The limits of fluctuation were set by the cost of transporting gold from one center to another. Thus if the costs of transport—mainly interest and insurance during transit—between London and New York amounted to 3 cents on the pound sterling each way, the rate would vary between $4.8965 and $4.8365. The former was known as the gold export point from New York and the gold import point to London. If an American debtor had to pay any higher than this to buy the sterling he needed in London, it would be worth his while to buy gold in New York and pay the costs of shipping it to London to pay his debt. In the same way if the rate fell below $4.8335, it would pay an Englishman who had a debt to settle in New York, to ship gold from London.

Within these narrow limits of the gold points the exchange rates were fixed as long as the various countries adhered to the gold standard. This was a great advantage from the viewpoint of international trade and investment. It was the closest approximation to a uniform currency the world has ever come. It eliminated the risk that the profits of a trading transaction would be extinguished by a sudden fall in the exchange rate, or that a foreign investment would lose a large part of its capital value in the same way. This stability of the exchanges was one of the main reasons for the great expansion of trade and the even greater expansion of international investment after 1870.

When the exchange rates were fixed in this way, any adjustment that became necessary to balance payments between national currency systems was thrown on to the prices of commodities and, as will be shown later, on to the rates of interest. For example, if there was a large harvest in the United States so that British imports of wheat called for larger sterling payments to be transferred into dollars, the demand in London for dollars would force up the price of dollars. Englishmen would then get fewer dollars for a pound sterling. If this dollar value of sterling was forced down to the gold export point from London, foreign exchange dealers would then present bank notes, directly or through their bankers, to the Bank of England and get gold to send to New York. The loss of this gold from the Bank's reserves would force it to contract credit and thus lower commodity prices until imports were checked and exports encouraged to the point where inward and outward payments again balanced.

This is an extremely simplified statement of what actually happened. If the currencies had consisted solely of gold coins the balancing process would have been direct and simple. It has already been explained in describing the classical price specie-flow theory of the balancing of payments. Assuming that no other money was in circulation as a substitute for the metallic standard, the relation between the available supply of money and the level of commodity prices was equally simple and direct. A reduction in the circulation would cause a proportionate fall in prices and vice versa. In these circumstances the stability of the exchange rates would be automatic. As soon as the actual rates departed from the mint par by more than the costs of shipping gold, there would ensue a movement of bullion or coin to remedy this difference.

By the time the international gold standard came into effective operation in the third quarter of the nineteenth century, these simple conditions had long ceased to prevail in the more advanced trading countries. Bank notes (bills) were in common use almost everywhere, and bank deposits subject to check were the medium through which the larger commercial transactions were made. The use of these supplementary moneys clearly influenced the value of gold as expressed by the level of commodity prices. In effect they multiplied the money that could be circulated on a gold basis. The amount of standard gold coin in circulation and the reserves of gold upon which paper money could be issued formed what is technically known as the "cash basis." Upon this basis a large and flexible "superstructure of credit" was built. The legislation governing the issue of paper money and the conduct of deposit banking, and still more the customary practices by which banking was conducted, differed from country to country. But, in all countries, the credit superstructure was flexible.

The international gold standard was essentially a monetary system in which gold had ceased to be the main circulating medium and had become the reserve and ultimate standard of value. The relation of the standard money to the price levels was complicated by this fact. Prices could rise by an extension of credit which need not always depend upon an increase in the supply of gold. The monetary steps necessary to maintain stability of the exchange rates therefore came to be the technical procedures for manipulating the credit superstructure.

The working of the international gold standard has so far been summarized and will be explained in more detail in later sections of this chapter, by emphasizing the relation between the available supply of money and the level of commodity prices. This was the relation which was emphasized by the classical and neo-classical economists. Modern economists lay greater stress upon the fact that an expansion of commodity exports placed a greater amount of purchasing power in the hands of the exporting groups so that there was an expansion of national income, multiplied in the national economy by the expenditures of these exporters upon local goods. In this view an expansion of commodity exports represented an addition to national income. On the contrary, an expansion of commodity imports represented what is now called a leakage of national income.

The inflow of gold which accompanied an expansion of commodity exports made possible an expansion of the credit superstructure. The outflow of gold which accompanied an expansion of imports necessitated a contraction of the credit superstructure. These changes in the credit superstructure accommodated both the increased or decreased purchasing power (the income effect) and the higher or lower levels of commodity prices (the price effect). Modern economists are concerned with the income effect but their nineteenth-century predecessors emphasized the changes in commodity prices. The exposition of gold standard practices given in this chapter follows the classical tradition for two reasons—because this makes possible greater simplicity of treatment and because the effect of changes in the credit superstructure upon commodity price levels was more important in the period during which the international gold standard was operative than it has been since the international gold standard ceased to operate in 1931.

A SUPERSTRUCTURE OF CREDIT

The evolution of paper money and of credit follows a very different course from that of the metallic standards. Historical origins can be traced far back in many countries, especially in respect to bank notes and to bills of exchange. The modern forms of these monetary devices, however, are not found in any country much before the nineteenth century. In many countries their development comes quite late in that century. There is no tradition of reliable paper money reaching back through the centuries and no psychological basis for popular faith in paper as a circulating medium, a standard of value, a standard of deferred payments, or a store of value. On the contrary, the advocates of gold can cite many historical cases of paper currencies falling into complete demoralization. Economists from the time of Adam Smith have been aware of the advantages of credit.[2] Enterprising merchants have never hesitated to make use of it. Indeed they have constantly pioneered new forms of trading upon credit. There is, however, a long record of disasters—John Law's Mississippi speculations, the South Sea Bubble, the assignats of the French Revolution, the greenbacks of the Civil War in the United States, and the debacles of many currency systems after the first World War.

There is still another respect in which the evolution of credit differs from that of the gold standard. It is a national rather than an international story. It is, therefore, at once more varied, more official, and more closely related to national needs and circumstances. The choice of gold as a monometallic standard, though consecrated finally by the action of the governments, was primarily the result of a preference for that metal shared by the traders and bankers of all the great trading countries. One of the merits of the gold standard in the eyes of its protagonists was that, once established, its maintenance could be left to the free operation of market forces with a minimum of government

[2] Cf. *Wealth of Nations,* Bk. II, Ch. II: "The gold and silver money which circulates in any country may very properly be compared to a highway, which, while it circulates and carries to market all the grass and corn of the country, produces itself not a single pile of either. The judicious operations of banking, by providing, if I may be allowed so violent a metaphor, a sort of waggon-way through the air, enable the country to convert, as it were, a great part of its highways into good pastures and cornfields, and thereby to increase very considerably the annual produce of its land and labour. The commerce and industry of the country, however, it must be acknowledged, though they may be somewhat augmented, cannot be altogether so secure, when they are thus, as it were, suspended upon the Daedalian wings of paper money, as when they travel about upon the solid ground of gold and silver."

interference. Moreover, the market forces were international and independent of the political pressures arising from the fiscal necessities of particular national governments.

This faith in an external and automatic agency of control over the mischievous interference of politicians with the law of supply and demand proved to be an illusion. The credit instruments which were developed to economize the use of gold were liable to abuse. National governments were forced first to regulate the issues of paper money, and later to control the use of bank credit. For the brief period from 1873 to 1914, they did so within the limits set by, and in an effort to maintain, the gold standard. But the control was always national and the divergences, both of national circumstances and of national controls, steadily widened.

As long as one great money market in which international trade and investment dominated national industry was able to exercise a predominant influence over the fund of credit available for trading purposes, the gold standard could be maintained by other countries accommodating themselves to the shifting pressures in that dominant market. All that was necessary was that those responsible for national monetary policies should regard stability of the exchange rates as the criterion of successful management. Whenever a situation arose in which a loss of gold from monetary reserves threatened to depreciate the exchange rate, the national authorities concerned took action to correct it. In most cases this took the form of refraining from taking action that might hinder market forces from correcting the situation automatically. No matter at what cost in lowered prices, bankruptcies, and unemployment, it was believed that the national currency must not be allowed to depreciate in terms of gold and, therefore, of other currencies.

It is necessary at this point to safeguard against the common misconception that London monopolized, or at least dominated, the foreign exchange market. Most Englishmen took for granted the virtues of their own sterling currency. They did their business and made their loans in sterling. Even when London accepted bills of exchange drawn to finance trade between the United States and China, for example, the bills would usually be drawn in sterling.[3] London was the

[3] Cf. H. Parker Willis and B. H. Beckhart, *Foreign Banking Systems*, New York, 1929, p. 710, in reference to the "stubborn fight for the introduction of the mark acceptance in overseas trade in place of the hitherto universal sterling bill," a fight which "lasted

principal trading, investment, and clearing center. Inevitably it provided the sterling counterpart of whatever foreign exchange transactions were made against sterling. But so large a part of the world's trade and investment was conducted actually in sterling that the transactions which required translation into or from other currencies could usually be left to the initiative of dealers in the countries concerned. It is therefore misleading to analyze foreign exchange dealings in terms only of the highly developed and peculiar structure of the London money market. In the time of the international gold standard the market for currencies was widely dispersed, and only in times of crisis, when it became necessary for foreign banks to buy sterling for clearing and settlement purposes, was London a large dealer.

The foreign exchanges were kept stable by other countries keeping their currencies pegged on sterling at the mint par, or at least within the gold points. This involved action to adjust credit conditions and commodity prices all over the world. Such action in New York, Berlin, Paris, and other centers was taken through the mechanisms peculiar to those markets. Analysis in terms of central banking policy, operating as in London through the Bank of England's relations with the short-term market and the commercial banks, ought not to be applied to New York where there was no central bank and the short-term market had a quite different character from that of London. Nor should it be applied to Berlin where the functions of banking had developed in closer liaison with the investment market, and the central bank was primarily an instrument of government policy.[4] Thus a brief examination of banking developments in the main trading countries will demonstrate how different were the credit superstructures built in different countries upon the common gold standard.

The British system of banking in the nineteenth century, despite its traditional forms and the historical accidents of its evolution, was a

for decades and, when the war came (1914), a point had just been reached at which the mark acceptance in direct transactions with German firms had partially established itself alongside the pound sterling." For the situation in the New York market cf. Margaret G. Myers, *The New York Money Market*, New York, 1931, Vol. I, pp. 349–50, especially the concluding sentence: "Dependence upon London became increasingly irksome to New York but it was not until after 1913 that this ceased to be the normal relation." Cf. also William Adams Brown, Jr., *op. cit.*, Vol. I, pp. 637–38.

[4] Cf. Charles A. Conant, *A History of Modern Banks of Issue* (6th ed.), New York, G. P. Putnam's Sons, 1927, p. 186: "The existing banking system of the German Empire is a part of the fabric of imperialism which was so industriously built up by Prince Bismarck from the beginning of his premiership in 1862 until his retirement from office."

smoothly working and efficient instrument. The Bank of England was a private corporation, but from its foundation in 1694 it had been the government's banker. There was therefore no problem, such as occurred in the United States, of the erratic influence exerted until 1914 by an independent treasury upon the money market. By reason of its close relations with government, the Bank of England enjoyed certain privileges, notably that of note issue. But, unlike the Imperial Bank of Germany, it was not dominated by government direction. Its policy was decided primarily by the merchants and merchant-bankers engaged in foreign trade and foreign investment.

After the Bank Charter Act of 1844, the Bank's monopoly of note issue put it in a position to control the cash reserves upon which the commercial banks built the country's superstructure of credit. The use of checks drawn upon bank credit came early in Britain. It developed in the seventeenth century, and by 1832, Charles Babbage could write in his *Economy of Machinery and Manufactures,* that "all payments are made through written orders called checks." [5] With the incorporation of the first joint-stock banks, outside London in 1826 and within the city in 1833, check banking spread rapidly. It was facilitated by the growth of industrial corporations after limited liability of stockholders was introduced in the late fifties, and still more after limited liability was allowed to banks in 1858, and reserved liability was introduced in 1879.[6] By this time the overwhelming bulk

[5] The word *check* has many meanings and a long history tracing back to the Persian word *Shah,* meaning king. It came into Arabian from the Persian, and was reintroduced into Persian in connection with the game of checkers (from which chess developed in India probably in the fifth century A.D.). The expression *shah-mat* (checkmate), meaning the king is dead, indicates the original use. The word in various forms was borrowed by the Romans from Persia, and was reintroduced by the Moslems into Spain. In course of time various meanings developed, connected with restraint, with the pattern of the checkered board, or with a countermove or counterpart. The original use of the word *check* to denote a monetary instrument referred to the counterfoil of a draft; but the meaning was transferred to a draft having a counterfoil, and thence to "a written order to a banker by a person having money in the banker's hands, directing him to pay, on presentation, to bearer or to a person named the sum of money stated therein." This usage was common by 1818 since a purist in that year complained that "this word is often corruptly used for the draft itself of the person on his banker." The English spelling, *cheque,* was originally a literary affectation, based on a false derivation from *exchequer,* the French word used for the checked table on which tax receipts were counted in the Middle Ages. It does not occur till toward the middle of the nineteenth century.

[6] The 1858 act was passed after the failure of several banks in 1857 ruined their shareholders, but the privilege was not used by the larger joint-stock banks until after the collapse of the City of Glasgow Bank in 1878. In the following year, the new form of "reserved liability" was created, by which uncalled capital to a certain amount could be drawn upon to repay depositors in the event of liquidation.

of payments was being made by check—bank notes and coin serving only for supplementary payments.

The amount of credit given by commercial bankers to their customers and available to be drawn upon by check was not independent of the amount of gold and bank notes in the country. By experience bankers had found that it was prudent not to extend credit beyond a certain multiple of their cash, including their balances at the Bank of England. The Bank of England kept gold sufficient to redeem the notes it issued. The commercial banks kept actual coin, notes, or deposits at the Bank which they could turn into notes, or if necessary into gold. This item, which appeared in their statements as "cash in hand or at the Bank of England," was gradually allowed by 1914 to fall to 10–11 per cent of the sight demands that might be made upon them. If at any moment it fell below the conventional percentage the banker would take steps to call in some of his loans and overdrafts, and would be prudent about making fresh commitments. There was, however, a considerable element of flexibility in the fact that both the amount of available credit and the rapidity of its turnover, varied with the state of business.

It was a peculiarity of the British system that the secondary reserves of the bankers, which were invested in the short-term money market, found their normal outlet in loans to the acceptance and discount houses which financed international trade. British merchants and manufacturers had gained a long start in the industrial revolution and were usually capable of financing their own commercial operations. The Stock Exchange and the banking houses which specialized in new capital issues were also strongly financed. The available short-term money in London was a very large amount since it consisted not only of the balances which formed the second-line reserves of the British banks, but also of the funds kept in London by colonial and foreign banks for the settlement of balances in the international accounts of their countries. So active was the money market that unused balances from many other sources found their way to London, where they were used primarily in the financing of international trade. It was always possible for banks or individuals to lend their temporary balances on very short terms to the discount houses which specialized in the discounting of commercial bills.

One other fact must be emphasized. With the great expansion of payments by check, the medium for payments was bank deposits rather than paper money or gold. The prices of commodities were quoted in units of the standard money, gold. But the value of that money in commodities fluctuated in accordance with the amount of credit available. This had a loose relation to the amount of gold in the reserves of the banking system. But it was the play of the commodity markets in the all-pervading credit medium which determined the value of gold rather than gold determining the level of commodity prices.[7]

It would be too large a digression from the theme of this volume to attempt even a brief survey of the evolution and characteristics of the different national banking systems, which in other countries departed widely in many important respects from this British model. Only those differences of development in the principal money markets which are important for an understanding of the international gold standard can be mentioned here. In the United States for example, there was no central bank. Also during a large part of the nineteenth century, the receipts and disbursements of the Treasury were administered independently of the money market. The banking system which grew up was one of local unit banks. Note issues were regulated independently of the credit system and of the external balance of payments. Most important of all, the chief outlet for the bank balances which were held in New York was in the call loan market—the market which dealt in short-term money which was always liable to be repaid at call. This market was engaged in financing domestic investment rather than international trade.

Until the passing of the National Bank Act in 1863, control both of credit and of note issue rested in the hands of the states. In 1811 sectional forces had defeated the attempts to develop the Bank of the United States, founded by Alexander Hamilton in 1791, into what might have become a central bank. In 1832 other sectional forces destroyed the second Bank of the United States that had been founded in 1816. The need of local unit banks to finance the development of new frontier areas was allied with fears of a banking monopoly. The Act of 1863 brought some order into the confusion of note issues; but banking remained primarily local without any centralized control over credit policy.[8]

[7] Cf. J. M. Keynes, *A Treatise on Money,* New York, 1930, Vol. I, pp. 32–33, with the title of D. H. Robertson's, *Banking Policy and the Price-level,* London, 1926.

[8] The main credit instrument in the United States has been the promissory note, rather than the overdraft. Bank notes in consequence have come to be called *bills.* This use

Quite early however, New York had developed into a convenient clearing center. As the western expansion gathered way and transport was cheapened by the construction of canals and railroads, the trade passing through the Port of New York outstripped that of Boston and Philadelphia. First the country banks of New York State, then those of the Middle Western states, of New England, and finally of the mid-Atlantic and of the Southern states, found themselves forced to keep bankers' balances in New York.

The outlet for these short-term funds was found in the call loan market. The primary credit need in a new and rapidly developing country was for long-term development loans and the first specialized market to develop in New York was the investment market. Call loans to dealers in that market were the obvious outlet for money that had always to be immediately available. The market for commercial paper was slow to develop and New York could not compete with London in the financing of foreign trade. Indeed the investment opportunities of the United States brought a flow of funds across the Atlantic and some of this flow found temporary employment at times in the call loan market. This market was engaged in financing security transactions. It used the short-term funds that were the banking reserves of the nation. The final responsibility for providing the banks with funds in an emergency fell upon the stock market.

The New York banks struggled with the necessity of handling the balances of their correspondents in such a way as to smooth out the seasonal and cyclical fluctuations in the demands for credit. They had no machinery through which they could act co-operatively and no power to regulate note issues or reserve requirements. From 1863 to 1913 the unregulated gold standard operated in the United States without organization or controlling mechanisms beyond the competitive forces of the money market. Where London operated on the credits which financed international trade, New York made its adjustments to international pressures largely through the investment market. Whenever London raised its discount rate, short-term credit

of the word *bill* is peculiar to the United States. In classical Latin the word *bulla* meant a bubble, whence, in medieval Latin, a seal, and therefore a document furnished with a seal (e.g., a Papal Bull). The word, which in modern English became *bill,* was used later for almost any paper (billet, whence billeting) or document (bill of lading, bill of exchange, bill of health, parliamentary bill). The bill of parcels, shortened to bill, came to mean an account rendered. American usage of the word to describe bank notes is derived from the documentary meaning.

was restricted in New York. This immediately caused security prices to fall all over the United States. There were other elements of instability—the inelasticity and instability of the monetary system for example—but the chief cause was the lack of organization which resulted in the country's banking reserves being used mainly in the speculative security market.

In other centers different factors operated, but the net effect, except in the case of Berlin, was to facilitate London's mastery over the short-term credit which financed the world's trade. Paris, after a slow recovery from the monetary disasters of the revolutionary and Napoleonic Wars, became once more a reservoir of cheap credit furnished by the savings of peasants and small capitalists. One clue to the economic development of France and to much of its politics and diplomacy is to be found in André Siegfried's remark that "every Frenchman wears on his mind the blue blouse of a peasant." In many respects France during the nineteenth century presented a striking contrast to the United States in monetary organization—a highly centralized banking system headed by the Bank of France with which the government had close relations; a central note issue which was not limited by any reserve requirements but could not exceed a total amount fixed by law; very little check banking but a very large central reserve both of gold and of silver; and low and stable interest rates. In nothing was the contrast so striking as in the plethora of funds coupled with a lack of enterprise outlets in France while in the United States there was never enough capital to meet frontier opportunities.

Banking proper was never highly developed in France and industry lagged behind that of Germany and Britain. French savings, therefore, went largely into fixed interest securities, usually French, Russian, or other government bonds, though some were tempted into fraudulent ventures. The policy of the Bank of France in this situation was to use its great influence in the money market to keep interest rates low and stable. Primarily its objective was to make available to local industry and commerce a steady supply of credit at moderate rates. During the third quarter of the nineteenth century it built up large gold and silver reserves. It did not compete with London in the financing of international trade, but at the approach of a crisis it was able to send gold in large amounts to the Bank of England in exchange for a portfolio of English commercial securities endorsed by the

Bank.[9] This use of a large metallic reserve to insulate the home market from externally caused fluctuations bears an obvious resemblance to the methods used after 1931 by the exchange equalization funds created in many countries to intercept the pressures on national credit conditions arising from shifts in the external balance of payments. It is very different from the technique of using bank rate, as in Britain, to force a deflation of domestic prices until import and export payments again balance.

Over a great part of Europe banking did not develop strongly until after 1870. Much of Europe was in a backward state of economic organization. In Russia the record is one of depreciation, both of the metallic currency and of paper issues, until the gold standard was adopted in 1897. In Italy after unification in 1870, a burst of speculative banking collapsed in the scandals of the 1890's. In Austria there was a quickening of economic development after the revolutionary year 1848 and many banks were founded in the fifties and sixties, but the vulnerability of Vienna to the economic and political difficulties arising in the Balkans made it the center from which crises were apt to spread. The Low Countries and Scandinavia developed more steadily. Credit associations and savings banks had developed, particularly in Denmark, after 1850. But until 1870 commercial banking had not developed to the point where it provided the essential credit facilities of industry and commerce. Belgium, however, had begun to experiment with banks which became typical of the continental development. These banks, in countries which were short of capital and had lagged behind in the Industrial Revolution, were more deeply involved in promoting industrial enterprises, and therefore were apt to be less liquid, than was the rule in England.[10]

Only in Germany during this period between 1870 and 1914 was a strenuous attempt made to compete with London in the financing of foreign trade. Germany had not developed check banking. One result of this fact and of the efficiency of state organization was the widespread use of postal clearing accounts for small payments. The device

[9] Cf. H. Parker Willis and B. H. Beckhart, *op. cit.*, p. 651, citing a Belgian economist: "This method," writes Professor Ansiaux, "does not aim directly to defend the par of exchange and still less the reserve. Its aim is to prevent monetary tension abroad. In this way, counterattacks, which might have taken place on the Paris market, were prevented, and French industry and commerce was able to profit from a moderate discount rate even in periods of crisis."

[10] *Ibid.*, p. 178.

of clearing payments through a central office was very familiar to the German people. The methods of its organization were highly developed long before the National-Socialist government extended it to international transactions. This is by no means the only aspect of economic life in Germany where administrative efficiency was used to compensate for the weakness of the private economic institutions that had developed in other countries with an earlier start and more abundant private wealth.

The first joint-stock banks had appeared in the German states about the middle of the century, but the banking system of modern Germany was created after unification in 1870. In that system the central bank, which was a private corporation but in whose direction the government had a decisive voice, played a strong role. It had a monopoly of note issue and it was able to foster and support the great joint-stock banks which were closely connected with the industrial development of the country. More than in any other country the banks served from the outset as the main source of capital, on long as well as short term, for both production and trade. Instances are not lacking where German banks, somewhat reluctantly, were persuaded by the government into foreign investments that buttressed the diplomacy of expansion. In the effort to expand foreign markets, German firms gave long credit and sought to encourage the use of mark in preference to sterling acceptances. Germany remained on the gold standard and conformed to the requirements of exchange stability, but the integration and government support of the banking system gave that system a resilience which was not always amenable to the pressures exercised by London upon the short-term money markets of the world. As the twentieth century opened, Berlin was beginning to compete with London at its most sensitive point, the financing of world trade. It seems probable that if war had not come in 1914, London would have had to share with Berlin the regulatory power over world trade and economic development which it had exercised so markedly in the nineteenth century. It is significant that the instrument which made possible this German challenge was an integrated credit policy under national direction.

THE MARKET FOR CURRENCIES

As the marketing process was extended in space and in time, an increasing number and variety of trading and financial transactions involved payments across national boundaries. However, no national currency is legal tender outside the boundaries of the state which issues it. Nor has there ever been a currency which has been universally acceptable in trading transactions. The nearest approach to such a universal currency was provided by the ready marketability of gold coins and of bank notes and credit instruments that were convertible into gold, as long as the countries of their origin remained on the international gold standard. This marketability, which ended in 1914, is the phenomenon to be explained in this section.

The use of credit instruments to avoid the expensive and cumbersome transfer of the precious metals was common from the twelfth century onward. A merchant in Venice might owe money for spices to a trader in the Levant while another Syrian merchant owed money to a Venetian exporter of cloth. If a connection could be made between these transactions they might be offset, and then no money need be sent in either direction. Rarely of course was it possible to find pairs of transactions that offset each other exactly. But middlemen with foreign connections would deal in bills of exchange and carry the balances due until they could be liquidated by further transactions or by shipments of the precious metals. In the fourteenth and fifteenth centuries the north Italian merchants were conducting much of their foreign trade by such bookkeeping methods, and a market for currencies, in which the transmission to Rome of Papal revenues was a considerable factor, had developed quite modern methods of operation.

Although this early trade dwindled, and the economic nationalism of the mercantilist period put obstacles in the way of exchange transactions, bills of exchange continued to be used. For the most part it was the merchants who sought means whereby they could avoid the expensive and risky shipment of bullion. They would do so by using the proceeds of export sales for the purchase of foreign goods that could be sold at a profit in their own countries. Thus at the end of the eighteenth century, New England traders would pick up sealskins in the South Seas or sandalwood in Hawaii, sell them in China, and bring the proceeds home in the form of tea, porcelain, and silks.

Wherever trade was more firmly established, the further step of selling claims on foreign funds to other merchants became possible. The shippers of cotton, tobacco, and wheat from the United States to Britain would advertise that they were willing to sell their claims to payment. These claims would be bought by importers who owed money to British manufacturers from whom they had bought goods. From this to the development of a specialized market in foreign currencies is a relatively short step. By 1840 that step had been taken in the United States. Certain merchant houses began to specialize in the buying and selling of bills of exchange, and then to create bills in advance of anticipated payments. As the dealing in foreign exchange thus began to grow into a complicated business, it was inevitable that it should pass into the hands of specialists. Such an evolution was virtually complete in the United States by the 1880's.

The foreign exchanges are best treated as a specialized market in which different national currencies were bought and sold at prices which varied, according to demand and supply. It was an essential and even central aspect of the market described in the preceding chapters. It should be emphasized that this dispersed and highly technical market, elements of which were to be found in every center of international trade, was not organized, either in the sense of being deliberately created, or in the sense of ever having a formal organization or a clearing house. Like Topsy, it "never was born, never had no father nor mother, nor nothin'," but "was raised by a speculator, with lots of others."

The great bulk of payments on account of international trade was transacted in sterling, even when the trade itself did not pass through British markets. As long as the international gold standard operated, the play of speculation in the foreign exchanges—except in regard to certain unstable currencies—was confined within the limits of the fluctuations in currency values between the gold points. A large proportion of these fluctuations were seasonal and therefore calculable. They offered an opportunity for constructive speculation by specialist operators who could foresee and offset, and therefore minimize, market fluctuations. For the most part, the methods used in such speculative operations were first developed by specialists in the secondary money markets where currency fluctuations made the risk of loss or the opportunity of a speculative profit on a trading transaction very real.

Thus there were found indications of a well-established market in forward exchange in Vienna in the 1880's and probably earlier. Berlin also was buying and selling rubles for future delivery in the eighties, covering the exchange risk in financial transactions with Russia, and speculating in the depreciation of the ruble. While the British merchant was trading mainly for cash on both export and import account and while the London money market except for a few specialist brokers was conducting its transactions mainly in sterling, enterprising individuals in Vienna and other continental markets were finding ways and means of coping with and profiting from the fluctuating values of their own and other currencies.

It was these individual brokers and banks, mainly in the secondary money markets, who pioneered the technical methods of foreign exchange dealings. This was particularly true in regard to the transactions which hedged against exchange fluctuations by buying and selling currencies for future delivery. The stability of sterling and the fact that most trading transactions were conducted in sterling made it possible to use that currency as a peg on which to hang speculative operations in less stable currencies. Moreover, London played a rather passive role in the transactions by which the exchange values of different currencies were kept pegged on sterling, and therefore on gold.

The market for currencies before 1914, therefore, was primarily constituted by individual brokers or banks in the secondary money markets. Only toward the end of the nineteenth century were there active dealings on a large scale in London, and it was not until about 1906 that the British commercial banks entered the market.[11] Other markets, including New York, anticipated these London developments both in regard to activity and in regard to the participation of the banks. In our own time, this has led to the virtual elimination of the independent brokers in most markets.

One result of this marked modern tendency of the great commercial banks to squeeze out the specialized brokers has been to concentrate monetary dealings in institutions which are bound to conform to national credit policies. This is one of the ways in which the nineteenth-century process of multiple equilibrium, achieved by the interaction of many specialized markets operating internationally, has been subtly changed and has become more subject to national pressures. The ultimate end of this development has been the subordination of the specialized money market functions, particularly the market for currencies, to the influence and in most countries to the control of national governments.

[11] Cf. William Adams Brown, Jr., *op. cit.*, p. 637. The statement made by B. M. Anderson, and quoted by Brown (p. xvii) that "the foreign exchange of every country in the world was freely dealt in in London, and could consequently be made the basis of bank credit," was probably truer in 1906–14 than it had been earlier; but needs qualification even for those years.

In view of the importance of London before 1914, the slow development there of an active market for currencies needs some explanation. It is true that large foreign balances were held in London, either to be available for settling international payments or simply to be invested temporarily in the short-loan market. London obviously supplied the sterling necessary to establish these balances. Sterling balances could be created by foreigners selling gold or commodities to London or borrowing there. London's rather passive role was incidental to the dominating influence of sterling transactions in world trade and investment. It was this dominance which has led some authorities to describe the pre-1914 international gold standard as in all essentials a sterling exchange standard system.

The dominance of London in the financing of trade and investment was one of the major reasons why at that time it did not need to develop an active interest in the market for currencies. The initiative in exchange transactions and the evolution of the various forms of arbitrage and of forward exchange dealings came primarily from dealers in other markets who used sterling as a peg on which to hang their operations. Thus a broker in Vienna could sell rubles against sterling and offset the transaction by arranging to purchase rubles in Berlin for sterling, taking the profit by buying marks and selling them for Austrian crowns.[12] In the process the sterling transactions would be canceled out. No transactions with London need enter into the picture. Such dealings called for a quick calculation of the profits to be gained by a chain of transactions carried through with as much speed as was possible, given the existing communication facilities. They were immensely facilitated after telegraphic and cable transfers became possible.

This pegging of the exchanges upon sterling should not be interpreted—as it sometimes has been—as meaning that the London market was a regulating center of foreign exchange transactions. London did not act consciously as a regulator even of world trading credits, nor did the Bank of England regard itself as an international institution, a central bank of central banks. London was a broker concerned for its own solvency, all the more since it operated on slender reserves. The raising or lowering of the various rates of short-term interest or of the Bank rate reflected conditions in the London market itself. These conditions were closely related to world trading developments,

12 These transactions are explained in more detail below, pp. 386–89.

and those individuals whose decisions interpreted market forces were particularly interested in world trade and investment. But it would be a mistake to conclude from these facts that short-term interest rates in London were fixed by conscious effort to maintain a world-wide monetary equilibrium. They reflected market conditions and short-run expectations in London itself. This indeed was fundamental to and characteristic of the whole marketing process. There was little thought of regulation other than an implicit belief in the power of free competition to bring about an equilibrium of forces in the market.

Before 1914 the great bulk of the international trading transactions of the world were carried through and paid for in sterling. A concrete example will illustrate the way in which the payments for these international trading transactions were cleared. An American importer of silk from Japan would arrange with his bank to honor drafts drawn by his Japanese suppliers against shipments. The drafts would be in sterling and they would be cashed by the Japanese merchant in yen at a Japanese bank. The Japanese supplier would therefore be paid in yen and the American importer would later pay in dollars. The foreign exchange transfer would be left for the banks to arrange.

The importer's bank at Paterson, New Jersey, would work through a New York bank. The ultimate result was that dollars were paid to the American bank by the silk importer. The bank bought from a correspondent bank in London sterling to the amount desired, or drew upon sterling balances held there. At the other end of the world the opposite process would be taking place. The documents conveying title to a shipment of silk, together with the draft drawn for payment (already cashed by the Japanese silk merchant), would thereafter reach London, and the Japanese bank would be credited with the sterling due. This transaction would extinguish the American bank's holding of sterling, so that the second stage of the operation resulted in a Japanese bank holding sterling.

But there would be British importers of United States cotton who would pay for their imports by a check in sterling. This would replenish the American bank's sterling balances, against which it would pay dollars in New York to the cotton exporter. In effect the silk importer's dollars would be handed to the cotton exporter. In much the same way a Japanese importer of British textile machinery would pay in yen, thus replenishing the yen which had been paid out to the exporter of silk. The Japanese bank would then pay for the machinery in London by drawing on the sterling it had acquired in the silk transaction. The end result, after all these transactions had been concluded, was that no currency had left any of the countries concerned. A British bank would have the sterling deposits (now held to the credit of the British machinery exporter), a New York bank would have the dollars (now held to the credit of the U.S. cotton exporter), and a Japanese bank would have the yen (held to the credit of the Japanese silk exporter).

This is a highly simplified picture of the essential elements of the clearing process. It boils down to the fact that the dollars paid by the merchant in Paterson, New Jersey, for raw silk found their way to an American exporter of cotton, while the yen received by the Japanese silk exporter were offset by the yen paid by the Japanese importer of machinery. In the process of clearing through sterling, the British exporter of textile machinery to Japan was paid by the British importer of cotton from the United States. Each importer paid his debts and each exporter received what was owing to him in his own national currency.

If there had been at every moment an exact equivalence of transactions, the market would have been simple. But there was an immense variety and considerable fluctuation in the continuous stream of transactions. Besides commercial transactions of the type mentioned above, there were many others which involved payments from individuals of one country to those of another. A ship's captain would buy stores or have repairs made in a foreign port. Tourists would buy hotel accommodation, transportation and other services in a foreign country. Missionaries would draw salaries and expenses against the collections made for their support by the home churches. Governments would pay their embassy and consular staffs or make other expenditures abroad. Chinese settlers in the South Seas would send through Singapore a regular and heavy volume of remittances to their folks at home, and many recent immigrants to the United States would send money to their relatives in Europe. The considerable volume of foreign investment and later the interest due upon it had to be transmitted across national boundaries. When a British investor bought shares in an American railroad, he put sterling at the disposal of Americans. Then against these sterling funds they could draw in payment for British exports to the United States.

To meet these varied needs there was a gradual elaboration of credit instruments and practices. The small sums remitted abroad might go by international postal orders or the very similar express checks. These were issued at an exchange rate which was usually fixed for long periods at a rate somewhat higher than the rate for commercial transactions. Personal letters of credit or traveler's checks were available for the tourist trade, and there was a steady evolution of commercial forms and practices as means of communication were improved. The bill of exchange drawn specifically for each separate transaction gradually yielded place to various methods by which banks established their credit with foreign correspondents, and then drew upon this credit as goods were received or services rendered. Telegraph and cable services made possible great changes in what became essentially a double bookkeeping system in which payments and receipts in one center would offset receipts and payments elsewhere. After the transoceanic telephone came into use, these credit arrangements could be made orally and confirmed by cable or letter. International firms with foreign branches sometimes practiced their own offsetting arrangements.

Account must also be taken of the speculative dealings which endeavored to profit from the fluctuations in the exchange rates caused by the ebb and flow of trade, by seasonal pressures in different markets, or by any economic or political causes affecting the demand for particular currencies. This is the aspect of the market for currencies which most students have found bewildering. The mystery surrounding it is heightened by the fact that professional operators use a jargon of their own. In addition to such terms as *bull* and *bear,* there are unfamiliar terms like *arbitrage, agio* and *disagio, report* and *deport, spot* and *future exchanges, swap* and *deposit,* while more familiar words such as *premium* and *discount, over-* and *under-valuation,* and *parity* are used in an unfamiliar setting and often with a peculiar meaning.[13]

The real difficulty of the subject comes, however, from two inescapable facts. The first of these is that one currency is quoted in terms of another. The exchange rate is a ratio. Thus before 1914 a mark was equal in gold value to almost 24 cents. Equally 24 cents was

[13] *Agio* and *disagio* are terms still in use in continental Europe, and sometimes in English and American texts. They derive from early modern Italian money-changing and mean the premium or discount at which a currency stands above the mint par. *Report* and *deport* are used to mean the premium or discount of the forward over the spot exchange value of a currency. In English, *premium* is used to mean either agio or report, and *discount* to mean either disagio or deport.

equal to a mark. This was the mint par based on the gold content of the standard coinage. If at any moment the demand for marks was such that 24.1 cents had to be given for a mark, it would be said that the value of the mark had risen, or the value of the dollar had fallen. But sometimes the exchange rate was quoted differently. Thus one pound sterling was equal to 20.40 marks. If there was a strong demand for marks, the rate might go to 20.20. Thus the same phenomenon was expressed in two different ways. The value of the mark had risen. The American had to give more cents *for* a mark, and the Englishman *got* fewer marks for his pound. Therefore it is advisable not to say that the exchange rate had risen or fallen. But one should keep clearly in mind that however quoted the rates always express the value of one currency in terms of another and that this value is a reversible ratio.

The second difficulty is that the professional speculator made his profit by operating against the market. When the demand for marks was strong, the speculator would sell marks. When it was weak, he would buy them, always at a price. As a result of these speculative operations, the fluctuations in the exchange rates were flattened out. A clear example was provided by the seasonal demands caused by the shifting of the crops across the Atlantic. When the harvested wheat, cotton, and other crops were being shipped from the United States to Europe, there would be a strong demand for dollars, and the dollar would be worth more in sterling. But the foreign exchange operators would have anticipated this annual demand and would be ready to sell dollars and buy the holdings of European currencies which Americans were accumulating. They knew from experience that the tide would turn and that the later demands of American importers for foreign currencies with which to pay for imports to the United States would enable them to acquire dollar holdings at a cheaper rate.

The foreign exchange operators would also watch for opportunities to profit from momentary discrepancies in the exchange rates in different markets. These operations were known as arbitrage. They took many forms. The simplest, known as exchange arbitrage, would take place when the dollar-sterling rate was quoted at a slight disparity in London from the rate in New York. Thus if the rate in New York was $4.80 to the pound sterling, and in London it was $4.79, sterling would be sold in New York and dollars would be sold in London until the rates in both centers became the same. If the amount necessary to achieve this result was the sale of £100,000 in New York and of an equivalent amount of dollars in London, the operator's profit would be $1,000. Actually the exchange arbitrage transactions were much more closely calculated than this, and they usually involved three or more markets.[14]

Clearly such dealings called for expert knowledge, wide connections, and a rapid execution of quick decisions based upon precise calculations. The market for currencies was no place for amateurs. When they were drawn into it they almost always lost. The market was extremely sensitive. Any transaction would be likely to cause an immediate alteration in the exchange rates. Opportunities for arbitrage profit remained open only for a very short time after telephonic and telegraphic communications had been developed, usually only for a few minutes. The speculator had to be very sure of his information and calculations and to have prearranged channels through which to carry out his transactions.

When other forms of arbitrage are considered, the complexities become even greater. Broadly defined, arbitrage could take the form of trafficking between any of the different kinds of specialized markets. A speculator could buy or sell commodities in different markets so as to take advantage of differentials between the prices and the exchange rates that were quoted at a particular moment.[15] Sometimes these transactions would become very complicated, involving several currencies and commodity prices in more than two markets. Again if future transactions were involved, the element of time and therefore rates of interest, would also enter into the calculation. It was by such transactions that prices, interest rates, and exchange rates were kept in equilibrium within each country and internationally. The result was that commodities moved where prices dictated and also that short-term credit moved where interest rates attracted it.

Two specific forms of arbitrage are of special interest. The first was gold arbitrage. This was the mechanism by which the exchange rates

[14] If a New York operator sold £100,000 at $4.80, he would receive $480,000. His correspondent in London would sell $479,000 for £100,000. This would cover the New York transactions by a margin of $1000. Here would be his profit.

[15] Thus if the cable rates of London on Berlin, Berlin on New York, and New York on London were respectively £1 = M. 20.35, M. 1 = 23.9 cents, and £1 = $4.87, there would be a series of transactions by which a New York operator would sell £100,000 for $487,000 and arrange to buy £100,000 for M. 2,035,000, which amount of marks he could buy for $486,365, and thus make a profit of $635.

were kept within the points fixed by the cost of transporting gold from one center to another. In this process gold was distributed among the world's monetary systems as the needs of trade determined. As long as the international gold standard was in force, the price of gold was fixed as a certain value in the standard money of each country. If at any moment the rate of exchange moved much above or below the cost of buying and shipping gold, the arbitragers would at once initiate the necessary operations to ship gold to the center where they could sell it and make a profit by buying the currency of that country cheaply. This form of gold arbitrage disappeared when the international gold standard broke down. A new form of gold arbitrage, however, developed in respect to the differentials between the price of gold in the limited free gold markets and the exchange rates. This was a new kind of commodity arbitrage.

The second and for our purpose the more important form was interest arbitrage. It was possible to buy and sell currencies forward, for delivery usually one, two, or three months ahead. This market for forward exchange was like the futures markets developed in cotton, wheat, and other commodities. It added a time dimension which greatly multiplied the possibilities of speculative transactions that might turn a profit out of discrepancies in the various rates. The value of a currency sold for delivery at some future time (the forward rate) would normally be different from its value for immediate delivery (the spot rate). Arbitragers would compare this difference with the short-term interest rates in the markets concerned.[16]

As long as the international gold standard remained operative, the scope for interest arbitrage was limited. The possible variation of exchange rates in most countries was kept by gold arbitrage within the limits of the gold points for each currency. A situation rarely occurred when the risk of exchange fluctuation was so great that merchants wished to safeguard themselves against it, while speculators could

[16] It is necessary to avoid confusing forward exchange with exchange which is sold spot for delivery in 30, 60, or 90 days. The exchange rate on bills or drafts falling due at a later date is always the same as the rate for cables, or sight drafts, less the interest which is calculable for the time that elapses. This interest is calculated at the market rate as a discount from the face value of the draft.

The forward rate, for transactions which will become actual at a later date, may diverge rather widely from these spot rates if there is fear of currency depreciation or of interruption such as war or exchange control. Thus in the post-depression years, the French franc was often sold forward at very heavy discounts (deports); the speculators in fact betting that in three months the franc would have depreciated.

profit from going counter to the market. This is why these forward markets developed first in such centers as Vienna and Berlin where it was possible to dabble in less stable currencies, such as the ruble and various Balkan currencies. Apart from these markets the chief importance of forward transactions before 1914 lay in the effect of short-term capital transfers upon the balancing of payments. These are best dealt with later. It was not till the breakdown of the restored international gold standard in 1931 that the forward exchange market developed its full importance. For a time after the breakdown, exchange rates were very unstable. In these circumstances forward dealings were advocated as a means of protecting national price levels from fluctuations induced by exchange instability. However, the increasing efficiency of exchange regulations put an end to the possibility that interest arbitrage in developed forward exchange markets might serve as a substitute for exchange stability.

THE BALANCING PROCESS

The preceding discussion has covered all the elements which, in shifting combinations, entered into the clearing of international payments during the heyday of the international gold standard. Stress has already been laid on the spontaneous extension of the marketing process in space.[17] An elaborate series of commodity markets was the foundation of this whole clearing and balancing process. Imports were paid for by exports. Temporary adjustments in the balances of international payments would be made by means of short-term credit accommodation. Such credit transfers were not only effective in plugging the immediate gaps in the balances of payment, but, through their influence on credit conditions, they also wrought changes both in the national incomes of the countries concerned and in their price levels. These credit transfers, of vital importance in the short run, achieved their ultimate effect by inducing the changes both in the volume of trade and in the prices of commodities that were necessary to maintain the long-run equilibrium.

This is an important fact to remember. The international gold standard functioned satisfactorily as long as international trade moved freely in response to the shifting market demands as indicated by relative prices. No international monetary arrangements, whether based on gold or on any other foundation, can function satisfactorily

[17] See Chapter X, "The Network of World Trade."

unless reasonable flexibility of trading relationships can be once again created. Flexibility of trading relationships will need to be created by new methods—methods which will take account of the changing structure of production. For this flexibility is an essential condition of international monetary equilibrium.

Attention has also been drawn to the complex variety of transactions in the capital market as it developed in the last half of the nineteenth century.[18] Both the volume of investment and the rate of interest were elements in the balancing process. Indeed, account must be taken not only of new investment but of the continuous revaluation of existing investments and of the transfers of ownership which were the result of the international security transactions on the world's stock exchanges.

It was characteristic of the nineteenth-century system that new capital issues, as well as the revaluation of existing capital, were by-products of the balancing process. The volume of credit available for investment depended primarily upon the money market conditions which resulted from the financing of international trade. Thus the fluctuations of world trade were transmitted to the capital market and were there amplified into the irregular rhythm of the business cycle. Investment, national and international, was the result of individual decisions rather than of planned national programs. The situation was that investment fluctuated according to the superfluity or scarcity of credit in different money markets—and this superfluity or scarcity was created from time to time by the response of the money markets to the ebb and flow of commodity trade.

Between 1896 and 1914 when the international gold standard was functioning at its best, these cyclical fluctuations appeared to be diminishing in intensity. Crises were relatively short in duration and mild in intensity. The adoption of the gold standard by one country after another had caused severe price disturbances in the seventies and eighties. These disturbances had been accentuated by the necessity of credit contraction to correct the inflations which had accompanied the wars of the sixties. But the last of the major crises of this adjustment period came in the early nineties and with it came the end of a twenty-year period during which the average level of prices had been falling. Thereafter until 1914 cyclical fluctuations were cushioned by a steadily rising tendency of average price levels, occasioned by the perfecting of

[18] See Chapter XI, "Investment and Enterprise."

credit systems and by the more adequate gold supplies available after the South African gold discoveries.

It must be remembered that there was a peculiar combination of strength concentrated in the London money market. The greatest volume of commodity trade passed through the free-trade markets of Britain, and a great deal of the trade between other countries was financed through London. At the same time London was the greatest international market for securities and by far the most important capital exporting country. All the major factors of the balancing process came to a focus in the operations of the London money market. It was a unitary though infinitely diverse process by which the ultimate clearing of international transactions and the settlement of international balances was carried through in one dominating center.

Finally in this chapter, the evolution of the market for currencies has been outlined. Theoretically the exchange value of a national currency is also one of the elements which enters into the process of balancing international payments. If a currency is allowed to fluctuate freely in the market this does happen. But in practice governments have not found it desirable to allow their currencies to fluctuate freely. As long as the international gold standard was in effective operation, the exchange rates fluctuated only within the narrow limits set by the cost of shipping gold from one country to another. This stability of the exchange rates was the rock upon which it became possible to build an expanding volume of world trade and investment. When the exchanges were pegged in this way—whether the pegging is interpreted as having been a link to gold or to the dominating stability of sterling in terms of gold—any adjustments of national economies necessary to balance international payments had to be made through the credit systems. This occurred by the adaptation of commodity prices, and therefore the trade which responded to price signals, as well as of interest rates, and therefore investment in all its phases, to the shifting conditions of world markets.

It should again be emphasized that the balancing process was complex because it was free and involved so many elements. Among these elements the more important were: commodity prices and the volume of trade, interest rates and credit to finance both short- and long-term investments, the revaluation of old and the issue of new securities, and, within the limits of the gold points, variations in the exchange rates. The shifting combinations of possible changes in all these factors.

brought about by actual changes in demand and supply, and by the incessant play of speculation within and between a series of intersecting markets, inevitably evokes the use of such terms as fluid, rather than flexible. Indeed the metaphor which is most useful in this connection is that of a continuous stream of payments, dividing and eddying, but, even in the most stagnant pools, never entirely separated from the main stream which consisted of the payments for an expanding volume of international trade.

In this field of international payments, as in other fields of economic behavior, economists have searched for uniformities that might be reduced to a neat theoretical system. They have usually explained the relations between prices, interest rates, and the volume of trade and investment, by assuming the fully developed mechanisms of the London money market. These mechanisms played an important role and were decisive in the ultimate clearing of the balances of international payments. But they were unique. No other money market functioned in quite the same way, and most of them were embryonic. The summary of the balancing process which follows emphasizes first the role of the London money market in the clearing process.

But it goes on to illustrate how less developed countries adapted themselves by their own methods to the pressures imposed by London on their balances of payments. The main instrument at London's disposal was its control over the financing of international trade. It did not need to call in loans. It needed only to limit its extension of new loans. As bills of exchange came to maturity usually within three months, they were not replaced by new bills, or were replaced only at a higher discount rate. This was the means by which London could exert pressure both upon the prices of internationally traded commodities and upon the volume of credit available for international investment.

The Bank of England was concerned to maintain a balance between its gold reserve and the short-term funds that were invested mainly in the acceptance and discount markets, and the total volume of credit made available to their depositors by the British commercial banks. If the total volume of credit had swollen so that business was active and prices were rising, there would be a growing demand for bank notes and coin as till-money and for use in petty transactions. The first-line assets of the commercial banks consisted of their "cash in hand and at the Bank of England." If their credit advances began to exceed a conventional multiple of these reserves, notes and perhaps gold coin would be drawn from the Bank of England. Thus an *internal drain* for domestic purposes would ensue on the Bank's gold reserves.

Normally also a period of active business in England would mean a brisk demand for imported foodstuffs and raw materials. Thus the balances held in London by foreign and colonial banks would be augmented. Temporarily, these balances would find their way into the short-term money market where they would be used primarily to finance foreign trade, and secondarily for the promotion of new capital issues. As these balances were used to finance exports of British goods, the exchanges would turn against London. The foreign holders of sterling would draw upon their holdings to pay for the imports they had bought. The exchange value of sterling would then fall toward the gold export point from London and there would be the danger of an *external drain* upon the Bank's gold reserves.

The Bank would normally raise its rate of discount to protect its gold reserves or to check dangerous credit expansion. Before raising it against an external drain, many devices would have been used. On occasion foreign holders were persuaded to take balances out of the short-term market. More often gilt-edged securities were sold in order to acquire cash and thus to reduce the note issue. This had the effect of tempting short-term money into purchases of gilt-edged investment. Occasionally there were slight raises in the gold purchase price. These devices would have some effect on interest rates. But if the pressure persisted, the discount rate at which the Bank of England would take bills that the discount market was unable to handle would be raised. If the supply of short-term money was sufficient to take care of all the bills being offered, the rise in Bank rate might be ineffective. However, this was usually interpreted as a danger signal. The commercial banks and specialized houses would take warning and begin to restrict their dealings. But if short-term money remained easy, steps would then have to be taken to drive the market into the Bank. The usual means of doing this was by heavier sales of securities in the open market until the surplus short-term funds were mopped up. This would tend to drive interest rates up because there would be less short-term money available for investment, and the price of fixed interest securities would have to be lowered to attract purchasers.

As the London interest rates were driven up, speculators would buy sterling to take advantage of the higher interest rates paid on sterling invested in London. They would also operate in the forward exchange markets. Here they would borrow foreign currencies in other money markets at the cheaper interest rates in order to buy sterling which would earn higher interest. This would more than offset the higher exchange rates at which they would contract to sell the sterling for foreign currencies in a month or three months' time.[19] Such operations would have a double effect in bringing the rates of interest into equilibrium between the different money markets and also in bringing the exchange rates back toward the mint parity. In the Berlin market, for example, such borrowing of marks would raise interest rates and tighten credit. In London it would ease the strain that was developing. But these effects would only be temporary—a plugging of the immediate gap in the balances of payments. Any long-run balancing would have to take place through an adjustment of prices and incomes and therefore of the volume of commodity trade, and through long-term interest rates and the volume of international investment. This in turn would ultimately be reflected in actual imports and exports of commodities and services.

In his survey of the way in which bank rate operated before 1914 in the London money market, J. M. Keynes pointed out that bank-rate policy has been explained as aiming at three objectives—regulating the quantity of bank-money, protecting the country's gold reserves by regulating the rate of foreign lending, and influencing the rate of investment relatively to that of savings. Of these objectives the first two are readily recognized as aimed at correcting the internal and external drains on the gold reserves. The third objective cannot be dissociated from the other two in fact, since it carries the analysis of both the domestic and the external effect of a rise in bank rate beyond the first effect of causing a fall in British prices and total income.[20]

19 Thus if the short-term interest rate was 3 per cent in London, and 2 per cent in Berlin, a German operator could buy £100,000 and invest it at 3 per cent for three months, earning £750 interest, as against the equivalent of £500 in Berlin. To do this he would sell forward marks at any discount appreciably less than ¼ per cent. If for example the spot rate was M. 20.35 to the pound sterling, and he could buy forward marks for M. 20.33, he would pay M. 2,035,000 for £100,000 on which he could earn an added interest of £250, and buy back the marks for delivery in three months for £100,098, thus making a net profit of £152 or M. 3,093.

20 There was a controversy in the thirties between J. M. Keynes and R. G. Hawtrey concerning the effect of higher short-term interest rates. Hawtrey had argued that the major effect was to bring pressure upon the commodity brokers of whose carrying charges interest formed a large part. Keynes at first disputed the importance of interest charges. After Hawtrey proved their importance by statistical evidence, Keynes retreated

As Keynes has pointed out, the objective of bank-rate policy which was uppermost in the minds of the practical bankers who evolved it in the nineteenth century was its use as "a means of protecting a country's gold reserves by regulating the rate of foreign lending." This objective it fulfilled since in Keynes's words it proved "both an expedient and a solution. It supplies both the temporary pick-me-up and the permanent cure—provided we ignore the *malaise* which may intervene between the pick-me-up and the cure." [21] The pick-me-up was the relief given by the restriction of foreign short-term lending and by the attraction of short-term foreign credits to take advantage of the higher interest rates. The malaise was the deflationary effect of the higher interest rates on investment and employment. The cure lay in the adaptation of prices and of long-term investment, to a level where the credit structure was not too top-heavy for the gold reserves to support while maintaining the customary relations between the credit superstructure and its cash basis.

This adaptation had to take place both in Britain and in every other country which sought to maintain its exchange rates stable in terms of gold and therefore of sterling. While the international gold standard operated, London called the signals for these adaptations and it called them by reference to the strains on its credit structure resulting from the fluctuations of world trade and investment. This was the supreme link between world markets. And the fact that new long-term investment which was so intimately linked with employment was a residual factor caused the recurrent malaise to which Keynes refers. The nineteenth-century marketing process cleared through London, and those who were responsible for the monetary reserves supporting

---

to his main defensive position which was that he preferred to emphasize the effect of higher interest rates upon total demand rather than upon the prices of already produced goods.

From the viewpoint of international trade before 1914, there seems no doubt that the most important effect of higher interest rates was, as Hawtrey argued, upon the prices of internationally traded commodities. From the longer-run viewpoint of employment policy, however, the residual effect of higher interest rates upon the credit available for new investment was a major factor in business cycle fluctuations. The stability of the exchange rates on London called for pressures primarily upon the prices of traded commodities. This was the quick method of adjusting balances of payments, but it produced a secondary effect on investment which aggravated the swing of the cycle.

The references to this controversy are: J. M. Keynes, *A Treatise on Money,* Vol. I, Ch. 13; R. G. Hawtrey, *The Art of Central Banking,* London, 1932, Chs. IV and VI; J. M. Keynes, *General Theory of Employment, Interest, and Money,* London, 1936, pp. 75–76, and R. G. Hawtrey, *Capital and Employment,* London, 1937, pp. 111–31.

[21] Cf. J. M. Keynes *A Treatise on Money*, pp. 189 and 214.

the credit structure through which it cleared were from time to time forced to protect those reserves by inflicting on their own and other countries a sharp curtailment of investment to correct previous mal-investment.

In New York, Paris, and Berlin, and also in Zurich, Vienna, Brussels, and Amsterdam, there were money markets similar to that in London. Between them there were short-term credit transfers associated usually with interest-arbitrage in the foreign exchange market. In the twenty years before 1914 these short-term credit transfers became an important means of balancing payments in the short run. It has already been shown that in New York the available short-term funds found their main employment in the stock market. A flow of funds from New York to London would therefore cause a fall in the stock market. It has been shown also that Paris endeavored to maintain a stable discount rate and an even flow of short-term funds available to domestic producers and traders. It was the policy of the Bank of France to lend gold from its ample reserves to forestall, or at least to mitigate pressure on short-term interest rates in London. In doing so it endeavored to keep its own interest rates from rising in sympathy with London rates, rather than to take advantage of the higher rates ruling in London. Thus each national economy made its own adaptations, through its own peculiar institutions and mechanisms, to the pressures imposed on it by London's attempts to regulate the balancing of international payments.

If this was so in the case of highly developed money markets such as those of New York and Paris, it was much more clearly demonstrated in the case of countries which did not possess such highly developed monetary mechanisms. China, for example, remained throughout this period before 1914 on a silver bullion standard. The Chinese trade statistics before 1914 showed an excess of commodity imports over exports. But careful study shows that this was not on account of an import of capital. In fact, China made heavier payments on account of interest and debt repayment than it received in the period from 1873–1914. Yet there was a fairly steady import of silver—particularly when the price of silver in terms of gold, of foreign currencies, and of such moneys of account as the Haekwan tael declined after the great silver discoveries which led to the demonetization of silver in Europe and the United States. Prices and land values in Shanghai were responsive to changes in the price of silver.[22] Here then is a case where the balancing process operated not through the medium of credit as in London and other highly developed monetary centers, but actually through a flow of specie.

In India during the seventies and eighties the balancing process operated as in China through a flow of specie. But here the British civil servants who were responsible for the government evolved an ingenious system by which they regulated the sale of bills drawn upon a gold fund established at the Bank of England. They bought and sold these bills so as to maintain the exchange rate of the rupee stable in terms of sterling. This was the first experiment in what came to be known as the gold-exchange standard. The rupee exchange rate was held at a fixed parity. The reserves of gold or of exchange convertible into gold were held in London.

Other countries began to adopt a similar system, holding their reserves in London or in New York. The domestic business of these gold-exchange standard countries was conducted in a local currency, in the case of India at this time mainly in silver. The exchange value of the local currency was kept at par by inflicting upon exporters and importers such changes in the prices of internationally traded goods as were necessary to balance payments. Because the subtle complexities of the London money market were not available in these undeveloped countries to cushion and spread the shock of sudden price adjustments the impact of changes in their balances of payments fell crudely upon commodity prices, first of exported and then of local goods.

A very clear, and more sophisticated, example of this kind of national adjustment was provided by Australia and New Zealand. Their local prosperity rose and fell primarily in response to the receipts from their exports of industrial raw materials and foodstuffs. Australia and New Zealand were nominally on the gold standard but their currencies were in fact pegged on sterling. These countries had no central banks. Usually the commercial banks held some gold. They also issued bank notes. But the volume of available credit was not governed either by the gold holdings or by the amount of note issue. It was geared to the funds available in London from export receipts or from borrowing. A good wool season with high prices would result in an accumulation of sterling. After the wool sales the banks in Australia and New

[22] See above pp. 307–9.

Zealand would have increased sterling balances in London and correspondingly increased deposits to the credit of the woolgrowers in Australia. These deposits would be spent on local purchases and would pass into the hands of importers who would draw upon them to buy drafts on the London balances with which to pay for the replenishing of their stocks of goods. The interest rate was stable at a customary level. In these circumstances the balancing process responded to changes primarily in export prices and to some extent in the volume of exports, by an expansion of local credit. This led to an increase in the volume of imports and to a rise in import prices, as far as the increased demand from these countries influenced prices.

In Australia and New Zealand this swing of the cycle was amplified by the fact that the stock and station agencies—firms which extended credit to the farming community with which to buy stock, seed, implements, and supplies—did so by using their deposits with the commercial banks as reserves. There was therefore a secondary and potent expansion and contraction of credit. Despite this tendency to exaggerate the swings of the cycle (which was reflected back into the industrial countries in fluctuations of the demand for manufactured goods and for development loans) the Australian and New Zealand banks were strong enough after the nineties to tide over such crises without departing from the exchange parity on London. Australia and New Zealand were able also to maintain an unblemished record of payments on their large external debts.

The same kind of balancing process was carried through in most of the raw material exporting countries, such as Argentina and others in Latin America. A season of high export prices would build up surplus funds in London. These funds would enable the raw material countries to import heavily. But there was always an appreciable lag—usually a year—before payment for these imports reduced the London funds built up by the exports. The result was an alternating rhythm of high export receipts and heavy imports. If the imports caused too severe a strain on London funds, the banks in the raw-material exporting countries would find themselves with depleted sterling deposits. Then deflation would ensue. In many Latin-American countries this recurrent strain on London funds caused both defaults on interest payments and from time to time, exchange depreciation.

In none of these countries outside western Europe and the United States was there a developed money market before 1914. Some of them have in recent years established central banks. But a central bank cannot operate (except as an instrument of government finance) without a money market in which short-term credit is used as a flexible means of adjusting the monetary system to pressures on the external balance of payments. In the latter nineteenth century the banks of most countries kept their surplus funds in London where there was such an active short-term market. Except for a very few countries there is not much point in attempting to describe the process by which international payments were cleared and balances were settled, in terms of a transfer of short-term funds back and forth between money markets of equal development.

For most of the trading world, what used to happen was this. When the Bank of England raised or lowered its discount rate (and therefore all the short-term interest rates which clustered around it), the credit available to acceptance, discount, and new issue houses (and equally to brokers in the commodity and security markets) was restricted or expanded. This would have an immediate influence on the prices of internationally traded commodities and would soon begin to affect the balances held by foreign and colonial banks in London.[23] When this happened, not only the bankers in New York, Paris, Berlin, and other monetary centers would soon feel the effects of this credit restriction or expansion in London, but also wheat growers in the Middle West of the United States, the Danube Valley, and the Black Earth region of Russia; woolgrowers, dairymen, and cattle ranchers in Australia, New Zealand, and Argentina; and peasants and plantation workers in Asia. These effects would reach them through a contraction

[23] Cf. William Adams Brown, Jr., *op. cit.*, pp. 774–75: "In this pre-war system of foreign exchange markets all countries had a substantial interest in keeping their particular currencies as stable as possible in terms of sterling, and their success in doing so contributed to the stability of their currencies in terms of one another.

"One reason for this interest in keeping the London exchange stable was that the world-wide price-making forces of primary raw materials were brought to a focus in world markets in London and Liverpool. British consumer demand was a dominant influence in the formation of many of these prices, of which the price of wool is a good example. In addition, the British view of the prospects of primary commodities had a great psychological influence in other countries, and throughout the continent buyers and sellers followed the British traders' lead. The world prices established in the British markets were a common element in the price structures of many countries. Their fluctuations in response to world-wide supply and demand forces directly influenced the incomes of large groups of producers in many countries, and consequently the demand for many products not traded in locally. They affected domestic costs of production. The international influence of the London or Liverpool price of many important commodities was therefore a factor tending to prevent substantial divergence in the movements of general prices of countries adhering to the international gold standard."

or an expansion of income, in which a fall or rise in local prices was a large element. The effects would be transmitted to each national economy in various ways peculiar to its circumstances—rarely through short-term funds being diverted from or to the local money market. In most countries before 1914 such money markets did not exist.

CHAPTER XIII

THE NEO-CLASSICAL DOCTRINE

THE ELABORATION OF ECONOMIC THEORY

THIS CHAPTER is concerned with the development and restatement of economic thought after the death of John Stuart Mill in 1872. It is particularly concerned with the contributions then made to the theory of international trade. In this period the basic concepts of economic theory were elaborated by mathematical reasoning. Significant contributions were made to the theory of value. There was a growing body of economic literature, both descriptive and analytical. Statistical data also became more abundant, and new devices of statistical method were invented to extract the essential meaning from these masses of figures. The great achievement of this generation of economists, however, was the fashioning of a theoretical apparatus derived from the mathematical elaboration of the theory of value.

The re-examination of the theory of value, which was to yield the fruitful concept of marginal utility, continued the classical tradition of economics as a study of the distribution rather than the production of wealth. The ingenious but inadequate labor-cost theory of value worked out by Ricardo, and regarded by John Stuart Mill as final, had emphasized the quantity of labor necessary to produce a commodity. This formal theory was hedged with assumptions and definitions; but these were forgotten or minimized by secondary writers and popularizers. Simplified in this way it could be used by the defenders of the existing social order—including the institutions of property, contract, and free competition—to demonstrate that free competition brought to all the maximum satisfactions that were consistent with that order. The group of writers who came to be known as the Harmony School—including Frederic Bastiat in France and Henry C. Carey in the United States—thus used it in their criticism of socialistic attempts to interfere with the working of the free market. But Karl Marx used his version of this labor-cost theory of value to attack the existing order, and particularly the institution of private property.

As early as 1854 the German, Hermann Heinrich Gossen, had formulated the theory of the satiation of wants, which led directly to the concept of marginal utility. Since wants are satiable, the utility of each successive addition to an individual's stock of a commodity will diminish. The more he has, the less the utility of each additional unit. The utility of the last unit which he finds it worth while to buy (or to make) is the marginal utility of that commodity to him. Gossen's work had passed unnoticed; but in 1871 two books appeared in which this concept was independently stated. In London, Walter Stanley Jevons applied the concept which he called "final utility" to the determination of value. In Vienna, Carl Menger also developed a theory of value based on this idea. Jevons had previously announced his discovery in a paper printed in 1862 and reprinted in 1866. Leon Walras had been lecturing along similar lines for some years at Lausanne and published his results in 1874. Alfred Marshall also had been working independently at Cambridge and his subsequent work was influential both in refining the theory and in reconciling it with the main body of classical doctrine.

This simultaneous formulation of a fruitful new concept in four independent centers of economic teaching was immensely influential. The elaboration of the concept and of its applications first to the theory of value and then to other aspects of economic theory occupied the majority of economic theorists for the rest of the nineteenth century.[1] The elaboration of this idea lent itself to mathematical exposition by use of the differential calculus. In the next two or three decades there emerged a symmetrical and elaborate system of theoretical analysis. It was at first devoted primarily to an exploration of the forces determin-

1 Cf. Knut Wicksell, *Lectures on Political Economy*, London, 1934, pp. 1–100. This clear exposition of the stages through which the modern theory of value has passed, was translated from the second Swedish edition published in 1911.

ing the value of commodities in a market. Analysis of the demand and supply of an individual commodity led to the development of a theory of general equilibrium. Therein it could be demonstrated that the prices of commodities were interdependent, and were constantly tending toward positions in which marginal costs and marginal utilities were in equilibrium, so that demand and supply would be equated.

The demand for each commodity would be effective at the price where marginal costs of production equaled marginal utility. Therefore the purchasing power available for each commodity depended upon the purchasing power available for all. A complete series of interconnected equations could be worked out in a system of general equilibrium. Every price as well as every demand and supply schedule —for the factors of production as well as for commodities and services —was a part of this mutual interdependence. Equilibrium was never completely attained. There were always misfits and miscalculations, but as long as competition was free there was always a strong tendency toward a return to equilibrium.

It has often been stated that the application of the differential calculus to the consideration of marginal cost and marginal utility as determinants of value was comparable with earlier developments in the experimental sciences by which mathematical precision was given to previously vague ideas. The illustrations cited are usually drawn from the physical sciences.[2] This raises the question whether economic forces can be assumed to act with the uniformity observable in physical phenomena, and to be capable of being studied one at a time on the assumption that other things remain equal. The reformulation of the theory of value assumed the continuance of political and economic institutions.

The theory of general equilibrium took for granted assumptions regarding social and political institutions, such as private property, freedom of contract, and a stage of industrial technology in which free competition was dictated by the existence of numerous producers and consumers among whom effective monopolistic combinations were impractical. It was concerned with probing the conditions of equilibrium in a competitive society unhampered by political intervention. It also assumed that economic forces were atomistic and infinitely divisible although interdependent. A favorite analogy was that of likening economic forces to balls in a bowl. Each was self-

[2] Cf. Knut Wicksell, *op. cit.*, p. 38.

contained, but each rested in a position determined by the position of all. This analogy is a perfect illustration of the fact that the neo-classical analysis was postulated upon the assumption drawn originally from Newtonian physics, of separate but mutually interdependent atoms held in equilibrium by mechanical forces. Economic analysis was therefore developed, largely by use of the mathematics elaborated to deal with physical problems, in terms of equilibria reached and maintained by mechanical forces acting and reacting upon mutually interdependent phenomena. This was particularly true in the first formulation of the static analysis which explored the conditions of equilibrium at a given moment. The increasingly elaborate use made of algebraic symbols expanded by mathematical manipulation, and of geometrical diagrams, demonstrated the fact that the reasoning was implicit in the assumptions that lay behind the precise definition of the symbols.

For some time, particularly among the followers of Menger in Austria, there was a tendency to overemphasize the importance of utility. It was not long, however, before the concept of the margin which had been developed at first on the demand side of the value equation was extended to the supply side. Gradually the reasoning was transferred from the theory of pure value to other aspects of economic study. In addition to marginal utility and marginal cost, most modern texts contain references to marginal productivity of labor, marginal efficiency of capital, marginal propensity to consume, import, save, and invest, and marginal net revenue. The concept of the margin has indeed been extended through every aspect of economic theory.

This elaboration of economic theory has often been described as a process of intellectual tool-making. The neo-classical economists displayed a remarkable degree of concentration upon methods of analysis rather than upon observation and classification of economic phenomena. Alfred Marshall was lecturer at Cambridge from 1868 to 1877 and, after an interval at Bristol and Oxford, Professor of Political Economy at Cambridge from 1885 to 1908. He became the leading exponent and teacher of the neo-classical school. Like all great economists Marshall did not confine himself to the elaboration of theoretical concepts. But there was some tendency among economists in general to concentrate upon tool-making. A distinguished member of the Cambridge school which Marshall founded has been cited as defining the subject matter of economics as neither more nor less than its own technique. Detailed analysis was sometimes developed as a demonstration of mathematical symmetries rather than as a deduction from observed and tested premises. Marshall himself had warned economists not to "fall tacitly into the fallacy of regarding what is tractable to our intellectual machinery as equivalent to what is important," but his warning was not always heeded.[3]

One may search long in the neo-classical economic literature before discovering any disposition to test the assumptions of theory or to alter the conceptual framework within which theory was developing. This is partly because of the neo-classicists' preoccupation with the fashioning of analytical tools, but also because the established order of society seemed to be both stable and efficient. The nineteenth century had opened in war and revolution. It seemed to be closing in peace and prosperity. At its commencement, violent and disruptive ideas had been vehemently debated. The classical economists had been concerned with great social issues. In their analysis of these issues they had developed a new theoretical system. The neo-classical writers carried over the main assumptions of their classical predecessors. These had been derived from the political philosophy of individualism and the doctrine of natural rights which can be traced back at least to John Locke. In their elaboration of economic theory, however, the neo-classicists ignored the changes in technology and in political organization which were beginning to alter the productive process, competition, and the institution of property. A new chemistry and a new physics were developing rapidly in the third quarter of the nineteenth century. The discoveries of men such as the American chemist, Willard Gibbs, and the English physicist, Clerk Maxwell, were quickly turned to account in steel-making and in the electrical industries. Andrew Carnegie began to put together what ultimately became the United States Steel Corporation and John D. Rockefeller to organize the Standard Oil Company. At the same time, a new idealist political philosophy began to be influential in Britain, though not in the United States.

The neo-classical acceptance of the classical assumptions is all the more remarkable for two reasons. In the first place these new scientific discoveries resulted from a re-examination of the assumptions of Newtonian physics. Again in their writing on economic policy, the neo-classicists, and even John Stuart Mill, the last of the classicists,

[3] Cf. E. R. Walker, *From Economic Theory to Practice,* Chicago, 1943, Ch. IV.

showed that they were aware of the new idealist philosophy. This was based immediately on the work of the German philosopher, Immanuel Kant (1724–1804), but ultimately on the work of Plato. This new philosophy emphasized the vital relation between the life of the individual and the life of the community. The liberty of the individual was still stressed, but it was no longer an atomistic individualism.

The door had been opened to social reform through collective action. Toward the end of his life John Stuart Mill had endorsed proposals that paved the way for a considerable development of municipal and state socialism. But his theoretical explanation of economic behavior continued to run in atomistic mechanical terms. Alfred Marshall made a conscious effort to construct an apparatus of economic analysis that would be useful in studying economic behavior from this new viewpoint. The political idealism which was gaining ground in Britain accepted the individualistic principles upon which economic activity was organized. Nonetheless it recognized the necessity for limiting individual rights whenever they impaired the rights of others. Marshall shared this philosophy. But it is difficult to see where he questioned any of the fundamental political and social assumptions of classical theory. Like Mill, he recognized the new forces at work and made concessions to them in regard to social policy, but he could not incorporate them into his analytical apparatus. This was because that apparatus was built upon assumptions that he did not question.

Thus the neo-classicists accepted the institutions of society which they found operative in the legislation and equally in the public opinion of their time. The main body of economic writing was not concerned primarily with great issues of public policy upon which there was fundamental disagreement, but rather with the elaboration of theoretical analysis upon the basis of agreed premises. However, the idea that study of economic questions gave scope for many kinds of analysis, and particularly for empirical observation and description as well as abstract theory, was gaining ground. In the first half of the nineteenth century, a school of German historical economists had protested against what they regarded as the abstraction, individualism, and materialism of the classical English writers. They pleaded that economic activity was part of the organic life of society and could not usefully be studied apart from its institutional setting. Toward the close of the century, however, the controversy between their followers and the neo-classicists died down. It became evident that there was no essential contradiction between theoretical and empirical studies but rather that these approaches to the study of economic questions were complementary.

When Alfred Marshall published his *Principles of Economics* in 1890, he made it clear that he was sympathetic to these criticisms of the classical doctrines. After making sympathetic reference to the vigorous new work appearing in the United States and various continental countries including Austria, he wrote that "on the whole the most important work that has been done on the Continent in recent times is that of Germany." He did not abate the need for "a firm backbone of careful reasoning and analysis," but he paid a particularly generous tribute to "the brilliant genius and national enthusiasm" of Friedrich List, and acknowledged that the historical studies of the German economists "have greatly extended the boundaries of economic theory." Ever since, there has been little dispute that both analytical theory and comparative historical studies have useful roles to play in the development of economic thought.

The most important body of dissent from the doctrines of the dominant neo-classical school was that of the Marxists. The work of Karl Marx himself has already been discussed in connection with his dissent from the classical theory. This is its proper historical setting. Though *Das Kapital* was not published till 1867, Marx was concerned with the earlier classical writers and particularly with David Ricardo. His followers disputed the marginal utility theories of value because these struck at the labor theory of value which was the theoretical foundation of the Marxian system of thought. However, neither this protest nor the voluminous and vitriolic disputations which, in Germany particularly, divided the Marxist school are particularly relevant to a discussion of international trade. In recent years the victory of the left-wing revolutionary group and its subsequent consolidation of power in the U.S.S.R. have practically eliminated the influence of those Marxist determinists who were content to wait till the inevitable contradictions of capitalism should usher in the socialist order, and likewise of the revisionists who believed that the workers should organize actively to promote socialism within the framework of capitalist democracy. These disputations of the past are regarded as deviations from the Marxian orthodoxy which runs from Marx and Engels to Lenin and Stalin. In this revolutionary creed deviations are not permissible.

It was not surprising that the dominant neo-classical school of economists in England and the United States ignored the Marxian protest. As world trade developed, capitalism appeared to be solidly entrenched and to be extending its influence. London had become the organizing center of this expanding system of world trade and investment. The continental expansion of the United States where capitalism was even less questioned than in Britain was intimately connected with the world market. The capital necessary to develop industry and to build the railroads that spanned the continent was drawn in large measure from London. The increasing production, not only of cotton but of the agricultural produce of the Middle Western states, found important export outlets in the industrial areas of Europe. The urbanization of western Europe would not have been as rapid without these growing supplies of raw materials and food arriving from the United States. Nor would the westward expansion in the United States have been as rapid if western Europe had not provided export outlets. The California gold rush in 1849 and the expanded production of silver from the Rocky Mountain states in the sixties were important factors in the monetary disturbances which led to the adoption of the international gold standard.

Thus it was hardly to be expected that economic discussions would be concerned with examining the basic premises of an economic order which was still displaying expansive vigor. Even in the decade preceding 1914, when the political tensions were building up that would issue in the first World War, both economic theory and business practice continued to take for granted the political and economic principles upon which the classical system of economic thought had been postulated. Those principles—particularly the prevailing belief in free competition, private property, and free contract—became articles of faith among the merchants, bankers, and industrialists who were the organizers of world-wide trade and investment. Edmund Burke had been right when he concluded that the aristocratic, feudal standards which he called "chivalry" were dead and that the businessmen whom he called "sophists, economists, and calculators" would be the controlling agents in nineteenth-century development.

The developing countries of the New World had rejected the free-trade doctrine. The emergence in 1870 of a united Germany upset the balance of power in Europe and led all but a small group of western European countries to abandon the dream of universal free trade. In the decades following 1870, the countries which clung to free trade were forced to accept great modifications of their agricultural and industrial production. Yet there is abundant evidence that the wealth and prosperity of the free-trade countries continued to increase. One of the greatest achievements of this trading system was its capacity to absorb the shifts in national production that were a consequence of international investment in the development of new areas of agricultural, mineral, and industrial production. The tensions that led to the first World War were political rather than economic. Never before or since had there been such flexibility of adaptation in the economic relations between trading nations as there was between 1870 and 1914.

In the early twentieth century a succession of diplomatic incidents arising from colonial and naval rivalries gave warning that imperialist scrambles for territory and for political influence were creating an international situation that might lead to war. The expansionist ambitions of Germany in eastern Europe, north Africa, eastern Asia and the Pacific Islands had been kept within reasonable bounds as long as Count Bismarck remained Chancellor. But they had been given freer rein after his fall from power in 1890. There was a definite accentuation of political tension at the turn of the century when the subjugation of the Boer republics by Great Britain in the war of 1899–1902 was widely attributed—in Britain as elsewhere—to the influence of a small but powerful group of mining capitalists. This imperialist adventure contributed greatly to the recriminations and diplomatic crises that followed in rapid succession. Whatever the influence of vested interests may have been in particular incidents, prestige and power rather than national economic gain became the motivating considerations in diplomatic maneuvering. By 1906, it had become evident that an armament race was in progress and that the suspicions and fears aroused by the negotiation of alliances and counteralliances might create a situation where an unfortunate incident could precipitate war. Several such incidents were smoothed over by skillful diplomacy, but with increasing difficulty. Then on June 28, 1914, the assassination of an Austrian archduke by a Yugoslav nationalist led to diplomatic exchanges between Austria-Hungary, Serbia, and Russia. The commitments of the Triple Alliance and the Triple Entente came into play so that Germany and Italy were called upon to support Austria-Hungary while France and Britain were aligned with Russia.

Italy did not accept this commitment; but before diplomacy could find a solution, the German armies had marched into Belgium on August 4, 1914.

It is not necessary here to discuss the diplomatic background of the war, nor to assess the weight of economic factors in the political tensions that finally led to war. All that is necessary for an understanding of the development of economic theory in the prewar and immediate postwar years is to recognize the fact that the political and economic institutions of capitalist organization were not seriously questioned. There was no re-examination of the fundamental assumptions of theory. The neo-classical doctrine was still set in the mold that had been cast by David Ricardo at the beginning of the nineteenth century.

THE NATIONALIST CHALLENGE

Despite the changing facts of production, trade, communication facilities, and credit organization, and despite the considerable elaboration of economic theory in general, theoretical analysis of international economic relations continued to follow the lines and use the simpler concepts of classical theory. In no other aspect of economic theory was the neo-classical acceptance of classical assumptions more evident than in the field of international trade. The gradual divorce of the theory of international trade from the main body of economic theory became a source of concern to specialists in the field and attempts were made to restate it so as to incorporate the new statistical and analytical techniques. These attempts failed of their purpose because the main body of theory had been elaborated upon tacit assumptions that did not take into account the revolutionary social and political changes that were developing in the early twentieth century.

Economic theory was itself in need of fundamental revision. Therefore it could not be used to illuminate the intricacies of international economic relations. Whenever this situation recurs—as it has repeatedly in the history of economic thought—there is cause to suspect the validity of the theorists' assumptions. This is not to impugn their logic but merely to raise doubts concerning the relevance of their assumptions to actual conditions in the real world. One reason for the failure of the neo-classical economists to take a more critical view of the assumptions on which their theories were erected was that the main issue of international economic policy was regarded as settled. The benefits of free trade had been demonstrated. Departures from free-trade policy were regarded as political aberrations. For example, F. W. Taussig concluded his presidential address to the American Economic Association in 1904 with an emphatic defense of the doctrine of free trade. In his view, this doctrine, though rejected in the practice of most governments, was intellectually unassailable.

At the turn of the century, doubts as to the theoretical justification of free trade, and dissatisfaction with the dichotomy that had developed between international-trade theory and economic theory in general, were beginning to be expressed with increasing frequency and force. What had been merely doubt grew into certainty, after the attempt in the 1920's to restore the international gold standard collapsed in a great depression. The final issue of dissatisfaction with current theory was a revolt against the whole body of classical and neo-classical doctrine initiated in 1936 by J. M. Keynes.[4] This revolt was based upon a rejection of the reasoning by which the international gold standard had been justified. This reasoning was rejected as theoretically imperfect and disastrous in its consequences, and the criticisms of the neo-classical doctrine were expressed in extreme terms. There are indications of a recoil from these extreme criticisms. But it is now evident that we are launched again upon a period of economic controversy comparable with that which followed the close of the Napoleonic Wars. As in the past, the attempt to find more adequate explanations of the working of economic forces has involved reconsideration of the whole body of theory, not merely that part of it which is immediately applicable to international trade.

Up to and even after 1914, international economic relations continued to be analyzed by most economists in terms of the simple conditions assumed by Ricardo. Two countries *A* and *B* each producing two commodities *x* and *y* continued to be the starting point from which the theory of comparative costs was expounded, and the theory of comparative costs continued to be the justification for a separate theory of international trade. It is, of course, possible to cite exceptions to this sweeping statement. The German historical economists rejected

[4] As an example of the growing body of protest may be cited Sidney Webb's letter (27 July 1890): "I went straight to the Club and read right through Marshall's six hundred pages—got up, staggering under it. It is a great book, nothing new—showing the way, not following it. For all that it is a great book, it will supersede Mill. But it will not make an epoch in Economics. Economics has still to be remade." Margaret Cole, *Beatrice Webb,* New York, 1946, p. 43.

For the Keynesian revolt cf. Chapter XV, "Economic Nationalism between the Wars."

the Ricardian teaching. The ideas of Friedrich List gained ground in Germany after 1870 and provided a useful theoretical basis for policies of national development behind the shelter of tariff barriers.

In the United States, Henry C. Carey, the son of Mathew Carey, was a diffuse and voluminous critic of the free-trade doctrine. In so far as any continuous thread may be found in the varying interpretations which Carey gave of his free-trade position, it is to be found in Alexander Hamilton's theory of economic development. The younger Carey was well placed financially and moved in the more successful business circles. His free-trade philosophy was a peculiarly American version of laissez faire which, before the Compromise tariff of 1833 and after the crisis of 1847, included advocacy of tariff protection. He was innocent of the Hegelian teachings which in Germany confused the wealth of the community with the power of the state. Carey's argument was directed toward the development of a manufacturing economy, to be created by giving scope to free enterprise. The exploitation of frontier opportunities provided him with innumerable illustrations of the beneficent results to be expected from such enterprise, but his ideas are difficult to reduce to a coherent theory. More sophisticated teaching, such as that of William Graham Sumner, included the tariff as one of the most flagrant examples of state interference with free enterprise. But this part of the teaching was apt in the United States to fall on deaf ears.[5]

The main stream of economic thought in the United States, Austria, Switzerland, France, and even in Germany, as in England, followed the Ricardian tradition. The discussions of international economic theory in this period before 1914 may be considered conveniently in relation to three major questions.[6] In the first place there was a distinct clarification of the assumptions that underlie the theory of comparative costs. Secondly, there was much discussion of monetary policy and of its function in the clearing and balancing of international payments. The third and main subject of discussion was the division of the gains from trade among the trading countries. These subjects are dealt with in the remainder of this section.

For a generation after 1848 John Stuart Mill's *Principles of Po-*

[5] Cf. W. G. Sumner, *Protectionism,* New York, 1885, p. VI: "Protectionism seems to me to deserve only contempt and scorn, satire and ridicule. It is such an arrant piece of economic quackery, and it masquerades under such an affectation of learning and philosophy, that it ought to be treated as other quackeries are treated."

[6] Cf. Chapter VII, "The Classical Theory of International Trade."

litical Economy had gone through successive editions until it gained almost unchallenged authority. In 1873 however, J. E. Cairnes published a general treatise, in which he developed the Ricardian distinction between national and international trade. In so doing, he revealed more clearly the limitations of the comparative cost theory. Cairnes opened his preface with a declaration of orthodoxy. He accepted the assumptions, defended the methods, and arrived at the conclusions of the classical writers. But in so doing he sharpened the intermediate steps of the reasoning. In particular he defined international trade as "that portion of the trade of mankind carried on between localities sufficiently separated from each other, whether by moral or physical obstacles, to prevent the action, as between producers in the trading localities, of effective industrial competition." This definition, crystallized in a phrase as trade between non-competing groups, was merely another way of stating the Ricardian assumption that the factors of production could not be transferred between countries. But this restatement threw a flood of light upon the abstract nature of the theories derived from this assumption.

The obverse definition of national trade as "carried on under those more favorable conditions where industrial competition is effective" had already drawn much criticism. Walter Bagehot was driven to defend it by emphasizing the fact that economic theory consisted of abstract reasoning from a hypothetical model. In doing so he spoke of "English Political Economy" and recognized that "it is known everywhere as the theory of 'free trade,' and out of England Free-Trade is almost everywhere unpopular." But, he argued, this English political economy consisted of "an analysis of that world so familiar to many Englishmen—the great commerce by which England has become rich," and therefore "it assumes the principal facts which make that commerce possible, and, in the way of an abstract science, it isolates and simplifies them; it detaches them from the confusion with which they are mixed in fact." The pure theory of international trade,[7]

[7] Cf. Alfred Marshall, *The Pure Theory of Foreign Trade and the Pure Theory of Domestic Values,* London, 1930. The foreign trade chapter is a rigorous elaboration of Mill's theory of international values, and in connection with the most important group of cases examined Marshall states (p. 5) that "the chief importance of these results arises from the fact that they may be applied to the trade that a compact industrial group carries on with its neighbours." The classical and neo-classical theorists defined international trade as trade between noncompeting groups, but discussed it as competitive trade between individuals. Cf. Frank D. Graham, *The Theory of International Values,* Princeton, 1948, p. 6.

therefore, is a study of the economic relations of groups inside which competition is perfect, but between which industrial competition is not effective because the factors of production cannot be transferred.

The extent to which trade between different countries conforms to this pattern obviously varies considerably at different times and in different regions. John Stuart Mill recognized this fact when he pointed out that wherever there was effective industrial competition, as between England and the West Indies, the trade was not international in his definition, but "more resembles the traffic between town and country, and is amenable to the principles of the home trade." Cliffe Leslie and other critics of Mill were not content with this recognition of the fact that some inter-country trade was not international. They attacked the classical distinction between international trade and home trade as increasingly unrealistic. The later neo-classical writers retreated to Bagehot's argument which defines "a nation in the economic sense—that is, a group of producers within which labour and capital circulate freely."

Under the international gold standard the distinction between domestic and international trade in practice became increasingly difficult to sustain. Capital moved more and more freely. Skilled labor and for a time, during the great transatlantic migration of the early twentieth century, even unskilled labor became mobile.

Little need be added at this point to the discussion of monetary policy in connection with the balancing of international payments. Running battles were fought over the silver question in the seventies and the eighties, and there were voluminous controversies over bank-rate policy. The international gold standard was being fashioned as the monetary mechanism through which international payments could be cleared and balanced. It was an elaborate and delicate process by which pressures on the credit facilities in different countries might be used to keep equilibrium in the world-wide marketing process.

Modern economists have come to believe that even in the latter part of the nineteenth century when prices were more flexible and there was more disposition than there is now to allow gold movements to bring about changes in the credit structure and therefore in prices—even then the changes in national income were the most important means by which equilibrium was restored in the international balances of payments. The neo-classical writers did not develop this idea. They emphasized the fact that from time to time the pressures on credit facilities involved deflation of commodity prices. While reserves were being accumulated to operate the credit systems on a gold basis, the pressure on price levels was heavy and the agricultural interests in many countries protested vigorously. Later when the credit structures had been organized so that the scramble for gold abated, it became evident that the periodic necessity for checking credit expansion, though exercised immediately on commodity prices, resulted in secondary and more severe pressures on investment. There was an alternation of expansion and contraction in new capital issues, lagging behind the manipulation of short-term interest rates that was dictated by the fluctuations of the commodity markets. As long as the drift of prices was upward, the resultant investment crises were not unduly severe. In the disturbed economic conditions between the wars, this cyclical fluctuation of investment and therefore of employment imposed a strain on national economies that was politically intolerable. The neo-classical writers, however, added little to the classical exposition of the price specie-flow theory by which the classicists had explained the balancing of payments.

On the other hand, important contributions to the theory of international trade were made in discussions concerning the division of the gains from trade. These contributions were a continuation of the controversy raised by Colonel Robert Torrens in connection with which John Stuart Mill had developed his theory of international values.[8] Torrens had argued that, since the value of commodities in international trade was determined by reciprocal demand, the demand for imports would be increased if a country lowered its tariff. Therefore the country would necessarily purchase its imports at a higher cost in exports per unit. In technical language the terms of trade would be less advantageous to the country reducing its tariff. The whole theory of international values was clarified when Alfred Marshall worked out his diagrammatic apparatus in *The Pure Theory of Foreign Trade.* Marshall distinguishes a normal case in which "a decrease in a country's exports will cause her to obtain her imports on terms more advantageous, but not much more advantageous than before." He then considers the most important exceptional case in which "a diminution of the total exports of a country may cause these to be in such urgent demand abroad that she obtains in return for her diminished exports an increased instead of a diminished supply of

[8] Cf. pp. 199–202.

foreign wares." Finally he considers the possibility that increased production for export greatly lowers the cost of production per unit so that the fall in export values diminishes the total amount of imports received in return.

This treatment recognizes the elasticity of demand for commodities and the possibility of increasing returns (diminishing costs of production). Marshall's analysis is static and therefore does not consider the possibilities of the factors of production being transferred from one country to another. Within these limits he plots on a series of diagrams the range of possible reactions and indicates the positions of stable and unstable equilibrium under the different conditions he assumes.

This elaboration of the theory of international values was carried forward by C. F. Bastable, F. Y. Edgeworth, and others. It is evident that it represents a partial though valuable treatment of the subject and needs to be combined with a similar elaboration of the supply side of the equation, starting from the theory of comparative costs. The combination has emerged in recent years in the equilibrium theory, which is summarized in the last section of this chapter.

Meantime it should be noted that academic discussion of the forces determining international values, upon assumptions which accepted the status quo in regard to existing social institutions and the economic development of different countries at a given moment, led to attempts at measuring the terms of trade and the division of the gains from trade. The classical economists had displayed little interest in these questions. John Stuart Mill's vindication of free trade rests largely upon political and even moral grounds. His economic case was cosmopolitan: an eloquent argument for foreign trade on the ground that its advantage consisted in a more efficient employment of the productive forces of the world. The classical economists had been content to rely upon the competitive efficiency of individuals and industries and had deprecated attempts to regulate trade for national advantage. British merchants evinced a robust faith in their own competitive power. But in other countries this was regarded as a rationalization of the interests of the already strong.

Toward the end of the century, doubts concerning the net advantages of a unilateral free-trade policy were expressed more vehemently in Britain itself. The Colonial Conferences called in connection with the Jubilee celebrations in 1887 and 1897 resulted in pressure from the self-governing colonies for preferential treatment in British markets. A considerable body of British opinion supported by economists of the historical school advocated closer commercial relations within the Empire. The demonstrations of imperial solidarity during the Boer War encouraged the tariff reformers. But free-trade sentiment was still strong in Britain and a general election in 1906 resulted in a resounding defeat for the tariff reformers.

Among the controversial literature one brief document may be cited to indicate the shift in opinion that was taking place in Britain. The Conservative Prime Minister, A. J. Balfour, was a distinguished philosopher and President of the Royal Economic Society. In August, 1903, he circulated among his colleagues a memorandum which was afterward published. Approaching the question of tariff policy as a free trader, he rejected the extreme positions on either side. He rejected the cosmopolitan free-trade position on the ground that the benefit of the world as a whole was not necessarily identical with the benefit of each particular country in the world. Going on to argue that the failure of other great nations to follow her free-trade lead had placed Britain in a vulnerable position, he raised the question "whether a fiscal system suited to a free trade nation in a world of free traders, remains suited to a free trade nation in a world of protectionists." He realized, as subsequent events were to prove, that Britain was "hampered indeed by foreign tariffs, yet able, in spite of them, to carry on an export trade which, if it does not increase as we might wish, yet increases rather than diminishes, and an import trade of unexampled magnitude." [9]

Mr. Balfour's argument rested finally upon the last point—the dependence of a heavily populated country upon imports of food and raw materials, and the consequent necessity of keeping open some markets for its exports. What he was concerned with was Britain's dependence upon imported foodstuffs and raw materials which might become a source of difficulty as other countries closed their markets progressively to British exports. Therefore he pleaded that Britain should not continue to accept the free-trade policy as perfect, "merely because it is simple, unartificial, and, above all, familiar." In a word he asked for a return to tariffs for bargaining purposes.

The cause of unilateral insular free trade was lost when such calculations came to be regarded as significant. No country would con-

[9] A. J. Balfour, *Notes on Insular Free Trade*, London, 1903.

tinue to expose itself to the risks and fluctuations of a situation in which its rivals not only pursued the policy of fostering their industrial development (and in the case of Germany, its military potential) but did so by thrusting part of the cost on the free-trading country. Mr. Balfour wrote the epitaph for the laissez-faire, free-trade doctrine when he pointed out that

> the actual nations into which the world is parcelled out,—would never have come into being, and could never be maintained as they are, but at the cost of something which, from the point of view of pure free trade theory, must be regarded as economic waste. And inasmuch as they are thus a standing violation of cosmopolitan free trade (as thus defined) it is not surprising that in their efforts at self-preservation they have not felt themselves bound to consider only arguments drawn from cosmopolitan economics. They have taken into account, not always wisely, something more than the present pecuniary interest of individual consumers and producers, they have recognised that the state is something more than the individuals composing it at any one time, and that not only is it irrational to suppose that what is good for the wealth-producing capacity of the world must necessarily be good for each particular state; but that quite certainly it is not.[10]

Thus in the field of international trade, the institutional setting betrayed the assumptions upon which theory had been elaborated. Nations were not ready to accept the consequences of free trade. Moreover the theoretical structure was built upon assumptions that approximated the simpler conditions of the late eighteenth and early nineteenth centuries. It offered at first too simple an explanation of the forces determining the division of the gains from trade. And when these came to be analyzed more closely, the analysis lent encouragement to the forces of nationalism.

More important still, theory was confined to analysis of static conditions. It neglected the factors of change and development in a dynamic world. There is a piety of scholarship which shrinks from breaking with the terminology and conceptual framework of past theory. Marshall took pains to fit his analysis into the pattern worked out by Mill, as Mill had been careful to work within the Ricardian pattern. Bagehot, noting the increasing range and importance of capital movements, remarked upon the necessity for modifying the classical as-

[10] *Ibid.*, p. 5.

sumptions. In the late 1870's, he had written that "Ricardo formed, and others have continued, a theory of foreign trade in which each nation is bounded by a ring-fence, through which capital cannot pass in or out. But the present state of things is far less simple, and much of that theory must be remodelled." It remained for a later generation of economists to attempt this remodeling. Before this was attempted, revolutionary changes of economic philosophy and structure had followed in the wake of a destructive war.

THE NEO-CLASSICAL RESTATEMENT AND VERIFICATION

Before the war of 1914–18, restatements of the theory of international trade followed the Ricardian pattern. In Britain the free-trade policy seemed firmly settled. There was little inclination toward revision of the theory on which it rested. Over most of Europe, however, as well as in the United States, and in the new countries of European settlement, the protectionist doctrine gained ground. The slogans upon which this doctrine rested were political rather than economic, and it was on political grounds that the case for free trade was finally challenged in Britain. Friedrich List had been concerned to foster the union of German states and to stress the educational benefits of industrial development. Alexander Hamilton also had been concerned with the strength of the union. The historical economists of the later nineteenth century did not formulate an alternative to the classical economic theories. They criticized them as being too narrowly based.

Early in the twentieth century, however, an Austrian economist, Richard Schüller, put forward a theory of protection based on purely economic reasoning. He argued that the total income of a country may be increased if a marked expansion of production is stimulated by a moderate tariff, entailing only a slight rise in the price of the protected commodity and only a moderate burden on the consumer. The neo-classical criticism of this argument was able to demonstrate that the expansion of the protected industry, at any given moment, must either draw resources from already existing industries in which the country's comparative advantage is presumably greater, or it must call into production unutilized resources. Schüller was clear on this point, but he argued that underemployment of resources was the rule rather than the exception.

At first glance this argument bears some resemblance to the "field of employment" concept urged by Wakefield and, before him, by Alexander Hamilton, and accepted by John Stuart Mill. It has also been claimed that Schüller anticipated the position taken by the followers of J. M. Keynes in recent years. It is difficult to accept either of these parallels. Schüller's analysis was static. The argument of Hamilton and Wakefield was dynamic. It presumed the movement of labor and capital to develop the idle resources of a new country. The infant-industry argument, admitting the case for protection over a limited period of time in order to develop the potentialities of such a situation, had been accepted in theory by both the classical and neoclassical economists from John Stuart Mill on.[11]

In considering Schüller's argument it must be remembered that the existence of idle natural resources at any given moment does not prove that the national income would be enhanced by bringing these resources into production. In so far as Schüller's argument differs from that of Hamilton's infant-industry argument, it is based upon a very old but persistent fallacy. Land lies idle, waterpower is unutilized, minerals remain in the ground whenever at the prevailing costs of production it is cheaper to import commodities. In such cases, the country's labor and capital are more profitably used in other directions. It would not increase the national income to divert labor and capital from profitable export to less profitable domestic industries, in order fully to utilize a country's natural resources.

There is more point in Schüller's argument concerning the use of unemployed or underemployed labor. In most cases this is a question not of the total national income but of its distribution. There is no doubt that in a single industry employment may be preserved against competitive imports by the imposition of a tariff. There is equally little doubt that in certain circumstances a larger working population may be maintained at a desired level of wages by a protective tariff, the burden of which is borne mainly by export industries that

11 Most economists have admitted it as a theoretical exception to the rule of free trade, the practical importance of which is much exaggerated. Cf. F. W. Taussig, *Some Aspects of the Tariff Question,* Cambridge, 1915, Ch. II and Gottfried Haberler, *op. cit.,* pp. 278–85. The political leaders of the free-trade movement went even further. Cf. G. Armitage-Smith, *The Free-Trade Movement,* London, 1898, p. 153, citing Richard Cobden's statement: "I believe that the harm which Mill has done to the world by the passage in his book on Political Economy in which he favours the principle of Protection in young communities has outweighed all the good which may have been caused by his other writings." Cf. also John Bright's comment on Mill's theoretical objections to the secret ballot: "The worst of great thinkers is they so often think wrong." (G. M. Trevelyan, *Life of John Bright,* p. 174.)

provide relatively little employment.[12] Theoretically there is even a possibility that, in the short run, the employment of otherwise idle labor, or the maintenance of employment in an industry threatened by temporarily severe competition, may increase the national income. Against this theoretical possibility must be set the risk that attempts to maximize national income by tariff or other methods restrictive of trade may initiate a widening circle of tariff reprisals.

It must be concluded, therefore, that Schüller's attempt within the framework of the Ricardian static analysis to construct a theoretical basis for protective policies was based in respect of material resources on fallacious reasoning. In respect of labor, the classical economists would have regarded his contentions as theoretical curiosities with unwise and dangerous implications for practical policy.

The classical doctrine was not seriously undermined by economic criticism before 1914. The cases in which it could be demonstrated theoretically that a nation might gain from intervention in the marketing process were regarded as unimportant exceptions to a sound general rule. They lent support to the arguments of those who, primarily for political rather than economic reasons, rejected or questioned the free-trade doctrine. But economists continued to teach that the long-run advantages of international specialization outweighed the speculative possibilities of maximizing temporary positions of advantage at the risk of impairing that specialization. Those who dissented from the free-trade doctrine did not successfully dispute its economic logic, but put greater weight on political factors.

Even after 1918 there was a remarkable degree of unanimity among economists. This was evidenced by the practically universal agreement on the necessity of restoring the international gold standard as quickly as possible. Indeed it was not until well after the first World War had ended that economists succeeded in achieving the systematic remodeling of the classical theory of international trade that Bagehot had seen to be necessary.[13] Before F. W. Taussig put into final shape

[12] This case is argued by a group of Australian economists in *The Australian Tariff: An Economic Enquiry,* Melbourne, 1929. Cf. p. 140: "The advantage of protection is in the maintenance of a larger population than could have been expected at the same standard of living without the protective tariff. It is not an advantage to every part of the population, nor has it produced the maximum of income per head. But given the basic Australian objective of seeking the largest white population at the highest standard of living, we consider that the protective tariff has been an effective means of securing it."

[13] Cf. J. M. Keynes, "Reconstruction in Europe," *Manchester Guardian Commercial Supplement,* No. 1, April 20, 1922, p. 5: "I do not see how one can arrive at a real sta-

his systematic treatise, he and his pupils had undertaken a series of essays in the verification of international trade theory. These essays were concerned with the statistics of the prewar period in various countries. Necessarily, they took account of credit mechanisms and capital movements that had found no place in the classical analysis. In Taussig's restatement of the classical doctrine, therefore, the rigidity of the assumption that the factors of production were immobile between countries was relaxed. Nevertheless Taussig reasoned within the framework of the classical doctrine, and his work though published in 1928 must be regarded as belonging logically to the nineteenth-century school which is usually described as neo-classical.

Taussig's treatise began with an analysis of the conditions in which trade arises. Throughout this analysis, Taussig avoided the complications that arise in a money-economy, and made his argument in terms of barter—goods being exchanged for goods. He constructed laborious arithmetical tables designed to illustrate absolute, equal, and comparative cost differences. Whether these are stated in terms of labor cost alone, of real costs of production measured by some composite unit, or whether the obverse demonstration is made of the absolute, equal, or comparative advantages which a country enjoys in being able to produce more units for a given cost—the arithmetic is always an elaboration of Ricardo's. As Taussig pointed out, most trade arises as a result of absolute cost differences. Thus it is obvious that the cost of production of bananas in a tropical country, measured in labor time or in any other way, is less than the cost of production of bananas in a temperate climate.

He demonstrated that a country might find it advantageous to devote its limited resources to the production of the commodities in which it had the greatest comparative advantage. Thus assuming that labor and capital could not be transferred, a country might import goods which it could produce at less real cost, in order to concentrate upon the production of other goods in which it had an even greater cost advantage. Only in the case where the labor costs of different

bilisation except by re-establishing the gold standard in as many countries as possible," and No. 2, May 18, 1922, p. 67, in reply to M. Hanotaux: "No! The economist is not King; quite true. But he ought to be! He is a better and wiser governor than the general or the diplomatist or the oratorical lawyer. In the modern over-populated world, which can only live at all by nice adjustments, he is not only useful but necessary."

Marshall's *Industry and Trade* was published in 1919, and his *Money, Credit and Commerce* in 1923. The final systematization of neo-classical theory, however, was F. W. Taussig's *International Trade,* which appeared in 1928.

commodities in one country bear the same relation to each other as they do in another country, would there be no profit in trade. Taussig showed this theoretically by an arithmetical example where, in two countries each producing two commodities, the cost of the first commodity in each country was twice that of the second. This is the highly unrealistic case of equal cost differences. In the real world, with many countries and many commodities, and with many elements besides labor entering into cost, it would be virtually impossible to find no opportunities for trade.

The core of Taussig's argument was that the barter terms of trade are determined by reciprocal bargaining. This means that the quantity of exports necessary to procure a given quantity of imports will be determined, within the limits set by comparative cost, by the relative intensities of demand in each country. Thus the quantity of bananas exchanged for an automobile will depend upon the demand in both countries for automobiles and bananas.

As soon as an attempt is made to relax the assumptions upon which this simple, hypothetical reasoning was based, it becomes evident that the approach to international-trade theory from this angle is cumbrous. It becomes necessary to consider a whole range of countries producing a variety of different commodities. The labor-cost theory of value has been long since abandoned and if attempts are made to use labor cost as a symbol of real costs, in the sense of the quantities of the factors of production devoted to producing units of a commodity, there is no common measure of these quantities, except their value in terms of money. Taussig circumvented this difficulty by assuming that the structure of industrial production was approximately the same in the trading countries, both in respect to the grades of labor employed and to the capital equipment and organization combined with labor. He recognized that there was a great variety of labor and of industrial organization in each country. But he assumed that the variety followed roughly the same pattern in each country, and therefore he took labor cost as typical of all real costs. In so doing he begged what many economists would now regard as among the most perplexing and important questions of international-trade theory.

Many other modifications of the neo-classical theory are called for if it is to be useful as a tool with which to analyze the actual processes of international trade. Goods are produced under conditions of increasing or decreasing costs; demand varies with income and with price; there are large elements of imperfect competition (oligopoly and monopoly in the determination of prices); monetary policies, as well as prices, affect the national income; and the complicated processes of investment and the developmental (dynamic) consequences of the increasing mobility of certain of the factors of production need to be taken into account.

Conceivably it would be possible to modify the neo-classical theory so as to take all these complications into account. The result would bear about as much resemblance to the original as a moth bears to its parent grub. Most economists now prefer to adopt a more direct approach. There are some who would rest content with a theory of international prices, abandoning the attempt to analyze the factors determining those prices. More than the piety of scholarship, however, impels continued effort to work out a reasoned explanation of the conditions in which international trade arises. The theory of comparative cost in its neo-classical formulation may not be a satisfactory statement in modern conditions. But it deals with a question of real importance for which an answer should be found. The best use of the human and natural resources of the world, given the control of those resources by the states which constitute the governing authorities of different segments of the world's population, raises issues which go beyond the immediate forces of the market. The nineteenth century answered these questions in terms of maximum total productivity, assuming the status quo in respect to population, skills, industrial organization, and capital accumulation. This answer does not satisfy the twentieth century. The search for a more satisfactory answer goes on.

In the same way, the mechanisms created to clear and balance payments between national economies and the theoretical explanation of the processes by which those mechanisms operated are no longer adequate to the changed circumstances of our time. The essays in verification of the neo-classical theory of the balancing of payments and Taussig's summary of their major conclusions added considerably to our knowledge of the working of the international gold standard. In particular, the essays explored and measured the effects not only of gold movements and credit transfers in the ordinary course of trade, but the effects of international lending on commodity prices, on the course of trade, and on the terms upon which trade was conducted. They broke new ground in considering the balancing process as it operated when one or more trading countries operated under an inconvertible and fluctuating paper money standard. The results of these investigations were generally accepted and passed into the literature of economics.

In the years since 1914 however, great changes have taken place. The trade of a country on an inconvertible paper standard when the rest of the world and particularly the great countries are firmly established on the gold standard can throw light on modern problems. But these problems are different when virtually all countries are on inconvertible paper standards, and when the marketing processes necessary for the effective functioning of an international gold standard have been curtailed almost beyond recognition.

THE GENERAL EQUILIBRIUM THEORY

Early in the interwar period economists were giving up the laborious attempt to adapt the classical theory of international trade to modern conditions. This was so even before the systematic restatement of that theory had been completed. Attempts to explain value —objectively as created by labor or subjectively as the resultant of psychological preferences—had given way to the theory of general equilibrium in which the varied forces of supply and demand were regarded as interdependent. For the most part, the marginal utility explanation of value had been put forward as it applied to a single market; but the Italian economist, Vilfredo Pareto, the successor of Leon Walras at Lausanne, had shown that it could be applied to many interconnected markets.

Pareto published his *Cours d'économie politique* at Lausanne in 1896–97. He was able to show that the classical theory of comparative costs based on labor costs could not be transferred without confusion to a comparison of money costs in different currencies. He found that trade conducted in monetary terms did not behave exactly like barter trade because of the different reactions of money and prices in different countries. Thus he was aware of the unreality of the classical assumption that the effects of monetary policy can be ignored in the balancing of international payments. While Pareto himself did not apply his criticisms and suggestions to a positive reformulation of the theory of international trade in terms of the mutual interdependence of prices in different markets, it was inevitable that this application should ultimately be made.

Impetus was given the reconsideration of international trade theory by Alfred Weber's studies of industrial location. These followed the German tradition which had been set by Johann Heinrich von Thünen in his attempt to explore the implications of the advantages (rent) of situation. Von Thünen's study *Der isolierte Staat* postulates an isolated region of equal fertility with a market at the center in order to find what will be the factors determining the kinds of cultivation at different distances from the market. Alfred Weber had studied in more general terms the factors determining the choice of location for different industries, particularly the costs of transportation for different products. He left an unfinished study in which he argued that international trade should be treated as a special case of regional trade arising from the location of industry as determined largely by transport costs. Study of the factors which determine the comparative advantages of different kinds of production, regionally and internationally, provides important background material for a realistic theory of international trade. But analysis of international economic relations cannot be confined to the economic and geographical factors studied in a theory of industrial location. The recent development of national monetary policies has added force to the reasons already given for the rejection of Weber's thesis. The whole trading process—including investment, foreign exchange, and labor policies as well as price formulation—is affected by manipulation of the monetary systems to achieve desired political and social objectives.

One further source of the new approach to international economic relations is sufficiently important to warrant specific notice. The studies in verification of the classical theory undertaken at Harvard under Taussig's direction, enlarged the scope of that theory first in their emphasis upon capital movements and second in the studies of trade under inconvertible paper currencies. The former led to modification of the Ricardian assumption that the factors of production were immobile internationally. The latter set the theory of international trade again in a perspective wider than that of the international gold standard. Thus the way was opened for a theory of economic development, transcending the purely static analysis of the classical theory, and for a general treatment in which gold standard conditions constituted merely a particular case.

The reformulation of the theory of international trade also drew heavily upon the theorists who elaborated the general equilibrium theory of value. The work of Bertil Ohlin in particular, is avowedly an attempt to apply to international trade the mutual interdependence of prices worked out in the general equilibrium theory described in the first section of this chapter. Ohlin made use of this theory as it was developed by Knut Wicksell, Gustav Cassel, and later Scandinavian economists. While it could be argued that Ohlin's treatment was in completion of, rather than in conflict with, the classical theory, it did constitute a fruitful new method of attack upon international economic questions.

As economists applied the general equilibrium approach to the theory of international trade it became integrated once more with the main stream of economic thought. Thus they were able to use the elaborate apparatus—particularly of the theory of value—which was the main contribution to economic thought of the writers of the latter nineteenth century. However, what has been said of the political assumptions of economic theory in general and of the philosophy on which they rest is equally applicable to the general equilibrium theory of international trade. For this theory is based upon the assumption of free enterprise and freedom of the marketing process. Applied to the extension of the marketing processes as they developed in the latter part of the nineteenth century, it is a more satisfactory instrument of analysis than the classical theory. And in so far as the marketing processes remain free it remains the most satisfactory apparatus yet developed for an understanding of international economic relations.

The main propositions of the general equilibrium theory do not differ greatly from those of the classical theory. The same answers are given to the main questions, but these answers are both more general and more qualified. The analysis may start from the variations of productive factor equipment in different countries or from the prices of these productive factors. In either case it is concerned with applying to international trade the modern theory of value. This can be done, as Professor Haberler has shown, in terms of opportunity costs, or, as many economists following Professor Ohlin have preferred, in terms of general equilibrium or mutual interdependence of the prices both of commodities and of production factors. When approached in this way, analysis of international as well as national trade must be in terms of relative prices. Trade develops because variant combinations of the factors of production in different countries result in variant prices for different commodities. Interchange tends to equalize commodity prices in different regions, and also to equalize the prices of the factors of production. The prices of commodities, the prices of productive factors, the demand for and supply of commodities, and the demand for and supply of production factors interact in mutual interdependence. Pushed to its logical extreme such a theory may amount to little more than a statement that everything depends upon everything else. The real issues of international economic policy are to be found in the answers given to questions that may be asked concerning the particular combinations of productive factors which are the originating cause of profitable trade. How have these variations of productive factor equipment come to exist? Can they be modified? Moreover the actual processes by which general equilibrium is maintained need to be explained, and the hindrances to their smooth operation examined.

In Bertil Ohlin's *Interregional and International Trade* or in any modern text since the publication of Ohlin's work in 1933, the distinction between interregional and international trade in so far as economic conditions are concerned is shown to be one of degree rather than kind. There is regional specialization within nations. For example, the southern area of the United States differs a good deal from the industrialized northeast. The high agriculture of Iowa differs considerably from both. The mountain states and those of the west coast have their own characteristics. Nor are these differences merely the result of climate and soil conditions. In part they are the result of historical developments that have determined the number and character of the population, the social environment, and the accumulation of capital resources and special skills.

The monetary system is uniform throughout the United States. The barriers to interstate trade, though tending to increase, are not yet serious. There are no linguistic or legal barriers to movements of population or to investment. Yet in addition to transport costs, there are factors of inertia which hinder the free exchange of population. There are, in consequence, quite definite production advantages which differ from region to region. Thus trade between these regions has some of the characteristics of international trade.

On the other hand, there can be cited cases where transferences not merely of goods but of enterprise and certain types of skill, and of credit conveying command over capital resources occur more easily in international than in national trade. There was much more industrial competition between Japan and the area within range of the Manchurian ports and railroads than there was between this area and the Manchurian interior or the rest of China. Shanghai and Hong Kong had closer economic relations with San Francisco, New York, and London than they had with Peiping. Buenos Aires and Rio de Janeiro were definitely within the orbit of the North Atlantic trading world. Such situations tend to disappear as the sense of national unity develops. But in the latter part of the nineteenth century there was more freedom of international trade and international investment in many ports and coastal areas, and also in many areas of mineral exploitation, than there was freedom of domestic trade between these regions and their hinterlands.

In all cases of regional specialization within and beyond national boundaries, productive advantages arose from a favorable combination of productive factors—natural resources, climate, accumulated capital, special skills, and organizing ability. What Marshall called "the momentum of an early start" often gave advantages to an old-established region, particularly in manufactures where the external economies derived from auxiliary services and industries, developed banking, transport and communication systems, settled government and specialized education, were important.

It is an important aspect of the general equilibrium theory that these productive advantages are recognized as being variable. The nineteenth century was a period of incessant change. Many examples may be cited of the development of new production areas—cocoa in west Africa, sugar in many tropical islands, rubber in Indonesia, copper in the Belgian Congo, wool in Australia, silk in Japan, tea in India and Ceylon, petroleum in Venezuela, Borneo, Iran, Arabia, and elsewhere. Clearly the production pattern was flexible. Comparative advantage was variable and temporary, rather than fixed and permanent. It depended upon shifting combinations of productive factors. Technology, including the mechanics of transport, could bring into the market new sources of raw materials and cause older sources to become worthless for trading purposes. Skills could be taught and enterprise could operate in areas far distant from the original seat of their development.

The general equilibrium theory was able to take account of these facts of experience. The prices not merely of traded goods but of the instruments by which their production was facilitated, entered into the marketing process. Even if there was no actual movement of land, labor, capital, or enterprise across national boundaries, the prices of these factors of production would tend to be equalized between countries as a result of free commodity trade. The whole range of production and exchange tended increasingly to become interdependent. Wage rates affected and were in turn affected by the prices of commodities entering international trade. The structure of interest rates in all the trading countries became sensitive to international influences both vertically (within one country) and horizontally (between countries). If there was an unusual difference between short-term and long-term rates in one country, corrective movements would be induced by the transfer of capital from abroad just as an unusual spread between the rates for similar forms of credit accommodation would bring credit transfers from one country to another. This is not to argue that either wage rates or interest rates were uniform, or that the spread of wage and interest rates followed the same pattern in every country. National peculiarities led to characteristic patterns, and there were always differences of real wages and net interest and even greater differences of nominal rates. But departures from the patterns which themselves were changing toward uniformity would bring profit opportunities, and there was an increasing complexity of international credit transfers to take advantage of these openings.

It follows that the clearing and balancing of international payments departed more and more from the simple adjustments of national incomes and price levels generated by and in turn generating specie flows between countries. When the international gold standard was functioning at its best, gold had moved freely. More and more, however, this gold flow represented the distribution among national monetary systems of new gold coming from the mines. That distribution was affected by the balancing of international payments and played a part in that balancing. In times of crisis it even played a large part. Its role in the balancing process, however, steadily diminished as short-term credit transfers were increasingly relied upon.

As the balancing process became more flexible, involving both short-term lending expedients and longer-run adjustments of the productive and trading relations between nations, greater attention was given to the study of the clearing of international payments when they were in equilibrium, and also of the methods by which disequilibria were corrected. It was realized that the array of interdependent variables in the balancing process was extensive. First came the whole long list of tradable and potentially tradable commodities, both in respect to the quantities exchanged and their prices. These reacted on the prices of the materials, labor, and other factors entering into their production, and into the production as well of competing, auxiliary, and substitute products for many markets at home and abroad. Next came the quantities and prices of the invisible items entering into the balances of payments. Among these the most important immediately for adjustment purposes were the various forms of credit flows and the rates of interest charged for such accommodation. The volume and rate of interest for longer term investment and the prices of internationally traded securities, though separable in theory, were difficult to distinguish in practice from the shorter-term accommodation. All these elements of the capital market were closely connected with the credit regulation which was devised primarily to operate on the financing of international commodity trade. It was, therefore, a large keyboard on which the adjustment processes could play, and many of the keys were subtly connected.

As the balancing process became more delicate and intricate, it became more liable to instability. Greater importance attached, therefore, to the policies by which national monetary authorities attempted to regulate particularly the supply of short-term credit available to the markets. As long as national monetary authorities remained faithful to the international gold standard, their commitment to exchange stability provided a fixed point around which adjustment could take place. If the exchange rate of a country moved beyond the gold points, the loss or gain of gold reserves brought contraction or expansion in the credit structure sufficient to bring about the required adjustments of interest rates, income, and prices, and therefore of trade and investment. But there was much play in the balancing process before gold shipments occurred. The increasing intricacy of these adjustment processes was such that, for all practical purposes, the principal money markets of the world formed one integrated market. The commodity markets were less integrated, and their response to the shifting pressures necessary to maintain equilibrium in the national balances of payments was heavy and belated. The organization of national production and employment was even more sluggish.

It is obvious that the extension of international credit constituted a delaying operation, giving time for the country whose balance of payments was temporarily out of equilibrium to bring about the necessary adjustments of its credit structure, and therefore of its price and income situation. As long as exchange stability was unquestioned, short-term credit moved mainly in response to differentials in the interest rates. If New York was temporarily short of funds, a slightly higher short-term interest rate would attract funds from abroad. But this higher rate would also dampen speculative and productive activity in the United States. This would decrease imports and increase exports because purchasing power would be constricted and prices would fall. New York would therefore be able to accumulate from export proceeds the foreign exchange necessary to repay the short-term credit. An entirely different situation arose, however, when capital flight developed for fear of exchange depreciation, particularly after 1931. No rise in the interest rate was then sufficient to tempt short-term credit to the money market that was under strain. On the contrary, the worse the credit stringency became, the more capital fled the country.

Clearly also the international connections of the short-term money markets gave rise to subtle and intricate reactions in the main trading countries. To explore these reactions would involve an excursion into monetary theory that would take us too far from the immediate subject. It is sufficient to note here that the general equilibrium theory of international trade proved capable of comprehending within its analytical framework not only the barter of goods for goods, but the interconnection of the monetary systems of the main trading countries.

It does not require much reflection to conclude that the division of the gains from trade was revealed as a question incapable of a precise answer from a national standpoint. The barter terms of trade reflected shifts in the quantities of exports exchanged for imports. Interpretation of these shifts required great caution since many factors were operative. A volume of exports increasing at a faster rate than the volume of imports might mean that a country was having to part with a larger proportion of its national production. But it might also mean that its productive efficiency was increasing more rapidly than that of other countries so that it could afford to purchase larger imports even at a higher barter rate. The statistics used to measure the barter terms of trade were necessarily crude so that only approximate measurements of the shifts in trading terms could be obtained. Moreover all that was measured was the direction of the shift, not the division of the gains from trade. It could not be assumed that the division of the gain was satisfactory in the base period from which the shifts were calculated.

In addition, as long as exchange stability was unquestioned, short-term credit transfers and long-term investments across national boundaries blurred the balance of payments. Increasingly the statistics of current imports and exports told only a part of the story. The more closely linked became the markets of the world, the less possible it became at any moment to separate current transactions from those whose yield could only be determined in the future. As the twentieth century opened it became almost as difficult to estimate the division of the gains from trade between the more developed countries as it would be to estimate the division of the gains from trade between different regions in the same country. Calculations from the statistics of commodity trade omitted too many elements of the situation, and it was virtually impossible to get accurate statistics of the complex and variable movements of short- and long-term credit.

The simple fact is that the dream of a world-wide trading and financial system in which national boundaries would have little economic significance came close to realization between 1870 and 1914. The trading transactions and the investments of individuals and groups crossed national boundaries with greater and greater ease, in much the same way as individuals at that time were able to travel over most of the world without visas and in many countries even without passports. Ease of transfer implied laxity or absence of controls and therefore imperfect statistical registration. The reason why the theory of international trade could be integrated with economic theory in general was that the distinction between national and international economic transactions was becoming blurred. If this process had been followed to its logical conclusion, the theory of international trade might indeed have become merely an aspect of the theory of industrial location.

However, the nineteenth-century trading system came to an end by reason of the resurgence of nationalism, just as the medieval trading system had ended in conflicts between the city-states. Economists might argue that war was a great illusion which would end in ruin for victors as well as vanquished. But such logical demonstrations could not prevent the strivings for national power and prestige that ended inevitably in war. The forebodings of the economists were borne out. The nineteenth-century economic system did not survive the first World War, and in the revolutions and counterrevolutions that followed in its train a second and even more devastating world war was prepared.

The generation of conflict through which we are now passing resembles that which ushered in the nineteenth century in so far as revolutionary upheavals have coincided with marked advances in the industrial applications of scientific knowledge. The pace of industrial development has continuously accelerated, and there is far more cause to label the present period a scientific revolution than there was to call the period between 1760 and 1830 the Industrial Revolution.

But in other respects the present conflict differs radically from that of the early nineteenth century whose revolutions were aimed at assuring political and economic liberty by breaking through the outworn controls of a preceding age of regulation. The revolutions of our time have been protests against the philosophy and institutions of the system of individualism based on natural rights. They have aimed at the opposite values of social control, and they have created myths and utopias which differ radically from the nineteenth-century utopias of individual liberty. The impersonal forces of the market on which the laissez-faire economists relied to bring about a maximum of production and a distribution of income which, if not equitable, would at least be effective in maintaining high production, tend now to be displaced as political ideals by such objectives as full employment and social security.

Inevitably these objectives imply regulation. And the only mechanisms presently available for such regulation are those of the nation-state. The evidence for this is to be found on every hand, and nowhere is it more conclusive than in the field of international economic relations. Tariffs, quotas, exchange controls, planned investment, and monetary policies directed toward stabilizing the national income constitute a formidable reinforcement of nationalism in the economic sphere.

Economic theory has begun to rationalize the new objectives. Working from the concept of national income, it is beginning to explore the processes of social accounting within a framework of national planning. Whatever may be thought of the wisdom or practicability of such planning, the fact must be recognized that the nineteenth-century integration of market processes has been impaired by the emergence in every country of a greater measure of state intervention particularly in the monetary sphere. The degree of intervention varies from complete state planning—as in the U.S.S.R.—through various modifications of the social service state to national economies still operating largely on a basis of private enterprise. But in every country there has been an increased degree of intervention and, in all, the instruments of intervention have been national.

The remainder of this book is devoted, therefore, to analysis of the forces which have led to this situation and to exploration of the questions of international economic relations which it raises. Reluctantly the general equilibrium theory must be set aside as an apparatus more applicable to the marketing processes of the prerevolutionary period than to those of our own time. What must be studied is again—as it was in the age of mercantilism—the commerce of nations rather than international trade. A new effort, involving a fundamental re-examination of elements and principles and unlikely in the circumstances to yield any symmetrical theory capable of general application, must be made to piece together into a coherent pattern the confused intimations of the age that is struggling to be born.

PART III

WARS AND REVOLUTIONS

"THE actual interdependence of human life, of persons, classes, nations, far surpasses our awareness of it, and still more our arrangements for cooperation. Wisdom is largely the perception of this interdependence, and the endeavor to give it organs."

Charles Horton Cooley, *Life and the Student,*
New York, Alfred A. Knopf, Inc., 1927

"Dans une de ses spirituelles lettres à Mademoiselle de Lespinasse, Turgot disait: «Quiconque n'oublie pas qu'il y a des États politiques séparés les uns des autres et constitués diversement ne traitera jamais bien une question d'économie politique»."

Institut National de la Statistique et des Études Économiques, *Études et Conjoncture Économie Mondiale,* Nos. 7 et 8, Décembre 1946 et Janvier 1947, p. 7.

CHAPTER XIV

THE END OF LAISSEZ FAIRE

THE CALAMITY OF WAR

It is sometimes argued that harping upon the effects of a past war is merely an excuse for failure to take action based upon a realistic appraisal of existing conditions. Every economist must sympathize with this. The wars were fought and have passed into history. Their consequences cannot now be escaped. The only practical attitude is to accept and build upon them. Yet it must be recognized that war impairs the ability of communities to rise above their misfortunes and to take rational attitudes toward the problems of reconstruction. Students of society have long known that great wars have been followed by economic disturbances, by a decline of political and social standards, and by deterioration in the physical and mental qualities of the population.

When this is borne in mind the economic fumbling of the years between the wars is easier to understand. The record of this fumbling, if interpreted with due regard for the different circumstances of our own postwar period, helps to make clear the questions with which the second World War has confronted us. The direct economic consequences of the first World War were too vast to be coped with by the peoples immediately concerned. They were faced by shortages and breakdowns. Ill-fed and insecure, they watched governments fall and monetary systems deteriorate without having either the resources or the energy to do much about it. Organized economic activity depends upon co-operation, and co-operation requires faith in the mechanisms of exchange. That faith and the energy which it generates were lacking in the difficult years after 1918. More than ordinary effort was called for just when reserves of energy had been exhausted.

Most people were eager to return to the prewar economic arrangements that seemed to have worked so well. It was hard to realize that it would prove impossible to restore the prewar economic system. Throughout the official conferences and the unofficial discussions of the 1920's, there was a backward-looking attitude—an attempt to restore, reconstruct, and rebuild upon the old plan of international co-operation. Abandonment of government controls over production and prices, reduction of government expenditure and taxes, balanced budgets, removal of trade barriers, and a speedy return to gold as the basis for national currencies were almost unchallenged objectives.

In the more fortunate countries domestic controls were quickly removed. But greater difficulty was experienced in restoring the international gold standard, and little real progress was ever made toward the removal of international trade barriers. What was achieved in the 1920's was the restoration of private enterprise within the national boundaries of those countries that had escaped the worst ravages of war, not the restoration of the international marketing process. Such reconstruction as took place was rendered possible only by reversing the currents of capital investment. Europe had been the world's banker; but after the war, Germany and other central European countries borrowed heavily from the United States.

In an economic sense the world which emerged from war in 1918 had been transformed. A large part of Europe had been cut off from world trade for four years. In the first postwar years (1919–20) the impoverished European countries made great efforts to re-equip and restock their factories. Their peoples bid desperately for imports even at the price of a continuously accelerating depreciation of their exchange rates. The more they bought from abroad the greater became the strain on their balances of payments, and the lower in consequence the value of their currencies. The inevitable end of this spiral, and of the similar though slower internal spiral of prices and costs, was monetary depreciation. And this led quickly in the most weakened countries to hyperinflation and economic collapse. Foreign assistance, and in some cases foreign control, was necessary to stabilize the currencies and to resume trade again on a modest scale.

Changes in the political map of Europe also had far-reaching economic effects. By 1917 Russia had lapsed into economic disintegration and political revolution. The agent of political reorganization was a small group of exiled revolutionaries led by Nicolai Lenin. The German government had facilitated the journey of Lenin from Geneva to the Russian frontier in the hope that his activities would weaken their enemies on the eastern front. After a brief period of underground activity, Lenin and his associates launched the revolution which in November, 1917, established the U.S.S.R. At the close of the war abortive attempts were made by the allies to destroy the still weak Soviet state. Even after the futility of these interventions was realized, economic activity in Russia remained at a low level and the U.S.S.R. was almost completely divorced from the rest of the world. For some neighboring countries and for Germany in particular, the loss of the Russian trade was a severe blow. The U.S.S.R. repudiated the debts of the Tsarist government and for France this meant the loss of a substantial part of her international investments. The destruction of business enterprise and the confiscation of mining and other concessions owned by foreign capitalists was a heavy blow to influential business groups, particularly in Britain. But what was of more importance in the long run was the withdrawal of Russia from world trade, and the erection of a novel form of political and economic organization whose only economic contact with the outside world was through a state trading monopoly.

The peace settlement in 1919 created new nation-states in Europe. Finland, Estonia, Latvia, and Lithuania were carved out of Russia, and Austria, Hungary, and Czechoslovakia out of the Austro-Hungarian Empire, while Poland was restored as a sovereign state. Each of the new countries set about to equip itself with tariffs designed to develop a large measure of industrial self-sufficiency, and with central banks capable of financing that development. The result was a severe restriction of intra-European trade. The consequences were particularly unfortunate for the countries of the Danubian basin which had formerly been parts of a balanced regional specialization.

It must not be forgotten that four years of war had left their mark on the countries outside Europe. In most of them and particularly in the United States and Japan, the stimulus of war demands and the absence of European competition had led to industrial expansion. At the same time their capacity to export agricultural products and minerals was much increased.[1] Except in the United States and Japan, the industrial expansion was on a comparatively small scale. But it was important, both because it laid the foundations of further expansion and because it led to increased protectionism after the first postwar depression developed from 1929 onward. The nineteenth-century patterns of specialization as well as the circuits of trade had been broken in the war years.

By far the greatest development of manufactures took place in the United States which increased its share of world industrial production from 35.8 per cent in 1913 to 42.2 per cent in 1926–29, while Europe's share fell from 46.3 per cent to 40.7 per cent.[2] Moreover, the United States and the other countries of the Western Hemisphere increased their agricultural exports during and just after the first World War. Japan was able to increase its share of world markets, particularly for textiles. Its share of the world's industrial production more than doubled, increasing from 1.2 per cent in 1913 to 2.5 per cent in 1926–29. Many countries shared in the dispersion of the textile industry upon which Britain's industrial position had rested so heavily. Britain was hard hit also by strong competition in shipbuilding and by a heavy fall in ocean freights, as well as by increased competition in the coal industry arising from the wide use of petroleum and hydroelectrical power.[3]

The Bank of England resumed its nineteenth-century role as the controlling agency in the international capital market and took the initiative in arranging reconstruction loans immediately after the war ended and before the pound sterling was stabilized. The great relief effort of the United States had been mainly concentrated in the armistice period, January-August, 1919. In the years 1921–24 Britain lent abroad an average of £124 million yearly. Most of the first reconstruction operations in Europe were the result of this British

[1] E.g., the added value of manufactures in New Zealand increased from £10.5 million in 1910–11 to £24.9 million in 1920–21, and to £36.8 million in 1937–38. At the same time New Zealand increased its butter exports from 18,600 tons in 1913 to 21,500 tons in 1918, and, after a brief decline, to 83,700 tons in 1929 and a prewar peak of 148,000 tons in 1937.

[2] Including Britain, but not the U.S.S.R. In the 1930's, Europe's share continued to fall (to 30.2 per cent in 1936–38), but the industrial development of the U.S.S.R. from 4.3 per cent in 1926–29 (as against 4.4 per cent in 1913) to 18.5 per cent in 1936–38, caused a fall in the percentage share of the United States in world production—to 32.2 per cent in 1936–38. Cf. League of Nations, *Industrialization and Foreign Trade* (II Economic and Financial, 1945. II. A. 10), Princeton, N.J., 1945.

[3] By 1930 the world production of coal stood at the 1913 level; but the index of petroleum production was 365 as compared with 100 in 1913.

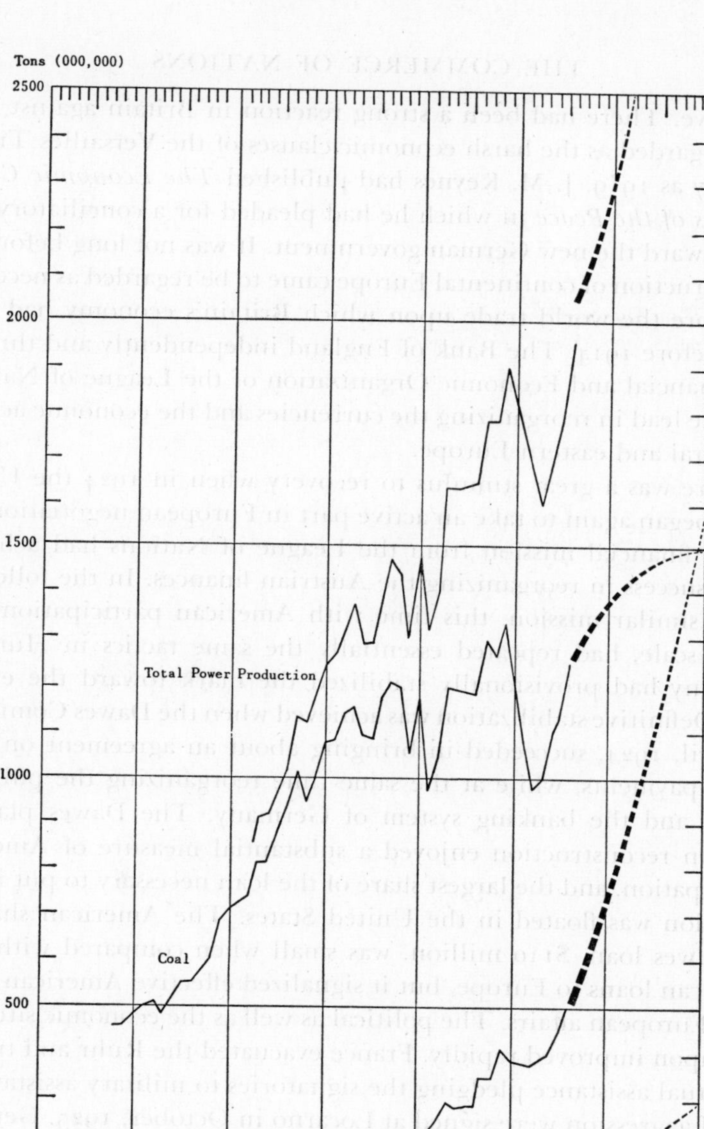

WORLD POWER PRODUCTION

The main sources of industrial power converted to the equivalent of coal consumption.

Source: Reproduced from League of Nations, *Report of the Committee for the Study of the Problem of Raw Materials,* Geneva, 1937, p. 44.

initiative. There had been a strong reaction in Britain against what were regarded as the harsh economic clauses of the Versailles Treaty. As early as 1919, J. M. Keynes had published *The Economic Consequences of the Peace* in which he had pleaded for a conciliatory attitude toward the new German government. It was not long before the reconstruction of continental Europe came to be regarded as necessary to restore the world trade upon which Britain's economy had been built before 1914. The Bank of England independently and through the Financial and Economic Organization of the League of Nations, took the lead in reorganizing the currencies and the economic activity of central and eastern Europe.

There was a great stimulus to recovery when in 1924 the United States began again to take an active part in European negotiations. In 1923 a financial mission from the League of Nations had achieved signal success in reorganizing the Austrian finances. In the following year a similar mission, this time with American participation on a minor scale, had repeated essentially the same tactics in Hungary. Germany had provisionally stabilized the mark toward the end of 1923. Definitive stabilization was achieved when the Dawes Committee in April, 1924, succeeded in bringing about an agreement on reparation payments, while at the same time reorganizing the public finances and the banking system of Germany. The Dawes plan for German reconstruction enjoyed a substantial measure of American participation, and the largest share of the loan necessary to put it into operation was floated in the United States. The American share of the Dawes loan, $110 million, was small when compared with later American loans to Europe, but it signalized effective American interest in European affairs. The political as well as the economic situation thereupon improved rapidly. France evacuated the Ruhr and treaties of mutual assistance pledging the signatories to military assistance in case of aggression were signed at Locarno in October, 1925. Germany entered the League of Nations and peace seemed at last to be assured in Europe.

Before 1925 recovery in Europe had been slow. Production in 1925 was little greater than in 1913 and trade lagged far behind. A League study had drawn attention to the fact that trade had recovered more rapidly in the Pacific than in the Atlantic area. But when the first exhaustion and psychological collapse began to pass away and conciliation paved the way for economic co-operation, the material damage, so much greater than in any previous war, proved capable of rapid repair.

There was a remarkable burst of productivity in the five years following Locarno and the Dawes plan. By 1929 all the measurements of world production were seen to have resumed their prewar trends of increase but at a more rapid rate. Almost a decade of economic development had been lost during the war and its aftermath, but by 1925 production was above the 1913 level and the accelerated rate of increase was beginning to carry it toward the level it might have reached had the war not intervened.

In the first years of relief and rehabilitation after the war there had been shortages of food, of raw materials, and of capital equipment. There was a market for practically everything that could be produced. After 1925 the shortages disappeared. Still there seemed to be a ready market for the restored production of Europe, as well as for the expanded production of the United States, Japan, and the rest of the world. The rapid recovery of the years 1925–29 seemed to mock the fears of those who had urged the necessity of adjustment to the changed pattern of production that had resulted from the war. It appeared as if those who had argued for freer trade as an indispensable condition of stable recovery had been doctrinaire theorists. Tariffs had not been lowered but on the contrary had been heavily increased in many countries. Yet trade increased faster than production during the upswing of 1925–29. Moreover it was no longer passing from the Atlantic to the Pacific. Europe was rapidly regaining its dominant position in world markets.

The explanation of these paradoxes is simple. The recovery was floating on a tide of credit expansion flowing from London to Europe, and from New York, independently and through London, to Europe. The United States was the chief source of this expanding credit. The reality and the extent of credit inflation in the United States was not recognized at the time. There was a sharp rise in the security and real-estate markets. The price levels of commodities, on the other hand, were relatively stable. Easy credit conditions also facilitated foreign loans which sustained levels of investment and of consumption that made unnecessary any real attempt to integrate the production patterns of the European and non-European countries.

A distinction should be drawn between the lending which took place for the most part by international agreement and under official auspices before 1925, and the much greater volume of lending after that date—for the most part negotiated by individuals and governments with private banking and issuing houses. The first loans were small and urgently necessary. They were used for stabilizing monetary systems, for relief needs and for restocking and re-equipment. It is possible to criticize some of the earliest methods of lending by which the exchange rates of the borrowing countries were pegged for a time at artificial levels. The plans of monetary reconstruction were on the whole both effective and economical. They were devised expertly and administered with a considerable degree of international co-operative discipline. Not only the League loans negotiated for Austria, Hungary, Greece, Bulgaria, Estonia, and Danzig, but those negotiated for Germany in connection with the Dawes and Young plans called for effort on the part of the borrowing authorities which had a tonic effect. The Blair loan to Poland also contained conditions regarding internal financial policy. The nominal value of these loans contracted by eleven European countries for currency stabilization and reconstruction in the years 1923 to 1931 was the relatively modest total of $827 million.

By contrast, the international lending after 1925 was on a much greater scale. Much of it was less economically negotiated and less efficiently expended. Much of this later borrowing was negotiated by national governments and municipalities with private banking and issue houses using the well-known methods of the nineteenth-century capital markets. Foreign lending became in large part a function of the credit inflation that carried the United States into a period of expansion which was not recognized for what it really was—a postwar reconstruction boom. Some of the foreign loans financed what can only be regarded as luxury expenditure, such as municipal improvements which turned out to be beyond the financial capacity of the borrowing countries. It is true that the financial capacity of these borrowers was much reduced by the extreme deflation of the 1930's. After the financial breakdown, it became easy to believe that the loans had sustained levels of consumption and corporate investment that were unwarranted by the productive powers of the borrowing countries. These loans enabled the borrowing countries to secure the foreign currencies, primarily dollars, with which to import heavily while postponing the effort to export. Conversely they enabled the lending countries to export heavily while postponing the necessity of receiving payment in the form of imports. Thus the credit flow papered the cracks in the structure of world trade.

The amounts were large. The foreign capital issues publicly offered in the United States alone between 1920 and 1931 amounted to $11,623 million. Of this total Europe took 40 per cent and North America (principally Canada) 29 per cent while Latin America, formerly the chief borrower from the United States, received only 22 per cent. In the six years 1924–29, Germany received a net capital import from all countries of over $4 billion, a greater net inflow of funds than the rest of the world in those years. Most of this great expansion of foreign lending, particularly from the United States, went to rebuild and re-equip Europe. Latin-American countries and the British Dominions continued to borrow in London and in New York, but some areas that had been safe and reproductive outlets for investment in the prewar period had a net capital export in certain of the postwar years. In the years 1925 to 1929, for example, the Dutch East Indies had a total net disinvestment of $223 million.

There was little recognition in these years of the necessity for drastic changes in the production and trading patterns of the great trading countries. Great Britain, the clearing center of the nineteenth-century trading system, had suffered heavily. Its overseas investments had been impaired, its shipping supremacy was challenged and the textile industries—which had been the mainstay of its exports since the Industrial Revolution—were met in almost every market by the subsidized competition of newly established national industries. The United States, on the other hand, had emerged as the greatest industrial country in the world and for the first time in its history a net creditor. Yet it maintained the policies appropriate to a developing and primarily agricultural debtor country. After the first postwar depression it raised its tariff in 1921–22, and again in 1930 the Hawley-Smoot Tariff Act raised duties to unprecedented levels. Germany, defeated and prostrate, strove with British and American loans to rebuild and regain its status as a great industrial power. Its immediate markets in central and eastern Europe were, however, intent on their own national development. In every country this effort to regain what had been lost but not to surrender what had been gained was evident. Prague, for example, became the commercial and financial capital of a new country, but Vienna strove to preserve its former greatness.

These realities of economic life were obscured by financial calculations and transfers. The ultimate economic reality is the production of goods and services that are exchangeable. The skilled and unskilled labor of human beings applied co-operatively to material resources constitutes production. Even before the boom broke in 1929, it was becoming painfully evident that this labor was being wrongly directed. Where there had been shortages, burdensome surpluses were beginning to accumulate, particularly in the basic foodstuffs. Underlying the violent fluctuations of the interwar financial crises, there was structural maladjustment. This was caused by the attempt to put the trading world together according to the nineteenth-century pattern, without taking account of the changes that had occurred during the war years when the pattern of trading specialization had been broken.

A TREND TO COLLECTIVISM

Throughout the nineteenth century, particularly in Britain and the United States, the economic functions of the state had been limited. Private enterprise had been relied upon to organize and regulate the varied aspects of economic and financial activity. Not only was the great bulk of production and commerce in private hands, the banking systems also were independent of government. There were exceptions to this general rule, notably in Germany where close relations had developed between government, banking, and business. But the extraordinary wealth and power of Great Britain and the still more extraordinary development of the United States were universally attributed to the freedom of private business enterprise enjoyed in those countries. The movement toward political democracy was associated with this freedom.

It was to business enterprise and to political democracy that most countries turned in 1918 to seek relief from the restrictions and inconveniences of the war years. This attitude was all but universal in the victorious Allied countries, despite the success of public controls and administration in promoting the war effort. Great hopes were expressed that a chastened Germany might choose this road to prosperity and peace. Government controls of domestic economic activity were removed quickly at the end of the war, and the United States took the initiative in disbanding the interallied councils set up to administer the financial, food, shipping, munitions, and raw-material resources of the allies. The markets were returned to private enterprise.

At the time there was little questioning of the wisdom of these decisions. In every country the people generally and businessmen in particular who were weary of war restrictions welcomed their abolition. It is important to understand clearly the limitations that the political and economic facts had imposed upon the desire to return to free enterprise. Within the United States, the reversion to free enterprise was virtually complete. But even there the economic functions and influence of government were enlarged by the heavier budget swollen by debt charges, veteran payments, pensions, and other war legacies. In most countries it did not prove possible to go as far or as fast as had the United States in demobilizing the wartime government controls of economic activity. The distortion of the economic systems was worse and the burdens placed on government were greater. Thus, although there was a considerable relaxation of controls, the economic functions of the state in all countries had been considerably enlarged.

Moreover this relaxation was essentially in respect to national economic activity. In the most important sphere of international economic policy, that of tariffs, the United States raised its tariff schedules in 1921–22 and again in 1930. There was a very marked and widespread increase of protectionism in Europe and elsewhere. Although the aim of policy was to give the freest possible rein to private enterprise, those countries which were hardest hit by the war quickly discovered that there were grave difficulties in the way of restoring competitive world markets. It was not possible to open national markets freely to international competition without inflicting heavy losses on politically powerful segments of the national economies. In the early postwar years quantitative restrictions on exports as well as imports were extensively used. These were relaxed when the European reconstruction effort, supported by American loans, got under way in 1924. But tariffs were raised to compensate for the abolition of quantitative restrictions. This persistence and stiffening of national controls over international trade contributed greatly to the collapse of the world trading system in 1931.

The vast flow of credit from the United States to Europe in the years 1925–29 masked the essential instability of the reconstruction effort. Some countries such as Australia and Argentina had found it difficult to borrow as much as they wished, even before the American lending began to dwindle as the boom rose to its height in 1928–29.

This cutting off of the American loan flow was the immediate cause of the crisis and financial panic which spread over Europe in 1930 and 1931 and caused the collapse of the international marketing system. But the fundamental cause of that collapse was the failure to allow competitive trade to readjust the pattern of world specialization.

It had never been practical to restore free enterprise suddenly after the war, without having first taken steps to create the conditions necessary to the functioning of international markets. The postwar scramble to get rid of wartime controls within national boundaries did not strengthen the private enterprise system in the long run. On the contrary, its ultimate result was a considerable enlargement of the functions of national governments in the economic field. This whole attempt to reconstruct the European economies by the extension of loans without taking the necessary steps to reorganize national economies to the point where the channels of world trade might safely be reopened was based on a miscalculation of the economic and political situation. This miscalculation, not by governments but by private enterprise, underestimated the importance of international trade in the world economy and the political strength of the resistance to a reduction of trade barriers.[4]

In every country economic activity was disorganized when the war mobilization came to a sudden end. War production stopped abruptly leaving surpluses of equipment and in some cases of goods. In the United States, for example, shipbuilding facilities had been created in excess of peacetime needs, and there was also a surplus of shipping tonnage much of which was unsuitable for peacetime transport. In Australia and New Zealand there were accumulated stocks of wool too great to be absorbed quickly even though markets were bare of raw materials. Many other surpluses of war goods were of little use in a peaceful world.

The national price structures were distorted. Because of the war-

[4] The loans which, for a short time, masked the inherent instability of the situation, ran up the annual payments due for interest and amortization to an annual total conservatively estimated at from \$2 billion to \$2½ billion. This was a large amount to be transferred even in 1929 when world trade was at its interwar peak of \$36.6 billion. It became an impossible burden when the total value of world trade fell in 1932 to \$13.9 billion. After the loan flow dried up, there was in 1930 a considerable extension of short-term banking credits, particularly to Germany.

Cf. League of Nations, *World Economic Survey, 1932–3*, Geneva, 1933, p. 269 and William Adams Brown, Jr., *The International Gold Standard Reinterpreted*, New York, 1940, Vol. II, pp. 1025–26.

time interruption of trade, commodity prices had diverged in separated markets. Average price levels were out of line with exchange rates. And different elements of the price structures were out of line in varying degrees. There was no exchange rate which did not call in every country for some adjustments in the price structures. Everywhere the pattern of production had been distorted in different degrees by large-scale government purchases, subsidies, and direct production aids. The pattern of wages and the location of employment had been distorted in consequence of the shifts in production needs. Where initiative was returned to private enterprise, the readjustments of prices and production were swift and severe. Most governments were afraid to face them.

Another difficulty in restoring private enterprise arose from the weakening of the prewar mechanisms for the clearing and balancing of international payments. In the postwar period they proved incapable of handling the great shifts called for in international economic relations. For many decades private enterprise had been geared to a virtually world-wide marketing process. In the latter nineteenth century a series of clearing and regulatory institutions had developed, each with its specialized functions, but all interdependent in delicate balance. Commodity exchanges—regional, national, and international security markets and other agencies of capital investment—the foreign exchanges, and the money markets of the great financial centers—all these were essential cogs in the machinery by which goods were exchanged, prices determined, capital allocated and the international balances of payments cleared.

These international connections had been broken or distorted by the war. The flow of trade along the main arterial system of the world's commerce had been short-circuited. Moreover the markets had grown apart. It was unrealistic to expect that they could again play their traditional roles in the world trading system. In fact, the prewar system of trade, payments, and investment was never effectively restored, though the outflow of credit from the United States for a few years masked its disappearance.

These difficulties faced by private enterprise throughout the world were difficult to recognize in the United States. Its situation was unique. Alone among the great trading nations it had suffered relatively little from its short and largely vicarious war experience. It was less dependent than any other country on international trade and its economic organization was intact. It is true that a speedy return to its competitive peacetime production and trade could not be achieved except at the cost of a sharp recession in 1920. Immediately after the war it had become necessary to shift labor from wartime to peacetime employment, to cope with the sudden falls in prices occasioned by the cessation of war buying, to refinance industry to meet new market demands, and to achieve a new equilibrium between costs and prices. Before these readjustments could be completed, heavy losses had been inflicted on some of the war-expanded sectors of the economy, and these losses had initiated a sharp decline in price levels and in national income. Moreover interest rates rose in 1919 and 1920, as the government relaxed its control over the monetary system and the capital market. There were serious declines in the prices of Liberty bonds and new industrial capital was more difficult and expensive to raise. There was sufficient resilience in the American economy to carry it quickly through this first sharp postwar depression. It was short, and once the readjustments had been made it became evident that inflationary pressures in the credit structure were strong.

Other countries were not as fortunately placed. Though Japan had made much profit out of the war of 1914–18, it had overexpanded its credit facilities. It had barely weathered the depression which became world-wide in 1920–21, when it was struck by the disastrous earthquake of 1923. The agricultural-exporting countries of Latin America and the British Dominions were also in a less favorable position than the United States because they were more closely tied to the European markets. The strain imposed upon Great Britain by the war was aggravated by the decision in 1925 to stabilize the pound sterling at its prewar parity with the dollar, since this involved what turned out to be a price and wage deflation more serious and lasting than had been anticipated. Throughout the reconstruction boom, 1925–29, the British economy was laboring in difficulties. Since it was difficult for Britain to export enough to pay for needed imports there was a constant tendency to lose gold from the banking reserves.

The most serious consequences of the war were to be seen in those countries where the mechanisms of organized economic co-operation, and even of government, collapsed under the double strain of impoverishment and defeat. After the collapse which made possible the Bolshevik revolution, Russia remained for long years in a state of virtually complete disorganization. Gradually the small group of convinced

Marxian theorists, by the use of ruthless methods, was able to create a new form of government and a new economic structure in which all power was centered in the state and from which private enterprise was completely eliminated.

New governments modeled on the democratic systems of the United States, Britain, and France came into power in Germany, Austria, Hungary, Poland, Czechoslovakia, Yugoslavia, Finland, Estonia, Latvia, and Lithuania. In all these countries the monetary systems had either to be newly created or to be reorganized after inflation. The middle classes everywhere had suffered heavily. The institutions which had mobilized and facilitated economic activities—banks, insurance companies, transport systems, commodity exchanges and the like—had to be reorganized. In these reorganizations national governments generally furnished initiative, capital, and guarantees.

Moreover the fiscal necessities of these countries played a large role in determining their economic policies. The search of governments for revenue is a principal clue to national economic policies in the reconstruction period. In some countries war expenditures had left heavier burdens of public debt than had been known since the Napoleonic Wars. In those where past debt had been liquidated by inflation, new debt was rapidly accumulated in the reconstruction period. National budgets remained after the war at levels far exceeding those of the prewar years. Not only heavier debt burdens but other consequences of the war, such as pensions and a widening range of social services, called for heavier taxation. Great Britain had its unemployment dole and Germany its expanded system of social insurance. The inevitable result was a much heavier burden of taxes. There was considerable reluctance to abandon an important source of revenue by reducing duties on imports and on exports. Income and property taxes rose steeply. Gone were the days when an addition of a penny in the pound sterling on the British income tax would give rise to prolonged and spirited debate.

The heavier direct taxation of the interwar period, reinforced by levies on corporations, interfered directly with the functioning of free enterprise. Government expenditures accounted for a larger proportion of the total national outlays. War finance had created vast amounts of new government securities, many of them on short term. If interest payments were to be kept at levels which would not unbalance the budgets, the manipulation of the short-term credit market through the issuance and redemption of government bills would require delicate handling.

Thus the prevailing belief that a quick return to private enterprise would rapidly restore prewar conditions was illusory. The springs of private enterprise had been seriously weakened, less in the United States than elsewhere, but in all countries in some measure. The clearing and regulatory mechanisms by which private enterprise had functioned had been strained. The distortions and disequilibria with which they had to cope after the war were immeasurably greater than they had been devised to handle. On the other hand, the functions of the state had been extended in new and old fields. Defense preparations called for massive appropriations. Their extension into new industrial fields created closer links between government and business. Germany reorganized its chemical cartels and created the I. G. Farbenindustrie. Britain created the corporation known as Imperial Chemical Industries and set about the development of an optical glass industry. Social security services were adopted in most countries, though not in the United States until after the depression of 1929–33 was well along. In the prosperity of the new era, the United States with its high productivity, low taxes, and lack of social security legislation was a nineteenth-century island of free enterprise in a sea of increasing socialization.

The unreality of the attempt to restore the free international trade and investment of the prewar period was quickly revealed whenever it appeared as if there might be a slackening of the credit outflow from the United States. Such a slackening appeared likely in 1927, but a chorus of appeals from Europe caused a withholding of the monetary restrictions that had been talked of as necessary to check the developing inflation.

Britain had continued its foreign lending after sterling was stabilized in 1925, despite the heavy strain on the British balance of payments. By 1927 a new element of strain had been introduced by the approach toward stabilization of the French franc. The level chosen was low and this added to the strain on sterling. The Bank of France accumulated foreign exchange which it could turn into gold on the London market. The Bank of England felt unable to raise its discount rate. Conversations between London and Paris in May were followed by discussions among central bank representatives in New York in June, 1927. It was agreed that France should transfer her gold purchases from London to New York, and that the Federal Reserve Bank of New York would take the lead in bringing about easier money conditions.

Thus was the fateful decision taken to continue with the reconstruction policies based upon lending from London and New York. In the long run it was an untenable policy.[5] As the rise in security prices became steeper in the United States, more of the currently available funds in the country were diverted into local investment. The inevitable crash came in October, 1929. It was not long before a bank panic began in Vienna in May, 1931, spread to Germany in June, and by September had forced Britain to abandon the gold standard it had fought so hard to restore.

The great economic depression which was ushered in by the 1929 break in the New York stock market marked the end of the first attempt at reconstruction after the first World War. The scope and magnitude of this depression were so vast that its consequences must be dealt with in many connections. It is no exaggeration to say that it has colored all subsequent economic thought and action. The whole effort at European reconstruction had depended upon a continued flow of funds from the United States to Europe. When the monetary consequences of the cessation of this American lending are studied, it will be shown that the London money market was particularly vulnerable to the ever-present possibility of a sudden withdrawal of short-term funds. In 1930, as the drying-up of American loans imposed upon the continental European countries the sudden necessity of balancing their external payments by means of their own resources, there came a scramble for foreign exchange.

Ultimately this was a scramble for gold or dollars, but most of the drain was concentrated upon London which had once again become the monetary clearinghouse for world trade. Short-term funds were withdrawn from London. Exports were increased from the debtor countries and at the same time these countries cut down their imports.

[5] Cf. William Adams Brown, Jr., *op. cit.*, Vol. I, p. 809: "Low interest rates made it easy to finance valorization schemes and price control arrangements and promoted the issue of foreign loans, particularly in the United States. Foreign loans in turn helped to maintain prices in many debtor countries and also prevented the growth of tariffs from checking the expansion of international trade. The continued extension of international credit was a dam that was holding back the onrushing torrent of economic readjustment. The strength of this dam depended upon the de facto cooperation of the center countries in reinvesting their currently accumulating credits in debtor countries. It did not long survive the completion of the gold standard facade."

The prices of agricultural commodities suddenly collapsed, and accumulated stocks of raw materials and foodstuffs were released on to the world markets. Every debtor nation tried to expand its exports even at the cost of lowering prices and in doing so added to the downward pressure on prices.

What is relevant for our purpose here is the extent of the fall in prices, the reduction in national income, the curtailment of manufacturing production, the loss of employment, and the shrinkage of international trade. Some illustrative figures may be cited from the *World Economic Survey, 1932–3,* published by the League of Nations in July, 1933. Average levels of prices in most countries fell precipitately from their 1929 peak to the lowest point in the depression which was reached at various dates from 1931 to 1933 in different countries. In the United States, for example, the average level of prices in February, 1933, was 38 per cent below the peak of 1929. Measurement in most countries is difficult since the gold standard was widely suspended after September, 1931, so that comparisons with previous price levels became artificial. The fall in prices of some sensitive commodities was much greater than the fall of the average price level. Coffee, for example, fell by more than 70 per cent. National incomes fell in most countries by 40 to 50 per cent—in the United States by the latter figure. Agricultural production was maintained. But world industrial production fell between 1929 and 1932 by 31 per cent, the fall in the United States being 46 per cent, a greater decline than in any other industrial country. The estimates of registered unemployed rose in early 1933 to 30 million, of whom over 13 million were in the United States. The value of world trade fell by 65 per cent between the first quarter of 1929 and the first quarter of 1933, the fall in United States imports and exports being greater than the average. Fragmentary as these statistics are, they reveal a collapse of the economic mechanisms so painfully restored between 1925 and 1929.

The positive steps taken by practically all governments to relieve unemployment and buttress price levels resulted in a great enlargement of the economic functions of the state. The great depression forced emergency action upon governments, even in the United States. By 1934 when the depression was brought under control, the international gold standard was gone. Governments everywhere had asserted control of monetary policy and had undertaken a vast extension of economic functions in many fields. The capital markets were controlled, exchange control was widespread and tariffs had been reinforced by import quotas and bilateral barter agreements. As an aftermath of the depression, a much greater segment of commodity prices had come to be controlled by cartel agreements or sustained by government guarantees. Social security legislation was becoming almost universal.

Thus the premature attempt to revert immediately after the war ended to complete freedom of private enterprise, without facing the readjustments that were needed particularly in the sphere of international economic relations, collapsed in the great depression. Freer trade would have caused the abandonment of uneconomic forms of production. Many of the war-stimulated industries would have had to close down. A new pattern of international specialization would have emerged. Clearly such developments would have created widespread temporary unemployment. But they were necessary if private enterprise was to function effectively on a competitive basis. The difficulties involved in restoring world markets had been evaded by resort to inflationary credit policies. The ultimate result was a substantial enlargement of government controls.

AN EVOLVING CAPITALISM

Private enterprise and free competition are not synonymous terms. In the latter part of the nineteenth century, businessmen and economic theorists often assumed that they were. They had faith in free competition as a regulating principle of organization and believed that private enterprise would necessarily bring competitive methods into play. In the disorganized interwar period it did not prove easy to restore equilibrium by competitive methods. The business world became skeptical of the quasi-theological faith in competition that had been almost unquestioned before 1914. Most of its leaders retained their belief in private enterprise. But they began to stress the destructive and inefficient aspects of free competition. They still criticized and resisted most forms of government intervention but on grounds of efficient operation rather than because of any great belief in the merits of competition as a regulating principle. Distrust of government policy determined by legislators elected on political issues and of executive action by government officials is quite compatible with loss of faith in the self-regulating virtues of a competitive economic system. It was this combination of ideas which led to attempts at industrial reorganization by business leadership. These attempts were far-reaching. They went beyond industrial and even national boundaries into business diplomacy.

New impetus was given to the trade association movement and to industrial agreements limiting the scope of competition and wherever possible eliminating redundant capacity. Voluntary limitation of output, price maintenance, combined marketing and research services, the pooling of patents and processes, standardization, comparative cost analysis, and similar attempts to reduce costs and secure the economies of large-scale production, were advocated by arguments stressing the values of co-operative effort and the disadvantages of unrestricted competition. These were not new arguments, particularly in Germany, but the circumstances of the postwar years made them more persuasive.

Generally these attempts to restrict competition by agreement were advocated as a means of reorganizing the older manufacturing industries which traditionally had consisted of a great number of small firms tenacious of their independence. Most of the European manufacturing industries and notably the British textile industries were of this character. The newer industries, particularly in Germany and the United States, by the very nature of their technology were bound to develop large-scale production methods. The mechanical production of mass-consumption goods had been developed to a high pitch in the United States not only in the automobile industry but over a widening range of standardized products. In Germany even before 1914, the electrical, chemical, and other industries in which the industrial application of scientific research played a large part had developed both large-scale units and co-operative cartel practices. In these scientific industries flow-processes paralleled the assembly lines of the mass-production industries.

There were many reasons why the economies of full-capacity production were more pronounced in these newer industries. They may be summed up by reference to the increasing importance of fixed overhead costs. The various factors entering into overhead costs derive primarily from the necessity of planning in great detail elaborate installations of equipment and integrated flow-processes which can be most effectively used in the repetitive production of standardized commodities and their component parts. The division of labor has been carried to great lengths in the final stages of production. But if these are to be smoothly integrated the prior planning must be meticulous.

In order to develop the materials, design, and planning for large-scale production of this type, it is necessary to organize expensive laboratories for scientific research. Even heavier expenditures are involved in the later research stage known as process development. There is a long interval between the laboratory demonstration of a new process and its application to commercial production on a large scale. In most cases a pilot plant must be erected so that by practical experiment, the new processes may be cheapened, standardized, freed of "bugs," and reduced to methods capable of operation by unskilled labor. Thereafter the process must be adapted to the routine of large-scale production for the market. It is not uncommon for these stages to take five or more years and to involve hundreds of thousands of dollars of expenditure for a single new process or product.

In these new industries the property right known as a patent has become an important factor in increasing the optimum size of a producing firm. Originally a monopolistic right to produce or sell some product, a patent has now developed into a right primarily to use certain mechanical or chemical processes. A basic patent indeed, tends to become a right to monopolize the industrial applications of a narrowly specialized field of scientific research. The complexity of modern machines and products is such that improvements of a specific part are seldom of any value except as applied to the whole. As the long list of patent records with overlapping expiration dates on many appliances will testify, the larger corporations are in a strategic position to utilize the subsidiary improvements to an original invention.

In addition to patentable devices, there is an increasing amount of know-how, i.e. technical experience specifically related to particular processes. The inevitable result is a differentiation of products. While there is monopolistic competition between them, each has a measure of monopoly increased by advertising. Since new processes must be patented on a world-wide scale to forestall litigation, and since they involve heavy advertising and other merchandising costs, the necessity for these expenditures has added incentives to large-scale operation. The exclusive licensing of patents and processes in defined markets rapidly developed during the interwar years into the most significant method of negotiating international marketing agreements.

This trend toward large-scale production and monopolistic development was further stimulated by financial reorganizations leading to control of business units by financiers rather than industrialists. This was not a new development. The trust movement in American industry was clearly evident in the last quarter of the nineteenth century. J. H. Clapham devoted the longest chapter of his *Economic History of Modern Britain* to the processes of amalgamation characteristic of the period in British industry. The cartel movement spread at the same time within Germany. But the abundant credit created by the method of war financing through the banks, coupled with the heavy burden of postwar taxation and with the emergence of surplus capacity in many war-expanded industries, gave impetus in the 1920's to the reorganization of production by financial combinations.

Outside the corporate organization of industry there were many consequences of the war mobilization which encouraged monopolistic trends. The financing of war production had linked industry with the banking system and had concentrated the credit functions in the commercial banks. These in turn were more dependent than they had been in the nineteenth century upon the exigencies of public finance. Rates of interest were neither as flexible nor as responsive to the needs of industry as to the needs of the treasuries manipulating swollen national debts. It became more difficult for small businesses to find venture capital. In this as in other respects, the United States was less affected by the first World War than were the other great trading countries.

Moreover the increased bargaining power of trade unions in the war period was reflected in an increasing rigidity of wage rates. This paralleled the increasing rigidity of interest rates, taxes, and other elements of overhead cost. Industry-wide bargaining developed in place of local negotiations that could be adapted readily to the circumstances of particular firms and localities. Inevitably these developments of the labor as of the capital market gave advantages to the larger corporations as compared with smaller production units.

Thus what was rapidly emerging was an industrial structure very different from that of the multiplicity of independent small producers upon which the faith in competition had been postulated. Industrial giants, endowed by their size with market leadership or even domination, began to be capable of maintaining the prices of their products by varying their output. The increasing secrecy of specialized technical processes restricted entry into many fields of production. Great corporations maintained expensive industrial research laboratories from which flowed a stream of specialized applications of scientific discoveries. Moreover the ability of these corporations to sustain the heavy costs of developmental research enabled them to derive the greatest advantage from the scientific research and training supported by the community as a whole.

This widespread movement toward industrial concentration in the stronger new industries coupled with industrial association in those which had formerly been keenly competitive was one of the most important developments of the first postwar decade. This was clearly reflected in the documents of the World Economic Conference in 1927. In Germany the movement was known as rationalization, and German experiments exercised a great influence on the surrounding countries. In Britain it was generally known as industrial reorganization. The trade association movement in the United States dated back at least to the 1890's. But it was greatly reinforced after the first World War and it exercised a great influence upon the industrial codes developed by the National Industrial Recovery Administration in 1933.

Primarily this was a movement described as fair competition, toward the abandonment of free competition and toward concerted action among producing groups. In the beginning it was a repudiation both of state control and of free competition—an attempt to obtain by agreement acceptance of industrial and trading practices that would limit destructive competition. But after the depression of 1929–33 it led to state-supported and state-enforced monopoly organization in many countries. It was helped along after 1931 by the increasing network of import and export licensing, of quota systems, and of exchange controls, all of which mushroomed after the breakdown of the restored gold standard. Limited state trading monopolies made their appearance and ultimately the conduct of trade came under bureaucratic regulation in many countries. But the roots of this trend to monopoly and to monopolistic association are to be found within industry itself rather than in state regulation.

It is not possible to give a simple comprehensive explanation for a world-wide trend that took such diverse forms as the development of integrated large-scale enterprises in most industrial countries and such varied legislative experiments as the national recovery codes in the United States, the German compulsory cartelization after 1933, the van Zeeland New Deal in Belgium, the Flandin decrees in France, the Italian corporative system, the Japanese experiments in voluntary and compulsory cartelization, and the state socialism of the U.S.S.R. There is an immense literature, descriptive and theoretical, concerning the decline of free competition between the wars and the emergence of varying degrees of monopoly, national and international. As early as 1927, D. H. Macgregor, with some exaggeration, reported to the World Economic Conference that the idea of regulating output by concerted arrangements between producers was no longer seriously opposed by economic theory or public policy. Despite the vehement opposition since expressed by many influential sections of American opinion, particularly to the arrangements loosely described as cartels, there is widespread recognition among businessmen and economists that the nature of industrial competition is changing. It must now be admitted that all over the world, and even in the United States, industrial as well as government action in recent years has amounted to a rejection of competition as a self-regulating and self-equilibrating principle of economic organization.

It follows that over a widening range of manufacturing production the price mechanism ceased to have the flexibility upon which was postulated the classical explanation of the balancing of international payments. The strains of adjustment to shifting pressures on the balances of payments became concentrated upon a narrowing segment of trade, and particularly upon those primary commodities such as foodstuffs and raw materials which by virtue of their dispersed production were not capable of organization along monopolistic lines. The processes of adjustment could no longer be cushioned, as they were before 1914, by short-term credit transfers in response to flexible interest rates.

Nor were the processes of adjustment spread as readily over the wage rates and living levels of the working population as they had been before 1914. In increasing measure, wages were fixed by contract for relatively long terms, often on a nation-wide basis, and were buttressed by a variety of unemployment benefits and social services. Labor became less mobile between industries and between regions. Statistical measurement shows that this was in fact a less hampering obstacle to adjustment than the rigidity of interest rates. But it was part of the retreat from the flexible, self-equilibrating price mechanisms of the nineteenth-century international marketing system.

The consequence was that the greater strains of adjustment in the postwar period were concentrated upon those segments of international economic transactions that remained adjustable—primarily the security markets and the trade in raw materials and foodstuffs. They were therefore reflected in more violent price movements. These price fluctuations were of a range and a rapidity unknown in the latter nineteenth century. For the incessant but relatively small adjustments of all sorts of prices—including the prices of capital and of labor—in interdependent markets all over the world, there was substituted a regulation of output in the large-scale manufacturing industries, stereotyped wage and interest rates, and, from time to time, sharp and necessarily large adjustments of raw-material prices.

The violence of these price fluctuations was greatly aggravated when the mechanisms of international adjustment broke down in the great depression that began with the sagging prices of agricultural staples in the Southern Hemisphere in late 1928, and took a sharp downward turn when the New York stock market crashed a year later. Despite emergency measures on an international scale, the depression deepened during 1930. In May, 1931, a bank panic started in Vienna and spread rapidly across Europe. When Britain abandoned the gold standard in September, 1931, the whole international payments system was thrown into confusion and prices fell steeply. The worst of the price decline was concentrated on raw materials and foodstuffs. It was natural that the idea should be put forward of international agreement to mitigate and control the sharp decline in the prices of staple commodities that were important exports of the raw-material exporting countries.

The idea was developed in two forms which shaded into one another. The first was an attempt by business leadership to arrive at international understandings and agreements designed to minimize competition. The later form was the comparable attempt to negotiate international commodity agreements by which the powers of government were invoked to compel dispersed and competitive producers to adhere to programs of production or export regulation or to price maintenance. Logically it is possible to draw a clear distinction between the private agreements and those negotiated by governments and to distinguish different types of agreements according to their legal structure. But in practice one type shaded into the other.

In Germany and some other countries cartelization was officially recognized and was even arranged in some cases by government intervention. In Britain, industrial reorganization, much of which was of the cartel type, took place sometimes voluntarily, but often with the encouragement of government agencies or as a result of legislation. After Britain reverted to protection in 1931, the tariff was used to compel such reorganization and to facilitate the negotiations, notably of the iron and steel industry, with international cartels. A long list of special acts may be enumerated in Great Britain and also in the United States, by which segments of industry have been carved out from the field of free competition.[6]

Whether the industrial arrangements by which competition was limited were administered by private initiative, or needed government support, is not very important from an economic viewpoint. In practically every case producers instigated the governing legislation and controlled the administrative devices set up to implement it. When the producers were strong enough to do so they spurned government support. But when a recalcitrant minority had to be coerced or when agreement could be reached only under the umbrella of government control and often with aid from the taxpayer, there was no hesitation in accepting it.

It is very difficult to arrive at any convincing estimate of the degree to which producers' agreements were effective across national boundaries. The most effective of them stopped trade almost completely, since it was usual to reserve to each corporation its own domestic market. As in the case of tariff measurements, completely successful trade barriers are not reflected in the statistics of the trade which re-

[6] Cf. *Memorandum on Regulatory Measures Affecting American Foreign Trade*, submitted to the National Foreign Trade Council, Inc., New York, 1944, and "approved for distribution in September 1944 for information and study by members of the Council and others interested." Section 6 cites the Interstate Commerce Act (1887) and Transportation Act (1920); Shipping Act (1916); Packers and Stockyards Act (1921); Capper-Volstead Act (1922); Perishable Agricultural Commodities Act (1930); Labor Provisions-Clayton Act (1914) and Norris-La Guardia Anti-Injunction Act (1932); Agricultural Adjustment Act (1933); National Industrial Recovery Act (1933); Communications Act (1934); Fisheries Cooperative Marketing Act (1934); Connally Hot Oil Act (1935); Poultry Amendment to Packers and Stockyards Act (1935); Interstate Oil Compact Act (1943) and State Tobacco Compacts Act (1936); Motor Carriers Act (1935); Bituminous Coal Act (1937); Civil Aeronautics Act (1937) and Small Business Mobilization Act (1942).

mains free to pass. Various attempts have been made to estimate from the trade statistics what proportion of international trade was subjected in the interwar years to some measure of monopoly control. Most of these attempts do not discriminate between the various forms and degrees of monopoly in regard to particular products at different times, and it is doubtful whether the resulting estimates mean very much. But students of the question agree that there was a remarkable penetration of monopolistic practices into world trade.

The belief spread that it was both wise and necessary in the interest of world prosperity and of world peace to negotiate international economic agreements by private treaty among business leaders.[7] The campaign for business diplomacy was actively promoted at the World Economic Conference in 1927 and in frequent exchanges of visits between national industrial groups both before and after this conference. However, experience has proved that there is no solution to the problem of international prosperity and peace along these lines. Rather, an internationally cartelized world would be likely to hinder adjustments to international equilibrium and would also be likely to intensify the power struggle. The result of such efforts would be to transfer power from political to industrial leaders, and this would lead inevitably to a revival of the corporative forms of government that in the past have proved a menace to peace. There is much to be gained from friendly contacts across national boundaries between industrialists, as there is between labor, professional, women's, and all other organized groups. But there is no reason to believe that any one of these groups can discharge the functions of government. There is, on the contrary, much reason to fear the concentration of political and economic power in the same hands.

The primary fact to be emphasized in connection with the interwar years is that no satisfactory solution was found to the questions connected with the clearing and balancing of international payments. The international marketing system of the latter nineteenth century was never restored after 1918. Distrust of government controls and their speedy abandonment after World War I did not connote a re-

[7] Cf. Eugen Grossman, *Methods of Economic Rapprochement,* Geneva, 1926, p. 29: "If a friendly atmosphere can be created by a series of agreements within the principal industries in Europe, we shall have penetrated to the cause of all armed conflict, as M. Loucheur suggested to the Assembly of the League of Nations in 1925, and more will have been done for the maintenance of peace than by any conceivable arbitration or disarmament conventions."

turn to free competition. The attempt by private enterprise with or without government aid to regulate competition within and between national economies proved a failure economically and a danger to peace. Cartels and other forms of industrial agreement were not able to develop a satisfactory substitute for the price mechanisms that had functioned with reasonable efficiency before 1914. The bargains of industrial groups could not replace the free play of demand and supply in broad competitive markets. Yet the very nature of industrial development had destroyed the conditions which made free competitive markets possible. The international trading methods of the twentieth century differ as markedly from those of the nineteenth as the latter did from those of the eighteenth. The questions arising from monopolistic competition remain with us, more urgently than after the first World War. And their solution is still to be found.

MONOPOLISTIC COMPETITION

Until very recently the main body of economic theory remained an elaboration of propositions concerning the determination of prices in free competitive markets. To illustrate these propositions the commodities usually chosen were agricultural products such as wheat or simple manufactures such as textiles. The markets analyzed were more typical of simple handicraft than of complicated machine production. This type of theory persisted despite the technical developments that created large-scale production units, the financial considerations that expanded them and the developing movement to limit what was termed cutthroat competition.

It is true that a distinguished line of mathematical theorists—Cournot, Walras, Jevons, Pareto, Edgeworth, and Marshall—had treated questions of monopoly value. They recognized that the single seller was in a different strategic position from that of numerous producers for a competitively organized market. They recognized also that a similar monopoly might arise on the buying side, though it was left for a modern economist to introduce the term monopsony to denote a buyer's monopoly. Duopoly (the sharing of a monopoly by two firms) and bilateral monopoly (the relations between a monopolistic buyer and a monopolistic seller) were discussed as special cases. Monopoly was always contrasted with competition, and the laws of monopoly price were distinguished sharply from the laws operative in free competitive markets. Moreover monopoly was usually discussed as an aberration from what was often described as healthy competition. Nineteenth-century opinion, colored by Darwinian theories of the survival of the fittest, had come to regard competition not only as the normal type of economic activity, but also as the type which had been proved by experience to yield the maximum attainable degree of social justice and economic progress. The notion that competition and monopoly are alternative forms of organization, with its corollary of approval of the former and condemnation of the latter, is characteristic of nineteenth-century economic thought. This notion still persists in some circles in the United States. Though the practice of business has radically changed, the symbols and slogans derived from the theoretical analysis of a past generation are still potent.

The preceding section of this chapter has outlined the trend toward industrial concentration which was a consequence both of changing technology and of the failure after the first World War to restore the competitive mechanisms of international marketing. This section is concerned with the reflection of these developments in contemporary economic writing. The voluminous and dispersed literature on this subject is reviewed briefly not to attempt a critical, still less an exhaustive, analysis of what has now become the main body of economic as distinct from monetary theory, but rather to indicate the significance of this economic analysis for an understanding of international economic relations in the modern world.

The principal body of this writing is concerned with the theoretical analysis of imperfect or monopolistic competition, supplemented in recent years by inductive studies of price behavior or price policy in particular firms and industries. Both of these categories are concerned with the working of the price mechanism. They constitute a refashioning of the theory of value which has always been the central preoccupation of economic theory. However, another and very large body of writing is concerned with questions of economic leadership and economic power, rather than with the determination of prices or the maximization of wealth. The bulk of the writing in these fields is to be found in the years following the great depression of 1929–33. This breakdown encouraged economists to question the adequacy of traditional analysis and predisposed them to be receptive to the ideas of monopolistic competition that were slowly being formulated throughout the first postwar decade.

Some of the impetus to restate theoretical foundations came by reaction from the economists who were described as institutionalists because they were concerned with the social setting, rather than the theoretical analysis, of economic phenomena. Thorstein Veblen and John R. Commons were particularly influential. The former was concerned to examine the actual working of economic processes, to seek for the location of power in the modern economic system, and to emphasize the subordination of the technician to the organizer. He stressed the growing dependence of modern industry upon trained engineers (to whom in later years should be added experimental scientists), but he pointed out that the overriding decisions of industrial policy lay in the hands of those who organized and controlled the business corporations. Commons also laid stress on the power element in economic organization.

Wherever economists were led to examine the applications of theory to practical situations, they encountered the facts of large-scale production—the complicated technology, the elaborate selling organization, the differentiated products carrying with them an element of monopoly, the uncertainties affecting profit expectations and therefore price policies, and the pervasive influence of overhead costs and unused capacity in the machine processes of modern industry. Whether stimulated by the criticisms of anti-theoretic schools, or by the challenge of an economic historian, or by attempts at experimental research in economic theory, they were driven to the conclusion that prices did not depend entirely upon automatic market forces but that management was able to exercise a considerable measure of discretion in selecting price policies.

The emergence of discretionary powers over prices inevitably connotes a widespread degree of dispersed monopoly in the industrial system. This is the result partly of new technical methods of production, and partly of the organization that mobilizes the resources necessary to plan and conduct production and selling by the new methods. The harnessing of new forms of energy capable of providing power for immense and complicated machines is the fundamental technical factor. But the devising of new administrative methods of planning and integrating the detailed operations of large-scale enterprises is at least as important. Both the new technology and its administrative organization have increased the scale of overhead costs and the importance of these overhead costs in determining price policies. As J. M. Clark pointed out in the study which is fundamental to the whole discussion of these questions of monopolistic competition, "Overhead costs are not exceptions to a general economic law: they are the general law. Dynamic economics must not merely take account of them, it must be built around them, for they are part of its essential framework." [8]

These overhead costs—the continuing expenses that must be carried whether productive capacity is used or unused—include heavy research and development expenditures which can be carried only by large concerns. The distribution of these costs over the prices charged to ultimate consumers gives those who decide price policies in these large concerns a discretionary power. It is this power which constitutes a major element of imperfection in modern markets. Competition remains but it is less and less of the type of atomistic competition between small-scale sellers and equally small-scale consumers who must accept the working of supply and demand in free competitive markets. On the other hand, it would be difficult to find examples of pure or absolute monopolies where a single seller may determine his price policy without taking into account those of other sellers. The price competition which exists is shot through with elements of partial and temporary monopoly.

The formulation of systematic theories of imperfect competition developed simultaneously in several centers. In recent years it has rapidly taken a central place in economic teaching everywhere, as did the theory of marginal utility sixty years earlier. A distinction may be drawn between imperfect and monopolistic competition. The former is the wider term, covering all imperfections of the market process. The latter is concerned solely with those imperfections which arise as a result of monopoly. However, monopolistic competition constitutes by far the most significant element in the new theories, and attention is therefore focused upon it.

The elaboration of complicated relationships between buyers and sellers with varying degrees of monopoly power leads to disconcerting theoretical conclusions. If competitive relationships are assumed, it is possible to work out a simple, systematic, and comprehensive theory which gives determinate relations between the demand, supply, and price for particular commodities. Competitive relationships, however, must be assumed to include not only flexible responsiveness of individual buyers and sellers to the price changes that are necessary to equate demand and supply, but a corresponding flexibility of production

[8] Cf. J. M. Clark, *The Economics of Overhead Costs,* Chicago, 1923, pp. 479 and 486.

costs and also complete freedom of entry (and exit) to the production and sale of the commodity concerned. The neo-classical theory as worked out by Alfred Marshall demonstrated that under completely free competition the price of a commodity would settle at, and if disturbed would return to, an equilibrium point at which the supply would be equal to the demand. It recognized that time must be allowed for the working out of long-run forces. It also recognized but dismissed elements of friction in the adjustment process.

However, it is these elements of friction that now hold the center of the stage. This is particularly true of those which spring from the dominance in many basic industries of large-scale producers whose overhead costs are heavy, who produce a variety of commodities over which those costs must be spread, and whose products are differentiated from those of other firms by special characteristics, by selling campaigns, and by advertising. It is clear that entry into or exit from these types of large-scale production is not an easy matter. In all three major aspects of competition—flexibility of prices, flexibility of costs, and ease of entry into the market—the new technology aggravates the elements of friction to a point where nearly all sellers of economic goods and services enjoy some degree of monopoly.[9]

But there remain to consumers wide possibilities of substitution in their expenditures. The particular markets into which the economic world is parceled are interdependent. A patented line of plastic doorknobs may have some measure of monopoly, but it must compete with glass and metal doorknobs and is in any case dependent upon the demand for other building materials. This twofold development, which has both generalized the notion of competition and introduced into it a bewildering variety of monopolistic elements in particular cases, has gone far to destroy the simplicity of value theories derived from competitive assumptions. The pure theory of monopolistic competition has been worked out mathematically on the basis of rigid as-

9 Duopoly is price determination where there are two competing sellers, oligopoly arises where there are a few sellers. Economists who delight in classificatory terminology and have some knowledge of Greek have invented many more such terms. The possibilities are considerable. The significant texts in this field are: Edward H. Chamberlin, *The Theory of Monopolistic Competition*, Cambridge, Mass., 1933, and Joan Robinson, *The Economics of Imperfect Competition*, London, 1933. Mrs. Robinson in her foreword mentions fellow explorers in Denmark, Germany, India, and the United States as well as England. R. Triffin, *Monopolistic Competition and General Equilibrium Theory*, Cambridge, Mass., Harvard Univ. Press, 1940, reviews the discussion out of which these publications emerged and notes the main contributions.

sumptions concerning the extent of monopoly and monopsony in typical and rather broad, simple cases.

The core of the theory lies in the assumption that individual firms will endeavor to maximize their profits, and that they have some power to arrange output, prices, and the content of the product offered, so as to maximize them. The implications of this statement are far-reaching for the theory of international trade. Price policies are determined not by the demand and supply for simple products in competitive markets, but with reference to the aggregate net profits of enterprises making a great variety of products. Thus there cannot be said to be a market for aspirin in the sense of the nineteenth-century market for wheat. Aspirin is one of many pharmaceutical products produced under conditions of joint supply. Monopolistic competition between chemical corporations results in a price structure for chemical products very different from that which was worked out for wheat upon the assumption that a great number of producers accepted the price fixed by supply and demand. Moreover the great modern corporations tend increasingly to spread across national boundaries either by the formation of international business enterprises or by forms of cartel agreement.

It is often said that the shift of economic analysis from questions of pure competition to those of monopolistic competition has been a shift toward a consideration of firms rather than industries.[10] In classical and neo-classical analysis, however, the term industry was implicitly restricted to a single homogeneous commodity. The shift has in fact been from a consideration of the market for a single commodity to the more complicated relations between large firms each producing a variety of commodities. Within each firm overhead costs must be spread over the variety of commodities it produces. What then becomes of the price theory upon which the neo-classical explanation of the balancing of international payments rests? What becomes of the theory of comparative cost when the cost of producing individual commodities becomes in large measure dependent upon the allocation of overhead?

[10] Cf. R. Triffin, *op. cit.,* p. 67: "By breaking up the Marshallian 'Industry' into individual firms, each of which has to solve for itself its own equilibrium problems, Professor Chamberlin and Mrs. Robinson could approach a problem largely neglected by particular equilibrium theory: the problem of the competitive inter-relationships between the firms."

The profits of a corporation will be maximized when it pushes the production and the sale of each commodity in each region of its operation to the point where the additional income gained by further sales would be less than the additional cost involved. This is the meaning of the statement that marginal net revenue equals marginal cost. It is demonstrable that a corporation which could accurately forecast not only its cost and the response of consumers to particular prices but also the policies of its competitors in respect to their products could maximize its profits by setting output and therefore prices at the point where the marginal cost, including selling cost, would be equal to the marginal revenue of each of its products.

Under conditions of pure competition each firm would find its marginal revenue and marginal cost equated and therefore its profits maximized at the point where demand equals supply at the price determined by the market. But this presumes flexibility of costs and output as well as prices. Under monopolistic competition on the other hand, the equilibrium which maximizes the firm's profit is reached at a smaller output and a higher price for the various commodities produced by a large corporation.

It is obvious that the blending of monopolistic and competitive elements in the determination of output and prices has destroyed the simplicity of price theories. The broad and necessarily vague relationships in the simplified types of situation selected for theoretical analysis can seldom be found in practical business experience.[11] After the first challenging statements of this new approach, the literature of monopolistic competition was plunged into terminological controversy (much of which is in the nature of translation from one language into another), and into the elaboration of particular small aspects of the theory. It is significant that the original works though frequently reprinted have not been significantly revised, nor has there been much attempt to work out the full implications of the new approach in other aspects of economic theory.

Meantime, however, a great and increasing number of inductive studies into the actual price policies pursued by particular enterprises

[11] Exceptions can be cited where a particular practical situation corresponds closely with a recognizable, and therefore relatively simple, category of theoretical analysis. It is noticeable that such situations are more often found in industries producing a single homogeneous commodity. The consideration of monopoly, duopoly, oligopoly, or a closer approach to pure competition in such cases becomes largely an elaboration of neo-classical analysis of monopoly value theory.

or groups of enterprises has been accumulating. They describe the organization of an industry with particular attention to the differentiation of its products, to the determination of costs and to the allocation of overhead costs, including research and development. An endeavor is made to determine the extent of price leadership or of rivalry among a few dominant sellers (oligopoly), and to locate the key decisions of price policy. In analyzing the pattern of price behavior, use is made of the "box of tools" devised by the theorists of monopolistic competition, which constitutes a point of reference against which actual price policies may be checked and from which ideas may be gleaned as to the significant facts to look for. The nature of these case studies is such that it is not possible to review them briefly. Nor would it be relevant here to do more than note that they have accumulated an imposing body of evidence that the office of the industrial executive, rather than the market, has become the birthplace of prices over a considerable and growing part of economic activity.

Economic theory has always tended to work almost exclusively from the concept of wealth.[12] The theory of pure competition assumed that individuals desire to maximize their income. It further assumed that the ownership and management of production were in the same hands, or at least that the vital decisions of policy were taken by proprietors rather than managers. The theory of monopolistic competition, on the other hand, assumes that each firm desires to maximize its profit. This raises questions of power and of executive leadership within the structure of the firm. The emergence of the corporations necessary to produce on a great scale and to sell on an even greater scale has created a situation different in important respects from that in which

[12] It should be noted that other concepts are beginning to make their way into the theoretical literature. Professor A. C. Pigou published his *Wealth and Welfare* as early as 1912, recognizing that social welfare was not coincident with individual wealth. *The Economics of Welfare,* London, 1920, was an elaborate attempt to apply theoretical analysis to the new concept. The third (1929) edition of this volume incorporated significant elements of the developing theories of monopolistic competition.

There has not yet been any systematic attempt to incorporate the concept of power into theoretical analysis. Bertrand Russell in *Power: A New Social Analysis,* New York, 1938, set out to prove "that the fundamental concept in social science is Power, in the same sense in which Energy is the fundamental concept in physics." In the field of international economics, Albert O. Hirschman's *National Power and the Structure of Foreign Trade,* Berkeley, 1945, sets forth a theory of international trade based upon the assumption that nation-states wish to maximize their military power. There is no comparable theoretical study of efforts to maximize the economic power of individuals or groups; but Robert A. Brady in *Business as a System of Power,* New York, 1943, has broken ground for such a study.

venture capital, and hence effective control over policy, was owned by those responsible for management of the enterprise. In the modern corporation, executive leadership tends increasingly to be separated from ownership by the stockholders. Analysis designed to locate the seat of power in the economic system tends to emerge as a promising method of analyzing the central, regulating mechanisms of economic activity. It is significant that even before the definitive works on monopolistic competition were published, a study of corporation structure had appeared which was to set in train an extensive literature on the location of power in the modern economic system.

Reference was made earlier to the movement in the 1920's which attempted to rationalize business leadership in most industrial countries. The belief grew that reliance on the automatism of the market was no longer possible. On the other hand, there was aversion to government regulation and still more to government operation. Therefore business leadership was urged to put its own house in order and to develop policies that would demonstrate the efficiency of private enterprise to serve the social interest. There was a confident note in this literature of rationalization, which even went to the length of offering "business diplomacy" as an effective means of reducing international political and economic tensions. After the great depression of 1929–33, however, the corporation as a dominant type of industrial organization was thrown on the defensive and business leadership was on trial.

As in the 1890's, the popular distrust of monopolistic practices was most evident in the United States. A succession of Congressional inquiries just before and during the second World War—the Temporary National Economic Committee (T.N.E.C.) on Concentration of Economic Power; the Nye Committee on Munitions; the Bone Committee on Patents; the Truman Committee on National Defense; the Kilgore Committee on Scientific and Technical Mobilization, and other investigating committees—accumulated a vast mass of information, charges, and views. Of these committees, the T.N.E.C., which arranged for the publication of a long list of monographs as well as several volumes of hearings, bore most directly upon the questions of concentration and location of economic power. No adequate evaluation of this somewhat unsystematic investigation has yet been made, though the opinion has been ventured that its documentation tends to exaggerate the extent to which the economy of the United States is permeated with monopoly. The crusade undertaken by the United States Department of Justice to enforce the Sherman Act has contributed both a series of semi-official monographs and a vast volume of evidence and documentation adduced in the course of judicial trials. Most of this is in the nature of a brief for the prosecution. It is only since the war ended that a more detached analysis of international cartel questions has become available by the almost simultaneous publication of several independent books on the subject.

The nearest approach to a comprehensive survey of this whole vast question of the power to make price policy in a system of monopolistic competition is contained in the work of Professor E. G. Nourse, entitled *Price Making in a Democracy*. The argument of this work is essentially based upon the author's "belief that the spontaneous and independent action of individual firms is capable of meeting the requirements of successful operation of our economy under a private enterprise system more fully and with less reliance on government aids, or with much less fear of government constraints, than is commonly supposed." [13] It is argued that the continuance of high production and employment levels depends upon maintenance of real purchasing power adequate to take goods off the market. The responsibility is thus placed upon management to follow output and price policies that will avert industrial depression.

This admonition to business leadership to follow in its own self-interest a low-price policy of maximum output is based upon the belief that the prosperity of the individual firm depends upon general prosperity. The finding of monopolistic competition theory is that the profits of an individual firm are maximized when output is restricted below and prices are maintained above the level at which demand and supply would be in equilibrium. It is clear that profits may be maximized in the short run by the exercise of monopoly power to charge what the traffic will bear. But against this must be set the fact that attempts to maximize profits in the short run inevitably result in periodic depressions. Whether business statesmanship, primarily in the great corporations that set basic prices, is capable of devising price and output policies that aim at less than maximum short-run profits in order to secure a greater measure of stability in the economic system and therefore greater profits in the long run, is a question the answer to which depends primarily upon the character and outlook of those

[13] Edwin G. Nourse, *Price Making in a Democracy*, Washington, D.C., 1944, p. 443.

who control management. It is not within the decision of stockholders.

Power in the economic system is now held uncertainly, and by undefined exercise of will, by a new class of professional business managers. On occasion, the maximizing of their personal incomes has conflicted with the maximizing of the profits of the firm. But power (and glory), as well as creative satisfactions, are among the motives which create their will to action. The fate of the private enterprise system of monopolistic competition will depend very largely upon the ability of these managers to understand the long-run forces that determine equilibrium and to weigh those forces against the short-run maximizing of profits and income.

CHAPTER XV

ECONOMIC NATIONALISM BETWEEN THE WARS

THE DEEP ROOTS OF PROTECTION

THE FIRST reconstruction effort broke down because of the failure to reduce trade barriers during the years when the American loans gave a breathing space that should have been used to restore world trade and to allow competitive trading to work out a new pattern of international specialization. It may be argued that this failure was inevitable, that the statesmen were wiser than the economists, and that the maintenance of trade restrictions was unavoidable in a world plagued by the economic consequences of a disastrous war. No one can say whether this was the case, or whether bolder statesmanship in support of the League efforts for freer trade might have proved successful. The fact is that the League efforts failed. There had been a dramatic shift in the balance of economic power in the world.

During the 1920's Britain had taken the initiative in reconstruction lending. The British were driven to this effort at international reconstruction because their economic livelihood had come to depend upon the world trade which their traders and investors had built up in the nineteenth century. In the attempt to rebuild world trade and to restore European production as a necessary element in that trade, Britain took risks that proved to be unsound. The United States, on the other hand, emerged from the war of 1914–18 by far the greatest industrial power in the world. Its balance of payments position had changed radically from that of a net debtor to that of a large net creditor on international account. If trade after the war had been as free of restraints as it had been before 1914, this shift in the balance of payments would have entailed either a sharp reduction of American exports, particularly of agricultural products, or a sharp increase of imports, or both. At a time when United States' exports of food and raw materials, as well as of manufactures, were so badly needed for reconstruction purposes, a reduction of exports was difficult to contemplate. And there was strong traditional resistance to imports.

An easy solution of the dilemma had been found by lending European countries the credit to buy from the United States the goods they needed and which Americans wished to export. By this loan outflow the day of reckoning was postponed for more than a decade. When it finally came, the reckoning was heavier since interest charges and debt claims had been added to the already large export balance both of manufactured and of agricultural commodities. The theory behind the reconstruction loans had been that they would restore the productive capacity of the countries devastated in war. Though a substantial proportion of the loans was spent in maintaining unwarranted levels of consumption, the productive capacity of Europe was substantially restored between 1925 and 1929. But little account had been taken of the necessity to adapt this reconstruction to the shifts in world production. Thus by 1929 the Danubian countries were again exporting wheat, while the industrial countries of western Europe were protecting their own increasing wheat production, even though at the same time the overseas exporting countries—Argentina, Australia, Canada, and the United States—had greatly expanded their exports.

If the trade barriers had been lowered in this first reconstruction decade, when American loans were available to balance international payments, competition would have rearranged the pattern of world production. Not only wheat but a great variety of other commodities would have been produced in low-cost areas, while their production in high-cost areas would have proved uneconomic. If this had happened, the sudden cessation of lending in 1930 would not have released large accumulations of surplus stocks of staple products on top of an already sagging market. Thus it is necessary to probe into the reasons why so little progress was made in the first interwar decade toward restoring world trade, and to discover how far trade barriers were responsible for this lack of progress. It is all the more necessary to consider these problems because the developments of our own time bear such an ominous resemblance in many respects to the first reconstruction effort after the war of 1914–18.

The restoration of world trade on a competitive economic basis is an essential condition of the success of the European Recovery Program. Hence it is important to discover what light past experience can throw upon the nature of the resistance offered to a reduction of trade barriers. Little effective progress was made before 1929 in the campaign for tariff reduction. The relative freedom of international economic transactions that was characteristic of the period preceding 1914 was never effectively restored. The reasons for this failure to negotiate a reduction of trade barriers call for analysis.

A preliminary point should be made clear. As a general rule tariff levels were not high in the first interwar decade. The real difficulty presented by tariffs and other trade barriers in these years was the use made of them to resist the adaptations of national economic production that were necessary if competitive world trade was to be reorganized. A tariff does not need to be high on the average to be destructive of trade. All that is necessary is that the duties charged on competitive products shall be raised when the domestic industry feels the effect of competition. This is the flaw in the argument so often advanced in the United States in favor of flexible tariff duties. If the duty is adjusted every time import competition begins to be effective, trade is killed.

In its changed creditor status, the United States should logically have moved toward lower tariff duties so as to admit a greater volume of imports. Instead the first postwar depression led to the Fordney-McCumber tariff of 1922. The average level of duties in this tariff was not very high, as compared for example with the average level of the Hawley-Smoot tariff of 1930. But the increases were shrewdly placed on the very imports that might have done most to right the balance of payments. Their effect was to reinforce the growing belief that British reconstruction efforts would have to be supported by American loans. The escapist illusions fostered by these loans were the major cause of the interwar failure to face up to the adaptations of national economic activity necessary to restore balanced international specialization. The American refusal to take payment for its much-needed exports by accepting a larger volume of imports diverted the

American exporters who needed European markets, and the European consumers who needed American food, materials, and equipment, to what seemed the only possible alternative—American loans to Europe.

Many other examples might be cited of tariffs which, though not very high, were destructive of trade. Until 1931 Britain remained faithful to its free-trade tradition, though a breach had been made in this tradition by the imposition in 1919 of duties in which preferential treatment was given to a limited number of imports mainly from the dependent colonies. In 1921 also, some duties were introduced into the British revenue tariff which were avowedly protectionist and were not countervailed by local excise taxes. They affected only about one-tenth of one per cent of the total imports, but they too constituted a precedent. The self-governing Dominions were clamoring for imperial preference but this would have involved the imposition of a protective tariff on foodstuffs and raw materials which were at that time on the free list. Britain was not ready to tax food and raw materials, and the Dominion demands for special treatment were therefore met by setting up research and promotion agencies—the Imperial Economic Committee (1924) and the Empire Marketing Board (1926).

On the continent of Europe, tariffs were not much higher in 1929 than they had been before 1914. Wherever specific duties were charged, calculated as a fixed sum per unit of the quantity imported, the higher price levels resulting from monetary inflation had had the effect of reducing the ad valorem burden of these specific duties. The French tariff, for example, consisted mainly of specific duties. As prices rose after 1919, these duties were increased in an effort to compensate for the depreciation of the franc and the rising price level. A parliamentary committee in 1926 reported that these increases did not compensate for more than half the rise in prices. On the surface, in the 1920's tariffs appeared to be moderate. But more detailed investigation reveals that the increases made in many countries were concentrated upon the import items which threatened to compete with newly established war industries. These were precisely the items that should have been adapted to the new postwar specialization. The smaller and mainly agricultural countries in Europe, as well as the British Dominions and Latin America, raised their duties on manufactured imports in an effort to preserve the local manufacturing industries that had sprung up in the war period.

The number of separate customs units in Europe had been increased from 20 to 27, and their new frontiers were longer by about 12,500 miles. The small new states created by the peace treaties tried to build up a measure of self-sufficiency. It was this erection of new trade barriers in Europe that gave rise to the maps and models showing tariff walls, and to the calculations of tariff levels which were among the most telling exhibits at the World Economic Conference in 1927.

Until 1925 Germany was not completely free to shape her own tariff policy. Then she began to increase the tariff protection given to the grain-growing areas east of the Elbe. It is one of the ironies of history that the year 1925—the first year of the restored gold standard—saw the beginnings of what became a steady trend to agricultural protectionism in Germany and elsewhere. Agricultural tariffs were then on the whole low. In many countries they were below pre-1914 levels. But from 1925 onward there was a developing agricultural crisis, the chief signs of which were a growing accumulation of burdensome surpluses and sagging price levels. By 1927 the index of the world stocks of agricultural commodities had risen to 146, and the price index had fallen to 81, as compared with the base period 1923–25 = 100. This was not yet disastrous, but the abundant harvests of 1928 and 1929 further weakened the agricultural markets. By the end of 1929 these indices were 193 and 64. At the depth of the depression in 1932 they reached 262 and 24.

This great maladjustment of agricultural production was one of the most significant factors in the opposition to freer trade, and in the crisis which finally broke the restored gold standard system. The political choice made by the German republic in electing to intensify the protection to grain growing on the Junker estates is typical of the almost innumerable similar decisions forced upon democratic governments by powerful political groups. The decision in Germany happened to be politically and economically significant, but it did not stand alone.

No aspect of economic policy between the wars has been so much discussed as this failure to reopen the channels of international trade. In addition to the voluminous writings by economists, there is a large body of documentation contributed to the conferences of the International Chamber of Commerce, as well as the studies of the Economic Intelligence Service of the League of Nations and the reports of the numerous official conferences with which these years abound.

The International Chamber of Commerce was itself a postwar phenomenon. Founded in 1920, it labored throughout the interwar years to apply the principles of private business to the current issues of international economic policy. It did so by striving to work out agreements on specific issues among the business groups concerned. Much of its work dealt with technical questions such as double taxation, commercial arbitration, customs formalities, international river communication, bills of lading, and the interpretation of most-favored-nation treatment. In these and similar fields a body of agreed rules, which inevitably recalls the Law Merchant of the early modern age, was hammered out in conference. It is interesting to note that much of this work has now been incorporated into the draft agreement for the International Trade Organization of the United Nations. In addition the leaders of the International Chamber of Commerce were active in propounding business solutions to the questions considered by the successive postwar conferences called to implement the European peace settlement. The Dawes plan to commercialize reparation payments was a case in point. The World Economic Conference called in 1927 to seek ways of promoting freer world trade also owed much to the initiative and interest of the International Chamber of Commerce.

The documentation of this conference still provides the most comprehensive survey of the international economic issues of the first postwar decade. The unanimous declaration of the conference that "the time has come to put an end to the increase in tariffs and to move in the opposite direction," was hailed as a great triumph for the world business movement. The Report of the Committee on Trade Barriers set up by the International Chamber of Commerce became the central document of the conference and, despite some expression of French skepticism, carried the day.

The power to take action, however, remained with national governments. All that the conference could do was recommend action, and no action was effectively taken. The best that could be negotiated was a brief tariff truce, a series of bilateral commercial treaties in 1928, and some mitigation of export prohibitions and import quotas. Before the echoes of the conference had died away, the deepening agricultural crisis presaged the collapse of the reconstruction effort. Within a couple of years the financial crises that ushered in the great depression put an end to all hope of freer trade.

The skepticism of the French delegates to the World Economic Conference was amply warranted, though the alternative policies they suggested were frankly pessimistic in regard both to world peace and to private enterprise. One element in the failure of nations to adopt policies that would have led to increasing economic interdependence was the fact that warning voices were raised against the strategic dangers of such interdependence. It began to be realized that trade carried with it an element of power and, in certain circumstances, of domination. The first breach in the British free-trade tradition, for example, was made in favor of certain "key industries" deemed essential for national defense. The French, Czechs, and other nations were equally alive to the increased importance in modern war of the chemical, optical glass, steel, and other industries.

The resolutions of the Economic Conference of the Allies held at Paris in June, 1916, before the United States entered the war, had foreshadowed the development of this element in postwar policy. The initiative in this conference was taken by the French government which was very conscious of the weakness of its strategic situation. The war of 1914–18 was to them a round in a fight that had started long before and could be renewed. They did not have the manpower, the industrial resources, or the equipment to fight again effectively. Therefore they sought means to prevent a reinvigorated Germany rising from defeat to renew its quest for power. In that quest Germany had made effective use of its trading organization. France was anxious to prevent this from happening again.

Despite the rather vague economic plank in the fourteen-point platform from which President Wilson later conducted the psychological offensive against Germany, the principles of this Paris conference were written into the Versailles Treaty—not as strongly or as permanently as the French had wished, but sufficiently to give color to the German propaganda against the treaty as a harsh peace. It was against these economic clauses that J. M. Keynes campaigned in his *Economic Consequences of the Peace.* Liberal sentiment in Britain and the United States quickly rallied to his point of view. The argument was clear enough. The nineteenth-century world trading system of which Britain had been the center could not be restored unless Germany once again was able to play an important role in European production and trade. The business world sought reconciliation with a democratic Germany. The French forebodings were borne out by the rearmament of Germany, even under a democratic government. Peace had not been restored in Europe.

It is not easy to assess the influence in practical policy of the various forces at work, and one should not exaggerate the importance of strategic and military factors before 1933. From his vast experience of international trade negotiations in this period, Sir Arthur Salter has painted a realistic picture of the root causes of their failure. This is in sharp contrast with the views of those who attributed the persistence of protectionism primarily to national rivalries and hatreds.[1] It is true that there was an undercurrent of emphasis on the strategic importance of certain aspects of trade and national production. The armed services were among the organized interests to which governments had to pay greater heed after the war. While strategic considerations were not absent even in the first postwar decade, they were not dominant until after the breakdown of the restored world trading system in the great depression of 1929–33. The major cause of the first wave of protectionism during the interwar years was the pressure upon national parliaments of those local interests which had been sheltered by wartime conditions and were threatened by import competition as soon as world trade began to revive.

Many of the new governments in Europe were weakly organized. Food shortages had made it difficult to act drastically against the great estates whose surpluses fed the urban populations of industrial areas. And when these shortages gave way to burdensome surpluses, it was difficult politically to refuse protection to the owners of these estates. The new governments were in many cases not able to organize effective administrative services. In many European countries this admin-

1 Cf. Sir Arthur Salter, *World Trade and Its Future,* Philadelphia, University of Pennsylvania, 1936, p. 39: "Each official was the prisoner of his own national system, each item of which represented a protection to some home industry which was supported by those who had secured its adoption. He was responsible to ministers who were the prisoners of the groups of organized interests in their respective parliaments. Each national representative, therefore, while urging that others should change their policies, felt bound to defend his own and had no authority to agree to change it. The greatest of all the difficulties in these negotiations was not that of a real conflict between divergent national interests and national policies, but that there were no genuine national policies conceived as a whole but only a series of national systems devised under pressure. And neither ministers nor officials were effectively masters of the national system so constructed. Always, as the negotiations proceeded, one felt that the dominant consideration in the mind of each national representative was not a conception of his nation's interests as a whole, mistaken or not, but a calculation of the pressures to which the national government would be subjected by organized interests in the respective parliaments."

istrative confusion and weakness enabled the compact vocal groups of interested producers to secure the protective aid which prevented the adaptation of national economies to the freer flow of competitive world trade. After 1925 there was a general tendency to remove the more burdensome trade restrictions such as export prohibitions and import licenses that had been imposed in the first postwar transition. But as these barriers were removed, higher tariffs were introduced to soften the blow to the local producers. Moreover governments everywhere desperately needed revenue, and tariffs on imports and in many cases on exports also were remunerative and easy to collect.

The decline of faith in the competitive system was a new and important influence on commercial policy as on all other aspects of government and business policies. In lectures delivered at Oxford in 1924 and in Berlin in 1926, J. M. Keynes gave authoritative expression to this growing skepticism. In tracing the origins of the laissez-faire philosophy and its connection with nineteenth-century economic practice, he was at pains to discard the metaphysical principles upon which the almost universal faith in free competition as a regulating force had been grounded. Keynes's statement is worth quoting: "Let us clear from the ground the metaphysical or general principles upon which, from time to time, *laissez-faire* has been founded. It is *not* true that individuals possess a prescriptive 'natural liberty' in their economic activities. There is *no* 'compact' conferring perpetual rights on those who Have or those who Acquire. The world is *not* so governed from above that private and social interest always coincide. The world is *not* so managed here below that in practice they coincide. It is *not* a correct deduction from the Principles of Economics that enlightened self-interest always operates in the public interest. Nor is it true that self-interest generally *is* enlightened; more often individuals acting separately to promote their own ends are too ignorant or too weak to attain even these. Experience does *not* show that individuals, when they make up a social unit, are always less clear-sighted than when they act separately." [2]

The conclusion of his argument was a plea for greater activity by government in setting the framework within which private enterprise might operate. This plea was typical of the thought of those who sought to take effective action, usually by monetary policy but often by trade restrictions, against the unemployment that persisted even during the

[2] J. M. Keynes, *The End of Laissez-Faire,* London, The Hogarth Press Ltd., 1926, p. 39.

reconstruction boom. It became irresistible when that boom collapsed.

Specific cases can be cited where tariff protection was advocated by socialist or planning groups as a necessary instrument of public control. The German agricultural protection, for example, though to the advantage primarily of the great conservative landowners, was imposed by governments of the left and justified as an essentially socialistic measure. In most countries it did not need parties of the left or of socialist convictions to introduce protective legislation on social grounds. In almost every country except the United States, social and political pressures led governments to accept the necessity of preventing a decline in wages and therefore of national income. There was widespread acceptance also of the social responsibility imposed on governments to safeguard workers against the hardships of prolonged unemployment. In part the resistance to imports came naturally enough from those interests directly threatened by imports. But this is far from the whole story. The economic uncertainty led to a general feeling of apprehension and distrust of the self-regulating mechanisms of competition.

In face of this combination of strategic fears, pressures of vested interests, administrative confusion, and loss of faith in the self-regulating mechanisms of free competition, the great international campaign for freer trade was almost entirely fruitless. The international gatherings which advocated freer trade, imposing and influential as they seemed to be, were in fact powerless. The pressures to which governments were responsive were not those of economic logic, but those of domestic politics. While an important segment of the business leadership of the United States was exerting its powers of persuasion and influence in the biennial meetings of the International Chamber of Commerce, the sectional pressures upon Congressmen were building up that were to issue in the Hawley-Smoot tariff of 1930. The battle for freer trade was lost not on the international, but on the home front.

The complete failure of the campaign for freer trade contains a lesson which needs to be emphasized and re-emphasized. That failure is all the more noteworthy since the League of Nations had seemed to offer a new focus of action and had developed what appeared to be a promising technique of expert leadership. Although the United States was not a member of the League, many American experts had participated in the work of its technical committees. In the later 1920's there had been a marked feeling of optimism and even of elation as these committees began to marshal expert leadership in a co-operative attack on world problems. In refugee settlement, public health, and the fight against the drug traffic, co-operative action had yielded substantial results. The financial reconstruction of Austria and Hungary had been a triumph for the new methods of consultative co-operation. When the League officials in 1927 summoned the World Economic Conference in a frontal attack upon trade restrictions they realized that they were attacking the citadel of economic nationalism. Success had seemed to lie within their grasp.

The debacle which followed so rapidly turned what had been a crusade into salvage operations. No action could be taken by governments before the agricultural depression brought prices tumbling and soon afterward security prices followed. A tariff truce confined to a few western European countries was hastily patched up in March, 1930, and existing commercial agreements were prolonged for a year. This was a sad retreat from the brave aspirations of 1927. Then when Congress passed the Hawley-Smoot tariff in the following June, it destroyed all hope of maintaining even this modest agreement.

In the final showdown, the issue was not technical but political. It was not a question of technical skill or logic but of political power and votes. The League was built upon national sovereignty. It had no power save that of persuasion. Action was the prerogative of national governments, and each government responded to political pressures exerted by local lobbies. The campaign against trade barriers failed because the protectionists worked on the home front while the internationalists were encouraging each other abroad. No national government was strong enough to resist the political pressures of the minority-interest groups. And thus no effective steps could be taken in any country toward realizing the ideal of international economic co-operation to which all gave eloquent adherence.

THE WEAPONS OF ECONOMIC WARFARE

The second postwar decade was ushered in by the great depression of 1929–33. That depression wrecked the European reconstruction effort as completely as a hurricane passing over a temporary housing project erected on inadequate foundations. Out of the wreckage governments fashioned trade into an instrument of economic warfare. Once it had begun, economic warfare became its own justification.

The development of totalitarian autarky in the 1930's was made possible by the failure of democratic governments to agree upon international economic co-operation in the 1920's. It is not easy to summarize the rapid and confused sequence of events that led from the optimistic campaign for freer trade in the 1920's, to a scramble by every government to erect emergency trade barriers in the early 1930's and after 1933, to the use of these emergency devices as weapons of economic warfare. Events in one country impinged upon those in other countries. Monetary, financial, agricultural, and commercial policies acted and reacted one upon the other.

However, it is clear that the agricultural crisis which had been building up during the years 1925–29 should have received more attention. Even while the stream of American loans was supporting high European consumption levels, surpluses of staple materials were accumulating. Prices of these materials were maintained with difficulty by a great variety of governmental devices such as commodity pools, guaranteed prices, parity prices, and export controls. Behind these as behind a dam, stocks were accumulating. Even before the break of the New York security market in October, 1929, Australia and Argentina were in difficulties with their balances of payments. As the investment boom in the United States spiraled upward during 1928 and 1929, it sucked in some of the credit that had been used to float foreign loans. The raw-material producing countries felt the effect of this drying-up of loans, even while Europe was still receiving large credits. The break on the New York Stock Exchange made it clear that the lending era had come to an end. The effect on agricultural prices was like the sudden bursting of a dam. Prices tumbled precipitously and enormous stocks were released in markets that were already saturated. By the end of 1929 the agricultural price index was more than a third below the average level of 1923–25; by the end of 1932 it had fallen by more than three-fourths.

This price decline was unprecedented in its steepness, and in its range. In many respects the most severe suffering was experienced by the efficient farmers of the New World countries who had been encouraged to extend their production to feed a hungry world at the close of the war. Within the United States the loss of export markets for many staple agricultural products—cotton, lard, and dried fruits, as well as wheat—contracted the national income severely and led to fierce competition on the local market. At the same time the manufacturing industries that had expanded their export outlets suffered a sharp reduction in sales both from the loss of foreign markets and from the abrupt decline of agricultural income within the United States. Unemployment in the cities kept pace with falling prices on the farms and an interaction was set up which created a deflationary spiral. There had been much speculation in farm lands as well as industrial securities. Many of the small unit banks had become involved in real estate and security loans that were frozen as values continued to fall. These developments culminated in the bank crisis early in 1933. After that crisis approximately five thousand banks, mostly the smaller local banks in agricultural areas, failed to reopen.

Outside the United States, all the agricultural-exporting countries were heavy debtors on international account. Their efforts to accumulate the foreign exchange necessary to discharge their debt payments by exporting foodstuffs and raw materials in even larger volume completed the demoralization of the agricultural markets. As the agricultural-exporting countries strove to counteract the price fall by exporting more, they poured a flood of agricultural exports over the modest tariff barriers of the major consuming countries. Just as this flood was rising to its crest, the United States in 1930 passed the Hawley-Smoot tariff. This was the highest tariff in its history and the first to raise really effective barriers against agricultural imports. The European markets were in any case the main importers of agricultural products, and to them the whole force of the flood was now diverted. They were swamped. Thus the pressure upon the agricultural-exporting countries to pay their debts became the proximate cause of the sharply increased tariffs that after 1930 followed each other in rapid succession in one country after another. It was also the cause of the introduction into many countries of import licensing and quota systems.

All but the strongest of these agricultural debtor countries were forced in the end to suspend their overseas debt payments. Flights of capital set in to those countries which remained on the gold standard—the United States, Switzerland, the Netherlands, and France. This added to the strain on the balances of payments of the debtor countries, especially after a bank panic began with the run on the Austrian Credit-Anstalt in May, 1931. To higher tariffs and quota systems were added a variety of controls over the foreign exchanges. The panic swept on till Britain was forced to suspend specie payments in September,

1931, and the international gold standard collapsed. A large volume of credit, held on deposit and transferred from one financial center to another in search of security, became a major cause of the breakdown of exchange stability in 1931. In 1932, after the British had successfully converted a large part of their national debt to lower interest rates and sterling appeared to be more stable, there was a large flow of this loose credit from New York to London. This was a major reason why the United States in its turn went off the gold standard in April, 1933.

Far more than the mechanisms of international economic co-operation was involved in the collapse. With the gold standard there tumbled the whole financial structure of postwar reconstruction and the political organization that had been built upon it.[3] The foundations of that structure had not been solidly anchored in the realities of the changed techniques of economic organization and the altered postwar relationships of the great trading countries. They gave way at the first shock of the crisis. The New York Stock Market crash had signaled more than the end of the new era in the United States. It released the forces that wrecked the whole effort to restore international economic activity by lending to weaker countries so that they might avoid the harsh necessity of paying the real costs of war. The flow of loans from the United States had begun to dwindle from the middle of 1928, and this had contributed to the strain on agricultural prices and on balances of payments. The decline of security values in 1929 doubled this strain, and the collapse of currencies in the summer of 1931 completed the breakdown.

During the ensuing two years there were developed a host of emergency devices of trade regulation, import quotas, exchange control, and bilateral clearing systems. When the flood of agricultural exports began to pour over the moderate tariff barriers of the western European countries, there was great pressure to devise more effective protection for the agriculturalists of those countries. Some commodities were subjected to import licensing and definite limits were set to the

[3] Cf. Sir Arthur Salter, *op. cit.*, p. 35: "Then came the sudden and devastating collapse in the economic life of the world, in its financial system, in parliamentary government, in the new structure of peaceful international relations. The world depression of 1929; the financial chaos of 1931; the new dictatorship in Germany of 1933 and its profound repercussions elsewhere; the diminished membership and reduced authority of the League as disputes and menaces alienated Japan, Germany, and Italy, came in rapid succession; and a new race in armaments, at once a reflection and a cause of political tension was inaugurated with the breakdown of the Disarmament Conference."

quantity that could be imported. This quantity was called the quota (in French, *contingent*). At first the list of such goods was small and comprised total or global quotas, not allocated between the supplying countries. But in most countries it was rapidly extended and national quotas had to be allocated. A variant of the quota system was sometimes introduced in the form of tariff quotas, by which a limited supply could be imported at a low duty, after which penal duties were applied to any further imports.

As it extended, this system of quantitative control became cumbersome and inadequate to cope with the adverse balances of payments of many debtor countries. Exchange control was therefore introduced in one country after another. In essence, a system of exchange control seeks first to monopolize all foreign exchange possessed by the residents of the controlling country. To do this it must license exports and insist upon exporters surrendering to the monetary authorities all foreign exchange they receive. It must try to prevent the illegal export of goods, securities, or other assets that can be sold abroad. It must also prevent the withdrawal of foreign balances from the country. Much ingenuity was displayed in the 1930's in the devising of means to get assets of one kind or another out of the countries which had imposed exchange control.

The foreign exchange which was gathered in was allocated for use abroad according to priorities determined by the monetary authority, usually for government purchases, debt payments, and authorized imports. The power to allocate means of payment gave the authorities a potent control over imports. Thus exchange control in most countries quickly came to be a more important instrument of trade regulation than quota restrictions on particular imports. The control of imports either by quotas or by exchange control is a two-edged device. A country can cut down its imports, but it cannot force its exports on other countries.

Economists have endeavored to analyze the economic effects as well as the incidence of import quotas and exchange controls. The difference between them and tariffs is that they operate directly to restrict the supply offered in a particular national market. An import duty operates upon the price of the taxed commodity. It is imposed at a sensitive point in the price mechanism, whence its effects are readily diffused over all the factors of demand and supply. If the tariff is high enough, it shuts out imports as effectively as any quota. However, circumstances may exist which allow the imports to continue, since the effect of the tariff is borne by the foreign exporter, or can be passed on by the immediate consumer. But a quota directly limits the permissible imports. No matter how prices are affected, imports cannot enter beyond it.

To trace the very wide variety of these price effects, according to the different circumstances of particular commodities, offers scope for much ingenuity of theoretical reasoning. Some commodities have a high elasticity of demand—a slight rise of price will cause a great fall in demand. For others the demand is less elastic. On the supply side there is the same variation. A slight rise of price may call forth a greatly increased supply, or it may call forth very little increase. These relative elasticities of demand and of supply for different commodities in the markets, divided as a result of the imposition of quotas, often give rise to peculiar results. Such analyses, while interesting in theory, do not usually take account of the most important characteristic of these new quantitative trade restrictions, namely, their flexibility and frequent changes. Tariff duties were as a rule stable over reasonably long periods of time. But quotas and exchange control allocations are temporary by their very nature and changeable by administrative discretion.

The new devices were introduced mainly for this reason. The case is very clear in regard to France which relied heavily upon import quotas while resisting exchange control. Even if the French tariff had not been bound by commercial treaties, it would have been difficult in 1931 and 1932 to raise duties to the levels necessary to check the flood of imports then pouring into French ports. Definite limits on the quantity of goods to be admitted seemed the only possible course of action. At first it was not easy to improvise the administration of quotas. How was the permissible total to be distributed among the various ports, among the various supplying countries, among various merchants in different parts of the country? How was it to be distributed over periods of time? Answers to such questions were found in due course. They all gave added power to the administrators. The difficulty of finding solutions that would be acceptable to all parties and yet limit imports sufficiently, led in many cases to provisional quotas renewed at short periods. Thus trade became much more dependent on arbitrary administrative decisions.

When Britain went off the gold standard in September, 1931, there was great confusion in the foreign exchange markets. London had never lost its predominance as a clearing center. International obligations were still settled mainly in sterling. This was particularly true of balances due in respect to commodity trade, since London was still a great trader and provided the short-term funds to finance a large proportion of world trade. Then suddenly the value of sterling depreciated. Foreign banks which had left part of their reserves in London for clearing purposes found the value of these reserves reduced and uncertain. In consequence a sort of paralysis descended on the financing and clearing of world trade. Even neighboring countries had been used to squaring their accounts through London, and had no other facilities for settling their international balances.

It was for this reason that the Swiss and the Austrians devised the first bilateral clearing agreement in November, 1931. This arrangement contemplated the collection in Swiss francs by the Swiss national bank of the payments made by Swiss importers for Austrian goods while across the border the Austrian national bank collected in Austrian shillings the payments due from Austrian importers for Swiss goods. The reverse payments to Swiss and Austrian exporters were made out of the national currencies collected. This simple device enabled some trade to continue. But it had the obvious defect that it required imports and exports to be balanced between pairs of countries. Thereby it reinforced the trend to bilateralism in trade.

There were some who hailed these cumbersome bilateral clearing arrangements as a brilliant new invention superior to the barbaric gold standard. In fact, the clearing of payments while the international gold standard was in operation had been a far superior offsetting or bookkeeping process. It was multilateral, flexible, and unofficial, and its bookkeeping was only remotely connected with actual transfers of gold. By contrast the systems of bilateral exchange clearing were very restrictive and clumsy. In due course skillful administrators were able to streamline them into reasonably effective methods of international payments, but they were far from being reasonable or effective at first. At the same time these monetary controls, necessary as they were to enable trade to continue at all in the chaotic price and exchange fluctuations consequent upon the breakdown of the gold standard, inevitably increased the power of the officials who were responsible for the allocation of foreign exchange. Imports were arranged not from the countries where prices were lowest, but from those where funds had been accumulated from exports.

These devices of import quotas, exchange control, and bilateral clearing were all introduced as emergency devices, and not as a permanent system. Throughout the crisis of 1929–31, governments and central banks had striven to prop up the weak spots in the world trading and financial structure and to prevent the final collapse of multilateral trade. The Bank for International Settlements which had been created in 1924 in pursuance of the Dawes agreement on reparation payments was active in promoting co-operation between central banks, but its powers and functions were limited. Like the League, it might in time have accumulated prestige and power. But the panic that swept over Europe in 1931 was beyond its infant capacity. The Bank of England and the Bank of France lent on short-term to central and eastern Europe, though the French authorities had made it abundantly clear that they believed Germany guilty of preparing a fraudulent bankruptcy, and French short-term capital imports which had to be offset by gold exports from debtor countries were among the chief disequilibrating factors in the crisis. There was much co-operation also from the commercial banks in New York. But the official attitude of the United States was still antagonistic to co-operative action. The United States Treasury maintained a sharp distinction between war debts and reparation payments, and the provincial outlook of Congress was dramatically demonstrated by the passing of the Hawley-Smoot tariff in the middle of the depression.

In these circumstances President Hoover's action in proposing a moratorium on war debts and reparation payments was courageous. The Austrian Credit–Anstalt's difficulties had been made public in May, 1931. It was known that many of the German banks had made advances in Austria and other southeastern European countries and that these advances had been frozen as a result of the banking panic which had started in Vienna. The panic spread to the German banks in June, and it was at this moment that President Hoover made his proposal on June 23, 1931. There was delay before the French government agreed to accept the moratorium, but early in July it went into effect. It helped ease tension somewhat, but it did not stop the run on the German banks, nor the extension of the panic to London. The

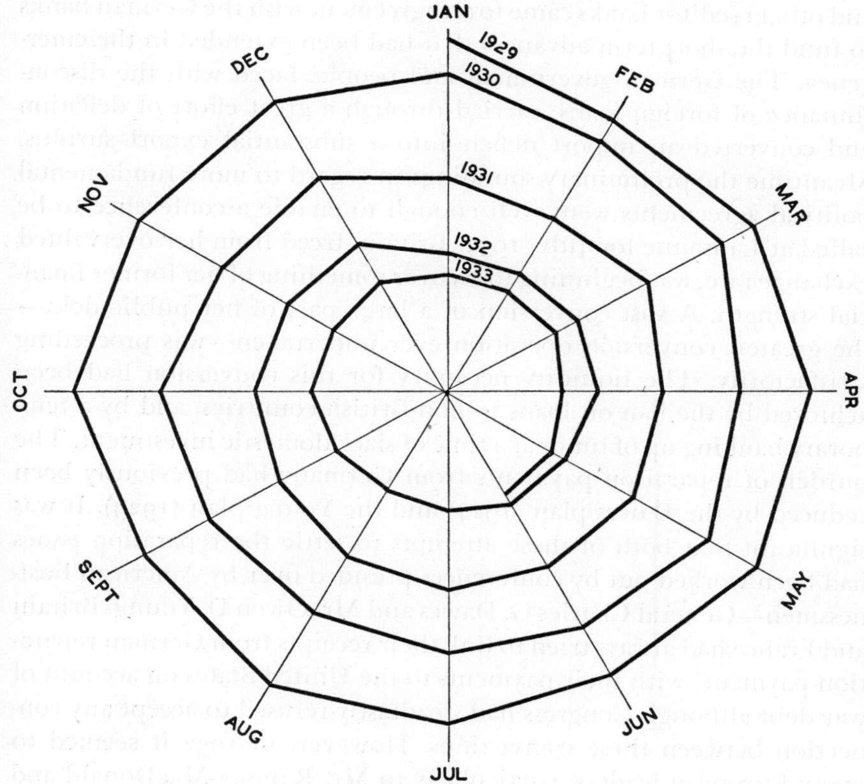

THE CONTRACTING SPIRAL OF WORLD TRADE

Read clockwise, this chart indicates how from 1929 into 1933 the value of world trade in each month was less than that in the same month of the year preceding.

Source: Reproduced from League of Nations, *World Economic Survey, 1932–3,* Geneva, 1933, p. 8.

crisis was not caused by reparation payments or war debts and could not be cured by their suspension.[4]

Negotiations went on. Representatives of the British, American, and other creditor banks came to an agreement with the German banks to fund the short-term advances that had been extended in the emergency. The German government and people, faced with the discontinuance of foreign loans, carried through a great effort of deflation and converted an import deficit into a substantial export surplus. Meantime the preliminary soundings in regard to more fundamental political agreements went well enough to enable a conference to be called at Lausanne for July, 1932. Britain, freed from her overvalued exchange rate, was beginning to recover something of her former financial strength. A vast conversion of a large part of her public debt—the greatest conversion operation ever undertaken—was proceeding satisfactorily. The liquidity necessary for this conversion had been achieved by the ban on loans to non-British countries, and by a temporary banking up of funds at a time of slack domestic investment. The burden of reparation payments from Germany had previously been reduced by the Dawes plan (1924) and the Young plan (1929). It was significant that both of these attempts to settle the reparation issues had been worked out by conferences presided over by American businessmen—General Charles G. Dawes and Mr. Owen D. Young. Britain and France had always tried to link their receipts from German reparation payments with their payments to the United States on account of war debt although Congress had steadfastly refused to accept any connection between these transactions. However, in 1932 it seemed to many European leaders, particularly to Mr. Ramsay MacDonald and to M. Edouard Herriot, the Prime Ministers of Britain and France, that the time was opportune to attempt a third, and final, settlement of war debt and reparation claims. The Lausanne conference was called for this purpose. The United States, however, refused to be a party to the Lausanne conference. Officially it maintained and still

[4] The present author went to Geneva in September, 1931, to write the first *World Economic Survey, 1931–2* for the League of Nations. His first impression of the effect of the Austrian crisis as recorded (pp. 72–73) was amply borne out by later events: "A crack had developed in the carefully constructed and patched façade of international finance and, through that crack, already timid investors and depositors caught glimpses of a weak and over-burdened structure. It was not only a bank that threatened to collapse, but the whole system of over-extended financial commitments which was the worst legacy of the war and of subsequent credit expansion."

maintains that war debt and reparation transactions must be considered separately.

The Lausanne conference did not indulge in the usual array of formal sessions breaking up into committees and sub-committees. It was conducted as a negotiating conference with visits between the heads of national delegations. What emerged was an agreement to which the French assented, that reparation payments should in fact cease. The basis upon which this reparation agreement was reached cannot be known until documents still held secret are revealed. No mention was made of war debts, but there were rumors that the United States might modify its attitude when a great conference met later to consider world economic co-operation. A temporary arrangement was in fact reached regarding the service of these debts—the last token payments ever to be made on these obligations were made just after the Lausanne conference.

It cannot be said that the Lausanne conference failed. It put an effective end to German reparation payments. One consequence of this, rightly or wrongly, was that after some further token payments Britain, France, and all the other European countries which owed war debts to the United States, with the sole exception of Finland, defaulted. The main achievement at Lausanne was the decision, in which the United States later concurred, to call a Monetary and Economic Conference. Preliminary meetings of experts, in which official representatives of the United States participated, were held at Geneva in November, 1932 and January, 1933. An annotated agenda was drawn up and the calling of the conference was left in the hands of the British Prime Minister, Mr. Ramsay MacDonald. This conference in the summer of 1933 proved to be the last attempt to bring international order out of the fast developing nationalistic chaos.

THE ANARCHY OF NATIONALISM

In the 1930's there was fashioned out of the ruins of international co-operation a more systematic economic nationalism than the mercantilists of the seventeenth and eighteenth centuries had ever been able to achieve. At the outset it was not a deliberate creation. In the early stages of the depression great efforts had been made to save as much as possible from the wreck—efforts which culminated in the calling of the Monetary and Economic Conference at London in the summer of 1933. After the breakdown of this conference most governments concentrated upon attempts to work out by national action means to insulate their peoples from the swirling panic which still lashed the international markets. Early in 1934, however, a new and formidable development became apparent in the German organization of commercial policy as an instrument of national power under the Nazi regime.

A knowledge of the political background is essential to an understanding of the failure of this London conference. On the initiative of the Canadian government, a British Commonwealth conference had met at Ottawa in July and August, 1932, immediately following the Lausanne conference. Great Britain had abandoned its free-trade policy by passing emergency customs legislation in the latter part of 1931 and consolidating this legislation in the Import Duties Act passed early in 1932. This historic reversal of British commercial policy not only transformed the British revenue tariff into a full-fledged protective system, it also re-introduced into it the principle of imperial preference. The Dominions had long since imposed higher duties on foreign than on British goods—Canada since 1898. Now the United Kingdom reciprocated. At the Ottawa conference in the summer of 1932 a series of reciprocal preferential treaties was negotiated between the different member states of the Commonwealth. Moreover, the dependent colonies were committed by Great Britain to the preferential system. This decision was greatly resented by Japan which had been a large exporter to the British colonial areas.

The decisions of the Ottawa conference were defended particularly by Mr. Neville Chamberlain, the Chancellor of the Exchequer, as a necessary prelude to the Monetary and Economic Conference held at London in June, 1933. The argument was that the conference would stimulate freer trade within the sterling area. In fact, however, it prepared an alternative to multilateral trade by organizing the nucleus of a regional trading area. This became evident in 1933 and 1934 when the British government proceeded to negotiate a series of bilateral trade treaties with Denmark, Argentina, Norway, Iceland, Sweden, Latvia, Estonia, Finland, and the U.S.S.R. All of these treaties were of the same general pattern. Tariff and quota facilities for British goods, supplemented by agreements to purchase definite quantities of particular products, were reciprocated by agreed import quotas and the promise of stability of duties and quotas. Britain was using its import market to negotiate an area of assured exports. The so-called sterling area so created was ill-defined. There was a solid nucleus of the British dominions and colonies—except Canada. After exchange control was introduced in 1939, these British countries pooled their exchange reserves. But there was also a considerable area outside the British Empire to which the British market was of dominating importance.

Two other historical facts need to be recalled briefly. Early in 1933 the National Socialist (Nazi) party attained power in Germany in a coalition with the Nationalists led by Herr Hugenberg. The control of the Reichsbank and with it of German internal and external economic policy passed into the hands of Dr. Hjalmar Schacht. When the London conference assembled in June, 1933. Herr Hugenberg and Herr Schacht sat as the representatives of Germany. In Berlin Herr Hitler was preparing the ground for his assumption of totalitarian power.

In November, 1932, the presidential campaign had seen the election of Mr. Roosevelt. The intervening months before the new administration took office in March, 1933, saw a notable deterioration of the economic situation in the United States. It culminated in the banking crisis of February-March. There was a lack of liaison between the outgoing and incoming administrations. When the Roosevelt administration finally took over it was preoccupied with domestic questions. The new Secretary of State, Cordell Hull, had definite views as to the importance of the London conference, which he attended in person as chief of the United States delegation. Nonetheless the American position was not prepared in advance except that Mr. Hull brought strong views as to the necessity of getting rid of the obstacles that were throttling world trade.

In late 1932 and early 1933 there had been a considerable movement of capital from New York, causing a heavy drain on the gold reserves at a time of acute depression. The prospect of a further gold outflow led President Roosevelt to abandon the gold parity of the dollar in April, 1933, just at the moment when Mr. Ramsay MacDonald was crossing the Atlantic to consult him about the date for convening the London conference. Though the agenda for the conference which had been drawn up in January was postulated upon a stable dollar at the old gold parity, the date of meeting was set for June 12, 1933, without any attempt to revise the agenda or to work out a new basis of agreement among the great trading nations. Meantime the domestic policies of the Roosevelt administration were directed toward public expenditures and monetary experiments designed to raise the price level and to stimulate recovery. In order to safeguard these experiments against the risk of gold being drained out of the currency reserves, the administration was reluctant to agree to any proposals for stabilization of the gold value of the dollar.

The London conference met therefore upon an agenda which had never been revised to take account of intervening events. The basic reason for its complete failure was that there was no readiness in any country to take the necessary steps to stabilize currencies, reduce tariffs, and get rid of the quantitative restrictions on world trade. It is true that the basic issues of the conference were never very clear. Currency rather than trade policy occupied the center of discussion. There was no longer the widespread belief in the gold standard that had made agreement on currency questions relatively easy at earlier conferences. By 1933 disagreement on currency policy was so marked that the more profound underlying conflicts on commercial policy never came into the open. France, Italy, Poland, and other members of the so-called gold bloc stood firm for a reversion to the traditional gold standard. At the other extreme the United States administration was experimenting with attempts to raise prices by daily raising the price at which the Treasury would buy gold.

It has sometimes been argued that the conference should never have met when it did. The political circumstances, it may be agreed, were unpropitious, and the confusion and cross-purposes within the United States delegation and between it and the administration at Washington paralyzed its great potentialities for the leadership which the conference so badly needed. But the political circumstances were not likely to improve. Hitler was already in power. The conference was perhaps called too late, in a sense more final than that in which all the interwar conferences were too late. Even at this eleventh hour the conference might have reached an understanding, at least among the American, British and western European peoples, if there had been a clearer realization of the international dangers ahead and if a more realistic search had been made for a prior basis of agreement on currency and trading policies.

A basis for currency stabilization might have been reached if the continental adherents of the gold standard had been less dogmatic in their orthodoxy, if the American delegates had had any forewarning of the lighthearted way in which their proposals would be scrapped in the presumed interest of an experimental domestic program, and if the British had displayed greater initiative or leadership in seeking a practical solution. While the overt disagreements at the conference were largely on matters of monetary theory, the real disagreements lay deeper. They were rooted in the domestic pressures on governments. In the United States the priority of these domestic considerations led to President Roosevelt's telegram which destroyed the last hope of agreement upon currency stabilization and so killed the conference. The depreciation of sterling, plus the protective tariff and imperial preferences which Mr. Chamberlain had achieved at Ottawa in filial piety, had placed Britain temporarily in a favorable bargaining position. In France, and the other countries of the gold bloc, monetary policy was primarily the concern of conservative investment groups.

The primacy of these factional and local interests was to the Russians merely a further manifestation of the Marxian doctrine that states are governed in the immediate interest of their ruling classes. Herr Hitler drew from this clash of interests the correct deduction that a determined nationalist drive in the economic sphere would encounter no serious challenge. The thorough technicians of Germany did the rest. Once the order was given and the goal was set, there were competent, even brilliant, craftsmen available to work out the details. It was less than a year before the master plan of a new German trading system was ready to be launched. This system was centered on Berlin and aimed at the triple purpose of equipping and rearming a militant Germany, extending its power and influence in strategic areas, and weakening the British power in Europe.

These German developments reveal one of the major difficulties in constructing a trading system to operate in a world where national governments exercise so much influence on economic activity. In the nineteenth century a private enterprise system developed and was able to operate through competitive world markets. Even then the conduct of trade carried with it latent elements of power. A small and poor country trading with a great creditor country whose market was all-important for its exports found its autonomy limited in respect to monetary and trade policy. The great importing country might not press its political advantage. But the weaker country felt insecure. The United States today does not intervene officially in the political arrangements of its good neighbors to the south. But one does not need to travel very far to discover that the sheer size of the Colossus of the North is a matter of concern to those good neighbors.

When failure was admitted at the London conference in 1933, every nation tried to safeguard its own economic stability and its own strategic security. The United States was the strongest world power, hardly conscious of that strength or of its responsibilities, but confident of its own self-sufficiency. Britain had finally rejected free trade and was busily engaged in building up a system of preferential trade within the commonwealth and empire and in negotiating bilateral arrangements with its chief customers and clients. The countries of the gold bloc led by France fought a losing battle to maintain their currency parities and the value of the investments contracted in them. The U.S.S.R. was not a great factor in world trade. But Germany in the West and Japan in the East embarked upon trading drives directed primarily toward neighboring areas of strategic importance to them. Here they pursued by economic means the objectives which Italy pursued in Ethiopia and Spain by direct military intervention.

This development of trading blocs led by great powers was the most significant economic development of the years immediately preceding the second World War. As always the breakdown of international law and economic order gave opportunity to the ruthless rather than to the strong. With all its defects the international gold standard system had been a system of world law and order. When it collapsed those states which followed by aggressive totalitarian methods what they conceived to be their own national interests could count upon the confused acquiescence of all but their prospective victims, and of influential segments of public opinion even among them. The story of the German drive in Europe and the Japanese drive in China is a story of a struggle for markets turning into a conscious and deliberate organization of trade as a preparation for conquest.[5]

[5] The elements of this organization have been put into systematic form by Albert O. Hirschman, *National Power and the Structure of Foreign Trade,* Berkeley, 1945, pp. 34–35. Summarized, the schematic tabulation of the principles of a power policy in foreign trade is:

I. Supply Effect
   - A. Concentration on strategic imports
   - B. Accumulation of strategic stockpiles
   - C. Redirection of trade to friendly or subject nations
   - D. Saving of trade routes against blockade

II. Influence Effect
   - A. 1. Increase the partner's gain from trade
     2. Increase the partner's adjustment difficulties

Preoccupied with their own domestic affairs, or with the organization of their own special trading areas, the democratic countries did not take effective steps to check the totalitarian policies of economic preparedness. Though the United States in June, 1934, passed the Reciprocal Trade Agreements Act designed to negotiate reductions in tariff barriers, the use made of this Act was not an effective counterpoise to the totalitarian trading drives. The very great potentialities of the method of bilateral negotiation to achieve an expansion of multilateral trade were demonstrated in a series of agreements with Latin America and some of the smaller western European countries. But the great proportion of world trade conducted by the sterling area made it necessary to reach agreement with Britain if world trade was to be restored. No such agreement could be reached till 1938. By this time it was too late, even if the agreement had been more far-reaching than it actually was. Failure to reach an understanding with the United States was part of the price paid by Britain for the Chamberlain protective and preferential policies. The Reciprocal Trade Agreement Act remains one of the most important instruments of economic policy at the disposal of the United States. It is the chief symbol of its policy of international co-operation in postwar reconstruction.

The only other significant approach toward a common front against totalitarian economic aggression was the cautious and belated Tripartite Declaration of September, 1936. Thereby the United States, Britain, and France simultaneously stated their intention to maintain exchange stability. This was a device by which it was made to seem respectable for France and its partners in the gold bloc to devalue their currencies to the level at which the dollar and sterling had settled—the old exchange parity but at lower values in terms of gold. It was hoped that France might thus escape from the continuous deflationary pressure on her economy, but the relief was only temporary. The political divisions in France, exacerbated by foreign propaganda and fifth-column activity, had gone too deep and had virtually paralyzed economic co-operation between management and labor. Further flights of capital and depreciations of the franc occurred with little real economic recovery. The outbreak of war in 1939 found

---

3. Create vested interests within partner country

B. 1. Trade with smaller countries
   2. Import so as to make these countries dependent
   3. Export highly differentiated monopolistic goods
   4. Develop transit trade

France virtually unarmed, by modern standards, and a prisoner of the Maginot mentality. The German techniques employed in their totalitarian drive on the economic front of war preparedness will be studied in war colleges for generations to come. But they have little relevance to any attempt to reconstruct a world trading system. While trade and investment conducted systematically by state regulation to maximize military power, by profitable means if possible but at a loss if necessary, are essential elements of economic nationalism, they constitute the complete negation of peaceful international economic co-operation.

Thus the decade preceding the second World War was one of economic breakdown and economic warfare. It is unfortunate that so much current economic analysis is postulated upon this pathological experience. The thirties was an abnormal, feverish decade in the course of which economic nationalism was rationalized. Because part of the program of war preparation was the utilization of resources and manpower, the militarists laid much stress on their ability to solve the problem of unemployment that had baffled the free economies. Too many economists were deluded into a scientific examination of their devices and techniques which were merely incidental to a strategic plan, which in turn was incompatible with either political liberty or free economic enterprise.

THE GILT-EDGED STANDARD

Of all the economic changes wrought by the war of 1914–18, the most profound was the subtle transformation of the monetary systems of the world. When the war ended there was virtually unanimous agreement among the experts that the international gold standard should be quickly restored. It was realized by some that concerted and speedy action was called for and that exchange rates should be adjusted to the shifts in purchasing power parities of the national currencies as reflected in price levels. More orthodox banking views, particularly in London, were reflected in the report of the committee presided over by Lord Cunliffe, then the Governor of the Bank of England, which in 1918 recommended unilateral return to gold at the prewar parity. There was no machinery readily available for international action. At the moment the inflationary dangers inherent in unstable paper currencies loomed greater than the need for international exchange stability. So great was the faith in gold, and so impressive were the examples at hand of uncontrolled inflation that national governments were more concerned to stabilize their currencies in terms of gold than to restore exchange equilibrium.

When the war ended in 1918, only the United States, and some of the European neutrals—the Netherlands, Sweden, and Switzerland—remained nominally on the gold standard. The history of the return to gold by one country after another in the years 1922–29 is long and involved. It is noteworthy that the countries which had suffered most from inflation were among the first to return to gold—Austria in 1922, Germany in 1923, and Hungary in 1924. Economists might plead for a general stabilization, in which the relations of prices in various countries might be taken into account in fixing the new exchange rates. The British authorities could wait till April, 1925, watching the movements of prices in the United States, before returning to the gold standard. But there was no confidence in credit issues or paper money in the countries that had gone through hyperinflation. A return to gold at almost any level seemed preferable to the dangers of further inflation. When Britain stabilized in April, 1925, all the countries in the British trading area followed suit. By common consent the restoration of the international gold standard was dated from this time. There were still important trading countries outside the newly restored area of exchange stability based on gold. One by one they too returned to gold, until by the end of 1928, the only important trading countries where currencies had not been stabilized on a gold basis, were Spain, Portugal, and Japan.

What had happened is most accurately described as a return to the gold basis for national currencies in the belief that, as before 1914, this would ensure exchange stability. No more striking illustration could be asked of the way in which symbols operate in public policy even after they have lost their essential validity. What was restored was the legal form of the gold standard. Those who could see beyond the symbols knew that the restored gold standard was a façade. They knew that the popular faith in gold as an assurance of both price and exchange stability rested upon an illusion reflecting prewar conditions that no longer existed.

In addition to the structural distortion and impoverishment of national economies which varied so greatly, there were differing degrees of inflation and of political stability in the countries returning to gold. Currency stabilization was a sovereign act, taken at the time and at the exchange level chosen by each nation. It is true that there was consultation among governments and central banks. There were a series of international conferences also among which that at Genoa (1922) was particularly concerned with currency questions. Nevertheless, the very fact that countries stabilized one after another meant that each successive stabilization was bound to disturb the earlier rates. Each country returned to gold at its own level.

Traditional banking beliefs and practices, rather than economic analysis, were the determining factors.[6] There was little statistical information at that time to work upon in calculating the balances of payments. The Economic Intelligence Service of the League of Nations gradually built up a substantial body of information in this field, but in the period of stabilization such information was scanty. The results were unfortunate particularly in the case of the British, who chose the pre-1914 parity for sterling. This proved too high to enable exporters to compete in foreign markets at the prevailing price level. The French, on the other hand, chose a low parity for the franc and so were able to allow prices to rise while the balance of payments remained favorable. In any case such statistical information, mainly in regard to price levels, as was available at the time of the first stabilizations was apt to be misleading. International trading competition had not been restored and thus there was little possibility of testing the workability of the exchange rates.

Moreover some of the most troublesome aspects of the international balancing of payments—the unilateral transfers on account of war debts and reparation payments—did not become an actual burden upon the international accounts until after stabilization of the main currencies. The German reparation payments were fixed as part of the currency stabilization worked out by the Dawes Committee in 1924. The British war loan payments to the United States were agreed upon in June, 1923. By 1926 a network of agreements with the United States, with Britain, and with France in regard to war debt and reparation payments was completed. Payments on account of these settle-

[6] Cf. William Adams Brown, Jr., *op. cit.,* Vol. I, p. 178: "The (British) will to maintain parity, or if forced to depart from it, to return to it, was the outgrowth of banking tradition, rather than of political expediency or of economic analysis. It may be thought of as the practical application on a grand scale of a deeply ingrained code of banking ethics. In this sense, it may be said that it was based fundamentally on moral considerations, combined with faith in the mechanisms of the pre-war gold standard based upon long experience."

ments were troublesome during the years of stabilization. The special pleading of Dr. Schacht blaming all Germany's difficulties upon them, rather than upon the war and postwar financial policies of Germany itself, is untenable. Both war debt and reparation payments were in fact paid only as long as the United States provided loans with which to balance the external payments of the debtors.

Throughout the stabilization period fears were expressed of a shortage of gold. Prices were high and the amounts of gold called for to support the credit superstructure necessary to maintain these price levels were greater than before the war. As the stabilization proceeded, one country after another adopted systems of note issue and of credit regulation that immobilized substantial amounts of gold to maintain the required reserve ratios. The inauguration in 1913 of the Federal Reserve System in the United States had begun this process. As new central banks were created in Europe after 1918, it was widely extended. Commercial banks did something to ease the strain on gold supplies by lowering their cash ratios. But this development weakened the control of the central banks over monetary policy and impaired the efficiency of the restored international gold standard. The increased importance of the commercial banks made for monetary nationalism especially since the distinction between deposit and investment banking became increasingly blurred even in Britain. Heavy tax rates made it profitable to finance industrial expansion out of bank loans rather than by floating new share capital. A central bank, therefore, had to proceed with caution before taking steps to correct a threatened disequilibrium in the balance of payments by raising interest rates.[7]

Before the sharp decline of prices in 1929, this fear of a gold shortage was not unfounded. Following the Napoleonic Wars and the Franco-Prussian War in 1870, a scramble for gold to reconstitute both circulating media and bank reserves had led, in these periods of increasing production, to long spells of falling prices punctuated by severe financial crises. World production of gold did not increase but after falling during the period of the first World War, remained stationary because of the high level of costs. The warning issued at the Genoa Conference (1922) that it was necessary to practice economy in the use

[7] Cf. William Adams Brown, Jr., *op. cit.*, Vol. I, p. 198: "The assent and cooperation of the joint-stock banks were becoming more than ever essential to the success of any credit control policy. The pre-war method of control indirectly through the short-term market had to be supplemented by a larger measure of direct agreement between the great commercial banks, the government, and the Bank of England."

of gold forestalled any attempt to coin gold for circulation. At the same time encouragement was given to the practice of holding substantial proportions of the central bank reserves in the form of foreign exchange balances. The situation changed abruptly after the fall in prices at the end of 1929 and after the collapse of the restored gold standard in September, 1931. Not only were the existing stocks of gold then revalued at depreciated currency levels, but the world production of gold increased sharply as its price in the new currencies jumped. And this increased price tempted a great volume of gold out of the hoards of the Asiatic countries.

It is important, therefore, to realize that the nineteenth-century form of the gold standard was restored in only a few of the major trading countries. Most of the European countries, and practically all of the countries outside Europe and the United States, held part or all of the reserves of their monetary systems in the form of short-term deposits abroad mainly in London and New York. This was an extension to European practice of the gold-exchange standard which had formerly been confined to colonial countries and not a restoration of the international gold standard. It imposed a tremendous responsibility upon London, and in less degree upon New York.[8] Until 1929 the price levels of most European countries had to be sustained by a great flow of loans which kept their balances of payments in equilibrium without the necessity of exporting heavily to pay for their reconstruction imports.

The whole intricate attempt to restore and maintain the international gold standard after 1925 has been described as "pegging operations on a vast scale."[9] It was essentially inflationary in its effects. In 1931 the Macmillan Committee was to emphasize the risks involved in Britain by the accumulation of foreign short-term deposits and foreign holdings of treasury bills. The risk became actual in the summer of 1931 when the sudden withdrawal of foreign-owned assets forced Britain off the gold standard. Then some countries, such as Czechoslovakia, Greece, and the Netherlands, which through loyalty or underestimation of the crisis had failed to withdraw their claims on London, suffered heavy loss of their monetary reserves when sterling depreciated. The Bank of England had constantly urged that short-term balances be kept in London to facilitate the clearing of

[8] For the origins of the gold-exchange standard, see above, pp. 397–98.

[9] William Adams Brown, Jr., *op. cit.*, p. 805.

international payments. In 1931 these balances were caught in the depreciation of sterling.

The preceding argument can be summed up in the statement that, one by one, most of the countries which pegged their currencies on gold did so by pegging their exchange rates either on London or on New York and by maintaining in those centers deposits or gilt-edged security holdings, in supplement of their gold reserves. In this manner there was a considerable double-counting of gold reserves, upon which were maintained a volume of credit and national price levels that avoided the necessity of readjustment to the postwar pattern of world specialization. The expansion of credit was greater than the growth of industry, real savings were less than real investment, and bank liabilities grew faster than bank capital. This whole inflationary structure was built upon international lending. This came from London in a measure which strained the British monetary reserves, and from New York in a measure which depended upon low interest rates and this in turn fostered a speculative security boom.

The hollowness of this façade began to be revealed in 1926–27 when France, approaching the stabilization of the franc at a low level, acted upon gold standard principles by turning its excessive holdings of foreign exchange into gold on the London market. By the test of prewar practice the French authorities were following orthodox procedure, but their gold purchases imposed a strain upon the London market. The Bank of England felt unable to react in the orthodox way by raising its discount rate to protect its gold reserve. By selling securities it did something to tighten credit so as to reduce the credit superstructure to a level commensurate with the inadequate gold reserve. But its powers in this direction were limited by the need of the Treasury to sell its bills and to keep interest rates low so as not to increase the budgetary burden represented by interest on a large amount of unfunded debt. The British commercial banks were so immobilized by their industrial advances that they could not tighten their lending without causing a severe contraction of industry which might have forced Britain off the gold standard.

The purchase of gold by the Bank of France was directed not so much against London as against Berlin. It was intended to force the Bank of England to bring pressure upon the Reichsbank to put a stop to the speculative operations by which Germans were building up balances abroad while borrowing in London and New York. The

French view was emphatic. It was that Berlin was reluctant to take over the foreign assets held by German citizens in order to place itself in a position to make reparation payments, because the German authorities were preparing to argue that these reparation payments should be reduced. The French insisted that the Reichsbank ought to raise its discount rate and thus recall these funds. But the British were reluctant to bring pressure on the Reichsbank because they feared it would check the economic recovery in Germany and in Europe as a whole.

The fact was that neither London nor Berlin was in a position to operate the gold standard along prewar lines. The French were theoretically and technically correct in their procedures. But their persistence would have brought about the collapse of the precarious international equilibrium in 1927, if the Federal Reserve System had not given it a further two years' lease on life by the decision in June, 1927, to lower discount rates. London was saved by this decision and could go on with its plans for European lending. The European countries, and Germany in particular, could borrow further and in greater amounts, in New York. Meantime France bought gold in New York rather than in London.

The elements of unreality in the British situation were clearly revealed in conversations between the Bank of France and the Bank of England in May, 1927.[10] Whereas before 1914, British industry had been more than able to finance itself—able, indeed, to provide large annual sums to the market for foreign investment—after 1918 it became heavily dependent on bank advances. In large part, also, the loans made by British banks abroad were a result of credit creation rather than of real savings. The credit superstructure, therefore, was precariously based upon a gold reserve which was less adequate for the enlarged credit structure, though greater than before 1914. It was still less adequate after the extension of the gold-exchange standard built up heavy foreign deposits in London. The commercial banks were now—to use a market expression—in the Bank in the sense that they were immediately sensitive to any action by which the Bank might try to regulate the external balance. Industry was certainly in the com-

[10] Ten years later M. Moreau, who was Governor of the Bank of France in 1927, revealed these conversations in articles contributed to the *Revue de Deux Mondes.* Cf William Adams Brown, Jr., *op. cit.,* Vol. I, pp. 453–58.

mercial banks to a greater extent than it had ever been in the nineteenth century.

The levels of economic activity and of prices in Britain were precariously maintained upon an inadequate gold reserve, and it had become necessary to avoid by all possible means any loss of gold which would cause credit contraction and so bring the whole structure down in a deflationary crisis. Mr. Keynes, with his acute and intuitive appreciation of the imponderables in any economic situation, published in 1923 his *Tract on Monetary Reform,* in which he made positive suggestions for the future regulation of money. It was significant that these were based upon the experience of Great Britain during the first difficult postwar years in controlling the domestic level of prices and insulating it from external causes of fluctuation. Keynes's suggestions were that monetary policy should be based upon the necessity for sustaining the domestic price level and that pressures on the external balance of payments should not be allowed to interfere with this purpose. He thought that policy to this end could be developed out of the practices that had been followed since 1918.

This recognition and rationalization of the extent to which British monetary policy since the war had been aimed at regulating the domestic price level was a startling break with traditional gold standard theory. It was also an indication of the marked degree to which the British monetary system had changed. No longer was the short-term money market primarily concerned with trade acceptances. Treasury bills and foreign deposits were its more important stock in trade. No longer was there a sharp separation between the foreign and domestic banking operations. The commercial banks financed British industry heavily and were in turn heavily dependent upon the short-term market which was the traditional mechanism for regulating both the external balance of payments and the supply of new capital issues.

At the time Keynes was writing, there was a considerable and influential body of economic opinion, strongly represented in banking circles, which did not shrink from the costs involved in a return to the prewar gold standard practices. This would have led to a general reduction of wages, unemployment, and a lowering of living levels. Such a return to prewar practice meant abandoning the tendency that had developed to concentrate policy upon the provision of credit adequate to sustain economic activity without regard to the external balance of payments. It meant regulating the amount of credit according to the pressures on the gold reserve caused by fluctuations in the balance of payments. In other words, it would allow credit to shrink and prices to fall if this was necessary to safeguard the gold reserves against an external drain. As Keynes recognized, foreshadowing the lines on which his theoretical outlook would develop, such a return to orthodox gold standard principles was bound to create unemployment. The decision in 1925 to return to gold at the prewar parity did involve just such deflationary procedures.

Even after the return to the prewar gold parity in 1925 the British situation was such that the Bank of England was not free to operate the restored gold standard in the traditional manner. A disturbing influence was exerted on British monetary policy in this period by the size, and even more by the structure, of the internal public debt. In 1924, less than 16 per cent of the total debt was funded. The floating debt, consisting mainly of treasury bills, was 12.6 per cent of the total, while short-term unfunded debt was 23.2 per cent, and long-term unfunded debt was 48.2 per cent. The Treasury was anxious to get the debt as quickly as possible on to a long-term funded basis so that it would not be faced with the frequent necessity of renewing short-term obligations with the risk that in a crisis the cost of such renewals would be a substantial rise in interest rates. On the other hand it could not run the risk of raising long-term interest rates by converting short-term obligations into long-term securities too rapidly.

It did manage gradually to shift the major part of the debt on to a long-term basis and funded some of it. The technical skill displayed in handling this situation was remarkable. As occasion offered, the British Treasury converted the debt into less dangerous obligations. It took advantage of favorable opportunities as recovery proceeded to float new long-term security issues and cancel short-term obligations without raising interest rates and therefore imposing a further burden on the national budget. But interest rates could be kept at reasonable levels only as long as foreign short-term capital continued to be attracted to London in large volume.

The Bank of England was also engaged in promoting both directly and through the Financial and Economic Organization of the League of Nations an extensive program of European economic reconstruction. After 1924 American loans became available, particularly to Germany, in increasing volume, but the British lending program was also a heavy one. These reconstruction loans were necessarily long-term investments. At the same time the British exporting industries were engaged in a desperate effort to recapture the markets they had lost during the war and they were saddled with a high cost structure. The competitive strength of the major British export industries such as coal, textiles, and shipbuilding had been impaired by high wages relative to productivity, by obsolescent equipment, by high taxes, and also by protected and subsidized competition in their former markets. It was imperative for them to obtain long-term reconversion and reconstruction capital at low interest rates. The Bank of England, therefore, was impelled to avoid any action—such as a rise in its discount rate or the sale of securities—that would force the commercial banks to raise long-term interest rates and contract their bank advances. Any such action would have put a sudden stop both to European reconstruction and to British recovery. The deflation that accompanied the return to gold in 1925 had caused wage cuts and unemployment that led to the bitter general strike in 1926. Throughout the stabilization period there persisted a hard core of unemployment. This was the result of structural changes in world production and trade, and the Bank could not run the risk of worsening this unemployment by contracting credit.

However, the Bank was forced to provide gold for export whenever the sterling rate of exchange fell to the gold export point, as it constantly did between 1925 and 1929. The cash basis of the necessarily inflated credit superstructure was very narrow and was always threatened by foreign withdrawals of credit or gold. Moreover the Treasury had constantly to renew large issues of short-term obligations which mopped up a large proportion of the short-term credit in the money market. In these circumstances Britain was forced to the risky expedient of accepting and even soliciting foreign short-term deposits. A large part of these deposits consisted of nervous refugee capital—the so-called "hot money"—which was always liable to be withdrawn hurriedly in a crisis.

In the words of the Macmillan Report, London was "practising international deposit banking, as distinct from international acceptance business." She was accepting what were in effect loans liable to be withdrawn at short notice, in order to make long-term advances that could not be so withdrawn—borrowing short, in order to lend long. It was a precarious expedient, putting off the evil day when a choice would have to be made between cutting domestic costs in order to remain on the gold standard, or abandoning the program of international reconstruction upon which Britain's future prosperity depended. The major reason which impelled the authorities to run such a risk was the necessity of avoiding higher interest rates. These would have made the periodic renewals of the unfunded debt too heavy a burden on an already strained budget, would have plunged the national economy into severe deflation, and would at the same time have entailed the abandonment of the great effort to reconstruct the European economy and the world trading system.

In September, 1931, a sudden withdrawal of foreign balances placed the British authorities in the long-feared dilemma. The sequence of events is clear. The stoppage of loans to Europe had placed a severe deflationary strain on the borrowing countries. During 1930 there had been a large extension of short-term banking credits which temporarily covered the deficits in the balances of international payments. In June, 1931, also, the Hoover moratorium on reparation and war debt payments had further relieved the strain. But these unilateral obligations were not the major source of instability. Nor was it possible indefinitely to plug the gaps in the balances of international payments by extending short-term banking credits. The whole inflated structure of the restored European economies was out of equilibrium.

In May, 1931, the Austrian Credit-Anstalt was forced to reveal the extent to which its assets were tied up in frozen long-term advances. A liquidity panic—in all essentials an old-fashioned run on the banks—set in. It swept from southeastern Europe across Germany and by the summer had caused nervous British and foreign holders of short-term assets to begin withdrawing them from London. At this moment the Macmillan Committee drew attention to the danger to the stability of the British monetary system which these short-term deposits constituted and a Parliamentary inquiry (the May Committee) published its report into British public expenditures, recommending severe budgetary cuts. When reduced pay scales for the armed services were put into effect there was a demonstration on board some naval vessels. This the American and continental press reported as mutiny. This incident touched off a panic which caused such a withdrawal of short-term funds from London that between Wednesday and Saturday in the third week of September, 1931, the Bank of England lost gold to the extent of £43 million from its precariously low total of £120 million. Over £200 million had been withdrawn from London in the two months preceding September 20, 1931. The Bank of England had borrowed from French and American banks to meet this drain, but the final withdrawals left no option but the abandonment of gold.

The crisis had come. It was too late to restore equilibrium by raising bank rate and inflicting a deflation on the credit structure.[11] If bank rate had been raised earlier in an effort to correct the inflation in Britain, it might have attracted even larger amounts of foreign short-term refugee capital. Now it was not possible to stem the withdrawals. The slower-moving deflation of British costs and prices which might have reduced imports and encouraged exports could not possibly take effect in time to cope with the strain on the British balance of external payments. On Sunday, September 20, hurried consultations resulted in the proclamation of a bank holiday for Monday, and on that day a bill relieving the Bank of its obligation to redeem notes in gold was passed through all its stages in both houses and received the royal assent. Britain had abandoned the gold standard again.

This was the death knell of the attempt to reconstruct the European economy and world trade without making the adjustments of national economies necessary to adapt them to the changed international economic equilibrium resulting from the war of 1914–18. More immediately it was the end of the restored gold standard.[12] Before long the struggle for liquidity was transferred to the United States. When Britain went off gold it was followed by all the countries to which the British import market was of dominant importance. These included the British Dominions and colonies—though South Africa was fearful that gold might lose its prestige and therefore resisted depreciation until the end of 1932. The Canadians, caught between the United States and Britain, maintained their currency midway between the dollar and sterling. The countries which followed Britain off gold included most of the Latin-American, Scandinavian, and Baltic countries. By the end of 1932, the larger part of the trading world had aligned itself with Great Britain, and many of the largest agricultural-

[11] Cf. N. F. Hall, *The Exchange Equalization Account,* London, Macmillan Co., 1935, p. 13: "Orthodox critics who were shocked at the spectacle of Britain leaving the gold standard in 1931 with the Bank rate at 4½ per cent were too late with their strictures. The situation as it then existed was the result of a disharmony between the real and money rate of interest which had persisted ever since the war."

[12] Cf. William Adams Brown, Jr., *op. cit.,* Vol. II, p. 122: "The juridical concepts of gold as reserve and gold as standard in Germany stood out like the weather-beaten ribs of some old sailing vessel long since cast ashore by a tropical hurricane."

exporting countries had depreciated their currencies even below the British level.

United States exports were faced with severe competition all over the world and also with a vast proliferation of tariff, quota, and exchange restrictions. The economic effect of this loss of foreign markets was added to the continuous pressure upon the economic activity and price levels in the United States, as credit continued to contract. The efforts of the Federal Reserve Banks to check this contraction had been fairly successful during 1930. But there was an immense volume of speculative advances upon real estate and securities, as well as a great expansion of consumer credit purchases. The shocks to confidence transmitted by the Vienna crisis in May, 1931, and the British crisis in September, 1931, set off renewed spasms of contraction. Between June, 1931, and June, 1932, there was a great deal of hoarding of gold and currency, as well as withdrawals of foreign-owned dollars, so that the total monetary gold stock of the United States declined in those twelve months by $1,900 million.

The Federal Reserve Banks lowered their rediscount rates and bought over a billion dollars' worth of United States government securities between February and June, 1932. The Reconstruction Finance Corporation was formed to tide solvent enterprises over the crisis by advancing new credits to them. The Glass-Steagall Act passed in March, 1932, gave the Federal Reserve Banks greater flexibility of action in regard to the cover required against credit creation. The combined effect of these attempts to ease the credit stringency was felt in an easing of the deflation during the latter part of 1932, but all the water had not yet been squeezed out of the credit system. Bank failures which had been very numerous during 1931 began again to increase. Hoarding was resumed and there was a renewed movement of short-term funds to what now seemed the greater security of London. In the middle of February, 1933, the distrust of the banking system quickened to the same kind of run on the banks that had happened in one country after another since the panic of May, 1931, in Vienna. On March 4, the day of his accession to office, President Roosevelt declared a banking moratorium. And on April 19, the United States in its turn abandoned the gold standard.

Even then a small group of European countries headed by France struggled, at the cost of continuous deflationary pressure and severe curtailment of imports, to maintain the gold parities for their currencies. The restored international gold standard, however, had collapsed in September, 1931. It had never functioned with the same efficiency as in the prewar period because neither the domestic nor the international economic situations had the degree of equilibrium and the flexibility of adjustment necessary for its functioning.

Those who had put their faith in gold as a symbol and assurance of monetary stability found their faith betrayed by the operation of the international gold standard as it was restored and operated in the years 1925–29. During those years the national economies were again linked together by their adoption of the common standard, gold. But what was created was an interdependence of instabilities. In this period the international gold standard operated as a transmitter of those instabilities from one national economy to another. The inevitable result was reversion to monetary nationalism. It was vain for orthodox economists to tilt against this trend. They were correct in their argument that the new monetary practices were a powerful reinforcement of both economic nationalism and collectivism. Both these trends were deeply rooted in the distortion and impoverishment left by the war. Both were immensely strengthened when the nations chose in the great depression to protect their domestic economic activity rather than the international purchasing power of their currencies.

DIVIDED RESPONSIBILITIES

The full measure of the difference between the economic world of the interwar years and the pre-1914 trading world has yet to be taken. A vitally important aspect of this difference was a shift in the center of the world's economic gravity. The monetary consequences of this shift created a situation very different from that of the nineteenth century when the bulk of trading and financial transactions had been cleared and regulated through London. The London short-term money market dealing primarily in trade acceptances had been the balance-wheel regulating the whole international marketing system. After 1918 acceptances were less prominent in the dealings in this market, while treasury bills played a much larger role. The market had always drawn large amounts of foreign funds seeking short-term investment. But in the interwar period these foreign funds were of a different character and they grew to dangerous proportions.

This incapacity of London after 1918 to function as the regulating center of the world's monetary system was an important contributing factor to the collapse of the international gold standard in 1931. The other side of the story was the independent development of national money markets. New York competed with London in the discharge of many functions which before 1914 had been concentrated mainly in London where they were geared into the multifarious operations of the money market. It competed with London for acceptances and thus shared in the financing of world trade. More important was the greater prominence of New York in international lending on long term.

The difficulties that might be expected from this division of responsibilities in what had formerly been an integrated world trading and financial system had been foreshadowed in the crises that attended the outbreak of war in 1914. The clearing and balancing of payments had been perfected in the nineteenth century, nominally in terms of the ultimate transference of gold from the reserves of one national banking system to another. In fact, however, it was rarely necessary then to fall back on this final guarantee of adjustment. The new gold coming from the mines was distributed smoothly and efficiently among the world's monetary systems as part of a vast and complicated marketing process. Into this process many factors—the amounts and price levels of a widespread variety of commodity trading transactions, and the services connected with them; the temporary credit accommodation called for in different markets; and long-term investment in all its phases (payments on account of past investments, the shifting valuations and domicile of current securities, and the new capital issues needed in an expanding world)—were all geared.

This was an intricate mechanism in which the balance wheel constituted by the London short-term capital market was an important regulating contrivance. But this balance wheel could not function effectively when the mechanism was thrown out of gear. The attempt just before the outbreak of war in July, 1914, to deliver gold in settlement of balances was no more realistic than an attempt of depositors in a developed banking system suddenly to claim gold or legal tender currency would have been. There had been violent distortion of the exchange rates and of prices in the effort to settle balances by gold transfers; but "the crisis caused moratoria, suspensions of specie payments, and legal or de facto gold export embargoes in many countries."[13]

The gold standard did not break down in face of this demonstration of its dependence upon the marketing process and of the clearing of that process through London, but necessity compelled subtle changes in the methods of its operation. These changes differed a good deal from country to country. When the war ended and the still unshaken faith in the gold standard impelled a return to the prewar forms of currencies based on gold, this diversity of national policies created a larger demand for internationally acceptable means of payment.

Since there was not enough gold available at the current parity levels to serve this purpose and at the same time to reconstitute the metallic reserves of the countries as one by one they returned to the gold standard, a considerable volume of short-term funds came into existence. These funds were held as foreign balances either on deposit or in short-dated securities, in financial centers such as New York, London, Zurich, and Amsterdam which promised at least temporary assurance that their gold value would not be reduced by sudden depreciation, and that they could at need be converted into gold. The varying instability of the economic developments in the different countries made this fund a variable quantity. But it was always large, even during the period when the restored gold standard was in operation.

Its size was increased by the widespread adoption of gold-exchange standard practices, pursuant to the recommendations of the Genoa Conference, 1922. The funds, held mainly in London and New York by newly created central banks and also by many of the older central banks which were faced with the necessity of reorganizing their currencies after the war and the first postwar inflations, were always a source of danger to exchange stability. In a world in desperate need of capital for long-term investment, these foreign balances were necessarily held readily available. They were always liable to be transferred from one center to another at short notice not, as before 1914, in order to take advantage of higher interest rates, but rather to preserve their

[13] Cf. William Adams Brown, Jr., *op. cit.*, Vol. I, p. 27: "The crisis of 1914 demonstrated the dependence of the [prewar international gold-standard] system upon the regular and uninterrupted operation of the financial machinery of the City of London, and showed the difficulties that arise when an attempt is made to force gold to serve as a balancing item in international payments when credit is disorganized."

gold value. This fact limited the use of the discount rates which had formerly been the principal method of regulating the balances of payment. A rise in the discount rate might be interpreted as a sign of instability and cause a withdrawal of these balances instead of attracting them.

Also the distribution of their ownership had been changed. Before 1914, the short-term balances held in London for the clearing of international payments had corresponded roughly with the volume of trade conducted by the countries which owned them. After the war, the largest balances held in London and New York were those of European countries. They consisted of currency reserves and of flight capital, rather than of international till-money closely related to the reality of trading transactions.

Then again the use made of them had been changed. Instead of nourishing the market for trade acceptances, the demand for which was much smaller than it had been, they went into short-dated gilt-edged securities such as treasury bills, or were held as short-term deposits. And it was against these that the holding centers made long-term foreign loans. The gold-exchange standard, however, was always regarded as an interim stage toward the restoration of the true gold standard. A central bank which found itself as France did in 1926 and 1927 in a position to re-establish its gold reserves, was always liable to withdraw its holdings of foreign assets by buying gold.

London had virtually monopolized the financing of foreign trade before the war, so that there was always a considerable stream of self-liquidating commercial securities flowing through the short-term market. After the war, this stream tended to dry up. New York, which had large amounts of foreign short-term funds, sought strenuously to create an acceptance market. London tried to retain its market. But new methods of financing trade had come into use and both the quantity and the quality of the bills available deteriorated. In 1922 it was estimated that the amount of trading acceptances current in London was only half that of the prewar period, and many of them were of a quality less desirable than the prime paper of prewar days. The result was a significant change in the character of the discount market and of its operations. After the breakdown of the gold standard in 1931 this became very evident. The already excessive amount of potentially "unfaithful balances" was suddenly and greatly increased by the great volume of flight capital seeking to escape from currency depreciation.

The market operations in the leading financial centers, which had been the chief means of maintaining stability in the exchange rates, became instead the chief focus of speculation against weak currencies.

In the interwar period from 1921–22 onward, a new factor of instability at times of crisis was created by the extension of the market in forward exchange. Transactions in foreign currencies for delivery at a future date became a common method of hedging against currency depreciation. In stable periods—particularly from 1925 to 1929 when the gold standard was operating—the volume of these transactions was relatively small and the forward exchange market was in the hands of professional specialists. In times of currency instability—before 1925 and after 1931—the volume of these transactions was large, and forward selling of weak currencies became a common form of speculation. Before 1914 forward dealings in the foreign exchanges had been limited and mostly practiced in secondary money markets. After the war the exchange risks were greater and the methods of forward dealing were practiced much more widely. They provided traders with the means of hedging their exchange risks, but they greatly increased the amount of mobile short-term funds. There was a special source of weakness in this development. Forward exchange escaped from the forms and therefore from the control of the acceptance market. Formerly the finance bills needed to transfer short-term funds from one market to another had been drawn, accepted, and discounted like trade bills and were handled by professional operators. But now a telephone call was adequate to set transfers in motion, and amateurs entered the market.

In other respects also the connection of short-term credit transfers with actual trading transactions was weakened. Their control passed out of the hands of the experienced operators of the London acceptance market. Much of the foreign short-term money in London was held in the form of treasury bills. This made it difficult for the Bank of England to use the discount rate as a means of regulating the external balance. It also meant that the credit movements which affected the exchange market were speculative operations rather than trading acceptances. It was a significant change—this transfer to rather nervous European owners of refugee capital of the control that had formerly been exercised by well-tested methods, worked out from the experience of conservative banking institutions long specialized in the financing of international trade.

The significance of this growth of volatile short-term credit, responsive to the instabilities of national currencies and controlled by those whose major interest was to preserve the gold value of their assets, has been treated at some length because it provides the background against which the competition of the New York and London money markets must be considered. In the interwar period no effective mechanism existed for regulating the international distribution of the world supply of international currency, either in the form of gold or in the form of foreign balances that could be turned into gold. London had provided such a mechanism before 1914. No small part of the stability of the nineteenth-century system had derived from the fact that all the major elements in the marketing process—commodity trade and its financing, transfers of short-term capital, security transactions, interest payments—all came to a focus in the London money market. The balance wheel could operate as a regulator of equilibrium when all the wheels of international transactions were geared into a centralized mechanism.

Even if New York had been able completely to replace London as the focusing center, there would have been difficulties in the regulation of this volatile short-term credit. New York suffered from certain handicaps in its efforts to compete with London. It was first and foremost the financial center of a continental economic system, the vitality and the fluctuations of which exercised a predominant influence over its money market. It could not, as London did before 1914, regulate that market primarily with reference to the movements of its external balance of payments occasioned by international trade and capital transactions. The size of the domestic economy of the United States was such as to outweigh external influences on the monetary system. There was not, as in pre-1914 Britain, a volume of imports and exports which was large, absolutely and relatively, in proportion to domestic trade. Moreover the United States pursued a policy of high tariff protection until the Reciprocal Trade Agreement after 1934 began to reduce the excessive schedules of the Hawley-Smoot tariff.

Thus the international commodity markets of nineteenth-century Britain had no parallel in the twentieth-century United States. New York could not exert effective influence over the prices of internationally traded goods. Its efforts to gain a share in the financing of world trade met with only partial success. It did not have the far-flung trading and financial connections, the developed techniques and institutions, or the corps of banking and trading personnel expert in the local conditions of markets all over the world that London had built up in the course of the nineteenth century when it was the trading and financial capital of the world.

London after 1918 was hampered by an increased national debt whose structure required the maintenance of low interest rates in the short-term money market. It was also hampered by a shift which proved permanent in the methods of financing international trade, so that the short-term money market was largely deprived of its former grist. Finally it suffered from the loss of its former pre-eminence in world trade and from a crippling of its basic export industries. These changes brought about a fundamental refashioning of the methods of credit control. The forms remained but the substance had changed.

New York competing with London tried to develop an acceptance market, but without the steady flow of imports into free markets out of which London had built its acceptance business. The United States had become the chief source of long-term loan capital, and the New York securities market was actively competing with that of London. London was still the biggest securities market, but New York had become the greatest exporter of capital. This greatly complicated the control of the exchanges, since it is easier to keep the exchange rates stable when the principal market for international security transactions is located in the country which provides the bulk of new capital investment. The monetary policy of such a country can then be directed toward regulating the export of capital so as to equilibrate the international balances of payment.

The burden of international reconstruction between the wars fell mainly on London and New York. Competition between them for foreign short-term balances led to pressure in both to devise new methods by which these balances might enable them to lend long. It was this competition which was in large part responsible for the overlending to Europe in the reconstruction period. The circumstances of these two centers were vastly different. London maintained a precarious price stability at the current gold parity, with credit finely adjusted to the price level. It was driven to defend this parity by methods which in the nineteenth century would have been regarded as unorthodox. This situation became worse when continental operators used the securities market as a channel to make payments through London to

New York.[14] New York, on the other hand, had an inflationary credit expansion based on adequate gold reserves.

Thus the restored international gold standard could not operate from a single center. The necessity for international regulation was greater than it had ever been before. But in place of a centralized regulation it had to operate from several competing centers. It was more than a question of competition between London and New York. The development of nationalism in all countries reinforced by a strong collectivist trend, inevitably found its ultimate economic expression in the monetary sphere. The money market of every country in proportion to its strength tried to safeguard the stability of its national currency.

The activity of the secondary money markets was never a negligible factor and at times it became decisive. Attention has been drawn to the influence exerted on London and New York by the French attempt to operate on orthodox gold standard principles even prior to the stabilization of the franc. The pull of Berlin on the capital and exchange markets was also important. Indeed the development of monetary nationalism was so widespread that the restored gold standard was constantly being called upon to cope with a succession of nervous shifts of short-term credit. These resembled a series of sudden attacks upon exchange equilibrium, first from one quarter and then from another, rather than a steady and co-operative attempt at mutual reinforcement in order to maintain and adjust a stable equilibrium.

After 1931, the forces of monetary nationalism were unleashed in their full disruptive fury. The restored gold standard had been maintained by a series of improvisations which were adaptations and modifications of traditional practices within the framework of the prewar gold standard. After the depression set in, and particularly after the departure of Great Britain from the gold standard, there ensued a veritable anarchy of monetary nationalism. New devices of quantitative restrictions on imports, of exchange control, of bilateral clearing and bilateral barter trading were invented. For a time there was a chaos of improvised expedients. Gradually, trading blocs began to

[14] *Ibid.*, Vol. I, pp. 521-22: "The international movement of funds in and out of the London securities market was far more important than the international shifting of bank balances. It often assumed very great proportions and contributed to a fundamental lack of stability in the world's exchanges. A mechanism designed to provide clearance became a channel of remittance through which reparation payments, flights of capital, and private movements of capital passed without being properly related in either time or volume to offsetting flows of payment in the opposite direction."

form. These experiments—the sterling area, the gold bloc, and the German clearing system in particular—attempted to rebuild integrated monetary policy within regional areas of complementary trade. There was no hope in the 1930's of restoring either trade or investment on a world-wide basis. The best that could be attempted was a series of regional arrangements.

The world-wide trading and financial system centered on London, which had functioned effectively in the latter part of the nineteenth century, came to an end in 1914. The attempt to operate a similar system from many competing centers, but still without any formal organization for consultation and for clearing and regulating the balances of payments, collapsed in 1931. Neither of these alternatives can again be attempted with any reasonable hope of success. Yet the need for centralized mechanisms for the co-ordination and clearing of monetary policy is obvious to all competent observers. The remaining choice would seem to be the conscious organization of formal machinery on a truly international basis, for the continuous consultations and clearing procedures that are necessary if exchange stability is to be maintained. No one who is aware of the disorganization caused by the second World War and of the technical and administrative, as well as the political, difficulties involved in organizing formal procedures of international co-operation is likely to underestimate the magnitude of the tasks to be attempted. But the evidence of the last postwar period is very emphatic.

The clearing of international economic transactions cannot be left to take care of itself. No financial center now has the means or can count upon the acquiescence of other centers to do in the twentieth what London did in the nineteenth century. The attempt to work the clearing and regulatory procedures from competing centers, without over-all agreement and mechanisms, was proved a failure by the interwar experience. The advantages of international economic co-operation cannot be enjoyed unless national governments are prepared to submit to the discipline which such co-operation necessarily entails. New methods must be evolved to meet the unforeseen and unforeseeable situations that must inevitably arise in attempting to re-establish and to maintain equilibrium in the trading and financial relations of the nations. The only possibility of developing such methods lies in a more sustained organization of international monetary co-operation than was practiced before the second World War.

CHAPTER XVI

THE AFTERMATH OF WAR

THE EFFECTS OF WAR MOBILIZATION

THE UNPRECEDENTED mobilization of resources necessary to fight the second World War has had more far-reaching consequences than those which followed the war of 1914–18. In so far as policies are projected upon attempts to reorganize the prewar pattern of international specialization, which was itself an unstable patchwork of political and economic expedients dominated by war preparations, they are bound to fail. As in 1914–18, but in much greater degree, the war of 1939–45 distorted the price and production structures of every country, belligerent or neutral, and broke the patterns of international specialization and co-operation. The longer duration, the wider range, and the greater intensity of destruction in the second World War has made its economic consequences far more severe. At its close there was far less general acceptance of working principles of economic organization than there had been after the first World War.

There was therefore far greater difficulty in organizing such a concerted effort as was made in the 1920's to restore the practices and institutions of the more peaceful and prosperous pre-1914 world. If there was any certainty in the confused groping toward working arrangements for international economic and political co-operation, it was that an effort had to be made to devise practices and institutions which would take account of the revolutionary changes in technology, in the balance of power, and in the political attitudes to economic organization that were slowly crystallizing in the postwar world.

It should not be forgotten that the second world conflict came after the elaborate attempt in the 1920's to reconstruct the mechanisms of international economic co-operation had ended in utter failure, and after this failure had led in the 1930's to abortive attempts by national aggression—Japanese, Italian, and German—to create new systems of political and economic power. From the economic viewpoint the second World War should be dated from September 18, 1931, when the Japanese army launched its aggression in Manchuria. This aggression came at the moment when Britain, the center of the restored world trading system, was in the midst of a severe financial crisis. Three days later Britain abandoned the gold parity for sterling. These practically simultaneous events signaled the collapse of the political and economic reconstruction of which the League of Nations had been the keystone.

Political and economic events were interdependent. Despite the intervention of the League supported by the United States, Japan made good its conquest of Manchuria. The United States had participated for many years in the preparatory work for the Disarmament Conference which was called by the League on February 2, 1932. Four days earlier the Japanese Navy had shelled Chapei, an industrial area on the fringe of the International Settlement at Shanghai. Before the Disarmament Conference had made much progress, Japan, on February 24, 1933, withdrew from the League.

Herr Hitler had become Chancellor of the German Empire on January 30, 1933. He quickly consolidated his dictatorial power. On the morning of October 14, 1933, the British delegate had presented to the Bureau of the Disarmament Conference the last of many disarmament plans. That afternoon Germany withdrew from the conference and gave notice of its withdrawal from the League. The failure of the Monetary and Economic Conference at London in July, 1933, had precipitated a series of higher tariffs, extended quota systems and exchange controls. Early in 1934 the German government promulgated a new and drastic series of trade restrictions, designed to put the German economy on a footing of war preparedness. Within a year the German trade drive in the Balkans was under way, creating in central and eastern Europe an economic bloc tributary to the German rearmament program.

The pace of events constantly quickened. Italy attacked Ethiopia on October 3, 1935. The members of the League condemned the aggression and, on November 18, economic sanctions which stopped short of oil were put into operation. Italy withdrew from the League. When the ineffectiveness of the limited League sanctions became evident, Germany poured supplies into Italy. On July 17, 1936, civil war broke out in Spain, and both Italy and Germany supplied planes, munitions, and troops to the rebels while the U.S.S.R. supported the government. By this time the decline of the League had become clear. A weak policy curiously labeled non-intervention was advocated by Britain and France. Japanese troops used an incident at the Marco Polo Bridge on July 7, 1937, to launch their campaign in north China. Austria was next on the list, being absorbed by Germany on March 11, 1938. The German demands on Czechoslovakia were agreed to by the French and British Prime Ministers at Munich in September, 1938. This betrayal caused many Czechs to look eastward to the U.S.S.R., rather than to the Western powers, for support after the war. The subjugation of Czechoslovakia was completed on March 15, 1939. On April 7, Italy invaded Albania. During the summer Germany worked up the tension over Danzig that led to the invasion of Poland on September 3, 1939. Britain and France declared war at this point in order to honor their treaty obligations to Poland.

Even this bare catalogue, which omits many stages in the aggressive diplomacy and forceful action that prepared the second World War, is sufficient to indicate that grave economic damage had been done before 1939. Without entering into detail, attention may be drawn to three major aspects of the economic consequences of this long period of war preparedness. In the first place, war was prepared on the psychological and economic planes and the potential aggressors were reorganizing their economies on a basis of war preparedness long before the shooting war started. Trade had become an instrument of national policy in the totalitarian countries. Those countries ran down their stocks of civilian goods and diverted their manpower, scientific research, capital resources, and technical skills to war preparation. The shortages of consumption goods and food that became obvious in 1945 were worse in the totalitarian countries and in the countries of their victims, because of this long period of economic mobilization. Their commodity reserves and even private stores of materials had been reduced to vanishing point. Worst of all from the viewpoint of postwar reconstruction was the damage done to educational systems and to scientific and civic training by the militarist subjection of a whole generation.

In the second place, the attempt to turn the totalitarian countries into self-sufficient garrison economies did violence to their own economic and monetary structure, and to those of their former customers and clients as well. In many of the European countries fifth-column activity and propaganda created dissension and paralyzed the political and economic preparations for effective defense. The circuits of trade and specialization had been gravely impaired even before the war began. In place of the multilateral exchanges of world trade, bilateral barter agreements in which diplomatic and military considerations often took precedence over economic objectives became widespread in Europe and were extended to Latin America.

The third effect followed. Central and eastern Europe was detached in large measure from world trade to become the economic hinterland of the German war economy. This facilitated the Russian economic strategy after 1945 which aimed at attaching this hinterland to Moscow in place of Berlin. The penetration of German ownership into most of these central and eastern European countries made it possible for the U.S.S.R. to claim possession of many important enterprises as legitimate war booty. The complex problems presented by the impoverishment and division of Europe trace back beyond the war to the period of war preparation. As early as 1936, economists were drawing attention not only to the economic costs of rearmament, but to the even greater costs of the economic mobilization for war preparedness.

One further legacy of this period of war preparation must be noted. It can be argued that modern war calls for such use of scientific training and for such enormous economic supplies that only those countries which retain the flexibility and initiative that comes from free scientific research and productive enterprise can hope to wage it to a successful conclusion. There is an important element of truth in this contention. The course of the second World War proved that if not overwhelmed by surprise attack, the free economies could mobilize resources adequate to crush the most formidably planned military adventure by a totalitarian state. But stress must be placed on the proviso —if not overwhelmed by surprise attack. The United States was able eventually to mobilize the greatest and most adequately equipped military, naval, and air force ever put into action. But it was not able to do so for a considerable length of time. Until it was able to organize itself, and in doing so to draw upon the resources of the free world to forge its striking power, the United States could do little more than fight delaying actions and rely upon its allies holding firm.[1]

New scientific advances of which the atomic bomb is the prototype have now underscored the necessity for safeguards against sudden attack. There is no longer safety in isolation and no assurance that time will be available to mobilize the striking power of a free and disarmed economy. For the future, security considerations must enter into economic policy. There is likely in the United States to be a greater burden of armament than before 1939. More attention must be paid to strategic industrial planning and to building up stockpiles of strategic materials. And more concern must be shown to build up the economic and military strength of potential allies. Emphasis is laid upon these political developments because they now exercise a greater influence upon economic policy than before 1914 or even before 1931.

The first experiments in governmental trade controls were absorbed by national controls over monetary policy. These controls were gathered up in the period of war preparation by attempts at national planning which were inevitably linked with the increasing power of the great enterprises that were the custodians of a new technology. Technical and political reasons made it impossible after 1945 to go back to the forms of international trade that were characteristic of the period before 1914. The international markets through which dispersed producers supplied the consuming public had given place in many important industries to more direct contact between large-scale producing units and their agents, branches, or clientele. Governments intervened, directly or by their control over the monetary system, to regulate the production, prices, and interchange of goods. They inter-

[1] Cf. George C. Marshall, *The Winning of the War in Europe and in the Pacific,* New York, 1945, p. 1: "The Nation is just emerging from one of its gravest crises. This generation of Americans can still remember the black days of 1942 when the Japanese conquered all of Malaysia, occupied Burma, and threatened India while the German armies approached the Volga and the Suez. In those hours Germany and Japan came so close to economic domination of the world that we do not yet realize how thin the thread of Allied survival had been stretched.

"In good conscience this Nation can take little credit for its part in staving off disaster in those critical days. It is certain that the refusal of the British and Russian peoples to accept what appeared to be inevitable defeat was the great factor in the salvage of our civilization. Of almost equal importance was the failure of the enemy to make the most of the situation."

vened even more purposefully in the capital markets. International economic relations can no longer be studied simply as marketing processes. Account must be taken of the far-reaching consequences of national monetary and economic policies.

The great mobilization by which the United States became the arsenal of democracy strengthened and consolidated these tendencies toward centralized political control. In the United States itself much stress has been laid upon the immense productivity that made possible the fabrication of ships, airplanes, armaments, equipment and supplies of all kind. Private enterprise operating on government contracts proved capable of the productive effort demanded. The winning combination was a blend of bold planning and dispersed individual efforts within the broadly planned framework. Inevitably the planning involved a considerable extension of centralized controls. Automobile production was eliminated, gasoline was rationed, materials such as steel and rubber were allocated among the producers according to their capacity to meet the demands of the war effort. Price controls were supplemented by partial rationing over a wide range of commodities. Manpower was not conscripted for industrial employment, but wage and employment policies were determined primarily by the need for continuity of production. Monetary and fiscal policies were devised to stimulate production, to discourage certain types of personal expenditure, and to stimulate investment in war bonds. While the planning was looser and less restrictive in the United States than in most other belligerent countries, it constituted a very considerable extension of government controls over private economic activity.

The main instrument by which the United States became the mobilizing center of the allied war effort was the Lend-Lease Act passed on March 11, 1941, nine months before the United States was itself involved in hostilities. This act signaled the effective abandonment of the attempt to isolate the United States from the European conflict. From 1935 onward there had been a succession of Neutrality Acts. After a long period of public controversy, the Lend-Lease Act was passed to enable the United States to supply munitions, materials and food to any country that the President might designate as aiding the defense of the United States. This enabled the designated countries to concentrate their manpower and resources upon immediate military purposes while drawing from the United States the equipment and supplies necessary to sustain a long struggle. It enabled the United States to supply economic aid without involving these countries in the financial difficulties that would have resulted from the negotiation of war loans. Congress appropriated large sums to be used at the President's discretion in the purchase of supplies, and gave him full discretion to settle the time, manner and amount of repayment to be asked from the recipients.

An immense volume both of war materials and of civilian supplies was thus transferred to the allied countries. Until the Lend-Lease Act was passed, the allies had been forced by the modified "cash and carry" provisions of the neutrality legislation then in force to pay in dollars for all purchases in the United States and to transport these goods in their own ships. The main burden of finance and shipping had fallen upon Britain and France, though all the allies mobilized their dollar resources. The drain of dollars at this stage of the war before lend-lease was all the greater because, to secure certain types of equipment including airplanes, the allies had had to put up dollars for capital construction and equipment. Their exports were dwindling and their shipping receipts were falling. Full use had been made of the dollars derived from rubber and tin shipments from southeast Asia, and from shipments of copper from the Congo. Overseas investments had been impounded and had been sold or mortgaged in the United States to secure dollars. Britain had come close to the limit of its dollar resources when the Lend-Lease Act went into operation.

In the course of the four and a half years that followed, the lend-lease deliveries by the United States totaled $50–52 billion, including goods that were in process and were delivered on long-term credit arrangements after V-J Day. Of this total about two-thirds consisted of actual munitions, weapons, and military-type goods and services. These together with the food and other materials actually used in the course of the war, were written off as part of the United States contribution to the common victory. The lend-lease arrangements were not entirely one-sided, but represented a system of mutual aid—a pooling of effort. The United States received from its allies aid to the amount of $7 billion, while Britain also provided supplies for its immediate associates in the war effort. The net cost of lend-lease to the United States was thus approximately $40 billion, since against a total expenditure of $50–52 billion, it received $7 billion in reverse lend-lease, and recovered $4–5 billion through cash payments and the sale of production facilities in the United States.

Lend-lease was a vast operation for which no parallel can be found in history. It has repeatedly been recognized as a great, imaginative, and generous action which, at the moment when Britain and the allied governments in exile were hard-pressed before the United States entered the war, contributed much to their ability to hold on and ultimately provided the economic basis for the common victory. It may be argued that the United States gained much from the fact that its allies sustained the brunt of the struggle for over two years. But their leaders have always paid tribute to the scale of American help and the generosity of its extension in their most desperate need without haggling as to terms of payment. They have freely recognized also the magnanimous settlement by which the great bulk of the obligations was written off without any attempt at calculations of cost. It would have been impossible to value lives lost and benefits received. But the recognition of this fact by the United States and its unquestioning assumption of the heaviest monetary costs of the whole mutual-aid program removed from the postwar world what might have been a source of great misunderstanding and bitterness.

It does not detract from the success of the lend-lease program to point out that it was the heart of the mobilization effort which converted production and trade from peacetime to wartime channels. In its program of war production on its own behalf and to supply its allies, the United States drew heavily upon raw-material supplies from many sources. Command of the sea lanes enabled these supplies to be drawn from the whole free world. When necessary air transport was used to bring urgently needed materials such as mica from as far away as India. Thus the economies even of neutral countries were affected by the demands of war production. The trading circuits of the prewar world were broken and the United States became the focusing and clearing center of wartime world trade. The full extent of the resulting disruption of international specialization has not yet been revealed. After 1945, as after 1918, the shortages that followed inevitably upon a long war created a demand for internationally traded commodities that seemed inexhaustible. Nevertheless the disruption of trading channels and the consequent growth in many countries of local productive facilities for articles formerly imported must eventually cause con-

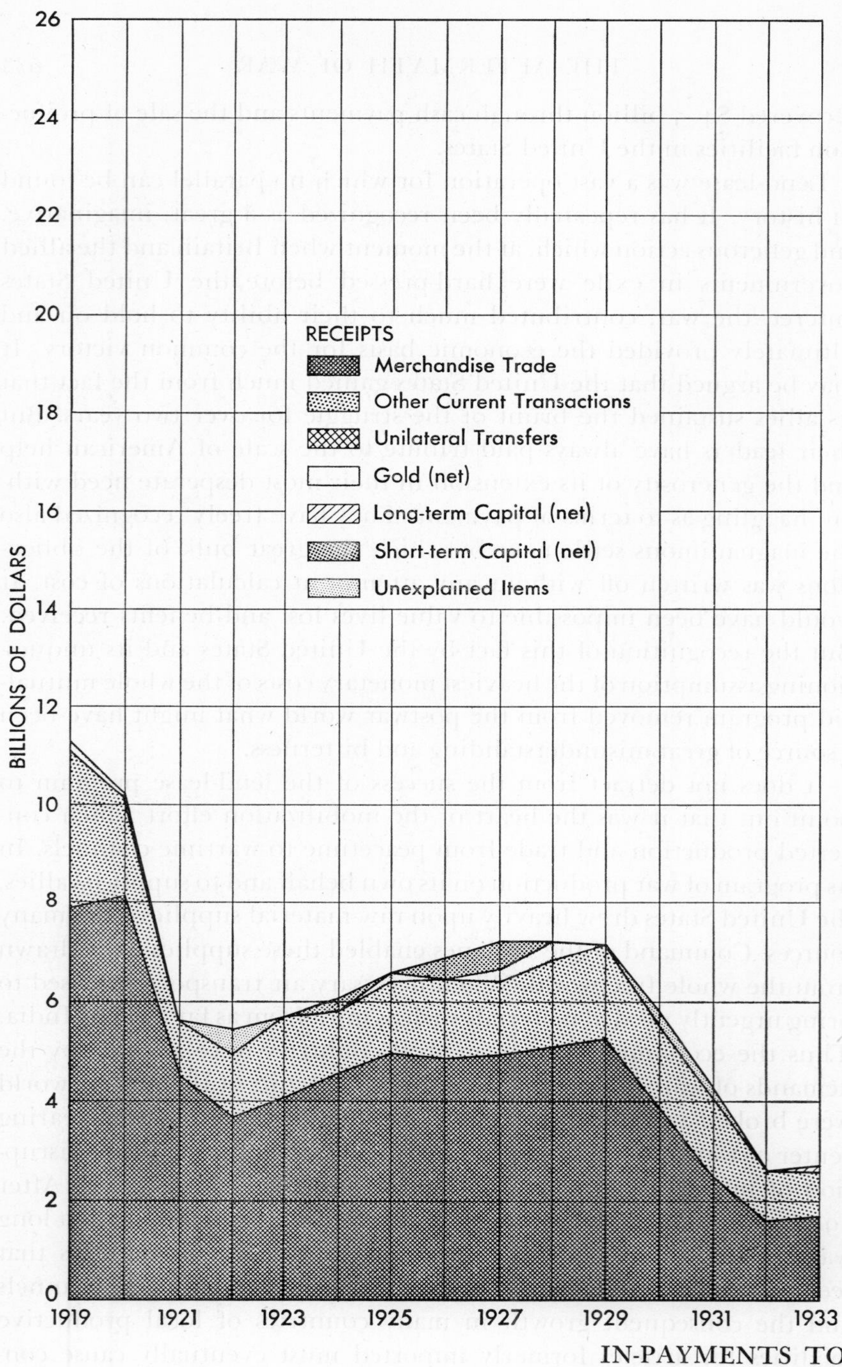

IN-PAYMENTS TO

Source: (1919–39) U.S. Department of Commerce, *The United States in the World* *International Transactions of the United States during the War 1940–45,* Economic March 1948, p. 18.

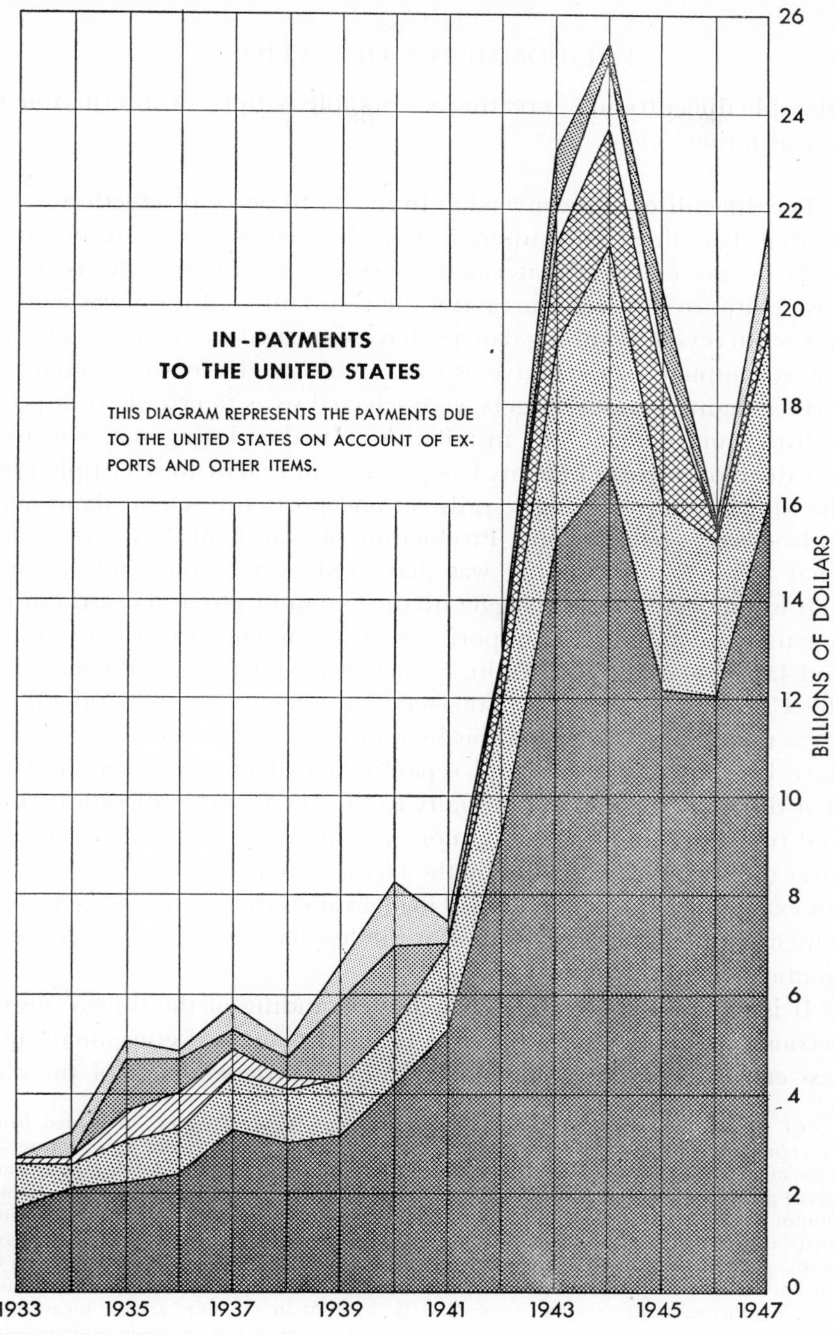

THE UNITED STATES

Economy, Economic Series, No. 23, Washington, 1943, Appendix Table I; (1940–45) Series, No. 65, p. x; (1946–47) *Survey of Current Business,* March 1947, p. 13, and

siderable difficulty in re-creating a workable pattern of international specialization.

The difficulties of reconversion from war to peace production were greater than those encountered after the first World War because of the greater extent of material damage suffered. Physical destruction was greater over a wider area and the resultant confusion was worse. As the surveys of bombing damage have shown, air bombardment was not as completely destructive as was often thought by the airmen. It was damaging because targets were selected so as to cripple transport facilities and damage key installations. In the closing stages of the war the movements of enemy troops and equipment were crippled by the blowing out of bridges, railroad and port equipment, dams and hydroelectric installations. Production of war materials was somewhat reduced and housing was destroyed over considerable areas.[2]

It is important not to exaggerate the extent of physical destruction, nor to overemphasize its importance. Many towns in Germany, Italy and Japan, and also in Britain, France, the Netherlands, Poland, and the U.S.S.R. were heavily damaged, but even in the worst-bombed areas the actual destruction was by no means complete. Nor would it have been incapable of rapid repair if it had not been for the fact that the hidden damage, especially to the key facilities of production and trade, was immeasurably more significant in this war. Recovery after the war was hampered by the fact that bottlenecks were created, for example by the destruction of bridges and other transport facilities, which crippled the effectiveness of the less damaged parts of the economic structure.

It is impossible to gain a clear understanding of the difficulties of reconstruction, even in respect to physical plant and equipment, unless emphasis is laid upon the complex interdependence of the ele-

[2] Cf. Henry Chalmers, "Current Trends in Foreign Trade Policies," reprinted from *Foreign Commerce Weekly,* February 9, 16, and 23, 1946, p. 10: "Even those European governments most eager to see their countries' foreign trade move back towards normal, were handicapped by the disorganized conditions left in the wake of the war—the destruction of productive facilities, the exhaustion of supplies, the disruption of transport and distribution channels, the scrambled ownership in industry, the inadequacy of foreign-exchange assets, the internal financial confusion, and often also the unsettled status of the governmental regime itself. These conditions were not equally serious in all countries, but, in practically all that had been directly involved in the war, a large measure of governmental control and even direct official intervention in foreign-trade arrangements seemed unavoidable, at least for a time." Cf. also Norman S. Buchanan, *International Investment and Domestic Welfare,* New York, 1945, p. 50.

ments in a developed economic organization. For instance it quickly became evident that one of the keys to recovery in Europe was an acute shortage of coal. However, before greater coal production could be achieved the miners needed more food and clothing and boots, and pit props had to be brought to the mining areas. Transport was not available, particularly in the important producing area of the Ruhr Valley, to bring in these necessities or to take out such coal as was mined. To repair railroad tracks and equipment, rebuild bridges, and restore canal services, steel was needed; but steel could not be produced without coal. Thus there was an entanglement of difficulties in restoring production.

There were two other costs of war which were more important than the damage inflicted by enemy action and these costs affected victors and neutrals, as well as vanquished. The first was the inefficiency caused by the fact that mobilization of resources for modern war had entailed neglect of the maintenance and repairs needed to keep productive facilities in working order. The United States' shortages of housing, automobiles, and rolling stock were the result of the impossibility during the war of replenishing working equipment. In the United States the shortages largely represented inability to keep pace with expanding demands—for power plants, for roads, for railroad equipment, for airports, for housing, and for similar conveniences.

In other countries, particularly in those which came under totalitarian domination in Asia as in Europe, the situation was indescribably worse. In many countries long years of preparation for war had depleted capital resources. For example, the railroads in Germany had been sacrificed while road construction was being developed in anticipation of a blitzkrieg. In many of the countries that had been occupied by Germany during the war, looting on a large and systematic scale had transferred movable assets and ownership of fixed equipment to the conquerors. In some of these countries, notably Manchuria, Russian occupation policies went far to complete the looting which the Germans and Japanese began.

Everywhere the capital equipment that was still intact functioned badly because of undermaintenance during the war period. One of the most significant illustrations of the neglect of maintenance and repairs was the damage done in southeast Asia. It was not as great in monetary terms as the damage in Europe, but it represented undermaintenance of mines, oil wells, and plantations, destruction of factories and transport facilities, and exhaustion of stocks that seriously hindered the reconstruction of world trade. Apart from the suffering imposed on great masses of people, it must be remembered that before 1941 the tropical countries had furnished, particularly to the United States, raw materials which were an important link in the chain of multilateral payments. The dollars paid out for such commodities as rubber and tin provided part of the means of payment, both for European purchases of American manufactures and for local purchases of European goods exported to the tropics. It is difficult to see how multilateral world trade can be restored, or even how western Europe can relax its trade restrictions until mines are reopened, plantations are cleared, irrigation and afforestation systems are restored, and ports, roads, factories and railroads are rebuilt in southeast Asia.

The second of these more serious costs was the running down of inventories. Long years of privation and regimentation while war was being prepared and fought, cleaned up not only the working stocks of raw materials, but the reserves of commodities in private ownership, down to the accumulations of rags, wastepaper, string, and scrap metals. Even before the outbreak of war, official collections in the totalitarian countries were mobilizing scrap resources. During the war heavy drains were made also on such capital resources as mineral deposits, forests, soil fertility, herds and flocks. War devours the seed corn of future generations. This depletion of working capital was one of the major costs of war and certainly one of the most troublesome elements in the first stages of reconstruction.

Attention must be drawn also to the very much greater distortion and impairment in the second World War of the non-material mechanisms of production and trade. Much greater structural shifts than after the first World War had to be reckoned with. The predominance of American industrial and agricultural capacity and the extraordinary development also of scientific research in the United States were the clearest indications of these structural changes. The other countries of European settlement overseas—Canada and the other British Dominions, and Argentina for example—had also taken great strides in industrial development, while increasing their agricultural output. They ranked after the war immediately behind the great powers—the United States, the U.S.S.R. and Britain—and ahead both of the heavily populated Asiatic countries and of the smaller European countries. Their increased influence in the various organs of the United Nations was a reflection of this fact. The U.S.S.R. was temporarily weakened economically, but its political influence had been immensely increased, in its own right and by virtue of the expansion of Soviet ideas buttressed by the strength of the Soviet armies in central and eastern Europe. Even though the eclipse of Germany and Japan might be regarded as temporary, it was clear that the economic world would have very different contours and that the currents of world trade would need to be adapted to these new contours. The trends of development that were noticeable after 1918 had been strongly reinforced by what happened after the second World War became inevitable.

On the other hand, there was a striking contrast between the monetary developments immediately following 1918 and those which followed 1945. The costs of the second World War were much heavier, budgets were more seriously unbalanced, and monetary systems were more strained. The Nazi government had transferred a large part of the inflationary financing of its war effort to the monetary systems of its victims. Yet it was a remarkable fact that, except for Greece, Hungary, Romania, and China, the price level nowhere escaped from control.

What was even more remarkable was the stability of the controlled exchange rates. After 1918, the currencies that were under strain had weakened faster in the exchange market than in the domestic markets. Their external purchasing power fell earlier and further than their internal purchasing power. Anyone possessing dollars in 1920 could change them into marks at a rate which enabled him to buy commodities cheaply even at inflated mark prices. At the close of the second World War the exact contrary was true for most currencies. Exchange rates were held firmly at parities which did not correspond with the higher price levels, so that the prices of goods and services seemed high when compared with dollar prices. On the other hand, the black markets in which currencies were exchanged at levels more nearly commensurate with the purchasing power parities were not large enough to affect the general situation. Controls were tighter than they had been in the years between the wars. This overvaluation of the exchange rates, and the tighter control of prices, was one of the main reasons why it was difficult to restore exports from Europe. Governments had learned how to control both domestic and external monetary policy. But the methods they had devised imposed great obstacles to the reconstruction of world trade.

This situation could not have been sustained as it was in the immediate postwar period, if it had not been for the fact that this time the United States remained actively interested in international co-operation. Of the $14½-billion international credits recorded from June, 1945, to June, 1946, the United States supplied over $9 billion. In addition there were large gifts to the allied countries, and even larger sums allocated from occupation costs to maintain the former enemy peoples at subsistence levels. The flow of exports from the United States ran at the $15-billion level, more than double the return flow of imports.

It is obvious that there were powerful forces making for monetary nationalism and that these forces had been greatly reinforced by the economic consequences of the war. During the war period, there had been a great extension of social-security services, in Latin-American countries as well as in Europe. Everywhere it had been recognized that large-scale and persistent unemployment would carry with it the danger of political revolution. Nowhere could governments afford to allow monetary deflation to create such unemployment. There was therefore little possibility of exchange controls being removed until substantial progress had been made both in national reconstruction programs and in the effective organization of international safeguards against sudden strains on the balances of payments. Moreover the burden of public debt had been greatly increased and the necessity arose of maintaining low and stable interest rates in order not to increase the strain on national budgets. Even in the United States, the size and structure of the debt was such as to impel watchful policies designed to keep interest rates low. Such controls over the credit system made it inevitable that the clearing and balancing of international payments had to be subject to an increased measure of government regulation.

The magnitude and complexity of these economic consequences of the second World War were aggravated by the fact that there was no peace settlement. Boundaries remained uncertain, self-government was not restored either to Japan or to Germany which remained a divided country. Meantime there was increasing conflict between the Soviet and democratic methods of organization on almost every issue arising in the peace settlement—in regard to the principles of international co-operation and to the government of strategic areas as well as to the treatment of the enemy countries. While the prospects of war were never imminent, the facts of conflict were continuously evident. Co-operative economic policies were dependent upon prior political agreement or compromise, and until a settlement could be reached economic recovery was hampered. The conflict was not confined to disagreements among the great powers. It was reproduced in sharp political disagreements within many nations. The total nature of modern war had fused the political and economic aspects of international questions. It had also blurred the distinction between international and civil war.

THE IMPOVERISHMENT OF EUROPE

The inevitable result of the economic effort which created the arsenal of democracy in the second World War was to enlarge the capital equipment and enhance the productive efficiency of the United States. To some extent these economic gains were shared by countries outside the zone of conflict, as were Australia, India, Argentina, Mexico, and Brazil—as well as by the European neutrals—though the dependence of most of these countries upon European markets for their exports rendered their postwar position precarious. The extraordinary wartime development of scientific research and its industrial applications in the United States were symbolized, but by no means comprehended, in the head start which the United States had gained in respect of nuclear fission.

In some measure this great advance in technology had been made at the expense of the European allies of the United States which had been under the necessity of sacrificing the civilian sector of their economies to the immediate needs of war. The close of the war found them in a desperate situation. There had been a great impoverishment of the European peoples who before 1914 had constituted the lending and controlling center of world production and trade. Their consumption of the bare necessities of life was reduced to subsistence levels. What was more important in the long run was the fact that their capital resources had been depleted while their industrial efficiency had been seriously impaired. Not only had past capital accumulations been destroyed or used up, years of industrial research and development had been lost. The glaring contrast between the enormous productivity of the United States and the reduced capacities of western Europe was one of the major obstacles to the restoration of international economic co-operation. This obstacle was reinforced by the fact that so large a proportion of the peoples of western Europe had lost faith in the principles of private enterprise that were still potent in the United States.

The industrial countries of western Europe, especially Britain, France, and the Netherlands, had sustained heavy losses in their overseas investments. Even before their colonial empires became directly involved in the Japanese war, they had sold many shares. There followed a great deterioration of fixed assets during the Japanese occupation. After the war, currency inflation, local conflicts and the emergence of nationalist movements further depleted the purchasing power of their remaining colonial investments. This was a particularly hard blow since they had relied heavily on the dollar earnings from colonial raw materials exported to the United States. Indeed the situation of Great Britain had been converted from that of the largest creditor to that of a heavy debtor. War purchases in India, Egypt, and elsewhere had resulted in blocked sterling balances owed to these countries amounting in the aggregate to approximately $16 billion.

The western European peoples are vocal. They have many connections with the United States. Some understanding of their difficulties was communicated to the American people and evoked a vigorous response. By far the largest volume of public and private relief expenditure immediately after the war went to western Europe. Individual gifts, army expenditures in the occupied areas, and organized war relief agencies found their chief outlets in those countries. The United Nations Relief and Rehabilitation Agency (U.N.R.R.A.) which went into action on November 9, 1943, spent the larger proportion of its available funds ($3,998 million), of which $2,700 million were provided by the United States, in western Europe. After U.N.R.R.A. closed its major activities on June 30, 1947, the United States continued its program of foreign loans and gifts. The largest single loans were those extended to Britain and France in the middle of 1946, amounting respectively to $3,750 million and $1,370 million. The first loans from the International Bank for Reconstruction and Development and the first purchases of dollars from the International Monetary Fund went to Europe also. In June, 1948, Congress authorized the first year's appropriations for the Economic Cooperation Administration amounting to $5,055 million.

There was little dissent in the United States from the view that reconstruction of the industrially developed areas of western Europe should be the first and main charge upon the resources available for postwar rehabilitation. The United States took the initiative in formulating plans for postwar reconstruction. The plans fell into three major categories—transitional measures of relief, intermediate programs of lending for rehabilitation, and long-term institutions designed to maintain international economic equilibrium. It is convenient to defer consideration of the long-term institutions, but it should here be noted that the practicability of the long-range program will be seriously jeopardized unless the major producing and trading areas, and especially western Europe, can be successfully rehabilitated. Until the concerted program of the European countries themselves and the effect of the United States co-operation with that program can be tested in practice, the longer-run proposals for international economic co-operation must remain speculative.

The transitional measures of relief undertaken at the close of the war, through the international agency of U.N.R.R.A., or unilaterally, proved to be inadequate both because the needs of the devastated countries had been underestimated and because the relief was not always successful in stimulating local production. The devastation wrought by modern war is even worse in the political and psychological spheres than in that of material facilities. A great amount of food, materials, and equipment was supplied, but numbed and dispirited peoples, hampered by political conflicts, were not fully restored to self-reliant productive effort. After two years of extensive relief, there was widespread undernourishment and a disappointing measure of agricultural or industrial recovery. The form of relief could be criticized, and its administration might not have been effective in some areas. The fundamental difficulty was its inadequacy to cope with the vast problems of distress and demoralization left by the most destructive war in history.

By the end of 1947, in addition to the net cost of lend-lease ($40 billion), military occupation costs ($2.8 billion), and its substantial relief contributions ($3 billion), the United States had extended $10 billion in rehabilitation loans, primarily to its allies, as well as other grants. Other New World countries, notably the British Dominions, had made gifts and loans comparable with their resources. These countries, together with Argentina, Sweden, and Switzerland were also advanc-

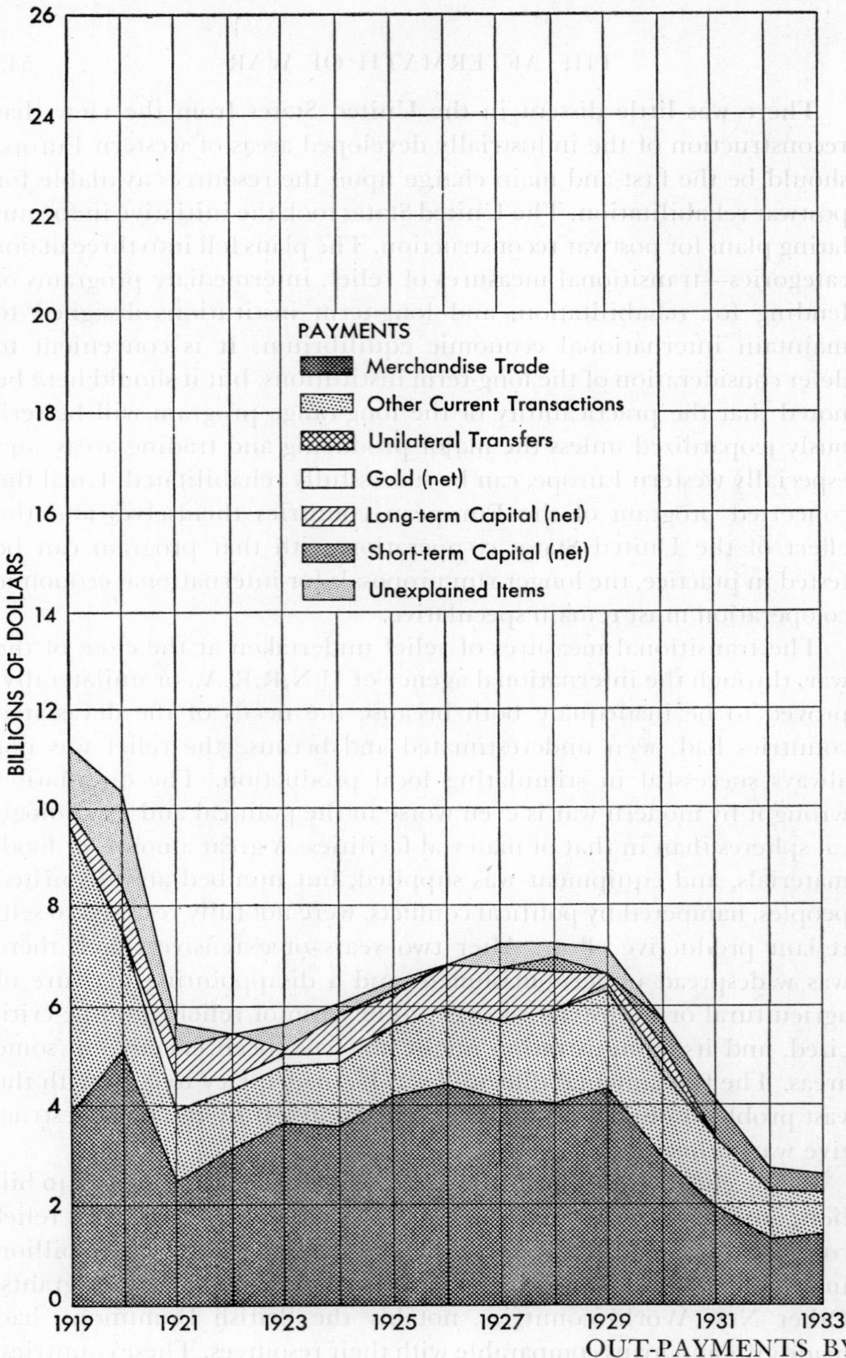

OUT-PAYMENTS BY

Source: (1919–39) U.S. Department of Commerce, *The United States in the World* *International Transactions of the United States during the War, 1940–45,* Economic 1947, p. 13, and March 1948, p. 18.

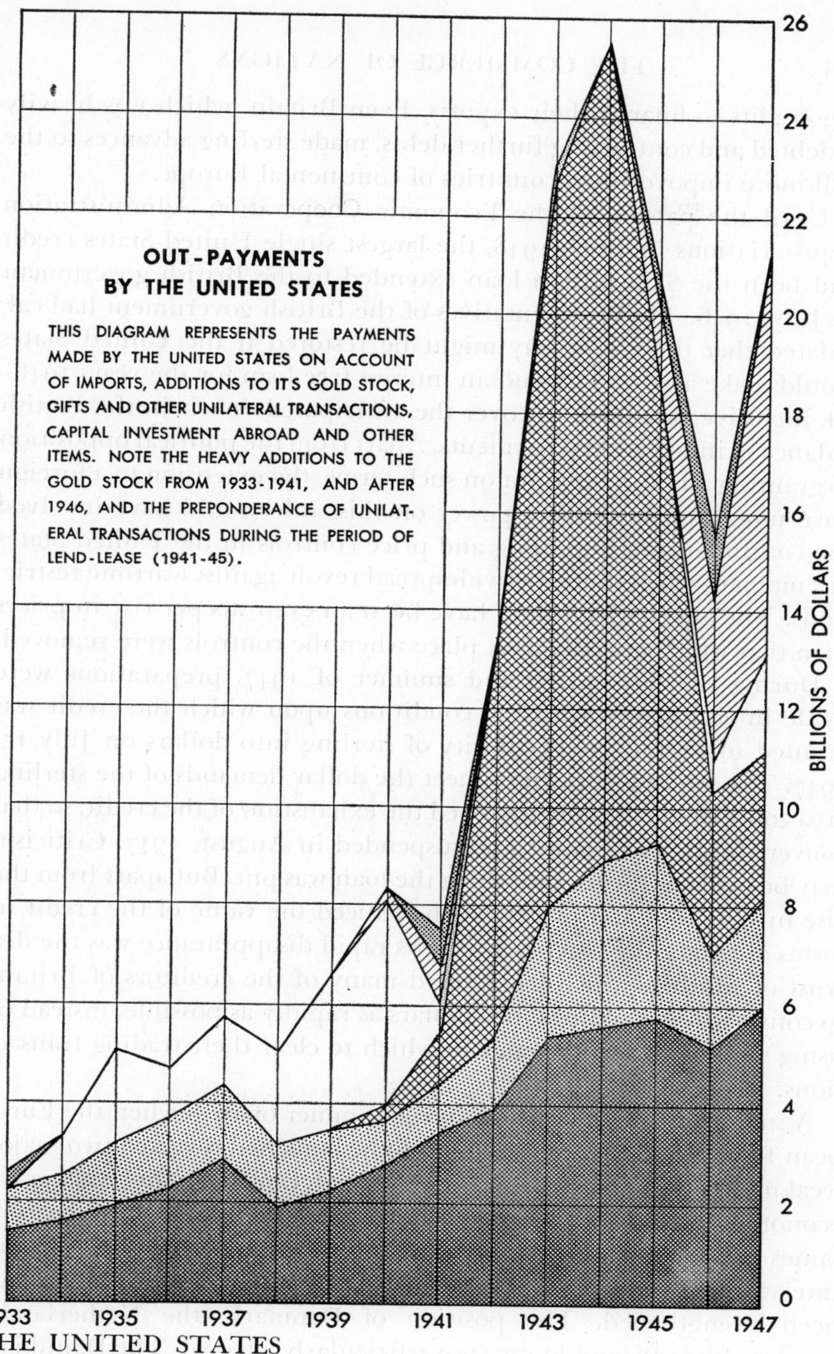
OUT-PAYMENTS
BY THE UNITED STATES
THIS DIAGRAM REPRESENTS THE PAYMENTS MADE BY THE UNITED STATES ON ACCOUNT OF IMPORTS, ADDITIONS TO IT S GOLD STOCK, GIFTS AND OTHER UNILATERAL TRANSACTIONS, CAPITAL INVESTMENT ABROAD AND OTHER ITEMS. NOTE THE HEAVY ADDITIONS TO THE GOLD STOCK FROM 1933-1941, AND AFTER 1946, AND THE PREPONDERANCE OF UNILATERAL TRANSACTIONS DURING THE PERIOD OF LEND-LEASE (1941-45).
BILLIONS OF DOLLARS
0
2
4
6
8
10
12
14
16
18
20
22
24
26
1933
1935
1937
1939
1941
1943
1945
1947

THE UNITED STATES

Economy, Economic Series, No. 23, Washington, 1943, Appendix, Table I; (1940–45) Series, No. 65, Washington, 1945, p. x; (1946–47) *Survey of Current Business*, March

ing credits to finance their exports. Even Britain, which was heavily indebted and contracting further debts, made sterling advances to the still more impoverished countries of continental Europe.

Until the passing of the Economic Cooperation Administration appropriations in June, 1948, the largest single United States credit had been the $3¾-billion loan extended to the British government in July, 1946. The representatives of the British government had calculated that their economy might be restored if the United States would make a gift, or extend an interest-free loan for the years 1946–50, inclusive, adequate to cover the anticipated deficit in the British balance of international payments. Apart from the political opposition to granting any such amount on such terms, the extension to a foreign government of purchasing power on this scale would have involved the continuance of rationing and price controls in the United States at a moment when there was widespread revolt against wartime restrictions. The alternative would have been an even steeper rise in prices than that which actually took place when the controls were removed.

During the late spring and summer of 1947, preparations were made in accordance with the conditions upon which the credit was granted to resume convertibility of sterling into dollars on July 15, 1947. The amounts drawn to meet the dollar demands of the sterling area countries materially hastened the exhaustion of the credit, so that convertibility had again to be suspended in August, 1947. Criticism may be made of the uses to which the loan was put. But apart from the rise in United States prices which reduced the value of the credit in terms of goods, the chief factor in its rapid disappearance was the distrust of sterling, which had caused many of the creditors of Britain to convert their holdings into dollars as rapidly as possible, instead of using sterling as the currency in which to clear their trading transactions.

A survey of western Europe in the summer of 1948 when the European Recovery Program was about to be launched revealed two major weaknesses. As after 1918, a demoralized Germany involved grave economic difficulties for all the neighboring countries whose economies had been closely linked with the German market. During the interwar and war period the German hold over these economies had been strengthened. The position of Denmark, the Netherlands, Sweden, Finland, and France was particularly affected. The Danubian countries had passed for the time being at least into the orbit of the U.S.S.R. There was a strong tendency also for the northern and western countries to look toward an increasing outlet for their exports in bilateral trade with Russia. This was evidenced by the Swedish trade agreement with the U.S.S.R. As long as the German economy was unable to function effectively, it was increasingly evident that there would be difficulty in the reconstruction of the European economies. Before the war, continental Europe bought more from Latin America, southeast Asia, and other raw-material and food-exporting countries than it sold in those countries. The decline of this great continental market was likely to affect the economies of the raw-material producing countries as soon as the first period of postwar shortages was past.

Even more important from the viewpoint of world trade was the postwar weakness of the British economy. The extent of this was revealed by severe winter conditions in 1946–47. Britain was still incurring a heavy burden of international indebtedness. She suffered from an inelastic demand for imports of foodstuffs and raw materials, and was therefore faced with the necessity of expanding exports on a scale that would have been difficult to realize in the best of circumstances. While calculations were necessarily theoretical, it was generally agreed that a substantial increase of exports would be necessary to balance the international accounts. The balance of payments was rendered more difficult by the fact that imports from the Western Hemisphere were 42 per cent of the total imports, while exports to that hemisphere were only 14 per cent of the total exports. The result was a severe pressure on dollar exchange resources. This situation was clearly explained by the British White Paper entitled *Economic Survey: 1947*.

We are now drawing some 42 per cent of our imports from the Western Hemisphere, which is now the main source of the food and raw materials that we must have. But we are selling there only 14 per cent of our exports. We are thus running large deficits with these countries. These must be settled in dollars or their equivalent. To much of the Eastern Hemisphere, on the other hand, we tend to sell more than we buy. In a world fully recovered from war, this would provide us with the means to settle our deficits with the West. But now many of the Eastern Hemisphere countries have no gold or dollars or essential goods with which to pay; to others we owe large debts which we shall have to repay gradually, and the surplus in our trade with such countries is used up in this way. We, therefore, shall not be able wholly to use our surpluses with Eastern Hemisphere countries against our deficits with Western Hemisphere countries. . . . This dollar problem within our total balance of payments can be wholly solved only by the economic recovery of Europe and the Far East and the establishment of equilibrium in all the major trading countries' balance of payments.

It was not possible to reduce imports in any great measure since they consisted largely of food and of raw materials. Some relief might have been given to the British balance of payments by a compounding and reduction of blocked sterling indebtedness. The Dominions—Canada, Australia, New Zealand, and South Africa—made substantial gifts to Britain.[3] The great bulk of this indebtedness, however, was owing to India, Eire, Egypt, Palestine, and other countries within the sterling area or on its fringe. Pursuant to the financial agreement negotiated in connection with the credit extended by the United States, Britain had been obliged on July 15, 1947, to seek adjustment of the blocked sterling credits. Negotiations with the owners of blocked credits brought no result, and therefore renewed emphasis was placed on the export drive.

If exports were to be increased, much effort had to go into production for the export market. British citizens and American tourists found that many goods on display in London shops were earmarked for export. Scotch whisky was scarce in Britain because it was shipped in large quantities to the United States. British automobiles and tractors were pushed on the American market to earn dollars, while gasoline was severely rationed in Britain to conserve dollar resources for more urgently needed imports. An effort was made to plan the British economy so that 25 per cent of British manufacturing capacity might be devoted to the production of exports. Since a large proportion of British production was for the home market, the industries which could export were forced to devote a much larger proportion than 25 per cent of their capacity to production for external markets. The British White Paper quoted above put the case bluntly: "There is nothing temporary about our need for exports; concentration upon

[3] Canada, in 1942, made a gift of $C1,000 million and in 1946 a loan, free of interest, of $C1,250 million; on May 13, 1947, it was reported that aid to Britain in cash and goods during and since the war totaled $C3,112 million; in 1947 Australia and New Zealand made gifts of £20 million and £10 million, respectively; in 1946 the Union of South Africa and its three protectorates presented Britain with a gold certificate for £985,000 and in 1947 South Africa made a loan of gold amounting to £80 million, at ½ per cent per annum. In 1948 Australia made a further Christmas gift of £8 million.

exports must become a permanent part of our normal industrial life. Without exports, we cannot get food and we cannot get raw materials, and without these, we cannot hope to increase our standard of living—or even maintain it."

The position of Britain was crucial. Despite its comparative weakness, it was still the strongest nation in western Europe, and by virtue of its large imports still the center of a great trading system. The social reforms and economic planning upon which it had embarked made necessary a strict control of imports. This control ran counter to the United States proposals to restore multilateral principles. In essence those proposals called for abandonment within a limited period of all forms of quantitative and monetary restrictions upon the flow of world trade. The objective was to restore competitive world markets. To this end, import quota and exchange control systems were to be abolished and tariff duties were to be reduced. All forms of discriminatory trade regulation, such as preferential tariffs and bilateral purchasing or trade agreements, were frowned upon.

For nearly two decades the European countries had relied upon these methods of trade regulation, rather than upon tariffs, to safeguard their balances of external payments. All of them in their impoverishment were planning very carefully the use of their limited resources. They were calculating national budgets of manpower, of raw materials, and of productive capacity in an effort to meet the minimum needs of their populations. This was as true of Denmark, of the Netherlands, and of France as it was of Britain. Until they could be reasonably sure of securing adequate foreign exchange to pay for essential imports of food and raw materials, they were reluctant to relax their quantitative and monetary controls over imports or to abandon their bilateral trading arrangements. Their major preoccupation was the rehabilitation of their own productive capacities to the point where they could maintain a minimum of subsistence equitably distributed. At the same time they sought to export enough to earn the means of paying for essential imports.

There were two sides to their embarrassment. The first was the limited market open to their exports in the United States. The world trading system of the past had been multilateral. The United States had bought raw materials mainly from the tropics, and had sold food, raw materials, and manufactures to the industrialized countries of Europe and to the recent European settlements overseas. At the same time it had imposed tariff barriers to the import of the most important products of the regions of recent settlement (for example, wool, butter, and meat), and to the manufactures of European countries.[4] In 1938 the best customers of the United States had been Britain (from which the United States bought 22½ cents for every dollar of exports); Canada (55 cents); Japan (53 cents); France (40 cents); Germany (60 cents); Netherlands (32 cents); Argentina (46 cents); Philippines ($1.09); Belgium (55 cents); Cuba ($1.40); U.S.S.R. (34 cents); South Africa (23 cents), and Australia (13 cents).[5] In only one instance—Cuba—among these countries did the United States buy more than it sold. These figures indicate that the re-creation of a world trading system could not be expected unless the United States was prepared

[4] Cf. League of Nations, *The Network of World Trade,* Princeton, 1942, p. 126, for the commodity trade of the United States in 1938, from which the following typical cases are taken. The list includes all countries where the balance exceeded $20 million.

	Import Balance ($ million)		Export Balance ($ million)
British Malaya	106	Britain	403
Netherlands Indies	41	Canada	208
India, Burma, Ceylon	37	Japan	113
Brazil	36	France	80
Cuba	30	Netherlands	66
		Australia	60
		Union of South Africa	54
		Argentina	47
		U.S.S.R.	46
		Germany	42
		Belgium-Luxembourg	35
		Venezuela	32
		Iceland	26
		Curacao	22
		Denmark	21
		China	21

[5] United States exports to and imports from these countries in 1938 were:

	Exports ($ million)	Imports ($ million)
Britain	521	118
Canada	468	260
Japan	240	127
France	134	54
Germany	105	63
Netherlands	97	31
Argentina	87	40
Philippines	86	94
Belgium-Luxembourg	77	42
Cuba	76	106
U.S.S.R.	70	24
South Africa	70	16
Australia	69	9

to take effective action to restore multilateral trade. This would have to be done by reorganizing productivity in the raw-material exporting countries. At the same time the United States would have to lower its tariffs and buy more from those to whom it expected to sell its exports.

The other side of the embarrassment of the western European countries was the fact that, before they could increase their exports, they were faced with the necessity of restoring and improving their former productivity, and lowering their unit costs of production. It is true that many of their typical exports—such as fine woolen cloths from Britain, and wines and perfumes from France—had competed on a quality rather than on a price basis, but after the war the volume of their production was too small and the prices of their exports too high to secure large markets even if United States tariffs had been reduced. In any case these European countries had to rebuild their stocks of raw materials, renew their equipment, and reorganize their productive and selling mechanisms, before they could expand their production and their exports. In most of them the currency was overvalued at the current exchange rates, so that the export prices were high in dollars.

It was to be expected that such difficulties would occur in the transition from war to peace. Beyond those immediate difficulties there loomed the fear that, as after the first World War, a succession of violent industrial fluctuations might occur. The quantitative and monetary devices by which trade is now regulated and restricted were imposed in the years of the great depression. In those years (1929–32) imports into the United States fell by about three-fourths. The United States was proposing that in return for tariff reductions and rehabilitation loans the European countries should pledge themselves to abandon the use of import quotas, exchange controls and exchange depreciation, bilateral purchase agreements, and all the other mechanisms of regulation that had been devised to protect their balances of payments in a crisis. Remembering their difficulties in the interwar years and fearing a repetition of those difficulties on an even greater scale, these countries were reluctant to give such a pledge unless they could be assured that the United States would join them in concerted measures to control cyclical business fluctuations. In the alternative they demanded the right in an emergency to take whatever steps might prove necessary to safeguard their economies from undue strains communicated through the balance of payments.

It was evident that the restoration of world markets depended in large measure upon the devising of national and international means to mitigate the severity of these periodic fluctuations of economic activity. If another depression should occur, comparable with that of 1929–33, no country could refrain from taking all possible steps to prevent mass unemployment within its borders. National action would be taken, primarily by monetary expenditures combined with national planning, that would involve resort to controls over external payments. International agreements to reduce tariff barriers and to eliminate quotas, exchange controls, and bilateral trading arrangements would not survive if such national steps were taken.

Meanwhile, measures had been undertaken to put relief and rehabilitation on to an organized basis. A concerted program of European recovery, aided by American loans and gifts, and worked out co-operatively between the Organization for European Economic Cooperation (O.E.E.C.) and the Economic Cooperation Administration set up by the United States, was inaugurated in June, 1948. Such a program had been suggested in the Harvard speech by Secretary Marshall in June, 1947. His suggestion was that the European powers should consult together in framing a concerted reconstruction effort and that the United States would be interested in co-operating with such an effort. The response was immediate and vigorous. The U.S.S.R. refused to enter into the co-operative program and brought pressure on its satellite countries to abstain. But sixteen western and southern nations created the O.E.E.C. and took part in the preparation of estimates of European needs. When the report of the sixteen-nation committee was presented to the United States, the President appointed three committees of officials and private citizens to examine it from the viewpoint of United States resources, of its prospective effects upon the United States economy, and of its necessity and adequacy. The investigations of these committees, supplemented by the personal experiences of influential members of Congress in Europe during the summer of 1947, provided a realistic basis for Congressional discussion of an effective European aid program.

There were two related but separate aspects of the recovery program that was finally evolved. The first, and in many respects the most important, concerned the proposals made for action by the European governments themselves. Each of the sixteen European governments, as long as it retained full sovereignty, was bound to carry the major responsibility for economic reconstruction within its territory. The United States negotiated separate agreements with each of these countries concerning the methods by which American aid would be handled. But in addition a permanent commission, representative of all sixteen nations, was created and equipped with a competent staff. The United States Ambassador-at-large responsible for supervision in Europe of the operations of the Economic Cooperation Administration maintained close touch with the Organization for European Economic Cooperation as well as with the individual governments.

The second aspect of the recovery program concerned the amount, character, and method of aid from the United States in supplement of European action. In the United States, the constitution of the Economic Cooperation Administration as a new organ of government was in many respects the crucial issue of Congressional debate. It was constituted as a public corporation on the pattern of the Reconstruction Finance Corporation and the Tennessee Valley Authority, with powers defined broadly by Congressional legislation and appropriations. The principle of aid to Europe had been broadly accepted. It was recognized that it must be furnished over a period of years, but each year's appropriation must be determined by Congress. Certain broad principles were laid down by Congress, as for instance the proportion of loans to gifts, but wide latitude in conducting specific transactions was given to the Administrator.

The Organization for European Economic Cooperation was not the only official agency engaged in exploring ways of promoting more effective methods of inter-European economic co-operation. The European Economic Commission of the United Nations (E.C.E.) was also working actively at Geneva with a competent staff. In an effort to break one of the most important bottlenecks in the postwar recovery of Europe, the Bank for International Settlements had developed new functions in respect to the clearing of trading balances and was engaged in devising methods for multilateral clearing between the European countries.

The coexistence of two bodies with parallel aims—the E.C.E., representative of all the European members of the United Nations, including the U.S.S.R., and the O.E.E.C., lacking the U.S.S.R. and its satellite countries—emphasized one of the dangers of regionalism. A somewhat similar situation arose with the Economic Commission for

Latin America of the United Nations and the economic activities of the Association of American States. Regional organization could be either a most useful supplement to world organization, or, on the contrary, it could develop into a substitute for world organization. In Europe as in the Americas, the United States was a member of both commissions, but in Europe the Organization for European Economic Cooperation was the channel through which the flow of United States aid was co-ordinated. Its creation outside the United Nations Organization reflected the impossibility of achieving co-operative reconstruction through any organization in which the U.S.S.R. possessed the power of veto.

As the impoverishment of Europe was more clearly recognized and the spread of communism became more menacing, a number of influential private groups began to work for closer integration of the western European countries. Official encouragement was given to this movement toward European union by the creation of the Organization for European Economic Cooperation, and also by statements of responsible United States officials. The fact that in every western European country responsible and influential leaders were willing to give time and energy to exploring the approaches to European union was an encouraging fact. But the complexities of the question quickly became manifest. There were some publicists ready to jump to the idea of a Customs Union which would turn western Europe into a great free-trade area. Others were thinking in terms of military alliance. Still others contemplated either political confederation or a complete federal union.

The more these proposals were explored, the greater the complexities that were revealed. The nation-states of Europe have a long history. Their economic structure was developed organically within the political institutions of national sovereignty. There were marked differences between them of economic organization, of labor supply, of living levels, of productive capacity, as well as inherited feuds and suspicions that lay deep in the consciousness of each national group. It was a remarkable fact that the risks of economic disaster and of communist infiltration had aroused leading Europeans to the necessity of rising above narrow national viewpoints. The willingness at long last to discuss a rational organization of European manpower and resources was a great asset. But it could not exorcize the very real difficulties confronting any such rationalization.

One important aspect of postwar development that had to be taken into account was the crumbling of empire. Western Europe for more than three centuries had drawn economic support from the trade and investment that had organized the resources of its colonial empires. Those empires were rapidly passing into history. Until an efficient economic substitute was found for imperialism, Europe would not be able to rely upon the raw materials or upon the profits drawn from its former colonies. It continued to consume more than it was producing. There was a large deficit in its balance of payments with the raw-material and food-exporting areas of the world. It was looking to the Economic Cooperation Administration to cover that deficit, and the United States was ready to appropriate dollars for that purpose over a reasonable period of time. The question was whether such emergency aid would be dissipated in maintaining traditional living levels and employment or whether it could be used as a lever by which to change the patterns of employment and stimulate production so that within a reasonable time Europe could again be economically independent.

The temptation was great both in Europe and in the United States to regard the Economic Cooperation Administration primarily as a channel through which the United States could send relief to Europe. The relief aspect of the program could not be ignored. Inadequately nourished workers were not capable of sustained effort and initiative. But mere relief was inadequate. The essential need was to reorganize the productive capacity of Europe. This involved insistence that the European governments set aside for capital development upon a co-operatively agreed program the manpower, resources, and credit necessary to create the productivity which would render them independent of further relief. Co-operative agreement involved the brushing aside of cherished national interests and prejudices and the planning of the European economy as a whole.

In planning particular projects of expenditure, the United States could make its aid conditional upon the ignoring of special interests. But if it did so it would lay itself open to the charge of economic imperialism. In calculating the amounts of relief to be granted, it could correlate them with the development plans in Europe rather than with the deficit in the European balances of payments. This would enforce a curtailment of imports for consumption and might be attacked as lowering living levels. It could insist upon using its available funds to provide loans for solvent capital projects rather than gifts for consumption needs. It could insist upon facilities being given for the technology and know-how of American private enterprise to associate itself with European enterprise as one of the most effective means by which productivity might be increased. But in all these matters it was evident that the actual arrangements agreed upon in detailed projects would need to come delicately close to interference with the domestic economic policies of the recipient countries.

Effective aid entailed using it as a lever to induce more rational and effective use of European manpower and resources. Lending or gifts which did no more than maintain living levels, prices, exchange rates, and export costs at levels that would prove untenable when the program came to an end would be merely an evasion of the real issues. Extensive reorganization of the European economy was necessary. This entailed the breaking down of national prejudices, the ignoring of special, local, and group interests, and the introduction on a large scale of improved production and marketing processes. The only way in which such a reorganization could be achieved was by consultative co-operation. In addition to the relief it brought to ease the suffering in Europe, the Economic Cooperation Administration had created mechanisms for the continuous exchange of technical assistance, know-how, and scientific knowledge. It offered Europeans an opportunity to realize the truth expressed by Friedrich List when he said that wealth is less important to a nation than the power of producing wealth.

THE CRUMBLING OF EMPIRE

The second World War and its aftermath threw into sharp relief significant shifts of power in the Western world. The extraordinary productivity and political prestige of the United States, the rise to world power of the U.S.S.R., and the impoverishment of western Europe were facts of tremendous importance. They marked the end of the era during which western Europe had dominated world politics and world economics. That the western European states would recover some of their former strength was more than probable. But it was highly improbable that they could ever regain the pre-eminence that had made them during the nineteenth century the organizing center of world production and trade and the focus of political world order. The basic economic trends were running against them. Power is based upon population, material resources, technical skills, and organization. In all these respects, the United States and the U.S.S.R. were more favorably placed than were the western European states. It would be an interesting exercise in political geography to map the centrifugal trends of economic and political power in the Western world. The concentration of economic and financial, and therefore of strategic and political, power in Britain reached its peak in the third quarter of the nineteenth century. Up to the first World War, Germany and the other states of western Europe gained an increasing share in that power. Two destructive wars then threw it to the United States and the U.S.S.R.

One essential element of western European economic and political strength had been the dominance of vast areas in Asia and Africa by trade, investment, and military force. The trade routes had led to the ports of western Europe. The economic development of the colonial world, including many countries that had retained their political independence but had yielded to economic penetration, was determined by the demands of a world market centered in western Europe. This nineteenth-century organization of world order was a remarkable achievement. Vast empires had been lightly held. A combination of naval force and skeleton garrisons at posts commanding strategic waterways had been sufficient to keep open the sea lanes. The threat of punitive expeditions had sufficed to maintain authority where it was directly exercised by European states and to ensure economic access where authority remained in the hands of local rulers. It is a significant fact that Britain, the greatest colonial power and the greatest trading country, did not find it necessary to resort to conscription before 1914. The real instrument of domination was economic power buttressed by skillful administration.

The crumbling of these imperial systems and of the world trading organization constituted a major element in the weakness of western Europe after the second World War. The system of world trade based upon the economic and often upon the political subordination of dependent peoples had been irretrievably wrecked. The distress of western Europe was aggravated by its inability to draw upon the raw material and food resources of colonial empires which had themselves been heavily damaged by the second World War, and which sought independent development as free nations.

This crumbling of empire posed difficult questions of policy for

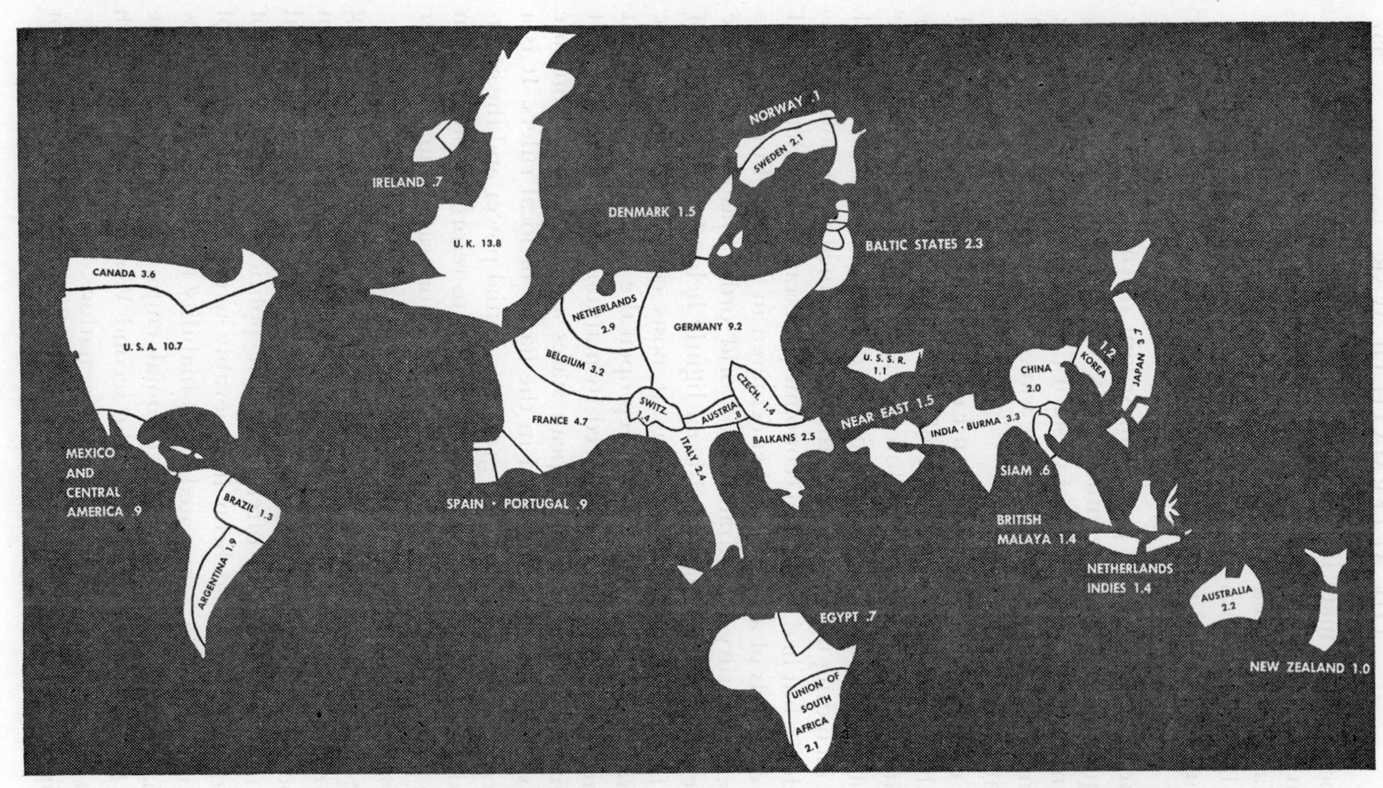

THE TRADING WORLD, 1938

The area of each country is shown proportionately to its share of world trade in 1938.

Source: Calculated from data in League of Nations, *Review of World Trade, 1938*, Geneva, 1939, p. 21.

the United States and the U.S.S.R. as well as for the western European powers. The American people were disposed by their own historical experience to sympathize with other peoples struggling for political independence. But a new and uncertain equilibrium of power was in process of being tested. The United States and the U.S.S.R., each in its own way, was taking the measure of this new power situation. The United States had pushed its defensive outposts to the boundaries of Asia. It was deeply committed to positive policies of economic assistance to western and southern Europe. In the Near East—the strategic land bridge joining Europe, Africa, and Asia—the richest known oil reserves essential for modern war were being developed, largely by American capital and enterprise. Free access to the eastern Mediterranean became a strategic necessity for the United States. The power struggle came to the surface in incidents that occurred in the borderlands of the continental mass controlled by the U.S.S.R. It was confused by a conflict of ideologies. The crumbling of empire created a great power vacuum in which the constructive forces of capitalism and the Soviet challenge to them were bound to compete for the allegiance of practically half the world's population.

What was at stake in the colonial world was not the territorial sovereignty over dependent peoples that traced back to the Portuguese and Spanish conquests in the sixteenth century. It was the economic organization of the colonial territories that developed during the nineteenth century, following the Industrial Revolution in Europe. The characteristics which distinguished this from earlier colonial development derived from the extension of the market in time and space which drew them into the currents of nineteenth-century investment and trade. Until the machine methods of the Industrial Revolution gave western Europe a decisive advantage in manufacturing production, the colonial economies had not been fundamentally affected by their political subordination to the aggressive Western powers. It was only when their arts and crafts were subjected to the competition of cheap machine-made imports that economic and social deterioration began to make this subordination felt in the daily lives of the working population. At the same time, there began the foreign processes of organization and investment that turned their agriculture more and more toward production for the world market.

These economic processes brought increased productivity. They dislocated the old and primitive systems of agriculture and handicrafts and went far to destroy the social discipline as well as the economic balance of the village communities. But they brought new methods and processes as well as products and organized them with the vigorous enterprise and scientific skills as well as the capital equipment of the Western world. It is true that these new processes remained dependent upon the fluctuations of effective demand in the world market. Shifts in demand for the natural product—as when the swollen production of indigo was displaced in a few short years by competitive chemical dyes—introduced a new kind and degree of economic instability. In the main, however, the impact of Western trade had been economically beneficial to the dependent peoples. The startling increases of population that took place throughout the colonies were evidence that the margins of subsistence had been raised. This indeed was one of the stark elements of tragedy in the immediate postwar situation. Numbers had increased because of improved methods of food production and because of heavy exports of raw materials, but the scientific knowledge, technical organization, and capital equipment which had made possible this increased productivity remained in alien hands. The colonial peoples faced a tremendous task in attempting to make themselves not only politically independent, but economically competent.

The outthrust of western Europe after the Industrial Revolution was primarily economic and only secondarily political. We can understand this if we recall what happened within the United States, where not only the Indians but the Mexicans in the West and Southwest were swept aside by the relentless enterprise of aggressive individuals in search of economic opportunity on the frontiers of settlement. This was the process of expansion—the moving frontier of trade, settlement, investment, and missionary enterprise—described by a historian of the British Empire as leading, wherever the local inhabitants proved recalcitrant, to territorial imperialism. During the latter part of the nineteenth century the economic frontier had moved steadily across Africa and Asia. A succession of colonial wars marked its progress. Despite the protests of liberal free traders, the great powers competed with each other for access to undeveloped areas of raw materials. Their competition had risen to a peak in the latter part of the nineteenth century, when vast new empires were carved out in Africa and southeast Asia and a scramble set in for spheres of influence in China. Behind this renewal of imperialism lay the triple search for markets, for raw materials, and for investment outlets.

The first World War had not greatly changed this pattern. Hostilities had been confined to Europe and the Near East. Germany was deprived of her colonial possessions and the Turkish Empire was broken up, but the great colonial powers—Britain, France, the Netherlands, and Belgium—retained undisputed possession of their empires. New forces, however, were at work. The prestige of the dominant Europeans had been undermined especially in the Far East by conflict among themselves and by the stripping of concessions and extraterritorial privileges from Germans and Austrians. The German colonies and substantial fragments of the Turkish empire had been distributed among the British, French, and Japanese empires. This was in the form of mandates subject to international supervision. The welfare of dependent peoples had been recognized as "a sacred trust of civilization." While the areas thus placed under mandate were relatively insignificant, the enunciation of the welfare principle encouraged the independent movements that were springing up among the more developed colonial peoples and gave impetus to experiments in "indirect rule" over the less developed peoples. Indeed it went far to change the spirit of colonial government everywhere. Throughout the interwar years the drift of policy was toward native welfare rather than the exploitation of trading and investment opportunities. In some cases notably Puerto Rico and the British West Indian islands, this involved substantial grants from the exchequer of the colonial power concerned. This policy was extended by the British Parliament in voting the Colonial Development and Welfare Act, 1940, and subsequently in the development of more elaborate programs particularly in Africa.

The effect throughout southeast Asia of the political and economic progress of the Philippine Islands after they had passed under the rule of the United States in 1898 should not be ignored. While criticisms have been made of certain phases of the administration of the islands, the broad fact stands out that it was directed toward preparing the way for independence. Inevitably there were Filipinos who chafed at the slowness of political emancipation and criticized the economic operations of American interests, though these never developed on a great scale. On the other hand, the inclusion of the islands within the

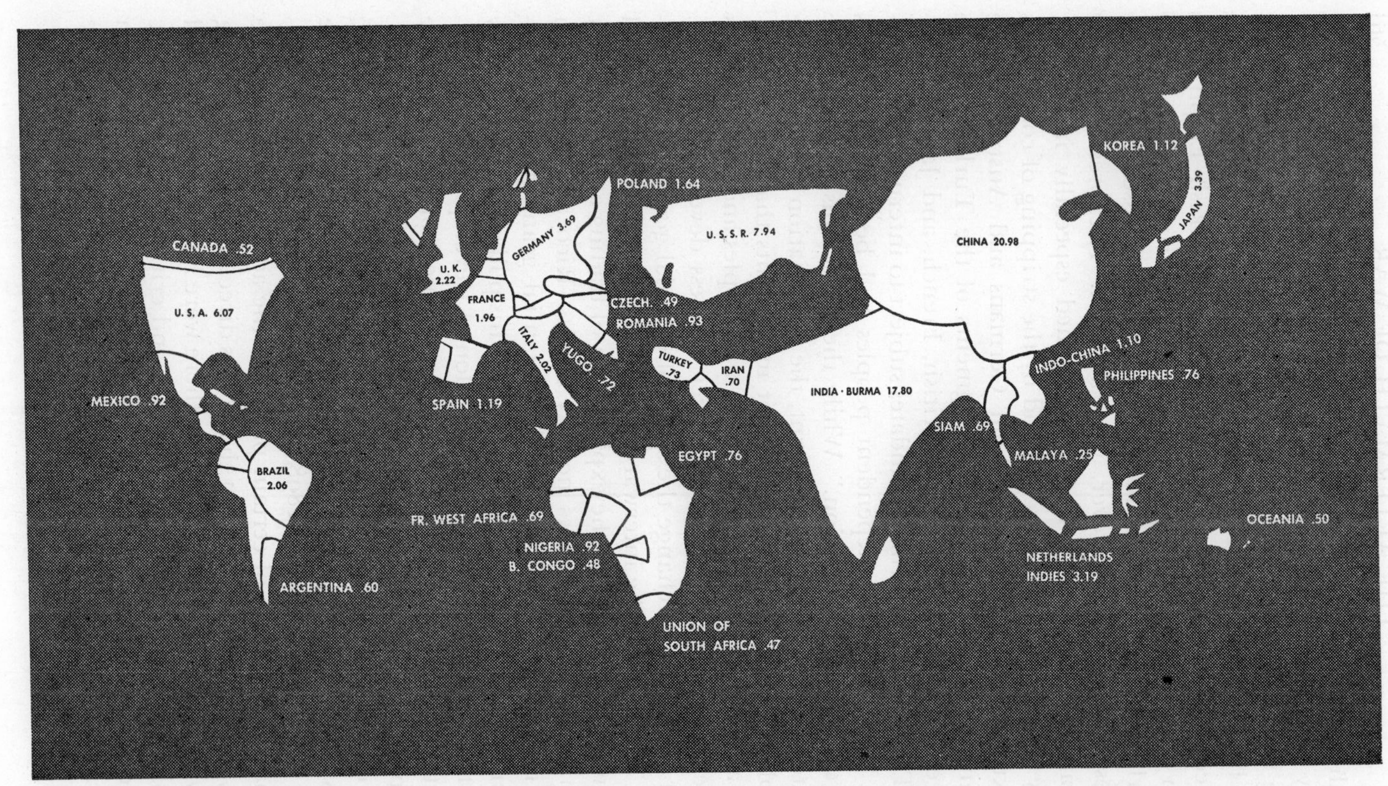

THE POPULATION WORLD, 1938

The area of each country is shown proportionately to its share of world population in 1938.

Source: Calculated from data in League of Nations, *Statistical Yearbook, 1939–40*, Geneva, 1940, p. 14 ff.

United States tariff area fostered economic development by giving Philippine exports free access to the United States market. Indeed the anxiety of competing interests to get rid of Philippine competition was a factor in the passage of the Jones Act of 1916 which promised independence to the Philippines "as soon as a stable government could be established therein."

After long delay the Philippine Independence Act, 1933, and the Act bearing the same title in 1934 authorized the calling of a convention to draft a constitution, republican in form and containing a bill of rights. It provided for a ten-year period of transition and the gradual withdrawal of privileged access to the United States market. This was accepted by the Filipinos, and on July 4, 1946, the Philippine Republic was inaugurated. Preferential treatment was provided for Philippine exports to the United States so that the islanders were not deprived suddenly of their greatest market. The preference is to be diminished until it finally ends in 1974. The feeling created by benevolent administration for half a century and by the generosity with which full independence was finally granted, while assuring the Philippine Republic of political and economic support, provided a notable proof of Edmund Burke's dictum that "not seldom in politics is magnanimity the truest wisdom." Filipino resistance on Bataan and in guerilla warfare throughout the period of Japanese occupation was in striking contrast with the almost simultaneous events in Singapore.

The effect of the second World War was, on the whole, to accelerate the trend toward colonial independence. Japan was stripped of all her conquests. The U.S.S.R. annexed the Kuriles and southern Sakhalin. Formosa and Manchuria were returned to China, and the Pacific islands were taken over by the United States under a form of mandate that enabled them to be used as advance military and naval bases. The fate of Korea, which had been promised independence, was still in the balance. But the net effect of the Japanese defeat had been to strengthen the forces making for independent nationalism elsewhere in Asia.

India achieved its freedom, though at the cost of partition. After decades of mounting pressure, the British government at last took farsighted action in refusing to delay its withdrawal, despite the difficulties involved in partition and the worsening of religious and racial riots. Instead, it took the initiative in 1946 in bringing to birth the new dominions of India and Pakistan, with the full understanding that at the end of a year they would be free to withdraw from the Commonwealth and set themselves up as independent states. Both chose to remain within the Commonwealth, though India has become a republic. Burma was constituted a self-governing dominion, but at the end of its first year of dominion status voted overwhelmingly for independence. Ceylon became a self-governing dominion. A new federal constitution with enlarged powers of representative government was negotiated for British Malaya, and the personal sovereignty of the Brooke family that had ruled Sarawak for a century was bought out, thus enabling Borneo to move further along the road to self-government.

In the Dutch East Indies somewhat similar steps were taken to separate the islands from the Netherlands control. An independent republic was proclaimed by Indonesian leaders and civil warfare was restrained only by an uneasy truce resulting from intervention by the Security Council of the United Nations. Meantime a Dutch proposal was advanced to constitute a United States of Indonesia, of which the new republic would be a constituent state. The French possessions in the Far East also revolted. The revolt was suppressed and the French government strenuously resisted the movement for self-government for Indo-China.[6] The French intention to maintain intact its imperial position in the Far East was demonstrated by a proclamation that the enclaves of Pondicherry, Yanaon, Karikal, and Mahé, which were all that remained of its once extensive Indian empire, would be preserved. No such announcement was made concerning the remnants of the Portuguese Eastern empire—Diu, Daman, and Goa in India, Macao in China, and part of Timor in Indonesia—but there was no evidence that they would be voluntarily relinquished. Despite these intransigeant attitudes, there could be no doubt that empire in the East was passing into history.

In the Near East the disposition of the Italian colonies in Africa was still undetermined but it was almost certain that they would be placed under some form of mandate. Trans-Jordan had followed Iraq,

[6] The agreement signed between France and the Viet-Nam (Annamese) leaders at Hanoi, March 6, 1946, recognized Viet-Nam as a free state with its own government, including parliamentary institutions, army, and finances; but within the Indochinese Federation, which in turn is a part of the French Union. Later France interpreted this agreement as applying only to a restricted area in Northern Annam.

Syria, and Lebanon in attaining its independence. Egypt had secured a notable revision of its treaty with Britain. The Palestine mandate held by Britain had been surrendered to the United Nations when Jewish resistance made it untenable. Before the United Nations had been able to implement the partition of the mandate, the new state of Israel proclaimed its independence. To the south, the Union of South Africa had proposed to incorporate within its territory the mandated area of southwest Africa, but this proposal was rejected by the United Nations Assembly. Indeed, the debate on this question led to what amounted to censure of the Union government's native policy in its own territory.

What bearing did these political changes have upon economic policy, and particularly upon the prospects of expanding world trade? It was clear that they had aggravated the impoverishment of western Europe and the demands made upon American resources for relief and rehabilitation. In particular they had aggravated the dollar scarcity which had made it necessary for the western European peoples to rely not only upon American food and raw materials but upon credit with which to buy them. In 1938, the United States had imported from India, Burma, Ceylon, and the Dutch East Indies raw materials to the value of $361 million. Ten years earlier, the imports had been $586 million, equal after the 1934 devaluation to $992 million of the present currency. In 1946 and 1947, imports from these countries were negligible. The decline of these dollar-earning exports was a severe blow, both to the colonial territories and to Britain and the Netherlands. The latter were forced to buy in the United States without the dollar receipts from colonial exports not only what they would normally have bought there, but much of what they could formerly buy in the colonies. This short circuit in the currents of world trade had crippling effects throughout the trading world.

Moreover there was a serious loss of capital assets. Immediately before the second World War and during its early stages before lend-lease began, the British in particular had drawn heavily upon such overseas capital assets as were realizable in order to secure dollars with which to purchase food, munitions, and equipment from the United States. Then came the Japanese conquests and a long period of occupation during which plantations and capital installations deteriorated. Wherever civil conflict ensued, as in the Netherlands East Indies, further destruction took place, some of it wanton and all of it bound to cause suffering to the local population.

Nor was it possible in the disturbed political conditions of most of these regions to expect renewed investment of private capital. The multilateral world trading system might have been restored in some measure if oil wells and refineries, tea, sugar, tobacco, kapok, and rubber plantations and factories, tin mines and smelters, could have been put into working order again. The exports of machinery and the technical services necessary for such reconstruction would have served to buttress the economic recovery of the European countries. The restored output of raw materials to the United States would have furnished dollars to pay for the imports the European countries must draw from the United States, while providing employment for the colonial peoples. But before this circle of mutually profitable investment and trade could have been restored, it was necessary to negotiate a settlement of political controversies and to reach agreement upon the nature and conditions of the investment to be made.

This was the nub of the conflict. For a century and more the dependent peoples had furnished labor for foreign-owned and foreign-directed enterprises. The impact of these enterprises had disturbed the self-sufficient village economies and had gone far to destroy the social structure which rested upon them. The most potent elements of disturbance had been the introduction of a money-economy by the recruitment of wage labor, and the use of land for large-scale plantations. The increased productivity resulting from more efficient Western methods of production and the use of capital equipment had been diverted in the past largely to the payment of dividends on the capital invested. That part of increased productivity which went to the wage earner had been swallowed in increases of the population. It was not possible after the war to go back to a primitive, subsistence economy. There were too many mouths to be fed. By some means or other these peoples had to continue their progress toward modern economic methods of production, or suffer hardship, disease, and famine on a scale that defies imagination. Throughout this whole region of eastern and southeastern Asia—one of the richest remaining areas of strategic raw materials—there was a confusion of policy in regard to economic development.

In some countries, notably the Philippines and India, there was a disposition to welcome private foreign investment, and to go a long distance in providing political guarantees for its profitable operation. It was highly unlikely, even in the most favorable circumstances, that alien capital would ever again be allowed to operate as freely and to draw such heavy dividends as in the colonial era. Nevertheless there was considerable scope for long-term direct investment with local participation in ownership and management. The credit of most governments in this area was too weak to warrant the expectation of loans on the scale necessary for large-scale economic development, but direct investment which carries with it technical skills and efficient management could be an effective force in training local technicians and managers. New forms of organization were needed in which national governments in default of local enterprise might join with foreign enterprises in creating mixed corporations for the development of specific products or services.

The economic development of these regions presented a challenge to private capitalism to demonstrate its realistic efficiency in coming to terms with a new political situation. New methods of investment and operation were necessary. It was no longer possible to develop production primarily for the world market. The insistent demand that the needs of the local communities take priority had to be recognized. Nor was it possible to retain ownership and management exclusively in foreign hands, however efficient they might be. One of the major objectives of the newly awakened nationalism was the training of technicians and organizers competent to hold their own in competition with the scientific West. The Asiatic peoples were not content to remain second-class world citizens. For a century they had paid the price of ignorance. Now that they had gained control of their own political destinies they were determined to learn the scientific and industrial secrets of Western efficiency and power. Here was an opportunity for the free enterprise of the United States. If ways and means could be devised to work with and strengthen the economic organization of the peoples with whose aspirations for national independence Americans were sympathetic, the American way of life would not only be consolidated at home, but be firmly lodged abroad.

Many of the leaders of the new nationalisms in the economically undeveloped countries placed their faith in government rather than business planning for development. There were great public works of national and often of strategic importance which had to be undertaken by government if they were to be undertaken at all. The capital costs were too high and the returns too slow for transport systems and hydroelectric dams to be constructed by private enterprise in weak and capital-poor countries. The basic heavy industries such as steel could not be left to uncontrolled private enterprise, if only because their location was strategically important. For such expenditures national governments turned first to the International Bank for Reconstruction and Development in so far as they needed foreign loans. In default of assistance from such an international agency, many of them sought to secure credits from agencies of national governments such as the Import-Export Bank of the United States. But if need be, they contemplated industrialization by the Soviet method of progressive, controlled inflation by which labor and materials can be diverted to national purposes while levels of living are kept low.

In the narrower field of commercial policy as well as the field of international investment, the crumbling of empire created difficulties for the United States. Even during the war, India had not been willing to subscribe to Article VII of the lend-lease agreements, by which the recipients of lend-lease agreed to pledge themselves to a reduction of tariff barriers and other impediments to the free exchange of goods. In the negotiations on the International Trade Charter during 1947, India was joined by other economically undeveloped countries in insisting upon recognition of the right of a developing country to establish infant industries by imposing not only tariffs, but quotas and other import controls. The United States, whose own tariff was developed in the first period of its independence primarily as an instrument of economic development, was in a weak position to oppose the arguments adapted from Alexander Hamilton's *Report on the Subject of Manufactures*. Provisions were therefore written into the Charter by which the right to protect infant industries was recognized, subject to consultation with the International Trade Organization.

The conclusion to be drawn from these facts would seem to be clear. As the world emerged from the debris and dislocation of war and statesmen approached the task of organizing international economic relations in the postwar world, they were confronted with fundamental changes in its political and economic contours. Any attempt at reconstruction of former relationships would inevitably have failed. The methods that had proved useful in the past had to be re-examined and adapted to the new situation. In many cases new methods had to be invented. If world trade was to be restored, the major responsibility and initiative fell upon the United States, which emerged from the war with unparalleled economic strength and leadership. That strength, however, had become more dependent than in the past upon access to raw materials and markets. War demands had made serious inroads upon the reserves of raw materials that are vital both for war and for peacetime productivity. Moreover, both industry and agriculture in the United States were geared to world markets.

Western Europe, the organizing and focusing center of world trade in the past, had been impoverished and weakened to the point where it was not only incapable of leadership but was itself desperately dependent upon American assistance. The colonial empires which had been tributary to its strength were in process of breaking away from their tutelage. As the former colonial peoples groped toward political independence, they were threatened by economic disaster because of the breakdown of the organization upon which their recent growth had been postulated. They could not revert to the primitive simplicity of village agriculture and handicrafts. There were too many of them. The only path for them to travel was toward more complete modernization.

Meantime the U.S.S.R. had extended the range of its influence and consolidated its power on the great continental mass stretching from central Europe across Asia. Only the peninsulas of Europe and Asia lay beyond the control of this heartland. At strategic points along its boundaries—Finland, Austria, Greece, Iran, Manchuria, Korea—incidents quickly occurred to demonstrate how, like wrestlers sparring for a hold, the two giant powers were testing each other's will and strength. As long as the Mediterranean was held, the mineral riches of Africa lay beyond the Soviet grasp. But other great areas of mineral wealth, the Near East and southeast Asia, lay in the no-man's land along its borders. The peoples of this area were slipping from the weakened hold of the western European powers and were striving to build an independent life for themselves. Thus much more even than the welfare of half the world's population was involved in the choice they would make of allies in their struggle for freedom.

THE SOVIET CHALLENGE

While the economic structure of the U.S.S.R. and its prewar economic achievements are reasonably well documented, there is a great lack of factual and statistical information concerning economic developments in the Soviet Union since the outbreak of the second World War. The rise of the U.S.S.R. to political and economic power was a fact that should have been clear to prewar analysts. At the close of the second World War, there was no longer any doubt that the Soviet experiment constituted a challenge to the capitalist system of imperfect competition—a challenge which had already exerted a considerable influence on political and economic thinking far beyond the boundaries of the U.S.S.R. itself. As this influence extended, it evoked emotional reactions so that even the most prosaic and best-authenticated facts became charged with controversial implications. Nevertheless, it would be unrealistic to omit from any study of international economic relations the significant fact that the U.S.S.R. had become a potent factor in world economics as in world politics.

To a historian concerned with the rise and fall of civilizations, the Soviet revolution appeared as the first powerful reaction to the impact of the Industrial Revolution from the world outside the dominant north Atlantic countries. Such a reaction would be likely to be followed by others no less significant. For at least three centuries and, since the Industrial Revolution with overwhelming power, the impact of the Western civilization upon the rest of the world had been irresistible. The Russian revolution being based upon a denial of the capitalist philosophy of individualism, constituted the first counter-offensive to this Western drive. The forceful superiority of the Western world had been derived from the applications of scientific knowledge to industrial production. However, these devices were not necessarily dependent upon the economic institutions and principles of private enterprise. It seemed entirely possible that further reactions against those institutions and principles might come from Asia, and that, in meeting such challenges the European countries and the United States might have to modify their institutions. The philosophy that lay behind the French Revolution in 1789 had achieved some of its most practical applications during the nineteenth century in Britain and the United States which were in a position to apply what was useful in that philosophy by evolutionary modification of their institutions. It could happen that the lessons of the Bolshevik Revolution, shorn of their destructive features, might exercise a similar revolutionary influence over the Western civilization in generations to come.

No one can understand the fundamental forces now at work in the Western world who does not realize that they are primarily the result of individual enterprise and the sense of individual responsibility. In the development of the Western world and its impact upon other societies, the philosophy of individualism found expression in every aspect of human activity—in political democracy and the religious reformation, as well as in an economic system built upon private enterprise. But it was the economic pressures which most directly affected the non-European peoples. It was too soon to conclude that the driving force of individualism had lost its impetus because at the close of the second World War it was faced with complex difficulties of readjustment.

There could be no doubt that the challenge to individualism was real. If this challenge was not met successfully, its failure would signal the end of the historical era during which international trade had been the potent means by which the dominant manufacturing countries had organized the economic life of the world. The straits to which the western European countries had been reduced by the second World War left the United States and a few smaller countries of the new world as the repositories of the individualist tradition. Less than 10 per cent of the world's population carried this responsibility. In the U.S.S.R. alone, almost 10 per cent of the world's people were committed to the alternative of organization by communist principles. The remainder of the world's population, including the 50 per cent who lived in eastern and southern Asia, would weigh the merits of these philosophies and of their application in economic life.

The philosophy of individualism had not gone unchallenged even in the nineteenth century. The commercial success which had accompanied the British experiment in laissez faire gave authority to the economic doctrine of competition. Attention has been drawn to notable bodies of dissent from that doctrine. The Marxian dissent became the creed of the Soviet experiment. That creed was primarily a philosophy of history and not a blueprint of economic planning. Its significance might be seen most readily in the conflict, which ran through all the major political disagreements of the postwar period, concerning the meaning of democracy. The philosophy of individualism, enshrined in the Constitution of the United States, interpreted democracy primarily in terms of individual civil rights. Numerous attempts had been made just after the second World War to draw up a bill of human rights that would safeguard individual liberties. Those attempts encountered a Soviet definition of democracy that was based primarily upon the Marxian analysis of history as a reflection of class conflict. In the Soviet definition, the toleration of minority opinion and action—one of the most cherished ideals of Western democracy—constituted anarchy rather than democracy. The reason for this was that in the Soviet view it permitted entrenched minorities to thwart the purposes of democracy.

When the leaders of the Soviet revolution took the responsibility for government in 1917, they did so in the belief that they were fulfilling a historic mission and inaugurating the dictatorship of the proletariat.[7] Marx, who was no utopian, had not sketched any blueprint of communist organization. He had prophesied that when the revolution actually placed the leaders of the proletariat in power they would have "to pass through long struggles, through a series of historic processes, transforming circumstances and men."

The leaders of the Bolshevik Revolution realized from the beginning that they could not retain control of the state and use it to reorganize the economy along communist lines if they allowed foreign trade to continue unregulated. As early as December 29, 1917, a decree was issued instituting a system of licenses for imports and exports. This system quickly proved unworkable. It was replaced on April 22, 1918, by a state monopoly of foreign trade.

The revolution had aimed at replacing the capitalist system by a completely new organization of society, in which the means of production would be nationalized and used according to a centralized plan. Its leaders, therefore, could contemplate neither foreign investment in Russia, a flight of capital from Russia, exports by private individuals, nor imports competing with the products of state enterprises and state-regulated production. The first requisite of a planned economic system was complete regulation of all economic transactions with the outside world. In the circumstances, this meant a virtually

[7] The original meaning of the word, from the Latin *proles* meaning offspring, was "the lowest class of the community in ancient Rome, regarded as contributing nothing to the state but offspring." As late as 1871, it was used in this sense: "Athens had her slaves, Sparta her Helots, Rome her proletariat." Hence it was applied in modern times, often with a hostile connotation, to the poorest class of the community. The growth of the capitalist system, however, specialized its meaning as "that class of the community which is dependent on daily labor for subsistence, and has no reserve or capital; the indigent wage-earners; sometimes extended to include all wage-earners; working men, the laboring classes." It is in this specialized economic sense that Marx used the word.

complete severance of external contacts. This was particularly so since the conclusion of peace with Germany by the Treaty of Brest-Litovsk (March 3, 1918) had been followed by refusal of the Western powers to grant credit or to accept payments from the Soviet government even in gold. In 1913 the value of Russian exports had been 1,520.1 million roubles; by 1919 it had fallen to 0.1 million roubles. Imports which in 1913 had been 1,374 million roubles had fallen in 1919 to 3 million.

This severance of external contacts lasted until the first temporary trade agreements were negotiated with Britain in March, 1921. At this time, the New Economic Policy was enunciated by which the pace of collectivization was temporarily slackened and some leeway was given to private traders. There was controversy within the Communist party concerning the wisdom of retaining the state trading monopoly by which all external transactions were conducted, or of abandoning it in favor of a system of tariff protection. The decision to maintain the principle of a state monopoly, even during the period of the New Economic Policy, was very significant. There had been administrative difficulties in organizing the mechanisms of the trading monopoly. Some leeway had therefore been given to co-operative and other organizations within the U.S.S.R. It was not easy, in default of a complete planning system, to co-ordinate foreign trading transactions with the greater freedom of private transactions allowed for a time in internal trade. In an effort to attract foreign capital, experiments had even been made with companies in which foreign investors joined with U.S.S.R. government enterprises to operate foreign trade concessions; but these mixed companies were always supervised by the Foreign Commissariat and were ineffective. As the U.S.S.R. consolidated its organization, both imports and exports gradually increased. They never reached the prerevolution levels.

In November, 1925, a significant step in Russian economic policy was taken by merging the commissariats of foreign and internal trade. This involved a shift in emphasis from the external to the internal aspects of economic development of the national economy. Thereby the advantages to be gained from retaining all foreign trade in the hands of a state monopoly and from gearing that monopoly to the needs of the planned internal economy became decisive. Such a monopoly protected the internal economy and its price structure from disturbing external influences. It enabled the authorities to regulate by administrative decision both imports and exports in accordance with the requirements of the planned development of industry or in conformity with foreign policy. It freed the monetary system from strains originating in pressures on the external balance of payments. In 1926 measures were taken to make the Soviet national currency a medium of purely internal transactions, with all foreign exchange transactions monopolized by the state bank.

The decision to maintain a state trading monopoly had been a necessary step toward the planned development of communism within one country. That development, which was to take definite shape with the promulgation of the first Five Year Plan in October, 1927, had been foreshadowed in the early proposals for economic planning during the first years of civil war and foreign intervention. Complete control of all foreign transactions left the way clear for planned industrial development, unhampered by any attempt to maintain a currency system that had to be regulated by reference to the balance of international payments, or by dependence of the national market upon the world market.

It is important to stress these decisions by which the autonomous development of the Russian economy was made possible. The national planning of production, employment, and prices called for a comprehensive and complicated system for the allocation of productive resources. It was not easy to integrate the plans for rapid industrialization, to arrange a smooth flow of materials, to provide the necessary labor in the areas where industry was located, to organize the production and distribution of food, clothing, and shelter, and to create an adequate system of transportation. An immense bureaucracy had to be organized. There was a shortage of technicians.[8] There was a great deal of resistance, particularly among the richer peasants, but this resistance was ruthlessly liquidated. There was no complication on the monetary side. The Soviet economists had worked out and put into practice much earlier than the monetary theorists of western Europe, a monetary system which adjusted the volume of purchasing power to the planned output at planned prices. This was a system of

[8] Cf. Stalin's speech at the First All-Union Conference of Industrial Specialists, February 4, 1931, cited by A. Baykov, *The Development of the Soviet Economic System,* Cambridge, 1946, p. 175: "Not until there are among us, Bolsheviks, enough people familiar with techniques, economics and finance, shall we have real unity of control. . . . We must master techniques, we must become ourselves masters of the trade. In the period of reconstruction technique decides everything."

progressive but controlled inflation, designed to limit consumption, and by taxation or specially designed consumption-traps (such as cheap travel) to draw private expenditures into channels that did not interfere with the main program of planned industrialization.

The result was in many respects an impressive achievement, though it has been exaggerated by the statistical methods used to measure it. The League of Nations statisticians have pieced together from Russian statistics an index of manufacturing production, based on 1925–29 = 100. This index rose from 10.5 in 1920 to 702.7 in 1938. Thus between the base period 1925–29 and 1938, Russian production increased sevenfold. In consequence of this rapid increase the U.S.S.R. took second place among the world's manufacturing countries, displacing Germany and Britain.[9] The index used may seriously exaggerate the increase of production. But no one questions the fact that the U.S.S.R. today is second only to the United States in total industrial production.

Despite the increase in heavy industry, the U.S.S.R. remained a country of low productivity and living levels. In 1926–29, a rough estimate of the dollar value per head of finished factory products other than foodstuffs placed the U.S.S.R. figure at $22 as compared with $254 for the United States. The rapid rate of industrial development in the subsequent period reduced the gap, but in 1938 the per capita manufacturing production in the U.S.S.R. was still only about one-fifth of that in the United States. Moreover a large part of its productive capacity was devoted to the heavy industries rather than to the consumption goods industries, so that the living levels of the population were lower than the indices of manufacturing capacity might suggest. It has been estimated that the average Russian must work 583 hours while the average American works 38½ hours to earn

[9] The percentage shares in world manufacturing production, as calculated by the League of Nations, *Industrialization and Foreign Trade,* Princeton, N.J., 1945, p. 13, were:

Country	*1870*	*1913*	*1926–29*	*1936–38*
United States	23.3	35.8	42.2	32.2
Russia	3.7	5.5	4.3	18.5
Germany	13.2	15.7	11.6	10.7
Britain	31.8	14.0	9.4	9.2
France	10.3	6.4	6.6	4.5

For a searching criticism of the statistical methods used by the U.S.S.R. to exaggerate the extent of its industrial development, cf. Seymour Harris, et al., "Appraisals of Russian Economic Statistics," *Review of Economic Statistics,* XXIX, No. 4 (November 1947), pp. 213–46.

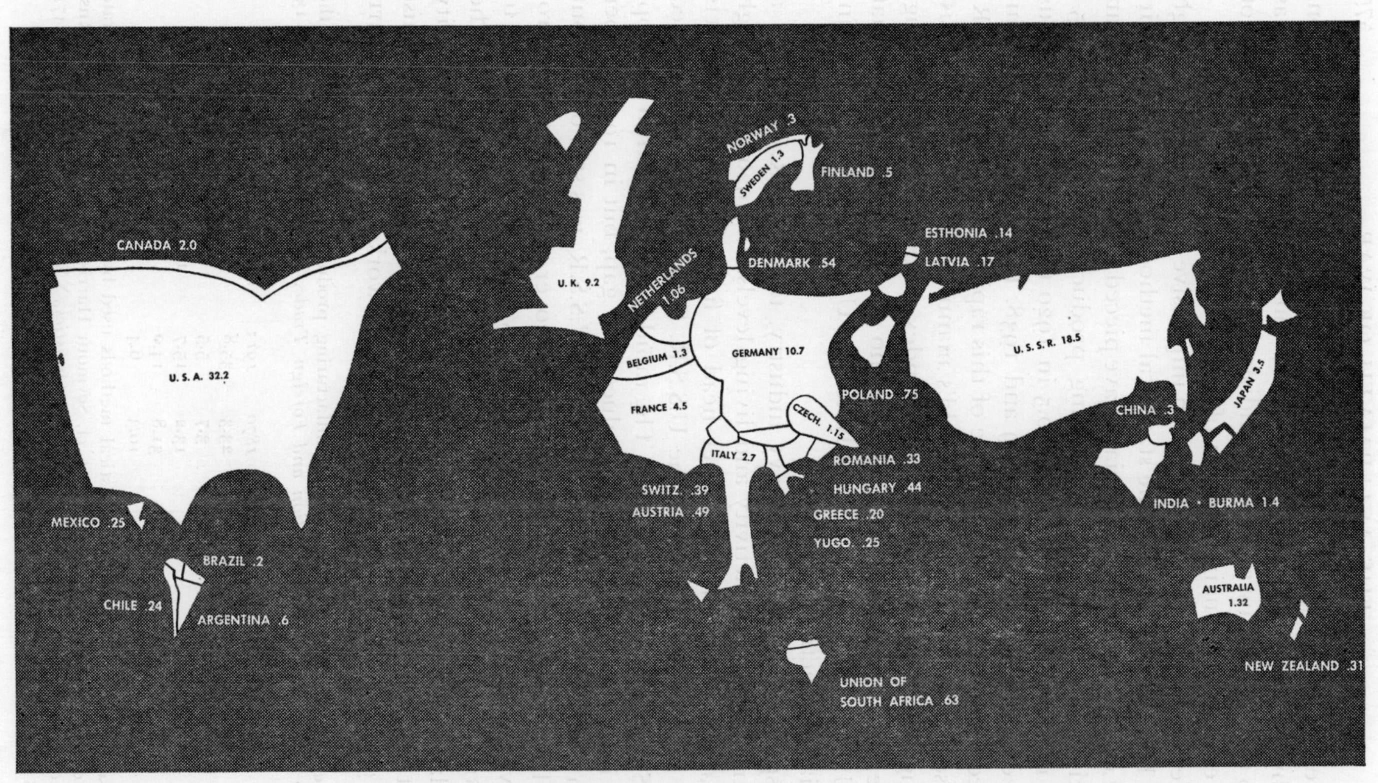

THE MANUFACTURING WORLD, 1938

The area of each country is shown proportionately to its share of world manufacturing production in 1938.

Source: Calculated from data in League of Nations, *Industrialization and Foreign Trade,* Geneva, 1945, pp. 13, 128 and 138 ff.

the price of a man's suit. While there must be a large element of uncertainty in such calculations, the differences are so great as to leave no doubt of the low living levels in the U.S.S.R.[10]

With vast territories, rich resources, and a large and rapidly increasing population, it needed only the accumulation of capital equipment and the acquisition of technical skills to place the U.S.S.R., despite its low living levels, second only to the United States in military power. The transformation of a peasant people into a potentially great manufacturing nation within one generation was a tour de force that will not be without significance particularly for other peoples in a backward state of industrial development.

The conduct of foreign trade from the inauguration of the first Five Year Plan in 1927 to the outbreak of war in 1941 set the pattern for Russian postwar policy. In November, 1930, the organization of the Commissariat for Foreign Trade had again been separated from the Commissariat of Supply of the U.S.S.R. The monopolistic corporations, into which the previous export and import joint-stock companies had been reorganized in February, 1930, now became the organs through which the Commissariat for Foreign Trade functioned. The import and export needs of different regions and industries were thus co-ordinated by the Commissariat and tied into the over-all plan of industrialization, the transactions being carried out by the export and import monopolistic corporations through the branches which they had been able to establish in various countries by treaty.

The onset of the depression had caught this reorganization at a critical point. It forced an effort to mobilize exports, even of goods that were in short supply on the home market, in order both to meet commitments for imports already contracted and to take advantage

[10] Cf. *United States News and World Report,* August 6, 1948. Other comparisons cited are:

Commodity	*U.S.S.R.*	*U.S.A.*
Cotton dress	32 hours	4½ hours
Man's shoes	108 "	9½ "
Automobile	3,750 "	1,085 "
Sewing machine	375 "	67 "
Radio	225 "	21 "
Wrist watch	337½ "	17½ "
Bicycle	467½ "	31 "
Red caviar	60½ "	12 "
Beer, 12-oz. bottle	1 " 40 minutes	6 minutes

of the low prices at which imports needed for the Five Year Plan might be secured. The volume of Soviet foreign trade rose to its highest levels in the crisis years 1930 and 1931. Thereafter it declined steadily.[11]

For a few months at the depth of the depression, increased Soviet exports caused a good deal of concern in some quarters. In order to obtain the foreign exchange necessary to pay for its planned imports, the U.S.S.R. had increased its exports and had lowered its prices particularly of grain, lumber, and oil. The concentration of these exports upon a few markets evoked protests from the rival producers in the markets most directly affected. But it must be remembered that Soviet purchases were a stabilizing influence in other areas. In 1931, the U.S.S.R. took about 90 per cent of the world exports of tractors and 55 per cent of all machine tools exported from the United States. In 1932, it took 81 per cent and 74 per cent, respectively, of all machine tools exported from Germany and England. This disturbance of world markets was a temporary phenomenon. As the depression passed away, Soviet imports and exports declined once more. During the depression there was an outcry against the low prices at which Soviet exports were offered; but it is now recalled that the U.S.S.R. also increased its imports in a period when world trade was being sharply curtailed. The moral has been drawn in some countries that a bilateral agreement for planned trade with the U.S.S.R. might be a good insurance against the possibility of future depressions.

A still further reorganization of the Russian state trading system was carried through in 1935. The main objectives of this were to give greater flexibility of operation to the trading corporations, and to transfer payments and negotiations from their foreign branches to the home offices in the U.S.S.R., thus reducing the administrative expenses payable in foreign currency, and keeping tighter control over transactions. As part of the over-all plan of industrialization, plans were drawn up for exports, for imports, and for the balance of payments over a definite period. The implementation of these plans in detail was made more flexible. But foreign trade remained, as it

[11] Cf. League of Nations, *World Economic Survey, 1931–2,* pp. 159–60. The physical volume (quantum) of Soviet trade is quoted by Baykov as follows:

Index of Physical Volume	*1929*	*1930*	*1931*	*1932*	*1933*	*1934*	*1935*	*1936*	*1937*
Exports	100	136	146	128	118	103	90	68	68
Imports	100	141	161	116	62	47	52	60	53

had been through the Soviet experiment, a subordinate and integral part of the planning of the national economy as a whole.

It has been claimed that this method of trading effectively correlated imports and exports and therefore avoided periodic strains on the balance of payments; that it provided effective protection for strategic and infant industries; that the calculation of import needs and export possibilities could be made in terms of national welfare rather than group advantage; and that economic policy was brought into line with other aspects of foreign policy. It is difficult, however, to draw any very clear conclusions from the Soviet prewar experience, since foreign trade was relatively small in volume, both as compared with that of other countries and as compared with pre-revolutionary Russian trade. A case could be made for the view that stability had been purchased at a high price in terms of progress, and that economic development might have proceeded faster if international contacts had been less restricted.

After the close of the second World War, the U.S.S.R. continued to rely upon centralized economic planning. Inevitably the war had caused heavy material damage—probably heavier in the U.S.S.R. than in any other theater. Many of the achievements of prewar planning, such as the Dneprostroi dam, had been destroyed. An effort was made to replace and supplement what had been lost. It was an ambitious effort. The magnitude of the war losses could be gauged from the targets set in the fifteen-year postwar plan. In that plan international trade played a role that was entirely subordinate. Russian expansion beyond the borders of the U.S.S.R. has attracted so much attention that it is important to stress the essentially nationalistic character of Soviet economic policy.

The extension of Soviet influence over eastern and central Europe led to parallel organization in those countries. The grain-growing Junker estates east of the Elbe—including the agricultural lands acquired by Poland as well as the east Prussian area acquired by the U.S.S.R.—ceased to be a source of food for the industrial towns of western Germany. The divided estates were used to support a greater number of families engaged in mixed farming. Any surplus of grain production for export was absorbed within the eastern European trading area. In the same way, the Danubian countries which formerly supplied western Europe with grain and other foodstuffs had less to export, and directed that export to the east rather than the west.

Within the zone occupied by the Russian armies, the U.S.S.R. insisted upon governments which were democratic in *its* definition. Those governments, whether they retained the forms of parliamentary democracy or were organized upon Soviet lines, established close economic relations with the U.S.S.R. Bilateral trade treaties which followed a common pattern were signed. The treaties usually scheduled the goods to be exchanged. The U.S.S.R. exported raw materials for the most part against machines and manufactures. It is true that the pattern was not invariable even in the first postwar year, since the U.S.S.R. agreed to supply Bulgaria with manufactures in exchange for tobacco and raw materials. In general, the Soviet Union drew heavily upon its resources east of the Urals—cotton, wool, and lumber as well as mineral ores—to pay for the capital imports needed for reconstruction.

The U.S.S.R. signed bilateral trade agreements during 1945 with Finland, Bulgaria, Yugoslavia, Romania, Poland, Hungary, and Czechoslavakia, and during 1946 with Iceland, Denmark, Sweden, and Norway. The closest trade relations were formed with Romania, Hungary, and Bulgaria by creating bi-national companies, with capital and management shared equally between the U.S.S.R. and the country concerned. In Romania, a bi-national company was created to control petroleum production, navigation, shipbuilding, hydroelectric production, air transport, lumber, glass, mining and metallurgical enterprises. In Hungary similar bi-national companies were set up to control bauxite, oil and petroleum refining, coal, power plants, machine and chemical factories, air and motor transport, to develop agricultural research, and to finance these enterprises through a joint bank. In Bulgaria, a bi-national company was formed to conduct mining. Such economic collaboration grew in part out of reparation claims or claims to German assets taken as war booty. It was obviously a powerful means of political as well as economic penetration. It could be a means of industrialization and of trade promotion as well as of close political and economic liaison.

The extent of Russian control over the countries which set up Soviet forms of government as did Bulgaria, Czechoslavakia, Hungary, Poland, Romania and Yugoslavia was difficult to appraise. A rift in communist unity had appeared in the summer of 1948 when the international organization of communist parties, the Cominform, denounced the leadership in Yugoslavia. However information was scanty and clouded by the forms of dialectical controversy peculiar to communist movements. There was evidently a struggle for personal power, complicated by nationalist differences and the outcome could not be foreseen.

The trade of the countries within the Russian military zone—Finland, Austria, and eastern Germany—was conducted by the familiar methods of bilateral barter and clearing agreements. In the spring of 1948 a communist coup had removed Czechoslavakia from this zone and made it an integral part of the communist bloc. The only other countries with which the U.S.S.R. managed to negotiate barter clearing agreements soon after the war were the Scandinavian—Denmark, Sweden, Norway and Iceland—and France. Before the end of 1947, Britain had been added to this list, but the French treaty was canceled. These bilateral agreements followed a regular pattern. They did not establish bi-national companies but scheduled the goods to be exchanged and stipulated the amounts to be traded over a period as long as five years. In the Swedish agreement there was also provision for a substantial credit against which the U.S.S.R. might buy machinery and other capital goods, to be repaid primarily by shipments of minerals and other raw materials. The volume of trade achieved under the Swedish agreement fell short of the planned amounts in the first years of operation. This was the result of disorganization immediately following the war. Also there was resistance within Sweden to the barter arrangements that had been made when the Swedish government anticipated that the United States would experience a sharp postwar depression as it did after the first World War.

There was no conclusive evidence that the U.S.S.R. would be able to develop the use of bilateral trade agreements as an instrument of economic policy outside the zone of its immediate strategic interest, or that foreign trade would be any more important to the U.S.S.R. in the future than it had been in the years between the wars. The most obvious explanation of Russian economic diplomacy since the war was that it had used every means possible of getting essential reconstruction imports from neighboring countries, without compromising the power position of the U.S.S.R. by bargaining for assistance from Britain or the United States. Considerable trade expansion might be undertaken at some future time. It was, however, unlikely that resources would be diverted to producing exports beyond the amount necessary to purchase essential imports. It was conceivable that the

U.S.S.R., once the worst pinch of postwar reconstruction was past, might pursue an aggressive trade policy as Germany did after 1933. But such a development seemed less likely than one in which other countries would seek to assure themselves of a stable segment of planned trade with the U.S.S.R.

CHAPTER XVII

NATIONAL ECONOMIC POLICIES

THE PARADOX OF PLANNING AND FREEDOM

IN FACING the new and more complex questions of economic policy in the modern world we must reckon with the fact that the institutions of government, as well as the location of population and industry, have developed to serve the needs of the past rather than the present. The whole administrative structure of government in democratic countries remains essentially as it was originally organized in the nineteenth century, a mechanism in which a premium is placed upon routine rather than initiative and enterprise. There are cases where the execution of new projects of government has been entrusted to agencies to which Congress has delegated large executive powers, and in the administration of which it has been possible to experiment with organization, personnel, and policies that approximate those of private enterprise. The Tennessee Valley Authority is such a case. But it has frequently happened that administrative departments recruited for routine operations have had responsibilities thrust upon them for the execution of which they must rely upon a temporary staff working within the established procedures of bureaucratic administration. The weaknesses of government economic intervention have come in large measure from the unimaginative use of unsuitable agencies originally created for entirely different purposes.

Before proceeding to examine the limitations upon effective national planning of economic policy after the second World War, it is necessary to state explicitly that the ideal of unrestricted freedom of enterprise leading to a competitive equilibrium was an illusion to which few students of society still clung. Enterprise had never been completely free of public control even in the nineteenth century, when the organizers of production by the new capitalist methods broke through the outworn system of state regulation. Their energy had been harnessed by legal, political, and social restraints. The laws of property and contract were fundamental to the capitalist system. To these there were gradually added safeguards for the protection of the economically weak who were unable by their own efforts to secure fair contracts with the strong.[1] The problem which always confronts society is to devise a form of social organization within which individual energy may be freed to serve the common good. The early nineteenth century laid stress on energy or enterprise, but was forced to realize that it must be harnessed and controlled. The twentieth century lays greater stress upon organization. In turn it may be forced to realize that effective organization depends upon its success in releasing energy.

At the opposite extreme from the anarchy of unrestricted energy is the exaltation of control or organization in the interest of something other than individual welfare—the interest of the state viewed as an end in itself. With its disregard of civil and political liberties the police state, whether organized for the aggrandizement of personal, group, or national power, or for the achievement of some ulterior, vague purpose such as the dictatorship of the proletariat is a perversion of organization. Like a cancer cell it develops without regard to the rest of the body politic. This philosophy, whether perpetrated by Hegel in the interests of the Prussian absolute monarchy or from the opposite angle by the followers of Marx in the interests of a supposed revolutionary mission, is bound to be rejected by all who value their freedom.

It is often argued in defense of this philosophy that the temporary suppression of civil and political liberties is justifiable, because the

1 It may be noted that Marx's attack upon the capitalist system postulated not only the degree of laissez faire in the labor market prevalent in British industry in his time, but the impossibility by political intervention of ever curbing injustice and exploitation. In fact the social history of the nineteenth century is largely concerned with remedying the abuses Marx attacked. Cf. K. R. Popper, *The Open Society and Its Enemies,* London, 1945, Vol. II, p. 117.

freedom they guarantee is formal and illusory unless it is completed by economic freedom. It may be conceded that the long struggle for political and civil liberties needs to be completed by the assurance to individuals of an economic status that enables them to make effective use of those liberties. But it is perverse to argue that the only way to achieve the economic freedom necessary to complete the political revolution is to abandon the political freedoms that have already been won. To acquiesce in the surrender of political and civil liberties in order to achieve vaguely defined economic liberties is not to forward but to betray the revolutions for which so much was sacrificed in the past.

Between these extremes of unfettered economic enterprise and organization for its own sake there is a whole range of situations reflecting freedom of enterprise and state intervention in combination. Every government today exercises its sovereign powers over economic activity. It does so by the enforcement of laws which govern the economic relations of its citizens, and also by its own activities in regard to such matters as taxation, monetary policy, and expenditures. The issue is not whether governments should intervene, but how and how much.

Immediately questions of economic intervention are raised, one important fact becomes clear. It is national governments with which we are concerned. There are no organs of world government and, as long as the world is divided by the conflict between communist and capitalist states, little prospect of developing world government exists. The United Nations and its associated institutions were frankly founded upon national sovereignty. They constitute machinery through which nation-states may co-operate if they so wish, but they have no power to compel sovereign states to co-operate. It is with the intervention of national governments to regulate private economic activity that we are concerned, and with the construction of international institutions through which national governments may consult and co-operate.

There are great differences in the democratic world in regard to the degree of intervention practiced by governments. The discussion which follows is confined to those forms of intervention that are compatible with the maintenance of political and civil liberties. It is not concerned with the authoritarian planning enforced by a police state. There is no reason to believe that such planning is economically efficient in the sense of releasing energy. But, even if it were, the suppression of individual liberties which it entails would be too high a price to pay. The evidence from such experiments as have recently been made in authoritarian planning—in Germany and Italy as well as the U.S.S.R.—is that two conditions are necessary for its execution. The authorities must be prepared to deal severely with those who even criticize the plans once adopted. And they must be prepared to insulate these national plans against disturbing influences emanating from foreign contacts. In practice this latter condition has meant placing foreign trade and all other foreign contacts under the strict supervision of state agencies.

The paradox of state intervention has been compared with the paradox of freedom. Too little restraint on individual freedom means the unbridled rule of the ruthless rather than the strong. Too much restraint may easily mean the rule of those who are able to gain control of the machinery of state. It is obvious that the concentration of political and economic power in the same hands is highly dangerous, and there is wisdom in watching carefully any such possibility. The political risks involved in large-scale government intervention are as important as the economic difficulties.

There is much confusion in the current controversies concerning the wisdom or unwisdom of national planning in a free society. Those who oppose the present degree of intervention which has resulted from the increase of state power since the first World War, are apt to underestimate the difficulty of restoring a larger measure of free enterprise. A simple illustration will demonstrate this. Opinion in the United States in trade union and agricultural as well as business circles is preponderantly opposed to government interference in the pricing process by which the production and distribution of goods is organized in a competitive system. But such government intervention is inevitable in the form of inescapable expenditures—such as interest on the national debt, veterans' allowances and pensions, social services and the cost of the armed forces—and of the taxation necessary to meet these expenditures.

Those who advocate an extension of government intervention so that it may become a system of complete national planning commonly underestimate the difficulties of planning and overestimate the instruments available for it. They are not content to invoke government authority to remedy flagrant abuses of the market process and to break through its bottlenecks. Their insistence is that such "planless planning" or piecemeal intervention is bound to be ineffective. Moreover, their advocacy of national planning is based upon assumptions that need careful scrutiny. Benevolence as well as wisdom in the planning authority is presumed. Such planning is also apt to presume the existence and validity of information that does not exist, or alternatively to stress the necessity for gathering such information in statistical form.[2]

The inadequacy of statistical information to explain current events is partly due to defects in the statistics but more seriously to the fact that statistics register the recent past rather than the present. It is necessary for planners to resort to the hazardous process of extrapolation. This means the projecting of estimates of future economic development and continuously correcting them. Those who control business enterprises constantly project such estimates for their own enterprises. In doing so they must take account of such estimates of national economic development as are available. Every improvement in the statistics upon which estimates of national income, employment, price levels, and other economic phenomena are projected, is useful, since these estimates must be one of the main bases for policy decisions both in private business and in government. Judgment as to the adequacy of statistical and economic knowledge for centralized national planning may vary. But any deficiency in such knowledge is less apt to lead to disaster if prediction is used as a basis for short-run and piecemeal decisions rather than for broad, long-run decisions involving the whole economic structure.

National plans whether partial or complete must safeguard themselves against strains arising from the balances of international payments. Theoretically national planning is compatible with international trade. In practice, such economic planning as has yet been attempted has led to increased restrictions upon international trade. This has been true of authoritarian planning, and of the partial planning in democratic countries. It was true of the national plans which

[2] Cf. Carl Landauer, "Prosperity, Democracy and Planning," in Abba P. Lerner and Frank D. Graham (eds.), *Planning and Paying for Full Employment,* Princeton, N.J., Princeton Univ. Press, 1946, p. 68: "National planning, therefore, is first of all a huge statistical job. A plan has to be compiled before it is carried out. Although this statement is certainly not more than a commonplace, it has often been forgotten, and much of the so-called 'planning' of recent years could with just a little exaggeration be described as attempts to carry out plans that did not exist."

were operating in the first postwar years in various western European countries. The dollar scarcity which became acute in the late summer of 1947 led to the imposition of severe restrictions on imports from the United States. In the same way, the national plans projected for such countries as China and India envisage a strict regulation of the balance of payments.

The condition in which national planning might lead to an expansion of international trade and a reduction of trade barriers has three aspects. It must be assumed first, that such planning would succeed in maintaining a stable level of full employment in all the planning countries; second, that all would plan; and third, that they would plan to increase international trade. This is essentially the obverse of the assumption that underlay the classical free-trade doctrine—that labor and resources displaced by imports would find alternative employment. The free traders were content to allow price competition to bring about such transferences through temporary unemployment and lowered prices. National economic planning does not contemplate the acceptance of any such necessities. Indeed, it contemplates continuous intervention designed to regulate the external balance of payments.

THE OBJECTIVES OF INTERVENTION

The first form of intervention after the Industrial Revolution to set limits to the working of free economic competition was the regulation of hours and conditions of labor. Statutes to establish and enforce minimum standards of industrial health and safety, hours and conditions of labor, holidays, methods of payment, and rates of wages, are now generally accepted in all democratic countries. Extensions of such legislative policy may still be debated, but seldom now on moral grounds. The wisdom of specific controls may be discussed. There may be grumbling about bureaucratic application of general principles in particular cases. But opposition to the enforcement of minimum standards of working conditions has passed into history.

In large part this came about because employers began to realize that efficiency is reduced and costs are raised by poor working conditions. On the other hand there is always some fear that labor costs may be increased beyond the levels of international trading competition. This fear remains a potent element in the cheap labor argument against free trade, but it has little basis in reality. As early as

1847, the British historian Thomas Babington Macaulay adduced the counterargument of efficiency that has proved unanswerable.[3]

Realizing that the freedom of contract in which they believed could not be achieved when workers dealt individually with factory employers, the classical economists defended the right of the workers to organize in trade unions. David Ricardo and J. R. McCulloch worked with Joseph Hume in the campaign for repeal of the Combination Acts by which until 1824 trade unions had been proscribed as illegal conspiracies. Subsequently legislation has been passed in all democratic countries to legalize and define the powers of trade unions, and this constitutes an even more effective form of intervention in the labor market than the passing of laws to enact minimum standards. The bargaining power thus assured to organized workers has been exerted primarily on the wage contract, but it has extended also to hours, holidays, apprenticeship, pensions and working conditions. This bargaining power has been a potent factor in raising actual working conditions beyond the minimum levels prescribed by law. As recent legislation in the United States indicates, there is room for controversy concerning both the legal rights guaranteed to trade unions and the use made of them by particular unions, but there is little disagreement now concerning the principle of unionism.

Inevitably organization was met by organization. The original reason for legalizing trade unions was to give the individual workers bargaining power equal to that of the employer. As the unions built up their industrial power, employers also organized on an industrial basis. As both labor and management began to exert political pressure, there developed organized groups to represent the political interests of agriculture. In most democratic countries today, economic policy is the result of bargaining, pressure, and conflict between these organized interest groups.

[3] In a speech on the Ten Hour Bill then before the House of Commons containing the well-known passage: "Never will I believe that what makes a population stronger, and healthier, and wiser, and better can ultimately make it poorer. You try to frighten us by telling us that, in some German factories, the young work seventeen hours in the twenty-four, that they work so hard that among thousands there is not one who grows to such a stature that he can be admitted into the army; and you ask whether, if we pass this bill, we can ever hold our own against such competition as this? Sir, I laugh at the thought of such competition. If ever we are forced to yield the foremost place among commercial nations, we shall yield it, not to a race of degenerate dwarfs, but to some people pre-eminently vigorous in mind and body."

The costs of industrial conflict between organized labor and organized management, though often exaggerated, have tended to mount, so that a new form of government intervention has developed in the public interest. Conciliation and mediation are the most usual forms of this intervention, but in some countries these are supplemented by voluntary or compulsory arbitration. Inevitably there tends to emerge a wage pattern—clearcut, as in Australia and New Zealand where the awards of the Arbitration Courts determining basic wage rates have the force of law, or vague, as in the United States where wage agreements are customarily set by the major units within each industry.

Two results follow from this trend toward collective bargaining under government auspices, or at least from the consciousness that public opinion is a factor in the bargaining process. In the first place, the individual worker tends to become more dependent on the organized group and less able to protect himself by individual contract with his employer, a dependence that is emphasized by union discipline exerted in a variety of ways. The second result is reduced flexibility of wage rates, individually and collectively. While this increased rigidity causes some difficulty in adjustment to shifts in the international balance of payments, theoretical analysis as to its effects on the business cycle is inconclusive, and the statistical evidence available does not seem to bear out the view that it increases the amplitude of business-cycle fluctuations.

The laws governing incorporation and particularly those which provide for limited liability and patent protection have set the pattern within which the large-scale corporations of modern times have developed and operate. The tendency toward industrial concentration would not have been possible without this kind of legislation. If a remedy is sought for bigness and for the monopolistic competition which results, it should be sought in a rewriting of the corporation and patent laws rather than in antitrust legislation. The increasing scale of modern business enterprises—with all the consequences it entails for the separation of management from ownership, for price determination, and for variability of output rather than prices—is set primarily by financial rather than technological considerations, and the roots of these financial considerations are to be found in the laws governing incorporation.

Still another form of intervention is to be found in the increasing tendency to create public regulatory bodies in specific fields of economic activity where the public interest is evident. For the most part, this regulation sprang from the defects of competition and the dangers of monopoly in what are now known as public utilities. The railroads provided an early example of the costs to investors and consumers of alternations of cutthroat competition and private monopoly. In the United States today the Interstate Commerce Commission, the Federal Trade Commission, the Civil Aeronautics Board, and the Securities and Exchange Commission may be cited as examples of federal bodies charged with specific regulatory functions.

Another aspect of this regulatory function is the provision of public service by government agencies. Many governments have taken over the operation of such public utilities as railroads, telegraphs, electric power, gas works, shipping, and correlated services such as trucking and insurance. This form of government intervention has been less evident in the United States than in most other countries. But even in the United States the government operates a long list of economic services, including the Panama Canal, the postal service, and shipping lines. There has been an increasing tendency for government operations to extend in the field of hydroelectric power. It is in the field of public utility operation that the greatest degree of political invention has been displayed, notably by the organization of public corporations combining public ownership and independent management and often crossing the boundaries of local government.

As the range of such government operations increases there is a tendency to restrict international competition. National enterprises as a rule give preference to local equipment and materials over and above existing trade barriers. Their prices or rates are often designed to promote national purposes as when, in the regulated bilateral barter trade of the interwar period in Europe, railroad freight rates entered into reciprocal bargains along with import duties, exchange rates, quotas, and subsidies. Nearly always such national enterprises are favored by special legislation or by direct or indirect subsidies such as the mail subsidies granted to United States ships. Inevitably, nationalization tends to reduce international trade. Where it is carried to its logical extreme in a completely socialized system, international trade is closely regulated. Then one of the most potent forces making for interdependence and co-operation in a peaceful world is weakened.

Of more fundamental economic importance than either the regulation of competition or the operation of specific industries, is the provision of services directly aimed at improving the quality of the population. Universal education, public health services, preventive medicine, low-cost housing, and various forms of social security services are now accepted as the responsibility of governments. In respect to education, the democracies have applied where it counts most an effective and practical communism—giving to each according to his need and taking from all in accordance with their ability to pay. The cost which has been growing rapidly and steadily is largely defrayed from general taxation. The high level of productivity where this investment in human capacity has been greatest proves the wisdom of the course followed. Following the same principle of investing in human capacity, democratic governments have intervened to promote health by medical and dental inspections, by the provision of school meals in certain cases, and by similar services.

Sanitary water supply and drainage systems, various forms of preventive public health action, the provision of public parks and facilities for cultural development, slum clearance and low-cost housing facilities are comparable extensions of economic intervention serving the general public interest. In the same way legislation has been passed for compensation to workers injured in industrial accidents, and for various types of pension schemes or insurance against misfortunes beyond individual control. Each extension of such intervention has been strenuously debated, as the need for some form of hospital and medical service is being debated at the present time. The social-service state is no longer a utopian speculation, but is being approximately realized in many countries. What has already been put into practice along these lines has a definite bearing upon international trade, since the costs upon industry directly and indirectly through taxation may affect at least in the short run the competitive position of a country on the international markets. If the levels of benefit are not set too high, the costs may be more than recaptured in the increased efficiency of the working force. It should be remembered in this connection that social security tends to strengthen the wage position of the organized workers and to increase the resistance to wage adjustments.

Finally it should be noted that there has been a constantly increasing tendency, particularly marked among the countries with high living levels, to restrict immigration on a selective basis. The immigration legislation of the United States is paralleled in many countries, and the nationalism of the totalitarian countries has been evident in the strict control of emigration, as well as immigration. It is even more difficult to get out of the U.S.S.R. than it is to get in. Moreover, the effort to restrict immigration is in most countries of high living levels strongly reinforced by protectionist devices aimed at restricting imports from countries with lower living levels. The burden of such import restrictions is borne largely by the more efficient export industries in the restricting country because their foreign markets are crippled. Such tariff protection further depresses living levels in the countries of low standards without effectively safeguarding the higher living levels of the protecting country.

All of the forms of intervention so far considered fall in the category of piecemeal social engineering, designed to remedy abuses and to create a society within which there is more equitable competition. Those who advocate national economic planning are emphatic in their view that such limited measures are inadequate and cannot function effectively in an unplanned economy. The advocacy of national planning is ordinarily based upon the belief that it will achieve a more abundant and a more stable economy, and also important subordinate objectives such as the conservation of natural resources. The chief driving force behind such proposals is clearly the painful experience of recent periods of economic instability and the belief that such instability is inevitable in an unplanned, competitive system. It is argued that the stabilizing of the economy will *ipso facto* eliminate the costs of periodic depressions and thereby make possible an economy of abundance. Among these costs unemployment ranks high, and it is full employment which is the major objective of proposals for national planning.

It is not possible to gainsay the importance of this objective. The advocates of free competition have long maintained and the classical economists always assumed that full employment would normally be achieved by the free play of economic forces in a flexible society. They were aware of the periodic fluctuations of business activity and employment in a cyclical pattern, but regarded them as temporary and self-correcting departures from a normal state of equilibrium characterized by an approximation to full employment. The experience between the wars of severe crises and, in some countries, of prolonged chronic unemployment on a large scale increased the desire of economists to investigate the causes which led to such deplorable results. In highly organized industrial societies mass unemployment is a political and social phenomenon of dangerous possibilities. It is improbable that free enterprise and free political institutions will emerge unscathed if another series of severe crises and prolonged mass unemployment should develop. There is general concern to forestall such a possibility.

During the violent fluctuations of the interwar years, analysis of the business cycle came to constitute a substantial body of economic theory. It had been possible for Marshall and his neo-classical disciples in the quarter-century preceding the first World War to present economic theory as an analysis of the forces determining a static equilibrium, to which relationships returned automatically if disturbed. The cyclical disturbances of those years were so mild that optimistic students of the subject concluded that they were coming under control.

The greater part of the theoretical discussion of business cycles in recent years has been concerned with the part played by credit. It should be noted that structural distortion, though sometimes affected by credit fluctuations, is not easily cured by credit policy. In these structural distortions which accompany a great war, credit movements are not the prime cause, though they may be the consequence, of distortion. Governments set out to mobilize the resources needed for war. In doing so they attract labor and capital and devote land to forms of production that are different from those needed in peace. It is not surprising, therefore, to find that business cycles have been of unusual severity in the periods following great wars.

The nineteenth century showed a clear alternation of periods when the general level of prices trended downward in a succession of sharp crises punctuated by mild recoveries and when the trend of prices was upward and the crises were mild. From 1815 to 1849 after the Napoleonic Wars, there was a long period of falling prices with sharp depressions in 1819, 1825, 1836, and 1847. It was the severe fluctuations of this period that led Karl Marx to conclude that capitalism would destroy itself in paroxysms of increasing severity. The next quarter-century, however, seemed to belie his prophecy. From 1849 to 1873 the trend of prices was upward and the depressions of 1857 and 1866 were mild interruptions of the general trend. In 1874, the first shock of reorganization, after the Civil War in the United States and Bismarck's triad of wars in Europe, ushered in another period of falling prices punctuated by the sharp crises of 1879 and 1890. Toward the close of this period, the stagnationist theory of a mature economy found expression once more as it always does in a period of violent economic fluctuation following rapid advances in technology.[4] The turning point came in 1895, and, from that year till the outbreak of war in 1914, the trend of prices was upward and the depressions mild. The severe crises of the interwar period in 1920–21 and 1929–33 were clearly aggravated by the structural distortions of the first World War.

The greater part of the theoretical discussion of business cycles runs in terms of the industrialized manufacturing countries where credit is highly organized and sensitive. However, fluctuations of agricultural and raw material production and prices play a large role in the periodic fluctuations of economic activity. Indeed the first explanations of periodicity ran in terms of harvest variations caused by climatic cycles. The great bulk of agricultural production which has entered into international trade in modern times has come from areas such as the United States and the British Dominions where farming is mechanized and makes full use of credit facilities. There is no reason, therefore, to seek for explanations of the cycle in agriculture radically different from those which affect industrial fluctuations.

It is important, on the other hand, to remember that world-wide distortion of agricultural production and prices was one of the major causes of the crises from 1929 to 1933. Economic policy in the interwar period was greatly influenced by agricultural interests. This is particularly true of the United States. In the nineteenth century the London merchant-bankers, whose primary interests were in world trade, held the strategic controls over international monetary policy. That power passed after the first World War to the United States, where agricultural interests exercise what in a crisis may become predominant political power. No one can understand the forces that

4 Cf. David A. Wells, *Recent Economic Changes,* New York, 1896, pp. 62–63: "There is very much that contributes to the support of the idea which has been suggested by M. Laveleye, editor of the 'Moniteur des Interests Materials,' at Brussels, that the industrial activity of the greater part of this century has been devoted to fully equipping the civilized countries of the world with economic tools, and that the work of the future, in this same sphere, must be necessarily that of repairs and replacements rather than of new construction."

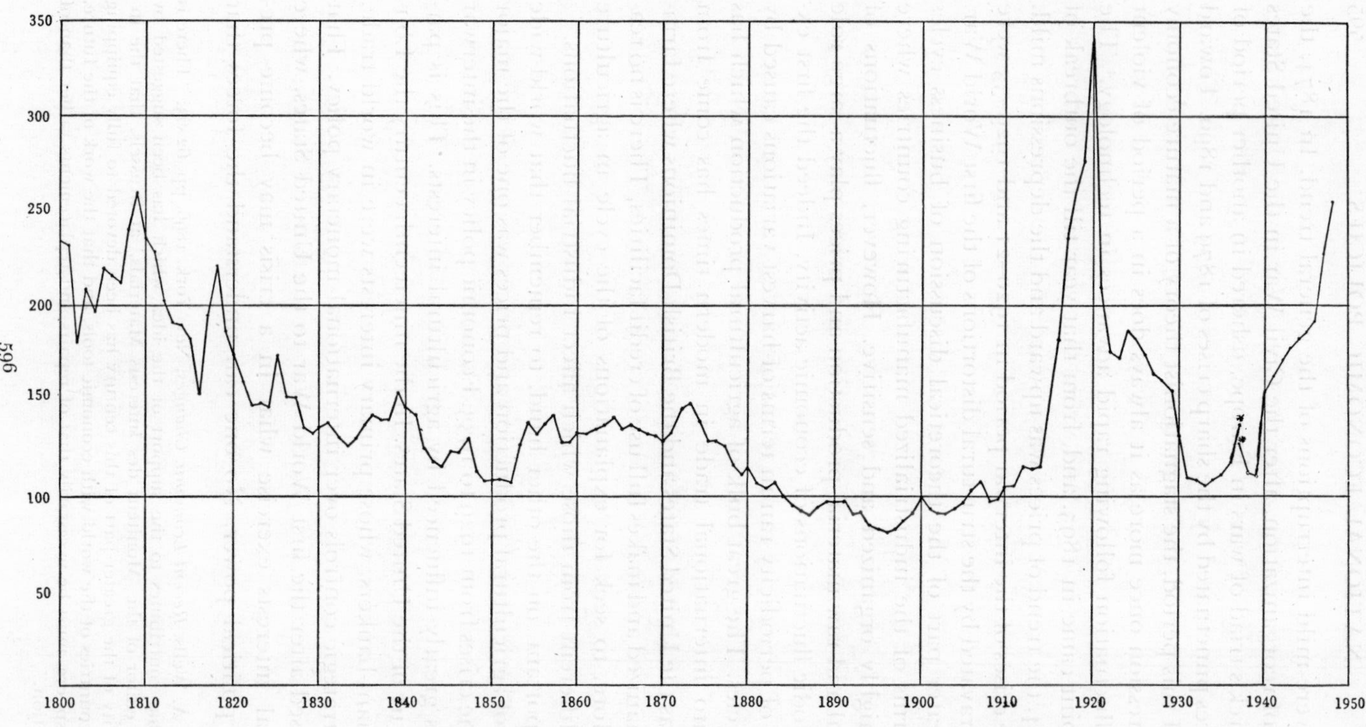

WHOLESALE PRICES IN GREAT BRITAIN, 1800–1948

Source: Walter T. Layton and Geoffrey Crowther, *An Introduction to the Study of Prices,* The Macmillan Co., London, 1938. Completed for 1937–1948 by plotting the wholesale price index of *The Economist* taken at mid-year and converted to base 1900 = 100.

determine policy in regard to the business cycle who does not study the currents of opinion reflected in farm congresses and agricultural journals, as well as in banking, industrial and economic literature.

Bearing these facts in mind, it is easier to understand the widespread expectation in Europe and elsewhere that it will be difficult for government or banking authorities in the United States to follow policies designed to prevent the upswing of cyclical development. Such policies demand firm pressure on interest rates, prices and through taxation on consumption levels. If a cyclical collapse of employment is to be avoided, it is necessary to damp down the period of expansion in which structural distortions occur. Whatever theory may be held concerning the ultimate causes of periodical booms and slumps, it is common ground that the most effective policy must concentrate on checking the boom before it causes such shifts of production and employment and such strains on costs and prices that a sharp restriction of production and employment leading to the possibility of widespread economic breakdown becomes inevitable. It is extremely difficult to envisage in the institutional setting of the United States concerted plans to raise interest rates, lower prices, and raise taxes in a period of expanding prosperity. Thus there is substance in the fear of other countries that involvement in the exuberant fluctuations of the United States economy may leave them defenseless in a crisis.

The proposals made for state intervention, designed to secure a high and stable level of employment, range all the way from observations of the trend of the cycle with the intent to recommend emergency action by governments and also by private economic interests to the laying down of general directives of economic organization and even to the detailed planning of national economies with power to enforce compliance. It would be easier to evaluate such divergent proposals if there were a greater measure of agreement upon the diagnosis of cyclical fluctuations, leading to surer prognosis of their development. There are many causes at work in the alternating periods of expansion and contraction of business activity, and the combination of factors operative therein varies from cycle to cycle. These facts do not warrant any great hope of finding simple formulae that will be applicable in all cases. But there are some aspects of the development both of expansion and contraction which seem to be common to all cycles and therefore suggest possibilities of remedial action. The general course of the malady is known, but experience has demonstrated that a variety of complications are to be expected from unpredictable combinations of causes, sometimes appearing suddenly and with far-reaching consequences. In these circumstances the most practical attitude would seem to be continuous study and readiness to recommend emergency action *ad hoc*.

This appeared to be the premise upon which the Council of Economic Advisers set up in the United States under the Employment Act of 1946 was operating. It was charged with the responsibility for diagnosis of economic tendencies, a responsibility which carried with it the duty of recommending to the executive branch of government appropriate courses of action and making its diagnosis of these tendencies clear to the public. Such a conception was modest, though responsible. Timing is of the utmost importance, both in early diagnosis and in giving time for recommendations to be weighed, and if adopted to take effect. To expect complete and unvarying success in diagnosis and still more in the recommending of practical action, would be asking for miracles. One may reasonably hope that constant watch by competent analysts may forestall many a dangerous development. In time such a watch may gain greater insight into the nature of the problem and win the confidence of those in government and business whose active co-operation is necessary if effective action is to be taken to control the instability of the economic system. This watch was installed at a crucial and dangerous moment when no one could be sure that the explosive elements in the postwar situation had not gone too far to be brought under control before the Council could effectively organize its procedures or mobilize the co-operative action needed to implement them. But the Council's procedures constitute a workable technique that should be continued. However, the chairman announced his resignation early in October, 1949, and it was not clear whether the Council would remain an instrument of economic analysis or become an instrument of party politics.

More active planning, such as that with which the British government experimented, did not suceed in avoiding acute difficulties. The preparation of an economic budget and the planning of a general framework of organization for the national economy, with due regard for available manpower and resources, was valuable in straitened circumstances where the national coat had to be cut according to the available cloth. The British procedure in 1947 was set out in two brief official papers. The first of these set out the general principles of planning for an economy of full employment but without resort to compulsion. The latter took stock of the manpower and resources available and set out the "targets and objectives for 1947."

The chief elements of the planning were stated succinctly.[5] General directives as to production and export targets were given, with fuller and more detailed planning for strategic industries—coal, power, steel, agriculture, transport, and building. Compliance with these directives was sought by resort to what was vaguely called "a number of methods, the combined effect of which will enable the government to influence the use of resources in the desired direction, without interfering with democratic freedoms." Broad objectives were set forth in relation to defense, payment for imports, capital equipment and maintenance, consumption, and public service, and these objectives were described as "very modest in relation to the nation's needs." The observation was added that "We cannot afford to fail on any of them. And they all depend upon coal."

Unhappily, it quickly became apparent that serious failure was imminent in at least the first four objectives. The government was forced to reduce its defense commitments, a shortage of dollars forced suspension of the convertibility clause in the financial agreement with the United States together with a sharp contraction of imports, the housing target was abandoned as impracticable, and consumption was cut down. It is of some interest to note that the principal difficulties of the planned program arose in connection with the international balance of payments, though the execution of the plan was clearly faulty at its critical points—manpower and coal. Subsequently the government took extensive powers to enforce compliance with its plans, particularly in respect to the transfer of labor from less to more essential industries.

In a planned economy there arises a problem not only of employ-

[5] Cmd. 7046, *Economic Survey: 1947*, pp. 5–6: ". . . the Government is seeking to develop a system of economic planning, of which the following are the chief elements:—

(i) An organization with enough knowledge and reliable information to assess our national resources and to formulate the national needs.

(ii) A set of economic 'budgets' which relate these needs to our resources, and which enable the Government to say what is the best use for the resources in the national interest.

(iii) A number of methods, the combined effect of which will enable the Government to influence the use of resources in the desired direction, without interfering with democratic freedoms."

ment, but of labor discipline. The compulsions for labor in the capitalist system are a combination of wage incentives and fear of unemployment. In a planned system the former is weakened and the latter disappears. But production remains essential. It would be premature to conclude that a war-weary and impoverished nation, which had borne more than its share of sacrifices in a destructive war, had demonstrated incapacity to plan because its first efforts in that direction failed to enlist the full co-operative effort necessary to realize the objectives. Subsequent modification of controls, coupled with the hope inspired by the beginnings of recovery, and the encouragement of American aid, called forth a magnificent collective effort of production. This difficult problem of labor incentives or discipline was by no means confined to the British plan.

During the war period, there arose among the workers in many countries an expectation that national planning would succeed in making postwar working conditions more stable and more remunerative than they had been during the interwar period. This expectation had been promoted by wartime prosperity as much as by wartime promises. Many governments had promised a wider variety of social benefits, including unemployment insurance, health and medical services, higher wages, shorter hours and better working conditions. To translate the higher wages into more abundant living—adequate housing, plentiful food supplies, cheap and abundant consumers' goods—required a great productive effort. This called for self-discipline on the part of the workers. That self-discipline and extra effort was not always forthcoming. In large part this was because of fatigue resulting from nervous and physical strain prolonged over many years. In part it was because a monotonous diet and a limited supply of drab austerity-type consumers' goods did not encourage greater effort, especially when taxes were high. A worker might just as well take out his satisfactions in leisure, when there was so little to buy if he did earn more.

In this connection, competent British economists severely criticized the sacrifices imposed upon the working population. The burden of their argument was that the government plans for capital development were too ambitious, that the present was being sacrificed to the future in a measure that entailed undue suffering and thereby made impossible the production necessary to realize the planned capital construction. A corollary to this argument was that the diversion of so much labor and resources to capital purposes, at a time when consumption goods were scarce, aggravated the inflationary pressures in the economy. The attack was leveled primarily at the policies of the Treasury in regard to public expenditure and taxation. In 1948, it was successful in bringing about some reduction of planned expenditure. While the need for modernization of equipment was very great, the critics of overambitious planning made good their point.

In large part, the difficulties of postwar planning arose from failure to secure a sense of participation in the national effort. Much merit has been claimed in this respect for the method adopted in 1946 by M. Jean Monnet in preparing a plan for reconstruction in France. In essence this program—which could hardly be called a national plan—was of the type of grass-roots dispersed planning by individual and group initiative, which had been advocated in the United States by the Committee on Economic Development. Regional and industrial groups made the first fact-finding studies and projected limited targets based on existing labor, equipment, and resources. These specific targets were built into a more or less co-ordinated national project. At this stage the needs for new capital investment, for more coal and electric power, and for careful regulation of the import and export balance were superimposed on the cumulation of specific plans. The important achievement was not the precise calculation of targets, but the degree of co-operation and the sense of participation gained among trade unionists and industrialists, as well as among government officials. The project as a whole was not devised by the bureacracy, but grew out of consultations among the rank and file of industry.

The importance of securing a widespread understanding and sense of participation in the formulation as well as the execution of any national plan is self-evident. It soon became evident in France that planning of this character throws into sharp relief a question of a different order. What was needed in the postwar state of disequilibrium was not a rebuilding on existing foundations, but a recasting of those foundations. The quickest but not necessarily the best way to restore a ruined city is to urge and assist each property owner to rebuild upon the city plan of the past. If such methods of reconstruction are followed in European industry and agriculture, without regard to the changes required to conform to the war-induced shifts in international equilibrium, there is grave danger that the mistakes of the last postwar period will be repeated. It is clear that the breaking down of economic barriers within Europe will not suffice. If the world is not to be faced once more with agricultural and industrial surpluses as it was from 1925 onward, an effort must be made to allow for the readjustment of production that would be brought about by competitive international enterprise. It was this which Lord Keynes had in mind when he wrote in his last published article that "in the long run more fundamental forces may be at work, if all goes well, tending towards equilibrium, the significance of which may ultimately transcend ephemeral statistics." This caused him to issue the warning that, "if we reject the [classical] medicine from our systems altogether, we may just drift on from expedient to expedient and never get really fit again."

The dilemma in which every country was placed after the war was the necessity of accepting as great a measure of adaptation to the new competitive situation as was possible without inflicting upon substantial segments of the working population such distress and unemployment as was politically intolerable. The pattern of employment which resulted from war mobilization had to be changed if it was to prove compatible with international competition. But the pattern could not be changed suddenly by allowing competitive forces to work freely causing bankruptcies and unemployment. It was evident that the battles of economic policy for some time after the second World War would be fought around the issues of unemployment. This in itself was an indication of a disorganized world. The decisions to be taken were decisions of national policy. The disorganization was largely the result of a breakdown in international economic relations, and the international repercussions of national policies had to be considered very seriously.

Before attempting to outline these international issues it is necessary to consider the instruments through which national governments might attempt to implement their policies. One instrument above all others was of particular importance. Monetary and fiscal policies were the most potent instruments available to national governments. Both had undergone revolutionary changes during the interwar period. With the development of central banking practice, and in the setting of swollen public debts and high taxation, governments everywhere had asserted a greater degree of control over the mechanisms of credit. This assertion of controls was the chief reason why the theories of the balancing of payments, which assumed semiautomatic adaptation of monetary supplies and price levels to the shifting currents of international trade, had become of doubtful validity. These positive monetary and fiscal policies, pursued independently by national governments aiming at definite objectives such as full employment, had to be reckoned with. Hence it becomes necessary to outline the development of monetary theory in recent years.

THE KEYNESIAN INFLUENCE

The first World War had caused important shifts in economic and financial power—particularly the rise of New York as a leading center. The gold standard system, under which stability of the exchange rates had been maintained by adapting national monetary policies to strains on the balances of payments, had broken down. In all the belligerent countries, the existence of swollen and largely unfunded public debts had created a budgetary situation that made it impossible to accept the sharp corrections of interest rates and price levels that would have been entailed by orthodox gold-standard policies. The United States was less affected than most countries, but for Britain in particular, the times were out of joint. It had been the financial and trading center of the world and its continued prosperity depended largely on regaining that position.

Thus the monetary history of the first postwar decade was largely concerned with the attempt to reconstruct the prewar gold standard, to finesse the weakness of the London money market, and to devise expedients by which conflicting policies in other financial centers might be reconciled without exposing this weakness. During this decade the British monetary authorities had been faced with a constant succession of urgent problems of short-run monetary management. In the middle of the decade they had taken the fateful decision to impose on the already weakened national economy a sharp deflation caused by a return to the gold standard at the prewar parity. This decision had been motivated largely by the desire to restore London's prestige and power as the leading financial center of the world. On March 5, 1925, the *Times* had argued that "once back on the gold standard we should find that foreign balances which have been kept in New York should return to us and our financial and monetary power would be greatly increased."

Even prior to the return to gold, the Bank of England had raised its discount rate in an effort to attract foreign balances. These foreign balances which were of a kind and a magnitude unknown before 1914, provide one of the principal clues to an understanding of the monetary controversies of the interwar period. It is also the key to much of the later developments in monetary theory. The dislocations of the first World War period and the uncertainties of reconstruction after 1918 had caused the nervous *rentier* capitalists of western Europe, who had inherited the financial claims upon continuing production built up in the prosperous decades when Europe was the world's banker, to concentrate upon preserving the capital value of those claims. In order to do so they turned them into cash or liquid balances and transferred them from one financial center to another in search of security rather than earning power.

The volume of funds thus hoarded was very large even during the years 1925–29 when the loan flow from the United States to Europe had enabled the gold standard to function and a considerable measure of reconstruction to be carried out. When this loan flow ended abruptly in October, 1929, and the strains upon the European economies—staved off momentarily by banking accommodation and the suspension of war debt and reparation payments—culminated in financial panic, the volume of these idle short-term international funds rose to larger proportions. At the beginning of 1931 they were estimated by the Bank for International Settlements as more than 50 milliards of Swiss francs (over $11 billion).

The importance of this problem of refugee capital or hot money, the idle balances of the international economic system, on a scale hitherto unknown, can hardly be overstressed. It was particularly harassing to the British monetary authorities who were striving desperately to restore the earning power of London as the financial center of the world, and at the same time to reconstruct the trading world in which that center might function profitably. The counterpart of the monetary difficulties presented by these idle balances was unemployment of resources and particularly of labor. Both had their roots in the dislocations and distortions of international economic relations after the first World War.

The course of the interwar monetary controversy can be illustrated from the development of J. M. Keynes's writings. Keynes achieved fame in 1919 with the publication of *The Economic Consequences of the Peace,* an attack upon the economic aspects of the peace settlement that rapidly became a best-seller. He followed up this work with a succession of books, pamphlets, official reports, journal and newspaper articles and letters which made him the most successful pamphleteer of modern times. His dominant interest lay in the formulation of policy rather than its rationalization in theory. One of the main characteristics of his intellectual adventurousness was his readiness to consider fresh solutions for the shifting aspects of a continuing problem.[6]

Flights of capital prompted by political and economic insecurity meant low levels of investment and hence unemployment. The British monetary authorities strove desperately to channel this hot money back into productive investment. In doing so they built credit commitments upon the insecure foundation of refugee funds. They were always conscious that the level of employment in England could be sharply reduced by a sudden withdrawal of this hot money. Keynes had foreseen these dangers and the argument of his *Economic Consequences of the Peace* had been a plea for restoring the kind of trading world of which Britain had for so long been the center and for a treatment of Germany which would enable her again to play her indispensable role in that world. He was, as E. A. G. Robinson points out, "primarily pro-English and pro-world," not "pro-German."

His other writings at this time, particularly the articles contributed in 1922 to the *Manchester Guardian Supplements,* had proposed a general exchange stabilization at parities appropriate to the changed postwar international equilibrium. From that time forward he consistently opposed all deflationary policies. His antagonism to the *rentier* capitalist which was to color all his subsequent work was expressed in a variety of arguments and proposals. In 1920 he had advocated either a capital levy or a reduction in the stipulated rate of

[6] Cf. L. R. Klein, *The Keynesian Revolution,* New York, 1947, p. 31: "It was not his theory which led him to practical policies, but practical policies devised to cure honest-to-goodness economic ills which finally led him to his theory." And E. A. G. Robinson, "John Maynard Keynes, 1883–1946," *Economic Journal,* March, 1947, p. 45: "A careful study of Keynes will, I believe, show him to have been remarkably consistent in his strategic objectives, but extraordinarily fertile in tactical proposals for achieving them. Like a resourceful tactician, he would probe, try to find the enemy's weak points; if repulsed he would quickly fall back and regroup and put in another attack elsewhere. But in the end his victory was complete. Full employment of resources has become the national objective; some would say it has obscured other objectives. Ordered flexibility of exchange rates has become the agreed world system. Low interest rates have become the official policy to the extent that former advocates now begin to fear."

interest on the public debt. This was consistent with his argument for the scaling down of reparation payments and war debts, with his advocacy of devaluation in the *Tract on Monetary Reform* (1923), and above all with the vehement fight he made in 1925 against the British return to the gold standard at the prewar sterling parity. It was significant that the argument of his *Tract on Monetary Reform* turned on the necessity of sustaining the British price level and the level of domestic employment. If the *rentier* claims on current production could not be reduced by direct methods, he was in favor of reducing them by stimulating a rise in the general level of prices, even at the cost of lowering the exchange value of sterling. In his view, it was worse "in an impoverished world, to provoke unemployment, than to disappoint the rentier." [7]

Unemployment persisted in Britain throughout the years of the restored gold standard from 1925 to 1931. In large measure it was structural, caused by the shifts of world production. The export industries did not recover their former place in world markets. Keynes continued to oppose any suggestions of deflationary policies, but he was searching for more direct methods of attack on the problem of chronic unemployment. He had become convinced that the classical policy of wage reductions would lead to severe industrial conflict without adding to employment opportunities. It was his view that wage reductions would diminish the national income and reduce employment opportunities because the reduction in the purchasing power of the workers would be multiplied by the reduced income of those who produced the goods they purchased.

The bitter general strike of 1926, which followed the deflation imposed by returning to the prewar gold parity, was broken, but it confirmed Keynes's prediction that the workers would resist lower wage rates with all their organized strength. The exasperation he felt with those who continued to offer the classical explanation of unemployment as caused by wage rigidities explains in large measure the violence of his later attack upon the classical theories. Before the economic breakdown in 1929–31, he had advocated a large-scale program of public works. As the depression deepened and he foresaw that it would develop into a long and severe process of cumulative deflation, he advocated still more drastic measures. For a brief period that came unfortunately at a critical turning point in British political

[7] J. M. Keynes, *Tract on Monetary Reform*, London, 1923, p. 40.

history, he was willing to throw overboard his free-trade convictions. Thus when it came to a choice between inflicting further deflation and unemployment on the British economy or sacrificing the attempt that had been made to restore the world trading system, he was ready to make the sacrifice. His advocacy of protection in 1930 and 1931 had been based on the belief that the adoption of import duties, in order to safeguard employment in the short run, to lower real wages, and to provide a flexible source of revenue, might avert the necessity of abandoning the gold standard. In the political circumstances of the time, his arguments were seized upon by those who were bent upon tariff protection. In the end both free trade and exchange stability were lost. While his advocacy of protection continued beyond the immediate crisis, he reverted to the free-trade position in 1944.

In the early years of the great depression, Keynes had continued to advocate monetary devices to lower interest rates and to force money into circulation. He had welcomed with relief the British conversion of 1932, by which £2,000 million of war loan had been converted from 5 per cent to 3½ per cent. He had been one of the first to recognize the turning point of the depression in the summer of that year. But the problem of idle balances and unemployment continued. There had been a great flight of capital from New York back to London after the depreciation of sterling in September, 1931. As long as the dollar remained on its old gold parity, the Exchange Equalization Account had been able to hold down the exchange value of sterling by buying the offerings of foreign currencies. Thus over £70 million was added to the Bank of England's gold holdings during 1932. But after the devaluation of the dollar in April, 1933, the value of sterling was no longer controlled. Before the end of 1933 it rose above the pre-1914 parity. It had again become evident that the maintenance of employment in Britain was threatened by the handicap imposed upon exports by an overvalued currency.

Keynes had thrown all his influence against proposals to stabilize the exchange rates at the Monetary and Economic Conference held at London in the summer of 1933. He was convinced that pegging the pound again on gold or on the dollar would revive the conflict between policies aimed at expanding employment in Britain and those dictated by the necessity to maintain stable exchange rates. In fact what happened gradually in the years that followed was *de facto* stabilization of the exchange rates practically at the prewar dollar-sterling parity.

In the meantime Britain had abandoned free trade. The British tariff had been developed into a formidable instrument for the protection of local industries, and new instruments of trade regulation had been adopted. Three such instruments were of particular importance. While the war-debt conversion was being prepared in the first half of 1932, a general ban had been placed upon the flotation of foreign loans, and although this ban was modified in October, 1932, in respect to loans within the British Empire, it was never lifted. Thus Britain had abandoned her traditional role as the source of long-term capital for countries outside the area of her immediate trading interests. Also the Ottawa agreements had been signed in July, 1932, so that the British Commonwealth and Empire had been turned into a great trading area within which trade was subject to lower duties than those imposed on imports from non-British countries. Then in the next few years a series of bilateral clearing and payments agreements was signed with the main suppliers of British imports in Latin America and northwestern Europe. Within this enlarged sterling area, including not only the British Dominions and colonies, but also those countries which had aligned their currencies with sterling, Britain was able to safeguard her essential markets.

It was more than a coincidence that the turning point in the development of the Keynesian economic theory may be dated from the latter part of 1933. Keynes was in the closest touch with events. His business activities made him keenly aware of the imponderables in the money market. Among those imponderables was the continuing and unpredictable influence of nervous, refugee capital upon the money market and upon the exchanges. He made it clear that it was not the flow of capital into industrial long-term investment that had determined his thinking. Rather it was the preference for liquidity shown by owners of monetary claims. This hoarding on a great scale was not only a continuing cause of chronic unemployment, but the cause also of potential exchange instability. Like the loose gun in Victor Hugo's novel, it shifted with the storm and threatened to sink the ship.

The subsequent development of economic theory in every country has been dominated by the theoretical form into which Keynes cast his rationalization of the questions raised by this problem of loose, uninvested funds. In order to shock professional economists into reexamining the assumptions of their thinking, he published in 1936 his greatest tract, *The General Theory of Employment, Interest and*

Money. Its main ideas had been crystallizing at least since 1933. They had been foreshadowed by journal articles, but they were couched in such provocative language that they produced the effect of an explosion.[8] The vast discussion which followed publication of the *General Theory* and the extraordinary flood of articles which appeared after its author's death in 1946 prove that he achieved his main object. Economic theory will never be the same as it was before 1936. But it would be a mistake to treat the *General Theory* as the final exposition of Keynes's own thought.[9] It was an attempt to force consideration of neglected economic issues by devising new theoretical tools of analysis. As its author himself once wrote: "The Theory of Economics does not furnish a body of settled conclusions immediately applicable to policy. It is a method rather than a doctrine, an apparatus of the mind, a technique of thinking, which helps its possessor to draw correct conclusions." [10]

Some economists still contend that there was nothing essentially novel in the Keynesian theory except the striking manner of its presentation, and the context of policy recommendations derived from it. Whether this contention is true or whether, as enthusiastic Keynesians maintain, a revolution had been wrought in economic theory, is not of great importance. What is significant is that the emphasis which Keynes placed upon maintaining the aggregate income of a com-

[8] In part Keynes's violence was a deliberate device to shock his fellow economists out of what he felt was a complacent tendency to accept the classical teaching without regard to the assumptions upon which it was based. These, Keynes felt, no longer corresponded with economic realities, and therefore led to disastrous policy recommendations. Cf. E. A. G. Robinson, *op. cit.*, pp. 40–41: "To the world outside, however, *The General Theory of Employment, Interest and Money* came as a shock. Keynes had meant to shock. An ordinary book, wooing with sweet reason, would not have fulfilled his purpose. . . . For if he was right in his analysis, the basic assumptions of the automatism of the economic system were at fault. Because he believed it necessary that economists should face these issues, he deliberately heightened differences and emphasised controversy."

[9] Cf. E. A. G. Robinson, *op. cit.*, pp. 41–42: "To those in Cambridge, the whole process seemed much more continuous, and both the *Treatise* and the *General Theory* appeared much more as instantaneous photographs of an athlete in action than as carefully posed studio pictures with every limb perfectly set. Already before the war, Keynes was moving ahead again, as in his contribution to the Irving Fisher *Festschrift* (*The Lessons of Monetary Experience*), and was finding himself prepared to accept certain developments or modifications of his ideas propounded by writers in England, America and elsewhere. It would be a disaster, and wholly alien to Keynes' own concept of the academic pursuit of truth, if the effect first of the interruption of the war and then of Keynes' own death were to be to establish for the first time a fixed and immutable creed that it is wrong to criticise or change or develop. I can conceive no memorial to Keynes' teaching that he would more passionately have assailed."

[10] Preface to H. D. Henderson, *Supply and Demand*, Cambridge, 1922.

munity directed the thinking of economists into this channel. He constructed a simplified model of the economic system. Necessarily this model was a kind of skeleton very different from the complicated body of individual transactions in the real world. The task of the theorist is to discover essential relationships among the abstract symbols that he uses to typify the aggregates and averages of economic activity distilled from observation of the endless variety of actual events. In order to do this he must select a relatively small number of symbols that throw light on the problem he wishes to study. Any number of such theoretical models can be constructed. Their usefulness depends on whether the factors selected for study throw light upon what happens in everyday life.

The heart of the Keynesian analysis lies in its emphasis upon the possibility that the demand of business organizers for capital goods may not be adequate. It may fall below the volume of capital goods that could be made available if real income was at a level calling for full employment of resources. If the organizers of industry do not anticipate sufficiently profitable and secure returns to warrant their embarking on adequate programs of new investment, the aggregate national income may fall to a level at which the capital goods produced equal their demand. This causes both underemployment of resources and a level of consumption lower than could have been achieved at full employment. It follows, in Keynes's view, that modern economies have an inherent tendency to self-degeneration. Savings will tend to increase relatively to total production, while the needs for investment remain a constant proportion of that total, so that a widening and dangerous deflationary gap develops. Keynes did not take into account the possibility that, once full employment is reached, higher per capita incomes will cause an increasing substitution of capital equipment for labor—unless improved technology with lower capital costs proves capable of meeting the increased consumer demands. If this possibility develops, there may be an increase in the rate of investment which will more than offset the tendency for savings to increase.

This type of analysis was in the tradition of economic theory and threw new lights into dark corners of the economic system. It also tended to obscure other important relationships than those emphasized by the setting up of the particular model that was investigated.

Hence it should be handled cautiously and be supplemented by close scrutiny of the assumptions explicitly or implicitly made in selecting the variables and setting up the equations in which their relationships were stated. Care should be taken also not to overlook the possibility that the composition of the aggregates may change with their size. It is very easy to focus attention on particular aspects of the economic system, such as unemployment, which are important in the circumstances of a given period, to the neglect of other significant phenomena, such as productive efficiency, price changes, and the structural stresses and strains within the aggregates and averages used as the elements of a theoretical model.

Thus employment turns out to have a very complex structure. Attempts to clothe such symbols as "income" and "employment" with concrete reality and to use these statistical estimates to predict economic developments were not conspicuously successful at the close of the war period, and there is much still to be done before analysis can be translated into policy. Unhappily decisions of policy based on statistical estimates that were falsified by actual developments greatly complicated the postwar situation. Moreover the Keynesian analysis as it was dynamized by Keynes's followers is predominantly concerned with short-run disequilibria. The secondary and often more important long-run repercussions upon economic activity of actions taken to achieve short-run objectives cannot be neglected with impunity. In both these respects the model of the economic system constructed by Keynes, and still more the models constructed by some of his followers, are apt to lead to policy recommendations that have a bias toward both nationalism and collectivism.

It is necessary to draw attention to some implications, not indeed of the theoretical apparatus which Keynes devised since this is merely an instrument of analysis, but of the use made of it in arriving at recommendations for practical policy. It is possible to claim the authority of the master for different policies, and to buttress that claim by reference to practical proposals to which he committed himself from time to time. There would seem little doubt that Keynes was a consistent liberal, opposed alike to financial privilege and state socialism. He was convinced that industrial capitalism, based on free enterprise, could and should be preserved. He saw the development of private financial control over industrial organization as a menace to the preservation of free enterprise, since it created the chronic unemployment that was eating away the moral fiber of the workpeople, and also destroyed the stability of international economic relations. In order to remove this menace he was prepared to use the powers of government drastically.

His authority has been invoked in support of the collectivist and nationalist elements of national economic planning, primarily by monetary manipulation. If full employment, in the strictest definition of that elusive phrase, comes to be regarded as the single dominant objective of economic organization, it is possible to use the Keynesian analysis to demonstrate that its achievement must entail socialization. In the same way, it is possible to demonstrate that the achievement and maintenance of full employment demand national planning which will involve manipulation of the balance of payments. That these were not the implications which Keynes himself drew just before his death is obvious enough from the closing paragraphs of his last piece of professional writing. Scattered comments for several years back warranted his statement that, "I find myself moved, not for the first time, to remind contemporary economists that the classical teaching embodied some permanent truths of great significance, which we are liable today to overlook because we associate them with other doctrines which we cannot now accept without much modification." The context of this remark made it clear that he had in mind "the sincere and thoroughgoing proposals, advanced on behalf of the United States, expressly directed towards creating a system which allows the classical medicine to do its work."

The proposals to which he referred have since been implemented by the *General Agreement on Tariffs and Trade* negotiated at Geneva in 1947, and by the *Draft Charter for an International Trade Organization* negotiated in 1948 at Havana. Keynes lent the full weight of his authority to these attempts at creating a freer world-trading system. While he was clear that exchange variation and over-all import control must be retained, he advised caution and moderation in their use so that they might not defeat, but "implement the wisdom of Adam Smith." [11] It is difficult to find in these wise words any support for economic or monetary nationalism. Neither the nationalist nor the collectivist elements in national economic planning can be reconciled with them.

11 Lord Keynes, "The Balance of Payments of the United States," *Economic Journal*, June 1946, pp. 185–86.

THE INTERNATIONAL REPERCUSSIONS OF PLANNING

The issues raised in this chapter had a very direct bearing upon questions of international economic policy at the close of the war. In the lend-lease agreements of 1942 setting down the principles upon which settlement of mutual obligations might later be made, the allied governments including the U.S.S.R. had agreed that at the close of the war they would take action to expand production, employment, and trade and would consult together regarding means to eliminate discriminatory trade policies and reduce trade barriers. In 1945 the United States government, in pursuance of this pledge, published its *Proposals for the Expansion of World Trade and Employment*. These proposals were accepted as a basis of negotiation by the British government, were made part of the Anglo-American financial agreement of December, 1945, and were formally approved in principle by the governments of France, Poland, and Czechoslovakia. They were later elaborated into the form of an international charter and submitted to the United Nations.

A preparatory committee of seventeen nations discussed this draft charter at a conference held at London in October-November, 1946. A second preparatory conference met at Geneva from April 10 to August 22, 1947, and agreed upon the provisional text of a revised charter. The twenty-three nations present signed a *General Agreement on Tariffs and Trade,* incorporating its substance.[12] Attached to the *General Agreement* was a schedule of tariff duties upon which substantial reductions had been made in an interlocking series of 123 bilateral agreements. This very considerable achievement constituted the greatest reduction of tariff barriers ever negotiated in a single conference. The parties to the Geneva negotiations with their dependent colonies conducted approximately 70 per cent of the total value of world trade, so that their action was an important step toward freer international co-operation. Subsequent negotiations concerning the International Trade Charter took place in the diplomatic

[12] Cf. United Nations, *General Agreement on Tariffs and Trade,* 4 vols., New York, 1947. The twenty-three countries were: Australia, Belgium, Brazil, Burma, Canada, Ceylon, Chile, China, Cuba, Czechoslovakia, France, India, Lebanon, Luxembourg, Netherlands, New Zealand, Norway, Pakistan, Southern Rhodesia, Syria, South Africa, Britain, and the United States.

For a summary of the negotiations and an analysis of the Geneva draft of the charter, cf. Carnegie Endowment for International Peace, *International Conciliation,* New York, No. 434, October 1947.

conference called by the United Nations at Havana from November, 1947, to February, 1948.[13]

The difficulties that confronted this conference largely reflected the clash of economic policies and philosophies which is the subject of this chapter. The United States sought to obtain agreement among the nations to allow a maximum of free enterprise to function in a world of expanding multilateral trade. It was extremely difficult for other governments to give firm commitments to abandon the controls they had established over external trade. Their difficulties arose largely from short-run disequilibria in their international balances. Their external trade controls were integrated with the national planning policies which many governments had adopted to cope with the economic disorganization caused by the war.

Any attempt to understand this confused situation must distinguish not only between the facts and the opinions held concerning them, but also between the short- and long-run aspects of the situation. These distinctions are necessarily somewhat artificial. The facts influence opinions, and the policies based on those opinions affect the facts. At the same time the short- and long-run considerations cannot be sharply separated. Nevertheless much of the confusion of controversy concerning commercial and monetary policy in the first postwar years arose from failure to make this double distinction. The result was that argument proceeded at cross-purposes. Hence an attempt must be made to separate the issues.

In the impoverished and distorted economic structure of the postwar world, the economic relations between the nations were such that an immediate postwar emergency had to be dealt with before long-run mechanisms could be installed with any hope of success. The proposals of the United States for freer multilateral trade involved the abandonment of controls over foreign trade and foreign payments that seemed to other countries to be essential instruments of national economic planning. Of more practical importance was the fact that those controls were the chief means by which the impoverished countries were attempting in the crisis of postwar reconstruction to cope with the strains on their balances of payments. The United States proposals for an international trade charter were never intended to cope with the emergency situation. The charter pledged its signatories to the principles of freer multilateral trade, but it recognized that

[13] See Chapter XVIII, "A Framework of World Order."

over a prolonged emergency period it was necessary to contemplate the use of quotas and exchange control.

The emergency was made evident by the increasing difficulty which many countries faced in finding dollar exchange to pay for imports from the United States. Behind this financial problem, there lay a much more fundamental economic disequilibrium. It was more than doubtful whether loans or gifts of dollars could bridge over the emergency unless they were used to help toward a permanent solution of the more fundamental problem presented by the gap between the productivity and living levels of the New World countries, particularly of the United States, and of the rest of the world including western Europe. This gap had never been so wide. Nor was there any sign of this situation being reversed. The United States had a long start in the new scientific technology. Its unparalleled facilities for applied scientific research and process development were steadily increasing its competitive advantage. In default of an imaginative program by which other countries might be helped to develop their productivity by the new technical methods, most of them were constrained to limit their purchases from the United States. At the same time they were being forced to draw upon their last reserves of gold and dollar exchange to pay for the imports which they could not do without. Hence each of them was watching anxiously the components of its national income, and particularly the balance of its external payments.

In all of the western European countries there had been a great impoverishment of equipment and material resources. Current production after the war ran at a low level. There was widespread acceptance of the necessity for national economic planning to maintain full employment at prevailing standards of wages and working conditions—standards which had been raised by comprehensive social-security legislation. In order to allocate the scarce supplies both of capital and of consumer goods and to prevent the abundant purchasing power from starting an inflationary price spiral, the existing price and rationing controls were maintained and even reinforced. At the same time there was pressing need to increase production and this called for large investment programs. But the rationing of scarce supplies, particularly of fuel and raw materials, handicapped productive efficiency. Insufficient reserves caused repeated interruptions of production. At critical moments these became serious, as was demonstrated in the winter of 1946–47 when a relatively small shortage of coal caused an extensive curtailment of power supplied to British factories. In these conditions, planned investment programs, though aiming at increased future productivity, reinforced the immediate inflationary pressures and made necessary even more stringent price and rationing controls.

In addition to the controls exercised over domestic economic activity, national economic planning had involved strict controls over the international balance of payments. Those controls were directed against any leakage of foreign exchange needed to pay for imports of essential food, raw materials, and capital equipment. They were also directed toward mobilizing the maximum receipts from exports, particularly from those exports that produced the foreign currencies needed to purchase essential imports. It was not surprising to find that when the dollar scarcity rose to a crisis in the summer of 1947, the British authorities withdrew permission for British tourists to use foreign exchange for their expenditures abroad and promoted a campaign to attract foreign tourists to Britain. At the same time they suspended the right of foreign holders of sterling balances accruing from current trade to convert their sterling into dollars, tightened the domestic rationing of foodstuffs, imposed heavy taxation on imported films and tobacco, refused any longer to supply gasoline to private automobilists, and introduced more severe import controls, particularly on the imports that had to be paid for in dollars.

The emergency postwar situation was rendered more difficult by this conflict between the philosophy and practice of national economic planning, which the western European countries used to cope with their immediate short-run difficulties, and free competitive enterprise, which the United States desired to restore as a long-run principle. The case for national economic planning was strongest in the short-run. On the other hand, a strong case could be made for allowing competitive forces to work toward long-run equilibrium. Those few economists who contended that it was possible or desirable for the western European countries to abandon their internal and external controls argued that it would in fact cause less social distress in the long run to accept a brief period of sharp unemployment while adjusting to a new competitive equilibrium than it would to maintain full-employment policies at the cost of drifting into regimentation at low living levels. This economic argument ignored political realities. These included the probability of severe labor conflicts, and even political revolutions, if an attempt were made to reach equilibrium at the expense of labor standards. On the other hand, it was necessary to remember that there was no long run in which short-run difficulties would disappear. There would never be an ideal period in which to face the costs of adapting national economies to the changed postwar international equilibrium. Unless resolute action were taken at the earliest possible moment to work toward such adaptation, it was almost inevitable that these temporary controls would harden into permanent regimentation.

At the opposite extreme from those who advocated a speedy return to free competition and an acceptance of its costs were those who criticized the United States proposals for freer multilateral trade, on the ground that these proposals could not be relied upon to ensure the maintenance of full employment. An increasing number of economists and political leaders in Britain and western Europe had come to defend policies of national planning for full employment not merely as a temporary necessity in the short-run emergency, but as a long-run policy to be developed and perfected. This view did not depend entirely upon the belief that a return to freer competitive trade would leave other countries defenseless against the strains imposed upon them by fluctuations in the economic activity and trade of the United States. But that belief was widespread and played a considerable part in buttressing the case for national planning.

It could be argued that internationally concerted policies of full employment would make possible a considerable relaxation of trade barriers. However, the possibility of securing international agreement upon such concerted policies was remote.[14] The advocates of national planning for full employment were not satisfied that countries which desired to pursue full-employment policies would find their balances of payments sufficiently safeguarded in a crisis by the limited facilities of international short-term credit offered by the International Monetary Fund. They were convinced that if full-employment policies

[14] Cf. the specific proposals made by the Australian government to the Twenty-Sixth Session of the International Labor Conference at Philadelphia in 1944. These proposals included regular reporting, commitment to confer, and consideration, in the event of a serious decline in employment, of measures designed to stimulate private investment, increase public investment, increase consumption expenditures, and expand overseas investment. The Australian resolution along these lines was rejected in committee. Cf. Allan G. B. Fisher, *International Implications of Full Employment in Great Britain*, London, 1946, Ch. VIII.

were not to break down in a great depression, the countries pursuing them had to be free to restrict imports. Their central thesis was that if full employment were to be sustained, it would be necessary to prevent the national income—this being the aggregate of demand which sustained employment—from collapsing in a crisis. They did not believe that within any country effective demand could be maintained by relying solely upon the central bank taking steps in a crisis to make credit cheap and abundant. They argued that it might be necessary for governments to put credit into effective circulation by embarking upon large public expenditures.

If this were done by one country alone, there would inevitably ensue a strain on its balance of payments which could not be met merely by short-term credit from the International Monetary Fund. Either the full-employment country would need to be free to restrict imports in order to protect its balance of payments, or it must be able to rely upon other countries, particularly the United States, being pledged to undertake public expenditures sufficient to maintain full employment within their borders. In this view, international agreement to maintain full employment would force every country to meet a threatened depression by embarking upon public expenditures of unpredictable magnitude. There were constitutional limitations that would make it impossible for any United States administration to assume such commitments. Even if public opinion could be brought in a crisis to support Congressional action in this direction, no administration could give assurances that a future Congress would implement such commitments.

Thus the international safeguarding of national economic planning to ensure full employment demanded international economic planning in the sense of commitments to take concerted action. Since the United States was not in a position to make such commitments, the possibility of a world system of planned full employment was ruled out. Two possibilities remained. Individual countries might follow policies designed to maintain full employment and might plan the necessary action to prevent strains on the balances of payments from jeopardizing their national policies. Or an attempt might be made to achieve multilateral trade based on concerted full-employment policies within a large region of like-minded countries.

There were many countries whose governmental structure was too rudimentary to enable them to follow full-employment policies.

Among these were India, China, and most of Latin America. Most of the "immature countries" to which loans and liquid funds might be directed by the International Investment Board projected by the exponents of international full-employment policies fell into this category. Their administrative backwardness might not be of great significance if they were part of an international system centered upon a mature country, prepared as Britain had been in the nineteenth century to accept imports and provide liquid funds, and also to furnish a stream of long-term foreign investment funds for this development. But the United States was for the foreseeable future the major source both of liquid short-term banking accommodation and of long-run permanent investment funds. With the United States outside any regional system that might be projected, it was clear that the organizing countries must limit the area of their operations to countries within their political influence and also within their economic and financial potentialities. In practical politics, the full-employment proposals of British planning economists seemed likely to reinforce the political plans of those who projected the formation of an enlarged sterling area.

Before dealing further with the proposal for regional agreement to pursue full-employment policies, it is convenient to consider the international economic policies that would be involved in any attempt to maintain full employment within one country, irrespective of the policies followed and of the fluctuations of economic activity in other countries. Such a national policy would strain its balance of payments merely by creating the domestic demand necessary to create full employment, or by maintaining that demand when there was a slackening of exports and an increase of imports caused by declining employment elsewhere. There were many examples in the interwar years of such unilateral policies—in Italy, Germany, Belgium, and France. Invariably before the point of full employment was reached, strains developed on the balance of payments and these called for restrictions on external transactions—to check imports or stimulate exports, or to prevent a flight of capital. In other words, there was a point at which it became necessary to limit the advantages accruing from international specialization, if national policies of full employment were to be pursued.[15] Moreover, such measures of intervention as worked through the price mechanism—import duties, export subsidies, cur-

[15] Cf. T. Balogh in *The Economics of Full Employment,* Oxford, 1945, p. 135.

rency depreciation, and the like—proved to be cumbrous and slow-moving. If intervention was to be effective quickly in preventing strains on the balance of payments from interfering with full-employment policies, it had to resort to more direct measures—quotas, exchange control, licensing, bulk purchases and sales, and bilateral trading bargains.

Any economist can demonstrate that an astute use of such devices, properly timed and skillfully administered, could influence the general conditions of trade in favor of the country imposing them. Apart from the administrative and political difficulties of ensuring that such action could be timed and calculated accurately and would not be merely a response to the pressures from interested groups, the advantages to be derived from such astuteness are minor when compared with the advantages of international specialization. It has been wisely said that "no country can, by being smart, juggle its way to prosperity while others languish." Nor could any country—particularly a great manufacturing country—count with impunity upon the chance that its competitors would not retaliate against its efforts to manipulate the terms of trade in its favor. It was possible that retaliation might prove difficult and dangerous.[16] But even if this proved to be the case, the ultimate result of national planning for full employment, pursued unilaterally by direct methods of regulating the external balance, was bound to result in a marked trend toward autarky. Inevitably it was also bound to involve an increasing degree of domestic regulation leading ultimately to authoritarian planning.

What was true of national planning was true in large measure also of the regional alternative. The larger and more self-contained the region, the greater would be the advantages of multilateral trade within its constituent units. Despite the growing mastery of chemists and physicists and biologists over materials, there was no region in the postwar world which was self-sufficient. Indeed interdependence became greater with greater progress in the mechanization of industry.

[16] Cf. T. Balogh, "The Economics of Retaliation," *Review of Economic Studies*, Vol. II, No. 2, 1944. It is of some interest to note that the assumptions made in this article are a reasonably close approximation to reality, so that one may read for country A, the United States, and for country B, Great Britain. This is a good example of much of the current literature which argues controversial questions of current policy in the guise of theoretical analysis, the definitions and assumptions being in fact rationalizations of a particular situation.

This was true even for the basic materials necessary to maintain industrial production and military power. It was still truer if account was taken of the levels to which productivity might be raised by international co-operation in contrast with the present low levels of postwar productivity. While the losses to be expected from a recurrence of severe cyclical fluctuations of industry and employment were greater than those to be expected from a curtailment of international specialization, it did not follow that a choice had to be made between a world of full employment, organized in autarkic national or regional units, and a world of multilateral trade afflicted with uncontrollable cyclical depressions.

A middle path was possible. It involved giving up some measure of dogmatic adherence both to the new creed of full employment and to the older creed of free multilateral trade. It was unlikely that either of these creeds could be fully realized in the confusion and change of the postwar period. In the short run there was great concern for employment—perhaps too much concern for employment and too little for inflation—particularly in the countries that had been impoverished by war. It was not wise, however, to allow the longer-run advantages of international specialization to be obscured by pressing immediacies.

There was no possibility that this middle way could ever be tried if, in their eagerness to establish overnight the perfect economic world of their dreams, those responsible for economic policy fell into the pitfalls either on the left or on the right. A planned world of full employment was not in the realm of political possibilities. Nor was a world of unqualified competitive equilibrium. Attempts to brush aside the war debris of disorganization and impoverishment in order to allow competitive forces to work freely would have involved such widespread suffering that it would not be long before even more stringent forms of national organization and control would become necessary. On the other hand, national policies, which in fear of temporary interference with ambitious social policies consolidated the national collectivism rapidly developing, would break the world into blocs pursuing trade by methods akin to economic warfare.

The international institutions, which were created as forums of consultation and as agencies of flexible adjustment to changing situations, had the means to ease countries over temporary difficulties. Those means, however, were inadequate and were never meant to cope with the immediate postwar strain. A great effort was called for —of self-help on the part of the countries impoverished and exhausted by the war, and of realistic, understanding generosity on the part of those who had escaped such impoverishment. The war in fact had not ended when victory was achieved over the enemy powers. Unless the mutual aid which made victory possible was continued until reconstruction was well advanced, the long-run mechanisms devised for mutual accommodation in a peaceful world would fail of their purpose and might never function in any effective way. Such mutual aid entailed both an absence of recrimination and a willingness to put on one side dogmatic adherence to theoretical objectives in favor of a co-operative effort to discover workable methods of international economic co-operation.

CHAPTER XVIII

A FRAMEWORK OF WORLD ORDER

THE UNITED NATIONS CONCEPT

THE MAIN EMPHASIS of Part III has been upon the disruptive effects of two world wars, upon the revolutionary changes in the technical methods and structure of business enterprise, and upon the increasing government intervention in economic activity. We are living through a period of revolutions and wars in which the processes of social change are quickened. New power alignments are developing. The confusion is the greater because a new aggressive philosophy of political and economic organization has emerged to challenge the fundamental postulates of the established order. It is reasonable to expect that the economic and political map of the world will register shifts in the location of industry, in political structure, and in the balance of power that will make the latter half of this century as different from the nineteenth as the latter half of the nineteenth was from the eighteenth century.

In these changes, the promise not so much of atomic energy as of the new scientific knowledge of which it is a by-product is balanced by a threat of scientific warfare. The choice between co-operation and violence becomes more significant with every advance in scientific knowledge. From any rational standpoint, war has become an anachronism. The supreme question confronting this generation is the challenge to create effective mechanisms for the pacific settlement of international disputes. Since these disputes originate in the complex relations between nation-states, the negative problem of preserving peace is part of the larger, positive problem of organizing peaceful international co-operation.

The United Nations and its associated agencies constitute the latest and most ambitious attempt to organize effective means of international co-operation. There is a long history behind them. Since the late nineteenth century, the increasing range of international contacts has evoked a large number of international associations both private and official. Some of the earliest were founded by the initiative of individual governments. Thus Belgium set up and carried the main burden of financing both an International Statistical Bureau (1885) and a Union for the Publication of Customs Tariffs (1890). The French government initiated the Office International d'Hygiène (1903) and the Institut International de Coopération Intellectuelle (1926). The International Institute of Agriculture at Rome, though founded in 1905 largely by the enthusiasm of an American, David Lubin, later derived its main support from the Italian government. Some of the earlier private associations pioneered the way for later official agencies. The International Association for Labor Legislation, founded in 1897, was the precursor of the International Labor Organization, which in 1920 was created as a semi-autonomous agency of the League of Nations and in 1945 became a specialized agency of the United Nations. There has been a constant tendency for official organizations to take over the work of private associations and for these official organizations to be grouped with the international institutions created to maintain peace. There remains a great variety both of official and of private international agencies in addition to the United Nations agencies.

The League of Nations was created in 1919 primarily as a mechanism for the collective enforcement of peace. In form it was a loose confederation of nation-states pledged to enforce the principles of pacific settlement laid down in the covenant. Though the covenant was drawn up by the victors, most of the smaller powers that had been neutrals during the war and all the defeated powers, including Germany, later adhered to it. Though individual Americans took an active part in League committees and the United States government after 1931 co-operated with many League activities, the United States never became a member. Germany was a member only from 1926 to

1934 and the U.S.S.R. from 1934 to 1940. There were other defections and the League never became the universal organization it was designed to be.

Though designed as an instrument of collective security, the League developed many technical activities during the two decades of its active existence. The organization of facilities for international co-operation in such fields as public health, the traffic in opium and narcotic drugs, the reconstruction of devastated countries, and the resettlement of refugees were among its most successful activities.

The League organization was unitary. All of its activities went to the Assembly through the Council composed of Foreign Ministers (or their deputies) who were preoccupied with political questions, such as disarmament or the successive disputes that threatened a breach of the peace. It could be argued that it was an advantage to leave final decision in the hands of political leaders, since technicians could not commit their governments. But many questions of international co-operation were not closely connected with the great issues of peace and war. Action by responsible political leaders was necessary but it was in such technical fields as agricultural, fiscal, labor, monetary, and tariff policy rather than in the high political questions with which Foreign Offices were usually concerned. The whole apparatus of national governments was involved, and effective international co-operation called for more elaborate mechanisms than could be provided by the simple unitary structure of the League.

The United Nations and its associated organs created in 1945 provided a much more elaborate series of consultative mechanisms. The great political issues of peace and war were entrusted to a Security Council. The issues of international co-operation were entrusted under the Assembly to an Economic and Social Council and a Trusteeship Council. Since conflict is easily dramatized and the issues of political conflict lend themselves to such dramatization, the proceedings of the Security Council received most publicity in the first years of the United Nations. The weight of the mechanism, however, was intended to lie in the Economic and Social Council and the Trusteeship Council. The work of these Councils was fundamental to the success of the United Nations because the whole concept of the organization was one of consultative co-operation between sovereign states rather than one of the collective enforcement of peace.

Like the League of Nations, but to an even greater extent, the United Nations was based upon a frank acceptance of national sovereignty. Its first formative years demonstrated that national governments intended to keep a tighter grip on its mechanisms than they had kept on the League of Nations. For example, there was less use of independent experts on committees and commissions, and a greater use of national representatives drawn from government agencies. Moreover, the influence of the great powers was more explicit and more extensive. In the Security Council particularly, the permanent members—Britain, China, France, the United States, and the U.S.S.R. —were given voting power that placed them in an entirely different position from the other members. The privileged position of these permanent members made it apparent that the United Nations concept was postulated upon their agreed action.

Since China did not command the resources of a great power, and Britain and France aligned themselves on all important policy issues with the United States, the unanimity that had to be secured before the United Nations could function effectively came down in practice to agreement between the United States and the U.S.S.R. As long as the U.S.S.R. found itself in a minority among the permanent members on the Security Council and in the Assembly, the veto which prevented action was that of the U.S.S.R. The Russians used their veto power more frequently and on relatively less important issues than had been contemplated by the framers of the Charter, but it was not difficult to conceive circumstances in which this right of veto might become important to the other permanent members—particularly to the United States. Public opinion in the United States might accept a decision of detail which the United States representatives had opposed, but it was difficult to imagine acceptance of such a decision on an issue vital to national security. For instance, if communist governments came to power in France and China, the United States would be placed in a minority on the Security Council. If a proposal were then advanced to hand over the control of all international waterways, including the Suez and Panama Canals, to a United Nations commission dominated by the U.S.S.R., the United States would certainly exercise its veto power.

Although the technical commissions and specialized agencies of the United Nations did not have the same voting arrangements as the

Security Council, their activity was hampered by the conflict of ideologies. There are some students of international affairs who believe that effective co-operation in technical fields must precede any attempt to organize collective security. This belief is based upon the theory that increasing awareness of the need for co-operation and mutual trust, developing from the habit of consultation and common action, will gradually engender a greater readiness to experiment in political as distinct from technical questions. The difficulty here is that all technical co-operation involves political considerations. The conflict between the Soviet concept of government and economic organization and that held by the rest of the world was so fundamental that it colored all technical discussions. The experience of the technical commissions and specialized agencies of the United Nations illustrated only too well the difficulty of organizing effective means of technical co-operation between nations that did not share a common political philosophy. Though some states in the Soviet zone became members of some of the specialized agencies, the U.S.S.R. abstained from active membership in all but three. The codes of economic co-operation which the specialized economic agencies had drawn up were open to adherence by all states, but they entailed acceptance of obligations postulated upon a political and economic philosophy which was rejected by the U.S.S.R.

The organization of the United Nations is shown by the diagram on pages 628–29. The U.S.S.R. was represented on the Security Council and its subordinate commissions, on the General Assembly and the International Court of Justice, on the Trusteeship Council, on the Secretariat, and on the Economic and Social Council and its commissions and subcommissions. It had also joined the three specialized agencies which could be described as clearing agencies for national services—the International Telecommunications Union, the Universal Postal Union, and the World Health Organization—but in February, 1949, it served notice of withdrawal from the latter. It had not joined any of the specialized economic agencies—the International Labor Organization, the Food and Agriculture Organization, the International Bank for Reconstruction and Development, the International Monetary Fund, and the International Trade Organization. While several states within the Soviet zone were members, the division between the Soviet and non-Soviet world, without Soviet par-

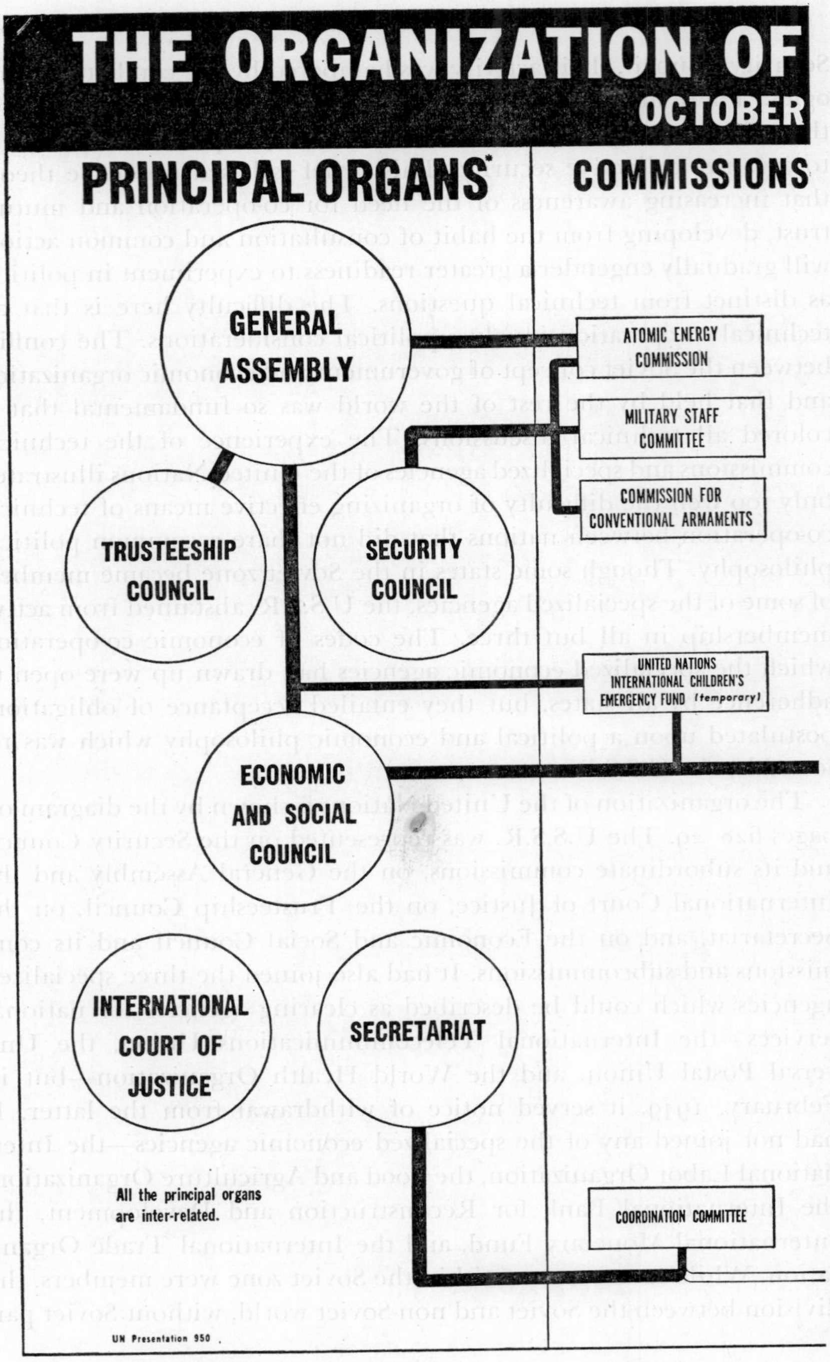
THE ORGANIZATION OF
OCTOBER
PRINCIPAL ORGANS*
COMMISSIONS
GENERAL ASSEMBLY
ATOMIC ENERGY COMMISSION
MILITARY STAFF COMMITTEE
COMMISSION FOR CONVENTIONAL ARMAMENTS
TRUSTEESHIP COUNCIL
SECURITY COUNCIL
UNITED NATIONS INTERNATIONAL CHILDREN'S EMERGENCY FUND (temporary)
ECONOMIC AND SOCIAL COUNCIL
INTERNATIONAL COURT OF JUSTICE
SECRETARIAT
All the principal organs are inter-related.
COORDINATION COMMITTEE
UN Presentation 950

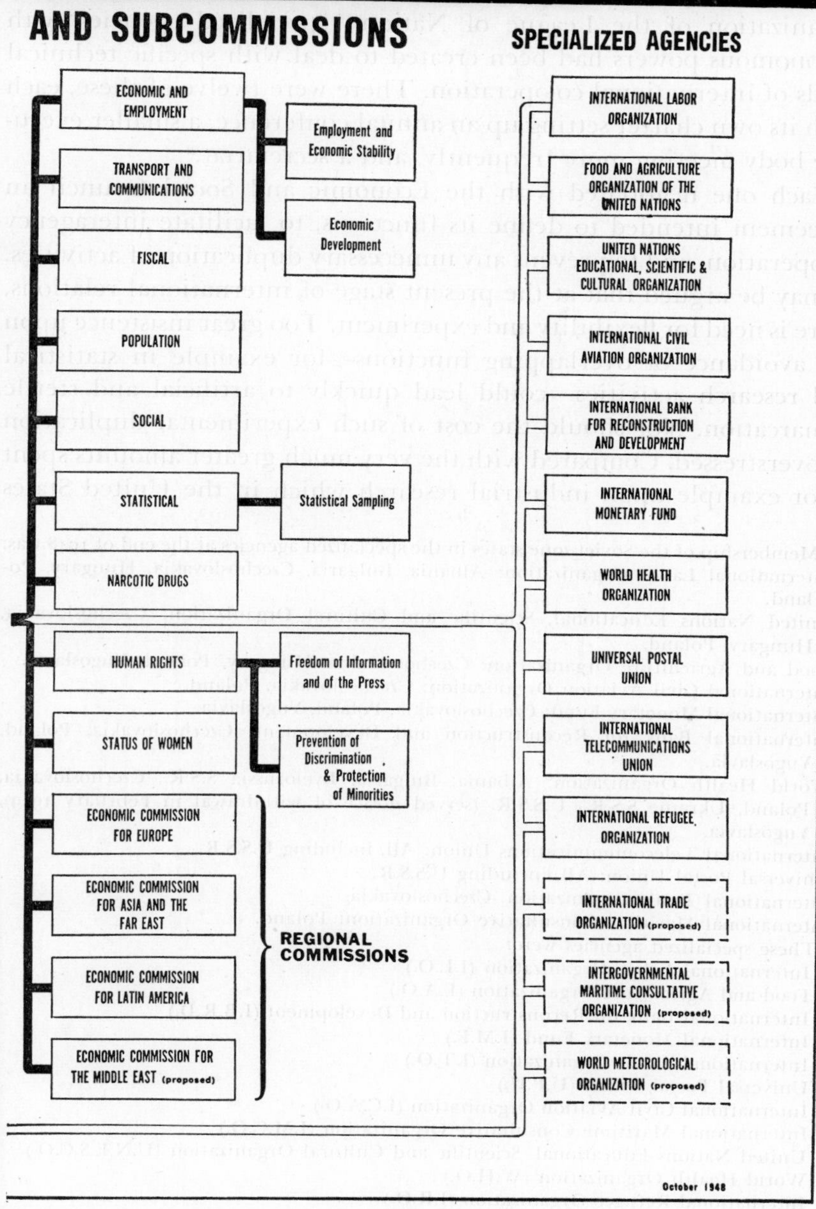
THE UNITED NATIONS
1948
AND SUBCOMMISSIONS
SPECIALIZED AGENCIES
ECONOMIC AND EMPLOYMENT
Employment and Economic Stability
TRANSPORT AND COMMUNICATIONS
Economic Development
FISCAL
POPULATION
SOCIAL
STATISTICAL
Statistical Sampling
NARCOTIC DRUGS
HUMAN RIGHTS
Freedom of Information and of the Press
STATUS OF WOMEN
Prevention of Discrimination & Protection of Minorities
ECONOMIC COMMISSION FOR EUROPE
ECONOMIC COMMISSION FOR ASIA AND THE FAR EAST
ECONOMIC COMMISSION FOR LATIN AMERICA
ECONOMIC COMMISSION FOR THE MIDDLE EAST (proposed)
REGIONAL COMMISSIONS
INTERNATIONAL LABOR ORGANIZATION
FOOD AND AGRICULTURE ORGANIZATION OF THE UNITED NATIONS
UNITED NATIONS EDUCATIONAL, SCIENTIFIC & CULTURAL ORGANIZATION
INTERNATIONAL CIVIL AVIATION ORGANIZATION
INTERNATIONAL BANK FOR RECONSTRUCTION AND DEVELOPMENT
INTERNATIONAL MONETARY FUND
WORLD HEALTH ORGANIZATION
UNIVERSAL POSTAL UNION
INTERNATIONAL TELECOMMUNICATIONS UNION
INTERNATIONAL REFUGEE ORGANIZATION
INTERNATIONAL TRADE ORGANIZATION (proposed)
INTERGOVERNMENTAL MARITIME CONSULTATIVE ORGANIZATION (proposed)
WORLD METEOROLOGICAL ORGANIZATION (proposed)
October 1948

ticipation in these economic agencies, would become sharper the more effectively they were organized.[1]

In an attempt to overcome the difficulties that arose from the unitary organization of the League of Nations, specialized agencies with autonomous powers had been created to deal with specific technical fields of international co-operation. There were twelve of these, each with its own charter setting up an annual conference, a smaller executive body meeting more frequently, and a secretariat.[2]

Each one negotiated with the Economic and Social Council an agreement intended to define its functions, to facilitate interagency co-operation, and to prevent any unnecessary duplication of activities. It may be argued that at the present stage of international relations, there is need for flexibility and experiment. Too great insistence upon the avoidance of overlapping functions—for example in statistical and research activities—could lead quickly to artificial and sterile demarcation. Nor should the cost of such experimental duplication be overstressed. Compared with the very much greater amounts spent —for example upon industrial research which in the United States

[1] Membership of the Soviet zone states in the specialized agencies at the end of 1948 was:
International Labor Organization: Albania, Bulgaria, Czechoslovakia, Hungary, Poland.
United Nations Educational, Scientific and Cultural Organization: Czechoslovakia, Hungary, Poland.
Food and Agriculture Organization: Czechoslovakia, Hungary, Poland, Yugoslavia.
International Civil Aviation Organization: Czechoslovakia, Poland.
International Monetary Fund: Czechoslovakia, Poland, Yugoslavia.
International Bank for Reconstruction and Development: Czechoslovakia, Poland, Yugoslavia.
World Health Organization: Albania, Bulgaria, Byelorussia S.S.R., Czechoslovakia, Poland, Ukraine S.S.R., U.S.S.R. (served notice of withdrawal in February 1949), Yugoslavia.
International Telecommunications Union: All, including U.S.S.R.
Universal Postal Union: All, including U.S.S.R.
International Trade Organization: Czechoslovakia.
International Maritime Consultative Organization: Poland.

[2] These specialized agencies were:
International Labor Organization (I.L.O.)
Food and Agriculture Organization (F.A.O.)
International Bank for Reconstruction and Development (I.B.R.D.)
International Monetary Fund (I.M.F.)
International Trade Organization (I.T.O.)
Universal Postal Union (U.P.U.)
International Civil Aviation Organization (I.C.A.O.)
International Maritime Consultative Organization (I.M.C.O.)
United Nations Educational, Scientific and Cultural Organization (U.N.E.S.C.O.)
World Health Organization (W.H.O.)
International Refugee Organization (I.R.O.)

alone was running at about a billion dollars a year—the $70 million of United Nations expense shared among all the members was not an excessive sum to venture upon a search for effective means of international co-operation.

The real risk was that efficiency would suffer in the dispersion of effort entailed in trying to do too much too quickly. In addition to the twelve specialized agencies, the Economic and Social Council of the United Nations had set up fourteen commissions and some of these had set up sub-commissions.[3]

These economic commissions dealt with questions handled by the specialized economic agencies. Thus the Economic and Employment Commission, with its two sub-commissions on Employment and Economic Stability and on Economic Development, was concerned with issues that were also of concern to the International Labor Organization, the International Bank, the International Monetary Fund, and the International Trade Organization. It was conceivable that the Economic and Social Council might use its commissions as the instruments through which to co-ordinate the activities of the specialized agencies. But it was also possible that competition and rivalries might develop.

The possibilities of duplication appeared even greater between the regional commissions and the regional organizations that had been created outside the United Nations and between both of these and

[3] The list which follows is sufficient to indicate the difficulty of classifying these commissions:

Economic Commission for Europe
 Inland Transportation Committee
 Coal Committee
Economic Commission for Asia and the Far East
Inter-American Economic Commission
Economic and Employment Commission
 Sub-Commission on Employment and Economic Stability
 Sub-Commission on Economic Development
Economic Reconstruction of Devastated Areas Commission
Transport and Communications Commission
Fiscal Commission
Statistical Commission
Population Commission
Social Commission
Commission on Human Rights
 Sub-Commission on Freedom of Information and the Press
 Sub-Commission on Prevention of Discrimination and Protection of Minorities
Commission on Status of Women
Commission on Narcotic Drugs
International Children's Emergency Fund

the specialized agencies set up to deal on a world-wide basis with labor, agriculture, investment, money, and trade. The main dangers to be watched in this confusion of competing regional and functional organizations within and without the United Nations were the strain that it imposed upon resources and personnel and the dispersion of effort upon co-ordination rather than its concentration upon specific activity. For the smaller members the cost could become a serious drain upon limited foreign exchange resources, particularly of dollars. If default in payment of contributions became widespread, a serious situation would arise. The League of Nations had faced such defaults, and this had been the primary reason why its activities had been restricted to a limited number of urgently necessary projects. Even more important than this monetary aspect was the strain placed upon the limited personnel. As the number of commissions and committees increased and met more frequently, the representation particularly of the smaller countries devolved either upon permanent delegates who were forced to act on questions where they had no particular authority, or upon junior officials without power to commit their governments. Responsible statesmen could not take the necessary time away from their own countries. Therefore discussions tended to become more academic, more prolonged, and less decisive.

The International Monetary Fund and the International Bank had their own funds and were able to operate without the handicaps imposed on those agencies which had to work on voted budgets. However, their activities tended to become more specialized and to be divorced from the general plan of consultation and co-ordination of policy under the Economic and Social Council. A considerable effort of integration was needed if international economic co-operation was to be effectively organized.

The oldest of the specialized agencies was the International Labor Organization. From its beginning in 1920 as a semi-autonomous agency of the League of Nations, the I.L.O. had given direct representation to organized labor and management as well as governments. This tripartite representation was maintained in the annual conferences, in the more frequent meetings of the governing body, and throughout the increasingly elaborate structure of committees and sub-committees. The United States had become a member of the organization in 1934. Its survival was largely due to the widespread support of numbers of trade union officials and employers, as well as government officials, who had participated actively in its work. Over more than twenty years, knowledge of its activities had permeated through these representatives to the organized trade unions and management associations.

The I.L.O. had been able to present to its annual conferences a long series of conventions setting up standards in regard to many aspects of labor and social legislation. These conventions were submitted to national governments for ratification. As they were slowly ratified, a minimum code of labor conditions was gradually evolved. Conventions representing the lowest common denominator of legislation upon which international agreement could be secured were the target at which I.L.O. activities were aimed. The record of success in hitting this target was relatively modest, but the most important achievements of the I.L.O. were by-products of these activities. One was the reinforcement of free trade unionism in many countries where labor organization was in its infancy. Another was the increased understanding of labor and social problems that was gained by those who participated in discussions of these problems with men and women engaged in the same kind of activities as their own. A continuous process of mutual education went on between the three major groups—government, trade union, and management representatives. Moreover, the specialized experience of the secretariat and the expert advice it could mobilize from individuals and agencies outside the I.L.O. were made available to any member-government that asked for it. Thus members of the secretariat gave expert assistance in setting up social-security administrations in several Latin-American countries. The I.L.O. had achieved its greatest successes by the methods of consultative co-operation and mutual education. It had no power except the power of persuasion. Its conventions could only be submitted to national governments for ratification and enactment as and if each government saw fit. Yet in the course of preparing these conventions, the I.L.O. had exercised a degree of influence upon public opinion and upon national governments greater than could be measured by the number of ratifications secured.

In two major respects, both of which illustrated its main reliance upon consultative procedures, the I.L.O. had extended its activities in recent years. Beginning in 1936, it had held a series of regional conferences. During the second World War also, it had created Industrial Committees to explore the possibilities of improving working conditions in specific industries such as textiles, inland transport, coal mining, metal trades, iron and steel production, petroleum, and building trades. This devolution by region and by industry went hand in hand with a broadening of the objectives of the organization as a whole. The conference held at Philadelphia in 1944 adopted a postwar program based largely upon the maintenance of full-employment policies. The conference held at San Francisco in 1948 was centered upon discussion of a proposed convention on the right of freedom of association of workers. That discussion clearly revealed the division between the concepts of freedom held by the Soviet and non-Soviet world. And it illustrated the fact that the more effectively the specialized agencies of the United Nations implement the principles of international economic co-operation in the non-Soviet world, the sharper becomes the conflict between that world and the Soviet system.

Nowhere was the difficulty of organizing effective international co-operation more evident than in the field covered by the Food and Agriculture Organization. The majority of the world's people are still engaged in agriculture. In the densely populated countries of Asia, proportions of the population ranging up to 80 per cent work directly on the land. Nonetheless these countries contribute little to the world exports of food. These come mainly from the highly organized and mechanized countries of the New World. There has always been a shortage of food in the world as a whole. After the second World War, this shortage extended even to the western European nations. The whole nexus of problems connected with agriculture—production, trade, nutrition, and health—called for scientific, economic, and political collaboration. Food is the first essential of human life. But man has not yet succeeded in organizing effective means of co-operating to meet this most primitive of his needs.

It was therefore a well-calculated decision to explore the possibility of postwar collaboration by calling an international conference on food and agricultural questions even before the second World War ended. After this conference at Hot Springs, Virginia, in May, 1943, there was a prolonged period of study by expert technicians before the Food and Agriculture Organization (F.A.O.) was officially created on October 16, 1945. More than forty governments quickly accepted membership. The declared purposes of the organization were to raise the nutrition levels and standards of living in all countries, to improve the production and distribution of all food and agricultural products, to better the condition of rural populations, and to contribute toward an expanding world economy. While these objectives commanded universal assent, finding effective means to implement them was no easy task.

Before this new agency could be well organized, the anticipated food crisis at the close of the war had become a stark reality. There was famine in India and China. Over most of Europe millions of people were on rations. The caloric content of their diets was often much below the minimum necessary for normal health. Deficiency diseases were widespread. Emergency steps had to be taken to ship food, particularly to Europe. The United Nations Relief and Rehabilitation Administration was created on November 9, 1943. But its program did not include the former enemy countries, and these had to be fed by the occupation armies. On June 30, 1947, the U.N.R.R.A. program was terminated and in its place the United States and other governments made emergency loans so that food could be purchased. In 1948, the European Recovery Plan began to function. At the same time a good harvest seemed to promise the end of the immediate postwar emergency.

There was a longer-run aspect of the world food situation which was more ominous. The population of the world was estimated to have increased by about 200 million in the decade preceding 1948. Many of the food-producing areas were in a disturbed political and economic situation. This was particularly the case in the rice bowls of the Far East—Burma, Indo-China, and Indonesia. On the other hand, as western Europe increased its agricultural production, the risk grew that surpluses of agricultural staples, such as wheat, similar to those which had caused the agricultural depression in 1928–29, would again begin to accumulate. The case for rationalization of the world's agricultural production and trade was a strong case on three counts.

The first was the world's essential poverty. This was indicated by the fact that before the second World War at least half the world's population was subsisting at a food consumption level too low to maintain normal health. The second was the growing danger of famine in the heavily populated regions of Asia, such as India, China, and even Indo-China, Burma, and Indonesia. The third was the risk of agricultural maladjustment in the richer third of the world—western Europe and the food-exporting countries of the New World—leading once more to economic breakdown and depression. In September, 1946, the Director-General of the F.A.O. submitted to the annual conference at Copenhagen the results of a World Food Survey, together with recommendations to set up a World Food Board. The proposal was that this board should be created to develop and organize production, distribution and consumption of the basic foods so as to provide diets on a health standard for peoples of all countries, and in doing so to stabilize agricultural prices at levels fair to producers and consumers alike.

The adoption of this proposal would have created a supra-national agency which could have functioned effectively only if national governments had been prepared to endow it with effective power and resources. Its organization would have been a vast administrative problem, since it would have required both regional and functional decentralization. It was certain that the U.S.S.R. would not co-operate, and practically certain that none of its satellite countries in eastern Europe would be allowed to co-operate. In practice the World Food Board would necessarily have become an agency of the western European consumers and of the agricultural-exporting countries of the New World. It would have constituted an enlarged version of the Joint Food Board which operated under the Anglo-American Combined Chiefs of Staff during the second World War. In the present state of most of the Asiatic countries, it would have been very difficult to organize the means whereby they might have participated effectively.

Moreover, a very large question of principle was raised. Was the time ripe to take such a long step forward toward world government? Should these vital issues of food, nutrition, health, and agricultural welfare be decided by expert, authoritative world government from above, or by the slower processes of consultative co-operation and mutual education between national governments? The decision was to continue consultative co-operation. This was made at a meeting of the Preparatory Commission on World Food Proposals in Washington from October, 1946, to January, 1947. Largely upon the insistence of the United States, the proposal to establish a World Food Board with powers to stabilize agricultural prices, to purchase and allocate supplies, and to set up food reserves was rejected. Instead, a World Food Council of eighteen nations was set up within the F.A.O. to keep the question of world food supplies continuously under review and to recommend to national governments such action as seemed desirable.

The F.A.O. had been created in 1945 as an agency for research and consultative co-operation among independent sovereign states. It had no operative functions and no power in its own right. Much of the world might go hungry and even lapse into revolutionary chaos before the research men and statisticians could begin to produce the information that would lead by consultative agreement to action by national governments. There was grave risk that the maladjustments of agricultural production might cause a world agricultural depression. It was also possible that increases in population might in time lead to an even more serious food crisis.

Before action could be taken to forestall such disasters, it was necessary to obtain more knowledge and a greater popular and official appreciation of the need for international co-operation. What the immediate postwar crisis demonstrated was not the need for supra-national authoritative organization. It was the need quickly to organize efficient research and public education. Action not based on adequate knowledge and understanding of the basic issues could be no more than palliative. While bringing temporary relief it might aggravate the crisis in the long run. Anyone who tried to answer accurately the simplest international economic question soon became aware that only fragmentary facts were available. No one knew within 10 per cent, how many people there were in the world to be fed. No one knew for large regions what increases of population were likely to result from the developing trends of increase. There were great gaps in information as to the world production and consumption of different kinds of food. On the scientific side there was much to be done in regard to such questions as nutrition, crop cultivation, and the study of plant and animal diseases. Education must accompany research. Even with an imperfect state of knowledge, production could be vastly increased if what was already known to scientists could be effectively implemented by those who cultivated the soil. But political action to organize more efficient production and a freer interchange of agricultural products could not be undertaken effectively until the urgency of taking such action was more widely understood.

Immediately after the second World War, the world was not ripe for positive policies of international action in these fields. The basic issues were not clear even to the informed experts. Such knowledge as they had was not widely enough diffused among those who wielded political power nor among the general public. From the long-run viewpoint the most important matter was to push ahead with the organization of research and consultative mechanisms while staving off emergencies by whatever national or international means seemed practicable. A sound argument could be made for doing as much as could be effectively done through the international agencies, but care had to be taken not to overload these agencies prematurely. And in an emergency it was often more important to have the job done quickly and efficiently than to insist upon doing it in a particular way.

Research and consultative co-operation have been the activities most necessary and most valuable in the development of international institutions. This is true even of the specialized agencies with operative responsibilities. Those agencies had been created to administer elaborate codes of international monetary policy, investment, and trading principles, and to function within those codes in ways that had not before been practicable. The most specific code was that which established the International Monetary Fund. But it was precisely in this highly technical field of international monetary relations that research was most needed, and that the informed judgment of practitioners constituted the largest element in that research.

There are no magic formulas of action. Issues have to be defined, and action has to be taken, according to the best judgment of those capable of weighing the imponderable as well as the measurable factors in a constantly changing and always sensitive series of complicated relationships. It was encouraging progress, therefore, when technicians drawn from a large number of countries, including all the countries most prominently engaged in world trade, found themselves in continuous consultation, and when their communications with responsible national authorities were reinforced by periodic official meetings.

It cannot be too often repeated that important contributions to political education derive from continuous consultative co-operation on issues of common concern. Both the I.L.O. and the F.A.O. found their most effective outlets in research, in the organizing of expert help to members requesting technical aid, and in bringing together expert official groups from different countries to explore problems of common concern. The trained and experienced international secretariats could throw a flood of new light upon the international relations between seemingly unrelated national facts. The publications of the Economic Intelligence Service of the League of Nations did so particularly in respect to trade and monetary developments between the wars. Much could be done by rendering more intelligibly comparable the national statistics relative to currencies, weights and measures, and the like. These are collected in a variety of tongues by differing methods and base periods, and with a bewildering variety of terminology. The international secretariats faced many difficulties in collecting these materials and translating them to a common and comparable basis. But they were able slowly to improve and make these national materials more adequate and comparable. If no other service could be rendered than this elementary one of collecting and shaping the bricks, a great deal would be achieved toward the building of more adequate international understanding.

THE INTERNATIONAL MONETARY FUND

Broadly speaking the new specialized agencies erected at the close of World War II followed the pattern of the International Labor Organization. Though the forms of organization differed somewhat according to the functions of the agency, there was a broad similarity among them—an annual plenary conference of all members, a smaller executive body meeting more frequently, and a permanent secretariat with large powers. The International Monetary Fund was created to administer an agreed set of principles and procedures designed to develop an international monetary system. It was given both operating responsibility and capital resources with which to discharge its responsibility. In three respects new ground was broken—an elaborate code was worked out to which the members pledged adherence, the administration of the code was entrusted to a specialized international agency, and that agency was given specific operating functions.

It was in July, 1944, that a conference at Bretton Woods, at which forty-four governments were represented, negotiated articles of agreement to establish the International Monetary Fund. It is important to stress the long discussions that preceded the Bretton Woods conference, because the fact is too often forgotten that international agreement upon complicated issues is not easily won. The first tentative formulations by United States and British officials of plans for postwar collaboration on monetary policy were published simultaneously in April, 1943. In the following months bankers and traders as well as economists and government officials in both countries took part in what was essentially a great debate in the democratic tradition. In May, 1943, two French economists published unofficially their suggestions regarding international monetary regulation, and in June a group of Canadian experts published a draft which combined the United States and British proposals. With the publication on July 10, 1943, of a revised draft of the United States proposals the debate took a more authoritative turn.

One aspect of this debate was the exchange of expert ideas necessary to arrive at a workable compromise between the governments concerned. After the main lines of the United States and British proposals became known and these draft proposals were published, consultations were widened to include some thirty countries. On April 21, 1944, following what was in effect a preliminary international conference, there was published a *Joint Statement by Experts on the Establishment of an International Monetary Fund.* This statement, which was based upon the United States proposals but incorporated the ideas of British, French, Canadian, and other experts, made it clear that agreement was possible among the responsible government officials. The next step was the calling of the official conference attended by forty-four governments at Bretton Woods in July, 1944. This conference made considerable changes in the draft articles of agreement. The final draft was a joint product. The good will and the desire of the governments to co-operate, combined with readiness to leave the technical methods of co-operation to be worked out by experts, made possible this instrument of collaboration.

The backing of informed public opinion was as necessary as expert agreement. There had been acute disagreement among economists, bankers, traders, and treasury officials on the major issues of postwar monetary policies. This disagreement reflected conflicting views as to planning and free enterprise, and became a rationalization of national situations. A large part of the public debate was thus aimed at mobilizing public opinion for or against the official proposals. This caused frequent international misunderstandings. The proposals for international collaboration had to be explained to public opinion in all the democratic countries. Many fears and some fallacies had to be cleared away before the Fund became acceptable to public opinion. The British fears were in large measure the reverse of those which caused opposition to the Fund in the United States. Thus when Lord Keynes, in the House of Lords, tried to calm British apprehensions that acceptance of the Fund agreement would entail a return to rigid gold standard principles, his remarks alarmed many in the United States who feared the degree of flexibility embodied in the agreements. These misunderstandings were inevitable in a long-range debate on highly technical issues which had to be interpreted to a non-specialist public opinion by newspaper men whose condensations of complicated arguments had in turn to meet press deadlines. Indeed it was a remarkable achievement to secure democratic assent to such a technically complicated agreement.

After agreement was reached at Bretton Woods, it had to be ratified by the governments of countries having at least 65 per cent of the subscription quotas. Ratification involved more than formal adherence to the agreement. There had to be an appropriation equal to the country's quota—in the case of the United States, $2,750 million. In every country the debate was renewed on the principles of monetary policy embodied in the agreement. The United States and a sufficient number of other countries took the necessary action, and the Fund was formally inaugurated in March, 1946. After an organizing period for the recruiting of staff, the executive directors notified the member-governments on September 12, 1946, that the Fund would soon be ready to begin exchange transactions. Each member-government was asked to communicate the exchange value of its currency. On December 18, 1946, it was announced that the initial par values of the currencies of thirty-one of the members had been accepted at the current rates. The Fund was ready to begin operations on March 1, 1947, and its first transactions were actually made in May, 1947. By the end of August, 1949, forty-eight countries had adhered to the Fund.

In order to understand the purposes for which the Fund was created, it is necessary briefly to recall the fact that the mobilization of economic resources for war had distorted the production and price structure of every country. War could not wait for taxes to be collected. It was financed largely by governments going into the market for manpower and resources with credit instruments that increased the supply of effective purchasing power. Therefore an effort had to be made both to control the prices of basic commodities that were important for production and the cost of living, and to ration the supplies of those commodities equitably. In due course, tax programs were put through to mop up some of the excess purchasing power that had passed into private hands as a result of government expenditures. The excess was considerable because the war expenditures generated a multiplier effect, and this was continuously renewed by fresh expenditures, so that taxes never caught up with the increased purchasing power. What economists call an inflationary gap developed between the total amount of effective purchasing power and the goods and services on which it could be expended. Hence there was a strong tendency for prices to rise. Where price control and rationing were reasonably effective over necessities, the purchasing power flowed into other channels. The governments tried to entice it into war bonds. Prudent people reduced their debts. But some of the purchasing power went into luxuries, and some went into various forms of speculation.

When the war ended in 1945, every country—victorious, vanquished, or neutral—found itself with a severe disproportion between the increased purchasing power and the available supply of goods and services. If this had been the whole story, the solution of the inflationary problem would have been relatively simple. By various means, such as special taxes, capital levies, and the cancellation of purchasing power, the supply of monetary instruments could have been reduced. Some of those means were used in various countries. The U.S.S.R., for example, felt strong enough to cancel much of the excess credit in the hands of its citizens by revaluing the rouble. But in democratic countries very limited use could be made of such measures to reduce the money supply. Nor could such measures have remedied the most important postwar monetary problem—the distortion of the price structure. Price controls and rationing had kept some goods and services, such as rental housing, and in most countries food and clothing, at prices below the levels they would have reached if supply and demand had been free to operate. After other wars the distortion of the price structure had been allowed to correct itself by the play of supply and demand. While this was again happening to some extent in the United States after the second World War, in most countries the price inflation was suppressed by price controls and rationing.

Unfortunately it was not possible to put the processes of war production and finance into reverse. Reconversion from war to peace required public and private expenditures. Sudden deflation was almost as much feared as inflation. In every country the monetary situation was such that to avoid the stiffening of controls on the one hand or inflationary increases of commodity prices on the other, a delicately balanced monetary policy was necessary. Such a policy called in varying combinations for the maintenance of high tax levels to mop up the surplus purchasing power, but it called also for the tapering off of price controls and rationing systems so that the play of demand and supply might divert resources from military to civilian needs. Where price controls and rationing were strengthened, they threatened to rivet upon many countries planned economies at low consumption levels. On the other hand, tax reduction and the abolition of controls in the United States ran the risk of leading to a period of sharply rising commodity prices followed before long by a sharp recession.

After the first World War, the widely varying degrees of monetary inflation and the different national policies followed in dealing with it had led to severe strains on the external balances of payments. After the second World War there was an even greater variety of national monetary problems, but exchange control was tightly administered and the exchange rates were rigidly held at controlled parities. Thus there was not much to be gained by seeking to apply the theories developed in previous postwar periods to the very different and vastly more complicated circumstances of our own time. Those who advocated a return to the international gold standard were repeating the prescriptions of the economists who had wrestled with the monetary problems created by the Napoleonic Wars. They ignored the economic and political experience that had accumulated in the meantime. In particular they ignored the developments of the interwar years. The series of uncontrollable inflations that had wrecked the monetary systems of many European countries in the early 1920's was still within the experience of many who survived the second World War. But even more recent was the deflationary pressure that had attended the restoration of the gold standard following those inflations and the cumulative effects of the prolonged depression that had followed the breakdown of the restored gold standard.

Much had been learned by economists, central bankers, and treasury officials both from the restoration of the gold standard and from its breakdown during the interwar years. New devices of monetary regulation, particularly the exchange stabilization funds modeled upon the British Exchange Equalization Account, had indicated the nationalistic trend of central banking practice. But more important than the technical devices of monetary experts had been the growth of public support for policies of monetary nationalism. After the breakdown of the restored gold standard in 1931, autonomous credit policies had been directed toward stabilizing the national economies and intercepting deflationary pressures exerted upon them by the external balances of payments. The rationalization of full-employment theories by J. M. Keynes and his followers had led to a considerable elaboration of monetary practice in which the attempt to forestall cyclical fluctuations of employment was a major objective. On the other hand, the restoration of multilateral trade was recognized, even by the exponents of monetary nationalism, as a desirable objective of postwar policy. Moreover the extension of international credits was an obvious necessity both for reconstruction and for development. But multilateral trade and investment could not be restored except on a basis of exchange stability.

The problem was to work out a plan of international monetary collaboration that would permit as free multilateral trade as possible without stripping the countries whose balances of payments were strained, of their safeguards against cyclical pressure on those balances. The greatest obstacles to freer multilateral trade were exchange control and import quota systems, but these were the main safeguards to which the countries with weak balances of payments had resorted. It was tempting but inaccurate to identify the advocacy of freer multilateral trade with United States policy, and the advocacy of exchange control and import quota systems with British policy. It was true that the most ardent advocates of freer multilateral trade were to be found in the United States, while criticism of the principle of non-discrimination was most vocal in Britain. Much of the controversy between those who advocated the extreme positions on either side was couched in theoretical terms, but it was transparently a rationalization of what were conceived to be national interests. On both sides of the Atlantic there were warning voices that the long-run interests of both the United States and Britain would best be served by co-operative consultation to work out a middle ground. That these counsels of moderation were more powerful though less vocal than the expressions of either extreme was proved by the agreement reached at Bretton Woods.

The Bretton Woods agreement accepted the long-run objectives of exchange stability and freer multilateral trade. At the same time it provided for retention of exchange control over a transitional period of adjustment and for emergency departures from exchange stability and from multilateralism in periods of crisis. The compromise was not completely satisfactory to any of the participating governments. Nor was it immediately capable of realization. The argument could be made that to stabilize the exchange rates and to lay down the broad principles of a permanent international monetary system before national currencies had been brought under control was like building the roof before laying the foundations of international economic co-operation. But some assurance of interim exchange stabilization was necessary to avoid the hardening of emergency controls into permanent systems of exchange regulation, or alternatively such a debacle of currencies as that which followed the first World War.

During the war and in many countries for the better part of the preceding decade, exchange rates had been maintained at arbitrary parities by rigid systems of exchange control. Payment for imports had been rationed. The mobilization of resources for war had been achieved by the lend-lease program which had short-circuited the payments problem. It was evident that the urgent need for imports after the war ended might lead rapidly to exchange depreciation in many countries. If the economies of the war-devastated countries were to be reorganized, it was essential to prevent the competitive depreciation that had contributed so heavily to the demoralization of currencies after the first World War. The only practical method of preventing this was by retaining exchange control. It would have been fatal to the prospects of freer multilateral trade if exchange control had been allowed to become permanent. Thus what the nations were invited to do at Bretton Woods was not to abandon exchange control forthwith, but to sign a declaration that they intended to move toward its abolition. At the same time a set of principles of international monetary co-operation was adopted for future application, and a mechanism was created to facilitate co-operative action and mutual assistance in adhering to those principles.

Before describing this mechanism and summarizing the principles laid down for the new international monetary standard, it is important to make clear the limits within which the Fund was constituted. Its primary purpose might be described as an international extension of central banking practice. It had wider powers than those pertaining to exchange stability, particularly in respect to its consultative functions. It was not created to monopolize or even to dominate the foreign exchange markets. The fear expressed in some quarters that the Fund might eliminate private foreign exchange transactions was based on a misconception of its functions.

There was more reason to fear that the Fund might have been used, in the transitional adjustments following the war, to meet deficiencies in the balances of payments arising primarily from the economic dislocations of the war period. It was not intended for this purpose. Indeed the articles of agreement stated that "the Fund is not intended to provide facilities for relief or reconstruction or to deal with international indebtedness arising out of the war." Thus the difficult monetary problems of the immediate postwar period—the British blocked balances, relief, reparation payments, and reconstruction credits—were deliberately excluded from the Fund's operations. In the months immediately preceding the inauguration of the European Recovery Program, and particularly in the last quarter of 1947, Britain, France, the Netherlands, and Belgium did draw upon the Fund for dollars. But when the European Recovery Program went into effect, the directors of the Fund expressed the view that recipients of aid under this program should refrain from drawing dollars from the Fund, so that its holdings might remain at a level which would enable it to function as originally intended to correct situations of temporary disequilibrium after the transitional adjustments of the first postwar period had been made.

It should be emphasized that the achievement of exchange equilibrium was dependent upon the prior achievement of price equilibrium in each country. The major postwar monetary problems arose from the dislocations of the price structure. These problems were national, and had to be solved by each country for itself. The European Recovery Program was designed to take the strain off the external balances of payments during an interim period while each of the participating countries put its own monetary affairs in order. The Economic Cooperation Administration of the United States stood ready to offer both technical assistance and financial aid, but the major effort of reconstruction necessarily fell upon the European countries themselves. Individually and in concert, they had to reorganize their industries on a peacetime basis and get rid of the price distortions that caused expenditures to be excessive in the low-priced avenues of consumption, while hampering the restoration of productivity in the high-priced but essential goods and services. This involved abandoning state subsidies to keep food prices low, reducing over-ambitious programs of investment in durable consumption goods such as housing, stimulating greater productivity in such basic industries as coal production, even if this entailed temporary surrender of some hard-won gains in hours and conditions of labor, reducing consumption of imports by allowing prices to rise, and stimulating production of exports by more efficient methods of organization. These were not easy prescriptions to follow. Until productivity was increased, particularly in the export industries, and excessive import demands were reduced, there was no possibility that multilateral trade could flow freely without causing strains on the external balances of payments. Until this was achieved, the mechanisms set up in the Fund to facilitate the maintenance of exchange stability would be unable to operate.

The mechanism devised to maintain exchange stability was called a Fund, upon the analogy of the national stabilization funds of the interwar period. However, this title did not describe accurately the way in which the Fund was intended to function. It is true that a pool of currencies was created, to which each member subscribed an agreed quota. A fraction of each country's quota was subscribed in gold and the remainder in the country's own currency. The total of these national quotas was the equivalent of $8,046 million, of which $1,436.6 million had been paid in gold, and $5,539.7 million in different national currencies, while unpaid balances of members' subscriptions amounted (as of the end of August, 1949) to $1,070.2 million.[4] Between March 1, 1947, when the Fund opened, and the end of August, 1949, seventeen countries had exercised their right of purchase, all of them purchasing dollars, while two also purchased Belgian francs and one, sterling. The Fund's holdings of gold were intact, but it held fewer

[4] The unpaid subscriptions were those of Bolivia and Honduras in regard to which certain legal points were outstanding, Panama in regard to which negotiations had not been completed, and Austria, China, Finland, Greece, Italy, Poland, Thailand, and Uruguay, for whose currencies no par values had been determined and whose subscriptions therefore were not due. Yugoslavia completed payment in September, 1949.

dollars and more sterling, Belgian francs, Chilean pesos, Danish kroner, French francs, Indian rupees, Mexican pesos, Netherlands guilders, Norwegian kroner, and other moneys. Each member had the right to purchase from the Fund foreign exchange with its own currency to the extent of 25 per cent of its quota in any one year or 100 per cent of its quota in all.

For such purchases no charge was payable for the first three months, but thereafter a charge of ½ per cent was made for the next nine months. Then this charge rose by ½ per cent each year, and by another ½ per cent for each 25 per cent of its national quota used by a country. This progressive scale of charges was intended to discourage a member from drawing upon the Fund except to meet a temporary deficit in its balance of payments while taking steps to remedy the causes of that deficit. If a member were to draw upon the Fund to the full extent of its quota, the charges would go up on a sliding scale to a level that would eventually become burdensome. In the first year of operation, the British, French, and Mexican purchases were close to the permissible 25 per cent of the national quotas. When the European Recovery Plan went into effect, no further purchases of dollars were made by the European countries.

Before the Fund began operations, much fear had been expressed that it would quickly lose all its gold and dollars in exchange for a collection of less convertible currencies. The precise language of the articles of agreement, giving the right to purchase foreign exchange, lent some credence to this fear, but in fact the right was used sparingly. This could be attributed in part to the fact that the countries most short of dollars had received aid from the United States in other forms. However, the failure of most countries to exercise their right of purchasing foreign exchange could be attributed to the procedures by which such purchases involved discussion and persuasion. Severer tests might be imposed upon the Fund in some future crisis, but it could at least claim that at their initiation it had taught its members to be cautious.

The most important part of the mechanism was not the fund of currencies upon which governments might draw in emergencies. It was the facilities created by the Fund for organized consultation. The annual meetings of the Governors gave opportunity for discussion among those responsible for monetary policy in the member-countries. In addition the eighteen Executive Directors held permanent appointments and were in continuous consultation. The importance of these positions had led to the appointment of responsible officials from the eighteen countries directly represented. Moreover the representatives of the smaller countries were empowered to cast the votes of the remaining members. Thus the Mexican Executive Director cast the votes of Mexico, Colombia, Cuba, Costa Rica, Dominican Republic, Guatemala, El Salvador, Honduras, and Nicaragua. In all issues before the Fund, the views of all the members were continuously represented.

Each country had undertaken to furnish national data upon its monetary situation and policies, including specific items of information, many of which had never before been available to an international organization. Some of these, such as estimates of national income, required the improvement of national statistical services. The net effect of this pooling of information for analysis by a competent secretariat was to furnish a picture of the interrelations of international payments more complete than had ever before been possible. The full-time Executive Directors of the Fund were not only kept fully informed, they were instructed as to the views of their own governments and of those governments whose votes were entrusted to them. These facilities for continuous informed discussion gave rise to the hope that the Fund might prove able to foresee and forestall the development of strains on the national balances of payments. The major influence likely to be exerted was by recommendation and persuasion, arising out of the methods of consultative co-operation.

The articles of agreement had also laid down a set of monetary principles to which members agreed ultimately to conform. In nontechnical language the main obligations assumed were to refrain from depreciating the exchange value of their currencies except in clearly defined circumstances, and then only by agreement with the Fund. They likewise agreed that after a transitional period they would permit their currencies to be bought and sold freely at the agreed exchange parities. In so far as current trading transactions were concerned, the members agreed not to impose exchange control and to avoid discriminatory currency practices. The broad obligation, therefore, was to restore free multilateral clearing of international payments at fixed exchange rates.

After a limited transitional period, exchange control was to be abolished, and the national currencies were to be made freely convertible into gold, or into other currencies, at fixed exchange rates. What was aimed at was the free multilateral clearing of payments and the exchange stability formerly assured by the international gold standard. If those objectives were to be attained, each national monetary authority had to keep its balance of payments in equilibrium. This meant that the national economy must be continuously adjusted to the international payments situation. The right to purchase foreign exchange from the Fund provided some flexibility of adjustment so that the more vulnerable national economies might not be subjected to sudden strains.

The exchange stability aimed at was not tied to gold. Nor was it to be absolute. A country under strain might revalue its currency once, up to 10 per cent, or after consultation with the Fund, by larger steps. Thus the currencies were to be adjustable by agreement. There was provision for simultaneous devaluation by raising the price of gold in all currencies. The intent was, while maintaining exchange stability as long as there were not heavy strains on the balances of payments, to escape from the rigidity of exchange rates in a crisis.

One of the main fears—particularly of British critics—was that the United States with its preponderant weight in the world economy would continue to be subject to violent cyclical depressions. It was argued that the more vulnerable countries could not insulate themselves against the disastrous consequences that could follow even the fluctuations which the United States in its strength and vitality could take in its stride, unless they were able to discriminate against imports from the United States and by bilateral purchase agreements assure themselves of stable imports. The framers of the articles of agreement of the Fund had tried to meet these fears by providing that if a particular currency became scarce, the other countries might be allowed to discriminate against payments in that currency. In plain words, this meant that if the Fund declared that there was a general shortage of United States dollars, and the United States did not make more dollars available, other countries might impose exchange control against the United States. Some of the critics were not satisfied with this provision. They felt that the influence of the United States was powerful in the Fund's decisions. Thus they feared that dollars might not be declared scarce until after other countries had been forced into deflationary policies.

All that can be said with regard to such fears is that they were hypothetical. If such situations do arise, the consultative mechanisms of the Fund will have failed. The true test of the Fund's potentialities does not lie in scrutiny of the text of the articles of agreement, but in evaluating the facilities for international consultative co-operation which have been set up. Experience rather than exegesis must provide the answers to questions as to what the Fund will do in circumstances at present unforeseeable. If the articles of agreement come to be administered in a legalistic spirit, they will certainly prove unworkable in a crisis. If, on the other hand, the mechanism of consultation develops as a flexible and adaptable instrument of international monetary co-operation, the worst fears of the critics may never be realized.

It is of some interest to examine the working of the Fund in its first stages of development. The available evidence in the first year of the Fund's operations was limited. The general adjustment of exchange rates had been postponed and exchange control was still the general rule. Three situations had arisen in which the Fund proved that it could approach national difficulties with sympathetic understanding and interpret the obligations of its members with flexibility. The first was that of Ecuador. In June, 1947, Ecuador introduced a new method of allocating its limited foreign exchange so that the exchange value of the sucre was different for essential, semi-essential, and luxury imports. This could have been held to contravene the article of agreement directed against multiple currency arrangements. But the Fund treated this case under another article and co-operated with the Ecuadorean government, approving the emergency arrangement for two years and sending a technical mission to assist in eliminating the difficulty.

In March, 1947, Italy had become a member of the Fund but had postponed a definitive valuation of the lira. In March, 1946, a special lira rate had been introduced for foreign trade transactions. One half of the proceeds of exports were surrendered to the Bank of Italy at an official rate and the remainder sold in the free market. After November, 1947, the official rate was fixed at the average of the free market rates in the preceding month. The Fund accepted these as transitional arrangements in terms of Article XIV, 2, making exceptions for countries whose territories had been occupied by the enemy. By June, 1948, the official and free market rates for United States dollars had become identical.

On January 26, 1948, the French government devalued the franc by 44 per cent. In doing so it followed the Italian precedent. The official rate of the franc was fixed at 214 to the dollar. But a free market was recognized in United States dollars, Portuguese escudos, gold, and later in Swiss francs. The reason for this free market was the desire to attract gold from hoards, to encourage the repatriation of French assets held abroad, and also to encourage the tourist traffic. The French authorities consulted the Fund, which was not opposed either to the devaluation or to the creation of a free market for the purposes noted above and for a limited period. But the Fund *was* opposed to the French proposal to allow exporters to sell on the free market half of the dollars, escudos, and Swiss francs received in payment for exports. Such a proceeding would enable speculators to traffic in the cross-rates—for example, the sterling rate in francs—and also in commodity arbitrage transactions, buying British, Belgian, and even Australian exports at the official rate and selling them half at the official rate, and half at the free market rate.

Despite the opposition of the Fund, the French carried through their proposal. Thereupon France was declared ineligible to use its resources. France retained its membership, but could not purchase any further exchange from the Fund. By June, 1948, the free market rate for the franc had settled around 306 to the dollar. The neighboring countries, particularly Britain, had protected themselves by tightening both their exchange and trade controls, so that the net effect of the French devaluation was a restriction rather than a freeing of trade. France had defied the Fund and in a strict legal sense had broken its agreement. In consequence it had lost the privileges but retained membership. If the emergency arrangements proved to be temporary, no great harm might result. The Fund had shown that it could be firm, as well as patient and sympathetic with national difficulties.

It was by the accumulated experience gained in handling such incidents that the Fund would succeed or fail in the long run. There was no foolproof formula of monetary management. Every incident had to be dealt with on its merits. The technicalities of monetary management were merely the surface outcroppings of real economic disagreements. Alfred Marshall once wrote that "the only very important thing to be said about currency is that it is not nearly as important as it looks." The controversies that continue to arise concerning the Fund derive from conflicts of economic policy involving national and group interests, rather than from technicalities. The fears that are expressed spring mainly from the belief that the Fund will be used as a means to prevent countries from following economic policies that they may feel necessary to safeguard employment and living levels.

The Fund is only the monetary instrument for facilitating a broad program of freer multilateral trade and investment. In the final act of the Bretton Woods conference, the monetary experts felt it necessary to incorporate recommendations to the national governments concerned with "creating in the field of international economic relations conditions necessary for the attainment of the purposes of the Fund and of the broader primary objectives of economic policy." Some of these recommendations dealt with measures to handle the transitional difficulties which the Fund was not designed to handle. Two were for long-run action intimately connected with the purposes of the Fund. The first of these was worked out at Bretton Woods in the articles of agreement upon which the International Bank for Reconstruction and Development was subsequently created. The other was left for action by the later conferences which finally evolved the International Trade Charter.

The International Monetary Fund was a regulating rather than a lending institution. To that extent it was misnamed. To concentrate attention upon the pool of currencies used as a means of short-term accommodation for countries whose external balances were temporarily strained was to misconceive its purposes and functions. The Fund would succeed to the extent that it was able, by consultation and persuasion, to limit the needs of its members to draw upon this pool. But it could not succeed merely by marking time. Unless a determined effort was made to persuade the countries whose balances of payments were strained, and whose exchange rates were arbitrarily maintained at overvalued parities, to revalue their currencies and reorganize their economies, the whole precarious structure of international economic equilibrium might come tumbling about their ears.

THE INTERNATIONAL BANK FOR RECONSTRUCTION AND DEVELOPMENT

At the Bretton Woods conference attention was concentrated upon the International Monetary Fund. The principles laid down for the operation of the Fund were more elaborate and gave rise to greater controversy than the relatively simple principles by which the International Bank for Reconstruction and Development was to operate. One of the significant developments of the conference was a series of changes in the earlier United States draft for the International Bank. This had gone through the same stages of discussion as those described in connection with the Fund. Largely on the insistence of the British and other western European representatives, who were not in a position to commit their countries to an international bank that might involve them in large capital exports, the functions of the projected bank were limited. Its resources for direct lending were reduced to a minimum, the major part even of the subscribed capital could be lent only by permission of the subscribing country, and the bulk of the authorized capital remained uncalled as a guarantee fund. Thus the International Bank became an institution to facilitate, encourage, and in some respects to supervise the revival of private international investment.

Because the Bank was set up with a large nominal capital, there has been much public misconception of its functions. It came into existence on December 27, 1945, when its articles of agreement were signed by the representatives of 28 countries. It began operations in March, 1946, by holding an inaugural meeting of its Board of Governors at Savannah, Georgia, and electing the first Board of Executive Directors. It was opened for business on June 25, 1946, but conflict developed in regard to its administration, and it was not until the positions of President, Vice-President, and Executive Director representing the United States were filled on February 28, 1947, and March 14, 1947, by men drawn from circles closely related to private banking in the United States, that it became possible to negotiate actual transactions. The first loan was granted to France on May 9, 1947, and the first bond issue was floated in the United States on July 15, 1947.

As of August 20, 1949, forty-eight countries had become members of the Bank. The authorized capital stock consisted of 100,000 shares with a par value of $100,000 each, purchasable only by members, and transferable only to the Bank. The total subscribed capital was the equivalent of $8,348,500,000. Of this amount only 20 per cent was paid in, and only 2 per cent was paid in United States dollars or gold by countries other than the United States. The capital paid in national currencies could not be lent except with the permission of the member-country concerned. Only the United States, Belgium, Canada, and the United Kingdom had given this permission, the United States fully and the others for small amounts totaling the equivalent of $12 million. As of the end of 1948 the capital available for lending was $753.4 million. This represented the 20 per cent of the United States subscription which had been paid in, plus $98.3 million which represented the 2 per cent of other members' subscriptions paid in gold or United States dollars plus $12 million worth of Belgian francs, Canadian dollars, and pounds sterling and $8.1 million net profits. The remaining 18 per cent of members' subscriptions (amounting to the equivalent of $915,858,000 in different national currencies) was not available for loans since the countries concerned did not feel able to export capital. Most of them in the years immediately after the second World War, were themselves heavy borrowers on capital account. The uncalled 80 per cent of authorized capital (amounting to the equivalent of $6,610,480,000, of which $2,540,000,000 was the uncalled subscription of the United States) was held in reserve as a guarantee fund against any losses that might accrue from the Bank's direct lending, participation in lending, or guarantees of private lending.

Thus the loanable funds immediately available were $753.4 million. To this the bond issues of July 15, 1947, had added $250,000,000. On May 25, 1948, the Bank announced that it had arranged to sell short-dated bonds to the amount of Swiss francs 17,000,000 (equivalent to $4,000,000) to the Bank for International Settlements. This was the first flotation of bonds on a market outside the United States, the proceeds being devoted to meeting part of the loan that had been granted to the Netherlands. Current transactions increased the loanable funds. By August 20, 1949, the International Bank had negotiated loans totaling $716.6 million, of which $2,000,000 was in Belgian francs and $4,000,000 in Swiss francs, so that the total of loanable funds remaining was $390 million. Loan applications were pending from a long list of countries—Bolivia, Czechoslovakia, India, Iran, Italy, Norway, Peru, the Philippines, Poland, and Turkey and several others—in addition to a proposed loan to the European timber exporting countries (Finland, Poland, Czechoslovakia, Yugoslavia, and Asia). The latter had been recommended by the United Nations Economic Commission for Europe as a means of increasing timber exports to the western European consuming countries.

These figures have been quoted to indicate the relatively small scale upon which the International Bank was operating. It was possible that as other member-countries became able to permit use of the 18 per cent of their subscriptions and with the flotation of new bond issues in the United States and other markets, the scale of lending would increase. The Bank, however, was limited by its articles of agreement to loans which did not exceed its total authorized capital ($8,263,100,000), and even this amount was inadequate for the needs of reconstruction and development all over the world.

One of the primary purposes of the Bank was to re-create the international flow of private investment. By its articles of agreement it was required to satisfy itself that the prospective borrower was not able to obtain the required accommodation on reasonable terms through private channels. Thus the Bank was designed to break the log-jams of investment. It was not to act as an international agency of planned investment or as an instrument of international lending to counteract depression and to maintain international equilibrium at full employment. In its cautious and practical evolution maintaining the closest touch with the private banking and investing circles upon which it depended for additions to its loanable funds, it had little resemblance to the international investment agencies pursuing contracyclical policies that figured prominently in the projects of full employment theorists. On the contrary, it was a severely practical institution. It took pains to emphasize its role as a catalyst of private enterprise and private investment and thereby to win the confidence of banks, insurance companies, and other institutional investors.

The first loans that it made were limited to specific projects. In no case was there granted the full amount requested. Thus on October 8, 1946, the French Minister of Finance had applied for a loan of $500 million. Before the loan was granted, officers of the Bank and consulting engineers had been given facilities by the French government to investigate the specific projects that were planned and the general economic situation in France. In subsequent loan negotiations these precedents were followed, and the Bank officers made public statements that they preferred to open informal conversations rather than to receive official requests for loans, in order that the form of loan assistance might be worked out co-operatively. On May 9, 1947, the Bank announced that it was granting its first loan, amounting to just half the amount originally asked, to the Crédit National. This was a semi-public corporation created to assist in financing the reconstruction and development of the French economy. Repayment was guaranteed by the French government. The loan was not granted as a lump sum but was to be disbursed as required to meet the cost of purchasing specified items of equipment. The Bank received full information as to these purchases and opened a branch office in Paris to check upon the receipt and installation of the equipment.

Thus it was evident that as in the case of the International Monetary Fund and the other specialized agencies of the United Nations, the processes of consultative co-operation would play a large part in the Bank's activities. Its fourteen Executive Directors, like those of the Fund, held full-time appointments. In their deliberations they were instructed as to the attitudes of the member-governments whose votes they cast. There was a strong secretariat, and intimate relations were maintained with the secretariat of the Fund so that there was a pooling of information. While the Bank also co-operated with the other specialized agencies of the United Nations and with the Economic and Social Council, its agreement with the Council gave it independence in respect of loan negotiations.

The principles upon which it operated had been made perfectly clear in numerous statements made as part of the educational campaign undertaken in connection with the first flotation of bonds in the United Nations. The "ultimate mission" of the Bank was stated in an address by its President on April 5, 1948, to be "to blaze the trail for private international investment." In this and other addresses by Bank officers, stress was laid upon the fact that the Bank did not desire to dictate to any member the methods of economic reconstruction and development it might desire to follow. At the same time the Bank would require frank, full, and continuing consultation on the general economic situation of any member-country contracting a loan as well as close supervision of the disbursement of funds.

The repeated statement that the Bank intended to play an active role in seeking out opportunities for assisting reconstruction, rather than to wait passively for members to request loans, indicated that a pattern for restoring international investment was to be developed. Coupled with the provisions of the articles of agreement requiring the Bank to refrain from making loans that could be supplied on reasonable terms through private channels, and the repeated emphasis upon the limited funds available for direct loans, this adoption of an active role implied an attempt to encourage national governments to create the conditions favorable for private international investment. The loans made by the Bank were designed to break bottlenecks of development. In addition to such positive action, the first annual report emphasized a desire to assist in removing deterrents to the free flow of private capital and with it of foreign technical, managerial, and administrative skills, to the underdeveloped nations. In this connection the Bank's services were offered in making recommendations for just settlements of debts now in default, for the achievement of sound budgetary and monetary systems in the prospective borrowing countries, and for the negotiation of conditions of investment which would assure investors of equitable treatment, while preventing exploitation or interference with national policies.

As the Bank was able to extend its operations, it would function both as a catalyst to facilitate private international investment, and as a mechanism for the continuous audit of past and prospective investment. Statements condemning improper lending as causing loss to individual investors as well as burdens to borrowers, were as emphatic as warnings against reckless borrowing. The Bank had an important role to play in this respect. If it could discourage excessive and imperfectly negotiated international investment, it would perform a service to both borrowers and lenders. If it could help to assure borrowers and lenders that the loans negotiated were within the capacity of the borrowing country to repay, that their expenditure had been effectively controlled, and that the purposes of the investment would benefit borrower as well as lender, it might be that a smaller volume of investment than in the past would produce greater benefits and greater stability.

However, the notion of using an international investment fund as a device to forestall the spread of cyclical depression found little response in the Bank's philosophy and practice. The Bank was in the business of promoting reconstruction and development, not in that of regulating the flow of purchasing power so that national economic activities might be kept at levels of full employment. Any contracyclical lending that might be undertaken would fall within the province of the International Monetary Fund. But it might be argued that the resources of the Fund and the mechanisms of its operation were inadequate.

In the past, international investment had been subjected to the irregular rhythm induced by the London money market's manipulation of the interest rates in an attempt to keep international trading transactions from clogging the markets. In these conditions, the fluctuations of international investment had aggravated the swings of the business cycle. It could be hoped that the close relationship between the International Monetary Fund and the International Bank might in the future minimize this tendency for international investment to aggravate the fluctuations of the cycle. In so far as the Bank succeeded in influencing investors and borrowers to be cautious in their commitments, and provided an international forum in which the flow of international investment might be kept continuously under review, it would help to stabilize the cycle. But it was highly improbable that the Bank would try to compensate for any weakness that the Fund might reveal in its attempts to handle strains on the balances of payment. Measures to cope with cyclical fluctuations did not lie within its field of activities as it was functioning in the first years of its existence.

THE INTERNATIONAL TRADE CHARTER

The last of the specialized economic agencies to which attention must be drawn was the most difficult to negotiate. The International Trade Organization was designed to administer an elaborate charter of international trading principles. Negotiations leading up to this charter began in November, 1945, when the United States published its *Proposals for the Expansion of World Trade and Employment.* Behind these proposals lay a series of developments in the commercial policy of the United States since the passing of the Reciprocal Trade Agreements Act in 1934. That Act, renewed in 1937, 1940, 1943, 1945, 1948 and September, 1949, had delegated to the executive branch of government power to negotiate bilateral agreements for the reciprocal modification of tariff barriers.

Though the driving force behind the reciprocal trade agreement program was Cordell Hull, the Secretary of State from 1932 to 1944, the administration of the program was shared by many departments of government. Mr. Hull, during a long period of specialized study of financial and economic questions while he was first a Congressman and later a Senator from Tennessee, became not only a convinced advocate of freer trade but also a tariff expert. As Secretary of State he devised and promoted the enactment of the Reciprocal Trade Agreements Act and created the Trade Agreements Committee on which all the executive departments concerned with economic policy were represented. This committee was formed to assist the President in negotiating the trade agreements.

In order to give full opportunity for interested members of the public to be heard before any agreement was negotiated, public notice was required of the intention to negotiate and of the commodities on which the United States might reduce import duties. Another committee—that on Reciprocity Information, on which sat many of the members of the Trade Agreements Committee—was set up to hold public hearings on each proposed agreement. After public discussion of the detailed issues involved, the Trade Agreements Committee formulated recommendations. When these were approved by the President, the Secretary of State was enabled to negotiate with the foreign country concerned. The result of these negotiations was an executive agreement. This was not a treaty, and hence it did not have to be submitted to the Senate, but became law when proclaimed by the President.

The Reciprocal Trade Agreements Act represented a most significant shift from the high protectionism of the Hawley-Smoot tariff. From August 24, 1934, when the first agreement was signed with Cuba, to September 12, 1946, thirty-two agreements had been negotiated. Each of these had involved detailed analysis of the trade of the United States with the countries concerned and public discussion of the items upon which the United States might reduce its tariff, as well as of the reductions in foreign tariffs that might be secured in return. Attempts at statistical calculation in this field are notoriously treacherous. But there could be no doubt that over a very large volume of trade affecting thousands of tariff items and the larger part of the trading world, significant reductions of tariff barriers had been achieved. Though other factors were operative, the fact that from 1935 to 1939 the increase in United States trade with the countries that had negotiated agreements was more than double the increase in trade with non-agreement countries undoubtedly reflected the influence of the trade agreement program. The fact that exports to the agreement countries increased by 63 per cent, while imports from them increased by 27 per cent, was proof that the United States negotiators had not been soft in their bargaining.

This background of reciprocal tariff bargaining had been influential in the negotiation of wartime financial agreements. The most important of these was Article VII of the master lend-lease agreement,

THE RECIPROCAL TRADE AGREEMENTS PROGRAM

The countries with which the United States had concluded agreements up to January 1, 1948, are shown in black.

Source: U.S. Department of Commerce, *Foreign Commerce Weekly*, Washington, November 22, 1948, p. 47.

signed on February 23, 1942, between Britain and the United States, setting forth the principles upon which lend-lease and reverse lend-lease would be conducted. This provided that the final settlement of lend-lease obligations should not burden trade between the two countries but should promote mutually advantageous economic relations. In language that was repeated in the agreements subsequently signed with all the countries receiving lend-lease, it was also agreed that action should be taken, "open to participation by all other countries of like mind, directed to the expansion, by appropriate international and domestic measures, of production, employment, and the exchange and consumption of goods, . . . to the elimination of all forms of discriminatory treatment in international commerce, and to the reduction of tariffs and other trade barriers. . . ." In other financial agreements—notably in the one negotiated with Britain in December, 1945, providing for a loan of $3,750 million—the United States expressed its intention to move toward a reduction of trade barriers and secured the promise of its allies to support its attempt to restore freer multilateral world trade based on equality of trading opportunity. Thus the *Proposals for the Expansion of World Trade and Employment,* out of which grew the International Trade Charter, were given formal status by being accepted in principle in this Anglo-American Financial Agreement.

It was understood that the machinery by which the United States would negotiate reductions in its own tariff on a reciprocal basis against reductions in foreign tariffs and elimination of other trade barriers would be that set up under the Reciprocal Trade Agreements Act. This was done at the crucial stage of the negotiations on the international trade charter which took place at Geneva from April 10 to October 30, 1947. At that time a series of interlocking trade agreements was negotiated among 23 countries covering more than 45,000 trade items and representing about half of total world imports. The contribution of the United States to this greatest of all tariff negotiations ever undertaken covered tariff items representing about three-fourths by value of the total imports into the United States in 1939. For more than half of its total imports similarly measured, the United States promised not to increase existing rates of duty or to take items off the free list; on about one-fourth, duties were reduced by varying percentages up to 50 per cent of their 1945 levels. No reductions were made on the remaining fourth.

These arrangements constituted a major operation on the United States tariff which would have been impossible but for the powers conferred on the executive by the Reciprocal Trade Agreements Act. On January 1, 1948, the new tariff rates were put into force in so far as they were of primary concern to Australia, Benelux (the Belgian-Netherlands-Luxembourg Customs Union), Canada, Cuba, France, and the United Kingdom, which had ratified the agreements. In so far as the new rates were of primary interest to the other participating countries—Brazil, Burma, Ceylon, Chile, China, Czechoslovakia, India, Lebanon, New Zealand, Norway, Pakistan, Southern Rhodesia, Syria, and South Africa—proclamation was withheld until those countries ratified the agreement. By June 30, 1948, all of these countries except Chile had ratified, the required 85 per cent of the foreign trade of all the negotiating countries had been accounted for, and the *General Agreement on Tariffs and Trade* went into effect. As with all the Reciprocal Trade Agreements, the lowered duties were extended by most-favored-nation treatment to all countries which extended most-favored-nation treatment to imports from the United States.

To understand how this great tariff agreement was connected with the negotiations for an international trade charter, it is necessary to pick up the thread of negotiations after the publication in November, 1945, of the United States *Proposals for the Expansion of World Trade and Employment,* and their acceptance in principle in December, 1945, by the British officials who negotiated the Anglo-American Financial Agreement. The next step was taken in September, 1946. There was then published a *Suggested Charter for an International Trade Organization of the United Nations.* Therein the proposals were put into diplomatic language. On February 18, 1946, the Economic and Social Council of the United Nations resolved to call a conference on trade and employment to consider the suggested charter. At the same time, the Council set up a Preparatory Committee of nineteen nations (which later became eighteen because the U.S.S.R. did not co-operate) to arrange the conference, prepare its agenda, and draft a charter.

This Preparatory Committee met at London from October 15 to November 26, 1946. There was considerable criticism and revision of the American proposals. In their original form, they had been confined to provisions setting up a freer system of multilateral trade based upon equality of trading opportunity. This official policy, first expressed in the Reciprocal Trade Agreements Act in 1934, had gained the support of influential circles of public opinion in the United States. For example, in June, 1945, the Committee on International Economic Policy—a United States organization which had grown out of the collaboration of the Carnegie Endowment for International Peace with the International Chamber of Commerce—published the first of a series of pamphlets entitled *World Trade and Employment*. This was based upon an early draft of the United States proposals which had not at that time been published. But it also incorporated much of the detailed work of the League of Nations and of the International Chamber of Commerce with respect to such technical questions as national treatment, unfair competition, valuation, marks of origin, customs formalities, double taxation, and commercial arbitration. The later official draft proposals and the charter based upon them included most of this work, which represented the efforts of practical traders and technical experts to formulate agreed solutions for troublesome procedural questions. Broadly speaking the United States proposals were in accord with the principles and practice of private multilateral trade. The proposed bargain involved substantial reductions in the United States tariff against reciprocal tariff concessions and the abandonment by other countries of the instruments of regulated bilateral trade such as quotas, exchange control, subsidies, and bilateral agreements.

There was widespread fear among the delegates to the Preparatory Conference at London that the United States might fall into depression after having insisted upon other countries giving up the controls over their balances of payments upon which they depended for the maintenance of high living standards at full employment. The original proposals of the United States urged that both trade and employment must be expanded. While the tenor of the proposals was expansionist, the specific obligations proposed were directed to the reduction of trade barriers. At London, an attempt was made to write into the international trade charter specific obligations to maintain full employment. The representatives of the United States were not able to accept such suggestions. The parts of the draft charter which dealt with this question were somewhat expanded, but the positive obligations inserted went no further than the provisions of the Employment Act of 1946, already in force in the United States. Each member of the proposed International Trade Organization was asked to agree "to take action designed to achieve and maintain full and productive employment and large and steadily growing demand within its own territory through measures appropriate to its political, economic and social institutions."

The chapter of the draft charter concerned with the economic development of underdeveloped countries was also greatly elaborated at London. In its expanded form, it became the subject of much criticism by business groups in the United States. Even so, the proposed functions of the International Trade Organization and the escape clauses as well—to which objection had been raised—did not go far enough to satisfy India and China and did not commit either the I.T.O. or its member-countries to any very precise obligations. At London, as in the later discussions at Geneva and Havana, economic development proved the most difficult of all the questions of trading policy. The provisions of the draft charter dealing with commercial policy in general, with tariff reductions, national treatment, most-favored-nation treatment, abolition of quotas, and reduction of preferences, abstention from subsidies and similar technical issues were elaborated to take account of particular national situations. The draft charter which emerged from the London conference embodied substantially the viewpoint of the United States.

The United States also resisted successfully the attempt of the underdeveloped countries to stipulate that the already industrialized countries should accept obligations to assist in the process of industrialization through the international mechanisms of the projected International Trade Organization. While no specific obligations were written into the draft charter, articles recognizing the need for elaborating a code as to the conduct, practices, and treatment of foreign investment went far to meet the views of United States business interests. The major conflict in this regard concerned the desire of the underdeveloped countries to be free to impose tariffs or quotas as a means of establishing and developing new industries. This point was to prove the most controversial of all the articles of the charter at the later Geneva and Havana conferences. At London the United States delegation successfully defended the principle that such departures from the main intent of the charter should not be permitted except with the consent of the International Trade Organization and then only temporarily and on a non-discriminatory basis.

After a drafting committee had met in New York early in 1947, the Preparatory Committee met again at Geneva from April 10 to August 22. The Geneva meeting had a twofold purpose. The original committee, increased to twenty-three countries by the addition of Burma, Ceylon, Pakistan and Southern Rhodesia, negotiated the *General Agreement on Tariffs and Trade.* To this reference has already been made.[5] This agreement incorporated practically all the provisions of the draft charter in regard to commercial policy, strictly defined. It made no reference to the chapters on Employment, on Restrictive Business Practices, or on Intergovernmental Commodity Agreements, but it did incorporate a provision that, with the consent of the other contracting parties, an underdeveloped country, in order to establish new industries, might be released from certain of its obligations under the agreement. Thus this *General Agreement on Tariffs and Trade* contained many of the essential elements of the original United States proposals. The United States, in return for substantial tariff concessions, obtained from twenty-two countries both reciprocal tariff concessions and commitments to move in the direction of private multilateral, non-discriminatory trade. These countries, together with the United States, conduct about 70 per cent of the total of world trade.

At the same time the Geneva revision of the draft charter as a whole represented substantial successes for the United States point of view. As the charter emerged it was considerably closer in spirit and in many detailed particulars to the original United States proposals than the London draft had been. The pressure exerted in the meantime upon the United States negotiators by organized business groups and Congressional hearings had had its effect. The Committee for Reciprocity Information had held public hearings pursuant to the Reciprocal Trade Agreements Act. On November 10, 1946, pub-

[5] See above, pp. 662–63. The signatories of the *General Agreement* were Australia, Belgium, Brazil, Burma, Canada, Ceylon, Chile, China, Cuba, Czechoslovakia, France, India, Lebanon, Luxembourg, Netherlands, New Zealand, Norway, Pakistan, Southern Rhodesia, Syria, South Africa, Great Britain, and the United States.

Other countries which took part unofficially in negotiations on the Charter at Geneva were Afghanistan, Argentina, Colombia, Denmark, Ecuador, Egypt, Greece, Iran, Mexico, Peru, Poland, Saudi-Arabia, Siam, Sweden, Turkey, Uruguay, Venezuela, and Yugoslavia.

In addition, the following countries took part in the final negotiation of the Charter at Havana from November 21, 1947 to March 24, 1948: Austria, Bolivia, Costa Rica, Dominican Republic, El Salvador, Guatemala, Haiti, Indonesia, Iraq, Ireland, Italy, Liberia, Nicaragua, Panama, Philippines, Portugal, Switzerland, and Transjordan.

At the completion of the Havana negotiations, Argentina refused to sign the final Act, and signature was deferred also by Poland, Saudi-Arabia, Siam, Turkey, and Yugoslavia.

lic notice had been given of the intention to negotiate with a group of nations at Geneva. A long list of tariff items upon which reductions of duty might be negotiated had been published. In view of the importance of the impending negotiations, a special effort had been made to ensure that all interested individuals and groups were given an opportunity to express their views. In addition, the Trade Agreements Committee held public hearings on the proposed draft charter in six widely separated cities from Boston to San Francisco. Hearings before the Senate Finance Committee also produced suggestions for amendment of the London draft, and the larger number of these were accepted at Geneva.

Thus the United States negotiators at Geneva were thoroughly informed of public and Congressional opinion in regard to the charter and were stiffened in their insistence upon returning to the spirit of the original proposals. There was little doubt that the broad sweep of the United States proposals for tariff reduction took most of the participants in the Geneva negotiations by surprise. The tariff reductions proposed were so substantial that many countries had to revise their first rather meager lists of reciprocal concessions. This fact influenced their willingness to accept in greater measure the United States proposals for a private enterprise trading system.

The tariff reductions and the *General Agreement on Tariffs and Trade* negotiated at Geneva stood on their own merits as an accomplished fact. As far as the United States was concerned, the *General Agreement* contained the substance of the charter. That agreement, however, was temporary and unlikely to stand except as part of the charter. The charter itself had to be submitted for final adoption by the Conference on Trade and Employment which the United Nations convened at Havana on November 21, 1947. At this conference, which lasted till March 24, 1948, the original negotiating group that had worked through the preparatory discussions at London, New York, and Geneva was merged in a full conference of sixty nations.

A strong group of Latin-American states led by Argentina revived the major issues, particularly those connected with economic development. Much pressure was exerted to permit underdeveloped countries to use at their discretion not only tariffs, but quotas, exchange control, preferential agreements and state trading devices to establish new industries. On this crucial point, the United States finally offered a compromise. The demand of the underdeveloped countries was accepted in so far as it did not "apply to any product in respect of which the Member has assumed an obligation through negotiations with any other Member or Members pursuant to Chapter IV." This diplomatic language means that for the large number of items included in the schedules of reduced tariffs in the *General Agreement on Tariffs and Trade,* and for all items that might be included in subsequent reciprocal agreements, the underdeveloped countries must seek permission from their trading partners before using tariffs or quotas to develop their own infant industries. But they were to be permitted under the charter to use tariffs and quotas to develop infant industries producing *other* commodities. Since the schedules of the *General Agreement* covered about half the world's imports and included most of the commodities in which United States exporters were interested, the compromise was not as damaging as it might seem to the United States program of multilateral competitive trade. On the other hand, numerous exceptions and escape clauses elsewhere in the charter appeared to give a considerable degree of freedom in regard to exchange control and quotas, as well as tariffs.

The voting power of the underdeveloped countries at the Havana conference was strong enough to force this compromise. It also forced a change in the voting arrangements for the Executive Board of the proposed International Trade Organization and made a strong case for a permanent Economic Development Commission. Some elements of the compromise were of questionable validity. The exchange control provisions of the International Monetary Fund agreement would appear to conflict with the Havana draft charter. The Havana conference itself, after elaborating the economic development provisions of the charter, felt it necessary to refer to the Economic and Social Council the question whether the International Trade Organization was competent to act in this field.

Moreover, in an effort to write a constitution that would take care of all national interests in hypothetical future situations, the conference had produced a very long and involved document, full of exceptions and escape clauses. Thus the original trading principles proposed by the United States were lost in a maze of dependent and conditional qualifying provisions. The underdeveloped countries were within their rights in asserting their voting strength at Havana. But in so doing, they had written into the charter a mass of exceptions. Since it is impossible in any case to write a charter that would provide ironclad rules for all possible trading contingencies, it might have been wiser to concentrate on the creation of consultative machinery to work out the detailed application of broad general principles.

As it left Havana the charter was a lengthy document of 106 articles and sixteen annexes. Many of the articles were divided into numerous sections and subsections. The first part of the charter dealt with Purposes and Objectives, Employment and Economic Activity, and Economic Development and Reconstruction. From a practical point of view this represented little more than an overly long preamble. Much of the language had caused objection in the United States. It threatened to give ammunition to the opponents of freer trading policies and thus to delay Congressional ratification.

However, a careful reading of these chapters would indicate that the only positive obligation in respect to employment used the language of the United States Employment Act of 1946.

The main body of the charter was the second part which contained the essentials of a trading code. The chapter on Commercial Policy, in particular, contained these principles of a possible trading code in respect to tariffs, preferences, national treatment, quotas, subsidies, state trading, freedom of transit, antidumping duties, valuation, import and export formalities, marks of origin and other technical questions of great importance to practical traders. The general principle of equality of treatment (most-favored-nation treatment) was qualified by a series of paragraphs intended to maintain existing preferential systems as they stood after the conclusion of the *General Agreement on Tariffs and Trade*. Another article asserted the general principle that quotas and import and export licenses should be abolished, but followed it with a series of exceptions. The most important of these was recognition of the right of a member to impose such restrictions when necessary to safeguard that member's balance of payments.

Another part of the charter which was whittled down was that dealing with cartels. The chapter on Restrictive Business Practices was reduced to an agreement whereby complaints might be made (by governments but not by private individuals or groups) against monopolistic practices which "restrain competition, limit access to markets, or foster monopolistic control, whenever such practices have harmful effects on the expansion of production or trade." The practices listed were those commonly regarded as cartel arrangements, but the language in which they were described carefully refrained from presuming that they did in fact restrict trade. A procedure of investigation and of co-operation to remedy any justifiable complaints was outlined, the actual working of which must obviously depend upon the vigor with which it will be administered.

The important chapter on Intergovernmental Commodity Agreements provided a mechanism by which countries interested in primary commodities might set in motion studies and conferences to negotiate commodity agreements. In general, the attempt was made to limit agreements that might regulate production or trade in raw materials to measures that would be temporary and would result in as little restraint of trade as possible. While recognizing that such agreements might become necessary, their negotiation was hedged about with safeguards against their being created easily in a manner that might be unduly restrictive of world trade. This was one of the more conservative chapters of the charter. It therefore ran the risk of not meeting the desires of the raw-material producing countries in case of an agricultural depression.

There was much in this second part of the charter which was valuable and acceptable to traders in all countries. The working definitions and principles constituted a modern trading code. The compromises between the predominantly laissez-faire position of the United States and the desire of most other countries to safeguard their balances of payments by the insertion of exceptions and escape clauses were unlikely to be fully acceptable to the more extreme advocates on both sides of the controversy. But any attempt at renegotiation would be likely to result in much the same elements of compromise. As a practical matter, the projected International Trade Organization would have no power to force adherence to these principles. Sovereignty remained in the hands of national governments. And it was questionable whether changes in the wording of the charter were as important as a serious attempt by the procedures of consultative co-operation to work out decisions of policy in respect to specific cases as they arose.

The third part of the charter set up an International Trade Organization as a specialized agency of the United Nations. The constitution followed the familiar form of an Annual Conference, an Executive Board with power to create permanent commissions, and a secretariat. As in the case of the International Monetary Fund, the I.T.O. would have a set of agreed principles of international trading to administer and would be entrusted with specific operative functions. Unlike the Fund, it would not call for an appropriation beyond the sums necessary to meet its annual expenses. The organization could not be created until sixty days after thirty countries had ratified the charter. Or, if this did not happen before March 24, 1949, until at least twenty governments had ratified. If this did not occur before September 30, 1949 (as was the case), the Secretary-General of the United Nations was directed to consult the governments which had ratified the charter as to further action.

The desirability of completing the structure of the specialized agencies by creating an International Trade Organization needs to be heavily underscored. Unless world trade could be reorganized on a multilateral basis, the transitional programs of interim aid to Europe and other areas would fail of their ultimate purpose. The specialized agencies already created could not function effectively unless trade flowed freely. Trade was the lifeblood of international economic co-operation in all its phases. Without an International Trade Organization there would be no mechanisms of consultative co-operation in regard to commercial policy except those set up by the *General Agreement on Tariffs and Trade* negotiated at the Geneva conference among twenty-three nations. And there was a serious risk that national autonomy in regard to tariffs, quotas, preferential agreements, cartels, and commodity agreements might result in a rapid spread of bilaterally regulated trade, which would imperil even this limited *General Agreement.*

Whether the International Trade Charter was ratified or not, the renewal of the Reciprocal Trade Agreements Act for two years in September, 1949, was essential for the ultimate success of the policy steadily followed by the United States since 1934. The reciprocal trade agreement machinery was the only means by which the countries that were not participants in the *General Agreement* at Geneva, including most of the Latin-American countries and most of the European neutrals, could be induced to reduce their trade barriers and to adhere to the principles of multilateral trade. Renewal of the Reciprocal Trade Agreements Act was the linchpin of the instrument which would complete the mechanisms of international economic co-operation.

With that pin securely placed in position, the International Trade Organization once set up could operate, but it would still be necessary to work out effective methods of using these mechanisms. The United Nations and its specialized agencies were merely instruments through which the nations might co-operate. The will to use them was more important than the perfection of their structure. But they could not be used with any hope of success unless an effective International Trade Organization took its important place among the other specialized agencies.

PART IV

THE MODERN PROBLEM

"To one who, like myself, has come into the social sciences from the natural sciences . . . there seems to be too much integration, too little differentiation; too much spinning of hypotheses without regard to their verifiability, too little humble spade work in digging out facts. If, in the social sciences and especially in economics, more attention were devoted to the recording of what seem important facts and to the analysis of their significance, I am confident we should not need to worry about theory. With an adequate body of facts, theory very soon becomes obvious to any first-class mind. We would then build up a body of theory that grows out of life, instead of closed systems largely unrelated to the world of reality. We would devote less time and ingenuity to such subjects as the theory of value and the concept of marginal utility, and more time to learning how men actually behave, and what has actually happened in the economic sphere."

Carl L. Alsberg, "What the Social Scientist Can Learn from the Natural Scientist" (reprinted in Joseph S. Davis (ed.), *Carl Alsberg: Scientist at Large*, Stanford, California, Food Research Institute, Stanford University, 1948).

"Alfred Whitehead concludes one of his books with the remark that exactness is the great illusion of our time. Arthur Eddington makes a similar comment on contemporary thinking by means of a metaphor which can be extended to illustrate the activity of the poet. Men, said Eddington, are fishermen in the boat of life, casting nets of a certain size into the sea of experience. Modern man, more than any other man, is occupied with the catch, with the counting, measuring, assorting, and classifying of what he can spread out before him, touch with his hands, and use. He is also fascinated with making generalizations concerning the number and character of the catch and in forming definitions and laws on the basis of these. Eddington uses the figure of speech to dramatize his view that this focus of interest has led to man's being absurdly unaware of such fish as are too small to remain in the net or so large that they will always swim at prodigious and indifferent distances from it. Not only do they run the risk of coming to false conclusions about the nature of what is in the sea, but, in placing so high a value on positive knowledge, they are likely to be found establishing a high degree of certainty about matters so unimportant that it may never make any difference to anyone whether they are certain or not."

Edith Henrich, "Poetry as Communication," *Pacific Spectator,* Vol. III, No. 2, Spring 1949, pp. 128–29.

CHAPTER XIX

THE ASSUMPTIONS OF A MODERN THEORY

THE NATURE OF THE PRODUCTIVE PROCESS

IN ITS EARLIEST statement, the classical theory of international trade was concerned with the exchange mainly of consumers' goods produced by small-scale enterprises for highly competitive markets. Wine and cloth were the commodities chosen by David Ricardo to illustrate his argument. His theory was postulated upon the assumption that what he called the factors of production—land, labor, and capital—could not be transferred from one national economy to another, while within each national economy there was free mobility.

Later writers of the neo-classical school relaxed these assumptions. There has always been a considerable degree of difficulty in shifting labor and capital freely within a country. On the other hand, shifts of capital and even of population have taken place at various times between countries, while international trade has brought raw materials to the country of most economical manufacture. Thus the early sharp distinction between interregional and international trade was abandoned, and theoretical analysis was widened to take account of the transferability of factors of production. In consequence, the discussions of international trade tended to become an aspect of the theory of the location of industry.

It became clear that there were differences in the degree to which the factors of production were transferable within and between nations. In particular, certain forms of capital were more transferable, both between regions, and internationally, than most kinds of labor. Thus questions were raised concerning the distribution of income among classes of the population. It could be argued that an export of capital from a country where real labor costs were high to one where such costs were lower would result in greater total production and higher profits. These profits as a general rule would ultimately return to and be spent in the creditor country whose national income as a result of the foreign investment would be higher. But it did not follow that the spending of this higher income would give employment to the same workers in the same industries as might have found employment if the capital had been invested at home. It was even possible that the profits might be spent abroad.

Discussion of these distributive questions (which had been excluded, *ex hypothesi,* from the earlier static analysis of the classical economists) was more indecisive and obscure than it need have been because of certain assumptions that were hidden in the traditional listing of the factors of production as Land, Labor, and Capital. This classification has never been a useful tool with which to analyze production because land, labor, and capital are not realistic categories from this point of view. They were derived from Ricardo's attempt to analyze not the production but the distribution of income. Thus they correspond broadly with the social classes of his England—landowners, laborers, and industrial capitalists. Quite early in the development of systematic economic thought, Jean Baptiste Say (1803) had used this distributive classification to analyze production in categories parallel with those used for the study of distribution. This was a false logical symmetry and the cause of theoretical confusion in later writings. It was particularly confusing because it treated capital as synonymous with enterprise and management. In effect it identified all the functions of business enterprise—planning, risk-taking, organization, technical direction, management, and selling—with capital ownership. As long as the organizing, directing, and innovating functions of economic activity were compounded into the single factor of capital and identified vaguely with the ownership of a particular kind of industrial capital, there could be no really illuminating theory of production. Instead there developed an identification of economic function with the class divisions of English society in the early nineteenth century.

A theory of production should explain the co-operative processes of economic activity. In its most general form, it should comprehend not only industrial but agricultural and marketing processes, and personal services as well as usable commodities, whether organized within a collectivist, a mixed, or a capitalist system of economic organization. Necessarily it must be conceived in terms of the production of values—time, place, and form utilities—rather than of commodities or services. The agents, elements, or factors of production in such a theory would be seen to consist of a wide variety of human faculties applied with the aid of accumulated capital assets to natural resources of many kinds within the framework of an organized society. Friedrich List had a glimpse of such a theory when he based his analysis upon the thesis that "the power of producing wealth is therefore infinitely more important than wealth itself," and went on to emphasize the importance of the social environment.

In his *Principles of Economics,* published in 1890, Alfred Marshall seemed to recognize the importance of the social environment as setting the conditions within which production must be organized, but the net result of his discussion was merely to add a fourth factor of production—organization—to land, labor, and capital. This new factor Marshall identified broadly with business management. Subsequent economic discussion has tended to cling to this classification, but to incorporate some of the broader social questions—such as education, scientific research, and industrial training—under the head of one or other of the traditional factors of production. While it is possible in this way to cover most of the important questions that List was concerned with in his emphasis on "the power of producing wealth," their dispersed treatment does not emphasize sufficiently the important role played in production by efficient and honest government, by impartial justice based upon a developed body of law which is strictly enforced, by religious tolerance and freedom from caste, and by adequate provision both for universal elementary education and for higher specialized training and research.

It may be objected that such questions do not lie within the field of economic study strictly defined. It is true that if economic analysis assumes the political and social environment in any particular country, that analysis may be confined, without any serious risk of misunderstanding, to strictly economic phenomena. However, in discussing the economic relations between citizens of countries with very different systems of political and social organization, there is a considerable risk that such analysis will be invalidated by failure to take into account the variant levels of efficiency with which economic activity may operate in different social environments. Much recent discussion of economic development in industrially backward areas is vitiated by such failure, because it proceeds from the viewpoint of the creditor rather than the debtor country. It tends to ignore the economic and social potentialities and consequences of investment in the receiving country. This is because the primary interest of the analysis generally lies in the effect of foreign investment upon economic activity, particularly employment, in the investing country. If attention is given to the development of the receiving country, it tends to assume the economic processes that are familiar in the political and social setting of the already developed and investing countries, rather than the processes actually at work in the undeveloped and receiving countries.

It is particularly important to take account of these political and social considerations at present when the nineteenth-century network of world trade has been destroyed. In building a new trading network it is essential to devise means whereby a stream of foreign investment may be directed to the balanced development of areas which in the nineteenth century were partially developed as sources of raw materials feeding into the north Atlantic industrial system. This is vitally necessary if we are to restore the raw material and food supplies upon which the already developed industrial countries have come to depend for their prosperity, and in some cases for their subsistence. It is essential also because the effective functioning of these developed industrial economies demands world markets for their manufactured products and capital outlets to stabilize their operation. Even more important is the fact that the former colonies and the remaining colonies are no longer content to remain passive under a high capitalist development of their export industries, while their domestic economy remains primitive. They seek the kind of development that will enable them to conduct specialized trade with other countries on an equal footing.

When this question is raised and plans are discussed whereby the less developed countries may borrow from those more developed the needed appliances and technical skills, account must be taken of political stability, of law and the enforcement of justice, and of social conditions affecting the availability of labor and managerial skills, as well as capital formation in these less developed countries. In recent years there has been a prolific elaboration of ambitious plans for industrialization and modernization of the industrially backward countries. Most of these plans have been abortive because they have ignored the political and social conditions necessary for their implementation. In this respect businessmen and investors have been more realistic than the theorists, albeit their realism has tended to take the negative form of abstention from taking risks.

Imperialism had at least this merit. It brought a measure of settled government to the less developed peoples. The government services, educational systems, agricultural development programs, railroads, irrigation dams, and other public works installed by American officials in the Philippines, by British officials in India, and by the Dutch in the Netherlands Indies, put those countries further along the road to economic development than any others in Asia except Japan. Now a substitute must be found for alien rule. The first requisite for economic development is social order which must be attained in large measure by the efforts of the colonial peoples themselves. International assistance, involving concerted action by the more developed countries to guarantee the defense and buttress the stability of independent but still weak governments, would be helpful. Technicians in the arts of government, serving as experts employed by the newly created independent states, could also render useful aid. But the achievement of modernization is mainly dependent upon the self-reliant activities of the peoples most concerned—the colonial peoples themselves.

If this preliminary condition of civil order can be achieved, attention may be directed toward the more effective organization of the factors of production defined in stricter economic terms. The most important and the only conscious factors of production in any country are constituted by its array of human skills. These are not determined by biological heredity. There is no master race.

The United States has at the present time an array of skills without parallel by the test of economic productivity. These have been produced from a population which is the result of mingling successive waves of immigrant peoples, the larger number of whom were certainly not selected on the basis of special aptitudes or skills. This mixed population in a favorable social environment has achieved, in quantity never before approached, the engineering and commercial skills essential to productivity. No summary statement can be adequate to explain this phenomenon. More adequate nutrition in a land of bountiful resources has played a large part by increasing physical and mental vigor. Universal education and increasingly heavy investment in specialized forms of higher education have also contributed heavily to greater efficiency. But further explanation is needed for the significant achievements of the United States particularly in the industrial applications of scientific knowledge. This explanation is found largely in the development of the special skill which may be called business organization or management. In itself a form of skilled labor, business organization develops most effectively where there is a variety of subordinate skills widely dispersed among the population, and where the labor force as a whole displays a high degree of generalized ability. Such are the conditions which prevail in the United States.

Many types of skill are readily transferable between countries. Something has already been done, much more could be done—by the established processes of education in both developed and underdeveloped countries—to train technicians to assist in the development of the latter. The weakness of colonial education has been its failure to train enough technicians and to extend its training far enough down the scale of labor. No small part of the difficulty now faced by the newly independent countries is caused by the fact that educational facilities have prepared students for political and legal activities, rather than for technical work in agriculture and industry. But in fact the only adequate training ground for industrial skills is industry itself. While there is every reason to facilitate the transfer of special skills by interchange of students and teachers, there is little possibility of developing modern methods of production unless not only managers but foremen and skilled artisans have opportunity to acquire practical experience by actual industrial employment.

The industrial development of the U.S.S.R. since the revolution in 1917 has thrown light on this question. One of the most serious bottlenecks encountered in this program of rapid industrialization was a continuing shortage of skilled labor. Much was done in a short time to change the outlook and develop the skills of what had been a dominantly peasant country, with all the dead weight of inertia, ignorance, superstition and tradition common to such communities.

Formal education and visiting specialists contributed to this program. But the most important educational instrument was costly and hard-won experience in industry itself.

While the possession of accumulated capital is an asset to any country, it is not, strictly speaking, a factor of production. The labor and resources of past generations—in reclaiming land from the sea or from marshes, terracing hillsides and building the soil, in planting forests, building roads, canals, railroad systems, factories, public buildings and homes—contribute greatly to the productivity of later generations. The vast changes wrought in the shoreline of a densely populated port area, water conservation and irrigation systems, hydroelectric dams, reticulating power systems, and networks of telephonic communication, are examples of such capital accumulation. Increasingly, capital accumulation tends to represent public rather than private expenditures. Though the construction works may deteriorate they are relatively indestructible, and they are almost completely incapable of transference from one location to another. The tasks of postwar capital reconstruction and development are primarily local in the sense of utilizing both local materials and local labor. The physical destruction wrought by the war, the undermaintenance and deterioration of capital equipment, and the depletion of working stocks brought about by the war must be made good by devoting surpluses of current production to their restoration. In the same way, new capital construction in developing countries demands both increased productivity and the diversion of the surplus labor and materials thus secured to capital construction rather than to consumption.

There are relatively narrow limits to the transferability of these capital assets between countries. It is true that some equipment can be transferred, but this is of little practical importance unless the receiving country already has or can acquire the technical skills necessary for its operation. Inventories can be restocked by drawing from more abundant supplies of raw materials in other countries. Substantial aid may also be given by the provision of foreign food and other consumption goods, so that local labor and materials may be diverted to capital construction. But such transferences of capital assets from richer to poorer countries are not the major need either for reconstruction of war damage or for economic development of industrially backward areas. The crucial need is the development locally of a continuing surplus of current production over consumption. This need is crucial in the construction and maintenance of capital equipment, and in the replenishment of stocks. If the necessary resources are borrowed, the production of a surplus is obviously necessary for the payment of interest and the repayment of the loans. To fasten attention on the accumulations of the past is to ignore the vital fact that these accumulations have been created and must thenceforth be continuously maintained and increased out of current surpluses.

Economic productivity consists of a continuing flow of goods and services. No one would deny that the equipment and resources available to American management and manpower enable them to produce more effectively. But it should never be forgotten that the present equipment is the accumulated surplus from past productivity and would quickly deteriorate if it were not maintained and expanded by continuing productivity. The present plight of the western European countries—they were so rich a short generation ago that they exported capital to the rest of the world—is evidence enough that present productivity rather than past accumulation is the important element in this equation.

There are those who would argue that an even more fundamental element of productivity than settled government, human skills, or capital accumulation is to be found in the natural resources available to a national community. Obviously there is an important element of truth in this contention, especially when those natural resources are considered in relation to population. Natural resources must be defined more broadly than land since they include such natural assets as position, climate, means of water communication, minerals, and sources of industrial power. Clearly the high levels of productivity, attained by the United States, by the British Dominions and by parts of Latin America, must be attributed in some degree to the fact that relatively small communities entered into possession of rich natural resources and were able to retain exclusive use of these resources. When these countries are compared with others, such as China and India, that suffer from heavy population pressures on limited natural resources, it is obvious that they have a considerable advantage.

But this argument can be pushed too far. There are many examples of industrious and frugal communities that have developed highly

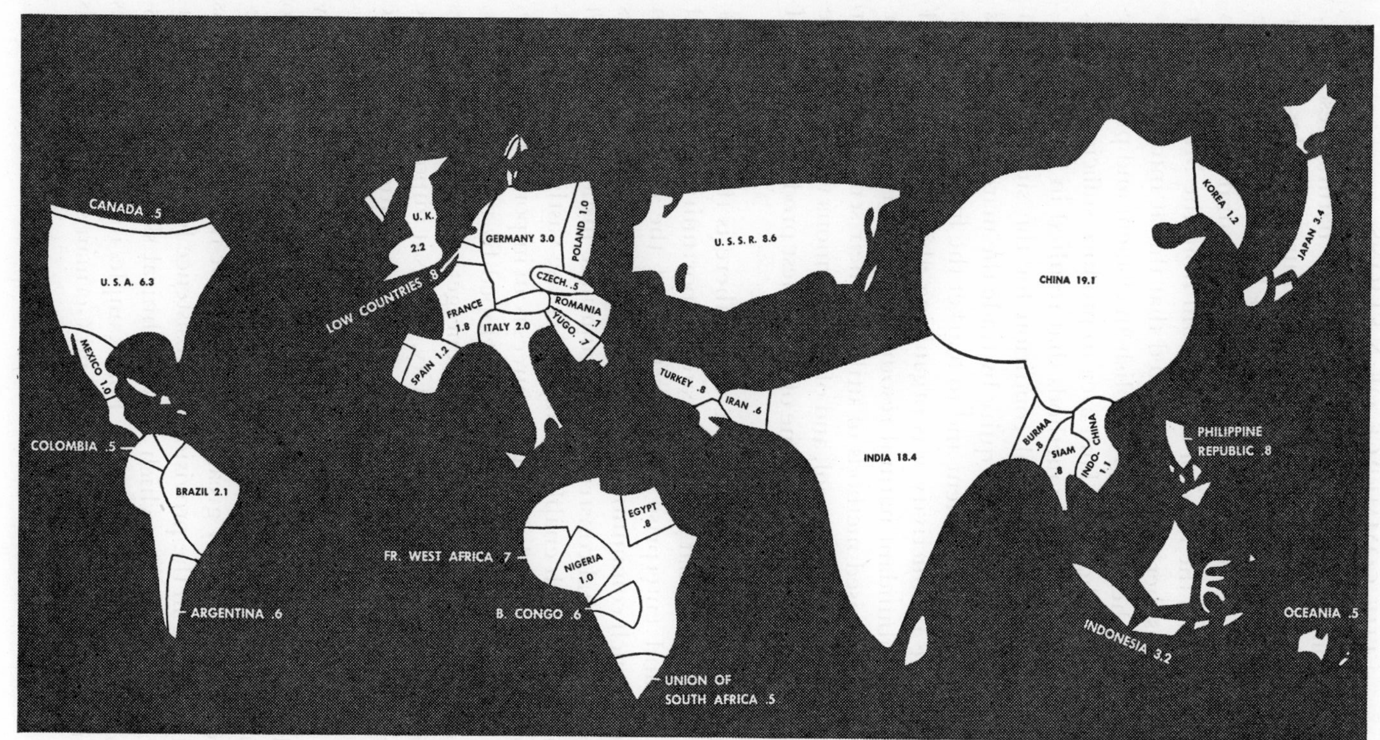

THE POPULATION WORLD, 1946

The area of each country is shown proportionately to its share of world population in 1946.

Source: Calculated from data in U.S. Department of State, Office of Intelligence Research, *Report No. 4192,* Washington, March 1, 1947, pp. 14 ff. (mimeographed).

productive economic systems with very limited natural resources. Switzerland, the richest country per capita in Europe at the present time, has practically no minerals or mineral fuel and little arable land. When Denmark was faced with an agricultural crisis in the 1870's, resulting from the flood of cheap grain from the Middle West of the United States, her people converted that threat into an opportunity by using the cheap grain to establish an efficient and productive pastoral industry. Without the land area to produce sufficient fodder, the Danes devised co-operative methods that resulted in high productivity. It is true that an essential condition for the success of such organization was the ability to acquire by trade the material resources lacking in the local environment and to market the finished products. The secret of the productivity was organizing ability and technical skill rather than abundant natural resources. This was as true of the Australians who devised methods of utilizing their semiarid interior plains for the production of wool, and of the Mormons who turned the Utah deserts by dry farming into one of the richest productive areas of the United States.

Human skills are most productive where there is the political stability and social order that give the greatest opportunity for individual development and enterprise to all sections of the community. In course of time such communities, by continuously devoting surpluses of production to capital construction, accumulate installations of real capital on a scale which enables them to increase vastly their productivity. The possession of abundant resources is an important advantage. But these resources often have to be developed by ingenious means, and the lack of them has not prevented energetic and skilled peoples from attaining high levels of productivity. Nor is it impossible for the peoples whose numbers are oppressively large in relation to available resources to improve gradually their skills and therefore their productivity. In the past the introduction into colonial countries of highly organized export industries has not led to capital accumulation or to educational expenditures that would have made possible the acquirement of technical skills by greater numbers. For the most part it has been swallowed up in the provision of subsistence for a larger population. There are means by which these technical skills may be transferred from one country to another. For example, in the United States both British commercial organization and German scientific methods were combined and transcended. However, such transference is not likely to develop where political instability and social tradition place serious obstacles to the enhancement of individual welfare.

In the long run each community achieves the level of productivity it chooses. For each generation the level is predetermined in large measure by the choices of former generations. But each generation can in its turn influence the levels attainable in the future. If it chooses the health, vigor, and training of its human capital as an objective more important than the maintenance of vested political interests or of archaic social customs, it can raise the productivity of the national community and thus set it on the way to progressively higher levels.

THE ORGANIZATION OF HUMAN SKILLS

In increasing measure economic analysis has come to stress the specialized and co-operative activity of individuals organized to produce a great variety of goods and services. This factor of organization comprehends but is broader than business management. Alfred Marshall started a trend in economic thought when he devoted as much space in his *Principles of Economics* to labor as to land and capital combined, and almost as much to organization as to all three. While he recognized that the organization of economic activity was important enough to be distinguished as a separate factor of production, he identified it as being virtually synonymous with business management. It will be argued here that in the new technology business management has come to approximate an aspect of government in the economic sphere, and further that the organization of economic activity in the changing circumstances of our time is calling forth the invention of new forms of management in which the demands both of public control and of private enterprise may be met. In a competitive economic system the forms of business organization are as diverse as the purposes for which production is organized. In our modern economy there is a great deal of economic activity organized through government agencies, or through a combination of public and private agencies.

Within the American pattern of organization, while there are many strands that are legacies of earlier economic organization, there are some of growing importance that foreshadow new developments. Agriculture ranges from share-cropping and subsistence farming to the highly organized and mechanized operations of a modern corporation. Retailing runs from the street stall and the corner shop to department stores and chain systems. There are relics of the gild system in some of the professions. Commercial agencies and some trade unions organize and even monopolize the market for certain personal services, while other forms of service remain competitive in unorganized local markets. On the other hand, there is a widening range of public services and enterprises, in which new forms of organization have developed, embodying characteristic elements both of government and of corporation enterprise. It is significant that the potentialities of atomic power should be in the hands of such an organization, and should lean heavily on the experience gained by the Tennessee Valley Authority. It is even more significant for our study that the Economic Cooperation Administration was consciously modeled upon these precedents and that of the Reconstruction Finance Corporation.

Many modern economists treat organization as if it were concerned primarily with the management of large-scale industrial production. Analysis of the economics of the firm has been developed mainly as the economics of the large corporation. The organization of personal services, agriculture, or government enterprise is apt to be regarded as secondary. This is a proper emphasis for the American economy, since the corporation is increasingly important in the economic structure of the United States. Moreover, there is a clear tendency toward concentration of productive power in the larger corporations. This concentration is matched by the consolidation of organized labor and by a trend toward the organization of trade associations and of agricultural interests on a national scale.

There is some tendency to exaggerate these developments. Statistical measurements of economic activity emphasize those forms of organization for which statistics can readily be compiled. Government intervention necessarily based on statistics, increases this emphasis. One result of this exaggeration of the part played by large corporations and groups is that the interests of the unorganized small producers and of the individual consumers are apt to be neglected in the formation of national policy. It is easy to get a picture of the national economy of the United States in which the subsistence farmers and the share-croppers, the independent craftsmen and repair workers, and the unorganized fringe of unskilled labor become forgotten men. In the statistics of production they may not loom large, but they form a large part of the population. On the international scale the larger part of the world's people fall into this category.

A most significant shift has occurred since 1914 in regard to the part played by business management in the national economies of the great industrial nations and in organizing world trade and investment.[1] Here we are concerned with the international aspects of the increasing power that has passed into the hands of those responsible for the executive management of great corporations. In order to understand the importance of this shift in the location of economic power, it is necessary to recall the fact that up to 1914 the major decisions that affected world trade and investment were taken by those who controlled the leading money markets and particularly the London money market. There were then few examples of large-scale industrial enterprises with international ramifications. The exports of manufactured goods from the industrial countries and of foodstuffs and raw materials from the agricultural countries were exchanged through the great network of international markets. The so-called international gold standard was essentially a commercial and financial system, in which the pivotal figures were the specialized bankers and brokers whose business it was to finance world trade and investment. These people regarded themselves as neutral interpreters of the market trends that developed from world-wide competition. It was their judgment of market trends that manipulated the short-term interest rates. These changes in interest and discount rates entailed price adjustments whose repercussions on national production and employment were world-wide. Moreover the amount and direction of international investment fluctuated with changes in these interest rates.

The merchant-bankers who dominated the Court of the Bank of England kept the sterling currency convertible and its slim reserves adequate, by decisions which affected the profit expectations and sometimes the solvency of investors, producers, and traders all over the world. Productive activity in all the trading countries was thus affected by these decisions in proportion as the national economies were geared to world trade. After the international gold standard broke down in the first World War, and more emphatically after the failure of its attempted restoration in 1931, the power of the London

[1] See Chapter XIV, "The End of Laissez Faire," for a discussion of the national aspect of these developments.

money market in regard to the regulation of world trade and investment largely disappeared. No other commercial or financial group has taken its place.

In the meantime the nature of large-scale industrial production and of the investment necessary to establish new enterprises has undergone a remarkable development. The power to organize world trade and still more to organize international investment has passed in large measure into the hands either of governments or of great industrial corporations. The governments have the political power. The corporations have the know-how. The great corporations of the United States, which since the second World War have been the main source of capital for foreign investment and the main repository of the new technology, have gained increasing importance and power in regard to foreign industrial investment and the reorganization of world trade.

Foreign investment has always carried with it economic functions that were particularly important in the relations between more developed and less developed peoples. The leading industrial country has always supplied not merely capital, but a large measure of the planning of new enterprises, the technical direction, and many kinds of skilled labor necessary for the operation of new processes. With the development of modern large-scale technology, the nature of these skills has changed.

The sixteen thousand British artisans who, it was estimated, slipped across the channel to France in the years 1822–23, in violation of laws passed to prohibit the export of know-how, were master-craftsmen skilled in the installation and operation of power looms, spinning jennies, and other new machines. Rather limited mechanical experience was the basis of their skill. This was true also of the construction foremen who formed the nucleus of the labor force organized in the third quarter of the nineteenth century by the great railroad contractors such as Thomas Brassey and Morton Peto. As mechanical methods of production became more complex and delicate and the scale of construction grew, engineers as well as craftsmen were needed. The chemical and electrical industries, pioneered in the latter nineteenth century by the Germans, depended on scientific research. Thus construction engineers and even salesmen began to need a general knowledge of scientific principles. The scope of scientific research and process development has never ceased to widen. In the decades preceding 1914, it achieved some of its most striking successes in agriculture, and particularly in colonial plantations. Sugar and pineapples in Hawaii, rubber in the Netherlands Indies, cocoa on the Gold Coast, tea in India and Ceylon, furnish examples of the scientific organization of new industries.

On the international as on the national scale, the organization necessary to create and manage new enterprises is no longer simply a question of obtaining access to credit, building a factory, installing power and machines, mobilizing a labor force, and establishing a system of distribution. These are still essential, but behind them lies a development of scientific research and its applications which grows rapidly in importance. The executive organizing functions are no longer in the hands of the owners of capital. They have become widely dispersed among specialized technicians of varied and complementary training and experience. As this happens, the planning and risk-taking decisions which are the main element in organizing economic activity become co-operative. Before final decision can be reached there is much prior investigation from different technical angles—reports, analyses, and committee discussion sifting the possibilities of alternative courses of action. In the hierarchy of a great corporation while the executive has final responsibility, his decisions are rarely taken without a great deal of consultation. The decision is thus largely predetermined in the gathering and presenting of the data upon which he must form a judgment.

It is sometimes difficult in a giant business to locate the seat of final executive authority. Power is an exercise of will. The management of industry becomes an aspect of politics in the sphere of economic activity. Those who reach positions of business power by whatever route—inheritance, salesmanship, financial skill, technical ability, or any other means—must control a large staff of trained and ambitious men of diverse ability and strong will. If the will and judgment of the individual making the ultimate decisions cannot dominate the technicians, his power will pass into firmer hands. There are two kinds of limitation on his power. Since he must take on trust many of the technical facts upon which he must base decisions, his success as an executive depends upon his judgment in selecting the technical staff. The second limitation is often overlooked. Planning, if it is to be realistic, cannot be far divorced from day to day operations. The formulation and execution of policy must develop out of the actual processes of production and marketing. These involve a considerable delegation of executive authority.

The direction of a great economic undertaking has many aspects of generalship. The executive must be free to deal only with the most crucial issues. He can seldom commit all his economic resources but must maintain flexibility and substantial reserves for contingencies. He must build up confidence in his leadership, not alone among the staff, but among the workers as well. He must delegate responsibilities, while retaining power to co-ordinate them. Co-ordination is achieved by persuasion rather than by the exercise of authority. In this way an understanding of objectives and a sense of participation are gained, and the further this can be extended down the line of responsibility, the better the results.

These changes in the character of executive management must be understood before any realistic approach can be made to the problems involved in the reconstruction of world trade or in the economic development of industrially backward areas. The new enterprises necessary for reconstruction and development of the world economy must be undertaken by teams of technicians. The executive is the co-ordinator and energizer of a dispersed process involving many skills, among which the scientific research and engineering skills tend to gain in importance. Investment, national or international, is no longer planned by the owners of capital or the specialists of the money market, but by government officials or by a relatively new class of business executives. The executive function has been discussed above in terms of the management of the corporations which are characteristic of business organization in the United States because these corporations have the power to play an important role in the economic reconstruction of our world, if only by reason of their possession of technical knowledge and know-how.

It should be recognized that this ability to organize and co-ordinate teams of specialists is not confined to the world of private business. There would seem no essential reason why forms of public enterprise could not be developed in which such organizing ability and drive might function. The executive organizing function is cultivated by the armed services. Many trade union leaders develop great skills in organization and management. Leadership is the essence of politics, but executive ability is rarer in politics than in business. The reasons for this are that the problems of organization are more difficult and there is seldom provision for competent staff work. Wherever political leadership has been effective in the economic field it has always used brain-trusts, usually recruited outside, though using the facilities of, the ordinary channels of government. Most party political issues do not lend themselves readily to such organization, so that executive leadership appears usually on matters that are somewhat remote from party politics. This is what occurs in times of national crisis such as a war, when partisanship is suspended.

It has become possible in recent years to envisage new methods by which the wide range of human skills necessary to the operation of great economic undertakings may be mobilized in the service of the community. Private corporations remain the most powerful of the institutions in which these skills are mobilized, but army engineers built the Panama Canal and government officials planned, let the contracts for, and have usually operated the great dams and power enterprises that have transformed large sections of the economy of the United States. The Manhattan Engineering District which organized the production of the atomic bomb was an example of public enterprise within which there was scope for private enterprise on a great scale. The Economic Cooperation Administration, set up to channel aid from the United States to Europe, has become the most significant factor in organizing trade, investment, and the international transference of technical skills in the immediate postwar period. Yet despite these examples, productivity and the know-how upon which it depends remain largely in the hands of the private corporations. Moreover this know-how and in particular the elusive qualities of business judgment and drive, as distinct from technical knowledge, is largely subconscious. It is the product of experience rather than of conscious reasoning. It can seldom be taught, though it can be learned.

The organizing leaders who rise to the control of big enterprises have one quality in common—will power. Within the limits of their operations, they also display shrewd judgment of men. It is not easy to find out their bases of judgment. If challenged, they will quite often fasten upon trivial evidence, though in fact their judgment is based upon unconscious associations of memory built up by practical experience. Their hunches are more often right than wrong; otherwise they would not be where they are. Once arrived, they may become fronts for more active and powerful minds within the organization. Nearly always they reflect its quality. The varied organizing skills over which they exercise co-ordinating control are a very important element in economic productivity, and the economic power that goes with the co-ordinating control is among the most important factors of production. Whether power in regard to the organization of international economic co-operation will pass into the hands of governments, or into the hands of those who exercise industrial leadership, or whether new forms of organization will emerge, giving scope both to public control and to the drive of executive leadership—this is a crucial question for the future.

The most fundamental issues of international economic conflict at the present time are those which arise in connection with this question of power in economic organization. These economic conflicts cross national boundaries. They are obscured by the conflicts of international politics, which are dramatized by the fact that nation-states are personified and their names are used as symbols. National security is always the overriding objective of national policy. In a period when there have been great shifts in relative power among the nation-states—such as always follow a great war—it is not clear what alignments will emerge to form a new power equilibrium. The confused groping toward such an equilibrium involves a testing of strength at various points, particularly in the no-man's land of influence over states that occupy strategic positions between the greatest powers. It may be hoped that the political power struggle can be contained within the limits of collective political institutions. But if this struggle continues to paralyze the working of those institutions, it is likely to result in an uneasy equilibrium of force in which a political accident may at some time suddenly precipitate hostilities.

No realistic analyst would underrate the reality of these political aspects of international conflict. Intermingled with them, however, are important issues of economic conflict. These economic aspects of the power struggle take many forms. In the former colonial areas there is a conflict between national aspirations for self-government and the maintenance by the citizens of the former colonial powers not only of property claims but also of economic power, in the sense of authority to decide the types of economic organization, and the allocation of available manpower and resources to different kinds of production. In the extension of economic aid from the United States to Europe it was urged that technical efficiency demanded that such aid be administered through a form of corporate action in which the technicians of American business might be able to insist upon effective organization of industrial reconstruction in the receiving countries.

The inventions, techniques, and methods of organization that hold the greatest promise of increasing productivity have their highest development in the countries where there is political freedom and a substantial measure of free economic enterprise. This is an important fact since not only higher living levels but the possibility of improved social organization and better opportunities for individual health, mental vigor, and cultivation depend upon the economic application of this scientific know-how. There can be little hope of expanding multilateral trade or of stabilizing employment at levels of high productivity unless a knowledge of these techniques can be diffused among the peoples whose economic methods are still on a primitive level of organization. These peoples need capital. They need still more the scientific skills whereby capital equipment can be properly used. For the most part these skills are in the possession of countries where they are mobilized for economic production by private enterprise. Among these countries the United States is pre-eminent. There is real validity in the argument that the extension of loans by the United States government to distressed peoples in Europe and Asia may only alleviate without curing their economic difficulties. The only means by which these countries may be put on the road to higher productivity is by the acquirement of improved technical skills and improved methods of economic organization. If these are to come from the United States, they must come in large part from the great business corporations which employ the experienced technicians whose accumulated know-how is the real secret of American productive efficiency.

There are those particularly among the organizers of industry in the United States, who hold firmly to the belief that scientific research, process development, practical know-how, and efficient organization of production and marketing cannot be developed except under the freedom of private enterprise. It follows logically that they consider it a necessary condition for the efficient transfer of such skills that the receiving countries shall abandon the impediments to private enterprise which the policies of nationalization and national economic planning represent at the present time in most European countries. It follows also in their view that the newly independent states of Asia must give up any ideas they may have of planned economic development, and allow private enterprise free scope to raise productivity by improved technical methods.

There are others who point to the wastes and instabilities of the capitalist system. They regard the stress laid upon the technical capacities of private enterprise in the United States as masking the desire to extend personal, institutional, and even national power to new fields of conquest. In this view there is a conspiracy among American businessmen and bankers, aided by government and the armed services, to extend their control over the national resources and policies of other countries.

It is not necessary to accept either of these extreme positions. Because the development of industrial production in the past has emerged as a by-product of private enterprise seeking the most efficient means of making profits, it does not follow that this is the only effective policy for countries which must now husband very carefully their limited margins of productive resources. Nor does it follow that countries which desire to modernize their economies must allow that modernization to emerge in the pattern dictated by private profit, particularly if it is the profit of foreign enterprises lodged within the national economy. The planning of economic policy in its broadest outlines at the highest political levels will not be abandoned.

On the other hand there is no reason why there could not be a great deal of flexibility in the detailed execution of policy within the general framework of national objectives. It is not necessary to identify national independence with rigorous and minute control over the economy. Indeed there is every reason to hope that practical agreement may be reached on methods whereby technical, as well as financial, assistance may be extended from the United States to western Europe without infringing the political independence or the economic autonomy of those countries. If this can be done, there seems no reason why less developed countries could not contract for similar technical and financial assistance in pursuance of their plans for modernization.

In the past, organization has been identified with capital ownership. But investment, whether national or international, can be broken up into many economic functions. A good illustration is provided by such public undertakings in the United States as the Hoover (Boulder) Dam. The decision to undertake this enterprise was made by a great engineer, then President of the United States. The planning and financing of the enterprise were undertaken by government agencies. Actual construction was contracted by a group of private industrialists who formed a joint venture for this particular task. Ownership and operation in this case remained in government hands. There are many possible combinations of these varied functions. There are many cases also of mixed corporations with both government and private capital, and some of these are international.

It is inconceivable that the twentieth century will remain bound to the forms of economic organization that were evolved in the nineteenth century. The mobilization of teams of technicians will become increasingly necessary as our knowledge of the fundamental relations between matter and energy extends from inanimate to animate nature and makes more evident the probability that both distinctions —between matter and energy and between inanimate and animate nature—merely measure our ignorance. As these technicians are mobilized the distinction which the nineteenth century drew so sharply between government and business is also likely to break down.

What will remain is the dependence of economic efficiency upon the organization of human skills. In the longer run it may be hoped that the division of the political world into independent and suspicious sovereign states may gradually be mitigated by an increasing degree of economic integration. In the meantime economic organization is hamstrung by this division and by dogmatic differences concerning the most efficient combinations of government and business. It is the tragedy of our generation that these differences are so confused, and exaggerated by national rivalries and suspicions that neither the economic nor the political issues can be met with intelligence.

MONETARY NATIONALISM

The management of the external balance of payments was a constant preoccupation of government officials, merchants, and economic theorists throughout the sixteenth, seventeenth, and eighteenth centuries. From the time the Spaniards first discovered gold on Hispaniola there was anxious debate in all the western European trading countries on how to manage the national economy, and particularly its external trade. Few then questioned the axiomatic assumption that government had a duty to regulate external trade so that it might yield a surplus of the precious metals. This was not because of a crude identification of money with wealth, though Adam Smith seized upon examples of this to ridicule the whole mercantilist argument. Rather it expressed the concern felt by merchants and officials lest the monetary circulation should be depleted so that prices would fall and production be impaired. Although the arguments used by the mercantilists were often crude and the expedients adopted to conserve monetary supplies were a mixture of confused thinking, graft, and selfish interest, their concern over the balancing of payments was real and well-founded.

In the middle of the eighteenth century, David Hume demonstrated that if governments ceased to meddle with the flow of specie, the precious metals would be distributed among the countries in accordance with trading needs. The lower prices and reduced incomes caused by an outflow of gold and silver would stimulate exports and check imports so that an active balance of commodity trade would then cause a return inflow of the precious metals. Thus the balance of payments could be left to take care of itself. Shortly afterward in 1776, Adam Smith launched his devastating attack upon the monopoly and inefficiency that sheltered behind the attempts of government to regulate external transactions. If war had not intervened in 1793, it is probable that the younger Pitt would have put Adam Smith's teachings into practice.

After the wars Ricardo returned in 1817 to the attack and used the violent price and exchange fluctuations of the war and immediate postwar period to demonstrate the validity of Hume's reasoning. Specie payments were resumed in 1819. It took a generation of controversy before tariff protection could be removed from the entrenched interests. But even the landowning interest was beaten by 1846, and Britain embarked upon her international crusade for free trade. Thenceforward, the concern that the mercantilists had shown over the balance of payments was treated by orthodox economists as an outworn illusion based upon fallacious reasoning. The prosperity of Britain, which became the industrial workshop of the world and financed world trade and investment through the free operations of the London money market, was regarded as a triumphant vindication of classical economic theory. Thereafter, despite the persistence of mercantilist practices in all but a few free-trade countries, the isolated economic theorists who suggested that national prosperity or security required governments to ensure that international trade and investment would not deplete the supply of circulating media and so induce deflation were regarded by the orthodox economists as monetary cranks.

The twentieth century has reverted to the mercantilist concern over the balance of payments. Modern economists have looked with more sympathy at the writings of the mercantilists and at those of Ricardo's critics. Lord Keynes has attempted to rehabilitate not their doctrines and certainly not their practices, but their awareness of problems which the nineteenth-century theorists assumed away. Malthus has been restored to fuller stature than Walter Bagehot was willing to accord him. Alexander Hamilton's plea for economic development is seen to embody a point of view that demands consideration. Despite his ill-judged politics, Friedrich List is likely to receive more attention from economists in the twentieth century than he did in the nineteenth.

This renewed interest in the balancing of payments is no mere swing of the pendulum in economic thought. While the necessity to safeguard national economic strength against undue strains arising from unregulated international pressures on the balance of payments may have been discarded in nineteenth-century economic theory, this idea never ceased to be influential in the practice of every country except Great Britain and a few small states of western Europe. Since the abortive attempt to restore the international gold standard broke down in the great depression of 1929–33, there has been a strengthening of mercantilist ideas in practically every country but the United States. Britain, long the bulwark of the free-trade doctrine, has become the source of monetary theories that have a distinctly mercantilist tinge. Before the war, Germany, Italy, and Japan developed policies of economic and monetary nationalism. The U.S.S.R. has gone further than any country in divorcing its domestic economy from the rigidly controlled direction of its external balance of payments.

The reasons for this reversion to monetary nationalism are not far to seek. In the first place national security, which could be played down in considering economic policy as long as the *Pax Britannica* of the nineteenth century lasted, is again an urgent consideration. As long as the outcome of the present power struggle is uncertain, economic policy will be affected by strategic considerations. The ideological war between the United States and the U.S.S.R. was fought on many fronts. To the discomfiture of the nation-states that were caught in the cross fire, this conflict rapidly rose to the point where they were forced to choose which camp they would shelter in. Domestic politics from Iran through Greece to Italy and France demonstrated this pressure. In the trade negotiations at Geneva, in the investigations of the Economic Commission for Asia and the Far East at Shanghai, in the sixteen-nation conference of western European states at Paris —in every discussion of international economic relations—this conflict had dominated the background and often the foreground of debate. Moreover the aftermath of the wars already fought made it necessary for most governments to be concerned over the monetary policies dictated by their domestic economic problems and over the strain imposed upon their economies by chronic weakness in their balance of payments position.

It was difficult for Americans to enter fully into an understanding of this situation. In possession of the largest gold reserves ever accumulated in one country, the United States drained gold from the last reserves of most other countries. It had the largest active balance of exports over imports that it or any other country had ever had. This balance was built up by the world's need for the agricultural as well as the manufactured products of the United States and by the inability of most countries to send exports in payment for these products. It was further swollen by invisible exports from the United States such as shipping services and capital investments.

The dollar was strong. For many years there had been no need to worry lest an outflow of specie should cause a contraction of credit and plunge the economy into deflation. When such a development had appeared possible in the early part of 1933, the gold reserves (then amounting to approximately $4 billion) had been promptly safeguarded by devaluing the dollar in terms of gold. The negotiators for the United States, who insistently urged upon other countries the desirability of getting rid of exchange control and quantitative import restrictions, were able to do so in the comfortable knowledge that no worries existed as to the continuing ability of the United States to trade without endangering the reserves upon which its currency system was based.

Another consequence of two world wars which made management of the external balance difficult for most countries was the heavy burden of debt charges, of payments and pensions to veterans, continuing military, naval, and air defense, scientific research into new weapons and the costs of occupation and relief in enemy countries. This burden was also felt in the United States. It was the main reason why taxation had been kept at a relatively high level and why the rate of interest was not allowed to rise. Though the low prevailing rates laid the base for credit expansion that constituted an inflationary pressure upon the price structure, the Treasury, which had control of short-term rates, was unable to allow them to rise because this would increase the budgetary burden. Thus the Federal Reserve Banks could not bring pressure on the commercial banks whose large holdings of short-term government obligations could be cashed if need be.

The credit system was therefore out of control by such processes as raising the discount rates and open-market operations, leaving only the manipulation of bank reserve requirements. This constituted a domestic problem of great importance to the United States. However, it did not cause difficulties in the external balance of payments and was not likely to do so unless price levels rose to the point—still far distant—where they induced a reduction of exports and an increase of imports large enough to cause an outflow of specie. Before that remote contingency, some strain might be caused if foreign holders of short-term obligations and credit balances took alarm and withdrew their funds, but refugee capital still sought refuge in the United States.

If these financial circumstances gave some cause for watchfulness in the United States, they did not make it necessary to impose rationing and price controls to prevent a runaway price inflation. It was still possible to allow the economy to operate freely in the expectation that production would keep pace with the expansion of purchasing power. In most other countries the inflationary pressures were greater in proportion to productivity. Also the chances of increasing productivity were limited by the acute shortages of equipment, raw materials, fuel, and reserve stocks of food and consumers' goods. These deficiencies had to be remedied by heavier imports before exports could begin to expand substantially. Governments therefore took steps to maintain the domestic price and rationing systems which restrained consumption, to control the balance of payments in an effort to mobilize every possible dollar that was received from exports of all kinds, and to prohibit all expenditures that might drain those dollars away to nonessential uses.

These dilemmas did not exist for the U.S.S.R. It had long ago divorced its domestic economy from dependence on a fluctuating balance of external payments, and had reduced those payments to a minimum. It was able also to carry through a drastic revaluation of the internal value of the rouble. Even if the western European countries had been willing to pay the price in the deprivation of civil liberties and in the loss of economic efficiency entailed by regimentation of their domestic economies on the Russian model, few of them were in a similar position to reduce their external transactions to a minimum. Thus the balance of payments on these external transactions remained one of their major preoccupations. In the case of those countries (among which Britain was the outstanding example) where a greatly increased population had come to be dependent upon international trade, the balance of external payments was the dominant preoccupation.

Another characteristic of the second postwar period, while not solely the result of two world wars, was greatly enhanced in importance by the dislocations of industry and employment caused by the wartime disruptions of international specialization. Employment and the welfare of the working population had become overriding policy objectives. The revolutions and counterrevolutions of the twentieth century had been facilitated by the suffering inflicted by unemployment upon articulate and politically conscious groups of organized workers. Revolutions seldom arise from proletarian initiative. But they always appeal to mass discontent and seek support in proletarian movements. The Russian revolution was launched and nursed to the stage of effective organization by politically active groups of intellectuals. The Fascist and Nazi movements drew their initial support largely from the middle and professional classes. However in totalitarian and democratic countries alike, the political power of the laboring population was such that no government could disregard the distress inflicted upon the workers by severe unemployment, lest their power be mobilized to overthrow it.

In this respect the situation was totally different from that of the mercantilist period. Labor was no longer a mere resource—a factor of production—to be kept abundant and cheap in the interest of national power. Organized labor had been courted by the belligerent governments during the first World War and had made considerable gains in political status and power. Though the Nazi and Fascist regimes destroyed trade unionism and the Soviet system assigned to it a subordinate role, the appeal made by these governments to the masses of the people was in terms of social security and welfare. The Nazis indeed had laid such emphasis upon this appeal that many foreigners had been deceived as to the true motives of their economic policy. There is little need to emphasize the great gains in political power that the labor movement had made as a consequence of the second World War. Even in the countries whose governments did not draw their main support from organized labor, the advances in social-security legislation were evidence of these gains, as for instance its spread in Latin-American countries during the war.

It is obvious that a highly precarious situation existed particularly in those countries where high levels of wages and employment and elaborate social-security services were maintained in face of acute scarcities of commodities. This situation was prevented from collapsing by the receipt of large imports from the United States and other countries whose agriculture and industry had expanded during the war. Those large shipments to Europe kept the exporting countries also at levels of economic activity that approximated full employment. While there was a considerable difference between full employment and scarcities on the one side, and full employment and abundance on the other, on both sides this full employment was maintained only by ignoring or postponing the problem of payments.

In the longer run, it was obvious that the postwar reconstruction boom would come to an end. This might occur gradually by production catching up with demand or explosively by credit expansion getting out of control. However, a third possibility could not be lightly dismissed. It was possible that, in order to throttle the credit expansion long before production caught up with demand, many countries might be driven to increasing regimentation both of their domestic economies and of their external balances. This could happen from an extension and consolidation of the emergency expedients that were being adopted to cope with the scarcity of dollar exchange.

The long-run problem of employment necessarily involved a large measure of reorganization of existing industries. The former export industries of the western European countries left high and dry by the collapse of international markets and the war industries that had to be cut to the size of peacetime requirements presented to planning authorities the necessity of direct action to prevent localized unemployment. The British case was very clear. A detailed survey of industrial areas by the Social Reconstruction Survey, instituted by Nuffield College at the request of the British government, argued that "planning for full employment and planning for correct location of industry necessarily go together; and both depend on key decisions in the field of international economic policy as well as on a correct dovetailing of the public and private sectors of home policy." [2] Population could not be moved en masse and, unless complementary industries could be located in what might become depressed areas, there was a real danger of substantial local unemployment even when the level of demand remained high in the country as a whole. Monetary manipulation could not be relied upon to shift people from their homes to the areas where industry had located itself to meet new conditions. Therefore if unemployment was to be avoided, the location of industry had to be fitted into where the people lived. It was easier to shift workers from one occupation to another than it was to shift families from one region to another. Thus, planning of the location of industry involved decisions as to the imports of raw materials and the exports of finished manufactures, and hence, a continuing control over the external balance of payments.

In recent economic literature the balance of external payments has been discussed mainly as an aspect of national monetary policy. It is true that fluctuations in prices, induced largely by instability of the monetary standard of value, have been a major cause of the great cyclical disturbances that have led to the most severe periods of unemployment in recent decades. This fact was well expressed by J. M. Keynes when he wrote: "Unemployment, the precarious life of the worker, the disappointment of expectations, the sudden loss of savings, the excessive windfalls to the individuals, the speculator, the profiteer—all proceed in large measure from the instability of the standard of value." [3]

Thus the balance of payments problems that arose after the second World War in connection with monetary policies designed to maintain income and employment called for careful consideration.

[2] Cf. M. P. Fogarty, *Prospects of the Industrial Areas of Great Britain,* London, 1945. Introduction by G. D. H. Cole, p. xxxiii.

[3] J. M. Keynes, *A Tract on Monetary Reform,* London, 1923, p. v.

The preceding pages have deliberately emphasized the structural dislocations of industry that were responsible for the hard core of unemployment in the interwar years. This stubborn maladjustment between the supply of labor and its skills, and the demand for them in areas and industries built up to supply markets that have disappeared, could not be cured by monetary policy alone. People had to be retrained in new skills. If they could not be shifted for family and similar reasons to areas of new industrial employment, then the industries had to be brought to them. The attempt by credit expansion to maintain a high level of demand, in order to avert the recurrence of unemployment in what had formerly been distressed areas, was bound to cause bottlenecks and an inflationary spiral of wage and price increases.

Because it was politically impossible to allow these areas to become economic slums from which at least the young and energetic workers had fled to seek employment elsewhere, it was necessary to reckon upon a continuance of economic planning for their rehabilitation. In the meantime, however, the national level of employment as a whole was in many countries precariously sustained by expansionist monetary policies. This was the case after the second World War in most of the western European countries.

It was easy to criticize this tendency to rely upon credit expansion. A good case could be made for disinflation and for a considerable relaxation of controls. But it would have been political suicide for any government to follow an abrupt policy of decontrol in respect to the external balance of payments. Instead most governments had to husband their limited exchange reserves and allocate them to the most essential import needs. The control of external payments was geared to domestic policies designed to nurse the level of employment while trying, by the direction of public investment, by raw-material and fuel allocations, by organizing labor mobility, and by retraining skills, to ease population out of and industry into the areas that threatened to become depressed. At the same time most governments were rationing scarce consumers' goods, controlling the prices of essential materials and consumers' goods so as to keep down production costs, and keeping wage rates from rising. Purchasing power was being drained off by high taxation while at the same time it was necessary to encourage by all possible means an expansion of production. Much of this increased production had to be diverted into exports so as to pay for needed imports. If the governments could obtain credit in various forms to postpone payment for imports, they gained a chance to carry through their programs of domestic reorganization without resorting to unduly drastic restrictions on imports. If it was not possible to secure foreign loans or if export receipts should fall as a result either of a shrinkage of foreign demand or of production difficulties at home, the authorities would be forced to clamp very severe restrictions on imports.

As long as such national plans were operative, it was essential that the reorganization of domestic industry should not be hampered by credit restriction. National monetary policies were therefore directed to maintaining an easy monetary situation. As a sculptor must keep his clay moist while he is moulding it into the desired shape, so the governments could not afford to have their plans for reconstruction hampered by a contraction of credit. If they could keep credit abundant and cheap without harsh restrictions on imports so much the better—always it was the domestic situation which dominated their thinking. All over the world the practice of monetary authorities accepted the necessity of allowing credit to adjust itself to what were considered to be the needs of national economic planning.

This fact calls for a revolutionary change in the most important of all the assumptions of the classical theory that explained the balancing of payments between national economies. Instead of the supply of money adjusting itself to trading needs as expressed by the pressures upon balances of payments, it had now come to be managed in each country by reference to the levels of prices and national incomes. Autonomous monetary policies were designed to keep national incomes stable at a high level which could permit at least an approximation to full employment. The external balance had to be adjusted to the level of national income, instead of national income being adjusted to the external balance.

This meant that the elaborate analysis whereby economists explained the price specie-flow theory of the balancing of payments was not relevant to modern conditions. That explanation had been simple when national monetary systems consisted primarily of gold and silver coin or of coin supplemented by paper money against which a proportionate specie reserve was maintained. It became more complicated when the great bulk of commercial transactions was settled by credit instruments so that the flexible relationship between gold reserves, paper money, and the credit structure introduced subtleties into the effect of specie flows upon prices. In that process, as long as the exchange rates were fixed by definition of the national currency units in terms of gold, the free exchange markets were the instrument by which national prices and production were continuously adjusted to the levels which enabled payments to be cleared.

The exchange rates are still fixed, though not in terms of gold. The markets are no longer free. The national levels of prices and production are maintained by credit policies which are governed by domestic rather than international considerations. If gold flows in as it did to the United States after the second World War, it has only a limited and mainly psychological effect on the volume of commercial credit. If gold flows out as it did from Britain and most other countries, this has no effect on the volume of credit in Britain or on the issue of bank notes needed for cash and till-money.

The balancing of payments is not brought about indirectly by adjusting the volume of credit and rates of interest in such a way as to cause a contraction or expansion of prices and production and thereby of exports and imports. Nor are temporary strains on the balance covered by higher rates of interest attracting short-term funds to the center which momentarily has difficulties in balancing its accounts. The whole price specie-flow mechanism is discarded in practice, at least temporarily. New methods of a more direct character are in use. The external balance is now like the bed of Procrustes to which travelers were fitted. Its size and shape are determined by national policy, and such external transactions as are permitted must be adjusted to it.

A VARIETY OF MIXED ECONOMIES

The economic and monetary structure of the trading world was never as uniform as the textbooks assume. However before the first World War, there was much more uniformity than there is now. Then there was a prevailing faith in competition as the regulating principle of economic activity. While this faith was not always clearly distinguished from mere opposition to government interference with private enterprise, it constituted a creed by conformity to which orthodoxy might be measured. Like all faiths, it was a source both of energy and of resignation. It was the mainspring of the vigorous but ruthless enterprise of the American frontier and of the London money market, of the great waves of migration that peopled the temperate zones of both hemispheres, and of the outflow of European capital and organizing skills that brought the outlying markets of Africa and Asia within the orbit of world trade. At the same time it served as the true opiate from on high that enabled the weaker competitor to accept his sufferings meekly.

For perhaps a decade in the third quarter of the nineteenth century it had looked as if the free-trade movement might spread until the whole trading world became linked in specialized interdependence. To the free trader the political concept of nationalism seemed an entirely laudable aspiration toward cultural and political unity, which bore little if any relation to economic development. He believed that national independence had little to do with the competitive processes by which businessmen would organize specialized production and commerce in a world of autonomous but interdependent states. This dream of universal competition faded in the late sixties when Bismarck's three sharp strokes created the German empire under Prussian leadership. This disturbed the balance of power in Europe and set free the fears, the suspicions, and the prejudices always latent in nationalism. A new era of national rivalries began almost before the free-trade initiative was well under way.

Inevitably these aggravated nationalisms blundered at last into the first World War. In the dislocation of economic relationships that ensued, a new dissident creed achieved expression. The leaders of the Allied powers hailed the Kerensky revolution in March, 1917, as a long-overdue extension of democratic principles. But the old Russia was too far decayed for any effective patching. In November, 1917, the mild reformists were pushed to one side by the disciplined and doctrinaire majority group of the Social Democratic party (the Bolsheviks) who held ruthlessly to revolutionary objectives and refused to compromise their principles. After many vicissitudes, the Bolsheviks beat back spasmodic counterrevolutions and Allied interventions, and succeeded in organizing a new and powerful state upon anticapitalist principles.

The emergence of the U.S.S.R. and its rise to power introduced a new element into international economic relations. The preceding nationalisms had accepted the competitive principle while controlling and modifying it. The U.S.S.R. rejected it, just as it rejected the pri-

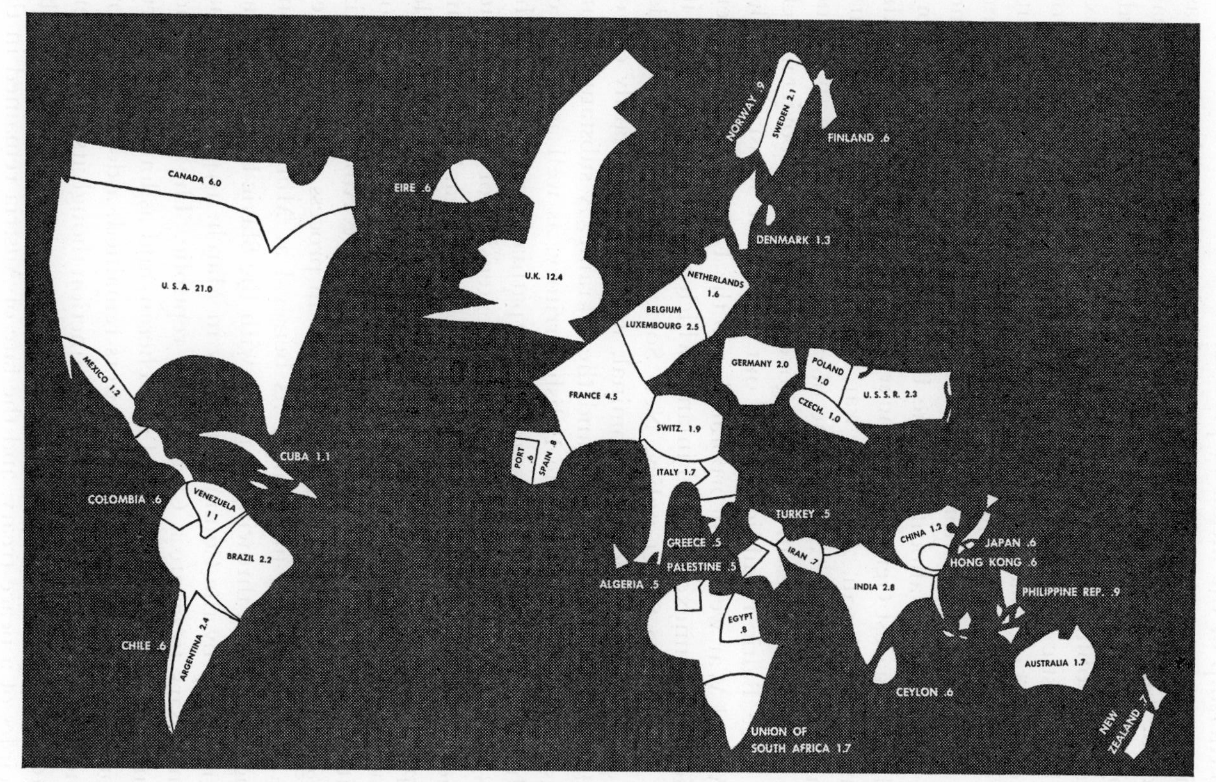

THE TRADING WORLD, 1946

The area of each country is shown proportionately to its share of total world trade in 1946.

Source: Calculated from data in International Monetary Fund, *International Financial Statistics*, Washington. November 1948, pp. 18–19.

vate ownership of the means of production and other fundamental principles of capitalist society. A planned industrial development was projected. This necessarily entailed close regulation of all external economic transactions. New devices of state trading were invented. Former debt obligations were repudiated, foreign enterprise was expelled, domestic monetary policy was divorced from the balance of payments, and international trade was reduced to the vanishing point. Thus was the Russian economy taken out of the world trading system.

In the military operations of the second World War, central and eastern Europe was allocated to the U.S.S.R. while the Allied effort was thrown against Germany on the western front, Italy in the Mediterranean, and Japan. After the war, the Soviet theater of military operations became the Soviet zone of occupation. Within that zone there arose intense pressure to create governments on the Soviet model. The three Baltic republics carved out of Tsarist Russia after the first World War were reincorporated into the U.S.S.R. Strategic territories were annexed from Finland, which must now conform in large measure to Soviet policy. New Soviet republics, whose independence in foreign policy is nominal, were created, mainly out of Polish territory in Byelorussia and the Ukraine. A substantial part of eastern Germany and some Polish territory, as well as a slice of Czechoslovakia lying northeast of the Carpathians, was added to the U.S.S.R. Poland was compensated by an extension of its boundaries on the west, and Germans were expelled from this area. In the Russian-occupied zone of eastern Germany, where lay the industrially developed areas based on the Silesian coal fields, there was every possibility of a separate government of the Soviet type. Albania, Bulgaria, Hungary, Romania, and Yugoslavia were in process of being sovietized. Czechoslovakia, mindful of its betrayal at Munich, had gone a long way toward throwing in its lot with the Slavic bloc, so that an internal coup by the Communist party in March, 1948, was all that was necessary to create a Czech-Soviet republic. The independence of Austria had been guaranteed at Teheran, and as long as the occupation forces of the four Allied powers remained, a democratic government on the Western model could function though its powers were limited. It had not yet been possible for the powers to agree on the principles of a peace treaty, and the fate of Austria remained in the balance.

The countries included in this Soviet zone of influence have not in the past been of major significance in world trade. Including the U.S.S.R., they accounted in 1938 for but 5 per cent of the total of world trade, and their percentage has undoubtedly decreased since the war. But the importance of this zone should not be underestimated. It constituted a large area with heavy trends of population increase, and with the only considerable European deposits of important minerals. For the most part its former trade had been centered on Germany and was with the industrial countries of western Europe. These central and eastern European countries had had little trade with the U.S.S.R. before the war and their commerce with the United States had been limited. To divert their trading connections from Germany to the U.S.S.R. required a tour de force of administrative regulation. However, it was doubtful whether the U.S.S.R. could act as the organizing center of this new trade group, and there was a clear tendency toward a limited resumption of the former trade between eastern and western Europe. If this tendency is thwarted by political direction it will be at the cost of greatly diminished trade and lowered living levels for both eastern and western Europeans.[4] The immediate effect of its enforced withdrawal from world trade was to complicate the provisioning of its former markets. New trade and payment circuits had to be built up by which food and raw materials in greater volume could flow from the United States, Latin America, and the British Dominions to the industrial countries of western Europe.

It was possible also that Soviet expansion had not yet reached its limits. Within Europe in the years following the second World War there was heavy pressure, exercised directly and through local Communist parties, upon Greece, Italy, France, and Turkey, but this

[4] The *Seventeenth Annual Report of the Bank for International Settlements*, Basle, June 1947, Ch. IV, brought together the fragmentary material available concerning the trade of these countries in 1946. Later material is contained in Economic Commission for Europe, *A Survey of the Economic Situation and Prospects of Europe*, Geneva, March 1948. The League of Nations' *The Network of World Trade* showed that in 1938 the exports and imports of the U.S.S.R. to and from these countries was negligible. Trade with the United States was greater but still small. The overwhelming bulk of the trade was with other European countries.

It was too early in the fall of 1949 to predict the future development of trade in this area; but there was every indication of the most strenuous effort being made to reorient trade of the whole region toward the U.S.S.R. The population of the U.S.S.R. and its eastern European satellites is now slightly greater than that of the 270 million in the sixteen European states which lie outside the Soviet zone. This discrepancy is bound to grow because the age grouping and present birth rates make inevitable a much more rapid population increase in eastern than in western Europe.

pressure was countered by economic aid from the United States. Across the Near East from Turkey to Iran, the U.S.S.R. had become a powerful neighbor of weak but richly endowed small states. The struggle for oil was complicated by the conflict between Jews and Arabs which inflamed nationalist feelings in the Moslem world from north Africa through Arabia to Pakistan. Communist parties were active in the independence movements throughout Asia. The Soviet zone of influence extended from Mongolia, Manchuria and northern Korea deeply into China. In October, 1949, the U.S.S.R. recognized the newly formed communist government of China, even before it had occupied the whole territory. It would require a greater effort than the U.S.S.R. could easily organize to develop all the opportunities offered in these varied situations. But compact and disciplined minorities had a chance after the war to make headway against weak ruling groups.

As soon as the war ended in Europe, a network of bilateral trade agreements had been negotiated among the European countries. In addition to the agreements centered on Moscow, there were three main foci in this network—Sweden, Switzerland, and Britain. All three had made it clear that their interim bilateral agreements were intended to be stopgap expedients pending the negotiation of a multilateral agreement for the reduction of tariff and other barriers.

The reconstruction of multilateral trade had been one of the major objectives of the foreign economic policy of the United States. With this end in view it had initiated the first international consultations at London in late 1946, and these were continued in a preparatory conference at Geneva. At Havana, the United Nations Conference on Trade and Employment had finally drafted the charter of the International Trade Organization. In order to gain the assent of the fifty-three signatory nations, the charter had had to be elaborated in even greater detail than in its original form, with numerous exceptions to practically all the major agreements of principle. This process of elaboration which had begun in the earlier London and Geneva consultations became even more pronounced at Havana. The reason was conflicts of attitude toward such questions as full employment and economic development. These conflicts were rooted in the great diversities of economic structure and of political objectives in the economic sphere. The negotiators for the United States had been able to resist the inclusion of any proposals binding its signatories to take concerted action of a planning character. This negotiating success had its price, which was the elaboration of escape clauses to enable other countries to maintain their full-employment policies, if need be by suspending their obligations to follow nondiscriminatory policies of multilateral trade.

Attention has already been drawn to the development of national economic planning in Britain and France. It should be recognized that the experience of these countries after the war was part of a trend that seemed likely to create a series of mixed economies whose economic structure would be located at various stages of government intervention between the completely planned economy of the U.S.S.R. and the almost completely private enterprise economy of the United States. It was difficult to draw any very clear line between state intervention designed to insure full employment, and that for national economic development. The Argentine five-year plan, for example, was described as one for economic development and industrial expansion and the Mexican six-year plan as one for industrialization and agricultural expansion. There was an ambitious plan on paper in China and there has been much discussion in India of the so-called Bombay Plan advanced by a group of Indian industrialists. In New Zealand a comprehensive plan had been outlined, covering all public and private construction activities and their co-ordination with national development and full-employment policies. The co-ordination was to be achieved through a Ministry of Works whose functions were projected along the lines of the National Investment Board proposed by Sir William Beveridge in his British study, *Full Employment in a Free Society*. It was evident that national economic planning was being focused on planned investment and that planned investment would entail continued control and regulation of the external balances of payment.

It would be premature to attempt an appraisal of all the many national plans. Most of them remained aspirations or by-products of emergency reconstruction activities, rather than rationally formulated long-range plans being worked out through appropriate mechanisms of government. There was more muddle than planning, more patching than reconstruction. It was necessary, however, to accept the fact that few countries would accept the assumption implicit in the proposals for the expansion of world trade and employment that were originally advanced by the United States. This assumption is that the removal of trade barriers would enable private competitive enterprise to restore productivity all over the world and that such restoration of productivity would not only be stable, but consistent with national prosperity and welfare in all countries.

The prevalence of all this politically motivated planning called for emphasis of the truth embodied in the United States' proposals, the fundamental importance of which was being underrated. Only in a world of expanding production and trade would national planning programs be likely to result in enhanced prosperity and individual welfare. Yet few governments felt able to risk giving up the safeguards upon which they had relied to protect their national economies from being plunged into deflation and unemployment by strains on the balance of payments. Few of the governments whose economies had remained underdeveloped were convinced that they could afford to allow the creation of transport and power systems, the construction of factories, and the improvement of agriculture to develop as a by-product of the competitive search for profits. Faith in the self-corrective automatism of the competitive system was at a low ebb. Governments which abdicated the responsibility for maintaining prosperity and advancing the development of natural resources were not likely to continue long in office.

It is significant that the crucial issue which arose at Havana in the negotiation of the charter of the International Trade Organization was the demand that countries pursuing policies of economic development should be free to use import quotas as well as tariffs, to protect their infant industries. Such a proposal had struck at the heart of the American plan. It could be argued that in the right hands a discriminatory trade policy, moderately and skillfully pursued, would result in less damage to world trade in a crisis than a doctrinaire adherence to a policy of nondiscrimination. But this argument was valid only on the assumption that an effective multilateral system for the clearing of payments could not be created, and that if created, it could not be reinforced by an adequate international reserve of liquid means of payment. The argument also assumed that those who discriminated would be both wise and skillful, and that they would be able to discriminate without provoking reprisals.

What was important in all these international negotiations was the implicit reservation of the right and duty of national governments to intervene in the competitive trading process. It became clear that a multilateral trading system must now accept this reservation. Action could be taken by national governments in many fields—by altering the exchange parity of the national currency, by imposing restrictions on capital movements, by discriminatory restrictions of imports from a country whose currency is scarce in world markets (most obviously from the United States), by bilateral agreements of a preferential character in regard to tariff duties, by import quotas or exchange allocations, or by bilateral purchasing agreements.

It had also become evident that there would be attempts to stabilize by bilateral agreement some part of the trade of many countries. In addition to the British preferential tariffs and marketing agreements, account must be taken of such experiments as the bilateral barter provisions in the Swedish trade agreement with the U.S.S.R., signed on October 7, 1946. While those negotiations were in progress, the United States expressed its concern both to Sweden and to the U.S.S.R. that this bilateral deal would conflict with the nondiscriminatory provisions of the proposed trade charter. Subsequently questions were raised concerning somewhat similar proposals projected in negotiations between Britain and both Canada and Argentina. Despite these protests, it seemed very likely that there would be substantial elements of planned bilateral trade within the framework of any multilateral trading system that might be developed. In 1948 it was estimated that 57 per cent of the total of British imports consisted of government purchases, largely through bilateral purchase agreements.

Quite apart from the existence of complete state trading monopolies in the U.S.S.R. and the satellite states of central and eastern Europe, the policies of partial economic planning pursued over a large part of the rest of the trading world presented great obstacles to the creation of a competitive multilateral trading system. The proponents of national economic planning projected a regional area of planned multilateral trade as a possible alternative to the world-wide multilateral trading system proposed by the United States. The difficulties involved in such an alternative would be almost as great as those in negotiating a world-wide system of multilateral trade. If such a world system cannot be created, the prospect would seem to be a widespread extension of bilateralism, within which rather narrow regional groups might develop triangular clearing arrangements, rather than a sterling area system of multilateral trade. This prospect was all the more likely since the resources for the economic development of industrially backward areas were not available in any quantity except from the United States.

The best chance to restore a world trading system to include the bulk of the world outside the Soviet zone was to implement the negotiations for a multilateral trading system based upon the United States' principle of nondiscrimination. In the difficult circumstances of the postwar world such a system might need to incorporate large elements of planned trade which are of the nature of bilateral barter. It would probably need also to provide for numerous exceptions to the rules of nondiscrimination whenever agreement to such exceptions was authorized by the International Trade Organization.

The alternative was an extensive complex of bilateral agreements, coupled with triangular clearings among limited regional groups, rather than a wide area of multilateralism based on sterling or any other currency alternative to the dollar. In any case, the disturbed political and economic circumstances of many developing countries made necessary emergency arrangements for such trade as could be carried on, while a wide and perhaps widening area on the boundaries of the U.S.S.R. was subjected to state trading monopolies. Thus it was not a simple or homogeneous free-enterprise world in which trade had to be reorganized. Rather it was a collection of independent nation-states pursuing a wide variety of national economic policies in which private enterprise and national planning were mixed in different combinations.

CHAPTER XX

THE BALANCING OF PAYMENTS

THE MONETARY MECHANISM

AFTER THE second World War the balancing of international payments had departed very far from the methods of the international gold standard. Under that standard, national currencies had been maintained at fixed parities within the limits of the gold points. Pressures were exerted upon national incomes and commodity price levels, primarily through manipulation of short-term interest rates. The prices of internationally traded commodities were competitive. Through them and through the effect of imports and exports upon national incomes, the whole structure of prices in one country was kept in flexible alignment with the price structures of other countries.

This balancing was continuous and involved the whole trading process. It could not be traced in the annual statistics which recorded the movements of goods and services. Nor was there any distinction between inert and balancing items in the transactions that crossed national boundaries. The quantities of goods and services exchanged, their prices, the transfers of credit on long and short term, interest rates, security transactions, and, within the limits of the gold points, the prices (exchange rates) of the currencies themselves were in constant flux. To an increasing extent the clearing and balancing of payments between countries approximated to the credit adjustments that went on within each country. The loss of gold from monetary reserves would bring about a contraction of credit and thus cause a fall in prices and in national income. Actual gold shipments were used only as the last resort in a persistent disequilibrium. For slight and temporary adjustments of a country's balance of payments short-term credit movements were sufficient to fill the need for means of international payment. They would be attracted by a rise in interest rates in the country that found it necessary to reduce prices and incomes. And thus in the longer run, payments on account of external transactions would be brought into equilibrium by increasing exports and reducing imports.[1]

It has been shown that this method of multilateral clearing and balancing of payments did not survive the first World War. The attempt to restore the international gold standard was not successful, because the flexibility of prices and interest rates and the relatively free movement of goods and services essential to its operation could not be restored. For a few years, the restored gold standard functioned with some difficulty. Britain was still the center of the world trading system, and London tried to regain its position as the leading money market. The drying up of the credit flow from the United States to Europe brought this experiment to an end. The financial panic that began in Vienna in May, 1931, and forced sterling off gold in September of that year, paralyzed the clearing of international payments. The total value of international trade in 1933 fell to one-third of the levels of 1929. New devices, primarily of bilateral clearing, had to be organized. There has never since been any possibility of restoring the nineteenth-century system of world-wide multilateral clearing and balancing of payments.

In the years that intervened between the great depression and the second World War a great confusion of practical expedients was devised for the balancing of payments between national monetary systems. These caused very important changes in the practice and to some extent in the governing legislation of credit institutions. With the further developments during and since the war, national monetary systems are now very different from those which functioned under the international gold standard. It is too soon to attempt a comprehensive survey of the many changes in the legal position and practice of central and commercial banks, in the methods by which foreign

[1] Cf. Chapter XII, "The International Gold Standard."

trade is financed and payments cleared, and in government controls over domestic credit policies and external payments. All these are still in rapid evolution. Until the first postwar crises are past and the relation of national institutions and policies to the new international institutions and treaty agreements has been tested, the best that can be done is to draw attention to some of the outstanding trends of development that seem likely to persist in the future.

To a considerable extent the great commercial banks have taken over the functions of the independent specialized operators who constituted the competitive markets in foreign exchange, bullion transactions, discounts, acceptances, and different forms of arbitrage. There is a connection between the increasing power of these great banks, and the government regulation limiting the transactions that formerly nourished these speculative markets. As these corporations swallowed up the bread and butter operations of the independent competitive brokers, government intervention became more necessary, because the brokers, deprived of their routine business, engaged more heavily in speculation, and more possible because these regulatory functions of the money market became easier to control when they were concentrated in a few powerful institutions. As these functions were concentrated in banks they were subordinated to national credit policy in general instead of working against its trend.

It is not easy to find a halfway house between free competition and complete state regulation. At present many of the financial transactions by which specialists in the money market used to correct disparities of demand and supply are either illegal or contrary to the policies of treasuries and central banks. This is the case particularly in regard to the capital transfers and arbitrage operations that used to restore equilibrium in interest rates and price levels. In recent years such operations have largely been used as a means of evading the restrictions on capital flight, or as a medium of speculative attacks on weak currencies. Bullion and forward exchange operations fall into the same category. Deprived of the legitimate operations that formerly gave them their livelihood, the specialist dealers found outlets during the 1930's for their working capital in such fields as speculation against weak currencies, outguessing the policies of exchange stabilization funds, operating on the minor exchange rates that were out of line with the pegging of exchange rates on the principal currencies, and finding loopholes in the exchange regulations as a means of getting funds out of countries threatened by exchange depreciation. In 1936 J. M. Keynes pointed out that the energies and inside knowledge of professional Stock Exchange investors and speculators had been diverted largely to attempts to outguess the general public in regard to its probable views as to the trend of security values. Other sections of the money market suffered the same kind of deterioration.

Many of the currency depreciations of the 1930's ought never to have occurred. Any sign of weakness in a currency, as for example a political crisis in France, was the signal for a concerted attack upon it by professional speculators. By what in effect was large-scale gambling on the chance that the franc would depreciate, it was forced to depreciate. Such destructive operations cost the speculators little, as compared with the gains to be made if the speculation was successful. They could put up relatively small amounts on margin to start a selling trend that would quickly be reinforced by a nervous public. The future value of the franc was thus forced down in the market by large forward or short sales. Nervous holders of francs sought refuge by buying international securities or by transferring their funds abroad. French exporters kept their receipts abroad in expectation of a depreciation of the franc. French importers were forced to sell francs to get foreign currencies and to hedge their prospective requirements of those currencies. The crisis would deepen in France as capital flight drained away exchange reserves until the pressure to depreciate became irresistible. After depreciation by buying francs at the new low rate the speculators could close out their transactions at a handsome profit. In Amsterdam, Zurich, Brussels, New York, and Paris, as well as London, these speculative transactions became destructive of international equilibrium.

Any consideration of the balancing process as it operated just before the second World War must start by recognizing that the specialized markets of which the money markets were formerly composed had lost their main purpose. In so far as they still operated in the balancing of payments, they were often at cross-purposes with the policies pursued by national agencies. Meantime the absorption of the international payments transactions by banks and government agencies had put these payments on a more routine basis. There was less flexibility in rates, margins were not calculated as finely, and the stream of payments moved more sluggishly. The concern of the banking institutions was the domestic market. Inevitably their conduct of international finance became subordinated to national credit policies. The result was the concentration of exchange transactions in state-controlled central banks, for which the commercial banks became merely the agents in dealing with the public. There was no longer an exchange market—no chaffering of competitive buyers and sellers. Gold and foreign exchange receipts were handed over to the central bank and rationed according to priorities determined, not by demand and supply, but by official decision. The official rates did not reflect market situations. Therefore they did not fluctuate. The stages through which this development passed varied from country to country. Attention may be drawn to some of the experiments which illustrate the interference with market forces in an effort to insulate national economies from strains on the external balance of payments. Those strains which arose from the violent fluctuations of income and employment during the great depression, and from the national measures adopted to offset them, were aggravated by three developments.

The first was the burden of external debt payments. These included long-term public debt, long-, medium- and short-term private debt, and even the short-term interbanking obligations, formerly of unquestioned liquidity. By means of moratoria and the blocking of external payments, relief—in some cases amounting to repudiation—from payments due on account of past obligations was sought. As clearing and payment agreements were negotiated, current trade took priority over past debts. While a creditor country which was also a great importer, could sometimes insist upon a proportion of export receipts being set aside to redeem debt, there was resistance on the part of the debtor country since it wished to use them to buy needed imports. There was a scaling down of the obligations, the market value of which had fallen heavily as soon as payment restrictions were introduced. Many countries used exchange control to negotiate a reduction of their international obligations. The freezing of the short-term accommodation that had been extended by foreign to German banks in the financial crisis of 1930–31, struck a mortal blow at the use of short-term credit transfers in the balancing process.

The second aggravation came from the international communication of frequent and violent price fluctuations—the attempt to recoup national income losses by increasing exports at lower prices. This took the form mainly of exchange depreciation in one country after another. One of the time-honored ways by which a country could attempt to redress its balance of payments was by devaluing its currency or by allowing the exchange value of its currency to depreciate without official devaluation. By this means exports were stimulated and imports checked. When Britain suspended convertibility in 1931, a great many countries followed suit. All the British Dominions and colonies (except South Africa and Canada) kept their currencies pegged on sterling, and many other countries for which Britain was a dominant market did so in fact if not in theory. Australia devalued its currency 20 per cent below sterling parity and a few months later New Zealand was forced to follow suit. Within a few days Denmark, and the other countries for which the British butter market was important, matched the New Zealand depreciation. By this time sterling had depreciated by 40 per cent from its former gold parity. Thus the New Zealand depreciation was nearly 50 per cent. The price of butter as measured in the currencies of countries which retained their former gold parity, was cut practically in half by this change in currency values. Hence a country like Switzerland was forced either to match the depreciation or to protect its price structure by excluding the imports of commodities supplied by the countries that had depreciated their currencies. All this led to a rapid extension of import prohibition and quota systems in an effort to divorce the domestic price structures from the effects of international price fluctuations.

The third aggravation of strain on the balances of payments has already been stressed in connection with the evolution of monetary theories. A great mass of short-term funds held in cash or readily realizable securities was liable to be moved rapidly, in search of security rather than profit, from one center to another. This was the most destructive of all the uncertainties of the interwar period. These idle funds could not be tempted into productive long-term investments. Attempts to use them as the reserves upon which currency systems were expanded, partly in order to make long-term foreign investments for reconstruction, exposed those systems to the risk that in a sudden crisis such reserves would be pulled from under the expanded superstructure of credit. This is what actually happened to one country after another in the panic months of 1931.

For a time after the depreciation of sterling there was much discussion in economic circles of the possibility of taking the strains upon the balance of payments by allowing exchange rates to fluctuate freely. Flexible exchange rates were advocated by many economists and some experiments were made in this direction. An exchange rate is a ratio. It is the price of one currency expressed in terms of another. If a national currency is to find the level which will equilibrate its balance of payments, it must have a fulcrum. This could happen when one country found the strain on its balances so great that it departed from the international gold standard and allowed the exchange value of its currency to fluctuate till it could be re-stabilized at a lower level. This was easy when the other currencies, particularly sterling, continued to maintain the former gold parity. When sterling carried most other currencies with it in the depreciation of 1931, the adjustment was sought by leverage upon the United States dollar and the currencies of the European gold bloc (France, Belgium, Netherlands, Switzerland, Poland, and Italy). The depreciation of sterling then placed British (and other) exporters at an advantage in neutral markets compared with American exporters. A British car costing £300, which competed on fairly equal terms in a Latin-American country with an American automobile costing $1,500 as long as the exchange rate was $4.8665 to the pound sterling, gained a great competitive advantage as the rate fell toward and even below $4.00 to the pound. Australian wheat and Egyptian cotton could undersell American wheat and cotton in world markets. Obviously the downward drift of sterling and its associated currencies was damaging to exports from the United States and it was stopped by the sudden devaluation of the dollar in April, 1933.

There was a clear recognition of the interdependence of currencies within large areas of close trading relationships. The British Dominions and colonies had followed sterling, except South Africa, which tried unsuccessfully to maintain its former gold parity, and Canada, which was caught between the British and United States policies. Most of the Scandinavian and Latin-American countries also pegged their currencies on sterling, even while some of them proclaimed, as Sweden did, their independence of action. In 1935 Belgium broke away from its European neighbors in the gold bloc and aligned its currency with sterling. In September, 1936, the Tripartite Declaration by which the United States, Britain, and France proclaimed their intention to maintain the exchange stability of their currencies, following an adjustment of the franc exchange rate, gave France and the other gold bloc countries the opportunity to do likewise.

One important result of the widespread currency depreciation in the 1930's was to give a lift to the gold-producing countries. As one country after another devalued its currency, the price of gold went up. After January 1, 1934, the official price settled at $35 an ounce, as compared with $20.67 before the dollar depreciated in April, 1933. The United States Treasury continued to buy all the gold offered to it. Naturally this encouraged gold mining. Most of the world's gold was mined outside the United States, in large part in the British Empire. The dollar value of the gold sold by British Empire countries to the United States rose from $118 million in 1929 to $2,616 million in 1939. This latter figure was greater than the total world production of new gold in 1939, indicating that reserves were drawn upon. The shipment to the United States of such large quantities of gold was a considerable help in balancing the international accounts.

These currency experiences demonstrated the narrowness of the limits within which the smaller trading countries were able to follow national policies which aimed at stabilizing their price levels and national incomes while allowing their exchange rates to fluctuate. Their economies are so interwoven with the economies of their principal foreign markets that stability in space is more important to them than stability in time. The influence of depression or prosperity in these foreign markets reaches them through so many channels directly affecting income, prices, and employment in their own economies that it cannot be circumvented merely by using flexible exchange rates as a shock absorber. There is more general recognition now that flexibly fluctuating exchange rates are impracticable. Occasional adjustment of an exchange rate which is out of equilibrium may be necessary. It is regarded as a surgical operation to be undertaken only in a grave emergency and after serious consultations as to its national and international repercussions.

In this period many countries experimented with exchange stabilization or equalization funds designed to give national monetary authorities means to meet sudden strains upon their balances of payments and thus prevent them from causing violent fluctuations in the national economies. There was nothing especially novel in these funds except that they recognized and separated the external use of currency reserves as distinct from their internal use as backing for the credit superstructure. Increasingly, credit policy in the great trading countries had been governed by domestic developments. An outflow of gold had not been allowed to restrict credit within a country. An inflow of gold, particularly when it was associated with flight capital, was regarded as a temporary acquisition. It was often segregated and sterilized. Many European central banks kept secret reserves against a sudden emergency. In other countries gold was held by commercial banks or other institutions apart from the currency reserves. There was a good deal of private hoarding.

After 1914 gold flows had ceased in large measure to play the role attributed to them in the classic version of the price specie-flow theory. The volume of credit was no longer proportioned to the size of the metallic reserves upon which the currency systems were based. It responded to the ebb and flow of production and trade within the country. That ebb and flow continued to be influenced by international pressures, but these were exerted directly through many channels, such as the volume of trade and commodity prices rather than through the monetary system. Frequent references to the balances subject to sudden withdrawal in a crisis indicated that there was hesitancy even in allowing short-term credit flows to affect the credit structure.

The segregation of a special fund for coping with sudden strains on the balance of payments was a development of orthodox central banking practice. The limits of its usefulness soon became evident. After the depreciation of sterling, the British Exchange Equalization Account was set up in expectation of a return flow of foreign funds. The only action that was necessary was to give the Treasury power to create sterling by issuing bills to a total of £150 million. This sterling was used to buy the foreign funds that began to flow back to London and to set them aside as a reserve of exchange assets. During 1932, a substantial reserve was accumulated and the exchange value of sterling was prevented from rising by the Exchange Equalization Account purchasing all offerings of foreign exchange with the newly created sterling.

In other countries such expedients did not fare as well. The special accounts could intercept and segregate an inflow of foreign funds. In the case of an outflow they merely acted as a pipe line from the currency reserves. When in 1934 the United States set up a Stabilization Fund from the profits of its devaluation, the mere fact of its existence made a currency war with Britain always possible. While the United States authorities acted with restraint, the mere existence of the Stabilization Fund was sufficient to check the depreciation of sterling. Now it is generally realized that competitive exchange depreciation, supported by what in effect are special funds for currency warfare, is an impossible policy for smaller countries and a costly and futile one for larger countries. While there is need for a reserve of liquid assets to be drawn upon to meet sudden strains on national balances of payments, this is best met by an international institution. The International Monetary Fund was created largely to set up a pool of currencies for this purpose.

It is significant that central banks have come increasingly under the influence and even the direct control of national governments. In the nineteenth century the state-owned central bank was an exception to the general rule of private ownership. Even during the interwar years authoritative opinion insisted that private ownership was necessary to enable a central bank to withstand governmental pressures. This cause has been lost. Of the 53 central banks operating in independent countries after the second World War, 32 were wholly and 8 partially state-owned. Most of the others were owned by public bodies other than the state, or were in process of being nationalized. All such banks created since 1937 were state-owned. The mere fact that the number of central banks has greatly increased since the first World War is indicative of the spread of nationalism in the field of monetary policy. The newly independent countries felt they must equip themselves with banks. While the attempt between the wars to give these newly created institutions some measure of independence reflected the distrust of governments prevalent after the postwar inflations, inevitably there had to be a close contact maintained between them and government treasuries. The pseudo-automatic principles of the international gold standard no longer prevailed and national monetary policies had to be managed with one eye on swollen national debts and the other on the external balance of payments. No government could allow a policy to be followed which increased its budgetary burden or threatened to start a deflationary cycle. In the statutes of all the new or newly nationalized central banks there was explicit recognition that the government had overriding authority. Care might be taken to prevent interference with detailed management and to preserve the bank's right to be heard, but there remained no doubt of the government's right to direct the bank's policy.

The functions of most central banks are not confined today to the art of central banking as it was expounded in the textbooks and actually practiced in the latter nineteenth century. This is evidenced by the illuminating statement made by the Director-General of the Bank of Mexico in August, 1946, in welcoming the delegates to the first meeting of central bank technicians from the countries of the American continent. Senor Villasenor referred to a modern central bank as being partly a central bank, partly a national bank, partly an instrument of industrial development, and partly a lender of last resort, and pointed out that it is a political as well as a technical organ serving the public interest. Thus central banks have become the institutions through which governments pursue positive monetary policies designed to achieve national objectives.

In most countries fiscal policy has become more important than monetary policy in maintaining the levels of national income and employment and thereby affecting the external balances of payment. Government expenditures, in many countries accounting for 20 per cent to 30 per cent or more of the gross national product, constitute a major influence in the total volume of spending—more direct than any central bank can exercise. No central bank, whether nationalized or not, is able to carry out a monetary policy contrary to the fiscal policy of the government. The monetary influence of a central bank is exercised largely through the advice it gives the government in regard to taxes, debt management, and current expenditures. Its central banking functions must conform with government policies. The most important operating functions of a central bank today are research and persuasion.

These changes in monetary mechanisms here briefly summarized are still in process of evolution. It is improbable that the different institutions of the money markets have settled down into their permanent relationship. The trend has run strongly toward the functioning of central banks under the aegis and in co-operation with national governments. There may be further important developments. In Australia and New Zealand which first broke from the interwar pattern of independent, privately owned, central banks, the first steps have been taken toward nationalization of the commercial banks. The Bank of New Zealand in which the government has had a controlling interest since 1893 has been nationalized. In Australia the Commonwealth government proposed in 1948 to nationalize all the commercial banks.

The virtual disappearance of the specialized dealers in the money markets, and these increased activities of central banks under government direction, underline the necessity to alter the major assumption of the classical theory of the balancing of payments—that monetary policy is responsive to the external balance of payments. Monetary policy is now responsive to national needs as interpreted by government officials. Among those needs the balancing of external payments remains important, but it is no longer the dominant consideration to which all other aspects of monetary policy must be adjusted. And thus it follows that the balancing of payments no longer takes place by flexible adjustments of national incomes and price structures pivoted on fixed exchange rates.

THE ECONOMICS OF INSULATION

To understand how payments are now cleared and balanced between national economies it is necessary to probe beneath the forms and practices by which they are made. The procedures developed in the nineteenth century still carry the bulk of private international trade and financial transactions. If there is an account to be paid in another country the simplest way to pay it is still to buy a draft from your local bank. The bank has correspondents and maintains balances in foreign countries. The legal instruments and forms of payments remain much as they were developed under the international gold standard.

It is worth while to emphasize these facts. A great fund of experience and a venerable body of precedents, established in legal and commercial usage, are embodied in this mechanism. There is a solid foundation upon which a new system of multilateral trade and clearings could be built. Those who spend their time and energy in thinking up new ways to meet old needs often underestimate the recuperative strength and economic validity of established institutions and practices. Before concluding too hastily that it is now necessary to abandon the methods evolved out of the practical experience of traders over the centuries, it is well to remember that the new methods of bilateral clearing have not yet been tested.

Much trade now proceeds as a result of government barter transactions. In addition national governments intervene by such methods as export and import controls, price subsidies, and exchange control to regulate the balancing process. Payments between some countries are cleared by bilateral arrangements between the governments concerned. Jurists have tried to graft these new practices on to well-tested legal ideas, but the rules of law so developed cannot be either as certain or as equitable as the older rules that were taken over from mercantile practice.[2] This type of clearing does not have a long history. It has never covered more than a fraction of world trade. There has not been enough experience yet to devise assured legal procedures and precedents. Still less has there been time to reveal the secondary economic consequences of channeling trade through bilateral accounts. Professor Gottfried Haberler has rightly pointed out that the government officials who introduced and administered exchange control and bilateral clearing arrangements were not conversant with the theory of the balancing of payments. They devised means to deal with some immediately urgent aspects of the balancing process. It was later found that their actions had far-reaching economic repercussions, so that "they had to discover step by step through bitter experience the principles of international trade—a wearisome process very costly to the economic system." [3]

It is with the economic rather than with the legal or bookkeeping aspects of the balancing process that we are concerned. An attempt must be made to answer the questions which the classical economists answered in their time by the price specie-flow theory.[4] How are payments made between national monetary systems? How are they offset and cleared? What corrective measures are taken when inward and outward payments fail to balance? What effects do these corrective

[2] The most thorough study of the legal aspects of exchange control and clearing is that of Rafael Lemkin, *La Réglementation des Paiements Internationaux,* Paris, 1939, which, unfortunately, has never been translated into English. As an example of the grafting of new practices on to older legal rules, cf. Poul Nyboe Andersen, *Bilateral Exchange Clearing Policy,* Copenhagen, Institute of Economics and History, 1946, pp. 100–1: "Originally the clearing system represented a retaliatory exchange blocking on the part of creditor countries against countries of Eastern and South Eastern Europe, and later on against Germany, too. This historical background probably explains the apparent inclination of jurisprudence to regard the clearing procedure as a special method of blocking the outstanding debts of a foreign country in favour of domestic creditors."

[3] Cf. G. Haberler, *The Theory of International Trade,* New York, 1937, pp. 89–90, and J. B. Condliffe, *The Reconstruction of World Trade,* New York, 1940, pp. 277–80.

[4] See Chapter VII, "The Classical Theory of International Trade."

measures have upon domestic economic conditions? Supplementary questions must be asked also regarding the part played by the precious metals in the balancing process.

In the United States there are still few restrictions on foreign payments. If one wishes to send payment abroad for a gift or a purchase there is usually no difficulty in doing so. A draft can be bought which will be honored in the receiving country. If a draft drawn in dollars is received in the United States from abroad the recipient can deposit it for his use in any way he likes. If the draft is drawn in foreign currency he can sell it to his bank for dollars. Neither he nor the bank has to report the transaction to the United States Treasury or surrender the foreign currency. There is no exchange control except for limited and specific purposes.

Elsewhere the situation is different. Elaborate sets of regulations govern the receipt and dispatch of foreign payments. These frequently changing regulations are intended to cover all possible transactions so as to prevent evasion. Visitors must declare all moneys of any kind in their possession as they enter and leave a country. This declaration is used as a check upon the amounts they take out when they leave. This is because the authorities are interested in preventing the national currency being sold abroad cheaply as a means of capital flight and with respect to other currencies because visitors must be prevented from taking more foreign exchange out of the country than they bring in. The larger payments made as a result of commercial transactions are subjected to more elaborate regulation. Such payments made either in his own or a foreign currency to the credit of a national must be reported. The foreign exchange involved must be surrendered to the monetary authorities.

Thus dollars paid for a draft or other credit instrument used to purchase French merchandise will end up in the possession of the Bank of France. If the American purchaser sends a check in dollars, the French exporter will sell it to his bank for francs, and the bank will in turn sell it to the Bank of France. It is illegal to hold such a draft for private purposes. If the draft is in francs, the transaction must be reported so that the Bank of France may check to see that the American bank has paid the equivalent dollars to its credit. A French importer, on the other hand, cannot obtain dollars except for specified purposes. While theoretically he may order goods from the United States, if he sends a draft in francs his supplier cannot change that draft into dollars except at the Bank of France, and the importer cannot get a dollar draft except for purchases permitted by that Bank. Receipts in foreign exchange must be surrendered to the central bank, and no payment involving foreign exchange may be made without its permission. The central banks are the agents of their governments. The increasing importance of their role in administering exchange control was one reason why it became necessary to nationalize them. All payments outside the national economy are subject to detailed control.

The essential step in establishing exchange control is to centralize the market for foreign exchange. Individuals may still deal with their banks, but the banks become government agents in so far as they deal in foreign exchange. Neither the individual nor the bank can shop around in an effort to buy foreign currencies cheaply or to sell them at a profit. The rate is fixed and invariable. Banks may buy as much foreign currency as is offered to them at this rate, but they must surrender all of it to the government. If they withhold it for sale at a price in local currency above the fixed rate to persons who hoard it or attempt to use it as a means of sending their funds out of the country, they do so illegally. No one may sell any foreign exchange except to the government, or with its permission. If foreign currency is needed for payments abroad, it will be furnished by the central bank only upon evidence that the purpose for which it is needed comes within the government regulations. In practically all cases which involve more than minimum amounts, decision must be taken by the central bank itself. This is a common and vexatious cause of delay. Even where, as in Canada, the commercial banks are allowed to provide foreign exchange for permitted imports, any transactions of a capital account nature require specific approval.

It is important to make a distinction between exchange control as exercised by a government which deals with the public through familiar market channels and the bilateral clearing systems in which the market mechanism is eliminated altogether. In the 1930's the number of countries that exercised exchange control grew very rapidly. Since the second World War, it has become all but universal outside the United States, Switzerland, Cuba and some other Latin-American countries. Before the war there were in existence also a large number of bilateral clearing agreements. The interest taken in these methods of bilateral clearing tended to exaggerate their quantitative importance. At their peak just before the war they did not account for more than about 12 per cent of the total value of world trade.

The essential characteristic of recent clearing procedures lies in the fact that they involve joint agreement between governments and are therefore bilateral by their nature.[5] The distinction between exchange control and bilateral clearing is that exchange control need not destroy the market mechanism for mutilateral clearings. Under bilateral clearing arrangements the market is broken up. International payments may be made through banks or directly by the clearing office. But the transactions between the two countries involved have no direct link with the transactions which either of these countries conducts with other countries. Bilateralism is simply another name for discrimination. Bilateral clearing is inevitably discriminatory. It is true that control over the exchange market always tends to be discriminatory; but it is at least conceivable that governments may exercise that control without being driven to bilateral clearing agreements, and therefore without destroying the possibilities of multilateral clearing. This possibility should be cherished as long as there is any hope of avoiding the fragmentation of the market that comes from bilateral clearing.

The multilateral clearing and balancing of payments under the international gold standard was pivoted on exchange rates that were fixed on the gold parities within the limits of the gold points. Nowadays the balancing of payments is pivoted on exchange rates that do not have even this degree of flexibility. Under the gold standard, any temporary disequilibrium in the balance of payments of a country was multilateral. That is to say, it arose from the international economic position of that country vis-a-vis the rest of the trading world. There was no bilateral disequilibrium.

If France was short of dollars she could buy them in London or Zurich with Swiss francs or sterling. If she was short of foreign exchange, it was an all-round shortage, not in respect to one currency, and therefore the disequilibrium to be remedied was in her balance of payments as a whole. If slight, this could be eased temporarily by bor-

[5] Cf. Poul Nyboe Andersen, *op. cit.*, p. 100: "A centralized market of foreign exchange is a corner stone of exchange controls generally. The clearing mechanism, however, takes a further step by abolishing altogether the exchange market, i.e. the possibilities of buying and selling exchange, and centralizing the payments themselves. The difference is, however, one of technique rather than of policy. What characterizes clearing rates policy as compared with non-clearing exchange policy, is not the centralization of clearing payments, but the facts that the clearing system is bilateral and has been established by joint agreement."

rowing on short term. In order to attract funds the short-term rates of interest would be raised. This would have the effect of crimping marginal credit transactions within France, so as to induce some fall in prices. This fall, reinforcing the restriction of national income caused by out-payments having been greater than in-payments, would in turn make France a good country to buy in and a disappointing market to sell to. The total value of in-payments would then rise and out-payments would fall, so that equilibrium would be restored. Security transactions would also play a role. Frenchmen pinched by the higher interest rates would be inclined to sell international securities and foreign investors would pick them up at a slightly reduced price.

Thus in all its ramifications, this balancing process assumed that, when the obligations of its citizens to make foreign payments outran receipts, a country would accept the necessity of lower prices and profits, some unemployment and lower wage rates. Membership in the gold standard club implied acceptance of the rules. The most fundamental rule of all was acceptance by each country of the automatic monetary adjustments called for by fluctuations in its balance of payments.

Long before 1914 it was evident that this necessity for adjustment to international pressures imposed limits on the conduct of national monetary policies aiming at domestic price stability. The art of central banking was developed to soften the harsh consequences upon a national economy of allowing the price specie-flow method of adjustment to operate crudely. It provided a cushion of credit expansion which would counteract to some extent the restrictive policies necessary to bring the balance of payments into equilibrium again once it had been disturbed. Such credit expansion gave time for price adjustments to be carried through without starting a secondary spiral of deflation. The main instrument of adjustment was the discount rate, which influenced the whole structure of short-term interest rates. A rise in this rate would make credit dearer and so check credit expansion throughout the national monetary system. However the higher rate would also attract foreign funds and thus offset in some measure the deflationary influence of the higher interest rates. In the highly developed money markets of northwestern Europe before 1914 these flows of short-term banking credits played a most important part in the balancing of payments, just as they do within the United States today. It is a mistake to exaggerate their geographical extent. Most of the countries engaged in world trade adjusted their balances by more direct methods.[6] The highly sophisticated art of central banking was confined to the very few money markets existent in creditor countries blessed with funds seeking temporary investment—such markets as London, Zurich, Amsterdam, Brussels, Paris, and to a less degree Berlin.

Even before the second World War began, the subtleties of credit flows between highly developed money markets had become of little relevance to the study of the balancing of payments. There was tight control of the foreign exchange markets, expressly designed to prevent such credit flows. During the 1930's they had ceased to be a means of correcting temporary disequilibria by attracting short-term funds to markets where a higher rate of interest could be secured, and had become a means of exporting capital from such markets and therefore of intensifying the disequilibrium. The same statement was true of forward exchange operations, which might have served as a useful means of correcting disequilibria and of giving some assurance of stable exchange rates to traders without pegging the rates to some absolute parity.

Monetary systems have now been divorced from their metallic bases. As long as the balance of payments of the gold-producing countries with the United States remains in deficit, and the United States is willing to buy all gold offered to it at the fixed price of $35 an ounce, the new gold mined will find its way to the United States. The small amounts which are bought in the Near East and Far East for hoarding at prices above those offered by central banks have little influence on the balancing process. The actual shipment of gold has little more effect on the balances of payment than an equal value of whisky or of woolen goods shipped. It does not bring about a reduction in paper money or in the credit structure of the exporting country, nor does it necessarily cause an increased circulation of paper money or an expansion of credit in the receiving country.

When gold is received in the United States, it is sold to the Treasury. This results in an equivalent increase of bank deposits. This can lead to an increase of member bank reserves with the Federal Reserve Banks. Unless offset this may lead to some secondary credit expansion; but such effects are small compared with changes in the money supply arising from other sources. Monetary authorities accumulate and hold

[6] Cf. above, pp. 396–400.

gold when they can because it is the only commodity for which there is an unlimited market at a fixed price. Whenever central banks sell gold it is to meet a deficit in their national balances of payments. The rest of the world sells gold to the United States because there is no other way in which desired imports can be paid for. Conversely when the United States receives gold it is in payment of an export surplus which has inflationary effects on the American economy.

How then are international payments now balanced? Balancing of payments takes place by rationing imports. This rationing is a combination of government purchasing, import licensing, and exchange control. The exchange rates are pegged at arbitrary levels. The paper money circulation is a function of the credit made available in each country, and this is now largely independent of any changes in the metallic reserves. Prices in each country are governed by national influences and diverge quite sharply from the movements of prices in other countries, often by multiples rather than fractions. Each national price system is insulated from every other. National markets are cut off from influences originating abroad. No longer are there any world markets for commodities. When individuals, corporations, or government agencies seek to export, they must make deals with those importers who are able to secure from their governments import licenses and foreign exchange permits. The officials who decide what can be imported do so by allocating the available foreign exchange among the purposes which have priority according to a more or less clearly formulated national economic plan.

Such rationing of foreign exchange has had the inevitable effect of further widening the disparities of prices in different national markets. It creates the peculiar situation that national price levels lose any very clear relation to the exchange rates or to price levels in other countries. This can be seen by comparing cost-of-living index numbers with the exchange rates now operative. In 1947 the Polish zloty was maintained for trade purposes at an external value in dollars and cents more than four times the value at which it would have stood if the cost of living in Poland had been compared with the cost of living in the United States. On the contrary, the dollar rate for sterling was only three-fourths of what would be indicated by a cost-of-living comparison. It took approximately five dollars and a half to buy in the United States the cost-of-living items that could have been bought in Britain for a pound sterling while the exchange rate was maintained at four dollars to the pound. If the comparison was made with wholesale prices rather than with the cost of living, the results would have been strikingly different in many cases.[7]

In most cases where the cost-of-living parity was below the exchange level, the cause was to be found in effective administration of price controls. Where, for example in Britain, the cost-of-living parity was lower than the wholesale-price parity, the cause was subsidies to keep down the cost of living. If the exchange market had been freed of governmental controls, the strong British demand for imports and her weakened capacity to export would have led to a scramble for dollars. This would have forced up the sterling price for dollars. Thus importers would have had to pay more pounds to get dollars with which to buy goods from the United States. If this had been allowed to happen the value of sterling in dollars would have fallen very fast and very far. Gold would have been drained out of the reserves of the Bank of England. Speculative sales of sterling would hasten this process.

In Britain imported goods would have become more expensive in sterling while British exports were cheap in dollars. Exports would have drained goods out of Britain. The result would have been an irresistible pressure on the British price levels. Sharp increases in prices would have made it impossible to maintain price control and rationing. In such cases there is always a lag in the purchasing power of wages and a still greater lag in the purchasing power of fixed-income groups. If the inflation did not escape from control, a new equilibrium might eventually have been reached at much higher British price levels, with sterling worth much less in dollars, with reduced imports and increased exports, and with the burden of fixed debt reduced in terms of purchasing power. In terms of community groups this would mean the impoverishment of the owners of monetary claims upon current production while speculative traders, manufacturers, and real property owners were enriched. After this equilibrium had been painfully reached such inward and outward payments as remained would again balance and the price levels would be in equilibrium with the exchange rate. All this assuming that the sacrifices imposed in the adjustment process had not led to reinstatement of exchange and price controls, or to a political revolution.

7 "Exchange Rates and the International Monetary Fund," in *Postwar Economic Studies,* No. 7, September 1947, Federal Reserve Board, Washington, D.C., 1947, pp. 26–27.

The answers to the classical questions may now be briefly summarized. The great bulk of international payments are made by various forms of draft or letter of credit. The forms and procedures by which payments were made across national boundaries, when the international gold standard was operating and long before that, are still in use. Obviously this was not wholly true of the export surplus of the United States which in the immediate postwar years was financed by loans and gifts, public and private. But the United States government was careful to use the channels of private trade as far as was practicable so that the larger proportion of payments across national boundaries was still using the time-honored instruments of the banking mechanism. There was a small but growing segment of trade in which payments were made directly by official clearing agencies.

The offsetting and balancing of these payments had raised new problems. The value of national currencies was no longer fixed within the gold points by the demand for and supply of the instruments of exchange. It was fixed and maintained rigidly at an arbitrary level. Therefore a balance had to be struck by regulating the transactions which give rise to international payments. No country could unilaterally control the demand for its currency which arises primarily from the desire of foreigners to pay for its exports. It could try to stimulate these exports by keeping down costs and therefore export prices and even by granting direct or indirect export subsidies. On the other hand, it *could* control the demand of *its* citizens for *foreign* currencies. Therefore exchange control systems operated to prohibit capital flight, to postpone or prohibit payment on account of past debt, to regulate or prohibit expenditures for foreign travel or payment for foreign services, such as shipping and insurance, and above all to limit payments for imports to the amount of foreign exchange that was available.

These various kinds of control over foreign payments, especially for imports, constituted the principal means by which payments were balanced. The main reliance was necessarily upon direct quantitative controls of imports. Domestic taxes which bore heavily upon the consumption of imported goods and services could be used as supplementary controls, but primarily the balance of payments was struck by issuing exchange permits and import licenses only up to the amount of foreign exchange that was available from export receipts, loans, or the realization of foreign assets. Necessarily this method of balancing tended to become bilateral—permits and licenses would be issued more freely for expenditures in countries which bought from the controlling country and therefore made their currencies available to meet these expenditures.

If a country was short of foreign exchange, corrective measures took the form of shutting down on imports. These corrective measures no longer operated directly on prices and indirectly on the quantities of imports. They operated directly on the quantities of imports and indirectly on prices. The effects on national price levels had been startling. A tariff duty acts on the price of the commodity imported, its effect being shifted smoothly—backward to the producer and forward to the consumer, and over a wide range of auxiliary and competing products and by-products. On the other hand, a quantitative restriction directly limits the supply of the imported product. A tariff has to be very severe to produce the restrictive effect of a quota. When supply is cut off, the price of that product in the importing country, if left free of control, will be determined by the elasticity of domestic production and by the elasticity of demand. If demand is inelastic as it is for most foods and for many raw materials, the quantity demanded being influenced only slightly by a rise in price, there will be a sharp rise in price. How sharp depends upon the elasticity of the domestic supply.[8] Inevitably, however, where demand is inelastic, the country imposing import restrictions will be tempted and even forced to subsidize home production in order to increase supplies, while controlling prices and rationing supplies.

Thus a network of government intervention is woven which insulates the domestic price of the controlled commodity from foreign competition. This intervention extends to substitute and competing products, to the materials entering into the production of the controlled commodity, and to those commodities into which it enters. Thereby the national price structure as a whole is increasingly isolated from

[8] In the country whose exports of the commodity are restricted by import control, the effect upon price will be determined by the possibilities of finding alternative markets, and of shifting to other forms of production. Generally the effect is to drive prices down heavily, thus accentuating the spread of prices between the importing and the exporting countries. There are cases, such as that of the quota imposed by Britain upon Danish bacon, where the demand of the importing country is inelastic enough to force prices up to the point where the exporters receive almost as large a total payment for a smaller quantity of goods supplied and are able to devote the productive capacity thus released to other goods. In this case the price of export bacon rose above that of domestic bacon. The right to export (which became known as the pig passport) was a marketable property which was bought and sold.

the effects of foreign competition. The whole pattern of production within a series of closed or partially closed national economies is divorced from any competitive tests of efficiency and ceases to reflect the comparative advantage of the country as measured by real costs of production. Instead it reflects the pattern of political influence exercised by organized groups within the particular national communities.

No national economy can be completely closed except by absolute controls enforced by police methods. As long as any importing and exporting continues, the balancing of international payments must remain a constant preoccupation. This balancing must be achieved primarily by controlling imports. It therefore constantly drives the national price structures further from international equilibrium. The extent to which it did so after 1945 was revealed in the comparisons of actual exchange rates and of the rates that would have reflected price parities at the level of wholesale prices or of the cost of living. Any arbitrary and sudden attempt to correct those disparities would have resulted in politically intolerable upheavals of prices, production, and employment in every national economy.

Government intervention in the process of balancing international payments had destroyed the international markets that were the greatest achievement of the nineteenth-century trading methods. A series of imperfectly isolated national economies had been created. The balancing of payments between those isolated economies required constant regulation, and that regulation increased their isolation. Control bred further controls. There was no end to this continuous deterioration of world trade based upon a territorial division of labor except resolute acceptance of the necessity to move cautiously but steadily toward abandonment of import and exchange controls.

Such movement toward freer trade would imply acceptance of the adjustments of prices, production, and employment thereby induced. No responsible economist could advocate that controls be suddenly abandoned so as to plunge every national economy into a chaos of readjustment to competitive efficiency. But there was good reason to advocate a reversal of the trend toward heaping new controls on to the old in order to keep payments balanced. If that reversal could not be negotiated, the result was bound to be increasing isolation of the national economies and increasing sacrifice of the advantages to be derived from international specialization and co-operation by way of trade.

BILATERAL CLEARING

The idea of offsetting payments by a bookkeeping process is familiar enough. An account may be paid by check anywhere within the United States. In every town there are regular clearings between banks, and out-of-town checks go to regional and national clearings. Every check finds its way home to the bank on which it is drawn, interbank and interregional transactions being settled by drawing checks for the difference between the total in- and out-payments. As with so many other trading and monetary devices, clearing was first developed in international trade. It was found safer and cheaper to work out a bookkeeping system of offsetting payments than to settle each transaction in coin. The medieval merchants in Europe discovered this fact, as did the Shansi merchants in eighteenth-century China. The first organized Bankers' Clearing House developed out of informal meetings between the collection clerks of London banks, somewhere between 1750 and 1770.

While there was never any formal organization of international clearings in the sense of a central clearinghouse, before 1914 international payments were cleared through the competitive institutions of the London money market. The clearing was multilateral, drafts and other credit instruments being drawn in different currencies and bought and sold freely. The flexibility and smooth operation of this multilateral clearing had only a remote connection with shipments of specie, even while the international gold standard was functioning. It was an integral and essential part of the international marketing process. In the latter part of the nineteenth century it was easier to make payments anywhere in the world than it has been since 1914. It was easier then to judge the credit of traders in remote parts of the world. This was not because of any magic in the gold standard. It was the result of a highly developed exchange of commercial information based upon a large volume of individual trading transactions.

It is important to make this preliminary point clear because there has been a tendency in some quarters to regard the bilateral clearing arrangements developed after 1931 as constituting a method of making foreign payments superior to the methods formerly used. Actually they are a retrogression in two important respects. They are bilateral rather than multilateral and they are segregated from the marketing process. A characteristic feature of the clearing arrangements that were developed after the breakdown of the gold standard in 1931 was the concentration of payments in a special office. This concentration was compulsory. The clearing was bilateral. And it could not function as a mechanism for balancing payments except by invoking direct methods of import restriction. Some economists have argued that clearing could be triangular or even multilateral, or at least that it could function multilaterally through a common clearing center.[9] However experience shows that in so far as clearing becomes multilateral it must approximate the methods practiced before 1914. On the other hand, to achieve the purposes for which it was used in the thirties, clearing must be bilateral. There is no experience of multilateral clearing except the informal competitive clearing of the gold standard mechanism. Such multilateral clearing could be organized without a return to gold as a standard of value. But even without gold this would necessarily entail adaptation of national price and production patterns to the shifting stresses of the international markets as reflected in national balances of payments.

Since 1931 a large number of bilateral clearing agreements have been negotiated and a considerable literature has developed around them. Attempts have been made to classify the different types of clearing agreements, but these classifications have rested upon formal rather than economic distinctions. A distinction can be drawn between private barter (compensation) and official clearing. This is based upon administrative rather than economic differences. When the clearing is confined to transactions arising out of commodity trade, the agreements are usually called Clearing Agreements. When payments for other than current trading transactions are included, it is usual to describe them as Payments or Clearing and Payments Agreements. A number of special kinds of barter agreements (such as the German Aski-mark transactions) were devised in the 1930's, and many such devices were invented after the close of the second World War in Europe. The important arrangements to study are the official agreements negotiated for the clearing of payments on account of bilateral trading transactions. If a new method of multilateral clearing cannot be created, it is probable that the number and scope of these bilateral clearing agreements will increase and that the bulk of international payments will come to be cleared through them.

[9] One of the earliest was Edgar Milhaud, *Trêve de l'or et clearing international,* Paris, 1933. (Earlier ed. privately printed, February 1932.)

An analysis of their operation will be clearer in the light of the circumstances in which they were introduced and developed. After Great Britain abandoned the gold standard, the Bank for International Settlements called a conference at Prague in November, 1931, to discuss how central banks could collaborate to combat the spread of exchange restrictions. This conference recommended the conclusion of "bilateral agreements as to allocation of foreign exchange, provided that such agreements confined the role of central banks to that of a clearinghouse, and did not import political aims into the direction of trade or interfere with existing commercial treaties." The first agreement made as a result of this conference was concluded between Switzerland and Austria. A proposal had been made by the President of the Austrian central bank that clearing balances should be cleared multilaterally through the Bank for International Settlements. This proposal was modeled on the arrangements embodied in the Treaty of Versailles for the liquidation of war debts. It was not approved by the conference, largely because bilateral clearing was regarded as an emergency device to enable trade to be financed until multilateral clearing could be reorganized.

In this first emergency period, it soon became apparent that the central bankers were concerned with other matters than restoring current trade. There were arrears of payments on trading account and also financial claims. In 1930 there had been a considerable extension of short-term banking accommodation to the debtor countries that had been hit by the sharp fall in agricultural prices and by the subsequent banking panic that began in Vienna in May, 1931. As runs developed on the banking system of one country after another, it had proved impossible for the debtor countries to meet all claims, so that much of this short-term banking accommodation had been frozen. The debts had not been repudiated. The foreign exchange necessary to repay them was not available so that interest and amortization payments in the national currencies were placed in blocked accounts in the national central banks. The first concern of the central bankers was to liquidate these blocked accounts. They were under heavy pressure also from bondholders and other financial creditors of the central and eastern European countries to find means whereby the debtor countries might resume payments on their long-term debts. Some of the creditor countries imposed unilateral clearing, amounting to a blocking of the payments for imports from the debtor countries in order to satisfy the claims of their creditor groups. Thus the first clearing agreements had the liquidation of these debt claims as one of their major objectives.

The ingenuity of Dr. Hjalmar Schacht gave a new turn to clearing procedures after the inauguration of the German "New Plan" in September, 1934. Most of the literature defending bilateral clearing as a device superior to the gold standard is the work of Nazi economists. Though clearing agreements were not confined to the German system, and other economists were misled into a serious examination of bilateral clearing as a means of organizing an expanding system of regulated trade, the spread of these agreements in Europe during the years 1934–39 cannot be understood except as an aspect of economic nationalism and economic warfare. *Wehrwirtschaft* (the economy of war preparedness) was the indispensable prelude and preparation for *Kriegswirtschaft* (war economy). A policy of provision as well as strategic considerations accounted both for the eagerness of German officials to secure imports and for their readiness often to accord quite favorable terms to their partners in the clearing agreements. Influence and power as well as imports were among their objectives. It is possible to exaggerate both the skill with which the Germans conducted these negotiations and their successes. Nonetheless it is obvious that the position they secured in many neighboring countries was ominous for the future they planned after victory.

During the war while Germany was dominant on the continent of Europe, trade was conducted almost entirely by bilateral clearing. As the Nazis had planned, Berlin became the center of a war trading system. Some attempt was made to arrange for transfers of clearing balances as an approach to multilateralism and there were isolated cases, for example in Denmark, where imports were obtained from a third country against a transfer of marks owing to Denmark on the German clearing. The exigencies of war prevented the Germans from pushing their bargaining advantage to an extreme or from organizing a new system of centralized clearing through Berlin. They were able to achieve some of their objectives in regard to the parities of national currencies, changing the value of those currencies in terms of marks to suit their purposes. However, in wartime these objectives had to be subjected both to the inefficiencies and pressures of wartime practice and to the changing needs of the military situation. There is little in the German war experience that is helpful in the conduct of peaceful trading relationships.

Since 1931 trade in many European countries and in many of the countries with which Europe trades has been regulated by direct quantitative controls and by quotas and exchange allocations, rather than by tariffs. The payments on international account have been centralized and foreign exchange has been allocated for imports to the amount and for the purposes decided by officials. There is no doubt that these arrangements made possible much trade that might not have been possible at all after the former methods of clearing through London broke down. The officials concerned became skillful in the handling of trade by these arbitrary methods. They were able with increasing success to overcome the administrative bottlenecks that were so obvious and so irritating. Some, notably the Czechs, were able to limit the extension of bilateral agreements and to maintain a considerable measure of free payments. Gradually there emerged a group of experts in the handling of regulated trade who met in frequent conferences during the 1930's. A new terminology began to develop together with what seemed to be agreement on the principles of regulated trade. Actually it was agreement on the tactics of regulation.

Inevitably regulation led to negotiated bilateral agreements. The peak number of such agreements was reached in the fall of 1937. There were 151 clearing agreements in operation between 38 different countries and 23 payments agreements between 24 countries. This seems a large number but one should remember that there were at least 60 independent countries in the world so that the maximum number of possible bilateral agreements was 1,770. The number actually negotiated was therefore about 10 per cent of this. While bilateral clearing became important in Europe, its importance in the total of world trade should not be exaggerated.

The clearing system so devised operated at first on what has been called the waiting principle in regard to the balance of payments. If a disequilibrium of payments developed so that the exporters of one country found that imports from the other country were inadequate to provide funds to meet the payments due, they were forced to wait until imports caught up with the situation. A simple illustration was provided in the German-Swiss clearing agreement. This provided for imports of coal and manufactured goods to Switzerland against exports of tourist services. The German authorities sold to their nationals coupons which the latter could present to Swiss hotelkeepers. The price of German coal was comparatively high and not much was imported. The Swiss hotelkeepers had claims on the funds in the Swiss Clearing Office, but the importers of coal had not paid in enough to meet all those claims. Therefore the hotelkeepers had to wait. In the meantime the arrangement to sell more coupons was suspended. Clearly the balancing of payments depended not only upon the quantities of goods and services exchanged, but also upon the rate at which Swiss francs were converted into marks, and upon the prices of the coal and of the hotel accommodation. In practice it was not possible to correct a disequilibrium except by direct action to restrict trade.

It was inevitable that this burden of waiting should be pressed on to the central bank of the clearing creditor country. Then emerged what has been called the financing principle. The first clearing agreements had been forced upon Germany; but the Nazi economists turned them into instruments for provisioning the effort at war preparation. For a time, the Germans were successful in thrusting the burden of financing trade on to their clearing partners. By buying freely on the clearing account, they built up substantial clearing debts. As soon as a bilateral clearing arrangement was negotiated, the Germans encouraged imports of goods from the other country that was party to the agreement. Soon the exporters in that country would have accumulated a large amount of claims on their central bank. But German exports were so slow that the importers of German goods in the other clearing country did not pay in enough in local currency to meet the claims of their fellow citizens who had exported to Germany. Thus there was a deficit in the clearing account. The counterpart of this was a surplus of blocked marks in Berlin, paid in by German importers over and above the claims made on these marks by German exporters. In the deficit country the exporters would clamor to be paid in their own currency. Ultimately the central bank took over this deficit and paid off the exporters. This created new credit to cover the deficit in the clearing balance.

During the war there was again a very large increase in the German debts on clearing account. Some of these debts even before the war were on account of investment, since the Nazi economists developed the fantastic theory that interest payments should precede capital investment and that the debtors should finance the creditor's investment. Their argument was that Germany would import heavily and so gain a favorable clearing balance. This balance it would use for investment in the countries from which the imports had come and which in fact owned the balances in the clearing accounts. According to the Nazi economists, the agricultural countries of central and southeastern Europe would thus advance the funds (including prepaid interest) which the Germans would use to make investments in their countries! This was represented as an advantage to the agricultural countries, since it freed them from the necessity of borrowing from Britain and the United States, which were not willing, as Germany was, to buy their exports.

The monetary system of a clearing creditor country was obviously disturbed. The deficit in the bilateral balance of payments on a clearing account had to be financed by the central bank creating new credit. Where this account was important in a country's trade, as for instance in Bulgaria's account with Germany, the necessity for the Bulgarian central bank to finance a large volume of exports to Germany in advance of receipts from importers of German goods entailed a considerable inflation of the Bulgarian currency. This affected the trade of the country as a whole, but had only a weak effect in balancing the clearing account that was out of equilibrium. In countries such as Denmark, where the clearing account represented a less substantial part of the total trade, the balancing effect of central bank financing on the clearing transactions was still weaker. There the central bank was driven to take counteraction to offset the disturbing effect of this credit expansion on the national price system and on the trade with other countries. The best account of the expedients to which these countries were driven, together with a detailed theoretical analysis of the effects of the financing principle, has been given by the Danish economist, Professor Poul Nyboe Andersen in his study of *Bilateral Exchange Clearing Policy*. The conclusion of his study is that there was a general trend in the development of bilateral clearing toward direct operation of the trading transactions by official agencies. Bilateral clearing led to bilateral planning, and such planning led to detailed control of the quantities, prices, and terms of payment in each separate trading transaction. This conclusion has been reached by every impartial student of bilateral clearing.

The consultative committees that were established between pairs of clearing countries to interpret clearing agreements, therefore, developed into actual trading groups. The mere fact that agreements were for short periods meant that negotiations were virtually continuous even where no formal committees were created. The word negotiation in many cases was a euphemism. The official negotiations over the terms and conditions of trade developed into a continuous wrangle. There is no balancing mechanism, no principle of adjustment or self-corrective tendency in bilateral clearing. On the contrary the institution of bilateral clearing inevitably strengthens the necessity for quantitative intervention, and this must take the form not of general principles but of detailed bargains in particular cases. Moreover such intervention must be discriminatory, since there is no point in bilateral clearing except to regulate trade so that payments may be balanced between pairs of countries. All the difficulties that arise in the trade relations between free and controlled economies are inherent in the adoption of bilateral clearing practices, since such practices must utilize discriminatory trade regulation as the principal balancing mechanism.

It is not surprising that those who defend bilateral methods display irritation with what they describe as the fetish of nondiscrimination, while the advocates of multilateral trade are insistent that there can be no compromise with the principle of equality of trading opportunity. The issue is clear-cut. Attempts by clearing methods to balance payments between each pair of clearing countries can be implemented only by an increasing degree of discriminatory trade regulation, using such methods as import quotas and exchange allocations. Any attempt to establish multilateral clearings—either by triangular arrangements or by facilitating transfers of clearing balances—involves acceptance of the pricing mechanisms and adaptations of the national economies to the competitive tests of efficiency imposed by these mechanisms. The principle of most-favored-nation treatment, equality of trading opportunity, or nondiscrimination, is inherent in multilateralism. Clearing, as it is proposed by the defenders of regulated trade, is therefore the negation of international specialization. The choice is between national and international, as well as between political and economic, criteria of trading. Bilateralism is necessarily a system of discrimination.

FIXING THE EXCHANGE RATES

The rate at which one currency exchanges for another—the exchange rate or the price of one currency in terms of another—is the pivot of the balancing process. In any circumstances—whether the exchange market is free or controlled, whether the clearing is multilateral or bilateral—this exchange rate is the most important single factor in the balancing of international payments. When the pound sterling was worth $4.03 the whole scale of British costs and prices translated into American money at that rate. When the rate fell to $2.80, the balancing of payments presented a very different aspect. All the international economic relations between trading countries come to a focus in this ratio. The most difficult decisions which national governments, in consultation with the International Monetary Fund, will have to make in the postwar adjustment will be those concerned with fixing a new workable system of exchange rates. In theory and in practice this is the core of international economic relations.

The articles of agreement of the Fund pledge the member-governments to co-operative international monetary policies. A pool of currencies has been created upon which members may draw to ease temporary strains on their balances of payments. The Fund was not designed to cope with the immediate problems of the postwar transition period. It was designed as a means of maintaining equilibrium once a workable equilibrium had been achieved. Nevertheless it provides a forum where national governments may discuss the difficulties involved in setting up exchange rates that will assist in establishing such equilibrium. Initially the Fund accepted the exchange rates in operation when it began business. It has already been necessary to adjust many of these rates. The timing and extent of such adjustment was the most complicated question faced by national governments and by the Fund since its inception.

This is not simply a monetary question to be solved by correct manipulation of the mechanics of the national monetary systems. The mechanics are important, but the exchange rate is the symbol and summation of the complex realities of a many-sided economic relationship. No lasting solution of this monetary conundrum is possible without solving these basic economic questions of which the exchange rate is the symbol and summation. When the French monetary authorities decide upon a figure at which francs may be changed into dollars, this decision not only involves how many dollars and cents will be given for a franc, but also how prices and wages will compare in France and the United States, what imports and exports will thereby be made possible, and in large measure what pattern of production and employment in each country will lie behind these imports and exports.

If the foreign exchange markets were completely free and competitive, the various rates at which the different currencies are exchanged would fluctuate like any other price, according to the demand for and the supply of those currencies. There have been times when economic theorists have flirted with the notion of completely flexible exchange rates responding in a competitive market to the fluctuating needs of foreign trade and investment. In practice the notion of complete flexibility has never been realistic. There has never been any experience in modern times of freely fluctuating exchange rates. There is much to be said for a greater degree of flexibility than exists at the present time, and it is possible to conceive a wider range of flexibility than existed under the international gold standard. A strong case can also be made for adjustment of the exchange rate in a crisis, rather than its maintenance at the cost of inflicting severe deflation and unemployment on a national economy. On the other hand, the case for stable as against freely fluctuating exchange rates is irresistible not only in theory but in practice.

The co-operative economic activity which in sum constitutes a national economy is an organic whole. Like any other organism it can survive only if it is stable. There must be balanced relationships between its constituent parts, the body economic relying upon automatic or semiautomatic corrective adjustments if these relationships are disturbed. No national economy is an economic island entire of itself. We live in a world of states whose national economies act and react upon each other, and the external forces which affect each national economy are communicated through the balance of payments and the exchange rate. Therefore, it is of the utmost importance that these joints of international economic relationships shall have the same kind of flexibility within a narrow range that physiologists emphasize as an essential means of preserving organic stability. There is no contradiction between the objectives of stability and sensitive flexibility within a narrow range. Indeed such sensitivity of reaction to external pressures is a necessary condition of stability. In this respect a strain on the exchange rate may be compared with a rise in body temperature.

As long as the international gold standard operated, exchange rates were determined within the limits of the gold points, in a highly competitive, individualistic, excitable and sensitive market. This sensitivity to shifting external conditions detected threats to the stability of a particular national economy and provoked adjustive reactions within it. The criticisms that have been leveled against this sensitivity are misconceived. It was the main service of the market—like the horns of a snail it telegraphed the dangers ahead of a sluggish organism. When the exchange rate is strictly and rigidly controlled there is no possibility of such reactions. This is prima-facie reason to doubt that exchange control is capable of serving as an efficient means of preserving stable relations between national economies.

The gold standard mechanism for the clearing and balancing of international payments—particularly as it functioned when restored between the wars—operated within limits of sensitivity that were too narrow. These limits were set by the cost of transferring gold from one monetary system to another. External pressure on the balance of payments would be met first by changes in the exchange rate within the limits of the gold points and this would cause reactions on income and prices as well as on short-term interest rates. But the pressures in the interwar years were very abrupt and very great. The road was rough and the shock absorbers worked stiffly. Whenever the pressures forced the exchange rates down to the point where gold flowed out of the banking reserves, this loss of gold set in motion deflationary forces of much wider amplitude than were necessary to correct a passing disequilibrium. There was not enough play in the joints.

If it ever becomes possible to restore a greater measure of free multilateral trade, it might be advisable to allow the exchange rates to fluctuate within wider limits than those set by the cost of the transport of gold. This is not a new idea. It was advanced by Robert Torrens after the Napoleonic Wars and by Lord Keynes after the first World War. If the exchange rates were free to fluctuate within somewhat wider limits, the market would give warning of strains on the balances of payments. This would set up reactions on national incomes, interest rates, and prices that would go some distance toward adjusting them to the strain. But there are disadvantages in such a proposal. If the limits within which an exchange rate is free to fluctuate were set too wide, the main advantages of exchange stability would be lost. A sudden shift in the rate might then be great enough to eliminate the profit on international trading transactions. It would also add an unpredictable element to the risks of international investment. It would be impossible to set limits of exchange flexibility wide enough to act as an efficient shock absorber for the recurrent pressures upon the balances of payments of the raw-material exporting countries and yet not so wide as to destroy the advantages of exchange stability. Any measure of increased flexibility that still preserved the essential stability of the exchanges could cope only with minor disturbances of international equilibrium.

In the postwar transition period, there was little point in trying this limited experiment in exchange flexibility. Most currencies were overvalued in terms of dollars. If the International Monetary Fund were to fix a zone instead of a point of stability, most of these currencies would drop immediately to the lowest point of the zone. This is tantamount to saying that the actual exchange rates were artificially sustained and the whole structure of rates was precarious. Yet there was no way of testing what might be a workable rate at which payments could be balanced without the necessity of restricting imports. The only way to determine what rate might work was to test it in actual trading. The sooner that could be done, the better.

Moreover, altogether apart from the disequilibria of the immediate postwar period, domestic and external stability must be regarded as alternative and often conflicting objectives of policy. Any attempt to maintain stable exchange rates as a basis for freer multilateral trade calls for the adjustment of the national economies in accordance with shifting pressures on their balances of payments. In the short run it is not possible both to maintain full employment *and* to keep the exchange rates stable and free. One or the other, or both, must be flexible. The practical problem of monetary statesmanship is to determine how much international trade can be developed at what risk to domestic stability. Or conversely, it is to decide how much control to retain over international trade to prevent unemployment from rising to intolerable levels.

Many economists now believe that the greatest defect of the international gold standard was that it communicated depression conditions from one country to another. They fear that depression will recur in the free economy of the United States. If other countries were pledged to maintain a free exchange market at stable rates on the dollar, the fear is that this depression communicated through the exchange rates would wreck the reconstruction of weaker economies. The argument that recovery from a depression is similarly communicated is regarded as scant consolation. If there was a reasonable degree of stability in international trade it could be argued that the dissipation of cyclical fluctuations over the whole trading world would diminish their intensity. Before 1914, this belief was firmly held. It was believed that a poor harvest in one country was corrected by heavy yields in another. Overexpansion of credit in one country was automatically communicated to all others. The sharp cyclical contractions of credit necessary to correct periodic overexpansion were spread in the same way. But many modern economists argue that there is an inherent tendency to depression—an a priori deflationary bias—in the capitalist system. The rhythmic cycle of economic fluctuations is beyond the control of any single country. During the interwar period the violence of these cyclical fluctuations was exaggerated by the attempt of every country to lever itself out of depression by exporting more and importing less. It is contended that the credit contractions necessary to produce these effects inevitably spread from country to country until depression became world-wide.

A corollary of this belief is widely held in the agricultural-exporting countries. It is that these countries are less able than their highly industrialized trading partners to defend their economies against deflationary strains on their balances of payments. Their national incomes are greatly influenced by export receipts, which are often derived from a few commodities subject to violent price fluctuations. Thereby the ability of their central banks to sustain the national economies is narrowly limited. Thus the burden of adjustment to shifting international situations is apt to be thrust on the economies least capable of protecting themselves by prompt adaptation. This argument is particularly pertinent in a period of violent change. In such a period the powerful countries have protected themselves by methods which have imposed heavy burdens upon their weaker trading partners.

No organism can adapt itself to external variations beyond a certain limit of tolerance. The body cannot react successfully to extremes of heat and cold beyond a rather limited range. The co-operative economic activity of a national economy can adjust itself only within a similar limited range. If it is called upon to react to such forces as were unloosed in the depressions of the interwar years the strain of adaptation is too great and leads to paralysis of vital functions. Moreover it is nearly always necessary to make a gradual transition from one set of conditions to another. It is the necessity of gradual adaptation that renders invalid the heroic prescriptions of laissez-faire economists who would cure the present distortion of exchange rates by an abrupt return to a free market.

Comparative stability is an essential condition of organic survival. Therefore by a series of approximations, an attempt must be made at a gradual adaptation of the exchange rates and of the national economic structures to the new postwar equilibrium of international economic relations. What that equilibrium may be it is not yet possible to calculate. Theoretical attempts at calculation of an equilibrium exchange rate must take into account too many independent and dependent variables which are political as well as economic to have any great chance of success. The modern theory of the balancing of payments takes into account not only the classical elements—interest rates, prices, and costs—but also more subtle considerations of elasticity in the supply and demand for imports and exports, and of the multiplier effect on the national income of increases or decreases of purchasing power. The theory of the multiplier was worked out by economists after the depression period 1929–33, when the problem of unemployed resources had been of the greatest importance in many countries.

An injection of purchasing power into the national economy, for example by increased government expenditures, is not exhausted by the first disbursement. The recipients of this income will in turn spend part of their increased income.

National income is increased by the receipt of greater payments for exports, regardless of whether this is the result of greater demand in foreign countries or of greater efficiency in the exporting country. The multiplier effect will be induced in some measure by this injection of purchasing power and will vary with the degree to which the increased income of exporters is saved, spent within the country, or spent on increased imports.[10] In calculating the probable effects of a new ex-

[10] For an account of the multiplier effect, cf. Stephen Enke and Virgil Salera, *International Economics*, New York, 1947, Chapter 12. In this account, the modern view is taken that increased exports represent an injection into, and increased imports a leakage from, the national income. For analysis of the various factors that enter into the determination of the multiplier effect in international trade, cf. Fritz Machlup, *International Trade and the National Income Multiplier*, Philadelphia, 1943.

change rate, it is not easy to give any realistic weight to these considerations. Some broad statements of the elasticity of supply and demand for imports and exports may be derived from statistical calculations of past trade, and these may be helpful in drawing attention to some characteristic features of the trade of particular countries. The multiplier analysis refines the familiar fact that a comfortable external balance generates purchasing power within the country. It does not add any essential truth to the theory of the balancing of payments.

In so dynamic and explosive a situation as the present, qualitative economic theory yields guidance for practical policies in the sense that it may serve to draw attention to factors that are easily overlooked in policy decisions, but it does not readily lend itself to practical calculations. The only practical way to approach a stabilization of the currencies is to test the market by establishing a zone of stability within which competitive transactions give some flexibility to the exchange rates.

There has been much discussion in financial and economic journals of the criteria by which the national governments associated in the International Monetary Fund might establish a system of rates and, as occasion demands, adjust the value of a particular currency suffering from a fundamental disequilibrium in the balance of payments. Too much of this discussion has proceeded purely in monetary terms. Economic activity comprehends more than the bookkeeping in which the accounts are kept. The credit systems in which economic activity proceeds, while themselves a potent cause of economic disorder when they are distorted by necessities of state, cannot be fruitfully studied apart from the economic activity which they register. Nor can the distortions of that activity be remedied by monetary means alone. There is fundamental wisdom in the remark attributed to the eighteenth-century economist who told the French monarch that he would restore order to the public finances and the monetary system if the king would adopt sensible economic policies. While the choice of workable exchange rates is a difficult and important decision, the restoration of exchange stability depends ultimately upon the domestic and external policies followed in the major trading nations.

There is general agreement among economists that an attempt by concerted action must ultimately be made to determine a series of exchange rates that will enable international trade to expand and yet not impose on any national economy severe deflationary pressures. In practical terms this means an exchange rate that will make possible a liberalizing and gradual abolition of exchange controls and quotas without plunging any country into such difficulties with its balance of payments that it must resort to sharp credit contraction and higher interest rates.[11] If international trade is to be restored on a basis of competitive efficiency of production in different areas, there must be adaptations of the present pattern of production and employment in every country. These adaptations, however, must be made gradually so that they do not lead to secondary spirals of deflation caused by an abrupt fall of national incomes. The balance of payments of each country must be watched carefully.

The best way to do this would be to fix a range of stability within which the International Monetary Fund would support the exchange rate while the exchange and quota restrictions on that country's imports were liberalized. If there developed a large and persistent deficit in the balance of payments causing a country to draw heavily upon the Fund, a prima-facie case would thereby be established for adjustment of the exchange rate to a lower level. There seems no practical alternative to this procedure. Any attempt to fix the exchange rate at a level determined by price or cost parities encounters insuperable difficulties in the present situation when prices are controlled. Nor is it possible, in the give and take of a multilateral adjustment, to make precise calculations of demand and supply elasticities, or multiplier effects. There will inevitably be some roughness in the adjustments which each country is called upon to make. An ideal solution is impossible after such an economic earthquake as the trading world has suffered in recent years.

In practice it will be necessary to concentrate attention upon a few key rates. The most important of these is obviously the dollar-sterling rate. There are large areas of stability in the currencies that cluster around the dollar and sterling. If a workable ratio could be found between these two major trading currencies, the two areas of stability could be joined into one. Other currencies need immediate adjustment. However, there is no set of ratios that will not entail adjustments of prices, production, and employment in every country.

If these adjustments are to be carried through swiftly so that multi-

[11] Cf. Arthur I. Bloomfield, "Foreign Exchange Rate Theory and Policy," in S. E. Harris (ed.), *The New Economics*, New York, 1947, p. 303.

lateral trade may be restored on a competitive basis, much of this adjustment must fall on the countries which have strong balances of payments. If this does not happen, and the burden of adjustment is thrown largely on to those countries that have slim margins of international means of payments, the relaxation of trade barriers must proceed slowly and cautiously. There is no way in which international trade may be expanded that does not entail considerable adjustments to a pattern of specialization which is now very different from that which prevailed before the second World War. If full employment is interpreted to mean that shifts of production entailing temporary and partial unemployment are to be prevented, it will be impossible to restore freer trade while maintaining full employment in every nation, or even in every major trading nation. It is perfectly possible to apply social-security measures to safeguard displaced workers and at the same time to forestall a secondary spiral of deflation, so that national economies do not collapse. Nonetheless shifts of employment are inevitable and desirable if economic progress is to be resumed.

The more quickly production in each country can be adjusted to the new patterns of international specialization, the less the costs of adjustment will be in the long run. The way to adjust is to allow trade to move freely. The way to discover whether the adjustments that are called for are likely to be too severe is to create a zone of stability within which the exchange rates are left to the play of market forces. If this zone is reasonably well chosen the effects of exchange fluctuation upon prices and production in the national economies concerned will not be beyond their capacity of adjustment. If a persistent disequilibrium appears in the balance of payments of any economy or if the effort to combat this disequilibrium entails a severe degree of unemployment, a case can be made for adjusting the exchange rate.

Such adjustment must be a matter for consultative and co-operative decision in the continuous discussions among members of the International Monetary Fund. In these discussions there is scope for the most elaborate and refined statistical calculations of all the elements that enter into the balance of payments of each country. The international secretariat of the Fund is capable of analyzing the relationships disclosed by these national statistics. The Fund has at its disposal a pool of currencies upon which its members may draw to maintain the currency parities agreed upon and the drawings will disclose strains upon the balances of payments at these parities. Thus the mechanisms are available for testing the workability of the exchange rates as they are exposed to the test of freer trade. However no mechanism will work unless the national governments are prepared to allow fluctuations of the exchange rate within a narrow range to cause the shifts of prices and production that are necessary to adjust to the shifting currents of freer international trade.

CHAPTER XXI

THE CASE FOR FREER TRADE

THE MODERN CRITERIA OF ECONOMIC POLICY

THE MAJOR QUESTIONS which must be answered in any restatement of the theory of international trade are the familiar three.

First, in what conditions does trade arise?

Second, how are the payments between national economies cleared and balanced?

Third, how are the gains from trade divided?

The answer of the classical economists to the first of these questions was their theory of comparative costs or advantages; to the second, the price specie-flow theory; and to the third, the theory of reciprocal demand. In the conditions they assumed, these concepts supplemented by an explanation of the distribution of precious metals formed a complete and logically integrated statement of international trading relations. The neo-classical economists refined this doctrine, and it was later developed into the general equilibrium theory whereby international trade was again integrated with the main stream of economic thought. But the conditions of modern trading activity differ from those assumed to exist by the classicists, the neo-classicists, and even by the more modern exponents of the general equilibrium theory. This difference is no mere matter of the untidiness of the real world in detail.

No one can gain insight into the essential relationships of a complicated mass of human activities if he attempts to deal simultaneously with all the variants of behavior. It is necessary to seek out the uniformities, the pattern that emerges as if from an aerial view in which the main ranges stand out while the minor spurs sink into insignificance. The criticism to be made of earlier theories is not of their abstractness, but of the pertinence of their basic assumptions in terms of modern reality. In a modern treatment of international trade emphasis must be laid on three important aspects in which the contours of international economic relations differ from those assumed by earlier economists. The first arises from the significant developments in the structure of economic organization resulting from new technical processes. The second is constituted by the increasing range of government intervention, especially in regard to monetary policy. Finally it is necessary to take into account national programs of economic development.

No longer is it realistic to assume that international trade emerges as a result of dispersed and competitive marketing processes creating a pattern of prices and production beyond the control of any of the numerous participants in its weaving and reweaving. That assumption ignores the positive economic policies of national governments and the imperfect competition of the great international economic enterprises that now dominate important segments of world trade. From the viewpoint of economic efficiency as measured by abundance, the political intervention of governments is more damaging to international specialization than the imperfect competition of great business enterprises. Even before the second World War D. H. Robertson had written that "in the economics of war the subtleties of comparative advantage become a foolish irrelevance." [1] This warning was abundantly confirmed. It is necessary to add that these subtleties may be brushed aside as irrelevant in the economics of national planning for full employment or economic development. Whether they are brushed aside in the economics of war preparedness depends upon how useful the subtleties are in the circumstances of particular nations. It will be argued later that freer trade is likely to be in the power interest of the United States.

With regard to the technical processes of modern production, emphasis has already been laid upon the increasing importance of

[1] Cf. D. H. Robertson, "The Future of International Trade," *Economic Journal,* Vol. XLVIII, No. 189, March 1938, pp. 11–12.

heavy overhead costs in modern large-scale enterprises. These make it difficult to determine the costs of individual products. Theoretical analysis assumes that such costs are determinable, but the unreality of this assumption is not the practical issue. The practical consequence of the joint costs in large-scale production is that international competition becomes less likely in individual products. A great manufacturing corporation is unlikely to invade the territory of another with a single commodity. Unless it is prepared to move in with a whole range of products over which its research, development, selling and advertising costs can be spread, it is likely to forgo passing opportunities of profit upon particular sales.

There are other consequences of the new technical processes of production. Professor Robertson also argued that the progress of scientific research and its applications sometimes widens the possibilities for international trade but at other times narrows them. Much of the recent discussion regarding the terms of trade between agricultural and industrial countries has turned upon varying estimates of the extent to which scientific research has increased agricultural as compared with industrial productivity. New types of wheat have been developed which ripen in the short but hot summers of the Canadian and Siberian subarctic plains. Other new types of wheat can be grown with scanty rainfall so that the margin of cultivation has been pushed further into the semiarid interior plains of Australia. In the tropical islands, scientific plant breeding, fertilizing, and control of insect and other pests have tended to cheapen the production of food and raw materials relatively to that of manufactures. Such developments encourage specialization and increase the scope for international trade. But the simpler machine processes of manufacturing industry can readily be learned by agricultural peoples and many forms—for example of textile production—have been widely dispersed since the first World War. In this case the scope for international trade is narrowed. Thus it is not easy to give a precise answer to the question whether scientific research has on the whole increased or decreased the scope for international trade, since the use made of research and inventions depends upon political as well as economic circumstances.

It has sometimes been argued that the increasing importance of technical and managerial skills which are readily transferable between countries tends to narrow the margins of comparative advantage. If a great part of the production cost consists of overhead—research, and development costs that may be incurred with almost equal effectiveness in any one of several countries—a relatively small shift in other costs may cause a very considerable shift in production, and hence very considerable dislocations of employment. This argument has been used in support of the case for conducting trade policy so as to maximize stability of employment rather than profits. But it depends for its validity upon the assumption that wages and other costs of production have developed rigidities that cannot be broken. If those costs were flexible, the slight shifts in comparative advantage would result in cost adjustments rather than in unemployment. If they are inflexible, it does not matter whether overhead costs are great or small—the crippling effect on international specialization would still follow.

International trade and the specialization of production upon which it depends are now influenced not only by such economic considerations as the maximizing of profits, but also by considerations of economic power. In the modern world there is a conflict of wills, a struggle for power between those who control the technical facilities for production and those who insist that decision in regard to reconstruction and development policies must remain in the hands of national governments. The full impact of modern technical efficiency cannot be quickly achieved except by application of the integrated resources and skills mobilized by business corporations. Until governments devise means of mobilizing effective teams of skilled organizers and technicians, the initiative that leads to economic progress will remain largely in private corporations. More and more international trade passes from the hands of specialist traders into those of corporation executives or of government officials.

In the first flush of the postwar years there were numerous opportunities for individuals and import-export houses in the United States to conduct a flourishing export trade. There were great shortages of essential commodities and in many countries military expenditures had placed dollar exchange in the hands of those who could profit by using it to import goods from the United States. But the opportunities for private trading specialists lasted only as long as the dollar accumulations. As early as the fall of 1947 this honeymoon was over and those who wished to enter international trade were beginning to find that employment openings for the future would be mainly in government agencies or in the export departments of great industrial corporations. After the devaluations of September, 1949, openings for small-scale trading enterprise were more abundant in organizing a return flow of imports to the United States.

It must be remembered that the classical theory of comparative costs was an attempt to explain the underlying reasons why individual merchants found it profitable to engage in international trade. The trade was conducted because individuals found they could profit by buying more cheaply and selling to better advantage abroad than at home. But an explanation was necessary for the fact that these price disparities existed between countries. It was found in the theory of comparative costs. Briefly stated, this theory was that if competitive trading was not interfered with by governments, the available labor and resources would be applied to producing those goods in which each country had the greatest relative advantage.

The later general equilibrium theory envisaged the possibility that labor and capital might be attracted to those localities which offered opportunities of profitable employment. In this way the equilibrium theory came to approximate a theory of the international location of industry. In doing so it abandoned the Ricardian explanation of international trade as arising from the comparative (real) costs of particular products and retreated to the more general case for international specialization as expounded by Adam Smith. Clearly this explanation of the international location of industry starts from the assumption that producers and traders will be free within broad limits to exercise their judgment and initiative. It also assumes that the objective they aim at is profit. It is conceivable that a national policy of economic planning might be motivated primarily by economic considerations. But in practice political rather than economic considerations tend to dominate such planning policies.

The most obvious case is that of a completely planned economy. Within the U.S.S.R. there is no possibility of foreign or of private economic enterprise. Nor does the U.S.S.R. allow its citizens to range other countries in search of profit opportunities. The industrial structure of the U.S.S.R. is not planned by a calculation of its comparative advantages in international trade. There are industries in the U.S.S.R., including some heavy manufacturing industries, where national production has been organized at high cost when imports could have supplied the materials or manufactured products more cheaply. There are other cases where labor and resources have been devoted to producing goods for export (notably gold) without any calculation of comparative advantage and sometimes under conditions that by capitalist accounting would have resulted in losses rather than profit. The gold-mining industry was expanded because certain imports, such as machine equipment, that could not be produced in the U.S.S.R. had to be paid for. As far as possible the payments were met from the sales of such Russian exports as oil, lumber, and furs that could be produced advantageously in the U.S.S.R. and met a ready market abroad. These did not suffice, and it was necessary to export gold since it was not needed as backing for Soviet currency. It was mined to provide a reserve of foreign purchasing power.

The planning of industrial development within the closed national economy of the U.S.S.R. has not been based upon calculations of comparative advantage in international trade. Individual profit is outlawed. Such trade as the state monopoly conducts undoubtedly drives as hard a bargain as can be made. The acquisition of equipment upon which industrial development can be based is sometimes necessary. But the motivation of such imports, and of the exports necessary to pay for them, has been provided by such ulterior objectives as strengthening the defensive power of the state, facilitating a planned program in which the training of technicians is an important element, and broadening the bases of industrial and agricultural productivity. Exports are kept to the minimum necessary to pay for imports as determined by the planning program. While import orders have often been placed where they might be construed as a means of cementing improved political relations, there is no evidence that such considerations have been allowed to interfere with the execution of the national plan for industrialization. Nor is there any convincing evidence that exports have been used for political purposes.

These facts are consistent with what can be gleaned from study of the location of industry within the U.S.S.R. New industrial cities have been built in remote regions. There has been a distinct eastward trend of industrial location and of population. In addition to the older industrial centers in European Russia, an attempt has evidently been made to create new areas of industrial concentration in the Caucasus and behind the Urals. Analysis of the principles that determined these plans suggests that they were largely motivated by political, strategic, and social considerations as well as by such economic factors as the proximity of raw materials, actual or planned, communication and transport networks, and population trends.

This case of the U.S.S.R. has been cited first because it throws into sharp relief some important facts common to all planning programs. The initiative of private traders and investors must be subordinated to the requirements of the national plan. Thus one of the major criticisms to be urged against the planning of international trade is that it stifles the private initiative which in the past has sought out profit opportunities and pioneered new markets. The control of investment is always an essential element of national economic planning. Even if that control is not complete, it is always necessary to take precautions against a flight of capital, and against the draining away of exchange assets by excessive imports. It is almost impossible to take these precautions without subjecting all payments for imports and exports to close regulation. Both investment and capital flight are normally carried in large part by commodity exports. Therefore in any system even of partial national economic planning, the private initiative of merchants must be subordinated to the plans of the officials. Their profit comes after defense, stability, full employment, and similar criteria of policy.

Not only industrial groups and workers faced by international competition and political leaders who are responsive to such pressures, but many economists now stress the fundamental importance of domestic stability rather than international specialization and dwell on the disturbing influence of periodic disequilibria in the external balance of payments of a country. They continue to advocate abundance and recognize that international specialization contributes to abundance. But they regard stability as the more important objective and make a strong case for it by arguing that in the long run specialization cannot be maintained if it causes heavy fluctuations of domestic employment and income. Upon these grounds they maintain that it will ultimately become necessary to work out an international trading code which is not based upon the competitive principle of nondiscrimination, but rather upon stable domestic employment and a steady flow of trade.[2]

[2] Cf. Sir Hubert D. Henderson, *The International Economic Problem,* Oxford, Oxford University Press, 1946, pp. 13 and 19: "Undoubtedly there is need to devise a code of good international behaviour to restrain the purely self-regarding policies of individual states, and to make them conform to the general welfare. But this code should be one which will

If, as seems likely, the tendency persists for countries to negotiate a substantial segment of their trade by bilateral barter methods within a multilateral trading system, it is obvious that private initiative will be largely superseded in this bilateral trade, and that the remaining trade will be exposed to more violent fluctuations. Thus, Britain draws a large part of its food and raw-material imports from the Dominions or from such countries as Denmark and Argentina with which it has bilateral arrangements. If, for lack of exports sufficient to earn the foreign exchange necessary to maintain the present volume of British imports, a reduction of imports becomes necessary, it must then be made in the segment of trade conducted with countries outside the area of bilateral agreements. In this case such trade as continued would do so under the bilateral agreements without regard to the principle of comparative advantage.

An even more important illustration of this tendency for planned trade to depart from the principle of comparative advantage was provided by the sixteen-nation plan drawn up at Paris in the late summer of 1947 in response to the suggestion of Secretary of State Marshall that United States assistance to Europe be made in accordance with a concerted program of European economic recovery. The first plan produced by the western European nations set targets for national production in each country. These were calculated not because those countries had a comparative advantage in producing the commodities in question, but because it was necessary to minimize the import requirements to be financed by the United States.

Another illustration of this tendency for planned trade to depart from the principle of comparative advantage was provided by the working of international commodity agreements in the 1930's. When burdensome surpluses of staple agricultural products and some minerals broke the international markets during the depression, there were negotiated arrangements to set aside stocks and withhold them from sale until prices rose, to regulate exports, and in some cases to regulate production. The quotas of continuing production allotted to

fit the conditions, the needs, and the aspirations of the modern world; not a code of Queensberry rules for an old-fashioned competitive prize-fight. It must leave countries free to regulate their economic life effectively, both in order to adjust their balance of international payments, and for such purposes as steadiness of trade and stability of employment. The trend towards an increasing degree of collective organization and State intervention in internal economic affairs must necessarily exert a far-reaching influence on external economic policies; and a wise code of international behaviour must be based upon an acceptance of that fact."

various countries and within these countries to various producers were based on percentages of previous production, modified in some cases by political bargaining. They did not eliminate high-cost production, but reduced the quotas of both high- and low-cost producers, the reduction in some commodities being greater proportionately in the low-cost than in the high-cost areas. Moreover, the quotas tended to stereotype the pattern of world production. There was no opportunity for the areas of low-cost production to win a larger share of the world market.

If such commodity agreements had been in force during the nineteenth century, it is highly improbable that the great expansion of international trade could have taken place. The greatest economic achievement of that century was the bringing of new areas of production into the world trading system. It was in this way that the great tropical plantations of tea, coffee, rubber, and cocoa, the grain-growing temperate plains of both hemispheres, the sheep and cattle pastures of the New World countries, and equally the manufacturing industries of the older industrialized countries were able to develop.

The case for international specialization rests upon two broad considerations. The peoples of the world are not equally endowed with natural resources, human skills, physical energy, and capital equipment. Moreover, these relative differences of national endowment are capable of gradual change as technical development progresses. It was the contention of the classical economists that the initiative of private traders competing in their search for profit would lead each country to specialize upon producing those commodities in which its natural and human resources gave it a comparative advantage. But it is necessary to realize that the national endowment of a country is not fixed even in respect to natural resources since new methods of cultivation or extraction have frequently changed the productive value of natural resources. The endowment of a country's human quality and skill is also capable of development, and capital equipment can be acquired by way of trade or of loans. Unhappily the co-operative economic relations which went so far in the nineteenth century to link the whole world in interdependent prosperity have been destroyed by war. The specialization remains, but the co-operation that was its counterpart is gone.

The classical and neo-classical analysis was of a static situation. Later economic analysis—for example the general equilibrium theory

—though capable of dynamic development, was concentrated upon calculations of marginal costs and revenues in the relatively short run. With the growing consciousness of national economic solidarity among many national groups, policy in regard to international economic relations has become less concerned with short-run calculations of immediate gain and more with long-run considerations of ultimate advantage. Thus international trade theory cannot ignore the dynamic requirements of national economic development, without ignoring much of present-day reality. Any explanation of it which ignores long-run considerations is bound to be incomplete and, if not carefully hedged, to lead to false conclusions. The territorial division of labor brought about by the relatively free trading methods of the nineteenth century was more than a reflection of the best economic use of human labor and of natural resources. As that specialization developed, it became an instrument of economic growth and change. While the economic theory of the nineteenth century may have been static, international trading practice was dynamic. The tacit assumption is often made by those who advocate policies of national economic development that governments take a longer view than gets into the market processes of a private economy. This assumption may hold true in some aspects of economic development, but there are many others where private enterprise is free to take a longer view than is possible to governments responsive to political pressures.

It would be possible to argue that those who now advocate regulation of the trading balance in order to achieve stability of employment are fighting a stubborn, rear-guard action to preserve the pattern of international specialization that was developed in the nineteenth century. In order to do this it has become necessary to restrain the competition that would create a new pattern of specialization by seeking out profit opportunities and organizing production where it will have the greater comparative advantage. This argument would doubtless be rejected by the advocates of national economic planning. They would maintain that they aim at freedom to change the past pattern along lines that will serve the national interest, rather than along lines dictated by external competition. But there is substance in the argument that they are resisting change.

The official policy of the United States since the passing of the Reciprocal Trade Agreements Act in 1934 has advocated the restoration of competitive multilateral trade. A very strong economic case can be made for this policy, on the ground of present efficiency and of future economic development. It is the same case as prompted Britain in the nineteenth century to lead the movement toward freer trade. The best economic use of the world's resources would be brought about in the long run by allowing competitive trade to create a new pattern of economic specialization. But it is obvious that such competitive trade would cause great dislocations of employment in Britain and other western European countries which in the past have built up trade connections in markets where at the close of the second World War they found themselves at a competitive disadvantage. Whether this competitive disadvantage as compared with the United States proved to be temporary or permanent, the people of Europe would strive to protect their export markets in countries from which they must secure raw materials and foodstuffs.

The trade relations between the United States, Britain, and Argentina illustrated an important aspect of this conflict between the attempt after the second World War to restore competitive trade and the desire to preserve the pattern of past specialization. The European and especially the British market remained the major outlet of such food-producing countries as Argentina. On the other hand most important Argentine products were either excluded from the United States market or were faced with strong local competition reinforced by protective tariff duties. Its import demands for Argentine beef and wheat gave the British government a powerful bargaining weapon in negotiating favorable terms for British exports to Argentina. The pronounced weakness of the British manufacturing industries at the close of an exhausting war had made it extremely difficult for them to compete on equal terms with United States industries. Until that weakness could be remedied, the British government would clearly use to the hilt the bargaining weapon represented by its import demand for Argentine products in order to get a preferred market for its exports to Argentina.

This might mean that Argentinians would be unable either to buy the American consumption goods they preferred or the capital equipment best suited to the needs of their program of industrial development. Indeed such a development of bilateral bargains would be injurious to all three countries—the United States losing part of a growing market, the British being forced to barter their exports for essential food, and the Argentinians having less ready access to the newest technical methods and appliances. The restoration of multilateral clearing by which each country's importers could buy in the cheapest market and let export outlets take care of themselves would obviously be desirable. But the postwar difficulties of the western European countries would have made such restoration extremely costly to them if it had been attempted before they could again bring their industries up to a pitch of competitive efficiency. Until that time they were bound to attempt to protect their markets and to oppose the premature relaxation of trade restrictions.

Any short-sighted attempt to brush aside the natural determination of the European peoples to live despite the handicaps imposed upon them by the war was likely to boomerang. The advocates of free competitive initiative had to reckon with the facts of life. Even Adam Smith had recognized that "humanity may require that the freedom of trade should be restored only by slow gradations, and with a good deal of reserve and circumspection," in cases "where particular manufactures, by means of high duties or prohibitions upon all foreign goods which can come into competition with them, have been so far extended as to employ a great multitude of hands."

In the short run over the larger part of the world outside the Soviet zone, a compromise had to be found between private enterprise and government planning. Private enterprise would aim at organizing production where the most favorable combination of the factors of production could be mobilized. In doing so it would reckon upon future as well as present potential. It would accommodate itself to the shifts in productive capacity brought about by the war and would test the competitive validity of those shifts. Much wartime industrial development would undoubtedly prove to be inefficient, but a good deal would survive. In Canada and Australia, India and South Africa, as in the West and South of the United States, there had been great strides in manufacturing efficiency. Economic development in areas of hitherto untapped resources, such as the oil of the Middle East and mineral deposits in parts of Africa, would loom large in the calculations. The organization of production and trade would function as an instrument of change and of growth.

Government intervention, on the other hand, was bound to be concerned largely with the preservation of employment in the areas and industries that had been developed to meet the needs of the recent past rather than of the present or the future. Its watchword must be reconstruction rather than development. The future envisaged by national planning policies was only too apt to be a perpetuation of past trends that had been exhausted. While each national plan projected rosy dreams of progress in the development of scientific methods, they were very apt to be dreams of improving the *status quo ante*.

Theoretically there was no reason why a national economic plan should not be as realistic as private enterprise in taking account of the changing international situation. In practice it was politically very difficult to carry through the changes in national economic structure that would be dictated by competitive efficiency. Such changes always entailed reconstruction of equipment and shifts of employment that bore harshly upon powerful groups in the community. There was reason, therefore, to suspect that the test of comparative economic advantage would be subordinated in national planning policies to such criteria as stability and full employment. This could be defended as a necessary compromise with the immediate postwar emergency. But it might develop into a continuing evasion of the necessity to conform to shifts in the international situation.

THE CALCULATION OF COMPARATIVE ADVANTAGE

The reason why governments intervene to regulate the profit-seeking activities of private traders is that with the present distribution of population and productive resources free competition would bring about great shifts in the location of industry and in employment opportunities. This was very evident, particularly in Britain, after the war in western Europe. The world trade of the recent past had been developed by those countries, which had specialized upon the manufacturing industries and increasingly upon the financial and commercial services called for by world trade. It was evident also in those raw-material and food-exporting countries that had directed their production largely toward the export market offered by the urbanized, manufacturing countries of western Europe. The specialization of many newly settled countries upon mineral, agricultural, and pastoral production had brought rich rewards and quick development.

To some extent those new countries had grown rich by exploiting the virgin fertility of their soil and by using up irreplaceable natural assets. But the main cause of their high productivity was their development of specialized methods of production for the export market. The disruption of multilateral trade since 1914 rendered precarious the high living levels attained by rapidly increasing populations in the countries of recent European settlement overseas, as well as in western Europe. Economists talked of such objectives as balance of payments equilibrium, a steady flow of trade, and stability of employment taking precedence over the restoration of multilateral trade. In so doing they were concerned with buttressing and preserving this pattern of past specialization or with its gradual adaptation along lines determined by national planning rather than with allowing competitive forces to create a new pattern.

Many international economic issues are raised by the mixed character of the competitive forces that would be set free if governments did not intervene to restrain them. Over a wide range of manufacturing industry and services, private enterprise now operates by the methods of imperfect rather than free competition. This development affects not only manufacturing industries, but it concerns also large-scale operations in mining, petroleum producing and refining, and many specialized forms of agricultural production such as sugar-growing and the processing of agricultural products.

There is an increasing tendency for the many financial and commercial services that were formerly conducted by competitive, small-scale enterprise to be provided by great corporations. Banks have created departments to handle security transactions, foreign exchange dealings, foreign credits and collections, insurance and similar services. Many manufacturing corporations, especially those which have established foreign branches, use their own facilities to conduct commercial and financial operations that in the nineteenth century would have been contracted out to specialist firms. The network of specialized commercial services and commodity exchanges that had been an essential feature of the competitive system has been seriously weakened. While the day of the specialized dealer, the compradore, the commission agent, the broker and the arbitrager is not yet ended, the openings for individual enterprise in these fields are much narrower than they used to be.

Thus our present concern is with the complications of international trading initiative and particularly with the difficulties in calculating comparative advantage, which flow from the organization of industrial and commercial enterprises by imperfect rather than free competitive methods.[3] A sharp distinction has been drawn between the kind of competition now prevailing between large corporate enterprises, and that which earlier economists studied as the competition between industries. The nineteenth-century economists assumed that the industries they wrote about dealt in specific, homogeneous commodities. While they were aware of the complications in costing presented by joint production of two or more commodities, their analysis of the market process ran in terms of a single commodity, such as wheat. This was particularly true in respect of international trade. The staple commodities of international trade were never in fact homogeneous. There are scores of varieties of wheat and cotton. But the device of averaging, or Alfred Marshall's device of a representative unit, could be used to study the market.

In considering the comparative advantage of a locality for the production of commodities entering international trade, the classical and neo-classical economists conjured up a picture of a great number of independent producers able to calculate the costs of producing a single commodity and without adverse effects on their profits also able to turn from one commodity to another as the market indicated. Even for agriculture, there was no analysis of the enterprise as a whole. It was assumed that a farmer was free to produce wheat or lamb in organizing his farm. However, it was the agricultural economists who first insisted that the enterprise must be regarded for many purposes as an integrated whole, rather than as the sum of its component parts. A farmer had to consider the economies of balanced production, crop rotation, and overhead costs, such as those involved in maintaining soil fertility.

In the modern manufacturing enterprises conducted by great corporations, the integration of processes and the importance of overhead costs grow steadily. The prime costs that can be most readily measured at the margin of profitability decline in relative importance. There is a tendency particularly in the corporations which manufacture such complex commodities as automobiles for durable consumption, and in those which manufacture chemical products, for the enterprise to spread over related processes.

The Ford enterprise incorporates within its major automobile plants, not only the assembling of parts—some of which are manufac-

[3] The theory of imperfect competition has been summarized earlier. Cf. Chapter XIV, "The End of Laissez Faire."

tured within the plant while others are bought from independent, specialized suppliers—but also installations which would formerly have been independent factories. Within it there are not only assembly lines, but furnaces to make steel, and the heat thus generated furnishes power to other parts of the enterprise. Junked automobiles furnish materials for the recovery of rare alloys, for polishing materials, and for glass. A glass factory makes all the glass used. There is a tire factory and many other subsidiary but integrated operations. The process extends beyond the boundaries of the parent enterprise. Ford ships bring ore and coal, sand, silica, and lumber from Ford mines and mills, some of which lie across the international border. As on the raw material, there are on the marketing side branches, assembly plants, and agencies abroad.

This type of organization takes many forms. In some cases there is a large central organization which manufactures the bulk of the product. In others a specially organized managerial corporation controls a network of semi-independent subsidiary enterprises. The interrelations between the parts and the whole enterprise often become so complicated as to defy diagrammatic representation. It is seldom easy to determine the location of power in these great enterprises. Since there is normally a large area of indeterminacy in the allocation of costs and the fixation of prices, it is important to discover not so much who exercises power in these respects, as what are the considerations which determine the decisions.

Though elaborate accounts are kept and the theory of corporate finance has developed rapidly, it is evident that there can be no very definitely fixed principles by which the exact marginal cost of specific parts, commodities or services can be determined. Apart from the difficulty of allocating to specific units of production the overhead costs of planning, management, capital construction, marketing, advertising, research, and process development, account must be taken of the fact that there usually develops an essential unity in the enterprise which cannot be mutilated by the excision of an operation that might be performed more cheaply by outside suppliers. Reorganizations do occur, but once an elaborate installation is in operation it must usually be operated, at least until it has been amortized to the point where extensive remodeling may eliminate obsolescent processes.

Research and process development offer peculiar costing difficulties.

successful experiment must offset the cost of failures. Moreover, it is often necessary, as research develops new processes, to load on to the price of a popular product as much as the traffic will bear, until its by-products are assured of remunerative markets. In any case the necessity of remaining abreast of a highly competitive situation among a relatively few great international enterprises may force the retention of a wide range of processes and products some of which are of doubtful profitability.

This greatly complicates the issues of tariff protection in the rapidly developing chemical industries. A French chemical concern may be faced with competition from Norwegian and Swiss firms, from I. G. Farben, from the British Imperial Chemical Industries, and from large United States corporations. The situation may arise where the French concern meets what it regards as unfair competition in a number of its major products. It is obvious that, by accepting imports at the cut rates, French consumers and industrial users of chemical products would secure an advantage. But the industry might be forced out of existence even for the production of the commodities in which it had a relative advantage if those articles could not be produced as part of a wide range of products. Indeed a situation might emerge where the lowering of tariff protection on some of these articles might render the enterprise as a whole unprofitable unless its remaining products could be sold at a very high price. If these remaining products were essential to other industries—as for example nitrates for agricultural fertilizers—a good case could be made for preservation of the whole enterprise by protecting the by-products from import competition. No doubt this argument can be used speciously. However, it illustrates the significant fact that competition between enterprises as a whole, as well as between their individual products, must be reckoned with.

Some important illustrations of this fact occur in the field of corporate international investment. Standard Oil of California and Texaco organized the Arabian-American Corporation (Aramco) to secure concessions in Saudi Arabia and other areas of the Near East. The development of these concessions included the building of a pipe line (with its appurtenant roads, railroads, airports, villages, schools, and repair shops) across the desert to the eastern Mediterranean. The construction was let to United States contractors, but much of the work was done with local labor and materials. While estimates of the costs of developing the new fields and constructing the pipe line are difficult to make, the total expenditure before oil could flow steadily in commercial volume across the pipe line has been estimated at about $200 million. The total investment planned was estimated at $1,750 million. Some of this venture capital was raised by loans from United States banks. Part of it was provided by the undistributed profits of the parent oil companies. Other Standard Oil corporations joined the original partners in the Arabian-American Corporation to make available undistributed cash (including Syrian pounds earned by sales of oil and not transferable into dollars) and to provide greater security for the bank loans. There were complicated relationships with the British, Dutch, and with other American oil interests in regard to prices, markets, refining facilities, and government contracts. The negotiations with various Arabian states were long and costly.

Such transactions raise a host of intriguing economic questions. It would be an interesting analytical exercise to trace the real incidence of this cost of construction, to discover what effect the increased credit made available for the purchase of equipment in the United States had upon the price of steel and other commodities, to calculate how far the accumulated profits ploughed back into this investment might otherwise have been used to increase stock dividends or to reduce the price of various petroleum products to the consumer. It would be more interesting and a more practical problem to determine how the costs of construction should be allocated against the hoped-for future production.

The setting of a price pattern for the various products and by-products of crude petroleum at the Arabian ports in comparison with the prices charged by Anglo-Iranian and other neighboring competitors, as well as with the price pattern set at other producing points—Venezuela, Borneo, Texas—is a task calling for long experience and shrewd judgment but not for theoretical economic analysis. There is a large degree of indeterminacy in the political and economic factors involved. Practical judgment must inevitably be conservative in the sense of allowing profit margins wide enough to meet unforeseen contingencies. In such a complicated series of decisions final judgment as to the profitability of the enterprise, which may be long deferred, cannot relate to particular products or processes. It must relate to the enterprise as a whole. While there are competitive elements in the dealings on particular products, the enterprise is a massive whole competing with others of like stature.

Another important factor complicating any attempt to calculate comparative advantage has been the great development of direct corporate investment in foreign countries, dictated at least in part by the desire to get behind tariff barriers or to cope with special tax situations. American automobile corporations set up Canadian branches to manufacture behind the Canadian tariff and within the British preferential system. Those branches may use parts manufactured in the United States or pay royalties on patents to produce the parts in Canada. What prices are fixed for these parts and royalties? Does the parent corporation charge what the traffic will bear? Or does it attempt to allocate to the Canadian subsidiary a proportionate share of its overhead costs? The principles upon which such an allocation may be made involve consideration of what can only be described as the politics of business. They may even be concerned with wider politics. In some instances the prices may be set so as to produce profits in the branches where expansion is desired. In other instances the different branches of the business make profits which conform to the pattern of taxation.

There has been considerable variation in the organization of foreign business outlets. When the I. G. Farbenindustrie operated in the United States it maintained with separate corporate structures a series of factories and a selling organization, retaining the essential know-how and the basic research organization in Germany. If it became necessary to change the production methods in the United States factories, formulae were worked out in the parent enterprise and introduced into the United States by sending across the necessary practical directions or the new raw materials, and, if necessary, the specialists with the knowledge to adapt the new processes. It was the competitive situation in the United States, rather than calculations of comparative cost, which determined policy. Knowledge is power and that power was retained in the parent enterprise.

Prestige is a factor in the international location of industry. Experimental ventures can nearly always be justified on the ground of prestige advertising or publicity. There is an element of emulation in such experiments. In a situation of imperfect competition, if one competitor engages in foreign investment or trade or even display, the others are often afraid not to follow suit. Strict attention by management to profits in the interest of the stockholders who own the enterprise would sometimes counsel more caution. It would be interesting to have an independent audit of the international trading and investing activities of some large corporations. Almost certainly such an audit would reveal cases where calculations other than those of profit were necessary to justify many activities.

While calculations have been made of the proportion of world trade that is subject to the restraints of monopolistic or cartel control, it is difficult to justify their basis. Such arrangements preclude the undertaking of transactions that would test the competitive situation of individual products. It is impossible to measure the trade which might have taken place. As in the measurement of tariff barriers, the absence of trade may be more significant than the amount which appears in the statistics.

It is obvious that among the great variety of products of great chemical corporations—acids and alkalis, dyes and drugs, foodstuffs and fertilizers, paints and plastics, and all the rest—tempting foreign trade openings must occur. But if an American corporation were to test the market in a British Dominion with a limited line of products in which it seemed to have a comparative advantage, it would have to market them expensively. It would almost certainly be faced with competition from a similar line of products marketed by Imperial Chemical Industries as part of a large established trade with the advertising and other costs spread over many products. The I.C.I. has well-established connections with distributors and customers, and a new competitor would have to break into the market and carry the costs of doing so on a restricted line of products. As a general rule, if it decided to extend its trade in this area it would normally be more profitable to do so on a front wider than the particular products in which the comparative advantage was clearest. In doing so, however, it would expose itself to the risks of intensive price competition in that market and to reprisals in other markets, perhaps including its own home market. While there are numerous exceptions, in general the industrial giants confine themselves to territories where they have a developed organization, thus respecting the territories of their foreign competitors. Opportunities for turning a quick profit are passed up. And these were the essence of a competitive trading system organized on the basis of individual commodity comparisons.

Instead, the corporations are apt to enter into patent and licensing agreements by which they exchange information in regard to research and process development and grant mutually exclusive licenses for the use of patents in their respective territories. Many such agreements were brought to light by the prosecutions instituted under the Sherman Act in the late 1930's by the United States Department of Justice.

A strong argument has been advanced that this system of exclusive licensing has increased production and trade. For example the International General Electric Company has participated in the formation of foreign enterprises, such as the Japanese corporation, providing not only capital but patents and know-how to create efficient productive arrangements in Japan. In this connection it is interesting to note that most of the prosecutions in such cases have led to a plea of *nolo contendere,* the corporations concerned acquiescing in a fine and an order directing them to cancel the agreement. Such proceedings preclude United States corporations from entering into further agreements for the licensing of patents by the effective sanction of contempt. However, since patents are of less importance than know-how, they cannot prevent the international exchange of specialized knowledge. Even if they could, the only result would be to widen further the disparities of technical development in different countries. There is no effective legal way by which corporations may be forced to compete commodity by commodity in international trade.

The prevalence of imperfect competition with its corollaries of indeterminacy in the costing of particular products and of hesitancy in entering markets on a piecemeal basis has an important bearing on this whole question of international disparities in technology. The extraordinary degree to which the United States has now attained competitive supremacy in the production of manufactured commodities, both industrial and agricultural, would not disturb the equilibrium of the balances of international payments as much as it does if international traders could pick off items in which other countries might compete. The tariff of the United States is designed like most others to prevent this happening. Imports would be easier if the tariff duties were not so high, if valuation procedures were less arbitrary, and if customs formalities were less complicated, and in addition if pressure were not brought to bear, comparable to that brought on the Swiss, to impose on exporters a voluntary quota for fear of provoking an agitation in the United States for higher duties.

In addition to such tariff barriers, commodity competition in many fields is made difficult by the corporate structure of manufacturing enterprises. There must be some automobile parts, for example, or parts of clocks and radios that might be supplied from foreign sources more cheaply than they can be manufactured by the automobile giants or their suppliers in the United States. However, the standardized processes of manufacture inhibit the use of any but standardized parts that can be supplied in large volume for assembly. In the electrical, chemical, and other industries the same difficulties confront the development of imports of uneven and unstandardized quality.

Thus international trade steadily loses its heterogeneous character. The commission agent picking up odd lots of varied commodities finds it harder to market them. The chemists find ways of rearranging the molecular structure of common materials so as to produce substitutes for many natural raw materials that formerly were indispensable and therefore had to be imported. The analysis of comparative cost in terms of these commodities must now reckon with the fact that uniform quality in large volume supplied over long periods of time from an assured source has become necessary for the manufacturing processes of great enterprises. This is true of intermediate processes and parts. As the Swiss manufacture of watch movements and radio parts has shown, it is not impossible to organize such standardized production in large and steady volume. But it is generally simpler for the mass production industries, when they need something, to produce it within their own organization, or to contract for its production according to their specifications among the network of suppliers who have grown up in the same industrial complex and are familiar with mass production methods, than it is to depend upon supplies bought in the open market.

New forms of international economic development have appeared. These are concerned with the export of know-how rather than capital. Hundreds of cases could be cited where American firms have made contracts with foreign governments and enterprises. Some call merely for engineering-economic surveys. Others involve the designing and sometimes the construction of plants. Nearly all provide for the licensing of processes and for the training of technicians. Very little capital export is involved in these new developments. They seem likely to inaugurate a new phase of international trade comparable with that launched by the British outflow of capital in the latter half of the nineteenth century. Many firms, operating by a great variety of methods, were engaged in these new forms of transferring technical skills to undeveloped regions. Immediately, the result could be a reduction both in foreign investment and in foreign trade. The new plants were for the most part financed locally and their production was for the local market. The ultimate result was likely to be a considerable stimulation of both investment and trade. But neither would be in the nineteenth-century pattern.

THE TRADE IN RAW MATERIALS

The staple products of the bulk trade of the nineteenth century—foodstuffs and raw materials—still accounted in the years just preceding the second World War for over 60 per cent of world trade. In many of the less developed countries and even in some of the highly developed countries of the New World, exports consisted almost entirely of foodstuffs and raw materials. In 1937 the percentage of total exports constituted by foodstuffs and raw materials ranged from 97 to 99 per cent in the Latin-American countries and from 93 to 99 per cent in various regions of Africa. It was 96 per cent in southeast Asia and in Australia and New Zealand; 82 per cent in the U.S.S.R., in the agricultural zone of central and eastern Europe, and in China; 79 per cent in India, Burma, and Ceylon; and 72 per cent in Canada. The corresponding figure in the United States was 50 per cent. Only in the highly industrialized regions of western Europe, where the percentage was 37 per cent, in Japan where it was 30 per cent, and in Britain 28 per cent, were foodstuffs and raw materials less important than manufactured exports. These figures offer striking evidence of the extent to which the trade of the world was centered upon western Europe and Britain and in minor degree upon Japan. They also show how large an area was affected by the violent fluctuations of agricultural and mineral prices in the years between the wars.

In the years ahead this experience of the interwar period is bound to be reflected in attempts to stabilize the prices and secure the outlets for these food and raw-material commodities that constitute the bulk of the exports from the whole world outside western Europe, Japan, and, since the war, the United States. The high production of foodstuffs and raw materials in the British Dominions and in Latin America has been directed in the past largely to the markets of Europe. The agricultural plantations in Asia—tea in India and Ceylon, rubber, sugar, and tobacco in the Netherlands Indies—have been developed largely for export. Mining enterprises in Africa, Central America, and southeast Asia have fed raw materials into the stream of world trade. In many countries peasant production has been drawn upon to supplement exports, as in the case of tung oil from China, rubber from the Netherlands Indies, and coffee from Brazil. The prosperity, even the subsistence, of hundreds of millions of people in widely separated areas has become dependent upon the prices which the produce of their labor can command in the distant markets of industrially developed countries.

It is significant that the prices, particularly of the staple commodities that can be produced in many countries, fluctuated during the interwar years more frequently and more violently than the prices of manufactured goods. The farmer cannot regulate his output quickly. As a general rule, he has no alternative means of livelihood and little reserve of purchasing power. When prices fall he is impelled to produce more and to sell more of what he produces. In order to gain as much total income as possible to meet the cash outlays to which he is committed, he pours increased quantities of his produce on to already glutted markets. In the nineteenth century the price fluctuations were less violent than they have been since the first World War. Moreover, there was an elaborate organization of dealers who made their profits in large part by cushioning price fluctuations, buying when prices were low and selling when they rose. These cushions are now much thinner so that even moderate sales may cause very large price declines.

What is true of individual farmers is true in large measure of agricultural countries as a whole. They were heavily indebted with fixed interest charges on their overseas debts, until they were able during the second World War to reduce this debt substantially. When their export prices fell in the oscillations of the business cycles, they were usually caught with large import orders so that there was a heavy strain on their balances of payments. They tried to maintain their credit by exporting more. But the more they exported, the more prices were forced down on world markets. These markets in any case were narrowed by the rapid growth of agricultural protectionism in industrial countries. In the 1930's particularly, the terms of trade were turned against the food and raw-material exporting countries by the Hawley-Smoot tariff, by the British protective tariff, by the programs of increasing agricultural self-sufficiency in Italy and Germany, and by the widespread use of quotas and prohibitions in other importing countries.

The territorial division of labor of the nineteenth century had been developed upon the assumption that the manufacturing creditor countries would provide expanding markets for the specialized products of the developing agricultural countries. Such specialization becomes impracticable when the importing countries of western Europe are unable to pay for imports, and the greatest industrial and creditor nation of the modern world, the United States, is also a great agricultural exporter. The international-trade theorists of the nineteenth century never contemplated a situation in which the greatest manufacturing nation of the world would also be one of the greatest exporters of foodstuffs and raw materials, and where the monetary and financial policies of this nation, now become the largest source of foreign investment capital, would be dictated not by international investment bankers, but largely by the dominant political power of organized farm groups intent upon maintaining both their domestic prices and their export markets.

In the years of scarcity that follow a great war the significance of this was easily overlooked. When the second World War ended there were glaring shortages of food and raw materials which seemed likely to persist for some years to come. The industrial urbanized areas of western Europe had been deprived by the war of much of their capacity to buy from abroad. Even if their capacity had been restored, the markets from which they used to draw part of their imports and to send a large part of their manufactured exports had been largely destroyed. Many of the Asiatic countries had been devastated, while others were suffering economic disturbances as the result of their attempts to install independent governments. In the British Dominions, to some extent in Latin America, and in India, great strides had been made toward industrialization. Eastern Europe was largely cut off from its former markets in the west and was in process of transforming its political organization. Part of the process was a redistribution of land and parallel agrarian changes that seemed likely to reduce the surplus formerly exported. If and when the iron curtain was lifted and trade began to move again within Europe, it was likely that the granary would be much barer than it used to be. Supplies were therefore short. Prices were high and likely to remain high for a considerable period.

Nevertheless, the policies followed seemed likely to result, as after the first World War, in the accumulation of what in the interwar period were called burdensome surpluses of the staple agricultural and mineral commodities. In Canada, Australia, Argentina, and many other countries as well as the United States, there was a greatly expanded yield of wheat. At the same time, Britain had embarked on a policy of increased agricultural production, intended to reduce its dependence upon imports. The plan for European reconstruction called for a restoration of cereal production equal to the virtual self-sufficiency of the late 1930's. The Italian battle for grain and the French policy of subsidized production were resumed. The voices raised in warning and in protest did not command much attention in the period of acute shortages immediately at the close of the war. But the time would come when the need to deal again with burdensome surpluses would vindicate them.[4]

The warnings were not against the introduction of improved production methods but against subsidies and price guarantees that stimulated the production of commodities in which the country did not possess a comparative advantage. Very clear illustrations of such agricultural stimulation could be found in the industrialized countries of western Europe. They practiced high farming in which a limited land area was made to yield heavily by intensive applications of labor, fertilizers, and capital equipment. In certain forms of agricultural production, such as stock-breeding and the cultivation of some fruits and vegetables, these methods were competitively efficient and were aided by proximity to the market. The urbanized population needed more of the protective foods thus produced. The grains, which could be more economically and efficiently produced by the more extensive methods followed in countries that had larger area and better climatic conditions, were also being produced in Europe under this regime of price guarantees and production subsidies.

A policy of territorial specialization was indicated by human needs

[4] Cf. *Economist*, September 27, 1947: "The state of the nation does not warrant a panicky attempt to get as much food as possible, as quickly as possible, quite irrespective of costs and consequences. It does most earnestly demand a progressive endeavor to raise by a parallel process both the output and the efficiency of British agriculture. . . . But to try and raise output by making bad farming pay is to risk creating costly inefficiencies which need never exist and whose existence will be a standing menace to the industry's stability. For if the expansion of agriculture is constructed on an unsound and costly basis, it will be dispensed with the moment circumstances permit; and if, as some say, the moment never comes, then it will be a perennial cause of national poverty."

as well as by the geographical distribution of natural resources. This specialization would give scope for European agriculture in the production of protective foods and for overseas agriculture in the production of staple foods.[5] Such a policy was thwarted by national programs of self-sufficiency whether they originated in short-run attempts to meet postwar deficiencies, in strategic programs designed in fear of war, in a desire to preserve the social structure and characteristics of peasant production, or simply in the dominating political strength of organized agriculture.

The root of this aspect of international economic disequilibrium was to be found in national policies. A great number of instances from many countries could be cited to illustrate the extraordinary extent to which domestic political influences continued to buttress programs of agricultural production that were ultimately indefensible from the long-run viewpoint of effective international specialization. Legislative programs supporting the price and thereby maintaining the production of cotton in the United States had gone a long way toward pricing United States cotton beyond the reach of important markets and thereby encouraging the production of cotton in other areas.[6] Similar support to the price of wool went a long way in 1945 and 1946, despite a high tariff, to price it out of the domestic market. The Commodity Credit Corporation was left with large stocks of

[5] This was the basic argument behind the League of Nations campaign for improved nutrition. Cf. F. L. McDougall, *Food and Welfare,* Geneva, 1938, p. 56: "The five aims of an improved level of nutrition, higher standards of living, a more prosperous world agriculture, freer international trade, and an increased volume of trade, together interlock to form lines of policy which should ensure economic and political stability to the nations prepared for such cooperation and if vigorously prosecuted should promote the peace so desirable but so difficult of achievement in the world today." Cf. also League of Nations, *Final Report of the Mixed Committee of the League of Nations on the Relation of Nutrition to Health, Agriculture, and Economic Policy,* Geneva, 1937.

[6] Cf. *Economist,* September 27, 1947, p. 531, for a table which may be summarized thus:

British Cotton Consumption by Growths

Types	*1939* %	*1946* %
American		
U.S.A.	45	25
Brazil	9	19
Other Sources	3	9
Egyptian		
Egypt	19	20
Sudan	6	12
Other		
India	11	6
Peru	6	4

domestic wool on its hands, until a disastrous drought in Australia in 1947 reduced world supplies and lifted prices to record levels. The example of sugar was notorious. Since the Napoleonic Wars when the production of beet sugar in Europe had been encouraged as an element of the economic reply to the British naval blockade, sugar had been the football of national politics in many countries. In 1882 an international convention regulating production quotas and prices had stereotyped the pattern of national production. Since that time there had been a political rather than an economic basis for the industry. The spread of prices that resulted—before the second World War the price of sugar in Hamburg was six times the price at which Java sugar could be delivered to Amsterdam—indicated the extent to which these political arrangements had departed from the principle of comparative advantage. Wherever a burdensome surplus had emerged in some staple commodity—coffee, rubber, wheat, and many other examples might be cited—there was in the background one or more national political situations that interfered with the competitive process and so made international consultations necessary.

When the great depression from 1929 to 1933 was marked by precipitous declines in the prices of internationally traded raw materials and foodstuffs, such consultations resulted in a variety of international commodity agreements designed primarily to raise prices. These agreements in many cases called for government intervention to regulate production or exports, to finance accumulated stocks that were withheld temporarily from the market, or to subsidize sales to preferred consumers at prices below the levels it was desired to maintain in the market. The occasion for such international consultations was always a market disturbance such as the interruption of established trade channels by a great war, or a sudden decline of prices in a sharp cyclical depression.

It had always proved difficult to work out bases of agreement satisfactory to the producing interests concerned, to say nothing of the consumers, except in cases where major producers were organized in large corporations domiciled in a small number of countries. Until the outbreak of the second World War the tin mines and rubber and tea plantations in southeast Asia were controlled from London and Amsterdam though the small-scale production of independent peasant and Chinese enterprises soon proved troublesome. It was relatively easy to work out an agreement between the small group of governments concerned—mainly the British and Dutch—even if other governments had to be brought in to extend the controls to minor areas of production. Agreement was facilitated because the continued operation of the plantations and mines of the major producing interests was important to the financial stability of the colonial governments. Indeed the international commodity agreements that lasted any length of time were generally in the nature of producers' cartels implemented by government action.

It was much more difficult to work out an effective international agreement in regard to a commodity such as wheat, produced by large numbers of independent, small producers in many different countries. The agreement entered into by the major wheat-exporting countries after the breakdown of the Monetary and Economic Conference in 1933 became a dead letter when Argentina disregarded the quota allotted to it. It had been imperiled before then by the fact that wheat from a large number of countries not party to the agreement began to appear in the world market. A similar situation developed in the middle thirties in regard to rubber and tin when peasant producers had to be restrained by legislation from exporting in excess of the agreed quotas. National subsidies and price-support programs always led to the necessity for international regulation of the market. Then in turn international regulation led to the spread of such national programs.

The experience of international commodity agreements was practically confined to the last decade before the second World War, and it was not till after the end of the war that this experience was subjected to critical analysis. The contemporary literature consisted largely of special pleading. Control schemes of many kinds were advocated to remedy the distressed situation of farmers in many lands. The purposes of these schemes were stated in unexceptionable terms by phrases carefully chosen to convey a sense of order, stability, regularization, and similar desirable achievements. Emphasis was placed upon such objectives as co-operation and research. The interest of the consumer in orderly markets was stressed. However, most of the agreements proved difficult to formulate and still more difficult to administer. Few of them survived their first contractual period and many broke down even before this period had expired. There is much less practical experience in the operation of these intergovernmental agreements than in that of the interindustrial agreements described as cartels. The more successful of the intergovernmental agreements resembled cartels in many important respects since the influence of large producers in a few countries was very considerable. Thus it is not surprising to find that whatever the objectives by which they were justified at their initiation, the maintenance or raising of prices and the curtailment of production were their chief results in practice.

As the second World War drew to a close there was increasing discussion of the need to organize commodity controls. It was recognized that a period of acute scarcity immediately after the war was likely to be followed before long by a period of surpluses of staple products whose prices are important to the prosperity and economic stability of the larger part of the food and raw-material producing countries of the world. International agreement based upon principles that could be accepted as mutually advantageous by consuming as well as producing countries was advocated as being preferable either to national action or to concerted action between groups of producers. The interallied mechanisms that had developed around the joint boards set up under the Anglo-American Combined Chiefs of Staff had been effective in mobilizing and allocating food and raw materials during the war. If they had continued their operations into the peace, they might have served as a pivot in the reconversion period. In default of such mechanisms many plans were projected for international commodity agreements and attempts were made to elaborate the principles by which such agreements might work to the benefit of both producers and consumers.

The most effective commodity-control schemes of the interwar period had been those dominated by the producing interests. Critical examination of their results indicates very clearly that they worked against the competitive principle. Their methods were primarily those of monopoly control directed toward raising prices, preventing the liquidation of high-cost enterprises, and hindering the rise or expansion of new producing areas. Thus they stereotyped the past pattern of geographical specialization.

The principal forms of international commodity agreements have been described by Professor Joseph S. Davis as the buffer-stock, the surplus-adjustment, and the commodity-control types. The buffer-stock idea has some points in common with plans to stabilize prices by using stocks of storable foodstuffs and raw materials as monetary reserves. It has many variants of which the proposals for stockpiling durable materials are perhaps the most practicable. Much could be done, particularly by the United States, to build stocks of durable materials for which it is dependent upon imports. If such purchases were timed so as to make dollars available to producers who were pinched in a crisis, the procedure might be used as a contra-cyclical policy. In the nineteenth century the free markets of western Europe often acted in this fashion since speculative brokers bought when prices fell and released their purchases as prices recovered. However, the limits of such policies are narrower than is sometimes thought. Except for a relatively few commodities storage involves heavy wastage, deterioration of quality and mounting cost.

The ideas of buffer-stock schemes, ever-normal granaries, or commodity reserves that were current after the second World War have not been worked out in practical detail. Nor has any of the projected or actual international institutions included anything in the nature of an operative commodity-control board. The broad idea of an international buffer-stock plan was advanced at the Hot Springs Conference which launched the Food and Agriculture Organization; but the conference was divided between this proposal and the earlier ideas embodied in a draft wheat agreement.

In 1945, the United States Department of State published its *Proposals for the Expansion of World Trade and Employment*. In the discussions of these proposals which subsequently took place at London, Geneva, and Havana, a narrower field for commodity agreements emerged in what Professor Davis has called the surplus-adjustment pattern. It was significant that this pattern emerged after a considerable measure of official and unofficial discussion, involving the policy of the United States, which since 1934 has been directed toward freer, multilateral trade. The provisions of the international trade charter which emerged from the discussions at London, Geneva, and Havana, in 1946, 1947, and 1948, incorporated a long chapter laying down, in considerable detail, the circumstances in which a commodity agreement might be made, the principles to which it should conform, and the national action required to ensure that the temporary disequilibrium of demand and supply might be remedied within the duration of the agreement.

The adoption of this chapter constituted a considerable victory for the official view of the United States. That view was not arrived at until after long and difficult interdepartmental discussions within the United States. The divergence of opinion within the administration was reflected by the proposal in 1947 to set up a World Food Board which had the support of some agricultural officials in the United States. This proposal would have set up an operative international body to distribute available food supplies. The surplus-adjustment theory, on the other hand, is based on the assumption that production and trade should remain in the hands of private enterprise and that any special international agreements that may become necessary in an emergency should be of limited duration and should be self-liquidating. This theory is compatible with world trade organized on the principle of comparative advantage. It is an attempt to afford a restricted opportunity for producers of goods in temporary surplus to liquidate their disequilibrium without hampering the expansion of competitive trade. As Professor Davis points out this may prove to be a counsel of perfection unattainable in a crisis. The international trade charter lays down strict conditions under which resort may be permitted to "the whole array of restrictive devices—export and import quotas, production restraints, price regulation, and reserve stocks." [7] The danger is that the devices will be used and the conditions ignored.

The commodity-control theory was illustrated in the negotiations for the international wheat agreement drafted as early as 1942 and advocated in many influential quarters as a model upon which other international commodity-control agreements might be based. Considerable opposition arose to the principles upon which this draft agreement was worked out. After much controversy it was renegotiated in March, 1948, by three of the major exporting countries—the United States, Canada, and Australia—and thirty-three importing countries of which the largest were Britain, Italy, France, the Netherlands, India, and Belgium. The importing countries agreed to purchase guaranteed quantities of wheat over a five-year period and the exporters agreed to sell those quantities, totaling 500 million bushels, at a fixed schedule of prices. An International Wheat Council would be created to administer the agreement. Essentially this constituted a price-supporting agreement by means of bulk-purchase arrangements.

It was submitted by the President to the Senate Foreign Relations

[7] Cf. Joseph S. Davis, *International Commodity Control Agreements: Hope, Illusion, or Menace?*, New York, 1947, p. 38.

Committee at the Second Session of the Eightieth Congress. The Committee deferred action until the next Congress, but expressed its "earnest belief that the principle of surplus marketing by international agreement is sound." After Senate ratification on June 13, the agreement was signed by President Truman and became effective July 1, 1949. On July 6, the International Wheat Council, representing twenty-two signatory nations, held its first meeting. It was made clear by this action that although the negotiation of such an agreement contravened the spirit if not the letter, of the International Trade Charter, there was enough political influence in the hands of organized farm groups to put through a series of international commodity agreements if agricultural prices should decline at all sharply.

The central core of controversy that runs through all the discussions of these and other variant proposals for international commodity agreements is the question with which this chapter has been concerned from many different angles. How can regulatory arrangements, national or international, be reconciled with the principle of territorial division of labor to maximize production and trade? The controversy comes to a head in considering the prices that it is desired to stabilize. In buying and selling, is the control organization to aim at adjusting demand to supply? If so, at what level of price? Or is it to aim at assuring to agricultural producers, threatened by international competition, a level of income comparable with that earned by more advantageously situated producers of other agricultural products? In fixing production or export quotas, in determining the acquisition or release of buffer stocks, in disposing of accumulated surpluses, the important issue is the price level to be aimed at. Competition would fix price levels so as to equate demand and supply. The purpose of commodity agreements is to the contrary. It is to protect producers from the effects of competition.

POLITICAL PRESSURES AND THE NATIONAL INTEREST

Just as long as governments intervene to protect the interests of groups of producers, the working of the competitive price mechanism is distorted. Competitive forces are also much hampered by the growth of monopolistic elements in business enterprise, and by government intervention designed to safeguard the national balances of payments. The fact must be faced that it has become increasingly difficult to find any economic test of efficient specialization.

There are some economists who protest that the notion of national planning upon a rational economic basis is an illusion. Economic theory, as they define it, and the competitive practices which it analyzed justify freedom of economic enterprise within a framework of social legislation, designed to maximize that freedom. Whoever tries to apply that theory to planning practices is bound to agree with Professor Ludwig von Mises that the result of government intervention is planned chaos. In large measure, this argument is a matter of semantics. In the nineteenth-century definition, economics was sharply differentiated from politics. It was a study of the activities of men in their search for wealth, whereas politics was concerned with their activities in seeking power. The science of economics when pursued in abstraction from politics yields a coherent body of logical theorems. These theorems state the relationships of cause and effect in a society whose members desire to produce wealth, unhampered by other motives. The art of political economy, however, must take account of criteria other than wealth. Among those criteria at the present time stability and security rank high.

There has been an increasing tendency to take more account of political and social forces and thus to broaden the basis of discussion. Of this Professor Pigou's significant title, *Wealth and Welfare,* first published in 1912, is an early illustration. The attempt to bring such concepts as welfare, security, opportunity for creative satisfactions, and status in society into consideration makes discussion more realistic, but it meets the difficulty that such concepts are not capable of quantitative measurement. The economic calculus cannot be applied to them with the same appearance of precision that results from its application to the single measurable concept of wealth. Moreover, the search for means of achieving such objectives as economic stability and security has led to group organization within society and this has greatly impaired the mechanisms of the market. It has also overburdened the machinery of government with economic tasks for which it was not designed.

Inevitably the politics of economic questions have assumed greater importance. This may be illustrated from many fields. Attention has already been drawn to the large range of indeterminacy in the fixation of prices and output under conditions of imperfect competition and to the responsibility thus thrown upon those who have power to decide within this range what prices and output shall be. Wherever such indeterminacy is found, the question arises as to who has the power to make decisions, and when power is under consideration, analysis enters the field of politics. There is also a large range of indeterminacy in regard to credit, fiscal, labor, and agricultural policy. The establishment of interest rates and of credit accommodation, of the tax structures, of wage rates, and of agricultural price supporting programs involves a mobilizing of will and a measuring of conflicting power interests. There is increasing recognition that, in this wide field of choice, economic behavior approximates to the strategy of a poker game. International politics aside, this development emphasizes the power struggle between organized economic groups. There appears increasing justification for Bertrand Russell's contention that power rather than wealth is the fundamental concept in social science.

The difficulty is to distinguish the major alignments in the power struggle. Individuals struggle for power within business enterprises, trade unions, and other organized groups. The leaders of these interest groups must maintain their leadership both by internal policies and by their representation of the group interest against that of other groups. These aspects of political conflict within a national economy are more important for an understanding of international economic relations than the divisions of party politics which are often confused by them. Except in a time of crisis they are more significant than the conflicts of international power politics.

Nor is it convincing to identify the positions of national representatives with a dominant group or class in each country. The United States negotiators who press for a recognition of free enterprise in the international trading charter, and for its implementation by tariff reductions, draw their support largely from public-interest groups, and to some extent from sections of organized labor and agriculture, as well as from those sections of business management interested in international markets. But they must always be conscious of the risk of being repudiated by a combination of craft unions, protected agricultural groups, and industrialists fearful of competition in their own markets. It is not easy to convince a particular group, such as the woolgrowers, that the loss they are likely to suffer is so much less than the gain other groups will enjoy that it is in the national interest for them to suffer. Thus the issue is decided not by economic calculations but by political influence. It is not possible to ignore political factors in considering economic policy.

What happens to the territorial division of labor when these political influences are taken into account? It is still an economic fact that specialization upon the forms of production in which each region or country has the greatest comparative advantage will lead to the maximum of world production, and therefore to the abundance which makes possible higher living levels. To ignore this fact is to risk abandoning all the gains from international trade that made possible the economic progress of the nineteenth century. There is much evidence that this retrogression is now taking place. No one can contend that France has any competitive advantage in the production of wheat, or Britain in the production of beet sugar, or the United States in the production of wool and almonds. All over the world, the power of government is being used to channel labor and resources into inefficient lines of production. The reason given is that it is in the national interest to interfere with the competitive economic market in order to achieve such objectives as economic stability or development, preparedness in strategic industries, a balanced diversity of occupations, or full employment.

Nearly everyone would agree that the general public interest should have priority over the profit of individual members of the community. But the crucial question is what constitutes the general public interest. Someone must decide whether the available labor and equipment in Britain shall be induced to dig coal, or be allowed to seek a livelihood in other fields of employment. In that decision account must be taken of the attitudes of the present coal miners and their leaders, of the consumers of coal, of the need for exports and for increased domestic consumption of a great variety of goods and services. Economic calculations must be made, but account must also be taken of the political power of organized groups and of the economic cost likely to be involved in enforcing decisions if some of these groups resist them as detrimental to their interests. Somebody must decide whether the scanty reserves of dollar exchange are to be used to buy cotton, food, steel, tobacco, petroleum, or films, and if steel is imported, whether it shall be allocated to the production of automobiles for export or to some other purpose. How are these priorities to be determined?

Past experience does not give any clear answer to such questions, but some tentative conclusions can be drawn from it. In all countries where representative political democracy prevails a determined minority may exercise political power out of all proportion to its economic weight in the community. Thus when there was a possibility of a tariff concession being negotiated on almonds in a trade agreement with Iran, the almond growers of California went to work. Through other farm groups they mobilized sufficient pressure to pass a resolution through both houses of the state legislature not simply to protest against this concession but asking for the repeal of the Reciprocal Trade Agreements Act. Almonds constituted seven-tenths of one per cent of the value of agricultural production in California, and one-twentieth of one per cent of the national total. Many Californian agricultural industries which had a far larger share of total production before the second World War had important export markets up to 40 per cent of their output. Important concessions had been secured for those industries in foreign markets in several reciprocal trade agreements. Nonetheless, they went along with the almond growers.

Then there is the problem of military security which inevitably ranks high among the elements of national interest. In the confusion of log-rolling and pressures from conflicting interests, it is difficult to calculate the balance of gains secured and losses sustained by different groups. But if a case can be made on grounds of defense or of economic aspects of preparedness, the appeal is strong to legislators and administrators. The armed services constitute a powerful interest group in most countries with access to the highest levels of administrative authority. Especially in times of international tension, if their influence is exerted in support of some economic policy, it is difficult to challenge. One consequence of national economic planning is the increased opportunity for influence which it is likely to afford to the armed services. The experience of many European countries in the interwar years supports this conclusion. The free traders of the nineteenth century were conscious of this connection between state regulation and defense. They identified their cause with that of peace and consistently opposed military and naval expenditures. It is not likely that merchants or economists will be able to ignore defense considerations as long as international conflict remains as obvious as it now is, and there is a danger that the influence of the armed services will increase in many economic fields. Besides the security aspects of atomic energy, their interest in many other fields such as rubber, oil, shipping, strategic minerals, and wool may be cited.

There is thus a temptation for minority group interests to appeal for special treatment on the ground of their importance for military security. Shipping is an important case in point, involving powerful trade-union as well as management interests. International competition in shipping is likely to result in a reduction of the United States mercantile marine. Construction costs in the United States are high. Much of the present shipping which was built during the war is likely very quickly to become obsolescent with other countries now building new and more efficient ships. The main disadvantages of American ships are in high management and port costs, the latter including the costs of labor conflict on the water front. However, recent experience has shown that modern warfare demands large fleet trains to provision the fighting ships, and even larger tonnage to transport men and materials to the theaters of operation and to provision allied peoples. Dockyard facilities are also important for defense. Thus the case for construction and operation subsidies to shipping rests ultimately on grounds of strategic security rather than economic efficiency.

These examples show that political factors make it difficult to formulate national economic policy upon any economic calculation of national interest. There is no statistical or other method by which the gains made and the losses incurred by particular interests may be calculated in terms of stability of employment or any other economic criterion. Decisions must be taken on the basis of judgment as to the importance of particular interests in respect to the criterion selected. The nineteenth-century economists were on surer ground when they rested their analysis upon productivity and were content to judge different forms of productivity by their ability to meet the test of international competition. The extent to which modern practice has departed from this test is indicated by the extraordinary divergence of commodity prices in national markets that now contrasts so sharply with the uniformity of prices in the international markets of the nineteenth century. As long as national governments intervene to protect the interests of different producer groups these disparities will exist and widen. The result is that production is organized in each country less as a result of its comparative economic advantages and more as a reflection of the political power that can be mobilized by different interest groups. The longer this trend continues, the more difficult it becomes to determine what the comparative economic advantages might be if these manifold forms of intervention were stripped away.

In view of the greatly accelerating pace of scientific discovery and its industrial applications, the future is more important than the recent past in calculating the bases of a national policy. But how can the possibilities of future development be estimated? A new form of power is being harnessed. In the course of the next two or three decades atomic energy will be used to supplement the energy derived from the burning of coal, oil and gas, and from falling water. Wherever bulky raw materials whose treatment calls for great quantities of power are located in areas distant from the forms of power now available, the energy released from small amounts of readily transportable fissionable material may cheapen production significantly. The repercussions will be felt in many aspects of production and trade. It will make possible significant changes in the location and structure of particular industries. Steam power, the internal combustion engine, and the harnessing of water power to produce electricity caused great shifts in the location of industry, in transport and communication, in the organization of production and marketing, in the processes of industry and in the nature of marketable products. Certain it is that the harnessing of nuclear energy will bring changes also.

Quite apart from this new form of power, great shifts in production are already well under way. The development of new industrial products and processes as the result of physical, chemical, biochemical, and biological research discoveries is proceeding very rapidly. The application of new methods, devised by chemists and physicists for the study of inanimate nature, to the study of animate nature promises to throw new light on the processes of growth. The vistas of research that are being revealed make it certain that industrial applications of the new knowledge will proceed at an ever more rapid pace. A policy that stereotypes the existing pattern of production is equivalent to contracting out of the possibilities of new methods and the use of new products. Nylon may be cited as an example of such a new product whose use is available as yet to only a small fraction of the world's population and may be withheld from consumers in most countries for a long time if the fabrics offered for sale in those countries continue to be produced from the old materials in order to safeguard employment as it is now organized.

In the past, and particularly in the nineteenth century, the economic map of the world was changed out of recognition by the development of new methods of transport and communication and of new industrial processes and products. The settlement of the temperate grasslands in both hemispheres was followed by an enormous development of tropical agriculture. Trade made the resources thus developed available to raise living standards everywhere. The older industrial countries were enabled to specialize upon the production of goods with which they could buy vastly greater quantities of more varied foodstuffs and raw materials of better quality than they could have produced for themselves. It is important to emphasize this experience. Comparative advantage shifts with scientific progress. Those countries which retain the possibility of flexible adaptation to these shifts are able to ride the tide of change. Those which, for reasons that seem imperative in the short run, pursue policies that hamper their adoption of scientific developments may find themselves caught for a long time in the shallows of lost opportunity. Instability and insecurity are economic evils, but stagnation may be a greater evil.

Few will quarrel with such general statements. A major difficulty in orienting wise national planning, at least in democratic countries, is to develop methods whereby out of the powerful political pressures that are often dominant there can be devised the means of experimental risk-bearing ventures. In the past such ventures have been undertaken mainly by those who have risked and often lost capital especially set aside for the purpose. Authoritarian planning systems do not have as much difficulty as exists in democratic countries in respect to these experimental ventures. It is true that examples may be cited of such ventures of public enterprise even in the United States which is preponderantly committed to the private enterprise system. Such imaginative and inventive experiments are for the most part in the public utility field as was the Tennessee Valley Authority. But it is difficult for a government department to set up a speculative fund, or to withstand criticism of a venture that fails. The private enterprise of the nineteenth century began and abandoned many such white elephants. It is more difficult for government servants to risk such a venture in peacetime. Notable achievements, such as the Panama Canal or the current expenditures upon atomic energy development, have strategic implications. Even the great hydroelectric enterprises, such as those of the Tennessee Valley, the Hoover, Bonneville and Grand Coulee dams, would have been difficult to justify as purely economic enterprises, apart from their conservation aspects.

It would not be too difficult to conceive of speculative enterprise being risked by governments if what was mainly concerned were great public undertakings of this character. However, the application of scientific research to industrial production must usually take the form of developments and adaptations of existing processes, involving the scrapping of plants and the shifts of employment that become obsolescent. Such undertakings require dispersed authority capable of rapid decision rather than the deliberate processes of debate. They call for industrial imagination and courage. This is difficult to visualize in governments subject to audit and sensitive to public criticism in the event of failures.

In the confusion that follows a great war, one may admit the political necessity of accepting the planned or piecemeal intervention of governments. Such intervention has a bias toward self-sufficiency and the avoidance of speculative risks. It is still important, therefore, to restate the principle of international specialization. Labor and resources should be organized to produce goods and services by the most efficient methods and in the most suitable regions. While visiting students may gain a sense of international co-operation and demonstrate it by digging with primitive tools through a Yugoslav hillside to construct a roadbed for a much-needed railroad, this operation is an inefficient expenditure of energy. A couple of bulldozers would be more to the purpose. It is important to provide employment for masses of workers in what might otherwise become depressed areas. It is even more important that the employment shall be productive in the sense of making the most efficient use of the available labor and resources.

This is the case for freer trade. In present circumstances it does not seem possible to those responsible for policy in many countries to allow international competition to furnish the test of efficiency. Nonetheless it is still important to insist upon the desirability of using labor and resources efficiently and to protest against flagrant violations of the principle of competitive specialization. In the absence of international competition, the technical processes of industry may become obsolescent. Even with the most efficient equipment and the best trained managers and workpeople, it cannot be said that an industry is efficient if it must be protected against external competition. A small country, such as New Zealand, may import the most up-to-date construction and industrial machines available for the production of refrigerators and tractors. However, it is impossible that such production to meet the needs of less than two million widely scattered people will be as effective as a comparable effort in the export industries like butter and cheese that produce on a large scale for export markets.

Thus there is a strong case for maintaining the maximum amount of international competition. If competition is restricted in the national interest however defined, the case for such restriction should be subjected to severe scrutiny. It is very easy for privilege, inefficiency and graft to take shelter under its banner. There is great danger in the easy acceptance of policies that limit international competition. If the greatest care is not exercised to safeguard against such tendencies, there will rise again the accumulation of bureaucratic incompetence that called forth the invective of Adam Smith. While the case for international specialization is now difficult to justify upon the logic of the comparative cost principle developed by the Ricardian school, the broader logic of the territorial division of labor remains valid.

Much could be done to safeguard against the dangers of national incompetence by organizing international mechanisms of consultative co-operation. A beginning has been made by the organization of such instruments as the International Monetary Fund, which is essentially a consultative body whose function is to forestall strains on the national balances of payments. The International Trade Organization could become a similar mechanism in the field of commercial policy. This is the main hope of avoiding excesses of economic nationalism in the near future.

However, international organization cannot solve what is essentially an issue of national policies. It can provide a forum in which these policies are discussed and in which their international repercussions are examined. It can pledge, as does the charter of the International Trade Organization, the contracting nation-states to follow the general principles of competitive multilateral trade and to refrain from policies inconsistent with those principles. But there is no power in such organization to prevent the adoption of national policies which conflict with it. Sovereignty rests in the hands of national governments. If they choose or drift without choosing into policies that flaunt economic realities, they will ultimately pay the price of devoting their productive energies to purposes that are not those in which they have a real advantage. The price may seem to be worth paying at the time. Or it may not be recognized in the effort to achieve other objectives. But it will become heavier as time goes by. It may be old-fashioned to insist that the classical economists laid hold of a vital principle when they enunciated the advantages of a territorial division of labor. It is certainly difficult now, in the absence of competitive tests, to clothe the theory of comparative advantage with any realistic and concrete meaning. But truth it remains that a country which ignores the principle that competitive efficiency should determine its economic organization has started down a slippery slope of political uncertainty and economic danger.

The nineteenth century case for freer trade was not made on national grounds. The element of national power was ignored. The cooperative economic advantages of world trade were presented as a practical alternative to the conflict of power politics. The merchants and economists, particularly of England, regarded their case as proven when the vast expansion of trade in the second half of the nineteenth century increased production in the world as a whole. They were content to see each country, and each industry and each individual therein, earn its share of this increased production by competitive efficiency.

The economic case for freer trade still rests upon the elementary truth that production will be increased by specialization. The conditions of modern industry and transport strengthen this case in many important respects. Despite the progress made by industrial chemists in producing synthetic materials, there can be little doubt that scientific discoveries have made the world more, rather than less, interdependent. It can be argued that these new scientific methods of production make possible a greater degree of self-sufficiency at least for big industrial countries. The case for freer trade, however, is a case for potential abundance rather than for a limited self-sufficiency. Improved methods of communication and transport as well as of production make possible the development of trade between remote regions so that the consumers of any country may have at their disposal the products of the whole world. We have not begun to visualize what improvements could be wrought in the living levels of all peoples if production and trade could be organized by modern methods freely and without regard to political boundaries.

CHAPTER XXII

THE GAINS FROM TRADE

NATIONAL INTEREST AND POWER

THE ANSWERS GIVEN by the nineteenth-century economists to questions concerning the gains from trade and their division among the trading countries must now be revised to take account of modern trading conditions which differ radically from the simple conditions of free competition assumed in their analysis. Part of the complication of the economic answer comes from the element of national power which they ignored. Thus the ground must first be cleared in that field.

The industries most vital for national security are those most dependent on international trade, such as the complicated machine industries that must draw their raw materials from widely dispersed sources. Ours is a mineral civilization, and we use up our mineral ores and fuels at a constantly accelerating pace. The older centers of industry have made the greatest inroads on their mineral reserves. Even the United States, which is richly endowed, has drawn heavily upon its reserves of iron ore, petroleum, and other basic minerals. It must reach out into many parts of the world for oil, tin, zinc, and a long list of alloy minerals. Unless peace can be assured by an equilibrium of power, preferably within a system of collectively guaranteed security, a struggle to assure access to essential raw materials could be a potent incentive to the nationalist policies that approximate economic warfare.

National power depends in large measure upon economic productivity. It has many elements—a strategic geographical situation to which must now be added room for maneuver and defense in depth, natural resources, and the size and skills of the population, including leadership. To an increasing extent military power depends upon economic strength. This is true in a double sense. Modern war calls for an elaborate organization of weapons and munitions and for a still more elaborate organization of transport, food, clothing, and engineering equipment in order to sustain military forces in the field and the civilian population in the occupied countries. It is also true that economic resources are potent weapons in the diplomacy of power-politics.

The second World War provided convincing evidence that a national economy could be organized in peace with the primary objective of mobilizing a striking force to overrun an unprepared opponent. The evidence was equally convincing that, given time to mobilize, the nations which in times of peace had devoted their resources to developing a free and flexible economic system could outproduce, outfight, and in the long run overwhelm those whose national economies had been regimented by war preparedness programs. There was little doubt in the years preceding 1939 that German economic policy was governed largely by strategic considerations. The domestic economy was made more self-sufficient. As far as possible essential imports were drawn from neighboring countries which were encouraged, bribed, and bullied into reorganizing their production to fit into the needs of German war preparedness. Substitute raw materials were developed to lessen the national dependence upon imports likely to be cut off in wartime. Roads were built to facilitate the rapid transference of troops. Trade was concentrated upon countries often by giving favorable terms where it was desirable to gain political influence. In the first years of the war these preparations yielded striking successes. But even before the Allied effort had reached its peak, the sacrifices of civilian reserves and scientific training over many years were beginning to weaken the German economy and hence its military potential.

It is evident from the published statistics of the Russian postwar plans, as well as from the successes of the Soviet armies in the second World War, that the economic organization of the U.S.S.R. also is largely governed by strategic considerations. The statistics reveal a high degree of concentration upon the heavy industries that are the indispensable means of producing war equipment. These industries are located as far as possible in areas that minimize their vulnerability to attack. Although the extent of industrial production may have been exaggerated by the methods used in compiling the statistics, it is substantial. On the other hand low levels of consumption indicate that the major production effort has gone into capital equipment rather than into consumer's goods.

Since the war ended in Europe a vigorous attempt has been made to integrate the national economies of the Soviet-occupied territories with that of the U.S.S.R. How successful this attempt may be in the long run it is not yet possible to judge. Yet it is clear that a potentially powerful grouping of peoples extending from mid-Europe across Asia is dominated by a country of large resources whose economy is organized on a basis of war preparedness. It is unnecessary either to exaggerate the efficiency and power of this grouping, or to attribute aggressive designs to the U.S.S.R., to realize that its mere existence poses questions in the field of international economic policy both for the United States and for all the other powers outside the Soviet orbit.

The further element must be added that scientific progress is constantly increasing the destructiveness and the speed of modern warfare. The symbol of these developments is the atom bomb. If another war should develop it may open with a sudden devastating attack at long range. Shock tactics have taken new meaning as the role of machines extends in attacks directed not so much against opposing armies as against the civilian bases of their economic support. The genie is out of the bottle and cannot be put back. The scientific formulae upon which nuclear fission can be developed are no secret. The engineering and mechanical gadgets that go to the production of an atomic bomb will become the property of any nation prepared to put the necessary expenditure of skilled effort into the experiment. The possibility of harnessing the energy liberated by nuclear fission is no longer a matter of dispute. The speed at which practical means may be found of transforming the heat into electrical power, or of using it directly, is still doubtful, and it is clear that for some time to come its use will be supplementary to other forms of power. But new fields of scientific knowledge are constantly being opened up. Industrial applications of this knowledge will follow. The nation that does not keep up with this scientific progress will be at an increasing disadvantage not only in direct military power but also in the economic productivity that is an essential support for that power.

In addition to the primary fact that scientific progress has reduced the protection formerly given by space and time to an economy that neglects defensive precautions, account must be taken of the long-run economic consequences of the scientific revolution now under way. The country which can take fullest advantage of scientific discoveries will gain in wealth and power. If some means were conceivable by which the danger of sudden devastating attack could be eliminated, the case argued by Adam Smith for setting constructive economic enterprise free of restraint would be irresistible. The facts must be accepted that there is no effective defense against paralyzing attack, and that there has been little perceptible progress in international negotiations to segregate the dangerous (war potential) aspects of nuclear fission under the control of an international authority. In these circumstances international economic policy must calculate how trading arrangements will affect national security in such a world.

For the countries that lie between the two great powers, this calculation will vary according to their commitments to one or the other principle of economic organization, and to their expectation of the ultimate success of the two great powers in implementing the principles of their policies. The withdrawal by Poland and Czechoslovakia of their acceptances to the Paris conference on the European Recovery Plan in the summer of 1947 demonstrated how little choice there was for countries in the Soviet zone of occupation. However public opinion in those countries might estimate the national interest, their governments were committed to a policy of collaboration with the U.S.S.R. that limited their participation with the United States in any recovery plans or freer trading initiatives. Unless those governments change, bilateral trading arrangements with the U.S.S.R. must remain the cornerstone of their economic policies.

The increasing dependence of most of the Latin-American republics upon the United States for imports as well as exports gives the latter a preponderant influence in their international economic policies. Even in those countries which assert most strongly their independence —as does Argentina—economic as well as political interest dictates a broad conformity with American policy. It is not so clear that the countries of western Europe are in this position. There is much reluctance on the part of substantial elements of public opinion in those countries to take sides in the power struggle in such a way as to become advanced bastions for either the U.S.S.R. or the United States. In Asia the issue may not seem as urgent, but in the long run it may become even more important than in Europe.

Economic policy is one of the major avenues by which influence may be gained over the countries outside the immediate Soviet and United States zones of influence. It is more important for the United States than for the U.S.S.R. This is because the United States is in a position to offer more economic aid, while it is handicapped by its political structure in pursuing effective policies of propaganda and political infiltration. The U.S.S.R. has convenient instruments of propaganda in the form of strong communist parties in other countries. To combat these directly would involve a degree of interference in the domestic politics of independent peoples that the United States would be reluctant and is ill-equipped to undertake. On the other hand, economic aid might alleviate the poverty which gives to the communist parties their most fertile field for propaganda.

In the long run, there can be little doubt that the organization of the widest possible area of freer trade is in the power interest of the United States. This conclusion follows directly from the nature of modern war. Military force is increasingly dependent upon economic productivity and scientific knowledge. The wider the market and the larger the scale of production, the greater the degree of specialized development that becomes possible. For a big and powerful country, such as the United States, this is a very great advantage. It is an advantage for peacetime prosperity, and even more for war, to have an automobile industry geared to world markets, with large numbers of trained engineers and technicians. This is true of all the industries that can be developed to their fullest efficiency only by large-scale production. Apart altogether from the desirability of preventing other countries in Europe and Asia from falling into the communist form of organization and so becoming advanced bases for the power policies of the U.S.S.R., the industrial development of the United States itself calls for export markets. The need for export markets in turn calls for aid to reconstruct the economies destroyed by war and to develop the countries of backward industry.

It calls also for the acceptance of imports to enable those countries to buy American exports and this entails some disturbance of high-cost American industries. Many of these high-cost industries will demand protection on the ground of their potential contribution to military power. Wherever a case can be made on these grounds—in shipping and shipbuilding, the production of rubber from oil, optical glass, precision instruments, and various chemicals—the most effective means of maintaining minimum facilities capable of rapid expansion is by direct government subsidy rather than by tariffs that hinder the growth of the strong exporting industries.

Stockpiling of essential war materials, particularly the durable materials such as the metals and rubber and to some extent wool, is eminently preferable to a protective tariff as a measure of defense. However, proposals for public action or for subsidizing private action to stockpile strategic raw materials encounter much opposition from domestic interests, coupled with a considerable inertia in official quarters. The same forces operate against an effective conservation policy to preserve intact the remaining reserves of scarce strategic materials, such as tungsten, mercury, and manganese. A vigorous and far-sighted economic policy would import, both for current consumption and for strategic stockpiles, all the durable materials that could be obtained from foreign and especially from potential enemy sources. It would minimize the use of scarce national reserves and develop production in friendly countries to which access could be reasonably assured.

Thus by the test of power-politics the United States stands to gain by promoting over as wide an area as possible the freest economic interchange. In so doing it would encourage the economic development of potential allies in any future conflict. Also it would develop to the maximum its own heavy industries. At the same time it would assure its access to important strategic materials. This would be a policy of enlightened nationalism, aimed at safeguarding the security of the United States by making it the center of a prosperous trading world. It would strengthen the power of all other countries prepared to trade with it on a co-operative basis by competitive principles. For in so doing the United States would identify the prosperity and the security of its trading partners with its own.

In many respects, the argument of the nineteenth-century free traders that abundance is the best guarantee of national security is still valid. To implement this argument in practical policy calls for more decisive action than the mere removal of barriers to trade. Positive action, requiring some measure of government initiative and participation, was found necessary if the western European nations were to cope successfully with the demoralization and distortion of their economic activity. Even more imaginative action is necessary if the newly won independence of the Asiatic countries is to be buttressed by effective organization of productive economic activity. The difficulties and the expense of executing such policies of reconstruction and development are very great. But the stakes in this power conflict are very high. For national security as well as for economic warfare, the United States, its own interest coinciding with that of all the other free countries, is bound to move toward a policy of freer trade.

A footnote needs to be added concerning the alternative. One reason why freer trade is important for the United States is that some choice must be made among domestic industries if a policy of protection is to be continued. The expansion of world trade is consistent with competitive methods. A policy of protection to special interests leads to lobbying and log-rolling and ultimately to government regulation of industry. These political maneuvers were carried to such extraordinary lengths in the framing of the Hawley-Smoot tariff of 1930 as to shock all those who were aware of the scramble for public favors. There was little consideration of the national interest as a whole. It was largely because of the disgust felt for these practices that Congress passed the Reciprocal Trade Agreements Act, 1934, by which the task of tariff revision was delegated to administrative agencies.[1]

The lobbying that is inevitable in the process of tariff-making is now mainly of historical interest. If a wide area of freer trade cannot be created, the methods of trade regulation will be more direct and drastic. There will be import quotas, export subsidies, exchange control. Instead of the tariff reprisals that marked the 1930's, there will be an incessant series of generalized reprisals, leading to complex bilateral bargains, the inevitable end of which is a steadily increasing measure of state control over the conduct of trade. This will involve at first the strengthening of the trade associations that alone have the technical knowledge to handle the detailed regulation. For a time the

[1] For the origins of this important Act, cf. Henry J. Tasca, *The Reciprocal Trade Policy of the United States,* Philadelphia, 1938. The delegation of power was limited to three years. The Act was renewed in 1937, 1940, 1943, and 1945. In 1947 the extensive use made of the delegated powers enabled the United States negotiators to conclude a series of agreements that reduced the tariff very substantially. In June, 1948, the Act was renewed for one year, and in September, 1949, for two more years.

illusion may persist that private industry can maintain its independence behind the shelter of government controls. However, the oft-repeated experience of bilateral quantitative trade restrictions is that they quickly lead to state regulation of domestic production and trade. While on the surface the structure of industry may not appear to change greatly, there ensue subtle shifts in the location of power to make decisions. The industry becomes dependent upon political decisions. In arriving at those decisions government officials are subjected to a variety of pressures—from the organized brokers, the specialized technicians, and the managers rather than from the consumers or stockholders.

There develops a curious combination of inside pressure by essential experts and political regard for organized groups. The organization of economic activity comes to reflect a pattern of political rather than economic power. There have been many recent experiments along these lines. In most the idea of national interest concerned with military force has predominated. In no case has abundance been realized. Always regulations justified by criteria of power, employment, or stability, have led to restrictions of the consumer's choice. More important still they have led to a channeling of activity which is incompatible with the flexibility and resilience that must be developed if scientific invention and economic productivity are to be maximized.

The domestic effects of regulation are of the utmost importance from the viewpoint of power. What we do to ourselves is more important than what we do to our trading partners and rivals in a period of economic warfare. If it is important to create a wide area of freer trade in order to build up a strong group of democratic countries, it is even more important to do so in order to avoid their being drawn into regimentation. Each one of them—including the United States—is most prosperous and most secure when it is freest, politically and economically. Given a two-power world, freer trade would strengthen the military potential of the countries that form the freer-trading area. It would not give assurance of peace. Nor would it provide security against sudden attack by atomic weapons. Nothing can. But freer trade over a wide area would stimulate the kind of economic development that would make the gamble of sudden attack less attractive, since it would enlarge the area from which effective counter-attack might be organized. The economic productivity and scientific progress generated by active trade would expand the economic strength of the United States and its associated countries. It would increase the area of their influence and give them assured access to the raw materials essential for strategic industries.

This is no new idea. Wealth and power have always been the aims of commercial policy. Sometimes they are incompatible. Then a country must choose between gain and security. Normally they run together. This becomes truer as the economic aspects of war loom larger.

DIVIDING THE ECONOMIC GAINS

In a private enterprise society it is not easy to define the national interest in any economic sense. What calculation can be made, for the United States as a whole, of the national economic interest as distinct from the national interest in strategic security? [2] The economic case for tariff concessions is that they are made upon high-cost industries. Thus consumers in America may get cheap Australian wool and consumers in Australia (which has its own automobile industry) may get cheap American automobiles. That there is more economical use of the world's resources and more productivity in the world as a whole, by opening up markets to the most efficient and lowest-cost producers, is incontrovertible in theory. But it is not easy to demonstrate this fact statistically in the case of such a country as the United States. Even if precise calculations could be made to show that what was lost by some local producers was less than was gained by consumers and exporters, the local producers would still clamor for protection and identify the national interest with their own.

On the assumption that competition was allowed to work freely, the classical economists were able to demonstrate quite conclusively that the economic gains from international trade were substantial. Practical experience bore out their theoretical reasoning. The immense increase in productivity which was stimulated by the trading expansion of the latter nineteenth century brought improved living

[2] Cf. Charles A. Beard, *The Idea of National Interest,* New York, 1934, p. 167: "The conception of national interest revealed in the state papers is an aggregate of particularities assembled like eggs in a basket. Markets for agricultural produce were in the national interest; markets for industrial commodities were in the national interest; naval bases, territorial acquisitions for commercial support, an enlarged consular and diplomatic service, an increased navy and merchant marine, and occasional wars were all in the national interest. These contentions were not proved; they were asserted as axioms, apparently regarded as so obvious as to call for no demonstration."

levels to larger numbers of people throughout the trading world. This was true of food, clothing, and shelter. The industrial workers of western Europe were able to buy tropical cereals, such as rice, sago, and tapioca. Even more important the railroads that opened up the Middle West, and other inland plains of both temperate zones, poured cheap grain into Europe. Bread, the symbol of prosperity, was made abundant and cheap. Even the lowest-paid workers could spare some income for the meats that came halfway round the world, for the oils and fats derived from tropical plants, and for the fruits of tropical plantations. Tea, coffee, cocoa, and sugar became plentiful and cheap. Wool and leather, cotton and linen, and even silk were made accessible cheaply to virtually all classes. Lumber from the northern countries, brick and tile, and iron roofing transformed housing facilities. The four-masted ships that sailed to Australia and New Zealand carried Marseilles tiles as ballast and brought back wheat to Europe.

The extent of these gains from trade became more obvious when so many countries were deprived of them by the breakdown of the trading system. To the nineteenth-century free traders it would have seemed incredible that the western European representatives who met at Paris in the summer of 1947 to concert a plan of reconstruction upon the basis of which they might receive economic aid from the United States, should have planned large increases in potato consumption; that England should need to ration tea and bread; that in western Europe as a whole the basic shortage of coal should be the result not of war destruction alone, but of inability to secure pit props, of inadequate food for the miners, of lack of leather to make their boots. No one with any knowledge of European recovery needs, or of the much more desperate needs of Asia, could doubt that measures to restore international trade would bring great gains. The needs in Asia for the simplest articles when the second World War ended were such that every ship leaving San Francisco for Manila carried carloads of cheap glass and crockery, destined for China. These were carried from Manila by Chinese traders who evaded import and exchange controls, and somehow managed to smuggle out of China means of payment that could be turned into dollars. The trade was for cash and the cash was forthcoming at Manila.

Even greater gains accrued in the nineteenth century from the trade in manufactured goods and from investment enterprises. The railroads of the United States, the irrigation projects in India, the

Assuan dam on the Nile, and other examples might be cited. During the nineteenth century the greatest gains derived by the United States from international trade were in the development of its resources. It is worth while to dwell for a moment upon the mutual benefit received in the nineteenth century by Britain and the United States from the rapid development of this trade between them, fostered by the investment of British capital in American enterprises. Britain grew rich not only by exporting manufactured equipment, such as steel rails and locomotives, and by drawing good interest from remunerative investments, but even more by gaining access to vast new supplies of food and raw materials to feed her growing industrial towns. The United States, on the other hand, grew rich by exporting and by borrowing to equip itself rapidly with modern means of production and transportation. As the frontier of settlement moved rapidly westward, the grains and animal products of the Middle Western states, the minerals of the Rocky Mountain states, the gold and later the fruit of California found export outlets largely through Britain. The market was always developing, and as population and income grew in the United States, local consumption accounted for a larger proportion of the goods produced until the United States itself became the most fully developed and productive community in the world. In the twentieth century it was equipped to do for other countries what Britain did for it in the nineteenth, and to earn as Britain did the rewards of high employment, rising wages, and cheapened costs—the essential elements of a continuing improvement in living levels.

The really strong case for freer trade at the present time—one that can be made on grounds of mutual benefit—is the case for the economic development of industrially backward areas. What is envisaged is not only the provision of richer and more varied diets, but also the transference of technical skills to peoples still living on the verge of starvation because their equipment and skills remain those of the wheelbarrow age. The most effective way in which the productive technology of United States industry can be made available to the populations of Asia and Africa—and even in the postwar debacle to those of Europe—is through trade, and through the investment which presupposes trade. This is a challenge to the inventiveness of private enterprise. Means could be found of constructing dams and railroads, of making the tropical jungles habitable, of restoring productivity to the seats of ancient civilizations such as India, Iran, Iraq, Palestine, and Egypt. With the scientific knowledge now available, the mineral wealth of Africa could be made accessible to the whole world and the Africans could achieve living levels more comparable with those of other countries. What was done with cocoa on the Gold Coast could be repeated with other commodities in other areas.

The chief obstacle to abundance is nationalism. Freer trade and interdependence are the alternative to policies of exclusive possession. The choice between these alternatives is tragically illustrated by the destructive conflict between Jews and Arabs that threatens to retard for a generation the possibilities of modern economic development in the Near East. The irrationality of such conflict is in sharp contrast with the imaginative proposal for the creation of an Atomic Development Authority. This suggestion, stemming from the initiative of scientists, was aimed at creating a supra-national rather than an international agency to develop the new form of power for the benefit of the world as a whole. Too much stress has been laid upon the negative aspects of this proposal—that is, the control of weapons utilizing nuclear fission. The imaginative vision that gave to the proposal its appeal, and will cause it to be regarded as a landmark in human history, was the leap to world government on a specific technical issue. If adopted this proposal could allay the fear of aggressive war and liberate all the energies that make for interdependence and hence for progress. These energies could transform the economic structure of the world through trade even more completely and quickly than they did in the nineteenth century.

An Atomic Development Authority would take a non-national view of economic development. It would place the power piles where they could be of most value not for a particular country but for the world as a whole. It need not be concerned with the vested interest of a particular region any more than the United States is concerned with the ghost towns of the former California gold fields. Population could be distributed, production could be developed and trade could be organized on a rational basis. The international secretariats of the League of Nations and of the United Nations caught a glimpse of these possibilities of a world organized sensibly instead of disorganized by jealousies, suspicions, and fears. The case for freer trade is part of the case for rational human behavior freed from the superstitions of national tribalisms.

The fate that befell the Atomic Development Authority is indicative of the difficulties that confront all rational proposals for co-operative international action. It quickly became a subject of suspicion and of striving for national advantage. Calculations of national advantage in negotiating arrangements for freer trade are of the same order. The important point to cling to is that freer trade would bring immense benefits not only to the United States, but to untold millions —benefits in productivity, in relief from burdensome toil and anxiety, in health and vigor and in the possibilities of training the creative skills. Freer trade could be a means of freeing large masses of men and women from degrading want and fear. The first steps toward such objectives are blocked by those who count the immediate costs of adaptation as more important than the chance of participating in a general improvement of well-being. Their attitude is exactly the same as that which prompted craft workers to smash machines in the early stages of the Industrial Revolution. Such fears are always exaggerated. There are always possibilities of adapting operations that seem to be endangered by trading expansion, and a case can always be made for public compensation where real damage is proven.

There is little value in trying to devise accurate measurements of the proportions in which the gains from trade are distributed between countries. Even under the simple conditions assumed by classical and neo-classical theory, there was no possibility of measuring the division of the gains from trade. Economists who have worked on this question echo the conclusion reached by Professor Viner in his minute examination of the theories worked out to measure the gains from trade, that they are ordinarily substantial but cannot be measured in any concrete way. They increase the real income of each of the trading countries unless the distribution of real income is so disturbed as to offset the greater quantity of goods made available by trade. In practice this qualification resolves itself into a question of employment. Freer trade will increase the national real income of all the trading nations unless it causes such an amount of unemployment as to set in motion a secondary spiral of deflation. At the present time when the patterns of national employment have developed independently and are out of equilibrium, this is a real and substantial risk. But this argument is not against freer trade in principle. It is against its sudden introduction without regard for its repercussions in an abnormal situation.

Uncompromising advocates of freer trade, and of private enterprise in general, are apt to brush aside this argument. However, two facts must be remembered. It is easier to rely upon competitive efficiency when there is little doubt of one's own competitive strength. And it is easier for a country which has ample economic reserves to risk a certain degree of temporary disorganization than it is for those countries whose margins are slim. In both respects the United States can afford in its own long-run interest to take risks at the present time. Its position is the same as Britain's when Cobden negotiated the 1860 treaty with France, giving substantial immediate reductions in the British tariff against the promise of future reductions in the French tariff. This promise the *Times* described as an I.O.U. Exactly the same charge was made against the reductions in the United States tariff by the trade agreements negotiated at Geneva in the summer of 1947 against graduated, and sometimes conditional, promises by other countries.

It is possible that the concessions made by the United States may turn out to be more substantial than those it obtained. If this is indeed the case, the greater share of the benefit from any future expansion of trade may accrue to the other countries. But the bargain will clearly be advantageous to the United States as long as it gets any share at all of the gain. Since it had a disproportionate share of the world's gold and continued to draw gold in payment for its exports, and since after the second World War those exports moved at unprecedented levels both absolutely and in relation to its imports, it was clear that the United States had to make larger concessions than its trading partners if the equilibrium of world payments was to be restored. Only after a considerable period will it be possible to estimate whether the trading equilibrium has been restored or whether the United States drove too hard a bargain for its own good.

Those countries whose productive efficiency had not kept pace with that of the United States, whose manufacturing equipment and raw material reserves had been reduced to dangerously low levels, and whose reserves of international assets were slim, were those which had to be careful not to lift their controls of the balance of payments incautiously so as to dislocate the precarious organization of production and employment within their borders. This is no argument for national economic planning. Even those British economists who were most aware of the need for transitional maintenance of controls found difficulty in setting out a convincing method whereby those controls could be made to serve the national interest in peacetime. In general terms it was easy to agree that government must set targets for the national economy. But those targets had to be achieved by the effort of private groups. Effective methods of developing unity of purpose and effectiveness of co-operation were not easy to discover.

It should be noted that the maintenance of controls over the external balance of payments, in order to safeguard against disruptive effects on the national economy in a period of strain, is quite different from the advocacy of such controls in order to extract the maximum advantage from trade. Commercial policy is a clumsy bargaining instrument. Even if, in the flux of trading, the manipulation of quotas and the allocation of exchange could be gauged with any accuracy, it is inconceivable that any country could pursue a policy of extracting the maximum advantage from every bargain without provoking the reprisals which would end, as they did in the 1930's, in a widespread restriction of trade. National struggles to get as large a slice as possible diminish the cake from which the slices are cut. Hereafter something more will be said of these too clever plans for trade manipulation. Here attention should be drawn to the fact that decisions in regard to economic policy are shared between individuals, organized groups, and governments.

The rational economic case for freer trade is a case for general abundance. There is no doubt that productivity would be increased by international specialization. Production, however, is now organized by larger units than those which operated in the nineteenth century. As long as output and prices were determined competitively by individuals and enterprises, no one of them big enough to dominate its market, and all of them forced to conform to the world market, it could be demonstrated mathematically that the gains from trade would be divided according to the intensity of demand within the limits of comparative costs of production. These limits were important. Within each community individuals would specialize upon the production of those commodities in which they had a competitive advantage. The bargaining of the market would determine the prices of those goods within the limits set by costs of production in the trading countries. If any attempt was made to set prices outside those limits either new competitors would appear or production would become unprofitable.

These market conditions have changed. Stress has been laid upon the increasing extent to which corporate organizations operating on a large scale now operate under conditions of imperfect rather than free competition, upon the increasing extent of government intervention, and upon the increasing influence of organized interest groups such as trade unions and trade associations. In a system of imperfect competition and still more in a system of government regulation, organized labor, management, and agricultural groups exercise decisive political pressures. How does all this affect the division of the gains from trade between countries?

The answer to such a question cannot be made in definite quantitative terms derived from statistical calculations. However, the nature of the answer, in so far as business organization is concerned, seems clear. It is—not much. The main outlines of the trading pattern are set clearly enough so that the instances of apparently arbitrary decisions fall within the broad pattern. It is very difficult to see how the monopolistic element in the decisions of a great corporation can affect very seriously the division of the gains from trade. When the Ford Company sets up plants at Antwerp and Copenhagen, the choice of these locations may be governed by a mixture of solid economic advantages and rather vague personal judgments. In the long run the gains from trade are shared between the country of the parent enterprise and those in which the products are consumed in much the same proportions as would be determined under completely competitive conditions. There are other automobiles—American, English, and Continental—and there are other means of transportation as well as alternative methods of expenditure for consumers. The monopolistic element has narrow limits in the general interdependence of economic activity. In not too long a run the business that does not show profit disappears, and the power of management to indulge personal notions or to experiment is severely limited by this fact.

The answer is not so clear in regard to government intervention whether partial or complete. In the case of great business aggregates such as corporations with branches in many countries, or groups of corporations joined by cartel agreements, the amount of trade affected is relatively small in the case of any one enterprise or group and the indirect pressures of competition are very real. No business grouping has yet appeared, except in some rather simply organized colonial areas, where the extent of monopoly has been such as to exercise a strong influence upon the terms of trade of that country. Moreover, a business must make profit. While it can exploit a favorable economic setting, it cannot and it does not try to fight against unfavorable economic factors. It does not try to manufacture for a market so small that the overhead costs become too heavy for profitable organization. It does not attempt to set up an industry in which economic advantages —such as cheap raw materials, low distribution costs, and skilled labor —are lacking. In other words, even the largest businesses conform to the basic economic pressures which operate in a competitive system.

Governments need not so conform. They are able to control the whole of a country's trade and, by manipulation of the credit system, to sustain prolonged industrial experiment within the country. State enterprises need not produce a profit, and they are largely immune from the indirect pressures of competition. Nevertheless the extent to which even a strong government can influence the terms of trade in its favor is very limited. What it *can* do is destroy the trade. One of the chief indictments to be made against government intervention is that positive results within a country are achieved only at great cost within and outside the country. The results are visible, but the costs may be hidden. The greater part of them are paid by the economically stronger groups within the regulating country, rather than by the foreigner.

Thus when the Swiss government in 1931 tried to protect local butter producers from the effects of currency devaluation in Denmark and New Zealand, the main burden fell not on the Danes and the New Zealanders, but upon the Swiss cheesemakers. Many examples could be cited in proof of the fact that government intervention to protect particular industries deemed important for national development has been mainly at the expense of its competitively stronger export industries. The majority statement of the Irish Banking Commission that the burden of industrialization was borne by Irish agricultural exporters parallels the confession of an Australian economist that in his nightmares he saw a sheep astride a precipice with the whole population of Australia clinging to its fleece.

Cases of colonial exploitation are not so rare. Exploitation is easier when economic dominance is backed by political power, but the exploitation is primarily a result of the economic rather than the political situation. Private individuals and companies, operating by competitive methods, have driven hard bargains with economically weak peasant producers in many Asiatic lands. This has happened both in colonies and in weak independent countries. The bargains have often been hardest where there was no government strong enough to restrain individual traders. Exploitation of this type is not a matter of private or government monopoly so much as of disparity in bargaining power.

The monopolistic regulation of trade as practiced by Nazi Germany had very limited success in manipulating the division of the gains from trade, except where the client countries were under military or political pressure. In theory the concentrated purchasing power of a state monopoly will give it some measure of monopsonistic (buying monopoly) control of the market. A large buyer may often squeeze a dependent supplier, but as long as that supplier has alternative outlets there are limits to the extent of the squeeze. The needs of a large buyer, moreover, may be imperative. This was the case with Germany in the prewar and war years. The need for food and raw-material imports was too urgent to allow her negotiators to insist upon the most favorable terms of trade, except where her political position was very strong. Even in the countries occupied during the war, as long as there was strong passive resistance that could not easily be crushed, it was more effective to get the needed supplies by offering favorable trading terms than to exploit the maximum advantage that could have been gained by force. What might have happened had a victorious Germany been able at her leisure to organize a new trading system centered on Berlin is quite a different matter.

Russian military and political dominance over the central and eastern European countries yields evidence that confirms this German experience. In the first months after victory a considerable volume of one-sided trade developed throughout the Russian zone of occupation and in those countries where governments of the Soviet pattern led by Soviet-trained communists had been installed. Wherever the national governments retained some measure of independence, as in Czechoslovakia, Poland, and Yugoslavia, there developed a strong tendency for trade to return to multilateral channels. As this happened the monopolistic buying power of the dominant trading partner was weakened.

The real problem for the small country is to maintain the possibility of alternative markets. As long as trade is multilateral, it can usually gain the maximum advantage in trade with larger markets.

If the small country can shop between at least two markets—as Denmark could before 1939 between Britain and Germany—it can secure favorable trading terms from them, for both exports and imports. It is in the position of the small, compactly organized business dealing with several large corporations. In that situation it can adapt its production and trade to the fluctuating possibilities of profit in the external market. This is not a matter of intervening to change the market or of isolating domestic industry from the effects of external change, but of flexible adaptation so as to profit from the change. A small country which practices a considerable degree of economic intervention or which isolates itself can do much damage to its own national economy without exerting much pressure on world markets while one which keeps itself flexible may profit considerably. The essential condition of successful adaptation is the maintenance of multilateral trading outlets. Bilateral agreements give to a great trading country the possibility in favorable circumstances of squeezing its weaker trading partners.

Thus as long as trade remains multilateral, the division of the gains from trade is not likely to be greatly affected either by corporate or by government monopoly trading. The real risk that is run in a policy of state trading is not so much that the terms of trade will be influenced by a government monopoly, as that there will be reduced trade which will be organized bilaterally. The state trading enterprise can do little to secure a more favorable division of the gains from trade unless it becomes the dominant partner in a bilateral bargain. What it does in striving after a more favorable division of the gains is so to hamper the trade that there are smaller gains to divide. There is nothing in the technology or the organization of modern production methods that even seriously weakens the classical economists' view that the most important objective of policy is to leave trade free to develop so that there may be substantial gains to be shared.

STABILITY OF INCOME AND EMPLOYMENT

A good case can be made for freer trade on grounds of power and abundance. The gains from trade will be greater and their division more equitable if trade is reasonably free. But this case is not convincing to those concerned primarily with economic stability. This raises for consideration the gains from trade as measured by employment and national income.

This test is the crucial one in many respects. While the popular slogan of full employment may be difficult to define, there can be no doubt of its political significance. It symbolizes widespread concern for economic stability, not necessarily as an alternative to but as a condition of abundance. This concern has three main elements. It includes the compassionate care for the welfare of displaced workers that has prompted economists since Adam Smith to justify exceptions to free trade on the ground of humanity. It recognizes the impairment of income distribution that has been noted as capable of nullifying the effects of abundance. And it goes further in its insistence that underemployment of resources will reduce effective demand and may set in motion secondary contractions of national income that will cause losses far outweighing any possible gains from international specialization. Thus it is intimately linked with modern explanations of the business cycle.[3]

The arguments for freer trade on the ground of abundance are cosmopolitan rather than national. They are concerned with long-run tendencies in an open world economy, rather than with short-run considerations in a closed national economy. But economic and political decisions are seldom taken on such long-run grounds. Ordinarily they are governed by immediate expectations of local gains. The general good has little appeal to a businessman whose investment is threatened by foreign competition, or to a worker who clings to his present employment because he must find food for his family next week. The gains from international specialization are regarded dimly by those whose interests must be sacrificed if such specialization is to develop. The most resistant obstacles to freer trade are rooted in a fear of cheap imports causing unemployment and loss to established interests. This fear is very great and in large measure is a fear of the unknown. The craft gilds and the gilds merchant long fought against national unification with its corollary of free trade within the national economy. There is no progress without some destruction of vested interests.

At a time like the present when economic relations are out of joint,

[3] Cf. Ragnar Nurkse, "Domestic and International Equilibrium," in Seymour E. Harris (ed.), *The New Economics*, New York, Alfred A. Knopf, 1947, p. 264: "It [The Keynesian approach] furnished at one and the same time an explanation of two related matters: (a) the adjustment process of the balance of payments and (b) the international transmission of fluctuations in economic activity and employment. The result has been a quite fruitful marriage of two subjects that previously led quite separate existences under the conventional names of international trade theory and business cycle theory."

the fear of international competition is enhanced and greater than the usual stress is laid on stability and security. No one can foresee what shifts in the location of industry and in production costs might result from freeing the channels of international trade. Currencies are still being revalued. The competitive efficiency of wartime developments has yet to be tested. In transport and communication, as well as in methods of production, a great scientific revolution is well under way. This is bound in the long run to bring about a new pattern of international specialization. Experience in somewhat similar periods of rapid and fundamental economic change suggests that those countries which anticipate and conform to this new pattern will gain a long lead over those which resist adaptation. The costs of adaptation always loom large in such a confused and uncertain situation. Without freer international trade it is not possible to test the potential gains and estimate these costs. And there is in most countries, and among important economic groups, a great reluctance to give up the controls of external trade behind which existing employment has developed and sheltered.

In theory full employment is consistent with freer trade. All advocates of national economic planning for full employment argue that the maintenance of high levels of demand will be reflected in large imports as well as in high domestic production. This is obviously true. The experience of the United States in recent years demonstrates the correlation between domestic prosperity and large imports. There is little dissent from the proposition that the most important contribution any country can make to international trade is to maintain its own prosperity at a high and stable level. This is particularly true for the great industrial countries. Their major imports are industrial raw materials the volume of which varies with the national income and the level of employment. It is of immense importance to the rest of the world that these imports be maintained at a high level. The country in which reasonably full employment is most necessary, if freer international trade is to be organized, is the United States.

However, it does not carry us very far to argue that if all trading countries maintained high levels of employment, trade would move more freely and it would be easier to get rid of trade barriers. In the flux of trade and particularly in its reopening after the disturbance of trading channels caused by a great war, it is improbable that full employment can be continuously maintained in all countries while competition is rearranging the pattern of international specialization. The assumption of doctrinaire advocates of freer trade is that in the long run it brings full employment. That of many modern economists is that in the same long run, full employment will bring freer trade. The main attack made by these modern theorists upon the argument for freer trade is that it ignores the unemployment caused in the short run by national adjustments to a constantly shifting pattern of international specialization. This charge can be reversed. Modern advocates of full employment policies only too often belittle the damage to international trade that is necessary if a country is to maintain itself in a continuous state of full employment.

While these policy objectives are not contradictory in the theoretical long run, they often do conflict in the practical short run. The practical problem for policy makers is to determine how much employment can be maintained with freer trade, or in reverse how much trade can be developed without causing undue unemployment. If policy adheres rigidly to either free trade or full employment as an article of faith, the other is likely to be sacrificed in a succession of short-run decisions. The only condition upon which both may ultimately be achieved is a reasonable flexibility which gives the greatest volume of trade at the least cost in employment. In practice this means either elaborate stabilization processes to regulate the external balance—processes which are difficult to administer without their degenerating into trade restriction—or acceptance of the necessity to adjust national incomes and employment to the shifting pressures of the international balance of payments. On the other hand, there must be readiness to devalue the national currency or to impose emergency import restrictions to prevent an adverse balance of payments inducing drastic deflation and widespread unemployment.

The doctrinaire free trader stands ready to plunge his country into severe depression rather than depreciate its currency or restrict its imports. The doctrinaire employment theorist stands ready to see his country sacrifice the advantages of international specialization rather than allow competition to reorganize the national economy consistently with its international trade position. This is another aspect of the many-sided conflict between energy and organization—a conflict that is real in the short run and unreal in the long run.[4]

[4] See Chapter XVII, "National Economic Policies."

What is called for is antagonistic co-operation—the reconciliation of complementary and co-ordinate objectives. Only the frustration of both, and disaster, can result if one objective is pursued to the exclusion of the other.

Consider the case of a small country which embarks upon a policy of full employment. Any such country that is socially and politically advanced to the point where full employment becomes a possible objective of policy is likely to have a relatively large volume of foreign trade. Its exports are likely to be specialized and directed to a few dominant markets. Its imports will be more varied and drawn from a somewhat wider area. This means that the country will have close international economic relations, particularly with its major markets. Stability of exchange and price relations with these markets will be of great importance. Therefore this small country will be sensitive to the fluctuations of income and of commodity prices in those markets. Most of the highly developed small countries have demonstrated that advanced social-security legislation is not incompatible both with high productivity and with a high degree of international specialization and dependence. Various forms of insurance and pension legislation now safeguard the individual against the consequences of economic misfortune beyond his or her individual control—against accident, invalidity, old age, widowhood, orphanhood, and unemployment. It is proposed to add to these social-security services provision for the maintenance of full employment.

In practice this means that the government must spend from taxation or credit creation, in order to provide employment whenever private industry proves incapable of providing jobs at current wages for all who are willing to work. If the expenditure is financed from taxation this amounts to a redistribution of income within the community. If it is financed by credit creation, the levels of income and—unless controls are imposed—the levels of prices will rise. This increased income will generate a demand for increased imports. If the unemployment has been caused by domestic reasons, this will mean only that imports are restored to their former levels. However, if the unemployment is a reaction to a fall in export receipts—and this is more often the case—the increased imports will then cause a strain on the balance of payments.

In the case where a small country suffers a loss of export receipts, ability to maintain national income at a level compatible with full employment depends upon the imposition of import restrictions. This is recognized by the exponents of full-employment theories. For a time the small country may bridge the gap in its balance of payments by drawing upon its liquid reserves of gold and foreign assets. In the future it may call, in such an emergency, upon the pool of foreign assets set up in the International Monetary Fund. But the limits of such emergency financing are very narrow. The next step it may take is to devalue its currency. This will tend to increase the sales of its exports and will also give to exporters a greater amount of local currency for a given sum of foreign currency. Devaluation will at the same time decrease imports by making them more expensive in local currency. This procedure, however, is apt to start a chain of reprisals.

In the depression of 1931 Australia, after losing gold and running down its sterling assets, devalued its currency by 20 per cent. It was not long before New Zealand followed suit and Denmark followed New Zealand. There was some relief to the important exporting groups in each country, which amounted in fact to a redistribution of income within the country. What pulled Australia out of the depression was a balanced combination of deflationary and inflationary measures within the country—wages and interest reductions combined with new credit issued by the Commonwealth Bank. It may be doubted whether even this well-planned and thoroughly publicized application of economic statesmanship could have been as successful as it was, if the strain on Australia's balance of payments had not been relieved by the depreciation of sterling and the subsequent debt reconversion and expansionist policies in her main export market.

There are few countries capable of executing the sophisticated economic policies advocated by the exponents of full employment theories. It has been argued that a single country can always pursue a policy of domestic expansion even when there is widespread depression and unemployment in other countries. This may be true in economic theory. But it is difficult to envisage China or India doing so, or even to assume that such countries in their present stage of development would be interested in the idea of full employment. Full employment is an industrial idea important only to countries with highly organized credit systems. These are the major industrial areas, such as the United States, the U.S.S.R., Germany, Britain, and

France. They also include many other countries—the secondary industrial countries of western Europe, the British Dominions, and some of the more advanced Latin-American countries—whose autonomy in respect of monetary policy is severely limited by the extent of their dependence upon export markets.

Full-employment policy may be discussed in three forms. The first is that all the major trading countries pursue full-employment policies, whether independently or by agreement. All maintain aggregate demand, and hence their demands for imported goods, at levels which make possible full employment in all countries without imposing strain on the balances of payments. This is the most desirable situation that can be envisaged. The situation of the United States is crucial, because it is the greatest industrial country and the greatest importer of raw materials. If its industrial activity were sharply reduced in a major depression, so that its demand for imports declined heavily, those countries where employment now depends in large measure upon the United States' demand for their exports would have to accept a large degree of unemployment or cut themselves off completely, as has Russia, from international trade. In the same way but in less degree, the failure of any other industrial country to maintain full employment would entail strain upon its trading partners.

There would be less concern about employment and less reluctance in other countries to remove import and exchange controls, if reasonable assurance could be felt that the United States would not allow a major depression to develop. It is constitutionally difficult if not impossible for the United States to enter into a binding agreement to maintain full employment.[5] But it is evident that the development of employment policy in the United States will be watched with anxiety abroad. The U.S.S.R., which ranks next to the United States as an industrial country, is not a factor in this situation, since it pursues a unilateral policy of full employment and its import demands are so small that they do not much affect the level of employment in other countries.

Some economists realize that there is no assurance that the United States can commit itself to international agreement to pursue full-employment policies, and lack confidence in the ability of private enterprise to control the national economy so that a major depression may be avoided. They have therefore been interested to explore a second

5 See Chapter XIX, "The Assumptions of a Modern Theory."

form of full-employment policy. This is the possibility that a more limited regional group of countries might form a multilateral trading area, mutually pledged to follow full-employment policies and to protect themselves against other countries—notably the United States —exporting their unemployment in a great depression. Such a notion appeals to some British economists who visualize Britain as the center of such a multilateral system. However, the risks and disadvantages of such an experiment for Great Britain are considerable. Its pattern of employment is the result of past developments in which Britain was the center of a world trading system, and more than any other country Britain remains dependent upon widely dispersed export markets and almost equally widely dispersed sources of imported food and raw materials. It would be difficult to organize the main British export outlets and sources of imports into a multilateral trading system pledged in a crisis to restrict imports from the United States.

The third, and this is the most limited possibility of full-employment policies, is that presented by independent national action. As the example of the U.S.S.R. demonstrates, it is possible to maintain full employment in one country, but only at the cost of sacrificing external trade connections. Should this alternative be followed by any appreciable number of countries, the regulations restricting imports would multiply and change so rapidly as to destroy any hope of rebuilding freer multilateral trade.

It is tempting to begin the theoretical analysis of full-employment policies upon the assumption that, to begin with, all national economies are in equilibrium at full employment. Equilibrium is defined as a balance of in- and out-payments without need either to deflate the national economy or to restrict imports. Starting from this ideal condition, the different causes of possible disequilibrium may then be examined, and it is not difficult to demonstrate that full employment can be maintained without disturbing the reasonably free flow of trade. If depression conditions develop within any country, they may be corrected by cheapening and expanding credit, and by government expenditures to provide employment. This will maintain import demands instead of forcing their restriction, and prevent the cheapening of exports which in effect amounts to exporting the country's unemployment and setting up an international chain of deflationary influences. If a country maintaining full employment is threatened with a surplus of imports by reason of depression conditions elsewhere, it may restrict imports to the customary level.

A more realistic assumption to make at present is that national economies are in disequilibrium at full employment. All are fully employed, but with few exceptions they have severe balance of payments difficulties. Save in few countries in- and out-payments cannot be balanced without a strict regulation of imports. Most of the important countries desirous of maintaining full-employment policies have already used up practically all their foreign assets and are able to finance their present regulated imports only by large loans and gifts from the United States. Therefore, the question to be answered is not how to maintain equilibrium at full employment. It is how to get back to some measure of equilibrium without causing widespread unemployment. In a very real sense most of the countries which are now at full employment have already exhausted all the theoretical possibilities of maintaining their international equilibrium. All of the countries with balance of payments difficulties have had severe budgetary difficulties. They have parted with their liquid reserves and have imposed exchange control, import quotas, and all the apparatus of quantitative import restriction.

This has been done already while external conditions are favorable. The United States and all the other industrial countries have high levels of national income. Therefore they have very high aggregate demand and import demands to correspond. This remained true, even though the mild recession in the United States during 1949 caused a fall in imports that was disconcerting particularly to the sterling area. Both for raw-material producers, such as the Latin-American countries and the British Dominions, and for such countries as Britain, which export mainly manufactured goods, export receipts are at high levels, but import restrictions are still necessary. Full employment is maintained at wage levels that could not be maintained if the balance of payments was not controlled. These national economies are like ships in full sail before a favorable wind, carrying every stitch of canvas that can be bent. If in a depression export receipts should drop sharply, much severer import restrictions would be necessary to keep the balance of payments in equilibrium. The theoretical analysis of full employment which starts from the assumption that national economies are in equilibrium at full employment explains what has happened up to the present. The question now arises, where do we go from here?

Part of the answer to this question lies in the steps being taken to reconstitute the export capacities of the countries whose balance of payments is adverse and to open wider export markets to them. The European Recovery Plan, including a considerable measure of continued material assistance from the United States but depending mainly upon the effort of the European countries themselves, will increase export capacity and reduce import needs. The trade agreements negotiated at Geneva in 1947 will open markets in the United States and elsewhere for that increased export capacity, and will also open wider markets for United States exports. These aspects of a general recovery program are interdependent. There can be no restoration of multilateral trade unless the capacity of the countries hardest hit by the war is restored. This involves not only a very considerable effort of self-help, but also the provision of strategic aid—food to improve diets and to make extra effort possible, equipment to restore key industries, and materials to restock inventories. Conversely the increased productivity will not be effective in solving balance of payments difficulties unless exports can be marketed. The reduction of trade barriers negotiated at Geneva will take time to become effective, since the hardest-hit countries will have to rebuild their export capacity and existing bilateral contracts will continue to channel trade to former markets.

Another part of the answer lies in realignment of the exchange rates. During the summer of 1949, it became evident that the fundamental disequilibrium in the international balances of payments could not be righted without a depreciation of most other currencies against the dollar. The opportunity for widespread devaluation when the International Monetary Fund fixed currency parities in December, 1946, had been missed. It could be argued that, so soon after the war, it was premature to fix new exchange rates. The Fund accepted the rates that had been operative. These were maintained only by rigid exchange controls. Despite national and international recovery efforts, the trade controls which continued to constrict trade within bilateral channels continued to tighten. The most obvious result of this bilateral balancing was the difficulty which Britain (and most other countries) found in closing what became known as the "dollar gap." This was not the only gap in the circuit of payments. There were shortages of Swiss francs and other hard currencies, and also of sterling and other soft currencies in many countries. The dollar scarcity was only one aspect of the failure to restore multilateral trade and payments. It was not possible to balance payments bilaterally without provoking a succession of financial crises.

In July and August, 1949, it became clear that the sterling area was facing an unusually severe crisis. Despite a substantial gain in national production and an increase of British exports amounting to 50 per cent above prewar, the drain on the gold reserves of the Bank of England was increasing. Production was going into domestic consumption, exports were going to Dominion and other sterling area countries rather than to the dollar area from which imports were badly needed. Sterling prices were too high except for buyers whose currencies were equally overvalued—who in any case had no option but to buy in sterling since they did not have dollars. The United States recession had reduced the American demand for such imports as rubber and tin, and this had aggravated the drain on the gold reserves. With the imminent prospect that this drain would force devaluation, orders for British exports dwindled. Speculation reinforced the pressure. Meantime imports had to be paid for. The decision to devalue was forced by these developments. Anglo-American-Canadian conversations in early September resulted in a series of arrangements to relieve the strain on the British balance of payments. The annual meeting of the International Monetary Fund gave an opportunity to clear the arrangements. On September 18, 1949, almost exactly eighteen years after the previous devaluation in 1931, the Chancellor of the Exchequer announced that sterling would be devalued by 30.5 per cent, the dollar value being reduced from $4.03 to $2.80, and the sterling price of gold being raised proportionately.

Simultaneously, or within a few days, a large number of other currencies were devalued. With the exception of Canada and Pakistan, the British Dominions—Australia, New Zealand, South Africa, India, Ceylon, and Southern Rhodesia—devalued with sterling. Australia whose rate had been 20 per cent below sterling did not take the opportunity to regain full parity. Canada, caught between the United States and Britain, devalued only by 9.1 per cent. All the non-self-governing British colonies followed sterling also. The same course was followed by Denmark, Egypt, Iceland, Iraq, Luxembourg, the Netherlands and Indonesia, Norway, Finland, Burma, Eire, Sweden, West Germany, and Hashemite Jordan.

There were some variants from this pattern. Belgium devalued only by 12.3 per cent. France (and her colonies) took the occasion to bring her multiple rates into a greater measure of uniformity, with the official rate falling by 22 per cent. Israel devalued only by 7 per cent, Italy by 11.5 per cent, Portugal by 13 per cent, and Thailand by 20 per cent. Greece, however, devalued by 33.3 per cent. Switzerland did not devalue but took the opportunity to bring the high exchange rate on financial, as distinct from commercial, transactions to parity again with the dollar.

Further devaluations were inevitable. Argentina announced on October 3 that the free peso rate would be devalued by 46 per cent, but that an elaborate sliding scale of rates would be set for particular import and export products. Not all the rates were announced, but for such exports as wool, edible oils, hides and quebracho extract, which were mainly exported to the United States, the devaluation was slight. British meat prices were unaffected. The effect of these complicated arrangements was to strengthen the detailed control exercised by the Argentine government over the terms of bilateral agreements for the sale of specific products. There was general expectation that Uruguay and other Latin-American countries would be forced to adjust their exchange rates also.

Broadly speaking, these events could be summed up as a world-wide depreciation of currencies against the dollar and the Swiss franc. Some minor currencies remained unaffected, at least for the time being, but the net effect of the changes was that exports from the United States were more costly in most currencies, while payments in those currencies were cheapened. The extent to which these exchange adjustments would be reflected in the prices of goods entering into international trade could not readily be estimated. It would take time for the adjustments to settle down. The expectation that all British goods sold in the United States would fall by 30 per cent was naïve. The wholesale price landed in the United States might fall, provided costs of production, including wages, did not rise in Britain, and providing also that the exporters did not conclude that demand was inelastic and could not be expanded by lowering dollar prices. The exporters of Scotch whisky and Canadian newsprint, for example, had maintained their dollar prices. Costs payable in dollars, including import duties, freight, advertising, and distribution costs, formed a substantial part of retail prices and these remained unchanged. It was possible that there might be a substantial increase of imports, less from Britain and western Europe than from the Dominions and colonies. Such materials as wool, rubber, jute, coir, possibly oil, would be sharply competitive with United States production. The more serious effect on United States production and prices would be felt on the export side, particularly by agricultural exports such as wheat, cotton, tobacco, lard, and dried fruits, but also by some manufactured exports.

Trade would be forced into multilateral channels to the extent that devaluation was not counteracted by inflationary pressures. Since the price of United States imports would rise in sterling (by 44 per cent), Britain would seek alternative import sources. At the same time, more export pressure would be directed to the high-priced dollar markets and away from soft-currency markets, not only by British exporters but by those of most other countries. If this redirection of trade led quickly to a loosening of quota restrictions, exchange controls, and bilateral purchase agreements, there would be substantial progress toward equilibrium in the international balances of payments. Encouraging steps had been taken toward the loosening of such restrictions in the trade between western European countries, including Britain; but the most important step to be taken was in the relaxation and gradual abandonment of bilateral bulk purchase agreements. The Argentinian action served notice that such relaxation would be opposed; but without it multilateral trade could not be restored. Unless it was restored, the devaluation would not solve the disequilibrium in the balance of payments.

It should be noted that devaluation aims at securing equilibrium, not by creating unemployment, but by reducing real wages and living levels. Living costs will rise and imports from the dollar area will be reduced. An attempt will be made to hold wages and profits at or near present levels. The costs of adaptation have been spread over the whole economy. But flexibility in this adaptation is also necessary. The effects of devaluation undertaken at full employment are quite different from those when unemployment is rife. It is not possible suddenly to increase production. Exports must be diverted from old to new markets, which necessitates changes in the industrial structure. This involves accepting some measure of transitional unemployment when workers must be shifted out of shrinking industries. Everyone accepts the inevitability of seasonal unemployment and no one expects painters to be regularly employed during the winter. The unemployment which results from adapting the structure of national industry to international trading competition must be accepted also—if there is to be any world trading system.

One unfortunate result of using such methods of government intervention as import restriction, price supports, and increased public expenditures, to avert passing and sectional forms of transitional unemployment, is that they are not then available to stave off a major depression. If called into use prematurely or too often they lose much of their potency. When a major depression begins to develop, the national economy needs a shot in the arm. Great public works can be launched. Industrial programs by great corporations, which are in the nature of public works, can be carried out to take up the slack of employment. Government can reduce taxes, and monetary authorities can make credit cheaper and more readily available. Bold and vigorous action of this kind previously concerted could go far to stave off such a general collapse as overtook the national economies in 1929–33. But such a program cannot be executed successfully if the reserves of government and business have already been frittered away in dispersed efforts to prevent minor unemployment in consequence of structural adaptations of the economy to the restoration of equilibrium in the balance of payments.

Together with national power and abundance stability of employment is a third co-ordinate objective of policy. It may sometimes be necessary in the interest of power to forgo the undeniable advantages of international specialization and freer trade. This may be the case also in regard to employment. Rather than plunge the economy into severe deflation, it is better to depreciate the exchange rate or restrict imports. However, the country which in peacetime can develop free and flexible enterprise serving a world, or at least a large international market, will have more power to mobilize in a war emergency. In the same way, such a country will not only attain higher living levels but will have a better chance of combating large-scale unemployment, if it keeps the powerful weapons of fiscal policy, exchange depreciation and import restriction in reserve against a really serious emergency than if it discharges them prematurely in a vain effort to avoid adapting itself to its international market needs. Otherwise, it will come to the emergency with no alternative but to tighten already imposed restrictions to the point where they sacrifice the advantages of international specialization. Full employment is not the alpha and omega of policy. It would be relatively easy to devise means by which everybody was fully and in the long run compulsorily employed and working harder for lower living levels. Real income levels are the more significant test of prosperity—not employment.

There is a growing consensus among economists that the free-trade doctrine based upon the tacit assumption of full employment ignores very real problems and that the extreme statement of the case for full employment ignores the risks involved in interference with multilateral trade. Discussion of these questions indicates the emergence of a middle ground. There is no predetermined formula for economic statesmanship in this field. Success in securing the long-run benefits of international specialization without inflicting severe short-run dislocations of employment on the national economies of the trading nations will be achieved, if at all, by consultative co-operation rather than by adherence to formulae or to institutional mechanisms.

Timing is always an important element in policy. Judgment in this respect and in regard to the weight to be attached to different factors in a complex situation is often more important than refined theoretical analysis. In dealing with large economic aggregates and with mass psychological reactions, considerable leeway must be allowed for administrative discretion. Since the governing decisions of economic policy must be prepared by consultative discussion over a long period and must then be given time to take effect, such decisions cannot safely deal with detail. Thus there is need for the framework of agreed principles and for the machinery to focus consultative co-operation that the specialized agencies of the United Nations were designed to provide.

ENVOY

THE THEME of this book has been that throughout recorded history new forms of trading have disturbed the established political order. Through all the groupings and regroupings of peoples, the shifts in power and the development of political ideas, the trader has woven and rewoven his web of international economic integration. This tendency toward integration has often been thwarted. The economic unity of the trading world has been broken at times as it was in the Dark Ages, when western Europe was cut off from contact with the more developed civilizations of Asia. Every stage in the economic expansion of Europe was connected with attempts to reopen the channels of trade with Asia. Again new forms of political power have sometimes destroyed the old economic order. More often the old order has mobilized its political strength to restrain new trading ventures. Yet the integrating tendency has persisted.

Once again the pattern of international relations is being rewoven. In this reweaving there will be fundamental changes of political and economic institutions. The main reason for the present confusion in the world is the collapse of western European leadership. The hegemony that western Europe had exercised over world economics and politics since the sixteenth century came to an end in 1914. After two destructive phases of this conflict, the countries of western Europe must themselves receive help to reorganize their institutions. They are torn by discords, which are reflected in the weakness of their moderating social groups and the increased strength of their extreme parties. But these discords echo more than the passing disruptions caused by two world wars. The fact is that the European system of world economic development has collapsed. Western Europe no longer holds the gorgeous East in fee. The western European countries have been living beyond their means. For more than a generation their living standards have been maintained and their international payments have been balanced by the sacrifice of past capital investment and by their receipt of loans and gifts.

The long succession of loans and gifts has come largely from the United States. There were the loans of the first World War and reconstruction period, the heavy outflow of commercial loans from 1925 to 1929, and, since the second World War, lend-lease, military occupation costs, relief and rehabilitation grants, loans from the Export-Import Bank and the Treasury, and more recently loans and grants from the Economic Cooperation Administration. The international institutions—the International Bank and the International Monetary Fund—have also acted as a channel through which dollars have flowed to Europe. A conservative estimate of the total net outflow of credit from the United States to Europe since the first World War would come close to $75 billion. Most of this lending was political rather than economic in character. A good case can be made for most of it. But, however good the case, such a credit flow was not likely to go on indefinitely. Whenever it stopped, as it did in 1929, the result was severe depression, unemployment, and lowered living levels. By far the larger part of the credit has been used to enable Europe to continue consuming more than it produced rather than to increase its productivity. Most of it is now written off or in default. No criticism is implied in these statements. Rather they are statements of fact. They are intended to point out the necessity to reorganize rather than to restore economic activity in the modern world.

Since the second World War ended in 1945, not only western Europe but most of the rest of the world has been dependent upon a continuing flow of foodstuffs, raw materials, and capital equipment supplied on credit by the United States and other New World countries. The statistics of world trade in 1947 told a melancholy story. Of the eighty-two countries for which statistics were available, all but sixteen were importing more than they exported. The United States accounted for more than 85 per cent of the total value of the export surpluses—its excess of exports over imports being $8,823 million. The countries next in line were Argentina with a surplus of $327 million, and Australia with $236 million. In 1948, out of 71 countries only 17 had active export balances. It is true that these figures record only commodity trade, so that they cannot be taken as an accurate picture of the world's balances of payments. However, there was no doubt that by far the larger part of the world was running into debt on current trading account, mostly to the United States.

Two broad conclusions may be drawn. First, the situation in the latter half of 1948, as the European Recovery Plan swung into active operation, bore an ominous resemblance to that in 1925, when the commercial flow of loans from the United States ushered in a few years of reconstruction and recovery. However, there was still time for the Economic Cooperation Administration to demonstrate that economic activity could this time be reorganized with such aid along lines that would enable the European countries to maintain their living levels without the need for subsidies by way of loan or gift. Necessarily, its first transactions had mainly taken the form of grants to sustain consumption levels, but the European economy had to be reorganized if it was to fit into the changed postwar world. Most European countries were producing more in 1948 than they had produced in 1938, but population had increased in the meantime. The recovery was uneven. The 1948 harvests were good but agriculture still lagged behind industry. Moreover, it was necessary not only to increase production, but to export a greater part of that production. There was real danger that the experience of high costs and shrinking markets which cramped exports from most European countries after 1925 might be repeated. Costs were high and creeping higher. As early as 1948 there was discussion in Britain of "frustrated exports," that is, goods produced for export under a national plan for which no markets had been found.

It was inevitable that the European balances of payment would come under heavier strain when the years of grace expired before interest and repayment fell due on the succession of loans. The strain would become cumulative as the scheduled payments increased. It was too soon to tell whether the United States would continue to make credit available over this period of strain. Though its price structure was creaking and there was in prospect a succession of price readjustments beginning with farm prices, national income and employment were at high levels and seemed likely to be substantially maintained as long as the international lending program continued on or about the present level. Therefore, it was probable that a few short years remained in which preparations might be made to face the necessary readjustments as the loan flow tapered off.

The second conclusion to be drawn from current trade statistics became more important. It was that a greater effort of constructive imagination than had yet been made was necessary to reorganize the free multilateral clearing of payments on account of world trade. Negotiations had been going on since 1945 to create an International Trade Organization but they had not been brought to a successful conclusion. It was true that, for 23 countries conducting about 70 per cent of the current value of world trade, the *General Agreement on Tariffs and Trade* negotiated in 1947 at Geneva had reduced tariffs and had set forth a basis of agreed principles for the conduct of multilateral trade. The tariff reductions had gone into effect but the agreement on trading principles was academic as long as quotas, exchange control, bilateral purchase agreements and the other instruments of quantitative trade regulation retained their validity and effect.

Even if this *General Agreement* could be brought fully into operation, its regional scope was limited. Twenty-three countries did not suffice to restore world trade. There were essential links in the chain of multilateral payments that lay outside the control of these twenty-three countries. Was it enough to restore production in Europe? The United States program of aid to Europe had been conceived in terms of military strategy. It is a cardinal principle of such strategy to concentrate force upon major objectives, even if such concentration must accept the calculated risk of an exposed flank. It is very doubtful whether this principle can safely be applied to the co-operative tasks of economic reconstruction. It may prove a fatal error to neglect any important segment of the payments mechanism.

Eastern and southeastern Asia was such a segment. Without exception the balance of payments of every Far Eastern country had deteriorated between 1938 and 1948. Though in most of these countries the higher postwar prices were reflected in increased export values, imports had increased more than exports. There were substantial increases of export values in the firmly administered colonial areas, Hong Kong and Malaya, and also in the independent areas of relative stability, Ceylon, India, the Philippines, and Siam. During the war there had been a considerable repayment of external debt, especially in India, but imports from the dollar area had to be restricted to avoid creating new debt. After the first World War, Japan and the Netherlands Indies had been the largest exporting countries in the Far East, but their exports are now reduced and their balances of payments are adverse. In 1938 the Netherlands Indies had an export surplus of $101 million. In 1947 there was an import surplus of $155 million, even though imports had fallen by 30 per cent in the meantime.

The collapse of empire in Asia constituted the Achilles heel in any attempt to restore western Europe and to rebuild a world trading system patterned on the nineteenth-century model. The political and economic situation there was a challenge to devise new forms of trade and investment, rather than to revive the pattern of the past. The notion that the United States could do in the twentieth century what Britain did in the nineteenth contained a large element of truth. There were many parallels between the economic position of the United States and that held by Britain when the machine processes of the Industrial Revolution gave her technical and economic leadership. The United States was impelled, as Britain was then, to lead in the development of world trade and investment. But the strength of nationalist sentiment was now such that trade could be revived only by dovetailing it with national aspirations. It was an illusion to believe that the leaders of the illiterate and poverty-stricken masses—in eastern Europe, the Near East, and Africa, as well as in Asia—would accept any attempt to reorganize trade and investment along nineteenth-century lines. For many centuries the economic life of the world had been dominated by the aggressive efficiency of western Europe and its offshoots overseas, but this dominance was already challenged. And it would meet with further challenge.

European capitalism had had long innings in such countries as India, Indonesia, Burma, and Indo-China, and the inhabitants of these countries were not prepossessed in its favor. There was a stirring of social discontent which gave vitality to nationalist movements in those countries. The leaders of those movements have been repelled by the Soviet disregard of civil liberties. But they have been impressed by the rapid economic development of the U.S.S.R. While many of them are aware that national independence is likely to result at the outset in some measure of economic inefficiency, they are resolved to create a new social order. And they are inclined, in Pandit Nehru's words, "more and more towards a communist philosophy." [1] It would be realistic, therefore, to accept the fact that any reorganization of international economic co-operation which is to command the support of these newly emancipated masses must give scope not only to their nationalism but also to their will to economic independence.

Any framework of international economic consultation and co-operation, if it is to survive, must be flexible enough to accommodate at once a shifting balance of power and a considerable shift in economic relations among the nations. Also it must be tolerant enough to accept considerable differences of political and economic philosophy among them. In so far as the world trading system has rested upon a division of labor between advanced industrial and creditor countries and backward raw-material producing and debtor countries, it must be refashioned. There will always remain scope for the territorial division of labor. But inevitably this division must come to be based upon differential advantages in natural resources rather than upon a subordination of skills. The prime factor of production is skilled labor. And of the human skills, the organization of technical knowledge is not only the most productive but that most readily transferable across national boundaries. The dominant white race has no monopoly either of technical aptitudes or of organizing capacity. It is unlikely that the newly independent governments of peoples that have hitherto been backward in economic development will be content to have their national economies remain at a primitive agricultural and handicraft stage of development. Nor will they be content to leave the ownership and management of their industries in foreign hands.

International trade has gone through many phases. In the first half of the nineteenth century, it was still an exchange of European manufactures for products of native origin—hides from California, spices from the tropical East, silks and porcelain from China. From about 1860, there was a clearly marked development when western European capital began to be invested in ports, railroads, and plantations all over the world. Production was then developed on a large scale for export to Europe. Mining enterprises together with tea, cocoa, coffee, sugar, rubber, jute, and indigo plantations, tin smelters in Malaya, and refrigerated meatworks in the Argentine with transport facilities to match, swelled the volume of world trade. This outpouring of

[1] Jawaharlal Nehru, *Towards Freedom,* New York, 1941.

capital equipment and organizing skills raised the totals of both exports and imports, but the colonial world became tributary to and dependent upon the enterprise of western Europe. This dependence has come to an end.

If international trade and investment are to be reorganized in Asia, it must be by methods that will give to these formerly dependent peoples the opportunity to develop their own resources and skills for their local as well as their export markets. The national plans now being drawn up lean heavily upon the Russian experience—not necessarily in the socialization of industry, but in the priorities of development and the location of strategic industries and above all in the training of technicians. If necessary, these underdeveloped countries will endure a transitional period of suffering and disorganization, during which such increased productivity as is made possible by forced savings and draft labor is withheld from consumption, in order to accumulate the capital equipment necessary for modernization. It is on this frontier of development that the greatest opportunities for the expansion of international trade will occur. These are the opportunities that call for new types of inventiveness and enterprise. There is greater scope than ever before for private enterprise, but it must be prepared to accept and to work within the new political order.

In the past, there has been a confusing conglomeration of economic functions—enterprise, the mobilization of resources and labor for the construction of capital undertakings, the actual construction, the ownership and the management of the enterprise once completed. In recent years in the more developed countries, particularly in respect to the greatest undertakings, there has been an increasing separation of these functions. Ownership and management are no longer synonymous terms. Construction is farmed out by both private and public enterprise. Public regulation of services affected with a public interest is increasing. This is particularly true where there is an element of monopoly in the service.

The potentialities of the new scientific knowledge will call forth new combinations of private and public enterprise. There is hardly any aspect of economic progress in which these elements are not intertwined. For example, in the recent development of California where population and productivity are increasing at a far more rapid rate than the average in the United States, there is a great deal of private enterprise. However, power comes increasingly from the great water conservation projects of the Federal government. In many respects the limiting factor in development is the availability of water. Behind the whole development, in addition to the applied engineering research of great corporations, lies the basic research and advanced training which is the product in the main of public educational institutions.

The distinction drawn so sharply between government and economic enterprise in the nineteenth century is breaking down. The particular forms of social organization which that century found convenient are not sacrosanct. Adam Smith, on the eve of the Industrial Revolution, committed himself to the dictum that joint-stock enterprise was an unsuitable form of organization for all but a limited range of routine economic activities. However, it was not long before this joint-stock form of organization became not only necessary, but the most progressive and efficient method of carrying out the large-scale undertakings made possible by the industrial application of new scientific discoveries. Those who still maintain that public enterprise is incapable of innovation, or even of efficient operation, except in limited and routine fields, may find their *obiter dicta* falsified by events.

The important objective in modern economic organization is the effective leadership of a general staff of technicians of diverse qualifications. The most dramatic example of such leadership and teamwork in history was the vast economic organization implementing the applied scientific and engineering research that produced the atomic bomb. It was a two-billion-dollar project that employed thousands of highly trained technicians and tens of thousands of employees. The planning was clearly an example of public enterprise. There were no high-salaried executives on the central planning staff, which was recruited from the universities, the services, and from private industry. There was a very considerable measure of private enterprise involved in the construction and operation of plants and also in the supply of equipment on contract. Those who participated in this undertaking as individuals or as executives of private industry gained insight and know-how in a new field of vast scientific and industrial possibilities. This was a momentous achievement, but it was carried to success in wartime when there was no political interference. The subsequent operations of the Atomic Energy Commission have been subjected to harassing criticism and investigation, rendering difficult the recruitment of scientists and thus endangering the whole enterprise.

A great variety of experiments might be cited to illustrate the fact that new forms of international economic enterprise are emerging. United States corporations are pouring capital into the petroleum-rich areas of the Near East, securing concessions from the local governments and letting contracts by which engineering firms build pipe lines, roads, airfields, port facilities, and schools. The Rockefeller interests are creating new local industries in Latin-American countries, with the active aid of the governments and the participation of local interests. It has become standard practice among many corporations not only to secure the participation of local capital in branch enterprises abroad, but to seek and if necessary train managerial staff from the local community. While private enterprise is developing new techniques, governments are also experimenting. Thus the Unilever interests are actively promoting economic development in British West Africa, and the Colonial Development Corporation set up by the British Colonial Office is also engaged in fostering new agricultural industries in central and east Africa. For this purpose it is using the most modern methods, such as aerial surveys, contour terracing, mechanical clearing, cultivation and harvesting, development of public health, scientific research, and educational institutions.

But the major challenge to the resourcefulness of the Western world lies in Asia. The circuits of world trade cannot be closed, and multilateral clearing of payments cannot be restored, unless practicable means can be found whereby the newly independent and sensitive governments of eastern and southeastern Asia may utilize the technical skills, the drive, and the organizing experience of the scientific West. In large measure the problem is one of utilizing the productive capacities of corporate enterprise in ways that are acceptable to the nationalism of these underdeveloped countries. Europe's problem of payments cannot be solved, nor can Japan's manufacturing capacity be restored, unless outlets can be found for their exports, particularly in Asia. At the same time it is necessary to develop an increasing export of raw materials from Asia to the United States. Thus the expansion of productivity in Asia is the key to this triangular development, in order that payments may flow from the United States to Asia, from Asia to Europe, and from Europe back to the United

States. Productivity cannot be expanded in such countries as India, China, and Indonesia unless capital, technical skill, and organizing drive are made available to them on a large scale. But the capital and organizing drive are not welcome on the old terms. New forms of co-operation must be developed which will strengthen the political independence and meet the economic needs of the Asiatic countries.

The Western world, and particularly the United States, has much to offer to these underdeveloped countries. The people of the United States, which was itself born in revolution, should be able to call upon their historical experience to understand the political and economic problems faced by such governments as those of Indonesia and India. Co-operation is made more difficult by the fact that leadership of many of the nationalist movements has fallen by default to nationals of the Asiatic countries who have been trained as instruments of communist world revolution. The power struggle takes many forms. The U.S.S.R. has gained an advantage by reason of having trained emissaries in good time so that they are now able to gain control of many nationalist movements. The surest way to lose the power struggle in Asia is for the United States to support reaction because it fears the spread of communism. To insist stiffly upon property claims built up under imperialist regimes and to support regimes or national cliques that cling to past privilege is to become an ally of the decaying past. The weakness, inefficiency, sensitivity, and often the pretentions of those who speak in the name of nationalism may be exasperating but the future lies in the development of productivity under national auspices. The British did more trade with the United States after 1776 than they formerly did with the colonies, and this could be true again, now that the independence of such countries as India is established.

The best way for the United States and western Europe to meet communist pretensions to leadership in long overdue social reforms is to take over that leadership. Social change will come. The masses of non-political but poverty-driven peasants may be inarticulate in their sufferings, but they will not always remain dumb driven cattle. Whether their power is ultimately exerted in a succession of social upheavals that destroy all possibility of co-operation with the technically efficient Western world, or whether it functions in the process of working out such co-operation, depends largely upon the imaginative insight and inventiveness of those who have the economic power to create new forms of international economic co-operation. This question is urgent. The infant United States responded to the encouragement and help that Lafayette brought in the critical and formative years of the nation, with a warmth of friendship toward France that lasted for generations. The weak fledgling governments of Asia need such encouragement and help now.

No one can foresee what may emerge from the confused situation created by the rapid application of new scientific knowledge to new industrial, transport, and communication processes, by the nationalist awakening of large masses in Asia, and by the competition for their allegiance between the aggressive individualism of the Western world and the equally aggressive and more coherent communism of the world revolutionary movement directed from Moscow. It is not difficult to suggest methods by which Western enterprise might effectively be employed in reorganizing international economic co-operation. The main instrument of economic development will be private enterprise; but public corporations and those combining elements of public and private enterprise are likely to play a larger role than heretofore in the planning and conduct of economic transactions which cross national boundaries. The practices of government, as well as of business, are likely to be transformed in the process. There will be devolution of government functions upon specialized agencies, and regional decentralization also. This double devolution may cross national boundaries as it has crossed state boundaries in the case of the Tennessee Valley Authority. New forms of organization more flexible in their operation are likely to be invented.

The forms of investment also are changing. Direct entrepreneur investment with varied forms of both public and private participation is likely to play a larger role in international economic development. Many contractual relationships—private, semi-public, and public—are likely to be tried out for a great variety of specific purposes. In these contracts, the training of local technicians and the transference of know-how will be an important consideration.

Some functions of government may be delegated. There can be regional decentralization. And as the functions of government are extended—for example in such fields as the generation of power—new institutions can be created to discharge these functions within the limits laid down by the central government. In the United States, in addition to the hierarchy of local government, a whole series of public agencies, corporations, and commissions, discharge governmental functions within the limits laid down by statute. Among these are the Atomic Energy Commission and the Economic Cooperation Administration. Congress remains the supreme deliberative assembly, but its overburdened calendar need not be cluttered by administrative decisions in technical fields. More and more it tends to become the dispenser and controller, rather than the sole seat, of democratic authority. The same kind of double devolution on a regional and functional basis is taking place in other countries. Other congresses, parliaments and presidia are coming to preside over similar dispersals of function among localized and specialized agencies. Inevitably there is a struggle for existence among these agencies and the pattern of institutional development varies from country to country. But in all it becomes more complex and less centralized.

Increasingly the application of new scientific discoveries to transport and communication brings the peoples of the world into closer contact on a wider variety of activities. As these activities cross national boundaries, these specialized agencies of national government must fit their policies together by consultative co-operation cleared through the international institutions which form a nexus in the United Nations. Thus the organs of national government tend to become the focusing centers of authority, intermediate between the ramifications of specialized national agencies, and the embryonic organs of world government.

It may seem theoretical at the present time to speculate upon possible developments of this or a similar nature. Nationalism is very strong, and there is still reluctance in many influential quarters to accept any hint of limits to the rights either of private business enterprise or of national governments. This outline of possible developments may not be a correct anticipation of future trends. It has been set down to convey some concrete notion of what historical experience suggests is likely to prove an inescapable development. The forms of organization that will be found suitable to the political and technical conditions of the near future will develop out of, but will differ radically from, the forms that have been evolved from the experience of the past.

It would be a mistake to prepare a framework of international consultation with codes of economic behavior that attempt to re-create the institutional relationships of the recent past. To make such plans at the close of a great war and in the middle of a period of accelerated social change would be equivalent to the mistake often charged against professional soldiers who are said in times of peace to prepare diligently against the preceding war. Since experience is the most obvious basis on which to plan, there is a natural temptation to prepare safeguards against the recurrence of preceding depressions and to plan for the restoration of forms of trading, investment, and monetary management that have become familiar in past experience but have little chance of being restored. The validity of the international instruments clustering about the United Nations will be judged in practice by their capacity to deal with situations and trends that cannot now be anticipated. It is unlikely that codes of international economic co-operation can be elaborated sufficiently to anticipate all future contingencies. It is still less likely that procedures can be devised to anticipate the proportions and relative weight of the problems that will arise. In all of them much scope must be allowed for "masterful administration of the unforeseen."

The primary importance of the codes, and of the institutions set up to interpret and administer them, will lie not so much in binding commitments to prearranged courses of action in particular circumstances, as in the procedures devised for continuous consultation and improvisation of policy. An overelaboration of written constitutions may in practice prove a handicap to growth and development. It is obviously necessary to lay down broad principles of common action, but it is equally necessary to provide for the flexible application of those principles to changing circumstances. In many ways the most important function that the new international institutions can discharge will be to provide means whereby greater insight may be gained into the realistic understanding of international relations. This was the most permanent legacy of the League of Nations experiment. Research studies by the secretariat can contribute to this insight, but the greater contribution is that made by continuous consultative co-operation among the technicians of national governments on matters of common concern.

The international organs of consultation must be talking-shops, even when they have specific functions to perform, as have the International Bank and the International Monetary Fund. While the talk may be highly technical and in some cases it may be secret, it is the making of contacts and the continuous exchange of information to be critically analyzed that is essential. Understanding must precede any attempt to formulate common policies of action, whether these policies be highly technical, as in the determination of appropriate exchange rates, or deal with large issues of public policy, as in the organization of social-security services. Research in its broadest sense and continuous discussion are the foundations of consultative co-operation.

It follows from this analysis that progress toward world government cannot be simply a matter of framing a world constitution, devising a code of international law, and organizing an international police force. Conceivably, authoritarian forms of world government could be established and maintained by militant minorities whose primary allegiance is to an elite organization transcending national boundaries, though at present this is unlikely. To some extent this has already happened where Soviet-trained leaders have seized power and organized dictatorships in the name of the proletariat. Democratic government, on the other hand, depends upon the consent of the governed. No system of democratic government is stronger than the loyalty it commands and the common will it can mobilize. Democratic forms of international co-operation must accept the fact that the dominant loyalties of the present generation are national. To build up a common will to enforce international peace and to create instruments of international justice must involve a transcending of national loyalties and a surrender or delegation of national sovereignties. Until the majority or at least an effective minority of men and women become citizens of the world, prepared in a crisis to subordinate their patriotism to the loyalty they owe the world community, democratic world government will remain a dream.

The alternative of co-operation between sovereign states is posed, on all major issues, by the impasse that developed after the war ended. The groups within the United Nations led by the United States and the U.S.S.R. have come to complete disagreement on disarmament, the control of atomic energy, and the organization of an international police force. It is true that there have been limited successes on incidents where the United States and the U.S.S.R. agreed on the action to be taken, notably by sending an international commission to implement a truce between the Dutch and Indonesians and by the stoppage of hostilities between Arabs and Jews in Palestine. But the shadow of increasing suspicion and conflict between the two great-power protagonists has made progress toward the organization of collective security impossible for the time being.

Outside the framework of the United Nations proper, there are three possible methods of negotiation between the contending powers. The first is by direct negotiation among the great powers in an attempt to reach a basis of agreement on the major issues of conflict. The second is by co-operation in regional organizations. The third is by co-operation in regard to the specific technical questions which the specialized agencies associated with the United Nations have been created to handle.

Little success had attended the first of these methods. The Council of Foreign Ministers of Britain, France, the United States, and the U.S.S.R. was created in July, 1945, at the Potsdam Conference. Quarterly meetings of this Council, which was intended to prepare the draft of peace treaties, were held until November, 1947. They functioned with increasing difficulty and adjourned their last meeting at Moscow without fixing a date to reconvene. In July, 1948, negotiations were resumed on the diplomatic level by the British, French, and United States Ambassadors calling upon the Soviet Foreign Minister. It was evident that progress in finding a basis for procedure was slow. The negotiations were secret but there was no resolution of the deadlock. Again in May, 1949, conversations were resumed. The blockade of Berlin was lifted and the Council of Foreign Ministers met once more.

The method of regional organization was tending to divide rather than unite the great powers. They were participating in some of the regional commissions of the United Nations, notably in the European Economic Commission, but the trend of organization was toward the creation of autonomous regional groups. The customs union formed by Belgium, the Netherlands, and Luxembourg (Benelux), and the growing sentiment for closer economic collaboration between the western European countries, were correlated with the extension of United States' interest in Europe. There was the negotiation of the North Atlantic Pact, and it became obvious that the power struggle rather than world co-operation was the dominating consideration in the European Recovery Program. In other areas regional arrangements were developing fast. The United States was a party to the Caribbean Commission and to the South Seas Commission, as well as the Association of American States. An Association of Asian States was emerging which was likely to be of increasing importance. The map of the world was being redrawn, not so much by the alteration of political boundaries as by a redefinition of the relationships within regional areas. There was likely to emerge a grouping of states very different from the pattern of independent nation-states upon which the nineteenth-century equilibrium of power rested. The formula by which India became an independent republic, but remained within the British Commonwealth was a good example of the ingenious political solutions that were emerging.

The remaining method of negotiation by co-operation upon technical issues could be a means of working toward world unity. However, the international agencies set up for this purpose revealed the deep gulf that lies between the Soviet concepts of political and economic organization and the concepts of the rest of the world. The U.S.S.R. had not participated in the work of these specialized economic agencies. In so far as they have been able to develop effective co-operation, it has been among the nations in the non-Soviet world.

This failure to find a basis of accommodation between the Soviet system and that of the Western world rendered the scarcely concealed conflict in Asia and the Middle East a matter of high political as well as economic importance. The Cominform was a living reality, maintaining connections with revolutionary groups in many countries. It was significant that when an attempt was made to discipline the government of Yugoslavia in June, 1948, resolutions condemning that government's intransigeance were passed in almost identical terms not only by the Communist parties of the neighboring Balkan countries, but also by those in distant countries such as China. The United States and the western European countries may stand ready to co-operate with the underdeveloped countries. But they need to do more than stand and wait. Enterprise entails action. Half of the world's population may wind up within the zone of Soviet organization unless the Western world bestirs itself to create more effective means of international economic co-operation than now exist.

BIBLIOGRAPHY

CHAPTER I: THE BEGINNINGS OF TRADE

Ch'ao-ting Chi, *Key Economic Areas in Chinese History,* London, 1936
Gibb, H. A. R., *Ibu Battuta: Travels in Asia and Africa 1325–1344,* London, 1929
Hauser, Henri, *Les origines historiques des problèmes économiques actuelles,* Paris, 1935
Hoyt, Elizabeth E., *Primitive Trade,* London, 1926
Kerner, Robert J., *The Urge to the Sea,* Berkeley, 1942
Mumford, Lewis, *Technics and Civilization,* New York, 1934
Newton, A. P. (ed.), *Travel and Travellers of the Middle Ages,* New York, 1926
Pirenne, Henri, *A History of Europe,* New York, 1939
Radin, Max, *Manners and Morals of Business,* Chicago, 1943
Ridgeway, William, *The Origins of Metallic Currency and Weight Standards,* Cambridge, 1892
Rostovtzeff, M., *Caravan Cities,* Oxford, 1932
————, *Social and Economic History of the Roman Empire,* Oxford, 1926
Selfridge, H. Gordon, *The Romance of Commerce,* London, 1918
Teggart, Frederick J., *Rome and China,* Berkeley, 1939
Thompson, James Westfall, *An Economic and Social History of the Middle Ages,* New York, 1928
Unwin, George, *Studies in Economic History,* London, 1927
Yule, Sir Henry, *The Book of Ser Marco Polo,* London, 1903

CHAPTER II: TOLLS, TARIFFS AND THE NATION-STATE

Brown, Richard (ed.), *History of Accounting and Accountants,* Edinburgh, 1905
Dowell, Stephen, *History of Taxation and Taxes in England,* London, 1884
Ehrenburg, Richard, *Capital and Finance in the Age of the Renaissance,* New York, 1928
Gras, N. S. B., *The Early English Customs System,* Cambridge, 1918

Gross, Charles, *The Gild Merchant,* Oxford, 1890
Isaacs, Asher, *International Trade* (Ch. III), Chicago, 1948
Jusserand, J. J., *English Wayfaring Life in the Middle Ages,* New York, 1925
Lipson, E., *The Economic History of England* (Vol. I), London, 1915
O'Brien, G., *An Essay on Medieval Economic Teaching,* London, 1920
Palgrave, R. H. Inglis, *Dictionary of Political Economy* (article on "Law Merchant"), London, 1926
Pirenne, Henri, *Medieval Cities,* Princeton, 1948
Pound, Roscoe, *Interpretations of Legal History,* Cambridge, 1923
Royal Institute of International Affairs, *Nationalism* (Chs. I–III), London, 1939
Tawney, R. H., Introduction to Thomas Wilson, *A Discourse on Usury,* London, 1925
————, *Religion and the Rise of Capitalism,* London, 1926
Unwin, George, *The Gilds and Companies of London,* London, 1938
Zimmern, Helen, *The Hansa Towns,* New York, 1891

CHAPTER III: THE EXPANSION OF THE WORLD

Buck, Philip W., *The Politics of Mercantilism,* New York, 1942
Cole, Charles W., *Colbert and a Century of French Mercantilism,* New York, 1939
Furniss, Edgar S., *The Position of the Laborer in a System of Nationalism,* New York, 1920
Gillespie, J. E., *A History of Geographical Discovery,* New York, 1933
Hamilton, Earl J., *American Treasure and the Price Revolution in Spain,* Cambridge, Mass., 1934
Hecksher, Eli F., *Mercantilism,* London, 1935
Ingram, J. K., *A History of Slavery and Serfdom,* London, 1895
Judges, A. V., *The Idea of a Mercantile State,* London, 1939
Knorr, Klaus E., *British Colonial Theories 1570–1850,* Toronto, 1944
Lucas, Sir Charles, *The Beginnings of English Overseas Enterprise,* Oxford, 1917
Madariaga, S. de, *Rise of the Spanish American Empire,* London, 1947
————, *Fall of the Spanish American Empire,* London, 1947
Morison, S. E., *Admiral of the Ocean Sea,* Boston, 1942
Newton, A. P., *The Great Age of Discovery,* London, 1932
Pohl, Frederick J., *Amerigo Vespucci: Pilot Major,* New York, 1944
Prescott, William H., *History of the Conquest of Peru,* London, 1848
Rose, J. Holland, *Man and the Sea,* Cambridge, 1935
Sanceau, Elaine, *Henry the Navigator,* New York, 1947
Schurz, W. L., *The Manila Galleon,* New York, 1939
Suviranta, Bruno Kaarle, *The Theory of the Balance of Trade in England,* Helsingfors, 1923
Sykes, Sir Percy, *A History of Exploration,* New York, 1934
Viner, Jacob, *Studies in the Theory of International Trade,* New York, 1937

CHAPTER IV: THE INSTRUMENTS OF ECONOMIC NATIONALISM

Andreades, A., *History of the Bank of England* (2nd ed.), London, 1924
Andrews, C. M., *The Colonial Background of the American Revolution,* New Haven, 1935
————, *The Colonial Period of American History,* New Haven, 1934–38
Beer, George L., *The Origins of the British Colonial System,* New York, 1908

Egerton, H. E., *A Short History of British Colonial Policy,* London, 1897
Harper, Lawrence A., *The English Navigation Laws,* New York, 1939
Hoon, Elizabeth K., *The Organization of the English Customs System, 1669–1786,* New York, 1938
Krishna, Bal, *Commercial Relations between India and England, 1601–1757,* London, 1924
Marshall, Alfred, *Industry and Trade* (App. D.), London, 1927
Morse, H. B., *Chronicles of the East India Company Trading to China,* Cambridge, Mass., 1926–29
Schmoller, Gustav, *The Mercantile System and Its Historical Significance,* New York, 1910
Scott, W. R., *The Constitution and Finance of English, Scottish and Irish Joint-Stock Companies to 1720,* Cambridge, 1912
Unwin, George, *Industrial Organization in the 16th and 17th Centuries,* London, 1904
Wilbur, Margaret Eyre, *The East India Company,* New York, 1945

CHAPTER V: THE EMERGENCE OF ECONOMIC THEORY

Bagehot, Walter, *Economic Studies,* London, 1880
Cannan, Edwin, *A Review of Economic Theory,* London, 1929
Cantillon, Richard, *Essai sur la Nature de Commerce en Général* (Henry Higgs, ed.), London, 1931
Clark, J. M., et al, *Adam Smith, 1776–1926,* Chicago, 1928
Gide, Chas. and Rist, Chas., *A History of Economic Doctrines* (2nd English ed., Chs. I–II), New York, 1948
Ginzberg, Eli, *The House of Adam Smith,* New York, 1934
Halevy, Elie, *The Growth of Philosophic Radicalism,* London, 1928
Johnson, E. A. J., *Predecessors of Adam Smith,* New York, 1937
Monroe, A. E., *Early Economic Thought,* Cambridge, Mass., 1927
Rae, John, *The Life of Adam Smith,* London, 1895
Roll, Erich, *A History of Economic Thought* (Chs. I–VI), New York, 1947
Smith, Adam, *An Enquiry into the Nature and Causes of the Wealth of Nations,* London, 1776
Toynbee, Arnold, *Lectures on the Industrial Revolution of the 18th Century in England,* London, 1884
Viner, Jacob, *Studies in the Theory of International Trade,* London, 1937

CHAPTER VI: LAISSEZ FAIRE: PRACTICE AND THEORY

The Industrial Revolution

Clapham, J. H., *An Economic History of Modern Britain* (Vol. I), Cambridge, 1926
Fay, C. R., *Life and Labour in the Nineteenth Century,* Part I, Cambridge, 1920
————, *Great Britain from Adam Smith to the Present Day,* New York, 1947
Hammond, J. L. and Barbara, *The Town Laborer,* London, 1918
————, *The Skilled Laborer,* London, 1919
Knowles, L. C. A., *The Industrial and Commercial Revolutions in Great Britain during the Nineteenth Century,* London, 1921
Mantoux, Paul, *The Industrial Revolution in the Eighteenth Century,* New York, 1927

Polanyi, K., *The Great Transformation,* New York, 1944
Usher, A. P., *The History of Mechanical Inventions,* New York, 1929
Wallas, Graham, *The Life of Francis Place, 1771–1854* (rev. ed.), London, 1918
Webb, Sidney and Beatrice, *The King's Highway,* London, 1913
————, *History of Trade Unionism, 1666–1920,* London, 1920

Growth of Population

Carr-Saunders, A. M., *World Population,* Oxford, 1936
Condliffe, J. B., *The Economic Pattern of World Population,* Washington, 1947
Malthus, Thomas Robert, *First Essay on Population* (reprinted), London, 1926
Mumford, Lewis, *The Culture of Cities* (Ch. IV), New York, 1938
Weber, Adna Ferrin, *The Growth of Cities in the Nineteenth Century,* New York, 1899
Winslow, C-E. A., *The Conquest of Epidemic Disease,* Princeton, 1943

The London Money Market

Andreades, A., *History of the Bank of England* (2nd ed.), London, 1924
Cannan, E., *The Paper Pound of 1797–1821,* London, 1919
Clapham, Sir John H., *The Bank of England: A History,* Cambridge, 1945
Crick, W. F. and Wadsworth, J. E., *A Hundred Years of Joint Stock Banking,* London, 1936
Duguid, C., *The Story of the Stock Exchange,* London, 1901
Hawtrey, R. G., *Currency and Credit* (Chs. XV–XVII), London, 1919
King, W. T. C., *History of the London Discount Market,* London, 1936
Shannon, H. A., "The Coming of General Limited Liability," *Economic History,* Vol. II, No. 6, Jan. 1931
Viner, Jacob, *Studies in the Theory of International Trade* (Chs. III–V), New York, 1937

The Classical Economists

Bowley, Marion, *Nassau Senior and Classical Economics,* London, 1937
Gide, Chas. and Rist, Chas., *A History of Economic Doctrines* (Part I, Ch. III), New York, 1948
Hollander, Jacob H., *David Ricardo,* Baltimore, 1910
Keynes, J. M., *Essays in Biography* (pp. 139–47), London, 1933
Mill, John Stuart, *Autobiography* (5th ed.), London, 1875
Seligman, E. R. A., "On Some Neglected British Economists," *Economic Journal,* Vol. XIII, Sept.-Dec., 1903
Viner, Jacob, "Bentham and J. S. Mill: The Utilitarian Background," *American Economic Review,* Vol. XXXIX, No. 2, March 1948

CHAPTER VII: THE CLASSICAL THEORY OF INTERNATIONAL TRADE

Angell, J. W., *The Theory of International Prices* (Chs. I–IV), Cambridge, Mass., 1926
Edgeworth, F. Y., *Papers relating to Political Economy* (Vol. II, pp. 3–60), London, 1925
Fay, C. R., "The Classical Theory of International Trade," *Southwestern Political and Social Science Quarterly,* Mar. 1928 and Mar. 1930

Mason, E. S., "The Doctrine of Comparative Cost," *Quarterly Journal of Economics,* Vol. XLI (1926–27), pp. 63–93

Mill, John Stuart, *Essays on Some Unsettled Questions of Political Economy,* London, 1844

————, *Principles of Political Economy* (Ashley ed., Ch. XVII–XXV), London, 1921

Senior, Nassau W., *Transmission of the Precious Metals from Country to Country* (reprinted), London, 1931

Taussig, F. W., *International Trade,* New York, 1928

Viner, Jacob, *Studies in the Theory of International Trade* (Ch. VI–IX), New York, 1937

Walker, E. R., "The Theory of International Trade," *Economic Record,* Vol. II, No. 10, May 1930

Williams, J. H., "The Theory of International Trade Reconsidered," *Economic Journal,* Vol. XXXIX, No. 154, June 1929

CHAPTER VIII: THE FIGHT FOR FREE TRADE

Reconstruction after Napoleon

Clapham, J. H., *Economic History of Modern Britain* (Vol. I), Cambridge, 1926

Corti, E. C., *Rise of the House of Rothschild,* New York, 1928

Hobson, C. K., *The Export of Capital* (Chs. IV–V), London, 1914

Jenks, Leland H., *The Migration of British Capital to 1875,* London, 1927

King, W. T. C., *History of the London Discount Market,* London, 1936

Robinson, James Hervey and Shotwell, James T., *History of Western Europe* (Ch. XXXIX), New York, 1946

Webster, C. K., *The Foreign Policy of Castlereagh, 1815–1822,* London, 1934

The Free-Trade Movement

Barnes, Donald G., *A History of the English Corn Laws from 1660–1846,* London, 1930

Fay, C. R., *Great Britain from Adam Smith to the Present Day* (Chs. I–IV), London, 1928

Halevy, Elie, *The Age of Peel and Cobden,* London, 1947

Hobson, J. A., *Richard Cobden: The International Man,* London, 1919

Holland, Bernard, *The Fall of Protection,* London, 1913

Morley, John, *The Life of Richard Cobden,* London, 1881

Trevelyan, G. M., *The Life of John Bright,* London, 1913

Commercial Treaties and Tariff Policy

Ashley, Percy, *Modern Tariff History* (3rd ed.), London, 1920

Culbertson, W. S., *International Economic Policy,* New York, 1924

Dunham, A. L., *The Anglo-French Treaty of Commerce of 1860,* Ann Arbor, 1930

Gregory, T. E., *Tariffs: A Study in Method* (Ch. XI), London, 1921

Grunzel, Joseph, *Economic Protectionism,* New York, 1915

Haight, F. A., *A History of French Commercial Policies* (Ch. II), New York, 1941

Isaacs, Asher, *International Trade* (Ch. XVII), Chicago, 1948

Röpke, Wilhelm, *German Commercial Policy,* London, 1934

Taussig, F. W., *Tariff History of the United States,* New York, 1893

U.S. Tariff Commission, *Reciprocity and Commercial Treaties,* Washington, 1919

Viner, Jacob, "Political Aspects of International Finance," *Chicago Journal of Business,* Vol. I, Nos. 2–3, April, July, 1928

CHAPTER IX: THE DISSENTERS

Economic Development

Carey, Mathew, *Autobiography,* New York, 1942

Eiselin, M. R., *The Rise of Pennsylvania Protectionism,* Philadelphia, 1932

Hill, William, *The First Stages of the Tariff Policy of the United States,* Baltimore, 1893

Kaiser, C. W., Jr., *History of the Academic Protectionist–Free Trade controversy in America before 1860,* Philadelphia, 1939

Sumner, W. G., *Lectures on the History of Protection in the United States,* New York, 1877

Taussig, F. W., *State Papers and Speeches on the Tariff,* Cambridge, Mass., 1893

The Colonial Reformers

Condliffe, J. B., *New Zealand in the Making* (Chs. I–III), Chicago, 1930

Fay, C. R., *Great Britain from Adam Smith to the Present Day* (Ch. II), New York, 1947

Guttridge, G. H., "Adam Smith on the American Revolution," *American Historical Review,* Vol. XXXVIII, No. 4, July, 1935

Harrop, A. J., *The Amazing Career of Edward Gibbon Wakefield,* London, 1928

Knorr, Klaus E., *British Colonial Theories, 1570–1850* (Part II), Toronto, 1944

Knowles, L. C. A., *Industrial and Commercial Revolutions in England during the Nineteenth Century* (Part VI), London, 1921

Mills, R. C., *The Colonization of Australia,* London, 1915

Wrong, E. M., *Charles Buller and Responsible Government,* Oxford, 1926

Socialism and International Trade

Beer, M., *A History of British Socialism,* London, 1920

Bloom, Solomon F., *The World of Nations,* New York, 1941

Menger, Anton, *Right to the Whole Produce of Labour,* London, 1899

German Economic Nationalism

Bowring, Sir John, *Report on the Prussian Commercial Union,* London, 1840

Bruck, W. F., *Social and Economic History of Germany from William II to Hitler, 1888–1938,* London, 1938

Gerschenkron, Alexander, *Bread and Democracy in Germany,* Berkeley, 1943

Hauser, Henri, *Germany's Commercial Grip on the World,* New York, 1917

Hirschman, Albert O., *National Power and the Structure of Foreign Trade,* Berkeley, 1945

Hoffman, Ross J. S., *Great Britain and the German Trade Rivalry, 1875–1914,* Philadelphia, 1933

List, Friedrich, *The National System of Political Economy,* London, 1922

CHAPTER X: THE NETWORK OF WORLD TRADE

Nineteenth-Century Trade Expansion

Högbom, Ivar, "Mineral Production," *Royal Swedish Institute for Mining Engineering Research, Proceedings,* Nr. 117, Stockholm, 1932

Knowles, L. C. A., *Industrial and Commercial Revolutions in Great Britain during the Nineteenth Century* (Part IV), London, 1921
League of Nations, *The Network of World Trade,* Geneva, 1942
Marshall, Alfred, *Industry and Trade* (Bks. I–II), London, 1919
————, *Money, Credit and Commerce* (Bk. III), London, 1923

The Marketing Process

Harrod, R. F., *International Economics,* Cambridge, 1939
Whale, P. Barret, *International Trade,* London, 1932
Zapoleon, L. B., "International and Domestic Commodities and the Theory of Prices," *Quarterly Journal of Economics,* Vol. XLV, No. 3, 1931, pp. 409–59

The Price of Progress

Bennett, Merrill K., "Population and Food Supply: The Current Food Scare," *Scientific Monthly,* Jan. 1949
Hailey, Lord, *An African Survey* (Ch. XVI), London, 1938
Jacks, G. V. and Whyte, R. O., *The Rape of the Earth,* London, 1939
Osborn, H. Fairfield, *Our Plundered Planet,* Boston, 1948
U.S. Dept. of Agriculture, *Soils and Men,* Washington, 1938
Vogt, William, *Road to Survival,* New York, 1948
Worthington, E. B., *Science in Africa* (Ch. V), London, 1938

CHAPTER XI: INVESTMENT AND ENTERPRISE

Bagehot, Walter, *Lombard Street,* London, 1873
Feis, Herbert, *Europe: The World's Banker,* New York, 1930
Foxwell, H. S., "The Nature of the Industrial Struggle," *Economic Journal,* Vol. XXVII, No. 107, Sept. 1917
————, "The Financing of Industry and Trade," *Economic Journal,* Vol. XXVII, No. 108, Dec. 1917
Frankel, S. H., *Capital Investment in Africa,* London, 1938
Hawtrey, R. G., *The Art of Central Banking,* London, 1932
Hobson, C. K., *The Export of Capital,* London, 1914
Iverson, Carl, *Aspects of the Theory of Capital Movements,* Copenhagen, 1935
Jenks, Leland H., *The Migration of British Capital to 1875,* London, 1938
Keynes, J. M., *A Treatise on Money,* New York, 1930
King, W. T. C., *History of the London Discount Market,* London, 1936
Lavington, F., *The English Capital Market,* London, 1921
McGrane, Reginald C., *Foreign Bondholders and American State Debts,* New York, 1935
Madden, John T., Nadler, Marcus and Sauvain, Harry C., *America's Experience as a Creditor Nation* (Ch. II), New York, 1937
Paish, Sir George, "Great Britain's Investment in Other Lands," *Statistical Journal,* Sept. 1909, Jan. 1911, and *Supplement,* Feb. 14, 1914
Remer, C. F., *Foreign Investments in China,* New York, 1933
Report of the Committee on Finance and Industry (Macmillan Committee) (Cmd. 3897), June 1931
Royal Institute of International Affairs, *The Problem of International Investment,* London, 1937
Viner, Jacob, "International Finance and Balance of Power Diplomacy, 1880–1914," *Southwestern Political and Social Science Quarterly,* March 1929

———, "Political Aspects of International Finance," *Chicago Journal of Business,* Vol. I, pp. 143–73 and 324–63

White, Harry D., *The French International Accounts, 1880–1913,* Cambridge, Mass., 1933

Wilson, Roland, *Capital Imports and the Terms of Trade,* Melbourne, 1931

CHAPTER XII: THE INTERNATIONAL GOLD STANDARD

The Battle of the Standards

Hawtrey, R. G., *Currency and Credit* (Chs. XVIII–XIX), London, 1919

Jevons, W. S., *Money and the Mechanism of Exchange,* London, 1875

Keynes, J. M., *Indian Currency and Finance,* London, 1913

———, *A Treatise on Money,* London, 1930

Laughlin, J. L., *The History of Bimetallism in the United States,* New York, 1900

Mar, A. del, *A History of the Precious Metals from the Earliest Times to the Present,* London, 1880

———, *History of Monetary Systems,* London, 1895

Marshall, Alfred, *Official Papers* (Chs. II–IV), London, 1926

Shaw, W. A., *The History of Currency, 1252 to 1894,* New York, 1894

A Superstructure of Credit

Beckhart, B. H. (ed.), *The New York Money Market,* New York, 1931

Bradford, Frederick A., *Money and Banking,* New York, 1937

Brown, William Adams, Jr., *The Gold Standard Reinterpreted, 1914–34,* New York, 1940

Hawtrey, R. G., *Currency and Credit* (Chs. I–V), London, 1919

Keynes, J. M., *A Treatise on Money,* London, 1930

Rist, Chas., *History of Monetary and Credit Theory from John Law to the Present Day,* New York, 1940

Willis, H. Parker and Beckhart, B. H., *Foreign Banking Systems,* New York, 1929

The Market for Currencies

Brown, William Adams, Jr., *The Gold Standard Reinterpreted, 1914–34,* New York, 1940

Cole, Arthur H., "Evolution of the Foreign Exchange Market of the United States," *Journal of Economic and Business History,* Vol. I, No. 3, May 1929

Einzig, Paul, *The Theory of Forward Exchange,* London, 1937

Goschen, George J., *The Theory of the Foreign Exchanges,* London, 1864

Southard, Frank A., *Foreign Exchange Practice and Policy,* New York, 1940

Towers, Graham, *Financing Foreign Trade,* Montreal, 1921

U.S. Dept. of Commerce, *An Introduction to Doing Import and Export Business,* Washington, D.C., 1947

The Balancing Process

Bloomfield, A. I., "The Mechanism of Adjustment of the American Balance of Payments, 1919–29," *Quarterly Journal of Economics,* Vol. LVII, 1943, pp. 333–77

Hawtrey, R. G., *Currency and Credit* (Chs. VI–X), London, 1919

Kemmerer, E. W., "The Gold Exchange Standard," in *Economic Essays in Honour of Gustav Cassel,* London, 1933

Paish, F. W., "Banking Policy and the Balance of International Payments," *Economica,* Vol. III (New Series), 1936

Prebisch, Raoul, *El patron oro y la vulnerabilidad de nuestros paises,* El Collegio de Mexico, Jornadas No. 11, Mexico City, 1944

Remer, C. F., *Foreign Investments in China,* New York, 1933

Tocker, A. H., "The Monetary Standards of Australia and New Zealand," *Economic Journal,* Vol. XXXIV, Dec. 1924

Whale, P. B., "The Working of the Pre-War Gold Standard," *Economica,* Vol. IV (New Series), 1937

CHAPTER XIII: THE NEO-CLASSICAL DOCTRINE

Neo-Classical Theory

Bastable, C. F., *The Theory of International Trade* (4th ed.), London, 1903

Cairnes, J. E., *Some Leading Principles of Political Economy,* New York, 1874

Edgeworth, F. Y., *Papers relating to Political Economy* (Vol. 2, pp. 3–60), London, 1925

Gide, Chas. and Rist, Chas., *A History of Economic Doctrines* (Bk. VI), New York, 1948

Marshall, Alfred, *Principles of Economics,* London, 1890

————, *The Pure Theory of Foreign Trade,* London, 1930

Pigou, A. C. (ed.), *Memorials of Alfred Marshall,* London, 1925

Schuller, Richard, *Schtutzzoll und Freihandel,* Vienna, 1905

Viner, Jacob, *Studies in the Theory of International Trade* (Chs. VI–IX), New York, 1937

Walker, E. R., *From Economic Theory to Practice,* Chicago, 1943

Wicksell, Knut, *Lectures in Political Economy,* London, 1934

Restatement and Verification

Beach, W. Edwards, *British International Gold Movements and Banking Policy, 1881–1913,* Cambridge, Mass., 1935

Taussig, F. W., *International Trade,* New York, 1928

Viner, Jacob, *Canada's Balance of International Indebtedness, 1900–1913,* Cambridge, Mass., 1924

White, Harry D., *The French International Accounts, 1880–1913,* Cambridge, Mass., 1933

Williams, John H., *Argentine International Trade under Unconvertible Paper-money, 1880–1900,* Cambridge, Mass., 1920

Wilson, Roland, *Capital Imports and the Terms of Trade,* Melbourne, 1931

General Equilibrium Theory

Ellsworth, P. T., *International Economics,* New York, 1938

Haberler, G., *The Theory of International Trade,* London, 1936

Harrod, R. F., *International Economics,* New York, 1947

Mosak, Jacob L., *General Equilibrium Theory in Foreign Trade,* Bloomington, Ind., 1944

Ohlin, Bertil, *Interregional and International Trade,* Cambridge, Mass., 1933

Whale, P. B., *International Trade,* Cambridge, 1933

Yntema, Theodore O., *A Mathematical Reformation of the General Theory of International Trade,* Chicago, 1932

CHAPTER XIV: THE END OF LAISSEZ FAIRE

The Calamity of War

Bresciani-Turroni, Constantino, *The Economics of Inflation,* London, 1937
Gathorne-Hardy, G. M., *A Short History of International Affairs 1920–34,* London, 1934
Gerschenkron, A., *Bread and Democracy in Germany,* Berkeley, 1943
Graham, Frank D., *Exchange, Prices and Production in Hyper-Inflation Germany, 1920–23,* Princeton, 1930
Keynes, J. M., *The Economic Consequences of the Peace,* London, 1919
League of Nations, *The Financial Reconstruction of Austria,* Geneva, 1926
————, *The Financial Reconstruction of Hungary,* Geneva, 1926
————, *Greek Refugee Settlement,* Geneva, 1926
————, *World Economic Survey* (annually), Geneva, 1932–42
————, *The Course of Control of Monetary Inflation,* Princeton, 1946
Madden, John T., Nadler, Marcus and Sauvain, Harry C., *America's Experience as a Creditor Nation,* New York, 1937
Mantoux, Etienne, *The Carthaginian Peace,* New York, 1946
Shotwell, James T., *What Germany Forgot,* New York, 1942
Wright, Quincy, *A Study of War,* Chicago, 1942

A Trend to Collectivism

Brown, William Adams, Jr., *The Gold Standard Reinterpreted, 1914–34,* New York, 1940
Feis, Herbert, *The Changing Pattern of International Economic Affairs,* New York, 1940
Hayek, F. A. von, *Monetary Nationalism and International Stability,* London, 1937
Hilgerdt, Folke, "World Trade in Fetters," *Index,* Vol. X, Feb. 1935, Stockholm
Keynes, J. M., *The Economic Consequences of Mr. Churchill,* London, 1925
————, *The End of Laissez-Faire,* London, 1926
Mannheim, Karl, *Man and Society in an Age of Reconstruction,* London, 1941
Mises, Ludwig von, *Bureaucracy,* New Haven, 1944
————, *Omnipotent Government,* New Haven, 1944
Robbins, Lionel, *Economic Planning and International Order,* London, 1937
Smith, J. G., *Economic Planning and the Tariff,* Princeton, 1934

An Evolving Capitalism

Berge, Wendell, *Cartels: Challenge to a Free World,* Washington, 1944
Berle, A. A., and Means, Gardiner C., *The Modern Corporation and Private Property,* New York, 1932
Borkin, Joseph and Welsh, Charles A., *Germany's Master Plan,* New York, 1943
Brady, Robert A., *Business as a System of Power,* New York, 1943
Burns, A. A., *The Decline of Competition,* New York, 1936
Bush, Vannevar, *Endless Horizons,* Washington, 1946
————, *Science: The Endless Frontier,* Washington, 1945
Commons, John R., *The Legal Foundations of Capitalism,* New York, 1924
Crum, W. L., *Corporate Size and Earning Power,* Cambridge, Mass., 1939
Davis, Joseph S., *International Commodity Agreements: Hope, Illusion or Menance,* New York, 1947

Galbraith, J. K., "Monopoly and the Concentration of Economic Power," in Howard S. Ellis (ed.), *A Survey of Contemporary Economics,* Philadelphia, 1948
Hexner, Ervin, *International Cartels,* Chapel Hill, N.C., 1945
League of Nations, *The Transition from War to Peace Economy,* Geneva, 1943
Lucas, A. F., *Industrial Reconstruction and the Control of Competition,* London, 1937
Lynch, David, *The Concentration of Economic Power,* New York, 1946
Mason, Edward S., *Controlling World Trade,* New York, 1946
Staley, Eugene, *World Economy in Transition,* New York, 1939
Stigler, George J., "The Extent and Bases of Monopoly," *American Economic Review: Proceedings,* Vol. XXXIII, No. 2, June 1942
Stocking, George W., *Cartels or Competition,* New York, 1948
———, and Watkins, Myron W., *Cartels in Action,* New York, 1946
Terrill, Robert P., "Cartels and the International Exchange of Technology," *American Economic Review: Proceedings,* Vol. XXXVI, No. 2, May 1946
Veblen, Thorstein, *The Engineers and the Price System,* New York, 1921

Monopolistic Competition

Bain, Joe S., "Price and Production Policies" in Howard S. Ellis (ed.), *A Survey of Contemporary Economics,* Philadelphia, 1943
Chamberlin, E. H., *The Theory of Monopolistic Competition,* Cambridge, Mass., 1947
Clark, J. M., *Alternative to Serfdom,* New York, 1948
———, *The Economics of Overhead Costs,* Chicago, 1931
Hamilton, Walton H., *The Pattern of Competition,* New York, 1946
Knight, Frank H., *Risk, Uncertainty and Profit,* New York, 1921
Nourse, Edwin G., *Price-Making in a Democracy,* Washington, 1944
———, and Drury, Horace B., *Industrial Price Policies and Economic Progress,* Washington, 1938
Robinson, Joan, *The Economics of Imperfect Competition,* London, 1933
Triffin, Robert, *Monopolistic Competition and General Equilibrium Theory,* Cambridge, Mass., 1947
Zeuthen, F., *Problems of Monopoly and Economic Warfare,* London, 1930

CHAPTER XV: ECONOMIC NATIONALISM BETWEEN THE WARS

The Deep Roots of Protection

Delle-Donne, O., *European Tariff Policies Since the World War,* New York, 1928
Hirschman, Albert O., *National Power and the Structure of Foreign Trade,* Berkeley, 1943
League of Nations, *The Agricultural Crisis,* Geneva, 1931
———, *Considerations on the Present Evolution of Agricultural Protectionism,* Geneva, 1935
———, *Report and Proceedings of the World Economic Conference, 1927,* Geneva, 1928
Liepman, H., *Tariff Levels and the Economic Unity of Europe,* London, 1938
Moulton, Harold G., and Pasvolsky, Leo, *War Debts and World Prosperity,* Washington, 1932

National Institute of Economic and Social Research, *Trade Regulations and Commercial Policy of the United Kingdom,* Cambridge, 1943
Ridgeway, George, *Merchants of Peace,* New York, 1938
Röpke, W., *German Commercial Policy,* London, 1934
Salter, Sir Arthur, *World Trade and Its Future,* London, 1936
Schattschneider, E. C., *Politics, Pressures and the Tariff,* New York, 1935
Timoshenko, V., *World Agriculture and the Depression,* Ann Arbor, 1933

The Weapons of Economic Warfare

Bidwell, Percy W., *The Invisible Tariff,* New York, 1939
Condliffe, J. B., *The Reconstruction of World Trade,* New York, 1940
Gordon, Margaret S., *Barriers to World Trade,* New York, 1941
Hoffherr, René, *La Politique commerciale de la France,* Paris, 1939
Jones, Joseph M., *Tariff Retaliation: Repercussions of the Hawley-Smoot Bill,* Philadelphia, 1934
League of Nations, *World Economic Survey* (annually), Geneva, 1932–42
Rappard, William E., *Postwar Efforts for Freer Trade,* Geneva, 1938

The Anarchy of Nationalism

Ahlers, John, *Japan Closing the Open Door in China,* Shanghai, 1939
Allen, G. C., *Japanese Industry: Its Recent Development and Present Condition,* New York, 1940
Asahi, Isoshi, *The Economic Strength of Japan,* Tokyo, 1939
Barnett, Robert W., *Economic Shanghai: Hostage to Politics, 1937–41,* New York, 1941
Basch, Antonin, *The Danube Basin and the German Economic Sphere,* New York, 1943
Baykov, Alexander, *The Development of the Soviet Economic System,* Cambridge, 1946
Bidwell, Percy W., *Our Trade with Britain,* New York, 1938
Kreider, Carl, *The Anglo-American Trade Agreement,* Princeton, 1943
Lauterbach, Albert T., *Economics in Uniform,* Princeton, 1943
League of Nations, *Commercial Policy in the Interwar Period,* Geneva, 1942
Lemkin, Raphael, *Axis Rule in Occupied Europe,* Washington, 1944
Mitchell, Kate L., *Japan's Industrial Strength,* New York, 1942
Nathan, Otto, *The Nazi Economic System,* Durham, N.C., 1944
Reveille, Thomas, *The Spoil of Europe,* New York, 1941
Schumpeter, E. B., *The Industrialization of Japan and Manchukuo, 1930–40,* New York, 1940
Tasca, Henry J., *World Trading Systems,* Paris, 1939
Taylor, George E., *The Struggle for North China,* New York, 1940

A Gilt-Edged Standard

Brown, William Adams, Jr., *The Gold Standard Reinterpreted, 1914–34,* New York, 1940
Gregory, T. E., *The First Year of the Gold Standard,* London, 1926
Hall, N. F., *The Exchange Equalization Account,* London, 1935
League of Nations, *International Currency Experience,* Princeton, 1944
Keynes, J. M., *A Tract on Monetary Reform,* London, 1923
Kock, Karin, *International Capital Movements and Economic Policy,* Bergen, 1939

Report of Committee on Currency and Foreign Exchanges after the War (Cmd. 9182), London, 1918

NOTE: Two volumes published under the aegis of the American Economic Association provide the best conspectus of developments in economic theory since the first World War. Howard S. Ellis (ed.), *A Survey of Contemporary Economics,* Philadelphia, 1948, contains several chapters directly relevant to international trade theory. Howard S. Ellis and Lloyd A. Metzler (ed.), *Readings in the Theory of International Trade,* Philadelphia, 1949, reprints twenty-three major articles selected by a committee of the Association. In addition it provides an extended bibliography of journal articles during the interwar years.

CHAPTER XVI: THE AFTERMATH OF WAR

The Effects of War Mobilization

Buchanan, Norman S., *International Investment and Domestic Welfare,* New York, 1945

————, and Lutz, Friedrich A., *Rebuilding the World Economy,* New York, 1947

Committee on International Economic Policy, *World Trade and Employment,* New York, 1942

Condliffe, J. B., *Agenda for a Postwar World,* New York, 1942

Hoover, Calvin B., *International Trade and Domestic Employment,* New York, 1945

International Labour Office, *Towards Our True Inheritance,* Montreal, 1942

Lasswell, Harold D., *World Politics Faces Economics,* New York, 1945

League of Nations, *Economic Stability in the Postwar World,* Geneva, 1945

Stettinius, Edward S., *Lend-Lease: Weapon for Victory,* New York, 1944

Tinbergen, J., *International Economic Cooperation,* Amsterdam, 1945

United Nations, *Economic Report: Salient Features of the World Economic Situation, 1945–47,* New York, 1948

U.S. Military Academy, *Raw Materials in War and Peace,* New York, 1947

The Impoverishment of Europe

Bank for International Settlements, *Annual Reports,* Basle, 1945–49

Basch, Antonin, *A Price for Peace,* New York, 1945

Dieterlin, P. and Rist, Chas., *The Monetary Problem of France,* New York, 1948

Dupriez, L. H., *Monetary Reconstruction in Belgium,* New York, 1947

Economic Commission for Europe of the United Nations. Research and Planning Division. *A Survey of the Economic Situation and Prospects of Europe,* Geneva, 1948

Fisher, A. G. B., *The Implications of Full Employment for Great Britain,* London, 1946

Foa, Bruno, *Monetary Reconstruction in Italy,* New York, 1949

Food and Agriculture Organization of the United Nations. *Report of the FAO Preparatory Commission on World Food Proposals,* Washington, 1947

Harris, Seymour E. (ed.), *The European Recovery Program,* New York, 1948

United Kingdom, *Statistical Material Presented during the Washington Negotiations* (Cmd. 6707), London, 1945

————, *Economic Survey* (Cmd. 7046, 7344, 7647), London, 1947–49

U.N.R.R.A., *The Story of U.N.R.R.A.,* New York, 1947

The Crumbling of Empire

Andrews, Russel, *Burmese Economic Life,* Palo Alto, Calif., 1947
Bonn, Moritz J., *The Crumbling of Empire,* London, 1938
Callis, Helmut G., *Foreign Capital in South-East Asia,* New York, 1942
Crocker, Walter R., *On Governing Colonies,* London, 1947
Fairbank, J. K., *The United States and China,* Cambridge, Mass., 1948
Grajdanzev, Andrew J., *Modern Korea,* New York, 1944
Gull, E. M., *British Economic Interests in the Far East,* London, 1943
Hailey, Lord, *An African Survey,* London, 1938
———, *The Future of Colonial Peoples,* London, 1943
Jacoby, E. H., *Agrarian Unrest in South-East Asia,* New York, 1949
Meyer, F. V., *Britain's Colonies in World Trade,* London, 1948
Mills, L. A., *British Rule in Eastern Asia,* London, 1942
Robequain, Chas., *The Economic Development of French Indo-China,* New York, 1944
Royal Institute of International Affairs, *The Colonial Problem,* London, 1937
Vlekke, Bernard H. M., *The Story of the Dutch East-Indies,* Cambridge, Mass., 1945
Wickizer, V. D., and Bennett, M. K., *The Rice Economy of Monsoon Asia,* Palo Alto, Calif., 1941

The Soviet Challenge

Baykov, Alexander, *The Development of the Soviet Economic System,* Cambridge, 1946
Carr, E. H., *The Soviet Impact on the Western World,* New York, 1947
Condoide, M. V., *Russian-American Trade,* Columbus, 1946
Fisher, Raymond H., *Agreements and Treaties concluded by the U.S.S.R. in 1945.* (Dept. of State Bulletin, Sept. 1946)
Harris, Seymour E., et al., "Symposium on Russian Statistics," *Review of Economic Statistics,* Vol. XXXIX, No. 4, Nov. 1947
League of Nations, *Industrialization and Foreign Trade,* Princeton, 1945
Letiche, J. M., *The Reciprocal Trade Policy of the United States,* New York, 1948
Schwartz, Harry, *Russia's Postwar Economy,* Syracuse, 1947

CHAPTER XVII: NATIONAL ECONOMIC POLICIES

Planning and Freedom

Clark, J. M., *Alternative to Serfdom,* New York, 1948
Fisher, A. G., *Economic Progress and Social Security,* London, 1945
Franks, Sir Oliver, *Central Planning and Control in Peace and War,* London, 1947
Hayek, F. A., *The Road to Serfdom,* Chicago, 1944
Henderson, Sir Hubert, *The Uses and Abuses of Economic Planning,* Cambridge, 1947
Jewkes, John, *Ordeal by Planning,* London, 1948
Landauer, Carl, *Theory of National Economic Planning* (2nd ed.), Berkeley, 1947
Popper, K. R., *The Open Society and Its Enemies* (Vol. II), London, 1945
Robbins, Lionel, *The Economic Problem in Peace and War,* London, 1947
Wootton, Barbara, *Freedom under Planning,* London, 1945

Objectives of Intervention

Beveridge, Sir William, *Full Employment in a Free Society,* London, 1944
Ezekiel, Mordecai, *Jobs for All,* New York, 1939
Fitch, Lyle and Taylor, Horace (eds.), *Planning for Jobs,* Philadelphia, 1946
Harrod, R. F., *Are These Hardships Necessary,* London, 1947
Hoffman, Michael L., "The Best Thing in France Today," *Harper's,* Sept. 1947
Lerner, Abba P. and Graham, Frank D. (eds.), *Planning and Paying for Full Employment,* Princeton, 1946
Monnet, Jean, *Rapport Général sur le Premier Plan de Modernisation et d'Equipment,* Paris, 1946
Oxford Institute of Statistics, *The Economics of Full Employment,* Oxford, 1944
Pierson, John H. G., *Full Employment and Free Enterprise,* Washington, 1947
Robbins, L. H., "Inquest on the Crisis," *Lloyds Bank Review,* Oct. 1947
Schumacher, E. F. and Kalecki, M., "New Plans for International Trade," Supplement to the *Bulletin of the Oxford Institute of Statistics,* 1943
United Kingdom, *White Paper on Employment Policy* (Cmd. 6527), London, 1944
Viner, Jacob, "An American View of the British Economic Crisis," *Lloyds Bank Review,* Oct. 1947

The Keynesian Influence

Burns, Arthur F., *Economic Research and the Keynesian Thinking of Our Times,* New York, 1946
Butlin, S. J. and Wilson, J. S. G., *The Life and Work of Lord Keynes,* Sydney, 1946
Dillard, Dudley, *The Economics of John Maynard Keynes,* New York, 1948
Harris, Seymour E. (ed.), *The New Economics,* New York, 1947
Hicks, J. R., "World Recovery after War," *Economic Journal,* Vol. LVII, No. 226, June 1947
Keynes, J. M., *The General Theory of Employment, Interest and Money,* London, 1936
————, *The Means to Prosperity,* London, 1933
————, et al., *Unemployment as a World Problem,* Chicago, 1933
Klein, Lawrence R., *The Keynesian Revolution,* New York, 1947
Robinson, E. A. G., "John Maynard Keynes, 1883–1946," *Economic Journal,* Nov. 1947
Robinson, Joan, "The Theory of Money and the Analysis of Output," *Review of Economic Studies,* Vol. I, No. 1, 1933

CHAPTER XVIII: A FRAMEWORK OF WORLD ORDER

Carnegie Endowment for International Peace, *Coordination of Economic and Social Activities of the United Nations,* New York, 1948
Finer, Herman, *The United Nations Economic and Social Council,* Boston, 1946
Goodrich, Leland M. and Hambro, Edward, *Charter of the United Nations: Commentary and Documents,* Boston, 1949
Halm, George N., *International Monetary Cooperation,* Chapel Hill, N.C., 1945
Hawtrey, R. G., *Bretton Woods: For Better or Worse,* London, 1946
International Bank for Reconstruction and Development, *Annual Reports*
International Labor Office, *Reports*
International Monetary Fund, *Annual Reports*
Knorr, Klaus E., "The Bretton Woods Institutions in Transition," *International Organization,* Vol. II, No. 1, Feb. 1948

Loveday, Alexander, "An Unfortunate Decision," *International Organization,* Vol. I, No. 2, June 1947
National Planning Association, *International Economic Collaboration: Role of the Economic and Social Council in the United Nations Organization,* Washington, 1946
Potter, Pitman B., *International Organization,* New York, 1948
Sharp, Walter R., "The Specialized Agencies and the United Nations," *International Organization,* Vol. II, No. 2, June 1948
Viner, Jacob, "Conflicts of Principle in Drafting a Trade Charter," *Foreign Affairs,* Vol. 24, No. 4, July 1947
Willcox, Clair, *A Charter for World Trade,* New York, 1949
Williams, John H., *Postwar Monetary Plans and Other Essays,* New York, 1944

CHAPTER XIX: THE ASSUMPTIONS OF A MODERN THEORY

Balogh, T., Note on Deliberate Organization for Higher Income, *Economic Journal,* June 1947
Barnard, Chester I., *The Functions of the Executive,* Cambridge, Mass., 1946
Belshaw, Horace, "Observations on Industrialization for Higher Incomes," *Economic Journal,* Sept. 1947
Buchanan, Norman S., "Deliberate Industrialization for Higher Incomes," *Economic Journal,* Dec. 1946
Cannan, E., *A History of the Theories of Production and Distribution in English Political Economy from 1776–1848,* London, 1893
————, *A Review of Economic Theory,* London, 1929
Davenport, H. J., *The Economics of Enterprise,* New York, 1913
Dobb, Maurice, *Capitalist Enterprise and Social Progress,* London, 1925
Drucker, Peter F., *The Concept of the Corporation,* New York, 1946
Fogarty, M. P., *Prospects of the Industrial Areas of Great Britain,* London, 1945
Folk, G. E., *Patents and Industrial Progress,* New York, 1942
Golden, C. S. and Rutenberg, H. J., *Dynamics of Industrial Democracy,* New York, 1942
Gordon, R. A., *Business Leadership in the Large Corporation,* Washington, 1945
Griffin, Clare E., *Enterprise in a Free Society,* Chicago, 1949
Holden, Paul, et al., *Top Management Organization and Control,* Stanford, 1941
Knight, Frank H., *Risk, Uncertainty and Profit* (6th imp.), London, 1946
List, Friedrich, *The National System of Political Economy,* London, 1928
Marshall, Alfred, *Principles of Economics* (Bk. IV), London, 1890
Mayo, Elton, *The Social Problems of Our Industrial Civilization,* Boston, 1945
Neumann, John von and Morgenstern, Oscar, *Theory of Games and Economic Behaviour,* Princeton, 1947
Ross, A. M., *Trade Union Wage Policy,* Berkeley, 1948
Schumpeter, Joseph H., *Capitalism, Socialism and Democracy,* New York, 1942
————, *Theory of Economic Development,* Cambridge, Mass., 1934
Slichter, Sumner H., *The American Economy,* New York, 1948

CHAPTER XX: THE BALANCING OF PAYMENTS

The Monetary Mechanism

Bloomfield, Arthur I., "Operations of the American Exchange Stabilization Fund," *Review of Economic Statistics,* Vol. XXVI, No. 2, May 1944
Dupriez, Leon H., *Des Mouvements Economiques Généraux,* Louvain, 1947

Hall, N. F., *The Exchange Equalization Account,* London, 1933

Keynes, J. M., *The General Theory of Employment, Interest, and Money,* London, 1936

Kindleberger, C. P., *International Short-term Capital Movements,* New York, 1937

Memoria de la primera reunion de tecnicos sobre problemes de Banca Central del Continente Americano, Mexico, 1946

Metzler, Lloyd A., "The Transfer Problem Reconsidered," *Journal of Political Economy,* Vol. L, No. 3, June 1942

Mikesell, Raymond F., "The Role of the International Monetary Arrangements in a World of Planned Economies," *Journal of Political Economy,* Vol. LV, No. 6, Dec. 1947

Nurkse, Ragnar, *Conditions of International Monetary Equilibrium,* Princeton, 1945

————, "Domestic and International Equilibrium," in Seymour E. Harris (ed.), *The New Economics,* New York, 1947

Robinson, Joan, "The Foreign Exchanges," in *Essays in the Theory of Employment,* London, 1937

The Economics of Insulation

Andersen, Poul Nyboe, *Bilateral Exchange Clearing Policy,* Copenhagen, 1946

Condliffe, J. B., *The Reconstruction of World Trade,* New York, 1940

Ellis, Howard S., *Bilateralism and the Future of International Trade,* Princeton, 1945

————, "Exchange Control and Discrimination," *American Economic Review,* Vol. XXXVII, No. 5, Dec. 1947

Gordon, Margaret S., *Barriers to World Trade,* New York, 1941

Hirschman, Albert O., *National Power and the Structure of Foreign Trade,* Berkeley, 1943

Lemkin, Rafael, *La Reglementation des Paiements Internationaux,* Paris, 1939

Schumacher, E. F., "Multilateral Clearing," *Economica,* Vol. X (New Series), No. 38, May 1943

Tasca, Henry J., *World Trading Systems,* Paris, 1939

Viner, Jacob, *Trade Relations between Free-Market and Controlled Economies,* Geneva, 1943

Fixing the Exchange Rates

Behrendt, Richard F., *Inter-American Economic Relations: Problems and Prospects,* New York, 1948

Bloomfield, Arthur I., "Foreign Exchange Rate Theory and Policy," in S. E. Harris (ed.), *The New Economics,* New York, 1947

Chang, Tse-chun, "British Demand for Imports in the Interwar Period," *Economic Journal,* Vol. LVI, No. 222, June 1946

Condliffe, J. B., "Exchange Rates and Prices," *Index,* Vol. X, No. 109, June 1935

Ellis, Howard S., "The Equilibrium Rate of Exchange," in *Explorations in Economics,* New York, 1936

Enke, Stephen and Salera, Virgil, *International Economics,* New York, 1947

Garnsey, M. E., "Postwar Exchange Parities," with comments by L. H. Dupriez, V. Salera and a reply, *Quarterly Journal of Economics,* Vol. LX, No. 1, 1945, pp. 113–35, 299–308, 622–23 and 624–30

Haberler, G., "The Choice of Exchange Rates after the War," *American Economic Review,* Vol. XXXV, No. 3, June 1945

————, "Currency Depreciation and the International Monetary Fund," *Review of Economic Statistics,* Vol. XXVI, No. 4, Nov. 1944

Hansen, Alvin H., "A Brief Note on Fundamental Disequilibrium," *Review of Economic Statistics,* Vol. XXVI, No. 4, Nov. 1944

Hazlitt, Henry, *Will Dollars Save the World,* New York, 1947

Metzler, Lloyd A., "Exchange Rates and the International Monetary Fund," in Federal Reserve Board, *Postwar Economic Studies,* No. 7, Sept. 1947, Washington, 1947

MacDougall, G. D. A., "Britain's Foreign Trade Problem," *Economic Journal,* Vol. LVIII, No. 229, March 1948

Machlup, Fritz, *International Trade and the National Income Multiplier,* Philadelphia, 1943

————, "Theory of the Foreign Exchanges," *Economica,* Vol. VI (New Series), No. 24 and Vol. VII, No. 25, 1939–40

Mikesell, R. F., "The Determination of Postwar Exchange Rates," *Southern Economic Journal,* Vol. XIII, 1947

Polak, J. J., "Exchange Depreciation and International Monetary Stability," *Review of Economic Statistics,* Vol. XXIX, No. 3, August 1947

Triffin, R., "National Central Banking and the International Economy," in Federal Reserve Board, *Postwar Economic Studies,* No. 7, Sept. 1947

Young, John Parke, "Exchange Rate Determination," *American Economic Review,* Vol. XXXVII, No. 4, Sept. 1947

CHAPTER XXI: THE CASE FOR FREER TRADE

Clark, J. M., *Alternative to Serfdom,* New York, 1948

Condliffe, J. B., "The Scientific Revolution," in *Proceedings of the 21st Annual Conference of the Pacific Coast Economic Association,* Dec. 1946

————, "The Value of International Trade," *Economica,* Vol. V (New Series), No. 18, May 1938

Davis, Joseph S., *International Commodity Agreements: Hope, Illusion or Menace,* New York, 1947

Eight articles on the "Principles of Trade," the *Economist,* Vol. CXLVI, 1944

Graham, Benjamin, *World Commodities and World Currency,* New York, 1944

Haberler, G., "Some Factors Affecting the Future of International Trade and International Economic Policy," in S. E. Harris (ed.), *Economic Reconstruction,* New York, 1945

Henderson, Sir Hubert D., *The International Economic Problem,* London, 1946

Hilgerdt, Folke, "The Case for Multilateral Trade," *American Economic Review,* Vol. XXXIII, No. 1, Part 2, Suppl., March 1943

International Labor Office, *Intergovernmental Commodity Control Agreements,* Montreal, 1943

Keynes, J. M., "The Policy of Government Storage of Foodstuffs and Raw Materials," *Economic Journal,* Vol. XLVIII, No. 191, Sept. 1938

League of Nations, *Final Report of the Mixed Committee of the League of Nations on the Relation of Nutrition to Health, Agriculture and Economic Policy,* Geneva, 1937

McDougall, F. L., *Food and Welfare,* Geneva, 1938

Robertson, D. H., "The Future of International Trade," *Economic Journal,* Vol. XLVIII, No. 189, March, 1938

U.S. Senate, *Executive Report No. 12,* 80th Congress, 2nd Sess., and *International Wheat Agreement: Hearings before a Subcommittee of the Committee on Foreign Relations,* May 14–17, 1948

Viner, Jacob, *International Economic Cooperation in the United States in the Postwar World,* Ann Arbor, 1947

————, "The Prospects for Foreign Trade in the Postwar World," *Manchester School,* Vol. XV, 1947

CHAPTER XXII: THE GAINS FROM TRADE

Beard, Charles A., *The Idea of National Interest,* New York, 1934

Brodie, Bernard, *The Absolute Weapon: Atomic Power and World Order,* New York, 1946

Condliffe, J. B., "Economic Power as an Instrument of National Policy," *American Economic Review,* Vol. XXXIV, No. 1, Part 2, *Suppl.,* p. 305 f., March 1944

Ellsworth, P. T., "Comparative Costs, the Gains from Trade and Other Matters Considered by Professor Viner," *Canadian Journal of Economics and Political Science,* Vol. V, No. 2, May 1939

Feis, Herbert, *Seen from E.A.: Three International Episodes,* New York, 1947

Fisher, A. G. B., *The International Implications of Full Employment in Great Britain,* London, 1946

Franks, Sir Oliver, *Central Planning and Control in War and Peace,* Cambridge, 1947

Haberler, G. (chairman), "Domestic versus International Equilibrium," *American Economic Review,* Vol. XXXVII, No. 2, May 1947

Hoover, Calvin B., *International Trade and Domestic Employment,* New York, 1945

Irish Free State, *Commission of Inquiry into Banking, Currency and Credit,* P. No. 2628, Dublin, 1938. pp. 23–118

Jones, J. M., *Tariff Retaliation: Repercussions of the Hawley-Smoot Bill,* Philadelphia, 1934

Letiche, J. M., *The Reciprocal Trade Policy of the United States,* New York, 1948

Nurkse, Ragnar, "Domestic and International Equilibrium," in S. E. Harris (ed.), *The New Economics,* New York, 1947

Polanyi, M., *Full Employment and Free Trade,* New York, 1945

Rothschild, K. W., "The Small Nations and World Trade," *Economic Journal,* Vol. LIV, No. 213, April 1944

Samuelson, P. A., "Welfare Economics and International Trade," *American Economic Review,* Vol. XXVIII, No. 2, June 1938

————, "The Gains from International Trade," *Canadian Journal of Economics and Political Science,* Vol. V, No. 2, May 1939

Schattschneider, E. E., *Politics, Pressures and the Tariff,* New York, 1935

Tasca, Henry J., *The Reciprocal Trade Policy of the United States,* Philadelphia, 1938

Wright, Carl Major, *Economic Adaptation to a Changing World Market,* Copenhagen, 1939

INDEX